COLONIAL VIOLENCE

DIERK WALTER

Colonial Violence

European Empires and the Use of Force

Translated by
Peter Lewis

HURST & COMPANY, LONDON

First published in English in the United Kingdom in 2017 by
C. Hurst & Co. (Publishers) Ltd.,
41 Great Russell Street, London, WC1B 3PL
© Dierk Walter, 2017
Translation © Peter Lewis
All rights reserved.
First published in German by Hamburger Edition.
Printed in the United Kingdom by Bell and Bain Ltd

The right of Dierk Walter to be identified as the author of
this publication is asserted by him in accordance with the
Copyright, Designs and Patents Act, 1988.

A Cataloguing-in-Publication data record for this book
is available from the British Library.

ISBN: 9781849048071

This book is printed using paper from registered sustainable
and managed sources.

www.hurstpublishers.com

CONTENTS

CONTENTS

INTRODUCTION

Afghanistan since 1999, Iraq since 2003, Mali since 2013—the continuing military interventions of Western powers in the Third World in
the opening decades of the twenty-first century now only make occasional headlines. In the interim, we have become used to Western
troops being permanently stationed in Africa and Asia, while even the
term 'war' (long proscribed in some countries, notably Germany, on
constitutional and historic grounds) is increasingly becoming commonplace to describe such armed deployments.

Yet recognition of this basic fact is at the same time intrinsically
bound up with the idea of a far-reaching change in our whole conception of war. The peripheral conflicts of current times clearly have little
in common with the traditional understanding of war in Western
modernity, which is still wedded to the idea of symmetrical superpower conflict as epitomized by the world wars that were waged in the
twentieth century. The armed forces of the USA and Western Europe,
which for decades were equipped and trained for highly intensive
mechanized warfare in the shadow of tactical nuclear weapons, continue to find themselves in a state of mental and organizational reori-
entation, given that the (often strongly politically driven) deployment
of limited troop numbers in poorly developed regions lacking in state
infrastructure represents a new and unfamiliar challenge for military
elites whose mindset is still shaped by the image of the Cold War.
Journalists, political scientists, soldiers and defence policy analysts are
in little doubt that the peripheral interventions of the twenty-first century represent 'new wars'.[1]

1

And yet a historically informed assessment of these conflicts appears to suggest the opposite: the current military incursions by Western forces into Third World countries follow in a long tradition. In the characteristic determinants of warfare, in their external appearance and in their conflict logic they are remarkably similar to the armed conflicts between European powers and non-European societies that erupted from the start of European expansion throughout the world. The conquest of the Americas and the maritime expansion that took place in Asia in the fifteenth and sixteenth centuries; the wars against the indigenous peoples of North America in the eighteenth and nineteenth centuries; the classic colonial wars during the 'age of imperialism'; the major wars of decolonization after 1945, the 'hot wars' of the Cold War fought out in the Third World: these all bear a striking family resemblance to present-day interventions, thus unmasking the concept of 'new' wars as at best short-sighted, characterized by a fixation on the core European image of warfare in the twentieth century, and at worst as journalistic sensationalism.

There is a reason why this family resemblance has gone largely unnoticed. The boundaries drawn between eras in academic studies militate against viewing earlier conflicts, even those of the Early Modern period, and those of the nineteenth and twentieth centuries together in the round. The year 1945, which ushered in the Cold War and the process of decolonization, is such a key cut-off point for the world of today that most people find it hard to accept any continuities that transcend this break. Moreover, imperialism, colonies, colonial rule and colonial wars have meanwhile had such a bad press that current conflicts have to steer clear of any association with these older structures and precedents, if only on the grounds of legitimacy. Correspondingly, most informed contemporaries would doubtless concur that the 'humanitarian interventions' and the 'War on Terror' of recent decades have few if any parallels in the campaigns of colonial conquest and punitive expeditions conducted during the 'age of imperialism', if only because there are no longer any Western empires that are taking possession of overseas colonies. Even in de facto protectorates like Iraq or Afghanistan, Western nations have refrained from redrawing the map of the world in the manner of the late nineteenth century.

INTRODUCTION

However, from the perspective of a longer-term history of the exercise of power and force in the modern world, such constitutional distinctions conceal certain fundamental structural continuities. One does not need to be a neo-Marxist to recognize that the world of the present continues to be shaped by the political, economic, military, legal, and cultural dominance of the principal Western powers.[2] Nowadays, the global reach of the 'World System' is almost total; within this system the Western industrialized nations (together with certain regional powers in the Third World) set the rules by which other nations have to play or—in the event that they prove reluctant to do so—with which they are encouraged to comply through political or economic pressure or, as a last resort, by force of arms.[3] All in all, this is undoubtedly an imperial structure, a power relationship between strong and weak collectives, between politically, economically and culturally expanding and dominant core societies on the one hand, and on the other peripheral societies that are structurally dependent on the former. Military interventions in this context are in essence intended to guarantee the inclusion or re-inclusion of these peripheral societies into the global system and to enforce its rules (international law) and values (democracy, capitalism and liberalism). Whether colonies come into being in the process is not of any great analytical relevance here, especially since, in the overall history of European expansion, formal colonial rule only ever represented the shiny obverse of the imperial medallion, whose less impressive reverse consisted of the prolonged economic dominance of the West over large parts of the world, imposed through political and military means.

This perspective, which instead of the global caesuras of the twentieth century places structural continuities in the foreground, may not perhaps accord with the political consciousness of today and its need for legitimation, but certainly does reflect the current state of research into imperialism, which increasingly regards the entire modern era as a 500-year-long history of European expansion throughout the world. Whereas in earlier studies dramatic parts of this process, supposed concentrations, were singled out as '(the age of) imperialism', in the last few decades, research carried out by Ronald Robinson and John Gallagher as well as Peter Cain and Anthony Hopkins has substantiated the thesis of continuity with earlier eras, at least in the case of British imperialism.[4] Likewise, in Germany, Wolfgang Reinhard has depicted the entire 500 years of 'European expansion' since the conquest of the Americas as an empirical entity.[5] Similarly, the imperial history of Spain also shows evidence of long-term continuities.[6]

Certainly, the 'peripheral approach' of Ronald Robinson, according to which imperialism was based primarily on collaboration with indigenous elites and formal colonial rule was just a stopgap,[7] and to a lesser extent the pronouncedly time-diagnostic and politically charged theory of 'neocolonialism' and dependency[8] prompt the question whether this technique of exercising power has ended with decolonization.[9] The most recent comparative studies of empires indicate that the global dominance of the West, not just in cultural terms but from the perspective of power politics as well, was not a phenomenon belonging exclusively to the past, but rather that the world of the present is shaped both by modern empires such as those of the USA and Russia and also by globally dominant supranational combines, which collectively in their foreign relations and internal structures behave just like empires.[10] Hence, it is possible to regard the whole of the economic and political genesis of the modern 'globalized' world as a conceptual entity—which does not, of course, mean that we should therefore ignore any breaks in this process.[11] Whether we then choose to use the term 'imperialism'—notwithstanding its centuries-old history as a term of political polemic—for this entire process, or prefer the seemingly more descriptive phrase 'European expansion' is really quite irrelevant.[12]

This process of Western penetration of the world was, as has often been remarked, extraordinarily violent. As Daniel Headrick has written: 'The history of Imperialism is the history of warfare.'[13] Even the starting signal for European expansion, the conquest of Central America, began with the virtual extermination by the Spanish (and by the diseases which they brought with them) of the indigenous population of most of the Caribbean islands.[14] Thereafter demonstrations of the deadly effect of firearms in order to intimidate and blackmail indigenous peoples, kidnapping, seizures of land, the destruction of homes and natural resources, plunder, punitive expeditions, the brutal suppression of revolts, full-scale wars, massacres, expulsions and even genocide became standard methods of expansion—and for the most part were also effective methods of combatting it. Violence was omnipresent in the extension of European power; it might even be said to have become a permanent state—from the late nineteenth century there are corresponding statistics which show that a rapid succession of military operations were carried out even in supposedly friendly colonies, often dozens within the space of just a few years. If we follow Gallagher and Robinson in their plausibly simple definition of imperialism as the political function of the incorporation of new regions into an expanding economy, then this political function in turn was clearly founded upon a prominent element of violence.[15] That does not necessarily mean that European imperialism was a military conquest—not least, the means to achieve this were lacking. But on the other hand, the process was inseparable from violence and war.

Thus, if we understand the process of European expansion as a conceptual entity, it also makes sense to examine its history of violence as a whole and to enquire whether any overarching patterns can be identified—in other words, whether the element of violence within imperialism may be seen as a form of conflict sui generis. This is the aim of this book. However, it is not driven primarily by this deductive perspective, but rather wholly inductively by empirical observations, and specifically by the aforementioned striking family resemblance of all the violent conflicts that have ensued within the scope of European imperialism since the sixteenth century.

This family resemblance begins with basic metropolitan prerequisites such as the extraordinarily limited level of resources for peripheral conflicts and continues with the way in which remote and undeveloped space on the periphery determined the reality of warfare, from the macro level of operational planning and logistics down to the micro level of tactics. The mostly very pronounced asymmetry of both sides' forms of social and military organization, of their respective capacities to mobilize resources and their notably different styles of waging war likewise fall into the category of family resemblance, as does the nature of war as a clash of different cultures of violence. At the margins of empires, war and peace were virtually inseparable from one another; conflicts often had neither a beginning nor an end, and no clear fronts either. The process of European expansion is inconceivable without transcultural alliances, and these lend the violent conflicts that erupted in these contexts a primarily political character. All these circumstances impact enormously on the structure of wars within the scope of imperialism, and reveal them to be fundamentally different in character to the major European wars that were being waged at the same time. In particular, these circumstances also go a long way towards explaining the conspicuous brutality of these violent conflicts without any recourse to national idiosyncrasies—namely because similar problems repeatedly led to similar solutions, and what is more ones that transcended both the spatial boundaries between empires and the temporal ones between eras.

It is therefore not our primary concern here to present a theoretical overview of the entire history of organized violence in the context of European expansion. Instead, the focus will be efforts to synthesize empirical observations in order to identify patterns which will show the violent elements of imperialism to be an identifiable structural phenomenon, and to give a coherent explanation for its logic of conflict. This will be the subject of the first chapter of this book. Chapter 2 addresses the question of both sides' war aims and attempts a tentative typology of the patterns of conflict arising from organized violence within European expansion. The frequent assumption that these peripheral conflicts invariably aimed at straightforward conquest and total control tends to hamper the identification of continuities, since this was at most the case only at the peak phase of formal imperialism, and even there not universally. On closer inspection, ostensible discontinuities become relative in the light of implicit and explicit legitimizations of interventions in the non-Western world across the centuries

'What happens when asymmetric military cultures confront one another? This question arose again and again during the four centuries after 1500, when Europeans expanded aggressively over the oceans into the Americas, South Asia, and Africa and encountered polities, societies, and military systems very different to their own.'[16] This observation by Gerald Bryant encapsulates the problems discussed in chapters 3 and 4 of this book. Indeed, alongside the general logic of imperialism and the projection of power into remote, undeveloped spaces, the difference in cultures of violence is undoubtedly the most striking feature of the military encounter between imperial and indigenous forces within the scope of European expansion. Where enemies had such completely divergent conceptions of the role of violence in human existence and of its permitted scope and its limits as the West and the majority of the rest of the world had in modern times, and where the means of violence and its organizational forms were so different, notions of essential otherness and cultural misunderstandings arose and contributed to the unchecked spread of violence.[17] This is the subject of chapter 3.

As Adam Hirsch has established in the case of New England in the seventeenth century, war between very different opponents gave rise to an intense pressure to adapt: 'Because military culture tended to express itself only in times of actual warfare [...], the acculturation process was not gradual, as in most other branches of culture, but "explosive", occurring at discrete intervals. This characteristic magnified the disorientation and misunderstanding that inevitably accompany the meeting of two disparate cultures.'[18]

While Hirsch highlights here the negative consequences of such a meeting, Robert Utley emphasizes the chances of a cross-cultural encounter (and its appeal to historians): 'War is an activity shaped largely by cultural influences. Thus people of differing cultures fight wars in greatly different ways. When two such peoples fight each other, as they have throughout history, they afford the student of military matters fresh and fascinating terrain to explore. The challenge is particularly inviting when the cultural gulf is large, when a people of simple technology and social organization are pitted against a people of complex technology and social organization.'[19] This of course was very often the case during European expansion. Chapter 4 thus treats the potential for development arising from this pressure to adapt and assimilate, showing how the conflicting parties at least in the long term adapted to one another or to the conditions of warfare by developing new weapons, tactics and methods or acquiring them from each other, and how they came to adopt a long-term approach to learning beyond the case in hand, with the result that imperial military apparatuses moved a step closer to gaining an understanding of how war against indigenous societies on the periphery could be regarded as a form of conflict sui generis—and finally how under certain conditions both sides produced genuine syntheses of cultures of violence.

Few people hitherto have attempted to investigate the components of violence within Western imperialism in a way that eschews imperial borders and strictly demarcated eras. In general, it is true to say that up until now not only the older periodization (colonialism, imperialism, decolonization) and academic demarcation of eras appear to have stood in the way of an overarching view of the history of violence in European expansion, but also spectacular historical turning-points, such as the development of weapons technology: it clearly makes a huge difference whether the West confronted the non-European world with arquebuses, machine-guns, F-4 Phantom fighter-bombers, or drones. The same is true of the changes that have taken place globally in how war is legitimized, particularly noticeable since 1945.

Accordingly, even most comparative studies of patterns of conflict in the history of violence during European expansion are closely tied to particular eras. The strongly theorizing paradigm of 'asymmetrical warfare' is almost exclusively applied to recent history post-1990 and is closely associated with the bold concept of 'new wars'.[20] For both of these terms, the (negative) point of reference is the highly intensive and generally symmetrical large-scale war in the Northern hemisphere, embodied in the two world wars of the twentieth century and the third world war that failed to materialize as the USSR and USA faced off. The fact that a change in the image of war is postulated post-1990 is in line with the shift in perception in Western public opinion from the centre, where arms build-ups and military crises have ceased, to the periphery, where armed conflicts still go on. Yet this premise rather tends to hamper an insight into more long-term continuities in the conduct of war on the periphery.

As regards the era of the wars of decolonization from 1945 until roughly 1975, comparative studies generally confine themselves to considering the development of such Western doctrines as 'counterinsurgency' and 'guerre révolutionnaire'. If older developments are included at all, then mostly this is solely in the national context and goes no further back than the interwar years.[21]

The very earliest era with which the comparative history of imperialist violence has engaged is its 'classic' phase from roughly 1880 to 1920, though this for the most part misses out the period of continental expansion by both the USA and Russia. The result of this is that, with very few exceptions, such clear parallels as those that exist between the Indian wars in the USA and the Western conquest of

Africa remain unmentioned. Comparative studies of the violence inherent in expansion which cover the Early Modern period or the early nineteenth century are extremely rare.

A further difficulty is added by the national fragmentation of research efforts, which has resulted not least in continuing attempts to explain the violence perpetrated in Germany's colonial wars as having its roots in the German military tradition, or German racial predispositions or a genocidal ideology peculiar to Germany.[22] If we set such explanations alongside the attempt, say, by Olivier Le Cour Grandmaison to interpret the brutality of the colonial conflict in Algeria and other French colonies from the nineteenth to the twentieth centuries as a special French way of waging colonial war, the senselessness of such narrow national approaches becomes apparent.[23] Even when, in the case of Germany, Susanne Kuß points to the specifics of individual peripheral theatres of war as an explanation for the nature of military operations in each of these places,[24] all this ultimately achieves is to lessen the gravity of national–metropolitan interpretative approaches, without however adding the essential rider that it was the general practice of Western expansion in the first place, the colonial situation,[25] that was responsible for the logic of conflict and hence for the violence of imperialism, and moreover that this was largely independent of the national military and ideological traditions of individual empires.[26] As regards the theoretical preconditions and the violent methods of imperialism, it is more appropriate to follow Robert Gerwarth and Stephan Malinowski in taking as our starting point a 'colonial archive'[27]— though even this, with its fixation on the West's role as the intentional perpetrator, neglects certain crucial basic conditions for the deployment of organized violence in European expansion resulting from its overall logic as a historical structural phenomenon.[28]

To be sure, cursory pointers to the more long-term continuities of violence in European expansion do occasionally appear in the body of research, and in particular to the enduring actuality of corresponding forms of war.[29] However, serious attempts to analyse this violence as a historical pattern that transcends eras and the boundaries of empires are rare. In fact, it is fair to say that Western military history has traditionally shown little interest in wars on the periphery.[30] Out of a total of 822 pages in Azar Gat's monumental work *War in Human Civilization*, barely two superficial pages are devoted to the phenomenon, while John Keegan's *History of Warfare*, which aims at being no less comprehensive, only mentions it in a few isolated subclauses.[31] Modern research into imperialism almost completely avoids the topic of warfare.[32] The sole attempt in book form at a systematic approach to the question of warfare between European and non-European forces that goes beyond specific continents and eras has been written by the ethnologist Lawrence Keeley.[33] Although diachronic studies of guerrilla warfare do generally include conflicts on the periphery, they do not systematically discuss their peculiarities.[34] In two separate studies, Bruce Vandervort has analysed imperial warfare in Africa and North America in the nineteenth century and pointed to important parallels.[35]

Almost all other comprehensive approaches are syntheses in the form of edited volumes, the great majority of which confine themselves to the peak phase of imperialism,[36] with some (mostly with a single thematic focus) treating the Early Modern period,[37] and only very few covering more than one era, at least as far as their stated agenda goes.[38] Now and then informative collections of essays appear, or even monographs on individual regions, colonial empires or eras,[39] along with some significant, if short, articles with a systematic focus.[40]

Essentially, though, by far the most common form of study in the literature on violent conflicts in the context of European expansion, as Jürgen Osterhammel has established with regard to the somewhat narrower concept of intervention, is the 'monographic case study',[41] a finding which in fact generally accords with a recent trend toward specialization in academic history.[42] This same trend clearly hampers a search for generalizations beyond the specific case, given that any such abstraction appears to be at variance with the aims of any individual case study, let alone a whole series of them. In contemporary historical research, the search for patterns or parallels[43] for a 'system that embraces a large number of instances'[44] has a truly hard time of it.

The body of literature on individual violent conflicts within the scope of imperialism is almost unmanageably vast. Accordingly, this book cannot be, and has no pretensions to being, a 'history' of organized violence in European expansion—particularly since such an account, in view of the omnipresence of the phenomenon, would scarcely be distinguishable from a history of the expansion itself. In an undertaking such as this, completeness could never be achieved, even if one spent decades amassing and evaluating all the research literature. Also, completeness is not the intention in the logic of this project, since I am not asserting that every single violent conflict within the scope of imperialism functioned in all its details in the manner described in this volume. I am certain that hundreds of empirical instances do not exhibit one or two of the characteristics discussed here, and presumably there are dozens that do not conform in several respects to the interpretation of conflicts within European expansion that is put forward. On the other hand, I would be extremely surprised if more than a handful of actual cases ran completely counter to the logic of conflict expounded in this book.

The purpose of the book is therefore not to provide conclusive answers for every individual case, but rather to develop a kind of ideal type (with variables) that generates further questions for research. The sheer volume of recurrent empirical observations on the history of violence in Western imperialism suggests that the interpretation of the extensive conflict pattern which links them, as well as the functionality of the internal logic of the history that I am attempting to present here, can also be generalized. This book makes a bid for incorporating such observations into the future empirical reappraisal of other conflicts, working from the assumption that the logic of the violent components of European expansion permits transferable conclusions. I put forward an interpretative framework for future researchers which is intended to relieve them of the necessity of constantly having to reinvent the wheel and in particular of having repeatedly to be surprised at the apparent irregularity and excessive violence of peripheral conflicts.

Accordingly the book operates with no clear definition, no explicit demarcation of the empirical instances that form the basis of my approach. The framework is provided by the historical structural phenomenon of imperialism or of European expansion, and the multifarious violent conflicts within this frame constitute the bulk of cases under investigation. Yet in essence I am interested in examining organized and transcultural asymmetric violence such as that which arises classically in the conflict between the West and indigenous collectives organized along state or tribal lines. If one considers the entire spectrum of violence within the context of European expansion as a continuum of intensity, at one end stand the West's warlike clashes with large and comparatively well organized and powerful empires such as the Chinese or Ottoman empires, or in the twentieth century with nation-states which at least superficially exhibit Western traits, such as North Vietnam or Iraq: in other words, roughly symmetrical conflicts that in many respects approximate to wars of the modern era in the West that are waged between states. At the other end of the continuum there is the largely unstructured everyday violence between individuals or small groups in regions that are remote from any formal state structure,[45] which, although an integral element of European expansion, lies beyond our conception of war. The primary interest of this book lies between these two extremes, in other words in the broad middle of the spectrum, where military representatives of the central states of the Western world are in conflict with non-European societies organized in some way or other as tribes, systems of feudal rule, proto-states, indigenous empires, or anticolonial resistance movements; where this struggle has an identifiable uniformity, logic and structure; and above all where it serves the purpose of extending or upholding the power of the Western world, and where the violence is organized and instrumental.

All the same, borderline cases are still included in the discussion, as long as they exhibit structural similarities. In addition to the aforementioned extreme ends of the spectrum—large-scale non-European empires and largely unstructured everyday violence—such marginal cases include:

- Conflicts between Western empires with massive indigenous involvement (such as the global wars of the eighteenth century, particularly those in North America);
- Conflicts with Western settlers (such as the American War of Independence in 1775–1783, the wars of liberation in Latin America at the beginning of the nineteenth century, and the Boer War of 1899 to 1902);
- Conflicts with other non-autochthonous peoples (such as the anticolonial revolts of slaves of African descent and freed slaves in the Caribbean in the late eighteenth and early nineteenth centuries); or
- Conflicts in the empire-like frontier zones of postcolonial nation-states (above all in South America in the nineteenth and twentieth centuries).

INTRODUCTION

I have omitted entirely any discussion of violent imperial expansion by non-Western empires such as China. This seemed to me to go beyond the scope of the framework and to distract from the coherence of the phenomenon. Restricting myself to violent conflicts within the scope of European expansion seemed justified to me because this process of expansion was the most extensive, protracted, and in its long-term effects the most significant and formative, the only truly global and collective such process. Moreover, European expansion was charged with the economic impetus of capitalism and a mix of ideological motivations based on religion, a civilizing mission and racism, and was underpinned by a discriminatory global legal system historically unique in its universality. These intensifying factors mark out European expansion among other imperialistic processes as being especially far-reaching and profound.[46]

The conflicts discussed here thus have no sharply defined external limits; they defy any clear historic demarcation beyond their location as instruments of power in the process of European imperialism. Their family resemblance makes them similar but not congruent. Not only are there many marginal cases in the context of European expansion, as we have already shown, but conversely some of the characteristics of the conflicts discussed here also apply to other campaigns across large areas (say, Napoleon's advance into Russia in 1812), other wars between states and sub-state actors (the Vendée Rebellion of 1793–1796 or the Peninsular War in Spain from 1808 to 1812), other trans-cultural conflicts (the Pacific War of 1941–1945), or even conflicts that have been construed as transcultural (the war between Germany and the Soviet Union, 1941–1945).

Nevertheless, I still maintain, and precisely because of the family resemblance, that the phenomenon exists, however vaguely it may be defined. The dynamic mix in which the particular characteristics of the aforementioned forms of conflict coalesce, and condition and reinforce one another is peculiar to the violent conflicts that took place in the context of European expansion. To hazard a simple comparison: a glance at a colour chart reveals there to be an endless number of shades of green: grass-green, which can be seen as a yellow; turquoise, which can be seen as a blue; greyish-green, which can be seen as a grey; and earth-green, which can be seen as a brown. And even though linguistics has demonstrated that there are languages which have no word for 'green', at the same time it has also proved that the speakers of such languages are clearly able to recognize green.[47] All these various shades ultimately show is that green cannot be clearly demarcated—and yet it still exists because at the root of our perception it is nothing other than simply green. In the same way—at least, this is the hypothesis of this book—the phenomenon of the violent conflict within imperialism exists as a pattern of conflict sui generis, as an intersection of all those conflicts in this context that do not have as much in common with other forms of conflict as they do with one another.

Is there a word for the phenomenon under discussion here? Of course, we could keep referring to 'organized violence within the scope of European expansion', but this becomes wearing after a while. 'Small wars'[48]—a commonplace term in Great Britain in the nineteenth century[49]—has the inherent problem of not only sounding pejorative but also of not fully conveying their peripheral nature. 'Asymmetric warfare' hits the mark pretty well, but in most people's understanding refers primarily to the combatants' respective military potential rather than to the transcultural aspect, and is furthermore, as a result of discussions over the past few decades in the political science arena, strongly associated with the modern era. 'Colonial war' has the advantage of being generally intelligible, but it is inevitably linked to the conquest or pacification of colonies, that is, with formal rule; as such, it might be argued that it is too narrowly associated with the late nineteenth and early twentieth centuries, and does not adequately reflect the 500-year history of European expansion, which for much of the time was conducted informally without the imposition of direct rule, but which was no less violent for that.

For the sake of simplicity and brevity, I will therefore adopt the shorthand designation 'imperial wars' for violent conflicts in the scope of Western imperialism.[50] However, in the context of this book the term is not central—it is simply intended as a loose neologism in an attempt to encapsulate the history of organized violence within European expansion as a conceptual entity.

Of necessity, this book tends towards a Eurocentric approach. Its focus is on the violent acts that occurred within the framework of a complex process. Granted, this process was played out by protagonists on both sides, or rather it had more than two sides, since it was just as strongly characterized by transcultural interactions and alliances as it was by intracultural divisions. But the process itself and the fundamental impulsion to violence ultimately derive from the foremost powers, the imperial powers, of the Western world. Europeans came to America, Asia and Africa, rather than the indigenous peoples of these continents to Europe, which thus makes every action on the part of indigenous peoples in this process, at least in the final analysis, a reaction to the reality of European expansion. Quantitatively, too, as Benjamin Brower has determined, 'the actions of European actors dominate the history of colonial violence.'[51]

Nonetheless, I have made every effort to include in this account a treatment of the indigenous side, its culture of violence, its scope for action and its adaptation to the challenge posed by European empires. The purpose of this book is to examine the interaction between cultures of violence. Yet the indigenous societies that clashed with Western empires over the course of European expansion were mostly pre-literate, meaning that what we know about them—apart from the oral history recounted by descended ethnic groups still in existence today, which can be, and has been, extensively evaluated by ethnologists[52]—derives mostly from the pens of European observers,[53] even though they in their turn tended to indulge in oral history too, like the Spanish in the wake of their conquest of the Americas.[54]

This situation regarding sources not only makes our viewpoint necessarily partial,[55] but at the same time also means that our picture of non-European cultures is already shaped by their reaction to European expansion. No Western observer ever reported on an indigenous society that had not already been affected and reconstituted by the shockwaves of the violent expansion of European imperial power. Trade goods, migrations, epidemics and secondary wars of displacement entered indigenous societies before any Europeans ever set foot there. Apart from a handful of archaeological finds, there is no historical record of the way the pre-Columbian Indians of North America waged war, and the same applies to an even greater extent to the Old World, which came into contact with these precursors of European expansion even earlier.[56]

For the purposes of both simplicity and lexical variation, over the following pages the terms 'Western' 'imperial', and 'European' will generally be used almost interchangeably to denote the globally expansive actor in this clash of powers, even though not all of these terms can be applied equally to settler communities of European extraction such as the United States (which are not European), Europeanized empires like Japan (not Western) or Western actors after the demise of colonial empires (the majority of which are at best only collectively imperialist). Moreover, at least since the East–West conflict (1917–1991), Russia is connoted less with 'Western' than with 'Eastern' (which is misleading in global historical terms given its clearly Western culture). Conversely, the terms 'non-European', 'indigenous' and 'autochthonous' are all used in a relatively undifferentiated way for the local, globally defensive actor, for which few other collective synonyms exist that are not widely regarded as pejorative.[57] Of course, it is open to question how indigenous the local combatants were in each case, in view of various indigenous peoples' own expansionist thrusts and migration movements (triggered not least by the incursions of Western imperialism). The non-European world was by no means static.

To call the non-European inhabitants of America before the twentieth century 'Native Americans' seems anachronistic to me, especially since the term is not—as we in Europe often wrongly assume—the most commonly used term even in the USA to denote people of indigenous descent, either by themselves or by others.[58] Instead, I have used the succinct term 'Indians' throughout.

1

WAR ON THE PERIPHERY

'War in Africa had a totally different character. It was most decidedly a war, a real war that was very hard, arduous and difficult, but sui generis.'[1] This claim, which appears in the introduction to a popular, memoir-based history of the war fought by the French in Algeria, is significant. Organized violence in European expansion—imperial wars, colonial wars, 'small wars'—is generally recognized as functioning quite differently to conventional large-scale wars between the Western powers, and might even be described as its structural opposite.[2] Such an *ex negativo* definition has long been the typical starting-point for any analysis of imperial wars, as illustrated by the following comments from the last hundred years or so:

'A comparative study of colonial wars requires two premises. The first is that colonial wars form a separate category. That is to say that they have something in common which distinguishes them from other wars—in short, that they are sui generis.'

Hendrik Wesseling[3]

'Colonial warfare is quite different from what is commonly known as conventional warfare.'

Jean Gottmann[4]

'Colonial war differs from the kind of warfare normally practiced in Europe by a number of special conditions in the way it is waged.'

Albert Ditte[5]

'Small war is a term which has come largely into use of late, and which is admittedly somewhat difficult to define. Practically, it may be said to include all campaigns other than those where both the opposing sides consist of regular troops [...] The teachings of great masters of the art of war, and the experience gained from campaigns of modern date in America and on the continent of Europe, have established certain principles and precedents which form the groundwork of the system of regular warfare of today. [...] But the conditions of small wars are so diversified, the enemy's mode of fighting is often so peculiar, and the theatres of operations present such singular features, that irregular warfare must generally be carried out on a method totally different from the stereotyped system'.

Charles Callwell[6]

What, then, do these 'special conditions' consist of, through which war within the scope of European expansion became the diametric opposite of major interstate wars of the modern era in the West? À propos of this, Gottmann took a classic approach in referring to distant lands, large uncharted tracts of territory, a numerically superior enemy familiar with the terrain, a yawning gap in civilization between the warring sides, and completely divergent war aims; the other three authorities cited here presented a fundamentally similar picture.[7] Later definitions of colonial warfare also drew on these sources.[8] Yet what they have in common is that they all take, at least primarily, the classic era of more recent European colonial empires and their wars of expansion overseas as their point of reference—in other words, the period from the mid-nineteenth to the early twentieth century. In truth, though, many of these 'special conditions' can also be generalized and applied to the whole history of the violent establishment and maintenance of the dominance of Western empires in the rest of the world.

What precise form did these 'special conditions' take over the five hundred years of European expansion? The physical geography of the theatres of operation determined the character of the fighting and in particular hampered the logistics of imperialism. The configuration of the two opposing armies was highly asymmetrical: fragmented indigenous societies with an extensive culture of violence encountered global empires with potentially almost boundless resources and the will to exert intensive force of the kind that had proved decisive in securing victory in wars waged in the West. In actual fact, though, the logic of the imperial system and the difficulties of projecting power onto the periphery limited the deployment of resources in those locations. As a result, a swift and decisive military outcome often proved impossible to achieve; instead, long-term and widespread conditions of violent conflict were much more typical of the margins of empires. Such conditions, and the attempts by empires to resolve them, form the subject of this chapter.

Spatial conditions

In order to visualize the dimensions of the geographical area within which imperial wars were often played out, it is not necessary to think straight away of the over 13 million square kilometres of Siberia, conquered by just a few Russians, or the 8,000 kilometres from the Urals to the Bering Straits, and take them as our yardstick.[9] Even the extent of the Congo Basin, most of which became a Belgian colony, was equivalent to that of Europe from London to the River Volga.[10] Likewise in the 1950s, Algeria, which rose up in revolt against its French colonial masters, was five times the size of the French metropole, which was itself at the time the largest country in Europe west of the Soviet Union.[11]

Distances were commensurate with these vast spaces. In 1533, during their conquest of Peru, the small band of soldiers commanded by Francisco Pizarro covered 1,200 kilometres along the ridge of the High Andes from Cajamarca to the Inca capital of Cuzco.[12] The goldfields of Cuiabá, which in the late seventeenth century were the scene of bitter fighting between Portuguese colonists and the Indian tribes who lived in the region, were located 3,500 kilometres by winding river from the nearest large settlement at São Paulo—a route that led through deep ravines and the Pantanal, one of the largest marshlands in the world.[13] The French Foureau-Lamy Expedition of 1898 marched almost the same distance from Algeria to Lake Chad, albeit on foot across the Sahara Desert.[14] As late as 1870—in the railway age—the campaign against the separatist Métis Republic on the Red River in Canada took a British column under the command of Colonel (later Field Marshal) Garnet Wolseley 1,000 kilometres across trackless wilderness full of mosquito-infested swamps and forests.[15]

Even though not all theatres of operation were enormous,[16] supply lines that stretched for many hundreds of kilometres through hostile territory in conflicts on the periphery were the rule rather than the exception.[17] And in many cases 'hostile territory' meant precisely that, and was not just a metaphorical abbreviation for 'territory occupied by the enemy'. In the words of the British Major-General Charles Edward Callwell, whose book *Small Wars: Their Principles and Practice* (1896) ran to several editions and remained for many decades the bible of imperial conflict, wars on the periphery were 'first and foremost campaigns against nature'.[18] Of course, some conflicts took place under temperate natural conditions, but much more often it was a case of inhospitable terrain, extreme climatic conditions and dangerous fauna and flora. In the Sahara, for instance, temperatures far in excess of 50°C by day alternated with night frosts, with both extremes sometimes coexisting shortly after sunset: the sand, heated by the sun, burned a person's feet, while their ears were already threatening to drop off in the icy night air. They also had to contend with sandstorms, tarantulas, sand fleas, lice, scorpions, poisonous snakes, jackals and hyenas as well as diarrhoea, cholera and malaria.[19]

Exceptional climatic conditions also characterized many campaigns in the US West. The Apache Wars took place in the scorched, malaria-prone deserts of Arizona, where temperatures reached 40°–50°C and there were hardly any sources of water but any number of thornbush thickets, snakes, scorpions, millipedes, tarantulas and the poisonous lizard species known as the Gila Monster.[20] Guns also became so hot that it was impossible to touch them.[21] By contrast, the campaigns against the Sioux in the North often brought conditions like those of the winter of 1876–1877, when blizzards and temperatures of between −40°C and −45°C filled the air with sharp shards of ice and left the troops with thick lumps of ice in their beards and the horses with icicles hanging from their nostrils.[22] During the Seminole Wars of the 1840s in Florida, heat, epidemics, foul stagnant water in the Everglades and the native saw-grass (*Cladium jamaicense*), whose serrated leaves caused cuts that became painfully inflamed, made the operation a living hell for US Army troops.[23]

The Caribbean also presented, alongside humid tropical heat, unfamiliar and dangerous flora and fauna: cactuses and other spiny plants, mosquitos, scorpions, giant crab spiders and millipedes, all of them poisonous.[24] In South America, Africa and Southeast Asia, the theatre of operations was in many places dominated by dense, sunless jungle, where undergrowth and creepers reduced visibility to almost zero.[25] In the Congo Basin, the trees grew 60 metres tall, while the dense forest understory reached a height of 5 metres. The Belgian troops who were supposed to patrol this virgin forest had to battle their way not just through mangrove swamps and sunken woods but also across tracts of dry savannah. They had to cope with searing heat, fevers, insects and unsanitary drinking water, while the constant high humidity rotted their boots and clothing.[26]

The uniforms and equipment of imperial forces, at least the regular troops, were often entirely unsuitable for such extreme environments.[27] This was true of the conquistadors of Pedro de Alvares during their invasion and conquest of Peru in 1534, who as well as having to deal with jungle warfare and volcanic ash raining down on them, also watched their weapons and kit rust before their very eyes; finally, in the cordilleras of the High Andes, a considerable number of them, along with most of their horses, succumbed either to altitude sickness or avalanches.[28] French troops in Haiti in 1802 were exposed to the humid tropical climate without any raincoats, sun helmets, tents or shoes, having instead been issued with heavy woollen uniforms, a situation that was all too symptomatic of Western military planners' lack of foresight.[29] For many decades, the standard-issue woollen uniform of the US Army was too warm for operations in the South, and too cold for the North, before pith helmets and cotton clothing were introduced for the former conditions and fur outer garments and long-johns for the latter, in around 1880.[30] Despite this, American volunteers who fought in the Philippines War of 1899–1902 still found themselves wearing thick wool uniforms.[31] Likewise, during the United Kingdom's intervention in Egypt in 1882, the standard uniform jacket, wool trousers and flannel shirts of British soldiers proved less than ideal, and were responsible for many men collapsing and being hospitalized with heatstroke.[32]

Other pieces of equipment and supplies also frequently proved wholly inadequate for extreme climates. On campaigns by the British in Africa in the nineteenth century, canned meat went off in the intense

heat, and drinking water was often boiling hot because it was transported in metal tanks on camel-back.[33] In the Sahara, sand clogged up
the firing mechanisms of machine-guns.[34] Even in the late twentieth
century, the damp climate of Guinea-Bissau hampered the logistics of
its Portuguese colonial rulers through the constant breakdown of
engines and other machinery.[35] In the 2003 invasion of Iraq, where
according to reports by Americans engaged in the conflict the heat
defied description, tank engines broke down through a combination of
overheating and sand.[36]

Many of the sites of imperial wars were breeding grounds for tropical diseases. The West Indies was particularly notorious, where during
the Napoleonic Wars British and French soldiers alike dropped like
flies.[37] Some 70 per cent of French reinforcements on Haiti fell victim
to a yellow fever epidemic within just a few months in the summer of
1802.[38] Spanish units stationed in Venezuela at the start of the nineteenth century were almost completely wiped out by diseases, suffering losses of some 90 to 96 per cent. Even in the 1890s, during the
Cuban War of Independence 22 per cent of the Spanish troops sent to
the island (and almost as many of the Creole adversaries) died of infec-
tious diseases.[39] However, nowhere was disease so rampant as in West
Africa, where malaria, yellow fever and stomach bugs produced one of
the deadliest climates in the world for Europeans. Every year, even as
late as the nineteenth century, around 20 per cent of all Europeans
here died of tropical diseases, while at the height of yellow fever epidemics, this figure rose to 60 per cent and more: In Sierra Leone, for
instance, in 1825 and 1826, 86 and 73 per cent respectively of the
foreign troops deployed there died. In certain locations, and especially
on campaigns, the death rate could even reach 100 per cent. Until the
mid-nineteenth century, the mortality rate as a result of disease was
heightened further by the primitive state of medical knowledge. In any
event, for those suffering from malaria, who were already dying of
anaemia and dehydration, the customary treatments of copious blood-
letting and laxatives to purge the body proved fatal.[40] Even when tropical medicine had at its disposal quinine as a means of preventing
malaria and a better appreciation of the necessity of maintaining
hygiene, it still depended to a very great extent on how effectively such
measures were implemented on the ground. In the British Ashanti War

of 1873–1874 where meticulous healthcare measures were supposedly put in place,[41] while only fifty of the 2,500 European soldiers deployed died of tropical diseases,[42] over 1,000 became invalids.[43] And in the French campaign on the island of Madagascar more than two decades later, a third of the troops still died of malaria, typhus and diarrhoea, presumably because of a lack of hygiene and too low doses of quinine, the intake of which was not monitored at this time.[44]

Even in less extreme areas of deployment, climatic conditions and illness still accounted in many imperial wars for high losses among the European troops sent there.[45] In the nineteenth century, the garrisons of remote and cut-off forts in North America (but also in Australia) suffered a high rate of attrition from scurvy, a vitamin-deficiency condition caused by malnutrition, at a time when the normal diet for soldiers on the frontier consisted of salt beef and hardtack.[46]

Extreme climatic conditions and epidemics were fatal not only for soldiers but also for their riding and pack animals, on which frontier logistics were deeply reliant until the late nineteenth century. In 1525 Hernán Cortés, the conqueror of Mexico, lost eighty-six of his valuable horses while undertaking a particularly arduous crossing of a pass in the Maya Mountains.[47] In 1864, most of the horses and draught oxen accompanying the Sully Expedition against the Sioux died of dehydration while crossing the inhospitable Little Missouri Badlands; the situation was even worse since a plague of locusts had stripped the land of all vegetation.[48] In the course of two French campaigns in the Sahara in 1900–1901, 25,000 out of 35,000 camels deployed died, which on top of everything had disastrous knock-on effects for the local economy.[49] In 1839, during the first Anglo-Afghan War, the Indian camels the British brought with them died because they were unaccustomed to the mountain climate, and also unwittingly ate poisonous vegetation.[50]

Sometimes the effects of climate on armies that were dispatched to the peripheries of empire were so dramatic as to have a decisive effect on the outcome of wars. The first British expedition to Nepal in 1767, which unwisely set off just as the monsoon season was starting, lost two-thirds of its troops to malaria and as a result suffered a crushing defeat at the hands of the Gurkhas, who beat the British with relative ease.[51] A British punitive expedition against the Ashanti in 1864 suffered much the same fate; it, too, was so badly decimated in the rainy season by diarrhoea and fever that it beat a retreat without having set eyes on a single enemy—defeated by hostile Nature alone.[52] This was the undertaking that prompted the Ashanti king Kwaku Dua to make the memorable comment: 'The white man brings his cannon to the bush, but the bush is stronger than the cannon.'[53] Little wonder, then, that the opponents of imperialism sometimes factored the effects of climate and disease into their strategic calculations.[54]

In many campaigns on the fringes of empire, the terrain could pose just as great a problem as the climatic conditions. Only very infrequently did it resemble the open plains, gently rolling hills and river valleys of Europeans' motherlands, with their intensive farming and extensive transport network, where waging war in the European style was so straightforward. This dream scenario of every colonial military officer was at least occasionally fulfilled for British generals in their campaigns against the Maoris in New Zealand.[55] Otherwise, though, the settings for imperial wars were as a rule inaccessible and undeveloped.

On the periphery, armies would sometimes operate in high mountainous regions whose dramatic landscapes were nothing short of spectacular. This was certainly the case in the British expedition to Abyssinia (Ethiopia) in 1867–1868, which saw the storming of the mountain fortress of Magdala—an 'inaccessible eagles's eyrie' set on cliffs over 100 metres high on the edge of a mountain plateau that rose 3,000 metres above the plain.[56] The Northwest Frontier of India too was dominated by 'steep and precipitous hillsides, interspersed by a succession of knife-edge ridges, rugged spurs, cliffs, and precipices.'[57] Even in the twenty-first century, the nearby Afghan highlands were only accessible to the US invasion forces via steep goat tracks across escarpments hundreds of metres high.[58] In New Mexico, the Hopi and the Zuni peoples resisted Spanish conquest until the eighteenth century by withdrawing to the steep plateaus, the so-called 'Mesas'.[59] In the Modoc War of 1872–1873 in northern California a lava bed, which according to contemporary observers resembled an ocean wave frozen in stone, proved impregnable to the US Army, even though it was only lightly defended.[60] Elsewhere, too, indigenous defenders profited from impassable mountain terrain.[61]

If high mountains were one classic nightmare scenario for Western armies of conquest on the margins of empire, the other was jungle. In

Malaya it covered 80 per cent of the colony (which measured half the size of Italy); here, visibility was restricted to about 20 or 30 metres, and in secondary vegetation to practically nil, and marching speeds under battle conditions ranged from one kilometre per hour in relatively open forest to 200 metres an hour in dense undergrowth, which soldiers had to hack their way through using a machete.[62] Jungles were a feature of many other colonial wars, as in Southeast Asia, Africa and Brazil.[63] Until the beginning of the nineteenth century, impenetrable virgin forest also covered large parts of North America east of the Mississippi, a factor which was tactically decisive in such imperial catastrophes as the devastating defeat suffered by the British commander-in-chief in North America, General Edward Braddock, at the Battle of the Monongahela (also tellingly called the 'Battle of the Wilderness') in 1755.[64]

Another form of terrain that characterized imperial wars was the desert, which played a key role not just in North Africa[65] but also during the first British invasion of Afghanistan, where the lines of communication to India ran for long stretches through the desert[66] and of course also, as mentioned above, in the southwestern United States.[67] Although the desert was—leaving aside sandstorms—relatively open terrain that offered no real tactical advantage to defenders, its sheer inhospitability was nevertheless strategically a decisive defensive factor, as Douglas Porch notes: 'The Tuareg did not even have to adopt a scorched-earth policy; nature had done that for them.'[68]

One final characteristic terrain was swampland, from the wooded prairies of Canada, where it impeded the suppression of the Métis Republic during the Red River Rebellion of 1870,[69] and the southern states of the United States along the Atlantic seaboard, where such terrain sealed the fate of the British forces under General Charles Cornwallis during the American War of Independence,[70] through the extensive swamps of Java[71] and the coastal mangrove swamps of West Africa[72] to the often immense rainforests in the Amazon Basin.[73] In Haiti, mountains and marshy mangrove forest even occurred together, cut through by labyrinthine gorges.[74]

These difficult types of terrain were virtually unpopulated, and provided very little in the way of sustenance, in some cases even no drinking water, and few other resources besides. Of course, this did not just affect the European troops, but because they were unfamiliar with the landscape and were not acclimatized either, it hit them considerably harder, especially when they were organized into large armies that quickly exhausted local resources. Difficult terrain also impeded orientation. It favoured the defenders, particularly when they utilized the terrain defensively and avoided pitched battles in the open. Landscapes that to all intents and purposes had no paths or tracks seriously hampered armies organized along Western lines, which often travelled with heavy weapons and elaborate logistical support, in a variety of ways. This meant that only small forces could operate in such areas.

Vision was severely restricted in mountains, forests and swamps alike. The indigenous adversary could, especially thanks to his superior knowledge of the terrain, easily conceal himself and launch attacks from cover and close proximity at any time; this terrain was therefore made for ambushes. Tracks through such terrain, insofar as they existed at all, were invariably narrow, winding and strewn with obstacles, thus forcing imperial armies to form narrow, long columns, which could easily be halted and attacked from the flanks. Space was usually lacking to deploy for battle—not to mention sufficient time to do so in the event of a surprise attack.

In firefights, mountains, woods, and swamps not only provided cover for indigenous combatants, but, in the case of tactical victory, they also made pursuit more difficult.[75] In mountains non-European fighters could exploit their freedom from heavy equipment by opening fire on colonial forces from positions on higher ground.[76] During the Soviet intervention in Afghanistan from 1980 to 1988, the mountainous terrain prevented the effective deployment of main battle tanks, which could not elevate their gun barrels sufficiently to bombard the Mujahideen on the slopes above.[77] The only viable strategy in such instances was airstrikes, which were first used in the final phase of the French conquest of Morocco in 1926–1934.[78]

Difficult terrain also posed huge problems for horses.[79] In the case of Peru, existing roads across the Andes proved useless, since the Incas had neither horses nor wagons and therefore constructed winding staircases rather than roads in the Western sense.[80] For heavy weapons like artillery pieces[81] or armoured vehicles, rugged terrain was often virtually impassable.[82]

If indigenous fighters wanted to avoid engaging imperial forces entirely or to limit themselves to small-scale guerrilla warfare, difficult terrain was the ideal ground for such tactics,[83] for example the high-lands of Central Mexico in the sixteenth century,[84] the swamplands of Florida in the Seminole Wars[85] or the jungles of Burma where, according to reports by commanders of imperial forces, enemy fighters would just vanish into the undergrowth.[86] This was especially true if the area in question was extensive. This made searching for an adversary 'who was difficult to get hold of and who when you did manage to melted away in your fingers'[87] into the proverbial hunt for a needle in a hay-stack,[88] as Curt von François, the former commander of German imperial forces in South West Africa, explained: 'A small native tribe like this can vanish entirely within their home area. If one needs to fight or punish them, and yet they refuse to be found, this is one of the hard-est tasks facing an occupying force. In these depopulated regions, you can never determine with any certainty from which direction you should expect the enemy to attack you.'[89]

Likewise, in the later wars against the Indians in the American West, the enemy tended to make himself scarce and to rely on the hostile nature of the landscape and the vast expanses, so that 'merely by keep-ing out of the way, the Indians allowed the enemy to defeat himself.'[90]

Logistics and mobility

Leaving aside engagements with the enemy—which in any case were extremely rare—the difficult terrain and the huge distances to be tra-versed were primarily a logistical problem for the armies of empire. As a rule, they operated in thinly populated areas, where the indigenous populations engaged in subsistence farming at best. Very small columns of troops were sometimes able to sustain themselves through indiscrimi-nate plundering of local food resources, as the Spanish conquistadors had done in North America; without the maize fields cultivated by local Amerindian tribes the conquest of this region would have been impos-sible.[91] Sometimes the target locations of imperial invasions were so rich in natural resources that an army without any well-developed logistics could survive there, as with the American destruction of the Iroquois nation in 1779.[92] But overwhelmingly the forces of empire were reliant, when operating on the periphery, on being supplied from fixed bases—ports on the coast or forts in the interior.[93] Firearms required ammunition, which in most cases could not be obtained locally. Reliable transport routes and large wagon trains for carrying supplies were therefore indispensable for Western armies in imperial wars.

However, on the fringes of empire there was mostly no question of properly paved roads in the modern sense. The routes that were marked on maps were simply the customary footpaths from A to B. Consequently, such 'roads' were unsuitable for heavier traffic, and at the first downpour (if not before) turned into bottomless morasses.[94] In reality, therefore, supply columns and heavy weapons were burdens that reduced imperial expeditions to a snail's pace. The customary image of colonial wars may well be that of a well-armed and disciplined European force driving back non-European 'hordes' in battle with relative ease, as in the classic painting 'The Battle of Abu Klea' by William Barnes Wollen (1896). But battles were exceptional situations. It would be more historically accurate to visualize imperial war as an endless column of ox-drawn wagons moving across country at a walking pace through deep mud.

For example, the British invasion of Zululand in 1879 took place across an area at least the size of Wales, in which there were no roads or tracks of any kind—'the theatre of war was largely a vacuum as far as modern communications were concerned.'[95] Since drought conditions prevailed and the Zulus had driven their cattle herds away from the area, the force commanded by Lord Chelmsford could not live off the land, and before it launched the invasion of Zululand only had enough supplies for forty-five days of campaigning. Added to this was the elaborate equipment of a nineteenth-century army on the march: every battalion of the line carried nine tonnes of baggage with it, with the tents alone weighing four tonnes and the reserve ammunition two. Oxen are reliable and undemanding, but hugely slow and need to graze for several hours each day. As a result, the army laboured across the difficult terrain at the speed of the slowest ox-cart. The rivers and crevices that criss-crossed the plateau land here produced chaotic tail-backs of ox wagons. And because of the drought, hundreds of these draught animals perished during the course of the invasion.[96]

Enormous numbers of beasts of burden were required to get an army on the move in India in the eighteenth century. It took no fewer than six oxen to carry the baggage and horse-fodder for a single caval-ryman or officer. A light 6-pounder field gun required thirty-five draught oxen, while a 24-pounder siege cannon needed 155. In addi-tion, to haul the forage for the team pulling the smaller gun required the services of another 105 draught oxen, while for the latter it took no fewer than 620—and this in each case for just a single artillery piece.[97] The crux of logistics using muscle power is that feeding requirements cause numbers to multiply exponentially. Where an expedition had to be self-sufficient, the draught animals carried their own fodder first and foremost, and their load capacity therefore lim-ited the expedition's range and endurance—to a single month if each pack animal only transported its own food requirements, which negated the point of military logistics.[98] Their range and time in the field were of course even shorter if the animals actually carried military equipment as well.

The resulting baggage trains were correspondingly vast, especially in India, where 'processional warfare' in the style of the Indian principali-ties generated veritable migratory movements of servants, labourers and itinerant merchants, all travelling in the wake of an army. These people were all lumped together as 'camp followers', whose numbers could reach many times those of the fighting men—ratios of 6:1 or even 8:1 are cited in the records.[99] The British Army of the Indus, which set off in 1838 on the first invasion of Afghanistan, embarked with 9,500 fighting men and 6,000 Afghan allies. But the soldiers were practically immovable because they were accompanied by an immense baggage train of pack animals (30,000 camels alone) as well as animals for slaughter, plus some 38,000 civilians.[100] Baggage trains like this ensured that the army only advanced at a snail's pace.[101] The British Army in India also exported this system to other frontier regions of the empire. In 1867 Sir Robert Napier landed in Ethiopia with 3,000 horses, 16,000 mules and ponies, 8,000 camels, 5,000 oxen, 44 elephants, 2,000 Bengali labourers, and 14,500 'camp followers'. The train of his 5,000-man strong fighting column was 11 kilometres long.[102]

The logistical effort was very much the same during the Indian Wars in the US West, where, because of a perceived 'ethos of war' (opera-tional thinking in the US Army revolved around great power wars which was in stark contrast to its actual duties on the frontier), heavy thoroughbred cavalry horses were fed on grain.[103] A horse that habitually lives on grain dies if it grazes on prairie grass. As a result, in order to carry the required forage when advancing west, the cavalry needed large columns of ox-wagons, which in turn had to be guarded by infantrymen, with predictable consequences for the force's mobility (though in this instance at least the oxen could graze on grass).[104]

In the early conquest of Latin America by Spanish conquistadors, the place of ox-wagons was taken mostly by local porters.[105] The same was true of Southeast Asia[106] and the malarial regions of Africa,[107] where African porters likewise greatly expanded the columns, slowing them down massively, 'so much so that some expeditions took on the appearance of leisurely promenades.'[108] In this context, it should be mentioned that the social costs for the home regions of the bearers, who were almost always forcibly recruited and who were usually treated appallingly, were immense, given their mortality rate of 10–20 per cent in the dry season and up to 40 per cent in the rainy season. This was compounded by the fact that the imperial armies press-ganged tens of thousands of such bearers, and sometimes (such as in East Africa during the First World War) even hundreds of thousands.[109]

In general therefore, at least until the twentieth century, in terms of their operational mobility, imperial armies of the periphery were relatively static. They would labour through the broad, inhospitable landscape like some ponderous dragon. This was primarily due, as we have seen, to the great distances involved, when local resources were lacking, and to the dire state of transport routes. Yet—as should have become obvious by now—the imperial culture of violence was also to blame.

The highly intensive style of warfare adopted by the West in the modern period was conditioned by the quest to deliver a swift and decisive coup de grâce in a set-piece battle. In addition, it staked everything operationally on a concentration of superior resources in combat, and tactically on a combination of moral shock (embodied par excellence in the bayonet attack by a body of infantrymen in close formation, or in the massed assault by heavy cavalry with sabres drawn) and intensive firepower (epitomized by platoon fire by the regular infantry, artillery bombardments, and later in machine-gun salvos and air-dropped bombs).

Moreover, until far into the twentieth century this search for a decisive outcome by means of intensive set-piece battles also contributed to a high number of losses of one's own men in a relatively short time.[110] This situation has changed in the meantime; since around 1945, at least for the governments of Western democracies, the avoidance of casualties is placed increasingly in the foreground on grounds of legitimation.[111] Instead, a decisive outcome is sought in the even more intensive deployment of firepower.[112] The best example for both of these requirements was the Vietnam War,[113] but also anyone recalling the Kosovo War of 1999, which was largely conducted from the air, or the carpet-bombing carried out by B-52s of the US Air Force at the start of the war in Afghanistan in 2001[114] will appreciate the key role played by firepower in modern imperial wars.[115]

The Western method of waging war thus historically goes hand in hand primarily with high material expenditure and secondarily—and above all in earlier times (since with growing firepower, materials can supplant troop numbers)—with the concentration of comparatively large armies in a quest for a decisive victory. Under the conditions existing at the periphery of empire, this meant that these armies became virtually immobile under the weight of their sheer numbers, plus that of their equipment and baggage train. The paradoxical effect was that, in searching for a swift decisive outcome in battle, the style of imperial warfare became so cumbersome away from the battlefield that the chances of ever joining battle became really quite remote, unless the enemy actively sought to engage.

Indeed, to some extent that also held true on the battlefield itself. In tactical terms, the heavy infantryman deployed by the West and the heavy cavalryman on his massive warhorse were also comparatively immobile. To press forward stoically under heavy fire in order to win above all a moral victory by vanquishing an enemy who was holding his ground, required many qualities, not least ruthless discipline, but these did not include agility. Accordingly, Soviet infantrymen in Afghanistan in the 1980s still went into battle wearing, in addition to their uncomfortable uniforms and bulky boots, flak jackets weighing 16 kilograms and carrying large quantities of ammunition, not to mention support weapons like heavy machine-guns and grenade launchers, which even without their tripods and ammo each weighed as much as two full beer crates.[116] It should have been obvious that the only way of attacking the enemy in such a manner would have been with his cooperation.

On the fringes of empire, in expansive areas and in difficult terrain and confronted with a more mobile enemy who avoided battle, the Western culture of violence often proved logistically, operationally and tactically counterproductive. There were naturally attempts at reform and improvement. The birch-bark canoe, adopted from Indians, revolutionized the mobility and supply of early European forces in North America, a tactic exploited especially effectively by the French in Canada, where settlements and roads were few and far between, but where there was an abundance of waterways.[117] During the later Indian Wars in the USA George Crook reduced the kit carried by his troops to the bare necessities and loaded it on to mules, thus bringing a marked improvement to the mobility and cross-country capabilities of his columns.[118] In the 1880s, the French colonial army introduced single-axle mule carts which at the cost of a small reduction in mobility, increased the load that an individual mule could carry by a factor of three.[119] However, it is not immediately evident how the logistical effort would have been significantly reduced by such a form of mechanization. Even in 1895, during the French invasion of Madagascar, a logistical force of 5,000 light wagons, 6,000 mules and 7,300 drivers was assembled to serve a fighting force of just 18,000 men.[120]

Above all, countless attempts were made to increase the mobility of Western troops through organizational measures: these included dispensing with heavy weapons and unnecessary baggage and the formation of smaller, where possible mounted, units. This all had a certain effect, but also often entailed a diminution of the direct military efficacy of the force, and hence recanting on the Western ideal of how to wage war, a psychologically difficult proposition.[121] Primarily for that reason, such experiments were mostly confined to units that had been specially formed for colonial deployment, and were only regarded as a compensatory addition, as mere auxiliaries, necessitated by the nature of the conflict and the terrain, to the regular heavy troops who would truly decide the outcome of the war.[122] Nor did such experiments resolve the problem of the immense vastness of the space involved.

One important means of improving mobility and logistics was the construction of roads in the wilderness. In many cases imperial armies were forced to hack out roads through jungles, build bridges across rivers and swamps and in some cases even make mountains passable before they could engage with their military opponent.[123] Yet road-building was not only a logistical necessity. It can also be seen as a symbolic and practical conquest of an alien environment that was predisposed to favour the indigenous enemy. Roads were a way in which empires could even the odds against a hostile environment.

This did not necessarily mean paved roads in the modern sense; in dense virgin forest, a broad lane of cleared undergrowth was sufficient to overcome many of the tactical and logistical disadvantages of the terrain and the sheer expanse of space. Roads through the jungle were therefore harbingers of the ultimate overcoming of indigenous resistance, as had already occurred in the Yucatán Peninsula in Mexico, among other places, in the seventeenth century.[124] Road-building represented an important aspect of British war strategy on the northern frontier of New York State in the eighteenth century (although a contemporary observer enquired whether the jumble of felled trees that resulted from hacking a path through the forest did not in fact facilitate ambushes by Indians).[125] In the nineteenth century it opened up the rainforests of Brazil, enabling Portuguese colonists to conduct a war of subjugation against local Indian tribes,[126] and in the twentieth century it made both the northwest frontier of India and the mountainous regions of Algeria accessible to motor transport and heavy weaponry.[127] Military historian Bernd Lemke has remarked appositely that the building of highways in modern wars fought on the periphery not only serves the purpose of winning the hearts and minds of the populace on the ground but also has the very practical ends of opening up the terrain in question and projecting power.[128] Following their conquest by Great Britain in 1901–1902, the Ibo of southeastern Nigeria were immediately forced to cut paths through the jungle 'in order to make the task of any future pacification forces easier.'[129]

Roads could even decide the outcome of wars: in 1831, harassing attacks in the jungle by the minor state of Naning, near Malacca in Malaya, so demoralized a British invasion force of 150 men that they disabled their own cannon and took flight. The following year, a 35-kilometre long and 200-metre wide 'road' was constructed through the jungle (its breadth indicates that this, too, comprised a cleared path hacked through the forest), and Naning duly fell.[130]

Occasionally action to overcome the challenges of the landscape went beyond road-building (which itself had already wrought considerable changes in cultural geography). Both in the Russian conquest of the Caucasus[131] and in the suppression of the Mau-Mau uprising in Kenya in 1952–1960[132] (as well as in an obscure case on the British Andaman Islands),[133] entire forests were clear-felled in order to deny the enemy any places of refuge. In the late twentieth century, chemical defoliation from the air achieved the same result at considerably less cost. The British thought about using this tactic against the insurgency in Malaya,[134] and it was notoriously enacted on a large scale in Vietnam (in conjunction with mechanical modes of forest clearance)[135] and, arguably less famously, by the French in Algeria, where some 70 per cent of the woods were said to have been destroyed.[136] Unlike in Callwell's account, the campaign against nature in such instances was construed as an active one. In the final analysis, enemy territory on the frontiers of empire ceased to be hostile if—in so far as this was possible—it was opened up to Western settlement and intensive farming, which automatically brought with them roads and other infrastructure improvements.[137]

Subsequently, the advent of the railway[138] facilitated logistics in the-atres of military operations on the margins of empire,[139] if only in the immediate environs of settled regions. In the war against the Herero and the Nama in German South West Africa in 1904–1907, operations away from the railway lines were still dependent on ox-wagons.[140] In this conflict, 4,000 troops with forty field guns needed thousands of local labourers and bearers and 20,000 pack animals.[141] At the end of the nineteenth century, the British Army excelled in field railway con-struction to support its military campaigns, especially in Africa;[142] this same strategy was subsequently employed by the Mexican Army in winning its war of conquest against the Maya in the Yucatán, where railway building enabled movement through the dense jungles in the same way that roads had done previously.[143]

In the later years of its conquest of the American West, the US Army relied upon steamships, which nevertheless had the disadvantage of tying logistics to navigable rivers and was not always necessarily faster.[144] In sub-Saharan Africa at around the same time, steamships became the most effective way of logistically penetrating the hinter-land.[145] Motor vehicles appeared at the beginning of the twentieth century, but their initial use was often compromised by their inability to negotiate difficult terrain and the lack of roads, or at least of prop-erly surfaced ones, on the periphery.[146] Even in Portugal's wars of decolonization in Angola and Mozambique in the 1970s, dirt roads presented a logistical headache even when they were not mined by local insurgents. In consequence, lorry convoys only managed an average of 20 kilometres a day.[147] This negated the advantage of motor vehicles, with the result that the 15 kilometres a day averaged by ox-wagons[148] or even the 10 kilometres a day achieved by Braddock's column as it hacked its way through the virgin forest to Fort Duquesne in 1755, do not look all that bad in comparison.[149]

The logistics and mobility of imperial armies in trackless wilderness on the periphery was only really revolutionized by the arrival of tactical air support in the second half of the twentieth century. The French had 400 helicopters in Algeria[150] and the Soviet Union set great store by airborne mobility in the mountains of Afghanistan.[151] However, this mode of transport remained too maintenance-intensive, scarce and expensive to be of much use on a day-to-day basis.[152] In each case, large bodies of soldiers cannot be supplied effectively from the air over a lengthy period, particularly if air superiority is not achieved, as shown conclusively by the defeat of the French by the Viet Minh at the siege of Dien Bien Phu in 1954.[153] At least the French troops manning remote and isolated outposts on the northern border of Morocco in the Rif War during the searingly hot summer of 1925 were able to receive vital supplies of drinking water in a novel way, with planes of the French Air Force airdropping blocks of ice to them.[154]

Yet all this technological innovation could do little to alter the sheer vastness of the space. The 900 kilometre journey from the port of St. Louis on the coast of Senegal to the main French supply base at Kayes on the Senegal River (now in Mali) was still the same distance by steamship. And the fact remained that the Senegal River was only navigable for a brief period at the end of the rainy season, and even then not every year. And Kayes only represented the beginning of the immense theatre of operations in western Sudan. From there, to penetrate further into the interior required taking columns of ox-wagons, though at least a railway had been built by 1887.[155]

The enemies of empire

Alongside spatial considerations, the forces that were brought to bear by either side also naturally determined the character of warfare conducted on the periphery. Let us therefore briefly consider the ways in which the warring parties organized themselves politically and militarily and mobilized the resources at their disposal.

> Let us take a brief look at history. The semibarbarous Tartars, the republics of antiquity, the feudal lords and trading cities of the Middle Ages, eighteenth-century kings and the rulers and peoples of the nineteenth century—all conducted war in their own particular way, using different methods and pursuing different aims.[156]

This assessment by the Prussian military theoretician Carl von Clausewitz of the relatively clear situation of Europe's Old World naturally applies in spades to the opponents of imperial encroachment in conflicts on all the other four continents. The mobilization of resources for war, the organization of military forces, the ability of societies to endure drawn-out conflicts, and not least the way in which war was waged—all these factors depend in large measure on the extent to which the actors involved constitute a state.[157] From the great empires of the Old and New World down to the numerous stateless societies on the fringes of their respective regional systems, the range of degrees of political organization is enormous. And the various ways in which the societies in question were constituted each entailed specific weaknesses and strengths when they came into conflict with the expansionist empires of the West.

For the purposes of this discussion, the opponents of empire may be divided into four broad categories:

1. Indigenous major empires and military monarchies;
2. Other monarchies and principalities of all kinds;
3. Stateless adversaries;
4. Modern (proto-) states;

The latter having in part evolved from secondary resistance movements, as an unintended consequence of imperial rule.

Of the major empires outside of Europe, four formed a special group, namely the Ottoman Empire, the Mughal Empire, China and Japan. They were so powerful that, generally speaking, every military confrontation with a Western empire took place on equal terms, a fact that threatens to violate the concept of an imperial war. Yet three of these four empires can in any case be ruled out of consideration as adversaries of empire: the Ottoman Empire because its direct military clashes with the West did not occur at the periphery but were fought as classic major-power conflicts in Early Modern Europe; the Mughal Empire because it was not a naval power and because it collapsed before European empires expanded on the mainland of the Indian subcontinent; and Japan because it had become for all practical purposes a Western-style empire itself before it first waged war with a Western empire (namely Russia, in 1904–1905). Japan should therefore rather be construed as an imperial actor rather than an indigenous opponent of empires.[158] As such, then, China remains the sole indigenous empire in a class of its own for the purposes of this investigation: an empire that was admittedly so powerful and populous that its ultimate subjugation by expansionist Western empires had to be ruled out de facto,[159] but which nevertheless was most definitely also the target of imperial violence, in the Opium Wars and during the Boxer Rebellion,[160] and which became the victim of the 'most gigantic of all colonial wars'[161] at the hands of Japan in the mid-twentieth century.

Yet even leaving aside the special case of China, the classic opponents of empires on the periphery also included some thoroughly impressive indigenous empires which in many cases exhibited high degrees of cohesion as a state. The Aztec and Inca empires were not only the virtually unchallenged supreme powers within their respective cultural spheres, but also highly centralized bureaucratic states with professional armies.[162] Furthermore, there were several other monarchies of this kind in Mesoamerica, notably the pronouncedly hierarchical Itza Empire of the Maya, which survived in a remote corner of the Yucatán Peninsula until the final years of the seventeenth century.[163]

Most significantly in this regard, in Africa north of the Sahara, Western imperial expansion in the nineteenth century encountered a series of aggressive jihad states, of whom Sydney Kanya-Forstner has written:

> Muslim polities, with their written languages, their heritage of state-making and the cohesive force of a universal religion preaching the brotherhood of all believers, could generally organize resistance on a wider scale than political units whose extent was limited by the ties of common ancestry. Muslims also had a strong incentive to oppose the advance of Christian power.[164]

What is not mentioned here is that religion frequently only provided the catalyst for what was in essence a social revolutionary impulse toward state formation, hence the decidedly aggressive impetus that characterized such movements, at least in their early formative years. These jihad states were expansionist military powers which in some cases brought vast regions under their control within the space of just a few years, and at the expense of politically less tightly organized opponents. In the West, one of the most well-known empires of this kind was that of the Mahdi in Sudan.[165] Yet the core region of this conception of statehood was in West Africa, where the Tukulor Empire in Mali, the Sokoto Caliphate in Nigeria and the Wassoulou Empire in Guinea (built around the dominant figure of the cleric Samori Touré) represented the archetypal jihad states.[166] They were organized around the army, and their raison d'être was military expansion—one principal reason why, as soon as the initial wave of conquest began to give way to a phase of the ruling elite seeking to consolidate its hold on power, their decline set in.[167]

Even without the impulse of Islam and social revolution, however, a number of pronouncedly military monarchies existed in both Africa and Asia, in which the king exercised a strongly centralized form of rule, holding the state together through his control over military assets and stabilizing his position through foreign expansion. In part, these states were straightforward dictatorships that were geared toward modernization, and which achieved an extraordinary degree of assimilation in the military realm. The fiercest opponents of European encroachment in India belonged in this category: the Marathas, Mysore under Haidar Ali, and the Sikhs.[168] There were similar military monarchies in Southeast Asia: Burma, Aceh and Mataram.[169] On the Guinea coast, Ashanti and Dahomey were examples of expansionist states of an older style, focused on the military, which as major regional powers could sometimes call upon gigantic mass armies but which did not attempt to keep pace with the West by implementing deliberate modernization programmes.[170] Finally, the military states of the Bantu-speaking peoples, which had developed from tribal groupings and which at the time when they first came into conflict with the West were mostly still quite new, were nonetheless very highly centralized. This category included the Zulu kingdom,[171] with its extremely mobile, cohesive and motivated regiments of Impi warriors organized into age-group cohorts (intanga), which were responsible for inflicting one of the heaviest defeats ever suffered by a British imperial force, at the Battle of Isandlwana in 1879. Other such polities were the kingdoms of the Nguni (in the hinterland of the Portuguese colony of Mozambique) and of the Hehe (in the interior of German East Africa), which were likewise organized according to the model of a military monarchy deriving from a tribal confederation, typical of southeast Africa.[172]

Given that major empires and military monarchies were, so to speak, the elite forms of indigenous statehood, the second category of adversaries of Western imperialism need not detain us for long. Large parts of the world beyond Europe were of course organized in some shape or form as states, and in general as kingdoms, principalities, feudal or aristocratic states and so forth, though these lacked either the cohesion of the major empires or the expansionist drive of jihad states and other military monarchies.[173] This did not necessarily mean that these states were unwarlike per se: sometimes, they were simply caught up in heavily fragmented regional power structures, in which no state was capable unequivocally of gaining the upper hand. This was true, for instance, of the decidedly militaristic states of Java in the Early Modern period.[174]

A similar position of average state cohesion and power is occupied by the piracy and trading empires which characterized, say, the east coast of Africa towards the end of the nineteenth century. Most of these were based exclusively on the slave trade, though others managed to sustain economic activity even after the abolition of slavery by trading instead in rare commodities such as palm oil.[175] However, because they did not have a tradition or conception of statehood that went beyond the simple mercantile motive of economic profit, such polities were lacking any stabilizing elements that might have enabled them to wage war long-term. One exception to this general rule was the Arab slave-trade empire in the eastern Congo, which was not only based on a flourishing farming economy but could also allegedly field an army of 100,000 men.[176] In one of the bloodiest imperial conflicts of all time, in the period 1891–1893 this empire was crushed by Belgian colonial troops.

The overwhelming majority of violent conflicts on the periphery were waged by imperial forces against indigenous groups whose levels of political organization were well below those of a state. These could range from societies of hunters and gatherers simply organized into family groups in areas of extremely low population density such as the Amazon Basin, Australia, Siberia, or the Pacific Coast of the USA[177] to larger groupings, which in some instances coalesced into fully hierarchical structures within permanent clan and alliance systems.[178] The details are the business of ethnologists, and it is of no consequence to us whether these more pronounced and durable social structures should be called 'tribes'.[179] What is of interest here is that this more rigid sociopolitical organization of societies that were actually stateless was often a reaction to contact with expansionist empires: anyone who is threatened needs to band together, and anyone who wishes to negotiate with a strong adversary requires a political organization.[180] It was not uncommon for stateless societies to be nomadic, such as the steppe peoples of Central Asia or the Tuareg of the Sahara.[181]

A special form of non-state (or in this case, perhaps more accurately sub-state) opposition was (and is) the secondary resistance movement against already well-established foreign rule, notably when this goes beyond isolated actions by autonomous local groups and mobilizes a supraregional and transethnic clientele. Up to the beginning of the twentieth century, such large-scale revolutionary movements mostly had a religious background and often went hand-in-hand with nativist and millenarian revivalist movements, which promised a return to an idyllic and blissful past before the advent of the white man: prime examples are the Pueblo Revolt in New Mexico in the late seventeenth century,[182] the prophetic movement among the North American Indians of the Eastern Woodlands, led by Tecumseh and Tenskwatawa at the beginning of the nineteenth century[183] and the Ndebele uprising of 1896 in the area that is now Zimbabwe.[184] Almost invariably, an important element of such collective movements was that their adherents were supposed to make themselves immune to the superior weaponry of the West through rituals—from the 'Cult of the Talking Cross' among the Maya in the mid-nineteenth century[185] through the 'ghost shirts' worn by the Sioux during their last stand against white domination in the 1890s[186] to the water cult of the Maji-Maji uprising in East Africa in 1905–1907.[187] The Mau-Mau rebellion of 1952–1960 in Kenya was a more recent example of a largely ethnically based movement that similarly sought to restore a pre-colonial past.[188] The effectiveness of groupings of this type was mostly short-lived, however, due to the fact that their promises of salvation quickly came to nothing and their supporters were often pursuing quite divergent aims.[189]

Clearly different in their structure are the modern political and proto-nationalist revolutionary movements, which from roughly the middle of the twentieth century onwards began in many cases to massively increase the costs of colonial occupation for the empires concerned.[190] An early example of this kind of indigenous movement, which set its objective not in a return to pre-modern dream worlds but rather in the overthrow of foreign rule using the methods of western modernity itself, is the Philippine Republic, which was suppressed by military force in 1899–1900 by the United States.[191] Modern resistance movements, archetypically epitomized in the national liberation fronts established in Indochina[192] and Algeria,[193] have also always been geared towards gaining the attention, and where possible the support, of public opinion around the world. Attainment of this goal was facilitated in 1919, when the principle of the self-determination of all peoples was first established,[194] and received a massive boost in 1945 by the general delegitimizing of colonial rule, the confrontation between the Western and Eastern blocs in the Cold War and the creation of the new forum of the United Nations:[195] international factors which—together with changing public opinion back in the mother nations of empire, where enthusiasm switched from colonies to consumer goods[196]—were ultimately far more relevant for the success of such independence movements than their political organization or military effectiveness.[197] The creation of a parallel statehood for the majority population under colonial domination was therefore not just a way of waging a (people's) war,[198] but also an important instrument in establishing a legitimacy to rule: in other words, a war of decolonization as a war of state formation, to borrow a paradigm of the Early Modern period.[199] At some stage, this search for legitimation also always entailed the transition to a conventional method of waging war with a demonstrative observance of the Western rules of engagement, thus establishing the resistance movement as a combatant of equal standing.[200]

At the latest from this point on, even sub-state violent protagonists, who began their operations within terror-cell structures, are in a state of modern (proto-) statehood and are hence in transition into the fourth of our categories of adversaries of imperialism. Alongside modern resistance movements, temporarily successful secessionist movements like the Yaqui Republic set up in the Mexican state of Sonora in 1875–1887,[201] or the Republic of the Rif under Abd-el Krim in Spanish Morocco in the 1920s,[202] may also form part of this hybrid group. These were proto-states whose national and international legitimacy was generally speaking of a lower order, though conversely they were much closer to actual statehood through their exclusive control over the territory they occupied.

Genuinely independent states in their modern configuration seldom formed the opposition to empires in anti-imperial wars, and when they did, the resulting conflict was in many regards almost symmetrical and hence a decidedly borderline case. The prime instances we might cite here are the internationally recognized centralized state of Ethiopia, which was heavily supplied with Western arms and which after its victory over Italy in 1896 remained independent as the only autochthonous African state until 1936,[203] and the South African republics governed by Boers of European extraction,[204] or post-1945 the exceptional situation of North Vietnamese participation in the civil war in South Vietnam, as well as Iraq during the two conventional wars of 1991 and 2003. The independence movement of the British Colonies in North America, however—another borderline case—should instead be assigned to the hybrid group of sub-state violent protagonists with a demonstrative search for legitimacy through parallel statehood.[205]

What role did statehood now play in the capacity of indigenous groups to resist imperialism? At first sight one might be tempted to say that states provide stability and legitimacy. They accumulate and organize human and material resources. They form professional administrative and military apparatuses. Statehood must therefore have hugely strengthened the resistance of non-European societies. In some cases, all this was undoubtedly the case; it was particularly true of instances where the indigenous building of a state had an additional identity-forming impetus, as with the jihad states, or where the accumulation of resources was transposed directly into military power by a modernizing dictatorship. But ultimately all that this route to statehood achieved was to enable an indigenous state to enter into a symmetrical conflict with the Western empires. And in the process it transpired that stability, legitimacy, mobilization of resources, bureaucracy and a professional military were only advantageous relative to the indigenous setting of such states: as a rule, the West remained clearly superior in all these realms.

The internal legitimacy of indigenous statehood (the external legitimacy was in any case only situationally acceptable at best to the empires) was often dependent upon military success. Indigenous states were often young, weak and decentralized; the largest of them were actually small empires in their own right, which as a result of conquest or alliances ruled over ethnically heterogeneous populations. In the case of a military defeat, which in itself need not have been decisive to the outcome of the war, these states would often collapse from within, because the ruling clan or the leading ethnicity had lost the aura of power and local groups found it expedient to make common cause with the prospective new principal power.[206] In the final analysis, the indigenous state was often a paper tiger, at least in comparison with the stable state tradition of the core states of the Western empires.[207]

For some indigenous societies that were strongly hierarchical, a well-developed state structure when in conflict with empires actually became an Achilles heel. The almost incredible model of the near total takeover of a complex state by taking its ruler hostage, a strategy that was improvised by Hernán Cortés in Mexico and perfected by Francisco Pizarro in Peru, could only work in a centralized state in which the ruler was deified and his word was absolute law. In full knowledge that their rulers no longer had any power of decision-making, the bureaucracy of these Amerindian empires continued to function uncomplainingly and so surrendered the states to the conquistadors—the perfect collaborationist regime.[208]

Not least as a result of this experience, for many centuries thereafter empires preferred states as their adversaries. A state was an identifiable entity. It had a rulership structure, a responsible leadership with which one could negotiate, upon which one could exert pressure and in the worst-case scenario even replace through a direct intervention. However, the ideal outcome was to seize the state intact—preferably through indirect rule, since that was a much cheaper option. A state had cities, fortresses and places of worship, whose occupation deprived it of its administrative, economic, military and legitimizing foundations. A state had an army that was recognizable as such, and against which one could engage in decisive set-piece battles.[209] And for the most part, such states were not sufficiently coherent and stable that empires would not be able to find within them allies who could be recruited for the empires' own purposes.

The ideal state to have as an adversary was therefore weak enough to be malleable, but on the other hand just stable enough to have the capacity to continue functioning even after a defeat. This would make the empire's victory complete and keep the follow-up costs down. Unsurprisingly, the real situation often looked quite different—the indigenous state turned out to be something of a chimera. It habitually collapsed, leaving behind a patchwork of quarrelling local groups, whose pacification after the unexpectedly rapid victory over the state was often protracted and arduous. This was one reason why the two-phase imperial war—first a war against a state, then a guerrilla war on a sub-state level—became such a standard model for indigenous resistance against imperialism (the other reason for a two-phase war, in cases where the state did not collapse, was a period of assimilation of the opponent's tactics after an initial phase of conventional warfare).[210] If the indigenous state was incapable of continuing the fight in this way under its own steam—as happened in the case of the Rif Republic, whose ethnic fragmentation in combination with the difficult terrain there would have suggested such an outcome—then it had clearly taken the process of statehood too far.[211]

In the long run, for indigenous societies that found themselves in violent conflict with empires, traditional statehood proved to be at least as much a weakness as a strength. On the other hand, from the point of view of empires, non-state opponents, especially nomads, seemed something very akin to terrorist cells. They had no supra-local political structure, no professional army, no government resources of a local nature and no complex economic systems; accordingly, it was very hard to bring pressure to bear on them or to conquer them.[212] Moreover, they frequently settled in inaccessible terrain on the periphery of the periphery: in dense forests, mountains, swamps, and deserts—in short in places where a lack of resources and transport routes made more sophisticated social organization and formal warfare in the Western style both unnecessary and impractical. For empires conquering a non-state adversary was a nightmare.[213] The only positive thing was that fragmentation into the smallest possible groups theoretically made it easier for empires to 'divide and rule' and to find allies—but in practice non-state groups often had so little to lose that they also had nothing to gain from an alliance.[214]

It has therefore been very appositely noted that it was often stateless societies who offered the most sustained resistance to conquest.[215] However, this was not always first and foremost a result of their intrinsic capacity to mount an effective defence. Sometimes, it was simply that the conquest of marginal regions lacking in any firm state structures was of low priority to empires.[216] The Aztecs were subjugated at the start of the sixteenth century, whereas the Apaches, who occupied the margins of basically the same cultural region, held out until the late nineteenth century, and this undoubtedly had to do with the fact that Central America contained fertile land and gold in abundance, while the Apaches inhabited an area of arid mountain valleys that were home to impoverished cattle rustlers.[217]

Autochthonous statehood that was weak or totally absent also had one other consequence: there was often no clear functional distinction between legitimate combatants and non-combatants. The implications of this for the rules of engagement within colonial wars are obvious and will form the subject of a later chapter.[218] Here it is important to note that in the absence of an official armed group on the opposing side, empires were ultimately confronted with a situation that in nineteenth-century Europe was commonly described as a 'people's war,'[219] as Hew Strachan has explained:

> Many opponents outside Europe were not soldiers, but warriors. They fought not as professionals separate from their parent societies, but as the representatives of those societies. [...] Moreover, many tribal communities were shaped and adapted primarily to meet the needs of war. When Europeans fought against them, they engaged not just armies but whole societies.[220]

This proved a decisive difference for the prospects of ending a war victoriously, since a state has responsible organs and can capitulate—and does so not infrequently—whereas an entire people cannot. Thus, to bring about a lasting peace, it has to be either subdued militarily—something only possible with sufficient manpower—or otherwise brought under control. I will discuss the problems arising from this at a later juncture.

The notion of a people's war begs the question what conception of violence and warfare the indigenous opponents of empires had, what importance was attached to force of arms in their worldviews, and how it was hedged around and defined. One immediate problem is that it is virtually impossible to generalize here. Of course, the culture of violence in major empires with professional armies such as Mexico and Peru has little in common with a stateless Amerindian group of fifty people—and yet both co-existed within the same cultural region and with only a marginal distance, in global terms, between them. All the same, certain patterns can be identified. These basically fall into the category of what Jürg Helbling has described as 'tribal warfare'[221] (some decades earlier Harry Turney-High referred in less politically correct terms to 'primitive warfare').[222]

In their observation of indigenous societies, Western observers were frequently struck by the apparent omnipresence of violence, whose forms far exceeded the measure of brutality that was still seen as acceptable in Europe, at least from the Early Modern period on. Torture, mutilation of the living, desecration of corpses, cannibalism, the slaughter of women and children—such violent practices among North American Indians, for example, horrified Europeans[223] and led them to wrongly conclude that wholly random violence had free rein in non-European societies,[224] a view that is still widespread today, at least in the popular imagination.[225]

It is certainly true that in many indigenous societies the use of weapons was an integral part of daily life. A sphere of warfare that was neatly separated from day-to-day civilian life, as in the modern Western world, was an alien concept in large parts of the world, where war was a permanent state of existence.[226] For the North American Indians of the Eastern Woodlands, violence against people and violence against animals had the same moral status, and war was a part of life just like hunting.[227] 'Tribal warfare' was invariably directed at the adversary's society in its entirety,[228] and its default objective was the total conquest of that society, albeit not through mass slaughter, but rather through absorption.[229]

Yet what most observers failed to recognize were the cultural limitations on this use of violence precisely because of its integration into daily life. Given that conflict was more or less a permanent state, it had to be demographically manageable. If stateless groups, each with only a small population, had slaughtered one another indiscriminately on a running basis, the world outside of Europe would have been depopulated long before the arrival of the first European imperialists.

Indigenous warfare was therefore generally subject to strict, often religiously codified rules, which were aimed above all at minimizing losses.[230] This did not necessarily mean that it was taboo to inflict relatively severe population losses on an adversary, but that occurred mainly when the possibility of retribution could be ruled out: hence the preference among indigenous fighters for night-time attacks or ambushes, in other words for situations in which their own losses could be kept to a minimum while those of the opponent stood a good chance of being maximized.[231]

Full-scale battles, as favoured by the Western culture of warfare, did not meet these requirements. Thus, when indigenous armies met one another on the battlefield, they tended either to engage in ritual show-piece combat[232] or to stage shows of strength as a kind of armed diplomacy, in which a demonstration of superior troop numbers or of impressive weaponry was designed to persuade an adversary to negotiate; this was the preferred military strategy of American Indians until well into the eighteenth century.[233] It rarely, however, came to a pitched battle, with the likelihood of high and potentially even comparable losses—this was a concept that would have struck most indigenous societies, with few exceptions, as completely absurd and positively suicidal.[234] This key requirement of avoiding losses at all costs also ultimately applied—albeit undoubtedly in a watered-down form—to most of the major empires and military monarchies that found themselves among the indigenous opponents of Western imperialism, despite the fact that—mainly in order to legitimate their authority—the general preference in their cultures of violence was for open warfare. This was true of the Aztecs, for instance, whose tactics were aimed, wherever possible, at outflanking and surrounding the enemy.[235]

This form of battle was at most only marginally concerned with the kind of frontal assaults and mass carnage that characterized the great set-piece engagements of Early Modern Europe: for instance, in the same decade as the conquest of Mexico, the combined forces of Spain and the Papal States suffered 65 per cent losses at the Battle of Ravenna in 1512, while the Swiss lost 50 per cent of their men at the Battle of Marignano in 1515.[236] Among indigenous groups, by contrast, the exceptions to the general imperative of avoiding losses are few and far between. The example that comes most readily to mind is the Zulu, who were prepared to incur heavy losses on the battlefield in order to vanquish their enemies,[237] but even their enthusiasm in battle was eclipsed by the stoical advance into certain death by line infantry, a standard tactic of European armies in the eighteenth and nineteenth centuries.[238] Similarly, in recent times and with reference to indigenous sources,[239] scholars have disputed the traditional view that battles in Southeast Asia during the Early Modern period passed off with relatively light losses, in the manner of 'tribal wars'.[240] This may, then, be another exception to the general rule; in all probability, there are also others. At least historically, the playing down of the degree of violence in battle in 'tribal' wars was the result of a body of source material that took the highly intensive battle-based warfare in the European style as its yardstick and ridiculed the notion of avoiding losses in conflict. A typical example of such an attitude was the New England commentator on indigenous warfare during the seventeenth century, Captain John Underhill, who contemptuously claimed that the Pequot and Narragansett Indians regarded battles as 'more for pastime than to conquer and subdue enemies', and added the jibe: 'they may fight seven years and not kill seven men.'[241]

Notwithstanding this, it is clear that the indigenous adversaries of empires—especially (though not exclusively) non-state opponents[242]—in the main avoided engaging in battle wherever possible rather than incur heavy losses, and instead relied upon concealment, ambushes and surprise attacks, on ruses such as feigned retreats, and on surrounding and 'cutting off' the enemy.[243] Since they were already using such tactics in wars within their own cultural sphere, it made perfect sense to employ them against the often better armed and trained imperial armies they encountered. Like the Turkmens, who when confronted with the Russian army galloped off on their light horses like 'a flock of wild geese',[244] many non-European opponents chose to avoid an unequal fight, and switched their tactics to ambush attacks,[245] and what is more long before the classic era of guerrilla warfare[246] epitomized by the Boers in South Africa,[247] resistance fighters in the Philippines (1899–1902)[248] and the Rif Republic in the 1920s,[249] the wars of decolonization,[250] or the peripheral conflicts of recent times.[251] In his classic documentary account, *Son of the Morning Star*, Evan Connell described the similar experience of US General George A. Custer, tragic hero of the defeat at the Battle of Little Bighorn in 1876, when pursuing Indians:

> Hostile redskins proved difficult to find, much less engage, because they would not stand up and fight [...]. They did what they often did when harassed: like an amoeba each band would divide, divide, and divide again, and again, and once again, leaving a less and less distinct trail, with the result that [Custer's] blue-jacketed cavaliers never could catch anybody to punish.[252]

This entirely understandable and pragmatic attitude was what the military forces of imperialism liked to portray as unfair and treacherous,[253] a view that still resonates in the mildly dismissive remark of Walter Laqueur, one of the most influential scholars of guerrilla warfare: 'Generally speaking, primitive peoples had an aversion to open fighting.'[254]

Furthermore, indigenous warfare was often drawn-out in a way that was utterly incomprehensible to Western military strategists. Their strategy was not to aim for a swift victory but for a certain outcome that entailed no great risk. This involved waiting patiently over a protracted period;[255] spells of war and peace would casually alternate,[256] frequently over decades,[257] and indeed were often barely distinguishable from one another.[258] This strategy was viable without any great logistical effort, and in actual fact had to be, because weak state organization and large tracts of land mostly lacking in intensive agriculture permitted the concentration of large unwieldy armies only in exceptional cases and for a short duration.[259]

Accordingly, indigenous modes of fighting were ultimately geared towards a high degree of mobility,[260] which in the absence of complex logistics was not only possible but also vital for the loss-avoiding style of warfare practised by most societies: anyone who plans to avoid a fight, to pre-empt his opponent and lay an ambush, and surround or surprise the enemy, needs above all to be quick on his feet. Indigenous warriors were precisely that. They travelled with light packs, lived off the land—usually by plundering[261]—and were extremely mobile and often mounted. They comprised both light infantry and light cavalry. As a result, their war was fought not in closed, tightly-packed formations, but classically in very loosely organized units.[262] Not least, this served to frustrate a weapon that the West deployed in the hope of gaining decisive superiority, namely artillery.[263] Non-European warriors were stereotypically portrayed as fleet-footed Woodland Indians or mountain dwellers, as nomads from the Central Asian steppes who could span their bows and shoot arrows while riding at full tilt, or as highly mobile horsemen of the Sahara, the great central plains of India or the American West, and as with all clichés much of this was certainly true.[264] Even the Zulu, who fought on foot in close formation, were still lightly equipped and in both operational and tactical terms highly mobile.[265]

Of course, examples can also be found to demonstrate the opposite. Aztec armies advanced at a snail's pace, despite a well-developed road network.[266] Likewise, the mass armies of the Indian princely states,[267] the Southeast Asian kingdoms,[268] and various other Muslim empires such as Morocco[269] were clearly lacking in operational mobility (though there were some remarkable exceptions to this)[270] yet on the battlefield even they proved light and nimble compared to the regular European forces opposing them. Even in the case of the heavy infantry that formed the core of the African armies of the Early Modern period in the Congo region, their lack of equipment strongly suggests that they—again in comparison with their European foes—were relatively agile.[271] In contrast, by all accounts, the army of the Incas had excellent operational mobility precisely because of well-developed logistical support, in the form of storehouses full of provisions and military materiel that were located throughout the empire.[272]

There were certain regressive developments. The more non-European armies began to conform to the European style of warfare from the eighteenth century on, and to adopt its forms of military organization, weapons and equipment, the more cumbersome their own logistics necessarily became, and the more their mobility declined.[273] As ever, the rise of symmetrical warfare was accompanied by a loss of significance of the characteristics that typified imperial wars. However, this development was often only a trend, since the assimilation was rarely total; instead, the Western elements tended to form a synthesis with the indigenous ones. For example, even in the symmetrical final phase of the war in Indochina, the operational mobility of the Viet Minh was still considerably greater than that of the French forces: this was one important cause of the French defeat at Dien Bien Phu.[274]

Yet despite the fact that the opponents of imperialism were often both operationally and tactically at an advantage thanks to their straightforward logistics and their uncomplicated mobility across the terrain, many of them were nevertheless lacking in strategic staying power. Relatively small societies that were not based on intensive agriculture and which were politically unstable or disorganized were seldom able to mobilize resources for warfare on a large scale and for the long haul. In particular, the subsistence farming that was prevalent across large parts of the non-European world was incapable of producing large food surpluses or of sparing a significant proportion of the male populace to take part in protracted campaigns.[275] Precisely in these areas, the core states of the Western empires were far superior, and had been so since long before industrialization.

The power of empires

The capitalist centralized state of the modern era in the West is a highly efficient bureaucratic machine for mobilizing resources, whose key objective is to project political, economic and military power. Until far into the nineteenth century the mobilization of people, military materiel and finances for war was virtually the sole justification for the existence of a state. The result was the emergence of instruments of power unparalleled in the history of the world. As early as the seventeenth century, even middle-ranking states maintained standing armies numbering in the tens of thousands; at the same time, the major European powers already had hundreds of thousands of men permanently under arms. In the nineteenth century, universal military conscription enabled the formation of extensive reserves of trained fighting units. The great wars of the twentieth century saw the mobilization of many millions of men. Naval forces had at their disposal battle fleets containing hundreds of ships. The financing of war through a system of government bonds, the economic muscle of large capitalist economies and an efficient bureaucracy as a central agency directing the mobilization and distribution of these resources all enabled the modern Western state to endure even lengthy conflicts.[276]

This kind of capitalist, bureaucratic, military state was at the heart of all Western empires of the modern age. Only a handful of societies outside Europe could compete with the scope, efficiency and endurance of this mobilization of resources. For this reason empires generally had a huge head start on their indigenous adversaries. Their human, material and financial resources ensured that they had far greater staying power in long conflicts, which would naturally overstretch less well organized societies.[277] As Brian Ferguson and Neil Whitehead have ascertained:

> The primary military advantage of any state is its ability to authoritatively direct and sustain massive force against a target. Even if indigenous fighters are able to repel state forces in open field combat, a state can send more men, and keep sending them, until native forces are routed. [...] European colonial and modern state armies have the additional advantage of being independent of labor demands for subsistence production, a major constraint on nonstate and ancient state forces, such as the Aztecs.[278]

Jaap de Moor has stressed the same point where the Dutch conquest of Indonesia in the nineteenth century was concerned:

> It was obvious that the Dutch could be beaten, despite their commitment of large numbers of men and heavy artillery. But it was even more obvious that they had the power to return to the battlefield after two, three or even more setbacks. If no garrisons were locally available, they ordered new, fresh troops from Java, or even from Europe. Dutch resources seemed inexhaustible.[279]

As already indicated here, often empires did not even need to take recourse to troops and finances from the European metropoles, bringing to bear instead the resources of their own overseas territories for further military expansion. This happened even as early as the Spanish subjugation of America, during which, in a permanent dynamic of expansion, each of the regions occupied became a new foothold providing personnel and finances for new conquests.[280] This system reached its peak in the British conquest of India, in which the tax revenue of defeated princely states enabled even larger armies to be raised, which then themselves had to expand, in a kind of fiscal and military *perpetuum mobile* that reached as far as the Himalayas.[281] In due course, British India not only itself became, by virtue of its own depth of resources, practically unconquerable by neighbouring states,[282] but also, beyond the subcontinent, a reservoir of manpower for the British conquest of Southeast Asia.[283]

In general, bureaucratic organization, a good communications network and naval dominance enable European empires to swiftly call up reinforcements from other peripheral regions in the event of overseas crises. Even with the comparatively archaic transport and communications technology of the seventeenth century, Francisco Pizarro still managed to gather together soldiers from Central America and even from Spain in a relatively short time to retake Peru following the rebellion of Manco Inca Yupanqui (1536–1544).[284] In later centuries such concentrations of overseas resources during crises could be achieved considerably faster and more effectively, as for example for the British intervention in eastern Sudan in 1884–1885.[285] One of the fundamental asymmetries of imperial warfare[286] consists of the fact that an isolated society with at best regional resources to draw upon would regularly confront a world empire with global resources. Moreover the vast bulk of these resources always lay beyond the horizon, at a safe remove from any attempt on the part of the enemy to seize them; this situation pertained at the latest from the sixteenth century onwards, from the moment that non-European powers definitively lost control of the oceanic trading network to the merchant fleets of the West.[287]

This in turn forms the basis of another form of asymmetry, namely that of risk. While the ability to project power far beyond one's own borders forms an integral part of the concept of a modern empire, from the Early Modern period onwards the seaborne empires of the West were at least in essence totally immune from attacks by their indigenous opponents. At most, their overseas offshoots were vulnerable, such as the British colonial settlements in North America and, to a lesser extent, land-based empires whose major cities were not shielded by an ocean (though the sheer vastness of a continent offered them protection). For centuries, the Russian frontier was threatened by raids launched by Steppe nomads.[288] In 1680, the Pueblo Uprising drove the Spanish completely out of New Mexico, and a fifth of the settlers were killed.[289] In North America, the frontiers of British settlements were rolled back massively on several occasions as a result of armed conflict with Indian societies, and not just in the seventeenth century, when white settlement was confined to narrow enclaves along the Eastern seaboard.[290] The Yamasee War of 1715 'nearly washed South Carolina off the map,'[291] and in the Seven Years' War (1756–1763) an area the size of Scotland was abandoned in panic (albeit only for a short time) following Indian attacks.[292]

Essentially, though, the maritime empires were invulnerable to overseas regional powers. The risk that they took in engaging in military clashes outside of Europe was always comparatively small, whereas for their enemies it was mostly a matter of life and death.[293] Even for Spain in its conquest of America, little more was at stake than a few conquistadors who were easily expendable, and who could at any time withdraw to their ships, which may indeed have been one reason why Cortés deliberately destroyed his before he set off with his force to conquer Tenochtitlan.[294] And ultimately the situation remains the same today: for all the capacity of global terror networks to expand the battlefield, and to inflict direct harm on the West even in its own home countries,[295] even attacks like that on 11 September 2001 are in the end only pinpricks that affect at most the feeling of security of the society that is attacked. That is not a trivial element, of course, especially regarding its effect on the internal composure of those societies; but even so it did nothing to alter the fact that the United States was able to invade Afghanistan with overwhelming military force, but not vice-versa.

An empire can therefore be seen as a practically invulnerable and almost inexhaustible machine for the generation of resources—and this without even mentioning so far the nature of these resources, plus the oft-cited (if not apposite on every single occasion) superiority of professional Western troops and Western military technology.[296] Furthermore, thanks to the bureaucratic organization and institutional stability of modern statehood—the 'everlasting nature' of the state—empires could hold out for longer.[297] They were able to pursue long-term plans for expansion with greater consistency. Repeated attempts at conquest, protracted imperial wars (against nearby and/or non-state adversaries) or serial imperial wars (against far-flung and/or state adversaries) with increasing outlay and continuing attritional wearing-down of the enemy are all characteristic of the institutional staying power of the 'everlasting' imperial state. Enemy victories were almost always merely a delaying of the inevitable; sooner or later, the empire would strike back with redoubled force.

Serial wars saw Russia conquer Eastern Siberia in the mid-eighteenth century[298] and Britain finally force the Indian princely states to their knees at the end of the same century.[299] The modern military monarchy of the Sikhs was made into a British protectorate in 1846 and three years later, after another war, was annexed to the British Raj.[300] The conquest of Indonesia by the Dutch lasted a whole century;[301] when the Balinese defeated a Dutch fleet in 1848, a larger fleet instantly appeared the very next year.[302] It took fifteen years of war before the French finally overthrew the West African state of Samori in 1898.[303] Even at the time, the British defeat in the First Anglo-Boer War in 1881 was regarded merely as a prelude to the decisive second round in 1899–1902.[304] The violent suppression of the Pampa Indians of Argentina, which was likewise concluded around this same period, had taken no less than 350 years all told.[305] The same applied to the conquest of Mexico, which began in 1519 and only truly came to an end in the nineteenth century.[306] And British and American colonial settlers and troops required 200 years altogether of serial wars and long-running conflict of a lower intensity to secure victory over the Indian peoples of North America.[307]

Perhaps even more starkly than the numbered serial imperial wars of the kind that became so typical of the long nineteenth century,[308] it is the length of these timespans which truly underlines the astonishing capacity of the 'everlasting' imperial state to wage long drawn-out wars in the service of expansion. As in the Roman Empire, so too in modern global empires the doors of the Temple of Janus—the 'gates of war' which stayed open throughout times of conflict—were never closed. In conjunction with their global depth of resources and their extensive immunity against counterattacks, it was above all this great endurance, this 'greater persistence in slaughtering their enemies'[309] that for centuries guaranteed empires a clear superiority over their indigenous opponents, who in addition to a paucity of resources lacked not least the institutional stability to wage this kind of protracted conflict. Fundamentally, therefore, empires were potentially invincible—provided the will to maintain imperial rule was present, as the body of literature on the subject makes abundantly clear:

Wars of resistance almost always ended with victory for the colonial state, particularly if it had acquired a clear advantage in weapons technology, was in a position to pursue a 'divide and rule' strategy, was resolute in its suppression of the native populace and was prepared to pay the price for this, whatever the cost. (Jürg Helbling)[310]

In the long run, the economic and technological resources of a modern European state could always be translated into an overwhelming local military superiority wherever the state was prepared to make the necessary commitment. (A. S. Kanya-Forstner)[311]

If the Europeans were prepared to make adequate efforts, their ultimate success was not usually in doubt. (P. J. Marshall)[312]

Limits to the projection of power

However, it did not ultimately turn out to be so simple. While these examples of wars drawn out over decades and centuries illustrate the ability of empires to wage protracted warfare, they also show that many imperial wars must have been anything but a walk in the park. For why would it otherwise have taken so long to suppress far weaker opponents? In actual fact, the empire at the periphery was often far from being a titan with unlimited resources to throw around. The huge accumulation of power by empires was actually dispersed across a number of obligations throughout the world, and was often only a theoretical proposition at any one location on the ground. In historical terms, the truly striking thing about the imperial presence on the periphery was how weak it could be.[313]

This began with the degree of control that the imperial centre exercised over its distant outposts. Before the world's oceans had telegraph cables laid across them in the late nineteenth century, the representatives of empires on the ground had to be furnished with extensive powers to act as they saw fit.[314] As late as 1870 it took eight months—even in the era of the steamship—for the British authorities in New Zealand to receive a response to a request of theirs from the motherland.[315] Less than a century earlier, a governor general in India had to reckon on a waiting time of two years or more before receiving a reply from London.[316] Under such circumstances, the military reaction to local crises was de facto totally removed from any decision by the metropolitan administration and of necessity lay instead in the hands of the governors or military commanders on the ground. Little wonder, then, that the impetus for violent expansion almost always came from the periphery. The 'men on the spot' exploited not only their effective freedom of action to present a fait accompli, but also their monopoly on information concerning local conditions in order to exaggerate the level of threat in the lead-up to action or to justify their actions retrospectively to a homeland or a domestic public that was often critical of expansion.[317]

A similar asymmetry in the decision-making process to the disadvantage of central political control also existed on the periphery of empire itself, where local bureaucrats or officers stationed on the frontier in their turn disengaged themselves, as the 'men on the spot,' from the political direction of their governors, picking quarrels and embarking upon military action on their own initiative. The more immediate perception of threat on the ground and military pressure for 'final solutions'[318] played a role in this, but also the desire to distinguish oneself through successful actions and enrich oneself with war booty. According to Kanya-Forstner, the French colonial army in the late nineteenth century elevated this form of career advancement to a point of principle and proceeded under its own impetus to conquer the Sahara.[319] As Douglas Porch has written in his work on this subject: 'If England acquired an empire "in a fit of absence of mind", as was often claimed, the French empire was acquired in an orgy of military indiscipline.'[320] French officers in Africa seemed in the process to have specialized in inventive excuses, like that of Colonel Louis Archinard who in 1889, having disobeyed orders by capturing the Tukulor Empire stronghold of Koundian in present-day Mali, after the event declared that he had considered the fortress a danger to security but for reasons of secrecy had been unable to solicit orders from his superiors.[321] Or Captain Gaston Cauvet, who in 1902 took it upon himself to send an expeditionary force into the Ahaggar Mountains (which came within a whisker of perishing there), and argued retrospectively that he had not disobeyed any orders, since he had not sought any in the first place.[322] The disarmingly casual message that Sir Charles Napier is said to have dispatched to his superiors in London following his unauthorized annexation of the Indian kingdom of Sindh (now in southwestern Pakistan) in 1843—'Peccavi', which is Latin for 'I have sinned' (= 'Sindh')—is clearly apocryphal and was most likely a satirical invention of the British press of the time.[323] It's a shame that this is so; this public-schoolboy joke, revealing a classical education, is just the sort of thing men like Napier, the proconsuls of this 'second Roman Empire', would have said.

The ultimate 'man on the spot' was perhaps the Spanish conquistador, whose urge to seize territory was driven unequivocally by personal financial motives, and who was completely cut off, in terms of both practical communication and any moderating influence, from an imperial centre that was a year away by ship.[324] The laws of the Spanish system of government allowed even official representatives of the Crown, at least on paper, to annul express prohibitions against conquest by means of legal faits accomplis: for instance, when Cortés defied orders in 1519 and invaded Mexico, he founded the city of Veracruz and then proceeded to seek retrospective sanctioning of his invasion from its municipal authorities[325]—given the importance that was accorded to purely formal acts of law in the Spanish Empire, this was no less significant than the absurd instrument known as the Requerimiento, the mere proclamation of which legitimized the war against the Indians.[326] Of course, the prime reason why Cortés got away with his insubordination was not this, but rather the extraordinary success of his adventure.

Ultimately it was this prospect of resounding success that motivated all 'men on the spot' to undertake expansion off their own bat.[327] In cases of doubt, they could always claim that they had been attacked or were acting pre-emptively to forestall an assault (if the worst came to the worst, they could even deliberately provoke such an attack). Such claims were hard to verify from the motherland, and most crucially took a long time to check.[328] Accordingly, the archetype of expansionist 'men on the spot' is evident everywhere, from the very earliest of the Portuguese adventurers in Africa,[329] through the Russian frontier with Siberia,[330] to India, where an entire continent with millions of inhabitants was ultimately conquered through local initiatives,[331] and beyond.[332] It was only the advent of improved communications technology from the late nineteenth century on that managed to reduce somewhat the scope for action of the 'men on the spot'.[333]

All the same, however little the administrators and military men on the periphery were kept on a tight rein in reality (indeed, for many centuries on scarcely any rein at all), they did remain fundamentally accountable and could at least in principle later be brought to book. The same could not, however, be said of the true troublemakers on many of the peripheries of empire: European settlers.[334] In the early days of colonization, they often lived in isolation on the edge of the wilderness, and their acts of violence against the indigenous population—motivated primarily by hunger for land or manpower—went unnoticed for the most part.[335] Even if the colonists were politically organized, this did not make supervision of the expansionist belligerence they engaged in for private ends any easier; on the contrary, self-government only served to strengthen the settler lobby and made the central government disinclined to disregard their demands.[336] In this case the problem was known about but ignored—at least just as long as the violent encroachments by colonists did not provoke an organized reaction by the autochthonous peoples. In the event that this did occur, the frightened colonists were then vocal in demanding military protection or even a 'final solution' to the 'native question.'[337]

And that was ultimately the crux of the violence that was unleashed by the 'men on the spot,' whether they were officials, soldiers or settlers: it was based on the local power resources of the imperial periphery, but could resemble kicking a wasps' nest. The military consequences swiftly overwhelmed the instruments of power of the original instigators of the violence, thus drawing first the colonial administration into the conflict, and thereafter the motherland.[338]

It would therefore be wrong to think of empires as monolithic violent protagonists deploying inexhaustible resources in a centrally directed manner. On the contrary, a marked divergence of interest between the centre and the periphery is frequently apparent, as indeed it also is—both on an imperial scale and on the ground in individual locations—between colonial administrations and actors on the frontier. The expansionist dynamism unleashed by armed conflicts emanated as a rule from the periphery. Yet it was the centre which primarily possessed the military means to bring serious conflicts to a swift conclusion, and these means, when set against an empire's global duties, were in short supply. Violent conflicts raged continuously on every periphery, sparked by land-hungry settlers, glory-seeking 'men on the spot' and of course by the general distortions brought about by foreign domination and economic exploitation, which went hand-in-hand with imperialism.[339] All these conflicts competed for the resources of the empire, not only against each other, but above all with the requirements for the defence of the homeland if it should become embroiled in a major war against other imperial powers. The security of the imperial centre was always the top priority of imperial defence strategy. Compared with this, all the conflicts on the periphery of empire—which after all, as we have already seen, hardly ever represented a serious risk to the homeland—were in the truest sense of the word peripheral.[340]

An additional factor was that, in the long term, imperial expansion had a fundamentally economic motive—enrichment through unequal trade and the exploitation of raw materials—an objective which costly military operations clearly obstructed. All the more so since they tended, thanks to their destabilizing effect, to result in the long run in formal rule, which was a loss-making enterprise, at least where state finances were concerned.[341] Leaving aside colonial settlements, the imperial system in the modern era was based by preference on informal dominion, and on the pursuit of economic interests through political means and military pressure, yet—wherever possible—without incurring the costs of military occupation and bureaucratic administration. The vast colonial empires which arose at the end of the nineteenth century were above all a chance product of global history, a result of a diplomatically relatively unique and chauvinistically charged competitive situation with strong peripheral pull factors; these polities actually contradicted the inner logic of imperialism, which was suspended here, albeit only temporarily.[342]

Consequently, not all imperial actors were so deliberately sparing with military resources as the semi-state chartered trading companies of the Early Modern period, to whom war (like governance) was positively anathema if it did not yield direct economic benefits.[343] Yet the maxim that dominion on the periphery should make the maximum profit possible with the minimum of cost was pretty universal for the empires of modern times. As a result, the general expectation was that the peripheries ought as far as possible to make do with their own financial and manpower resources and not have recourse to central funds[344]—which had the additional welcome effect that imperial expansion could proceed largely unnoticed by a potentially critical public back at home.[345]

Besides, there absolutely were some empires whose military resources for deployment on the periphery were genuinely scarce. By the seventeenth century Spain, which had been strategically over-stretched even in the late sixteenth century,[346] was a world power in decline, which found itself so overextended by wars against European powers, inflation and state bankruptcy that it no longer had any more resources at its disposal for maintaining firm control over its American dominions.[347] In the late twentieth century, Portugal had one of the largest remaining colonial empires, but was one of the smallest and poorest European nations, and was only able to wage three simultane-ous colonial wars in its African territories through a superhuman effort.[348] And in the eighteenth and nineteenth centuries, the United States adhered to a state ideology that demonized large standing armies in peacetime as instruments of despotism. For this reason, as well as fiscal considerations, the foremost power of the Western hemisphere maintained a miniature army that would have shamed a petty German principality at the time, and which was barely capable of guarding the frontier with the Indian territories—its only serious commitment.[349]

Yet even when the motherland was able and willing to commit supe-rior military resources to a conflict on the periphery, such a deploy-ment proved anything but uncomplicated. The difficulties of a transoce-anic projection of power were immense. Until the arrival of improved masts and rigging in the eighteenth century, putting to sea in the open ocean in large warships was only really possible in the summer months. Prevailing winds restricted the area within which larger undertakings could operate: thus, it was easy to sail to the Caribbean from Europe but far more challenging to reach the North American mainland. The distances were huge, international voyages took months and the food supply for such periods was difficult to ensure, especially for large bodies of troops. Scurvy and pestilences took their toll. In fact, the transportation by sea of European units to Asia in the eighteenth cen-tury had to factor in such high losses during the long voyage itself as to render the enterprise pointless as a general rule.[350] And for a long time, the projection of maritime power was severely restricted in regions that had a paucity of natural harbours and the coastline did not lend itself to easy landing, as was the case along large stretches of the West African coast.[351]

Steamships made the situation easier,[352] though even as late as 1870 the transportation by sea of a military detachment from England to New Zealand in under three months was considered remarkably quick.[353] The carrying capacity of vessels remained small and ocean voyages were still an arduous business, while the unloading capacity at the end destination was generally a bottleneck except for where proper port facilities had been built.[354] To transport 62,000 men and 36,000 animals for the expedition to Abyssinia in 1867, the British Army needed almost 300 ships. For disembarking in the shallow Bay of Zula in Eritrea, jetties several kilometres long and a field railway had to be constructed.[355] Essentially, the availability of strategic air transport first made the swift intercontinental transfer of large military detachments in times of crisis practicable—something that did not happen until the late twentieth century, and even then such operations overstretched the capacities of virtually all combatant nations except the two super-powers.[356] It is perhaps worth recalling that only a very small propor-tion of the US forces deployed to fight the third Gulf War in 2003 were airlifted. The large majority came by sea, and their disembarkation was severely hampered by the limited capacity of Kuwaiti ports.[357]

Moreover, what was difficult when attempted across oceans some-times verged on the impossible when tried across continents. Before the building of the Trans-Caspian and Trans-Siberian railways between 1880 and 1904, it took Russian troops a year to reach Central Asia and eighteen months to get to the eastern border of Siberia. Anyhow, the logistical restrictions on deploying large troop contingents to Central Asia were insuperable in view of the fact that the wells there could only provide a few hundred men a day with water.[358]

Troop numbers, population and area

The projection of power on the periphery was therefore considerably more difficult than frequently assumed. Armed forces on the periphery invariably remained small; certainly when measured against troop strengths in the motherlands, and those deployed in the wars fought by empires against other major powers, and also relative to the numbers of their indigenous adversaries, to the populations over which they ruled, but above all when set against the area over which they were supposed to have dominion.

Some statistics illustrate vividly what that meant in practice. Around 1900 the United Kingdom maintained a standing army of well over 200,000 men on the Indian subcontinent—the largest colonial army of all time. But India had 300 million inhabitants.[359] Across all of its sub-Saharan colonies, from Sudan to South Africa, in 1902 Great Britain could call upon just 11,500 men.[360] In Nigeria, 3,000 colonial troops 'controlled' 775,000 square kilometres of territory with a population of 24 million.[361] And fewer than 13,000 soldiers were stationed in the whole of French West Africa including the Congo, an area far larger than Europe.[362]

The situation was much the same in Germany's colonies: 250 police troops 'governed' Togo, an area the size of Bavaria and Baden-Württemberg put together;[363] in Cameroon, just three companies were responsible for a tract of land around the same size as the whole German Empire in Europe, while in German East Africa, fourteen companies controlled a territory seven times the size of Great Britain, to use a comparison first made by Lewis Gann and Peter Duignan.[364] By the mid-nineteenth century, the US Army had on average one soldier for every 100 square kilometres in the West.[365] Along the Pacific coast, 6,000 regular soldiers were responsible for a third of the entire surface area of the United States, or 3 million square kilometres.[366]

Often, the tactical numerical ratio did not look much different. In 1879–1880, two US cavalry regiments (fewer than 2,000 men) and 1,000 Mexican soldiers set out to hunt down the Apache leader Victorio in an extensive search operation that took in the US states of New Mexico and Texas as well as the Mexican states of Chihuahua and Sonora, a total area of roughly a million square kilometres.[367] In Angola a Portuguese battalion was once responsible for covering 12,000 square kilometres.[368] One of the earliest local administrators of Kenya summed up the incredibly thin presence of imperial instruments of power on the ground in his domain thus:

> Here we are, three white men in the heart of Africa, with 20 nigger soldiers and 50 nigger police, 68 miles from doctors or reinforcements, administering and policing a district inhabited by half a million well-armed

savages who have only quite recently come into touch with the white man, and we are responsible for the security in an area the size of Yorkshire.[369]

Even the large troop numbers that were mobilized for the great imperial wars of the twentieth century were often not so impressive when set against the vastness of the tracts of land involved. To be sure, at the height of its commitment in Vietnam (South Vietnam was barely half the size of Germany), the USA had 500,000 men stationed there. But the French deployed roughly the same number in Algeria, a country that was fourteen times larger than South Vietnam. Likewise, Afghanistan is at least four times the size of South Vietnam,[370] but throughout the 1980s there were never more than 100,000 Soviet troops operational there at any one time—so, in relation to the area, approximately twenty times fewer than American troop numbers in Vietnam. No wonder, then, that the Soviet Union never managed to gain complete military mastery over the country:[371] 'the immense and stark territory of Afghanistan swallowed the invaders up.'[372] As the most recent conflict there shows, the same goes for the 50,000 NATO troops stationed in Afghanistan as part of the International Security Assistance Force (ISAF).[373]

Regarding these ratios of imperial instruments of power to the area and the population of the theatres of deployment, which are absolutely typical of the situation on the colonial periphery, it will come as no surprise to learn that the armed forces of empires were generally inferior in size to those of their military opponents. Granted, the figures in this area should always be treated with a degree of caution, since they rely upon data gathered by contemporary commentators, who had an understandable interest in exaggerating the strength of their adversary in order to enhance their own glory[374] (or alternatively to excuse defeats). As a result, there has been a propensity right up to the present day to compare unlike things, such as the actual strength of imperial troops on the ground with the total potential military strength of an enemy society, a strength that could never be actually mobilized, let alone made available at the same time and in the same place. This was true, for instance, of the assertion that the army of the Dutch East India Company (VOC) in the seventeenth century amounted to 10,000 men, whereas the warrior caste of the Malabar Coast alone numbered one and a half million;[375] or of the claims that the British overran

Sokoto with just 600 men, 'yet Sokoto had an army estimated at nearly 30,000,'[376] that the Belgian colonial forces in the Congo, with 10,000 mercenaries and militiamen, defeated the slave empire of the Arabs, which 'had the capacity to field 100,000 men,'[377] or that Southern Rhodesia was conquered by fewer than 700 British settlers and police troops, despite the fact that the Ndebele ruler King Lobengula 'had over 17,000 warriors.'[378] These formulations already indicate that the figures for the opposing side are somewhat hypothetical. Moreover, the literary-mythological trope of the 'magic of the minority,' as Jürgen Osterhammel has fittingly put it,[379] also played a role here; this has given rise to such founding legends as that of the 800 Russians who under the leadership of Ermak are reputed to have conquered Siberia,[380] or to the classic question: 'How could 500 Europeans conquer Mexico?'[381]

Notwithstanding these reservations, there are some comparatively reliable figures which do actually corroborate the claim that imperial armies were clearly numerically inferior on the periphery. Thus, we know from data from both sides that the Portuguese really did embark in 1511 with a force of only around 1,000 men to attack Malacca, which was defended by 20,000 men.[382] It is also evident from the colonial wars fought by Germany in South West Africa in 1904–1905 that the Herero initially outnumbered the German expeditionary force two to one; and that, according to the most reliable figures, in confronting and suppressing a popular uprising in East Africa in 1905–1907 several thousand German troops killed some 180,000 Africans; and that the total strength of European troop contingents in China represented just a fraction of that of the Chinese standing army.[383] In the Indonesian War of Independence from 1945 to 1950, 140,000 soldiers of the Dutch Army faced around 350,000 indigenous fighters.[384]

However, imperial forces at the periphery were not always massively outnumbered. In exceptional circumstances, the numerical ratio could be almost symmetrical or sometimes even heavily in favour of the Europeans. Historically, most of the old colonial settlements are examples of this opposing tendency. In places where a sparse indigenous population made settlement at all possible in the first place,[385] such as in North America, on the Cape of Good Hope or in Australia, the demographic victory of the settlers was essentially a foregone conclusion. Epidemic diseases also contributed to this imbalance.[386] Even though the formerly popular notion that diseases imported from Europe depopulated entire continents with millions of inhabitants within just a few years has since been debunked, not least by microbiologists,[387] local epidemics certainly did, for instance, help colonists gain a foothold in New England and in the medium term to become the most numerous ethnic group.[388] It was only as a consequence of this demographic victory, which saw massive expansion of the settled areas at the cost of the autochthonous population, that serious military confrontations ensued, whose outcome at this juncture could generally be in little doubt. Wherever empires were demographically massively superior on the ground, it was much simpler to assert this superiority in tactical military terms.

The best documented example of such a situation are the British colonies in North America, which later became the United States.[389] Even as early as 1640 (after just three decades of colonization), there were many more colonists in the settlement of Virginia than there were Powhatan Indians—8,000 as against barely 5,000.[390] In King Philip's War (1675–1676) settlers in New England enjoyed 'overwhelming advantages in numbers'[391] over the Indians, since in the fifty years since the founding of the colony the settlers' population had risen to 52,000, whereas that of the local Indians had fallen from 144,000 to just 10,000.[392] By 1770, there were only about 150,000 Indians left between the Mississippi and the Appalachians, including perhaps 25,000 warriors;[393] at the same time, the United States already had 2 million inhabitants.[394] And by 1860, before the outbreak of the major Indian Wars, there were already about as many whites in the state of California alone as there were Indians in the whole of the West (around 360,000 in each case). At this time, the total population of the USA who were of European extraction numbered 27 million.[395]

Conditions were similar, albeit on a smaller scale, in Tasmania: when the government there proclaimed the 'final solution' of the 'native question' in 1830 and 2,000 soldiers, policemen, settlers and convicts combed the island to root them out, only around 200 of the original population of thousands of Tasmanians were still living on the island.[396] Things were not quite so drastic on New Zealand, where in 1840 there were still only 1,000 settlers as compared to 100,000 Maoris, yet by

1856 these respective figures had changed to 40,000 and 50,000.[397] In the Maori Wars of the 1860s, 18,000 imperial troops were ranged against 5,000 warriors.[398]

Essentially in such cases, the demographic trend alone proved the decisive factor, and the armed confrontation only a postscript. Not only did the European population explosion on the ground cancel out the usual numerical restrictions pertaining on the periphery; settlement also altered the living environment of the indigenous population so radically that their socioeconomic structure simply collapsed and in its wake so did their political organization and social identity too. It did not even take an actual act of genocide involving huge population losses to achieve this, though such losses did generally occur in the long run anyway. Gaining the demographic upper hand and Europeanizing the land through massive settlement and destruction of indigenous livelihoods was in effect the only way for empires to secure a lasting and irreversible victory.[399] (The fact that the victorious settlers then for the most part went on to disengage themselves from the motherland is another story.)

Thus, alongside the Indians of the USA, to whom the coup de grâce was delivered not just by demographic factors but also by the construction of the railway in the West and the mass slaughter of vast herds of American bison,[400] other indigenous groups who were conquered through colonization included the Amerindians of Central America, whose decline came about through destruction of their culture and demographics, but above all as a result of mixed marriages,[401] and those of South America, for whom plagues, forced labour and the general disruption of communities were the deciding factors.[402] Other groups depleted in this way were the San of the Cape Colony in South Africa,[403] Australian Aborigines,[404] and the nomads of the Russian steppe frontiers.[405] Naturally, all these processes were not free of violence—quite the contrary, in fact. But the decisive blow ultimately fell not as a result of military action, and the situation on the periphery was largely resolved through demographic and socioeconomic developments.

To a somewhat lesser extent, this also applied to Algeria, where French settlement definitely underwent an explosion under colonial rule, particularly during its final years: in the mid-nineteenth century there were 100,000 settlers, by 1870 250,000,[406] 833,000 in 1926, and finally by 1954, the year that saw the start of the Algerian War, 984,000 (79 per cent of whom had been born in the country).[407] And yet the colonists in Algeria never even came close to constituting a majority of the population: though the numbers of indigenous inhabitants initially fell in the mid-nineteenth century as a result of the war of conquest from around 3 million to some 2 million,[408] by the 1920s this figure had risen once more to 5 million, and at the outbreak of the War of Independence stood at 9 million.[409] The settlement of Algeria made the country a headache in terms of colonial administration but never won the country for the French.[410] The same could be said of practically all the other colonial settlements of more recent times, where the colonists always remained in a minority.[411]

The second instance in which an empire on the periphery was not numerically inferior came about when the metropolitan administration chose to turn the logic of imperial conflict on its head by sending massive military forces to avoid a conclusive defeat. Early examples of this were France, which as early as 1847 dispatched over 100,000 troops—a third of its army—to hold Algeria against the insurgency of Abd el-Kader and his force of barely 50,000,[412] and Russia, which around the same time crushed the Murid revolt in the Caucasus, which involved no more than 20,000 indigenous fighters, with 150,000, possibly even as many as 200,000, men.[413]

But first and foremost, it is the major colonial wars of the long twentieth century which fall into this category: the Cuban War of Independence of 1895–1898, in which Spain deployed 200,000 soldiers against a force of 'patriots' seldom larger than 50,000;[414] the Second Anglo-Boer War of 1899–1902, where 450,000 troops of the British Empire fought against some 60,000 to 70,000 Boers;[415] the Rif War in Spanish Morocco, in which Spain was initially unable to prevail despite fielding 150,000 men against a few thousand Berber fighters—and which it finally won in 1926, after joining forces with France, at the unbelievable cost of deploying no fewer than 500,000 troops against an enemy force of 12,000;[416] and the Italian invasion of Ethiopia in 1935–1936, to which Mussolini committed 400,000 soldiers and huge quantities of military equipment, including 250 tanks, 350 aircraft, 1,100 artillery pieces and 10,000 machine guns.[417] The trend continued post-1945, with the Malayan Emergency (involving 120,000 soldiers and police against 10,000 insurgents),[418] France's war in Indochina (456,000 against 350,000),[419] the Algerian War of Independence (462,000 against 60,000 to 90,000)[420] and the Vietnam War (500,000 against 240,000).[421] Finally, in the wars of independence fought by the Portuguese colonies in Africa, Portugal sought to overcome some 27,000 rebels with a force that ultimately numbered 150,000 men (70 per cent of its entire army).[422] Another possibly less relevant example are the 60,000 British troops who at the end of the 1930s attempted in vain to pacify the Northwest Frontier of India against barely 4,000 tribal insurgents.[423]

What do all these conflicts have in common? In almost all of them, empires found themselves facing (proto-) states or transethnic, proto-nationalist independence movements, the suppression of which took enormous effort (and often still failed). In addition, from the mid-nineteenth century onwards, these wars took place under hugely improved conditions regarding communications and transport, which generally speaking simplified the projection of power over large distances. Yet neither of these factors can explain why imperial powers were prepared to pay this price, in contradiction of the normal logic of imperial conflict. This motivation plays the far greater role.

Firstly, the conflicts in question were often ones which for an empire either on the wane or on the rise were fraught with considerable foreign policy prestige: for Spain, France, Portugal, and to some extent also Great Britain after 1945, it was a matter of proving that they were still leading powers;[424] for Italy in 1935, it was the urge to become one for the first time. Secondly, the regions concerned were sometimes on the fringes of huge contiguous mainland areas already dominated by an expanding power (the Caucasus, Northwest Frontier) or ones which like Algeria were situated close to the motherland and/or were considered an integral part of it;[425] this heightened the security risk and the claim to sovereignty (and made the projection of power easier). Thirdly, in many of the conflicts cited, larger strategic interests appeared to be threatened, which went far beyond the local significance of control over the region in question; this was the case in South Africa, where in the perception of the British 'official mind' nothing less than the long-distance securing of the sea routes to India was at stake.[426] A similar view was taken of the Northwest Frontier, which as part of the 'Great Game in Asia'—that is, the imperial conflict with Tsarist Russia—was deemed to secure India from Central Asian encroachment. And in particular after 1945 strategic concerns were a prime consideration for all those countries in which Western hegemony was challenged by a communist-inspired national uprising. Through such concepts as the 'domino effect', the Cold War made almost every anticolonial fight for independence into an existential struggle of global significance.[427]

All the same, one should not let oneself be deceived by the figures quoted. Even in the great nation-building wars in the West in the nineteenth century, millions of well-trained soldiers faced one another, while in the two world wars of the twentieth century, the combatants numbered in the tens of millions. While the imperial wars of the same era that were fought with a more intensive projection of power as their goal may have involved several hundreds of thousands of troops, these numbers still remained comparatively small, not only in relation to the resources mobilized for a major-power conflict between imperial motherlands, but also above all when measured against the immense tracts of land and population size on the periphery. A country many times the size of an industrialized European nation could not be militarily suppressed even with a million troops or more, especially not where the indigenous populace staged a guerrilla or popular war. Besides, such wars were merely exceptions in a period in which most military interventions on the fringes of empire continued to be far smaller affairs.[428]

Controlling a region

Yet aside from the (few) qualifications just discussed, imperial instruments of power on the periphery were always extremely meagre compared to the strength of the enemy and the space involved. This would have been a challenge even in a symmetrical war of set-piece battles. However, in colonial warfare the scarcity of resources was exacerbated by both the vastness of the space and the cultural propensity towards violence of the indigenous enemy. If the latter elected to wage a 'tribal'—i.e. a guerrilla—war, the armies of empire were forced to provide military protection for their lines of communication and their supply depots, lest any operation come to grief simply from a failure of logistics—as happened, for example, to a British punitive expedition against the Cherokee in 1760–1761.[429] And in view of the immense distances, guarding an army's logistical support often required such large numbers of troops that only a small proportion were left to engage in combat operations. An extreme example is perhaps the Second Anglo-Boer War, in which 400,000 men guarded the lines of communication, while just 40,000 actually fought.[430] But in other campaigns too (precise figures are available primarily for the nineteenth century), securing supply lines frequently absorbed over half of the fighting men deployed in the theatre of war, and sometimes considerably more.[431]

Surprisingly, in spectacular violation of the customary precautions taken when waging war in Europe, Western commanders in imperial conflicts often chose to divide their already small armies, a radical departure from the maxim which stated that instruments of force should always be concentrated, a cornerstone of the Western military tradition. Essentially three reasons lay behind this decision, two of which had to do with logistics and mobility. For one thing, smaller columns were easier to provision on the periphery, since they did not place too heavy a demand on the food resources foraged from the land. In other words, advancing in separate columns broadened the logistical basis while at the same time increasing mobility as a result of having reduced the baggage train. Secondly, dividing the army was often a highly practical move, since the cumbersome baggage and heavy equipment could be left behind temporarily under guard, making the combat troops into a light 'flying column' which for a while could either operate independently in logistical terms or live off the land, and so became a faster and more mobile force.[432] Only the third reason was an operational one in a narrower sense, namely when it was a question of trapping the enemy in a pincer movement between several columns in order to force him to engage in combat (a tactic especially favoured in the Indian Wars in the USA).[433] Yet a problem that often accompanied this tactic has been highlighted by Douglas Porch in his analysis of the French conquest of the Chaouia region of southern Morocco in 1907–1908: 'Converging columns worked only if there was something to converge upon.'[434] Not infrequently, by the time the units arrived, the enemy was long gone.[435]

The purpose of dividing columns was therefore to overcome the inherent sluggishness of imperial armies under the logistical conditions on the periphery and to increase the chances of forcing the more mobile enemy to stand and fight. What was anathema in European warfare was seen as positively good form in colonial conflicts.[436] Of course, it could still go wrong, particularly if the sometimes repeatedly divided columns eventually became so small that even an opponent who would not otherwise necessarily have engaged in combat saw an opportunity for an easy victory.[437] Or if the assumption that the enemy wanted to avoid doing battle was wrong from the start, as happened in two classic defeats of the West in imperial wars. While searching for their respective enemies, both George Armstrong Custer, probably the most famous US general of the Indian Wars, and Lord Chelmsford, the British commander during the invasion of Zululand, split up their forces into tiny bands that were ultimately no match for a concentrated adversary that had no reason to avoid a battle. In this way, Chelmsford lost half of his troops at the Battle of Isandlwana in 1879,[438] while three years previously at Little Bighorn in Montana, Custer had lost most of his men, and his own life in the bargain.[439]

If an opponent consistently avoided engaging in battle, or if an empire simply could not relinquish its claim to rule in a particular colony, the imperial army was confronted with a remit that went even further than just protecting its own logistical support, onerous enough though that task was already. As a general rule, it found itself obliged to assert extensive control over the indigenous population and the area they inhabited by showing a physical presence on the ground, and to prevent enemy attacks as well as provide constant protection for government institutions, commercial enterprises, infrastructure facilities and settler communities.

To guarantee this protection, empires often made use of fortification complexes, which had the same rationale on the fringes of empires as similar installations in the Early Modern period in Europe—namely, to establish control over an area using a relatively small number of troops. This trend was instigated by Spain in the sixteenth century in Mexico, but in time all imperial powers sought to secure or even extend their frontiers by erecting forts or fortified blockhouses.[440] Up to the twentieth century, these installations remained a standard feature of warfare, by then often combined with barbed-wire fences and minefields. In their attempt to gain control of large tracts of territory in the Second Boer War, the British built 8,000 blockhouses and put up 6,000 kilometres of barbed wire.[441] In Algeria, France's attempt to gain mastery over the region degenerated by the late 1950s into a 300-plus-kilometre-long electrified fence along the border with Tunisia, reinforced with minefields, barbed-wire entanglements and artillery emplacements and defended by 80,000 soldiers with tanks and helicopters: the so-called 'Ligne Morice', named after the French defence minister of the time.[442] In Libya, likewise, the Italians built a fence of their own; theirs was 270 kilometres long.[443]

Of course, static defensive duties and fortified installations kept a lot of troops tied up. A host of very small garrisons or forts were typical of colonial settlements in particular; indeed, the colonists clamoured for such defences.[444] For a long period in 1857, the British could not manage to assemble large military detachments to confront the Indian Rebellion, despite the fact that there was a standing force of 40,000 European troops on the subcontinent and reinforcements kept on arriving from other parts of the empire, for the simple reason that defence of the areas not affected by the uprising took precedence over suppressing the revolt.[445] Similarly, during the Cuban War of Independence the Spanish had barely 2,500 troops available to actually combat the rebellion, due to the necessity of protecting the sugar-cane plantations and manning static fortress complexes.[446]

In the major imperial wars of the twentieth century against sub-state guerrilla movements, the costs of maintaining control over a region entered the realms of the unrealistic. In Palestine in the late 1940s, 90,000 British troops tried to protect railways and oil pipelines from sabotage.[447] Toward the end of the conflict in Indochina, the French commander-in-chief Henri Navarre had a vast force of 456,000 men at his disposal; however, they were so comprehensively tied up defending static targets that in practice, sufficient troops were never available for offensive operations—in its physical domination of the country, the imperial army had effectively immobilized itself.[448] A decade later, the same situation also prevailed in Algeria, where at the height of the conflict around 470,000 French soldiers were still unable to assert any genuine control over the country.[449]

Ultimately, securing a large area against a popular or guerrilla war that cannot be decided by set-piece battles is always a task that is alien to military thinking, takes up a huge number of soldiers and is more of a police operation. General Charles Gwynn, whose 1934 book *Imperial Policing* was the British Army's first standard work on counterinsurgency tactics, therefore acknowledged the necessity of stationing troops across a wide area in order to protect government institutions and people's lives, but at the same time warned against using this as a reason to avoid taking decisive military action: 'The military view is, that once essential measures of security have been taken, further protection and the prevention of disorder is best provided by taking positive measures against the hostile elements. Anything that savours of passive defence encourages the other side and wastes power.'[450]

Likewise, the latest US Army manual on counterinsurgency (2006) gives great prominence to the insight that control of a foreign country depends less on the ratio of one's own troop numbers to the number of insurgents and more on the ratio of troops to the local population.[451] Where a conflict cannot be resolved by decisive battles—a typical situation on the periphery—colonial war amounts to an attempt to establish military domination over an area and control over its populace.

Grey areas

Given all these circumstances, it was only natural that empires should find it hard to bring a conflict on the margins of empire to a swift and permanent conclusion. In fact, it was often difficult even for contemporary observers to say when a particular war had begun and ended, or indeed if it had come to an end at all—or ultimately even to define what a war actually was. Analytically, this difficulty still remains today in many cases. The blurring of temporal (and spatial) limitations and legal as well as conceptual definitions is a key characteristic of imperial wars.[452]

A major reason for this is the aforementioned lack of central organization on both sides. Empires had only very loose control over their frontiers, especially over settlers; the indigenous side, meanwhile, was in most cases either non-state, or its statehood was weak and decentralized. These are in and of themselves not exactly ideal preconditions for containing violence, which on the frontier could erupt at any time as a result of conflicts over land, resources or manpower, even though the potential adversaries would have had a clear interest in such containment. But, as we have already seen, the truth was that violence formed an integral part of daily life, particularly for non-European societies, and most especially for non-state ones, and was not hived off into a separate political sphere by virtue of the state having a monopoly on violence, as in modern Europe.

Correspondingly, where empires were concerned, the fringes of their domains were regularly treated like frontlines, or at best like zones of occupation: a properly constituted civil administration was frequently only installed very late and even then was very poorly staffed in the main and scarcely present in daily life—in actual fact, much less in evidence than the armed forces. Even after centuries of colonization, the supposedly French Algeria still resembled a 'leopard-skin', on which the few French cities represented the 'spots' of civil government, while the background was territory nominally under military control,[453] with the result that, in large parts of the country prior to the War of Independence (1954–1962), the populace had never set eyes on a European.[454] In 1900, Nigeria was being run by a grand total of nine British colonial officers, and although this figure had risen to forty by 1903, this was still to govern a population of 24 million. Even after the colonial administrations of all empires had been massively expanded in the mid-twentieth century, large colonies were still governed by a few hundred political administrators; if one also counted all the doctors, teachers, foresters, land surveyors and other quasi-executive civil servants, together with indigenous employees of the state, the figures were still only in the low thousands—comparable with, say, the local government employees of a mid-sized town in England. If, on average, there was a population of several thousands for every one imperial soldier, then for every colonial civil servant the figure was several tens of thousands—54,000 for example in the 1930s in Nigeria.[455]

The colonial state was therefore for a long time a military state. For long stretches the military were the de facto rulers on the imperial frontier, with officers attending to administrative duties and administration and pacification being seen as two sides of the same coin; military and police duties were barely distinguishable from one another.[456]

These circumstances essentially made violence on the periphery an intrinsic social condition there. For the imperial machinery of power, if only because of its numerical weakness on the ground, resorting to a demonstrative and exemplary use of force was the most significant and often the only way of exercising authority, and given the dominance of the military, violent solutions were frequently the obvious answer to all problems.[457] Settlers felt themselves anyhow to be in a permanent state of siege and in most cases did not need any special reason to take up arms against their indigenous competitors for scarce resources. And of course it was not uncommon for the latter to respond in kind, while the colonial state looked on helplessly, or rather turned a blind eye.[458] Where the economy of a colony was based on forced labour, coercive violence against the indigenous population was likewise a daily occurrence.[459] Moreover, until far into the nineteenth century the institution of slavery represented a permanent structure of violence inherent within the colonial order.[460] Individual, structural and collective forms of violence were therefore endemic on the frontier and did not necessarily have to result in open warfare.[461]

Little wonder, then, that it remains difficult to this day to distinguish the outbreak of an actual war against the backcloth of a permanently high level of violence or at least propensity for violence on the frontiers of empire. Take, for example, the case of Spanish conquistadors in New Mexico, for whom it was quite normal to enforce their demands for provisions, gold or sexual services in Indian pueblos by force of arms, understandably sometimes leading to acts of violence on the part of the Indians against individual Spaniards, which in turn provoked the Spaniards to extirpate entire villages.[462] Another instance is that of Brazilian coastal settlements in the seventeenth century, where the warlike Tupi countered enslavement into forced labour in Portuguese sugar mills with attacks on colonists, which prompted punitive expeditions against whole communities (which yielded yet more slaves as a by-product);[463] or the circumstances that led to the Cherokee War of 1759–1761, namely a series of isolated violent conflicts between settler militias and Cherokee warriors who were allied with Great Britain, which escalated through vendettas and attacks on individual settlers to hostage-taking and punitive expeditions, until finally the British Army intervened.[464] Still other examples are the Indian Wars in the USA, which were often sparked by such trivial matters as theft or differences of opinion over the outcome of a sporting competition;[465] or Sierra Leone, where passive resistance against the new Hut Tax of 1898 escalated via stone-throwing at police troops to an open attack on a column of British soldiers.[466] In Tunisia in 1951–1952, a general strike, mass arrests, acts of sabotage, violent clashes between demonstrators and the military, political assassinations, and violence by settler militias all coincided.[467] When and where did the war begin there? It was never officially declared in any event, and whether the country was actually in a state of war lay in the eye of the beholder. One should therefore regard actual imperial wars rather as temporary concentrations in space and time of an endemic state of everyday violence on the margins of empire.

This view is also corroborated by the sheer volume of recorded military actions, which fundamentally indicate a permanent state of war. During the Raj, the British Indian Army put down no fewer than seventy-seven major rebellions.[468] Between 1893 and 1911, it took at least thirty military operations to pacify the British colony of Kenya.[469] Likewise, for the period 1891–1897 alone, sixty large-scale campaigns had to be fought to secure German East Africa,[470] with a total of 231 being conducted between 1889 and 1910.[471] The annals of the US Army register more than 1,000 clashes with Indians between 1866 and 1891.[472] Meanwhile, the official history of the West African Frontier Force, the British military authority in Nigeria, records nineteen numbered campaigns for the years 1900–1906 alone, with such fundamental and diverse objectives as 'to subdue the Munshi', 'to bring to heel the slave-raiding Emir of Yola', 'to avenge the death of Hon. D. Carnegie and to prevent repercussions by rapid action,' 'to prevent and punish outbreaks of intertribal warfare,' 'to seize a pirate chief,' 'to subdue the Dakakeri owing to their lawless behaviour in attacking caravans' and 'to bring under control the country lying to the south of latitude 6.30 N.'[473] This varied mixture of territorial control, war, deterrence, and police actions was the real state of affairs for imperial armed forces on the periphery. Imperial rule was rule through violence, of a constantly low and not infrequently also of a much higher intensity, with real imperial wars remaining rather a matter of perception, as Hendrik Wesseling has emphasized: 'Presumably it is not correct to consider colonial expansion as a series of individual wars. In fact it was a permanent process of warfare which periodically exploded into a series of spectacularly violent incidents which excited the imagination of the European public and therefore were recorded as wars.'[474]

Imperial wars are also hard to pin down in definitional terms because the legal parameters for defining a state of war on the periphery often did not exist or were deliberately blurred by empires. Thus, even in the Early Modern period, empires mostly insisted upon stigmatizing their opponents as rebels against a legitimate authority,[475] the legitimacy or at least legality of which the imperial authorities themselves had manufactured by passing one-sided—or in any event for the opposing side unintelligible—acts of law. One such legal instrument was the Spanish *Requerimiento*, a call to indigenous peoples to immediately submit to the historically founded and canonically legitimate authority of the kings of Castile. Merely the act of reading this decree in public—in most cases both inaudible and totally unintelligible even in linguistic terms to its intended audience, leaving aside their appreciation of the legal ramifications of non-compliance—automatically legitimized a war of annihilation against anyone who rebelled,[476] 'surely the crassest example of legalism in modern European history.'[477] Similar acts of law included the treaties by which the Indians of Louisiana subjugated themselves to Louis XIV, whom they had never heard of and would never hear from again.[478] Then there was the construct of the *terra nullius* (land devoid of ownership), which ignored all indigenous sovereign rights and was typical of colonial settlements.[479] Finally, and above all, there was the drawing of boundaries by means of treaties between imperial powers—on a grand scale, of course, after the Berlin Conference on Africa of 1884–5[480]—which legally made indigenous societies subjects of this or that empire, against their will and in most cases without their knowledge; it also summarily deprived them of the *ius ad bellum*, the right to wage legitimate war against occupation[481] (and at the same time also the privileges of the *ius in bello*, or customs of war).[482]

This expansion of juristic claims to rule over unconquered and not infrequently unknown regions and peoples created a confusion in terminology that has lasted to this day. It suggests an apparent legal clarity, where the transition from the external to the internal, from hegemony

to rule—as on all imperial frontiers—was ultimately fluid.[483] The customary distinction between a war of conquest fought between states
on the one hand and (subsequent) pacification or fighting against an
internal insurrection on the other, as classically formulated by Charles
Callwell,[484] is based on a fiction of international law, which even prior
to the effective occupation of large parts of the world had little significance at the conference tables of Europe, and virtually none for the
actual structure of conflict on the ground. Could a conflict that would
normally have been properly described as a war against a non-European people suddenly become a 'police action' merely by dint of the
collapse of an indigenous state or the imposition of a protectorate
under the threat of violence? This situation might perhaps look somewhat different in the case of a revolt following several centuries of
colonial rule recognized in practice—but then again, apart from in
colonial settlements where there was a demographic preponderance of
colonists, colonial rule was hardly ever effectively recognized. What
the imperial authorities saw as a rebellion would have been construed
by the indigenous actors as a legitimate exercise of a sovereign society's
right—one they had never waived—to wage war against aggression.

Consequently, such semantic-legalistic subtleties could, and can, do
little to explain the reality of the balance of power and the conduct of
warfare on the spot.[485] However, they did establish an intellectual tradition which, up until the late twentieth century, implicitly took the
imperial side and led to armed conflicts in existing colonies, including
even interventions into territories beyond, being described not as
wars, but as criminal insurrections (as with the Philippines War
of Independence),[486] as simple 'upheavals' or 'affairs' (the Boxer
Rebellion),[487] 'states of emergency' (the insurrection in Malaya and the
Mau-Mau insurgency), or 'incidents' (Algeria). These were clearly
designed to downplay the significance of the enemy (and to ward off
any ill effects from the colonial economy, since insurance policies were
generally rendered null and void in the event of war).[488] The Law of
Armed Conflict appeared to support this position through the Hague
Conventions of 1899 and 1907, which were entirely premised on war
between states.[489] Only after 1945, once substate groups engaging in
wars of liberation had been recognized by the United Nations as legitimate combatants, was this legalistic sham brought to an end, at least on

paper[490]—only to make a comeback in wars of the present, which likewise sometimes cannot afford to be deemed legal, in constructs such as 'unlawful combatants.'[491]

The opposing side also made every effort to put obstacles in the way of a clear distinction between war and peace. In particular, American Indians 'could change with bewildering rapidity from friend to foe to neutral, and rarely could one be confidently distinguished from another.'[492] Often, within the same small group, there would be a faction in favour of peace and one for war, with the former engaging in negotiations even while the latter carried out raids. That the US forces should at some stage switch over to holding the entire group responsible for attacks was understandable, if not always helpful; but for long periods of time, it was truly impossible to say if a certain group was at peace or at war with the United States.[493] The Cherokee Nation v. Georgia decision of the US Supreme Court in 1831 that devised the mystifying construct of 'domestic dependent nations'[494] turned the Indian nations into subject peoples internationally while at the same time making them sovereign treaty partners rather than US citizens internally, and thus only added to the confusion. All the while, of course, the Indian Wars too were not officially regarded as wars.[495]

So, given that peace and war on the periphery were legally and practically barely distinguishable from each other,[496] we should not be surprised that many conflicts dragged on for years, or decades or even centuries without coming to a clear conclusion. In Mexico the series of campaigns of subjugation and revolts that began immediately after the Spanish conquest, had still not ended by the nineteenth century. In the Yucatán, it even took until the 1930s before peace was concluded.[497] In Brazil, the warlike Chavante and Canoeiro peoples resisted colonial rule from the late eighteenth to the mid-twentieth century.[498] From the beginning of the French occupation of Algeria in the mid-nineteenth century until their withdrawal more than a century later, a virtually constant state of war existed in the country,[499] 'a war without end, which erased any distinction between a state of war and a state of peace.'[500] The same was true of Morocco, where France's conquest began in 1844 and only ended officially ninety years later in 1934, shortly before the end of colonial rule there.[501] Frontier conflicts in Australia rumbled on in some cases for centuries at a low intensity.[502]

Even some of the wars of decolonization of the late twentieth century only came to an end after decades (long after the withdrawal of the original colonial power): Angola suffered twenty-seven years of war, and Indochina thirty.[503]

Many imperial wars that were somewhat more clearly defined carried on for years or even decades beyond their official end—which in most cases was unilaterally set by the imperial power.[504] This was the case, for instance, with the Italian occupation of Ethiopia in 1935–1936, which for face-saving reasons Mussolini declared at an end after just seven months[505]—in George W. Bush's words, 'mission accomplished.'[506]

The fact that so many imperial wars were seemingly unending was also due to the fact that the bases for a negotiated settlement were mostly lacking. In many cases there was no-one with whom one could have meaningfully negotiated about a cessation of hostilities, and even when negotiations took place, their outcome seldom had any durability, for various reasons: because the underlying structural conflict remained unresolved; because one of the parties could or would not monitor observance of the agreed terms of the settlement; or because these had become obsolete with the collapse of the indigenous state. In particular, the conflicts of interest between settlers and the local non-European population, which due to their nature did not allow any compromise, either proved intractable to lasting resolution through negotiation, or foundered on the impossibility of actually holding settlers to the agreements.[507] As with the containment of violence, so did ending wars also presume a responsible state organization with a monopoly on the use of force, which simply did not exist on either side on the periphery. No wonder, then, that peace agreements often had more of the character of a ceasefire.[508] Besides, not infrequently it was the empires themselves which, however much they wished on the one hand to bring a war to an unequivocal end, made this impossible on the other by delegitimizing their enemy and imposing unacceptable conditions. Peace treaties presumably had their best chances in relatively symmetrical situations, in other words between locally comparatively weak empires and strong opponents, as in the Early Modern period in Africa.[509]

Decision at all costs

A major military operation launched in 1970 as part of the Portuguese war of decolonization in Mozambique against the FRELIMO guerrilla movement was actually called 'Nó Górdio', 'Gordian Knot': an almost Freudian pointer to the mindset of the military planners behind it.[510] Conflicts on the margins of empires mostly defied a clear and swift military solution. Yet the highly militarized frontier was the domain of the armed forces. And as the heirs to a culture of violence which had made the search for a decisive outcome by means of intensive military operations into the *ultima ratio* of war and which abhorred long wars of attrition, they were generally not given to accepting such a situation uncomplainingly. The 'military mind'[511] rebelled against any acknowledgment of the de facto powerlessness of the armed forces and opposed political solutions;[512] instead, it sought to use all means at its disposal to deal the 'knock-out blow,'[513] and this remains essentially the case to the present day.[514] 'Military officers intend to conduct "rapid, decisive operations" to produce "decisive victory". Much emphasis is put on being "offensively minded". Who, after all, would want to conduct "slow, indecisive operations" [...]?'[515] As Kanya-Forstner has said of French officers in the Sudan: 'Their overriding concern was with security; and the only way to preserve security, they argued, was to crush all oppposition, real or merely anticipated.'[516] This sounds like the Vietnam War, where the head of operations of the US Army once summed up the military strategy as follows: 'The solution in Vietnam is more bombs, more shells, more napalm... till the other side cracks and gives up.'[517] The obsessive quest for a decisive solution at all costs became the characteristic signature of imperial wars.

It became an obsession of the military to force a decisive confrontation, compelling the enemy to engage in battle, a battle that the imperial forces would try to ensure was as decisive, that is as devastating, as possible. All their thoughts and actions turned on the objective of breaking the vicious circle formed by an elusive enemy, territory they could not control, and a long drawn-out conflict. As Charles Callwell decreed in around 1900: 'the enemy must be brought to battle, and in such manner as to make his defeat decisive.'[518] This had been the quintessence of all military logic for imperial wars in the centuries preceding Callwell's book. Callwell went on:

Battles, then, are the objects to be sought for by the regular [imperial] troops, and since the enemy as a general rule shirks engagement in the open field, the strongest grounds exist for tempting him to fight [...]. [...] Battles being so desirable and so difficult to bring about, it stands to reason that when a conflict does occur the opportunity should be taken full advantage of. It must be fully realised that mere defeat of the adversary is not enough, the opposing forces should be beaten so thoroughly that they will not offer further opposition. They must if possible be in a military sense destroyed. Decisive victory is to be sought for and not merely success.[519]

Nothing tells us so much about the actions of imperial commanders on the periphery as the fear that the enemy might actively choose to avoid giving battle and thereby prolong the war indefinitely. 'For there is nothing worse than a long African war,' wrote one company commander of the German Schutztruppe, by way of explaining his preference for the 'short, sharp shock.'[520] Hence the stubborn conviction that 'the enemy must be brought to battle,' a maxim that the military 'men on the spot' proceeded to follow blindly, even when indigenous opponents did not make the slightest effort to avoid a fight. 'The enemy must be brought to battle' meant, stereotypically, always attacking, not just when necessary but also quite consciously without gathering any intelligence, in order to give the enemy no prior warning, and of course without paying any heed to his strength or his intentions. In any event, it was taken as read that the enemy had superior numbers, and any opportunity to lure him into a fight was simply too good to pass up: 'What a beautiful chance for a fight,' enthused Colonel Dixon S. Miles, when a group of Mescalero Apaches tried to offer their surrender in January 1855, 'The troops will never get such another.'[521] The key thing to note here is that the commander seriously contemplated refusing to accept a surrender in favour of a chance to defeat a concentrated and visible enemy in battle, just in order to finally make up for the frustration of never being able to deal a decisive blow.

No wonder that this fanatical zeal for going on the offensive, for chasing an opponent who was always thought (however wrongly) to be evading battle, was responsible for some of the most catastrophic tactical defeats suffered by imperial forces on the periphery,[522] primarily those inflicted on Custer in 1876 and Chelmsford in 1879. Both were in pursuit, with divided columns, of a numerically massively superior opposing force and stubbornly ignored every indication that the enemy might not in fact be on the run, but was liable at any moment to turn and attack them.[523] For Western commanders in imperial wars, the fear that the enemy might escape was so great that all military common sense was cast to the winds.[524] In the Boer War—which was after all against an opponent of European origin with tactical cohesion and excellent modern firearms—this fear resulted in massive losses for the British when they launched senseless frontal assaults against fortified positions.[525]

In operational terms the obsessive quest for the decisive battle led, as we have already seen, to the concept of a concentric advance in divided columns, to attempts to control swathes of territory, to restless protracted campaigning even in the subtropical high summer, the tropical rainy season or the Northern winter under the harshest conditions, in order to try and catch the enemy at all costs.[526] Yet this obsessive search for a decisive outcome also lay behind the ludicrous plan hatched by Henri Navarre, the French commander-in-chief in Indochina, to have thousands of airborne troops parachuted into Dien Bien Phu, 450 kilometres behind enemy lines, to try and force the Viet Minh to engage in battle and inflict a decisive defeat on them—the objective of forcing the Viet Minh to accept battle was met but, as is well known, the second objective failed signally.[527] Beyond the narrow military sphere, the fanatical search for a decisive victory was a fundamental reason for broadening the scope of the war, expanding the war effort to target the enemy's food resources, settlements and civilian population, and even going as far as conducting total war against entire societies.[528]

Finally, in strategic terms, the delusion of being able to break out of the vicious circle of indecisiveness with one liberating blow prompted a search for 'final solutions', for the complete destruction of indigenous political organizations and for the total subjugation of peoples. Unacceptable ultimatums and the refusal to enter into any peace negotiations that fell short of unconditional surrender were typical above all of the end phase of the carving-up of the world that took place at the end of the nineteenth century.[529] When, for example, the French invaded Dahomey in 1893, they repeatedly rejected a series of increasingly desperate concessions by the ruling Fon monarchy, only finally settling for the banishment of the king, annexation of half the country and the installation of a puppet regime in the other half.[530] Even as early as the Maori Wars in the 1840s, the British responded to their adversaries' restricted use of warfare with an intransigent campaign of ruthless subjugation.[531] During the conquest of America, all imperial players, but especially the English settlers there, resorted to uncompromising wars of annihilation[532] against their Indian neighbours.[533] Forced relocation or physical eradication could even sometimes be set as objectives in place of political subjugation, at least where stateless opponents were concerned.[534]

Cooperation

As a solution to the difficulties of imperial warfare on the periphery, the attempt to achieve a decisive outcome at all costs was problematic to say the least. In each case, the intensity of violence increased massively, the prospects of success were dim and even in the best circumstances the peace of the graveyard was bought at the cost of an undesirably high outlay in resources. Even so, empires apparently 'won' imperial wars with regularity (I will discuss exactly what that means presently), and in the course of these conflicts they repeatedly won battles—in so far as any battles were fought. And all that despite the relative smallness of their force compared to the vastness of space on the fringes of empire, not to mention on the field of combat.

It was only in the older colonial settlements, where the autochthonous population had already been demographically marginalized, that the West managed to attain a parity in the numbers of fighting men (as, say, in the USA)[535]—or even superiority (as in the Cape Colony and New Zealand).[536] Otherwise the non-European adversary was generally massively in the majority, even on the battlefield. Many historical accounts confirm this, though it should be borne in mind that these are based overwhelmingly on data supplied by the imperial commanders. But even taking this into account they present an unequivocal message. One can go back through history, from the wars of decolonization, where in 1954 at Dien Bien Phu there were ultimately 7,000 French troops ranged against 50,000 Viet Minh (who also possessed four times as many artillery pieces),[537] through numerous battles fought during the conquest of Africa, in which European soldiers were faced with five to ten times as many enemy warriors (and still triumphed, save for a handful of exceptions),[538] and similar instances in the Far East,[539] to the eighteenth century in Southeast Asia, where the troops of the British East India Company triumphed time and again over Indian armies which outnumbered them by a ratio of 7:1 to 10:1,[540] and finally back to the seventeenth century in Southeast Asia, where their Dutch rivals performed similar feats of arms.[541]

However impressive such relative figures may be, they nonetheless remain within the bounds of the credible and above all of the explicable. Discipline, drill and modern firearms made it perfectly possible for armies on the European pattern to emerge victorious against indigenous adversaries who were clearly numerically superior but far less well pre-pared and equipped for battle.[542] It may have been the case that not all of the enemy army joined battle, at least not at the same time; a large army is always more difficult to coordinate than a small one, and the techniques of leadership were not always very refined on the indigenous side. And then there is the fact, as mentioned, that the figures for the numbers of enemy soldiers are not firm statistics.[543] In all likelihood, things will have played out here in the manner outlined by G. J. Bryant:

> The reported numbers in 'country' [local] armies in standard accounts always need to be treated with greater caution that the better documented British head-counts, as the statistical source is often a guess by a Company officer who might have had a vested interest in exaggerating the size of the force he had just beaten or which had just beaten him, or who had mistak-enly included camp followers who were often less distinctive from proper soldiers in country armies.[544]

Furthermore, it was presumably not just in India that incidents like the Battle of Plassey in 1756 occurred, where the Bengali Army, which was confronting the 3,000 soldiers of the East India Company, may well have numbered close on 50,000 men at the outset, but even right at the start of the battle was rife with disunity, betrayal and desertion and began to disintegrate (British bribes played a significant part in this).[545] Plassey was a political and moral victory which one does not have to seek to explain tactically.

The notion should not, therefore, be dismissed out of hand that Western armies on the periphery regularly succeeded in beating enemy forces that were five or even ten times larger. The only problem is that relative troop numbers were also regularly reported from the violent history of European expansion that should begin to raise doubts over the sanity of those reporting them. To be sure, there were well-documented examples like the one that is perhaps the most stereotypical battle in a colonial war—namely the defence of the mission station at Rorke's Drift in Zululand on 22–23 January 1879—where a total of 152 British soldiers really did fight off three Zulu regiments, which must have numbered some 4,000 men.[546] But unlike the battle at Isandlwana, which took place on the same day, the defenders at Rorke's Drift had improvised defensive emplacements and a very narrow front to hold, circumstances that maximized the firepower of their Martini-Henry rifles.[547] The mother country, which in the light of the dreadful defeat at Isandlwana badly needed heroes, decorated no fewer than eleven of the defenders of the mission with the highest British military honour, the Victoria Cross—more than in any other battle in British history.[548]

There may well have been other similar instances from this era where highly disciplined and perfectly drilled professional Western troops armed with modern weapons encountered relatively loosely organized opponents who massively outnumbered them, but who overall were nonetheless not equal to them.[549] But are we really prepared to believe that in the Early Modern period, a few dozen European soldiers repeatedly defended tiny strongholds for weeks on end against tens of thousands of indigenous foes?[550] When over 20,000 Maya surrounded around 100 Spanish conquistadors in the open in 1517 at Chanponton in the Yucatán—in other words without the protection of a fortified position—is it even conceivable that fifty Spaniards broke through the encirclement and survived?[551] Even more absurd is the claim that, at Vega Real on the island of Hispaniola on 27 March 1495, 200 Spanish foot soldiers and twenty cavalrymen, together with twenty armoured war-dogs, surprised 100,000 Indians in their camp, they encircled and annihilated them—surely not only a military impossibility but quite clearly a geometrical one too.[552]

These kind of absurd relative troop numbers are especially prevalent in the history of the Spanish conquest of Peru. If we are to believe the Spanish sources and the accounts that are based on them (and, indeed, no other information is available)[553] Francisco Pizarro, with just 106 men on foot and sixty-two on horseback, conquered a major warlike empire which had at least two (and possibly as many as nine) million inhabitants, and could field a professional army of 100,000 soldiers.[554] At Cajamarca these 168 Spaniards are said not only to have taken the Inca ruler Atahualpa prisoner in the presence of his main army of 80,000 men, but also to have slaughtered 7,000 people, including most of the noblemen of the Inca Empire, within the space of an hour.[555] Supposedly, then, each Spanish soldier would have had to have killed more than forty people in short order; as George Raudzens has remarked, this would surely represent an all-time face-to-face killing record.[556] At the battles at Vilcashuamán and Vilcaconga, which took place during the advance on Cuzco, we are asked to believe that several thousand Inca launched surprise attacks downhill on the small band of Spanish conquistadors, and were fortunate in the one case to have killed just one Spanish horse and in the other five Spanish soldiers, while themselves sustaining casualties in the high hundreds on each occasion.[557] Later, during the siege of the occupied city of Cuzco by Manco Inca Yupanqui, 190 Spaniards are reputed to have held out for a year against anything between 100,000 and 400,000 Inca,[558] with the ensuing battle being decided when sixty-two Spanish horsemen sallied forth and, attacking uphill, captured the huge fortress of Sacsahuaman and cut down at least 5,000 of its defenders.[559]

These figures cannot be regarded as anything other than pure fantasy, and it is genuinely hard to understand why they are still cited in histories as though they were true. Indigenous armies in the Early Modern era numbering in the hundreds of thousands are an impossibility, if only from an organizational and logistical perspective. By the mid-nineteenth century, in an age of railways and telegraphs, it was an extraordinarily difficult task, even in highly developed regions in Central Europe or on the eastern seaboard of the USA, which had intensive agriculture and a dense transport network, to coordinate and above all to feed armies that numbered in six figures.[560] No one who is aware of this would still think for an instant that such a thing might have been possible in the Peruvian High Andes in the sixteenth century.

In any case, as Wolfgang Gabbert has shown, the Spanish:

> generally lacked the means of determining the numbers of their enemies more precisely. It was in their interest to give a high estimate in order to make their own feats of arms seem as impressive as possible. Finally, where many Spanish sources were concerned, it was a case of documents that

were meant to justify the compilers' own actions to the Crown and to substantiate their claims to the largest possible bounty.[561]

Another factor that came into play here was the sense of religious calling. For Spaniards of the sixteenth century, spiritual heirs of the Reconquista—the retaking of Spain from the Muslim Moors—it was nothing less than an article of faith, proving their divine mission, that they in their small bands should vanquish enemy hordes at least a hundred times larger, and so that was what they wrote in their reports.[562] Subsequently, this incredibly intuitive image, this 'loose but strong archetypal narrative'[563] of the dramatic struggle of the 'handful against the horde'[564] became the guiding theme of the European triumph in the conquest of the world, and has remained rooted in popular culture ever since. One need only think of the countless Hollywood Westerns from the twentieth century,[565] or more recently of the US blockbuster movie *Black Hawk Down* from 2001, which portrayed American troops as heroic individuals battling to the death against an amorphous mass of murderous, fanatical Arabs yelling unintelligible slogans.[566] One could easily scale down the figures cited in most accounts of the Early Modern period from the simply incredible hundreds of thousands to a sensible count of thousands without violating the source's power of veto. Sheer common sense also exercises a power of veto, and we can state with a high degree of certainty that these figures were never meant to be taken literally.[567]

Nonetheless, one continues to be confronted by the apparent fact that, in the conquest of Peru, but not exclusively there, a very small number of Spaniards triumphed over genuinely large Indian armies. One of the foremost experts on Early Modern military history, John Guilmartin, does not seriously question the figures given in the sources, but instead seeks to explain them by pointing to the penetrative power of steel swords, the protection afforded by steel armour against what were primarily Stone Age Peruvian clubs and slingshots, the skill of the Spanish in swordplay and finally the initiative, cohesion and tactical integration of the small band of conquistadors. Additional factors, according to Guilmartin, were the shock effect, mobility and virtual invulnerability of the horses the Spanish brought with them— due to the absence of any pikes on the opposing side, who did not have the wood for them.[568]

But even if Pizarro's conquistadors had been 'Terminators' wielding flashing steel swords, who could kill Indians as though on a conveyor belt until they dropped from exhaustion, as Guilmartin seems to imply,[569] their numbers, as attested in the sources, were still so small that they would in the long run have inevitably succumbed to an enemy force with even a hundredth of its reported strength. No matter what advantages a steel sword offered, it wasn't a machine gun, but a weapon for close-quarters combat, and a Spaniard with a sword could only kill one Indian at a time. What were the thousands (if not hundreds of thousands) of others doing in the meantime? Did they wait patiently until their turn came? It is worth noting at this juncture that Atahualpa's army was not some easily demoralized rabble of tribal warriors but a highly cohesive professional army that had just won a civil war and that did not, for instance, flee at the first encounter with the interlopers, but rather put up stiff resistance to them over a number of years. Yet this force was supposedly incapable of summoning up the small degree of coordination required to simply crush the little band of Spaniards just by their sheer weight of numbers?

And as for the shock effect of the Spanish horses: couldn't ten determined men manage to bring down a horse? With ropes, for example, which the Inca undoubtedly knew about, having used them in their rope bridges? And even if ten couldn't do it, then surely 100? And couldn't ten or a hundred men strangle, pummel or trample to death a fallen rider lying on the ground even if he did have armour and a sword? Instead of stylizing Pizarro's conquistadors into one-man killing machines, we should perhaps be looking for a simpler explanation.

For it may be the case that it wasn't just 170 Spaniards who overran the Inca Empire—at least not all on their own. The sources and the secondary literature based on them contain some hidden but revealing hints. At the beginning of 1534, the Inca general Quisquis, commanding 7,000 men in two columns, attacked the small Spanish garrison in the strategically located town of Jauja. The coordination went awry, and the 1,000-man strong encircling column reached Jauja first. They were driven back at a bridge by 'ten light horsemen' and 'some peon cross-bowmen', who then proceeded to cross the bridge and launch a counterattack[570]—so, a total of around fifteen or twenty men against a thousand, a ratio of around 1:65 or at best 1:50.

Thus far, this account echoes those from Cajamarca, Vilcashuamán and Cuzco. But the following day, when Quisquis's main column arrived from the other direction, 'twenty light horse and twenty peons with two thousand friendly Indians advanced to engage it.'[571] These allies reduced the relative troop strengths to a more credible ratio of 1:3. It is perfectly possible to imagine a horde of 2,000 Indians supported by forty grimly determined, well armed and fully armour-clad conquistadors repulsing 6,000 Inca warriors at spear-point, especially in a defensive position in a mountain valley.

The 'friendly Indians' in question here were the local Huanca people, who were rebelling against Inca rule and so made common cause with the Spanish. And that was the decisive factor: with the gambler's luck of a great adventurer, Pizarro happened to invade Peru at the moment when the Inca Empire had just come through a civil war. After the Inca emperor Huayna Capac died of the plague, the succession was disputed between the commander of the army, Atahualpa, and his brother Huascar; Atahualpa had emerged victorious from this clash just before the arrival of the Spanish, but the empire was torn apart and the scars caused by Atahualpa's punitive campaigns of revenge were still running sores. Many of the followers of Huascar (whose execution Atahualpa ordered, even while he himself was already Pizarro's prisoner) and many local ethnic groups who were antagonistic anyway to Inca rule did not need much persuasion to hail the Spanish as welcome allies.[572]

Therefore there can be no question of just 170 Spaniards conquering the Inca Empire. They merely had the good fortune to become a significant political factor in Peru, not least as a result of their bold coup against Atahualpa, and with the added bonus of the military and psychological impact of their modern weapons and horses to tip the scales in the civil war there. Their victory was not a directly military one, but rather a political manipulation of the military balance of power. All logic suggests that the absurd numerical ratios, which are still trotted out even nowadays, along with the huge exaggeration of the enemy's strength, simply resulted from the Spaniards' reliance on Indian allies. The fact that they were not keen to talk about them,[573] preferring instead to cultivate the myth that a handful of Spanish conquistadors, by the Grace of God, were able to overcome 100,000 Incas, is unfortunate for later historians, if understandable on a human level. There was no earthly reason to mention the matter of local cooperation to the Spanish public. 'Two thousand friendly Indians' is a kind of Freudian slip. A similar kind of nonchalant inconsistency is evident in the accounts that Pedro de Alvarado, a companion of Hernán Cortés, wrote about the battles during the conquest of Mexico, where he initially speaks about Cortés' 250 Spanish soldiers, only in the next breath to mention in passing their 5,000 to 6,000 Amerindian allies. Matthew Restall has said of this: 'There is no doubt that the Spaniards were consistently outnumbered by native enemies on the battlefield. But what has so often been ignored or forgotten is the fact that the Spaniards tended also to be outnumbered by their own native allies.'[574]

Likewise, Mexico was not conquered by 500 Spaniards either (who in any event actually numbered more like 1,500). The Aztec Empire, like that of the Incas, was a fairly unstable hegemonic structure, within which numerous constituent ethnic groups had not yet got over their recent forcible incorporation and who consequently gave an enthusiastic welcome to new allies—especially ones who came with firearms, steel armour and horses. The conquest of Mexico was a foregone conclusion the moment the country's second most powerful city-state, Tlaxcallan, entered into an alliance with Cortés. The Aztecs were toppled by hundreds of thousands of their Indian neighbours and vassals, while the conquistadors, who made up less than 1 per cent of the allied armies, acted merely as their shock troops.[575]

Moreover, this model can be applied elsewhere, not least precisely because the successors of Cortés and Pizarro (and every colonial conqueror for centuries thereafter who saw themselves as following in their wake) henceforth deliberately went in search of the faultlines in indigenous societies, the local equivalent of the Tlaxcaltecans, who could be mobilized to fight against the ruling power.[576] And they found such groups—every time without fail. No indigenous state in the New World—or for that matter scarcely any in the rest of the non-European world—was so stable, and no rulership so uncontestedly legitimate, that there were not other groups in existence who saw the arrival of heavily armed foreign adventurers who were clearly no strangers to violence as an opportunity to reshuffle the pack. If it wasn't an ethnicity that had recently been subjugated or a social group that was keen to advance itself, then it was a powerful grouping at the court or—very frequently—a contender for the throne. And even if a state was not divided against itself, it could be relied upon to have envious neighbours who would readily band together against it. A civil war or a power struggle could be found almost everywhere.[577]

Of course, these willing allies of empires were entering into a pact with the devil. For however much they may have profited initially from such an alliance,[578] after the regional ruler had been toppled, or at least once they had ceased to be of use, they regularly became the next victim,[579] as for instance in Brazil, where it became a virtual patent formula of the colonists to stir up one Indian group against another, in order to then occupy the land of their former allies who had been weakened by this conflict, if need be with the help of those who had originally been their enemy.[580] It is true that this ingratitude on the part of empires did not always manifest itself in the immediate and total subjugation of their former friends. It could instead result in an increasing lack of independence and a creeping process of destabilization, as in the case of the Indian princely states that allied themselves with the British East India Company.[581] But it was extremely rare for states that threw in their lot with empires to profit from the deal in the long run.

Often, the cooperation of subgroups or individuals did not pay off because, at the time of crisis or immediately thereafter, European settlers or imperial armed forces on the periphery exacted collective punishment and no longer made any distinction between friend and foe. In suppressing the Pueblo Revolt in 1680, the Spanish began by burning down the villages in the south of New Mexico, which had lived in peace with them or at least remained neutral, for the sole reason that they presented the easiest targets.[582] Similarly, after the Creek War in 1814, not only the hostile Upper Creek Indians, but also the Lower Creek, who had been allies of the victorious United States, were stripped of their land.[583] In 1883, the rebel Apache leader Geronimo was deported to Florida from the US Southwest, but alongside him too the Apache scouts who had helped the US Army track him down and arrest him.[584] In both South and North America, it was often those Indian groups who were on friendly terms with the colonial authorities who were for that very reason the first to fall victim to settler violence in times of heightened tension, simply because they were easily accessible: they lived close to European bases and believed that they had no reason to be armed and mistrustful. You couldn't tell by looking at the scalps that were delivered to the authorities in return for bounty payments that many of them came from people who had naïvely thought that they were living in peace with the empire.[585]

Indigenous alliance partners were guilty of underestimating empires across the board, since in most cases they did not have the slightest inkling of how absolute the will to rule of these newcomers was—after all, their numbers had hardly been impressive at the outset—or how destructive it was to local diplomatic customs and power structures, or above all how vast the reservoir of resources and stable authority was that the colonists could draw on. In fairness, even with a stretch of the imagination, the everlasting imperial state's enduring and uncompromising urge for conquest[586] was not plain to see in the small band of conquistadors.[587] The objective that Cortés pursued of complete subjugation and territorial domination over Mexico clearly surpassed the Aztec ruling elite's powers of imagination, who thought in terms of loose hegemonic systems.[588] Even subsequently, when the Europeans arrived with large armies, their unscrupulous willingness to overturn established systems and to strive ruthlessly after domination went far beyond the comprehension of many non-European societies opposing them, as Dirk Kolff has explained with regard to the British conquest of India in around 1800: 'Whereas the British were out for the subjugation and disarmament of the Indian princes and war-lords, the latter could only conceive of military enterprise as a means to refurbish the alliance systems that had always been the essence of Indian politics.'[589]

With regard to local alliances with empires, it has become commonplace to speak of 'disunity'[590] within the indigenous population. Not only is this an interpretation after the fact, which in addition draws upon an idealization of the modern nation-state, but also the moralizing undertone is of little help in understanding the circumstances of conquest. Empires encroached as outsiders upon long-established regional systems of diplomacy and structures of power and authority, in which they were an alien and at first peripheral factor. The true fault lines of conflict were familiar to the actors on the ground and were of far greater relevance than any relationship to the newcomers.[591] Developing a concept of indigenous solidarity towards this new power

factor would have meant suddenly gearing all strategic political thinking to the new situation, and for the actors involved there was for the
most part no immediately apparent reason to do so.[592] For a
Tlaxcaltecan, for instance, a Spaniard was not at first sight any more
strange, and in any event not any more dangerous, than an Aztec.[593] In
so far as the conquistadors were perceived as a significant power factor
at all, in the fragile balance of power that existed on the ground in
Mexico, they appeared as more of an opportunity than a threat. In any
event, the key thing was to prevent them from making common cause
with the indigenous enemy.[594] The North American Indians of the eighteenth century, who had already been in contact with European
empires for a longer period, had become somewhat shrewder by this
time and preferred entering into alliances with the weaker power in
any given location.[595] The Arikara, Pawnee and Crow peoples joined
forces with the US Army in the 1870s not because of any lack of solidarity within the Indian community, but because they had been sub-
jected to pillage and suppression by the expansionist empire of the
Sioux on the Great Plains for the preceding half-century. For them, the
United States was in actuality the less dangerous neighbour.[596] It took
a long time, sometimes centuries, for the necessity of intra-indigenous
alliances against the imperial powers to become apparent, and in many
cases it was then already too late.[597]

Alleged 'disunity' among the opponents of imperialism is thus of
little value as a reprimand. Analytically, one can, of course, demonstrate that much of the non-European world, compared with the
empires that were centred on modern Western nation-states, was positively atomized—a handful of comparatively unstable major empires
and fragile hegemonic structures, a few (mostly small and heterogeneous) states and countless non-state groupings, who were often in a
state of long-term conflict with one another. This world was eminently
dividable, or rather it was already divided before Western empires
came on the scene and exploited these divisions as an instrument of
control in their expansion. The imperative of the dominance of the few
over the many, namely 'divide and rule', suggests an excess of manipu-
lative power that often belies the real situation on the ground. Almost
every imperial war was a local affair to begin with and was often for a
long time a civil war between indigenous groups.

Across the board, imperial expansion throughout the world was based on the exploitation of conflicts between indigenous groups—and on indigenous manpower.[598] This can be demonstrated with statistics from across the centuries of European expansion. In the Early Modern period, the Spanish, Portuguese and Dutch routinely deployed armies in the Americas and Asia which consisted of between several dozen and a few hundred Europeans on the one hand and many thousands, sometimes as many as 10,000 or 20,000, indigenous allies or auxiliary troops on the other—not counting bearers and slaves.[599] One might sometimes have been tempted to ask exactly who were whose auxiliaries.

The mass armies that were deployed in India from the eighteenth century on consisted overwhelmingly of sepoys. Even as early as 1783, the British East India Company had a force of over 100,000 men, 90 per cent of whom had been recruited from the subcontinent.[600] At the Battle of Buxar in 1764, which secured Britain control over Bengal, the British fielded a force of 900 Europeans and 7,000 sepoys.[601] In the nineteenth century the ratio for India overall remained roughly of an order of magnitude of 1:5 or 1:6. In 1808, there were 25,000 British soldiers as against 155,000 Indians; shortly before the outbreak of the Indian Rebellion in 1857, the respective numbers were 45,000 to 232,000. After the mutiny, though, the proportion of European troops was drastically increased in order, as David Omissi has put it, 'to guard the guardians of the Raj'. By 1863, there were 62,000 British troops to 125,000 sepoys, and despite the continuing growth of the Indian Army this ratio of 1:2 remained the same until the twentieth century, when it gradually decreased once more to 1:3.[602] This relative high proportion of European troops—naturally as a result of the mutiny—made India relatively unique in the history of empire.

The military expansion into Africa at the end of the nineteenth century likewise relied to a large extent upon African troops. At most there was a hard core of European units, especially in French West Africa (10–20 per cent),[603] but as a general rule only the cadres were Europeans—typical of this, for example was the Belgian 'Force Publique' in the Congo, which on the eve of the First World War comprised 18,000 men under 400 European officers and NCOs.[604]

In the Caribbean, all empires recruited auxiliary troops and regular detachments alike from among the population of African origin on a grand scale, both in order to quell uprisings and to fight in the conflicts that erupted between European empires during the Revolutionary and Napoleonic Wars (1792–1815).[605] The situation was somewhat different in North America, where, due to the lack of a strong settler presence,[606] it was primarily the French whose empire and ability to wage war depended on alliances with the indigenous population.[607] Correspondingly the ambush that annihilated Braddock's army in 1755 was organized and executed by 100 French soldiers with 150 French-Canadian settlers and over 6,000 Indians.[608] But North America in the eighteenth century is a special case anyhow, since here it was first and foremost the conflict between empires (the English and French) that prompted the deployment of regular forces and strong contingents of settler troops.[609]

In general, most of the more well-established colonial settlements were less dependent upon transcultural alliances and indigenous manpower, at least in the long term. The more strongly pronounced the demographic preponderance of Europeans, the more they could do without indigenous cooperation. This is not, however, to say that no transcultural alliances of any kind were forged with the imperial power in colonial settlements. Whether or not it was absolutely necessary, an alliance was always cheaper and at least temporarily more helpful than a unified indigenous front. Yet the colonies of New England in the seventeenth century mistrusted Indian allies, with the result that in the eighteenth century, the British in North America were noticeably more hesitant about entering into alliances, and introduced them on a far more limited scale, than the French (except for during the American War of Independence).[610] Likewise, the young United States largely dispensed with indigenous auxiliary troops, and completely with any regular colonial forces, in the West. While some limited experiments were conducted by the US Army with companies of Indian scouts during the final phase of the Indian Wars, these were swiftly abandoned.[611]

During the Maori Wars in New Zealand, where 17,000 troops from Britain and other imperial forces were deployed, the 1,000 Maori who fought for the British Crown only played a subsidiary role at most.[612] An analytically especially confusing case is the Second Anglo-Boer War, in which a total of 5,500 Boers ultimately fought on the British side (granted, this figure only represented a third of the numbers ranged against the British in the field), as well as 120,000 African troops—yet as many as 14,000 Africans actually fought for the Boers against the British.[613] Occasionally at the end of the nineteenth century, when such things mattered, the principle of conquest by proxy was compromised by the idea that the prestige of the white race demanded that a victory should be won by white and not coloured troops; among other incidents, this determined the high proportion of British troops involved in the Ashanti War of 1873–1874 and the participation of large numbers of Italian conscripts in the failed invasion of Ethiopia in 1895–1896.[614] Similar considerations evidently motivated the US general Nelson Miles, who disbanded the Indian Scouts so that white troops could secure victory in the West.[615]

The deployment of indigenous manpower was in many regards a very economical system, almost a guaranteed success, as in India,[616] which according to John Robert Seeley 'conquered herself',[617] or early Spanish America, about which Philip Powell has written:

> In a very real sense the Indians of America were the conquerors—or destroyers—of their own world to the advantage of the European invaders. Time and again the story was repeated: Indians conquered other Indians to enable Europeans to control vast New World areas. Much, or even most, of European conquest in America was aided and abetted by the Indinas' [sic] fighting their own race—a fight that was supervised by handfuls of white men who astutely profited by long-standing native rivalries or the basic enmity between nomadic and sedentary Indian peoples.[618]

Things were much the same in Africa, as David Killingray explains: 'Indeed, most of West Africa was conquered, subjugated and policed by black armies led by a handful of Europeans.'[619]

Nothing chimed so well with the overriding imperialist rationale—namely that peripheries should above all be profitable, incur minimal costs and be as little trouble as possible to the metropole—than the policy of conquest by proxy. The indigenous population formed the bulk of every imperial army, with relatively few Europeans making up the shock troops,[620] the 'spearhead,'[621] the 'cutting edge'[622] or the 'disciplined, uniformed core of the violence.'[623] The advantage of indigenous manpower did not just reside in the fact that it was available in great quantity on the spot, and was both undemanding[624] and comparatively cheap,[625] which accorded fully with the logic of the imperial system.[626] Above and beyond this, local allies were acclimatized and far less susceptible to tropical diseases (a decisive factor in the West Indies and West Africa).[627] They also knew the locality and were familiar with the terrain and natural conditions, local customs and traditions of violence, in the face of which Europeans were often baffled if not downright helpless. In short, indigenous auxiliaries were specialists in colonial warfare.[628] Another key factor vis-à-vis the philosophy of 'divide and rule' was that their collaboration with the empire lent stability to foreign rule and divested any concept of solidarity between indigenous groups against imperial domination of some of its legitimacy.[629] Not to mention the basic fact that anyone who fought for the empire on the ground meant one less person fighting against it.[630]

With the establishment of an imperial presence, indigenous allies of empires underwent a series of stages of declining independence.[631] They started out as allies on an equal footing and with their own political aspirations, so long as the imperial power remained weak. As the empire gained in strength on the ground, so they increasingly forfeited their negotiating position and were reduced to the status of irregular auxiliary forces—fighting within their own, ethnically homogeneous units, no longer for collective political objectives but at best solely for personal economic goals, such as the plundering of enemies' resources.[632] Ultimately the regular colonial soldier, who had been recruited either as part of a contingent or individually, went on to serve as a mercenary in European-trained and -led and deliberately ethnically mixed detachments.[633] The original model for this was provided by the sepoys of the French and then above all the British armies in India.[634] The fact that the indigenous soldiers' individual skills as specialists in local fighting conditions were of necessity lost in the process of regularization later led to some particularly interesting discussions within the colonial military in the light of the guerrilla wars waged by their indigenous adversaries—an approach that relied heavily on good knowledge of the local terrain.[635]

Besides, however much the colonial soldier represented a pillar of the imperial system, he was nevertheless deeply mistrusted, an attitude that did not just begin after the sepoy revolt that culminated in the great Indian Rebellion in 1857. In conjunction with a racism that grew ever more intense as the nineteenth century progressed, such mistrust was of course the reason why colonial soldiers could become NCOs in the main, but very rarely officers (and even then only subalterns for the most part);[636] why they were not issued with modern firearms, particularly machine guns (a clear exception to this was the Force Publique in the Belgian Congo);[637] and above all why there was a distinct preference for deploying them away from their home regions.[638] In particular, this mindset was responsible for the imperial military's obsession with so-called 'warrior races', which in practice was used to denote groups from the periphery of the periphery: backwoodsmen who were far removed from the imperial system, who remained unaffected by its cities and power struggles and who for that reason became its willing enforcers—a pragmatic piece of ruler's logic but one that was overlaid with racial stereotypes and romantic fantasies about unspoiled primitive peoples.[639] Often, empires only began to row back from such security measures towards the end of their period of rule, when they were forced to take account of indigenous nationalism and when external dangers, in the age of world wars and the Cold War, seemed to require the creation of mass indigenous armies in the colonies.[640]

Occasionally colonial troops were more closely integrated into the imperial military system and became fully fledged imperial troops—in other words, an empire's manpower reserve, which could be deployed beyond the region from which it came.[641] A prime example of this was the British Indian Army, the 'foreign legionaries of the Empire'[642] for the whole of the Indian Ocean region (even though the Hindus in the Bengal Army had religious objections to undertaking sea voyages, a situation that led to strikes within the military prior to the Burmese War of 1825),[643] which saw fighting on behalf of Great Britain in two world wars, in theatres of conflict ranging from the Mediterranean to the Far East.[644] Within the larger force, the Nepalese Gurkhas were especially loyal, even playing an active part in suppressing the 1857 Indian Rebellion.[645] Yet Africa too formed an important manpower reserve for the British Empire: during the Second World War, 120,000 Africans served in Asia, and after the Indian recruiting pool dried up after independence in 1947, for a brief period there was even discussion about forming a standing African Imperial Army.[646] As early as the beginning of the nineteenth century, the British Empire used African-Caribbean troops in West Africa, largely because of their lesser susceptibility to tropical diseases than European soldiers.[647]

The later Spanish Empire employed Filipinos as auxiliary troops,[648] while in the early twentieth century soldiers from Mozambique served in all Portuguese colonies, as far afield as the Far East.[649] The French deployed their colonial troops not only on other continents, principally in Asia, but also regularly in major wars in the European theatre, including the Franco-Prussian War of 1870–1871 and both world wars[650] (215,000 men for the First World War alone, for which recruitment to the Tirailleurs Sénégalais unit increased by 1,300 per cent, from 13,000 to 180,000),[651] as well as a spell of duty as an occupation force in the Rhineland between the wars.[652] But after 1945, the imperial powers once more fell to worrying that their dependence upon non-European manpower in the wars and above all the fact that indigenous troops had been used against European adversaries may have helped to undermine the prestige of the white man. The collapse of colonial empires seemed to be proof positive of this.[653]

However, there were instances of the transcontinental deployment of imperial allies or auxiliaries long before the establishment of formal overseas imperial armies: for instance, Indian mercenaries took part in the Portuguese capture of Melaka (Malacca) in 1511,[654] and slave warriors from West Africa defended the Portuguese possessions of Ormuz (Hormuz) and Macao.[655] Tupi Indians from Brazil fought for Holland in Angola and El Salvador,[656] Amerindians from Central America served in Peru and even in the Philippines for Spain,[657] and following his alliance with Pizarro, Manco Inca Yupanqui sent 12,000 of his men to Chile under Spanish command.[658]

Alliances with the imperial power characterized the imperial system and the organized use of violence in pursuit of its aim to the very end, up to the time when transethnic, proto-nationalist independence movements began increasingly to strip colonial rule—and with it indigenous collaboration with foreign dominion—of any legitimacy it may have had.[659] The stereotypical response of imperial forces was to spread propaganda claiming that resistance movements were tribal, so denying their nature as legitimate national movements, or to rob them of their political legitimacy (say, by smearing them as communist during the Cold War).[660] At first, this tactic was successful: not infrequently socially conservative sections of the populace in particular tended to prefer the paternalistic imperial order to the radical proposals of nationalist movements that were often socially marginalized, especially when those groups espoused terrorism as a method of persuasion.[661] Collaboration with the imperial power commanded even greater support if the empire announced its intention of granting independence at some later date. In those cases, it became no longer a matter of supporting foreign domination but instead one of fighting for a moderate rather than a radical form of nationalism.[662]

Accordingly, the wars of decolonization were primarily intra-indigenous civil wars, in which local actors pursued their own political ends and empires—for all the resources that they sometime expended on the more significant of these conflicts—were mainly just the factor that tipped the balance locally.[663] Of the 375,000 men who fought for France in Indochina in the summer of 1953, only around 80,000 (21 per cent) came from the motherland. Some 66,000 (18 per cent) of them were Africans and foreign legionaries—hence imperial troops. The vast bulk, however—almost 230,000 (61 per cent)—were Vietnamese, Laotians and Cambodians, who went to war to defend their own vision of Indochina.[664] It was a similar story the same year in Malaya.[665] In Algeria, at least 1.5 million of the country's 9 million Muslims were on the French side, and in 1961 more Algerians were actually under arms fighting for France than for the independence movement[666]—though the bulk of the fighting in this particular conflict was done by conscripts from the metropole: of the 415,000 men in Algeria in the autumn of 1957, 86.1 per cent were French.[667] The same had also been true of the Indonesian War of Independence, in which two-thirds of the 140,000 Dutch troops belonged to the regular army and just a third to the colonial army. Of this latter force, only 60 per cent were indigenous recruits—even so, this still meant that almost 30,000 Indonesians fought against independence, and except for on Java and Sumatra, local support for the colonial power was almost total.[668]

Likewise, the Vietnam War was not fought primarily by the US Army; its 500,000-plus force was eclipsed by a South Vietnamese Army that was a million strong in 1970.[669] At the start of the 1970s, there were twice as many African auxiliaries fighting alongside 150,000 troops from Portugal in the country's African colonies.[670] And for the 100,000 troops that the Soviet Union sent to Afghanistan, there were twice that number fighting for the socialist regime in Kabul.[671] In actual fact, it is fair to claim of recent conflicts, like the wars in Afghanistan and Iraq, that they are primarily indigenous civil wars with the involvement of key powers of the Western global system. Alliances and auxiliary troops play just as significant a part in these conflicts as they did in previous centuries.[672]

Yet alliances were by no means the sole preserve of the imperial powers. As we have seen already, there were repeated alliances between ethnic groups, sometimes on a large scale and with significance far beyond the region, even though they proved in the long run to be heterogeneous and unstable, not least because they were often a belated response to a long-established imperial hegemony.

However, in their struggle against imperialism it was immeasurably more important for indigenous societies to find a more powerful alliance partner—in other words another Western power. That was the case above all in regions and times of intense and open conflict between the Western imperial powers.[673] Classic examples of this are North America and South and Southeast Asia in the seventeenth and eighteenth centuries, where the British and French, the Spanish and the Dutch were locked in fierce conflict, a situation that gave non-European peoples a great deal of room for manoeuvre.[674] Yet there were also other instances such as the war between the Netherlands and Portugal for control of Brazil in the late seventeenth century, which promised to liberate the Indians from their state of helpless surrender to Portugal, but only temporarily and with bloody revenge being wreaked upon them subsequently for their 'betrayal'—quite apart from the fact that, during the brief period when the Dutch were in charge, they treated the Indians no differently than the Portuguese had done beforehand.[675]

During the First and Second World Wars, anticolonial revolutionary movements were able to turn respectively to the Central Powers and the Axis for help; however, the support they offered, especially in the 1940s, was more hypothetical than actual.[676] The Cold War presented even more effective alliance options, as the two blocs competed to find client regimes in the Third World; as a result, their respective local adversaries in imperial conflicts worldwide could pretty much automatically count on gaining a strong alliance partner.[677] At the same time, from 1945 on the forum of the United Nations ensured that wars of decolonization were no longer automatically regarded as internal conflicts and hence were not seen as the sole concern of individual colonial powers.[678]

As a rule, though, from the beginning of the nineteenth to the middle of the twentieth century, empires did not actively contest one another's peripheral interests and refrained from stirring up the 'natives' against their Western rivals. Effectively, this resulted in a monopolization of foreign relations across large parts of the non-European world, something that Johan Galtung has identified as an essential structural feature of imperialism:[679] the complete diplomatic isolation of a peripheral region.[680] This meant that strong alliance partners were no longer accessible to the indigenous side and the only diplomatic option, if one did not intend to fight against the imperial power, was to form a debilitating alliance with it. This was the situation already facing the North American Indian tribes, at least those east of the Mississippi, by the late eighteenth century, when France and Spain quit the scene in 1763, and Great Britain departed in 1783 (definitively in 1795 with the signing of the Treaty of Grenville), meaning that for better or worse the indigenous population was now at the mercy of the United States.[681] On the islands of Indonesia, local societies found themselves cut off from the rest of the world by Dutch maritime power as early as the eighteenth century.[682] The 'alliance imperialism' espoused by Britain and America from 1898 onwards effectively consigned Latin America to the sole hegemony of the USA.[683] In the Cold War too, it was perfectly possible, albeit with some effort, to screen off at least smaller-scale conflicts from international public scrutiny.[684]

In practice, cooperation between the imperial powers could even go beyond non-intervention. Active collaboration ensued between Western empires to the detriment of non-European societies, and not just with regard to China, which in practical terms could never be conquered by any single nation.[685] In smaller wars as well, in Africa among other places, the imperial powers extended limited military assistance to one another.[686] At least in some cases multilateral wars were also fought outside of Asia, as for example in southern Brazil in the late eighteenth century (where otherwise, typical of the age, bitter rivalry between Portugal and Spain was the norm, leaving the Indian groups there plenty of room for manoeuvre);[687] in the joint deployment of US and Mexican troops against the Apaches in the 1870s;[688] in the collaboration between France and Spain in smashing the Rif State in 1926[689] (with the poison gas used in the conflict supplied by Germany);[690] and in 1957–1958, when the same two countries joined forces to defend their West African colonies against the expansion of Morocco.[691] Generally speaking, since the end of the Cold War, the key powers of the Western alliance have also found themselves in the same camp, united against attempts by peripheral states like Iraq, Afghanistan[692] and Libya to opt out of the global system.

Political warfare

The problem of differentiating between a state of war and peace on the periphery, the difficulty of resolving conflicts militarily, and not least the importance of local cooperation point to the great significance of the political sphere in the waging and resolution of these conflicts. For ultimately, even with armed local assistance, large regions could not be conquered in a purely military sense, still less held for any significant length of time, against a non-state adversary in difficult terrain. The cost of doing so would have proved prohibitive. No foreign domination by a tiny demographic minority over an overwhelming majority— which was the reality of colonial rule everywhere except for a handful of older colonial settlements—was conceivable in the long term without the cooperation of at least a significant proportion of those being governed. Due to the numerical weakness of its bureaucracy and its enforcement agencies, the colonial state was based primarily on ruling alliances with sections of the indigenous society.[693]

The aim of every imperial war was therefore ultimately the creation of conditions that facilitated a recognition in principle of Western dominance without the need for a permanent deployment of force— even if this dominance remained sufficiently fragile to require in practice the occasional exemplary show of force to underline it. No colony ever had the same thoroughgoing system of governance as a modern Western state.[694] Exceptions such as India,[695] which was ruled for a long time by Great Britain at comparatively great administrative and military cost, nevertheless prove the rule by virtue of the significant role played by coercive force even there;[696] even more so in the way that colonial rule collapsed so rapidly in India, once the cooperation of the bulk of the community was no longer forthcoming, from the mid-twentieth century on.[697] In the end, imperial rule on the periphery always functioned through a precarious balance of carrot and stick, in other words from the more or less voluntary cooperation of social elites or specific ethnic groups on the one hand, and on the other a permanent threat of retribution alongside the occasional demonstrative show of physical force so as to underscore Western dominance in both principle and practice.[698]

This balance of political and military measures in the sphere of general policy extended into the military realm in two ways: firstly, as we have seen, through military cooperation between indigenous groups or individuals—as allies, auxiliaries or colonial troops—and secondly through accompanying political measures for military operations—in other words through political warfare. In doing so, the military attempted in the most diverse ways to create the political conditions for a military victory; for a victory in imperial conflict which, due to a lack of resources and opportunities, could otherwise not be achieved at all, or at least not quickly.

Two misconceptions should be avoided regarding political warfare in the context of imperial conflict. One problem arises from the modern label given to political warfare, namely counterinsurgency, and in particular with the slogan that the British Army coined during the Malayan Emergency of 'winning the hearts and minds'[699] of the indigenous population. This creates the impression that the objective of political warfare is to foster a cooperative relationship with the civilian populace, to understand their culture, to win them over by being friendly, and to convince them of the well-meaning benevolence of colonial rule. This assumption would not only be unrealistic but would also represent a fundamental misunderstanding of the remit of the military and its own conception of itself. Seen in this way, political warfare would be a lengthy administrative and social process rather than a short-term military and political one, and could not be meant seriously or be at all plausible without placing the whole institution of foreign rule in question.

Tracing the roots of the slogan 'hearts and minds'—which as far it can be ascertained appears to originate neither from Malaya nor from the Northwest Frontier of India,[700] though most definitely from the British officers corps—brings to light the dual nature of political warfare. During the American War of Independence, the British commander-in-chief Sir Henry Clinton spoke of the need 'to gain the hearts and subdue the minds of America.'[701] This formulation sounds a lot less idyllic. Like imperial dominance and colonial rule as a whole, political warfare too is a combination of carrot and stick. Aside from all myth-making about benevolent military development aid, the aim of counterinsurgency is to make foreign rule or at least supremacy sufficiently bearable politically that the military can do the rest, namely enforce the exercise of that rule where necessary.

More specifically, the objective of counterinsurgency is to prevent a proto-nationalist feeling of solidarity against imperial rule developing across ethnicities within the indigenous population, by offering a few strategically selected groups incentives to cooperate (even if these only take the negative form of not imposing sanctions) and by showing the populace as a whole clearly and credibly that the imperial power is both willing and able to maintain its dominance. Alongside the use of propaganda and psychological warfare,[702] this is achieved by military means, since these are the quickest and clearest way of underlining an empire's claim to power; especially under the premiss that the 'natives' only understand the 'stick' anyway—a fancy shared by many colonial masters.[703] Both—cooperation and proof of credibility—ultimately serve to persuade the majority of the populace of the wisdom of collaborating with the imperial authorities and to isolate the insurgents who would remain the minority,[704] as Charles Gwynn explained in his classic 1934 study *Imperial Policing*:

> The admixture of rebels with a neutral or loyal element of the population adds to the difficulties of the task. Excessive severity may antagonise this element, add to the number of the rebels, and leave a lasting feeling of resentment and bitterness. On the other hand, the power and resolution of the Government forces must be displayed. Anything which can be interpreted as weakness encourages those who are sitting on the fence to keep on good terms with the rebels.[705]

Finally the aim of certain political or administrative measures is actually a straightforward military one, for example creating structures of settlement that deprive the insurgents of support.

What clearly emerges from this is that counterinsurgency is a political means of achieving a military objective: it is designed to facilitate military solutions to a political problem—namely the imposition of foreign rule. And therein lies the second misconception that must be avoided: political warfare is not about a victory of politics over the military, or a buckling of the military in the face of political logic. Quite the opposite, in fact: political warfare represents a victory of the military over politics. Counterinsurgency incorporates political measures into the military sphere, subjects them to military logic, and makes them into ancillary methods for achieving a military victory— nowhere is this so pronounced as in the French tradition:[706] 'Politics becomes an active instrument of [military] operations.'[707] Political warfare targets the entire indigenous civilian population as an object of military operations, not primarily through force of arms, but certainly through free military disposal over the civilian sphere. In essence political warfare thus follows the same logic as widening the scope of warfare by subjecting entire indigenous societies to physical violence[708]— in effect, it is its mythologically improved, less bloody (though still not entirely bloodless) flip side.

Political warfare may be read as the politicization of the military; but especially under the conditions existing at the fringes of empire, this process can go so far as to actually amount to a complete militarization of politics, at least in times of crisis: in the final analysis, counterinsurgency is the military state in its purest form, the perfection of a state of affairs that is in any case already well established on the highly militarized frontier. Little wonder that the merging of the civilian administration and the military to the point where military supreme commanders are appointed to govern with dictatorial powers—a role encapsulated in the English term 'supremo'—is a typical scenario for the colonial state of emergency.[709] The fact that, in a functioning Western state system, the military is nevertheless naturally subject in the final instance to civilian control does not play any significant role regarding the actual authority it exercises on the colonial spot.[710]

What, then, are the practical ways of conducting political warfare? In a very general sense we can surely include in this category all measures aimed at sowing division within the indigenous opposition, such as the creation of incentives to split certain segments off from the resistance movement, to win over the undecided, and to isolate the insurgents. A classic policy in this regard is to grant the majority of the population privileges that temporarily make the yoke of colonial rule easier to bear, while at the same time using ruthless brutality to make an example of individual opposition groups and above all their ringleaders.[711] If the indigenous population can be persuaded that cooperation brings rewards, whereas resistance will be bloodily suppressed, the choice is simple for all but the most determined opponents. The conciliatory offers can take a number of different forms, beginning with public honours and distinctions (which cost nothing) and material gifts[712] through administrative concessions,[713] local easing of the state of emergency for cooperative regions—a measure from the counter-insurgency bag of tricks used in the Malayan Emergency[714]—and participation in the political process plus the promise of self-government,[715] to expensive modernization measures such as road-building, supplying running water, and providing hospitals, schools and subsidized markets for colonial goods.[716]

These measures are of course ambivalent—over and above the material incentive for the civilian population, they are already aimed at bringing about consciously planned social change as a way of reducing the problems faced by the military in governing on the fringes of empire. This opens up a broad field of military social engineering,[717] in which economic advantages are not meant solely to win round a populace to imperial rule but also to alter their entire way of life: by turning nomadic groups into settled populations and persuading them to take up farming or paid employment, making them dependent upon markets and guaranteed trading links, and binding them to the Western way of life through religion, ideology or the economic system.[718] Small wonder, therefore, that the warfare waged by the Spanish and Portuguese in the Americas for so long went hand in hand with missionary activity, which in addition proved a wonderful means of driving a wedge between Indian peoples.[719]

For centuries, a fundamentally more invasive standard method of political warfare on the margins of empires was forcible resettlement. The local civilian population was transported from difficult terrain that favoured resistance to agrarian population centres which were chosen primarily for their remoteness from any hotspots and for being easy to monitor—which is why they often resembled detention camps—and only secondarily for their appropriateness to the kind of farming and the way of life practised by those who had been forcibly relocated. This system, which in some cases affected millions of people,[720] was generally speaking designed to be culturally genocidal[721] and was in actuality responsible for human tragedies on a vast scale: the Catholic mission settlements in Central and South America in the Early Modern period;[722] the North American Indian reservations of the nineteenth century;[723] the catastrophic relocations that took place on Cuba in the 1890s;[724] the concentration camps set up by the British in the Second Anglo-Boer War, in which 10 per cent of the interned Boer population perished;[725] and the camps and 'new villages' established during the great wars of decolonization in the 1950s, of which those in Kenya during the struggle against the Mau Mau Uprising have since been pilloried as 'Britain's Gulag'.[726] The internment of civilians has been described as the 'moral/military equivalent of the World War II practice of bombing cities.'[727]

For the perpetrators, however, the policy of resettlement was first and foremost a sweeping instrument of political warfare. Those affected were alienated from the environment in which they had grown up, their social structures were smashed, they were compelled to modernize and were more controllable, and ultimately resettlement was also a way of asserting control over an area. But above all it ensured that the basis for resistance was removed in its place of origin, by depriving it of its firm footing in the local populace, together with any economic support and protection from exposure to the authorities. For military commanders, forcible resettlements were the ultimate means of draining the 'pond' of the local population,[728] in which according to a famous saying by to Mao Zedong, the guerrilla swam like a fish in water.[729] Forced relocations represented a fulfilment of military commanders' dreams of an effective and violent elimination of social structures that stood in the way of swift victory on the battlefield, while at the same time, as a forcible implementation of the civilizing mission, they were also an investment in the future.[730]

There were also cases of violent deportation or expulsion where destruction (largely) dispensed with any counterbalancing element of enforced modernization or reconstruction,[731] though such instances belong more in the category of an erosion of the limits of warfare. At this point, the parallels again become apparent between political and total warfare, which in equal measure make the whole of the enemy's population into the focus of the war effort. It should be noted that population management still forms part of the repertoire of imperial warfare today—though it now functions without any large-scale resettlement, relying instead on bureaucratic and technological methods.[732]

Warfare against nature itself, which we briefly touched upon earlier, pales when set against such violent alterations in human geography, but it does belong in the same context. On the other hand, there was an ever more drastic way of waging political warfare, in the form of settlement policy. This was aimed at a permanent solution to the situation on the periphery through the settlement there either of colonists from the motherland or at least of settled indigenous soldier-farmers who were beholden to the imperial authorities.[733] In this way, the fringes of empire were transformed at first into a more friendly environment for imperial military expeditions and in the long term into firmly established outposts of the empire. Of all the means of political warfare, settlement policy alone (provided it was successful) went beyond the narrow realm of mere ancillary measures to military operations: it created long-term conditions under which imperial wars would in the long run become increasingly unnecessary, because the empire had scored a demographic victory over its indigenous adversary, who was either displaced or assimilated.[734]

Of course, political warfare was not a miracle solution. It could not (and cannot)[735] be employed indiscriminately in all circumstances and locations, in fact quite the opposite: since it relies at least in part upon coercion, as in the case of resettlements, it often required military force in the first instance before it could become of use to the military. Moreover, its effectiveness was geared rather to the long term, and its durability was hard to predict. For instance, when the Amerindians later slaughtered the Western missionaries in order to preserve some vestiges of their original way of life, the supposed political solution once again became a military problem.[736]

Even though political warfare took place under a military aegis and served military purposes, it was nevertheless a learning process.[737] As a general rule, it ran counter to military thinking. Compared with a rapid victory on the battlefield it appeared indirect, arduous and unmilitary. It is therefore hardly surprising that time and again military establishments proved resistant to the temptation to engage in political warfare, even when it was conducted under military auspices. This was especially true of the metropolitan military establishment, which was committed to seeking a decisive outcome in a large-scale war within a separate military sphere and which, when faced with operations on the periphery quite evidently had no appreciation of the necessarily political nature of such conflicts.[738] The quintessential example of this was, and remains, the US Army, which even in such clearly political wars as those in Vietnam and Afghanistan, nevertheless relegated political warfare to the margins of required military tasks.[739] By contrast, this was emphatically not the case with the British and French armies in the late twentieth century. However much the doctrines of 'guerre révolutionnaire'[740] and counterinsurgency were ultimately based on coercion and military domination, and however little they represented patent remedies for every situation (which would only come as a surprise to those who had already fallen hook, line and sinker for the myth of apparent miracle solutions), they nonetheless did demonstrate that the militaries of both of these great colonial powers had at least recognized that different parameters applied in imperial conflicts.[741] The same can also be said of Portugal to some extent, yet here too with the caveat that political warfare continued to go hand in hand with the use of brutal force against civilians.[742]

And this is perhaps the essential point that should be borne in mind when considering war on the periphery: it is political warfare par excellence.[743] The self-imposed task of empires, to establish permanent foreign dominion across a wide area and over large numbers of people while deploying the minimum of resources, has always of necessity been primarily a political one. In the absence of a responsible Western state structure and massive troop deployments, Clausewitz's rationale for waging war—'to compel our enemy to do our will'[744]—only applies on few occasions. Military operations on the periphery were at most able to create conditions in which alliances with the imperial power appeared promising—or in which major changes in a region's natural environment and demography became feasible. But such operations alone almost never decided the outcome of imperial confrontations.[745]

Ultimately, we must recognize that, at least under certain conditions, imperial wars could not be won in a military sense, even with accompanying political warfare. Accordingly, the Malayan Emergency—still the archetypal military counterinsurgency operation—was ultimately won politically through the promise of independence, a pledge that brought key parts of the Malay elites over to the British side and at least neutralized the majority of the population. It requires some thinking outside the box for the colonial power to see its withdrawal as a victory—even though in this case it makes perfect sense, since in the wider context of the Cold War a friendly, independent Malaya was far preferable to a socialist satellite Malaya as far as the British were concerned. But this was primarily a political solution that was also implemented militarily, and at best only secondarily a military victory.[746]

Conversely, it must be said of the Algerian War of Independence that France's military victory was achieved by such drastic means that, in the internal and external political circumstances of the 1960s, it amounted to a political defeat.[747] And in the absence of any political solutions, Portugal's near-victory in Angola and Portuguese Guinea (Guinea-Bissau) remained an irrelevance at the very least.[748]

Conclusion

Organized violence within the framework of European expansion obeyed its own logic, which with few exceptions still characterizes the shape of Western military interventions in the rest of the world nowadays. Difficult terrain favouring the defenders, and the lack of well-developed roads or sufficient provisions hampered logistics, restricted the size of armies and resulted in a relatively high cost for securing supplies and lines of communication. Security preferences, the stipulation that imperial dominance on the periphery should above all bring economic gain rather than loss, and the difficulties of projecting power across great distances led to imperial armed forces on the fringes of empire always being comparatively small. As a result of both cultural preferences regarding violence and purely pragmatic considerations, the indigenous enemy mostly tended to avoid engaging in battle with the interlopers, opting instead for a war of ambush. For this reason, and also because of a lack of any clear indigenous state structure, the forces of empire generally found it impossible to secure a swift, decisive and enduring military outcome.

As a consequence of all these circumstances, Western military forces on the margins of empire were faced with the necessity of controlling vast areas and large populations with minimal troop numbers, yet without any prospect of bringing the conflict to a quick conclusion. Temporal unboundedness thus became a key characteristic of imperial wars: a drawn-out series of violent conflicts which often merged into one long war of attrition. All the more so since—in view of the permanently high level of violence on a heavily militarized frontier and as a result of the refusal to acknowledge that indigenous peoples were engaged in a legitimate war—it was extremely hard to determine where wars began or ended.

These circumstances had three far-reaching ramifications for the nature of warfare on the periphery. Firstly, Western commanders used maximum force in an attempt to break the vicious circle of indecisiveness and force a clear military victory—a subject we will return to presently. Secondly, the cooperation of indigenous peoples and individuals played a far greater part in the conduct and outcome of wars than the technological superiority of Western forces themselves. And thirdly (partly as a result of the second factor) conflicts on the periphery were characterized as primarily political wars, in which force of arms always needed to be embedded in non-military measures if it was to play a significant role in any resolution—a recognition that encouraged the military to venture into the sphere of politics in the context of waging political warfare—and in which lasting resolutions of conflicts could practically never be attained through military operations alone.

2

OBJECTIVES AND LEGITIMATION

The first Europeans in New Zealand were killed and eaten by the Maoris.[1] But this kind of spontaneous and cannibalistic xenophobia was not the norm. Many of the earliest contacts between the pioneers of Western imperialism and indigenous societies were decidedly peaceful;[2] indeed, the first Europeans to set foot in North America could not have survived without at least partly voluntary contributions of food by their Indian neighbours.[3] However at some stage there always came a point when the representatives of expansionist empires wanted more than the non-European societies were prepared to give; more food, more land, more raw materials or more control. Mistrust and misunderstandings between the two sides led to encroachments, and then to individual and collective acts of violence.[4] No instance of contact remained peaceful in the long term, and some escalated into fundamental conflicts in which the imperial outposts—at least in their imagination—and indigenous societies, in their case often all too literally, had to fight for their very survival.

In the preceding chapter, I spoke about the unqualified urge of empires for conquest, a desire that often went beyond the compass of indigenous societies' comprehension, given that their war aims were primarily of a far more limited scope. This was true in so far as many non-European violence-based cultures did not consider war to be the coercive *ultima ratio* beyond diplomacy but instead to be an integral

115

part of it. For instance, military campaigns in India in the Early Modern period were displays of strength designed to cow any potential opposition rather than attempts to solve conflicts through the use of force.[5] Likewise, for North American Indians limited acts of violence from time to time were meant as an offer to negotiate—in other words, an implicit plea for talks to commence by demonstrating what could otherwise happen.[6] This was no contradiction in a society in which force of arms was an intrinsic part of everyday life anyway.

It is also true that such niceties were often lost on Europeans at the periphery; alternatively they chose to ignore them and to resort at the slightest provocation to intransigent campaigns of annihilation, not least as a result of the fundamental vulnerability of their position as a minority community on the ground. A good example of this was the Northern War in New Zealand in 1845–46, which saw the Maoris engaged in a struggle which they considered to be primarily symbolic against curtailment of their administrative autonomy, while at the same time fully intending to maintain their economic relations with the British. The British, on the other hand responded without further ado with a campaign of (military) annihilation.[7]

It therefore seems easy to concur with statements such as this by Wesseling: 'In colonial wars [...] war aims were absolute. Colonial conquerors came to stay. Their aim was the permanent and total subjection of the population.'[8] Yet the idea of empires' unqualified urge to conquer can at best only be applied as a generalization over the long term. The motives that lay behind individual military engagements, the circumstances which triggered violent conflict and the war aims in each separate case were frequently more limited, even on the imperial side—not least because military conquest and cost-intensive formal rule, as we have already observed, were not necessarily the primary aim of imperial dominance on the periphery. On the other hand there was sometimes a very definite impulse towards annihilation on the part of the indigenous opponent; at least, this factor lay at the heart of the rhetoric of the Nativist and millenarian revivalist movements, which as a reaction to an already existing hegemony made it their stated objective to wipe out or expel all Europeans.[9]

In addition, the origins, motives and immediate causes of conflict could take on a very complex form in certain instances. The Yamasee

War in South Carolina, for example, was a result of the long-term economic dependence of the Indian peoples of that region on British merchants. But the actual catalyst for the outbreak of this conflict in 1715 was the situational breakdown of transcultural diplomacy, which itself was ultimately a consequence of the chance circumstance that two British Indian agents could not abide one another.[10] Another pertinent example is the Maji-Maji War in East Africa in 1905–1907, in which African groups across the length and breadth of the colony took part for quite diverse reasons, which in part had nothing to do with the German presence in the region, but which lighted upon this factor as a natural focus.[11]

Of course, that the cases are complex is true of any war, and it is impossible to generalize on that basis. A further problem resides in the fact that the true motives of combatants may sometimes either completely defy historical analysis, due to there being no record of them in the sources, or be difficult to distinguish from the officially stated motives, as Jürgen Osterhammel rightly points out: 'The great uncertainty of interpretation derives from the lack of congruence between the aims, ideologies and outcomes. The true intentions were often not those that were publicly proclaimed and broadcast, and the actual result could, in the manner of unintended consequences, take a totally different direction.'[12] This was particularly true of those violent conflicts that went hand in hand, on the imperial side, with a major effort at justification and which not infrequently created the impression that the empire in question was waging a more or less altruistic war—on behalf of indigenous peoples on the periphery, whether they appreciated it or not.

Finally, generalization is also hampered by there always being (at least) two sides to any conflict. It is true that the representatives of empires were frequently the original instigators of violence, if only because it was they who had come to the Americas, Africa or Asia with the intention of asserting their interests and claims on power rather than the other way round. However, this cannot alter the fact that empires far preferred—not least because of the limited instruments of power available to them on the ground—to pursue their objectives without recourse to open conflict if at all possible. The result was that it was often the indigenous side that, in reaction to these aims, first took up arms. This makes the identification of clear patterns of conflict more difficult than it might first appear. For instance, while it is almost imperative that a violent 'uprising' by an indigenous population should be followed by a violent 'pacification' on the part of the imperial power—a case of action and reaction—the converse is not necessarily the case: a 'pacification' could take place even without an (acute) violent rebellion, and could be intended as a preventative measure or serve the purpose of establishing and legitimizing authority. Although in principle a typology of patterns of conflict should be conceived in terms of both parties to the conflict, violent motives did not exist on both sides in every case.

Fundamentally, however, it is not only the lack of sources concerning the actual motives of the indigenous side which is responsible for the fact that typologies of imperial armed conflicts are, without exception, constructed from the imperial side. There is also the apparent diffuseness of these motives. Even where there were concrete catalysts for violent action, the deeper rationale could sometimes be defensive in an unspecific sense, aimed at the defence of a hereditary way of life and independence of action, which were under threat more in structural terms, even though the representatives of empire formed the immediate manifestation of this threat. Ultimately, therefore, it is only right that the scope and aims of imperial acts of violence should be more reliably distinguishable and classifiable (and hence provide more material for a typology) than those of the opposing side. Accordingly, this is how the relevant literature on the subject has proceeded hitherto. Classically, Charles Callwell distinguished between: 1. (External) 'campaigns of conquest or annexation'; 2. (Internal) 'campaigns for the suppression of insurrections or lawlessness'; 3. Campaigns of punishment and retribution; 4. Wars 'to overthrow a menacing military power' (both of the foregoing without any intention of conquest) and 5. 'Wars of expediency undertaken for some political purpose'.[13] John Bodley, by contrast, recognized only punitive expeditions and wars of annihilation.[14] Osterhammel, meanwhile, has divided interventions on the periphery into those designed to seize territory, 'Big-Stick' campaigns, secessionist endeavours, and humanitarian missions,[15] while most recently Michael Hochgeschwender divided colonial wars into wars of conquest, wars between states, and 'wars of liberation or decolonization.'[16]

Some of these attempts at categorization have in common the problem that they ascribe too great a definitional importance to the distinction between internal and external conflict. As we have already noted in the previous chapter,[17] such a distinction was a legalistic or legitimizing construct enacted by empires, which actually did not play any significant role for the pattern of conflict on the ground, beyond juridical justification of the refusal to accord *ius in bello*, the laws of warfare, to an 'internal' adversary. Instead of focusing on internal and external, conquest versus suppression of insurrection, we should concentrate primarily on the aims, scope and duration of imperial military action, and secondarily on the motives of indigenous adversaries. In other words, what did empires hope to achieve with their deployment of force on the periphery?

Limited objectives

Perhaps it would make sense to organize imperial war objectives according to what these empires planned to do with the indigenous societies against which they went to war, and hence how invasive or permanent the intended results of their acts of force were. It was certainly not in every instance, in fact not even the general rule, that empires aimed for a 'permanent presence' or 'total subjugation'.

On the contrary, the aims of military campaigns on the periphery began (in ascending order of invasiveness) with quite marginal and not primarily power-political motives. Let us not forget that, aside from colonial settlements, the representatives of empires were mainly only present on the spot for the sake of economic profit. Correspondingly some military actions took place, especially in the Early Modern period, for the sole purpose of improving the political environment for trade. Thus, the first Europeans in West Africa hired themselves out to wealthy local potentates as mercenaries to fight in wars within Africa, in order to win the favour of local rulers on whom they were dependent for the establishment of trading bases.[18] Samuel Champlain joined the Algonquin, Innu, and Huron tribes, on whom the French fur trade depended, in a war against the Mohawk, and his successors proceeded to build France's Canadian empire through alliances and the supply of weapons to halt the advance of the expansionist Iroquois.[19] On Java, the

Dutch repeatedly involved themselves in disputes over succession, in order to ingratiate themselves with the ultimate victor, a plan which did not always meet with success: far from being grateful for the Dutch East Indies Company's support during a war of 1677–78 and granting it trading rights, King Amangkumrat II held it against the organization that it—displaying its customary business acumen—had tried to sell him a crown for his coronation.[20] Yet the Dutch were more successful with their interventions in the eighteenth century and managed to establish something akin to what would later become known as a collaborationist regime.[21] On the Indian subcontinent, various trading companies that had secured privileges for themselves—most notably the British—began to intervene with force of arms in succession disputes, which their Indian allies were happy to recompense them for with money and favourable trading conditions, but which they were ultimately to pay for with the loss of their independence.[22] Indeed, even leaving aside immediate economic advantages, certain military actions were primarily aimed at winning over an alliance partner, as in the case of Cortés, who had undoubtedly come to Mexico with the aim of conquering the country. The fact that his conquistadors carried out a slaughter among the unarmed populace of the Aztec vassal city of Cholollan was—at least according to the interpretation of Ross Hassig—a loyalty test for the Spanish that would irrevocably align them with the cause of their powerful ally Tlaxcallan.[23]

It was not uncommon for trading companies, and later in part also for imperial forces on behalf of their country's merchants, to establish a dominant position against their rivals in a particular location through the use of force. This particular concern entailed quite limited military engagements, which saw harbours blockaded or seized, bases established or those of the competition burnt to the ground, crops destroyed, and warships positioned in order to assert local trading privileges. This armed pursuit of commercial interests was typical above all of early imperial involvement in India and Indonesia, as well as of the early phase in the European expansion through West Africa.[24]

Another form of minimally invasive intervention were demonstrations of military might, the sole object of which was to show off empires' power and thereby ensure that that same might did not have to be deployed in earnest—a central instrument of control of large regions with minimal physical means of coercion. Thus, in 1525 Cortés progressed relatively peacefully through Yucatán with a force of 230 Spaniards and 3,000 Mexicans, as a way of underpinning his claim to power, which for the time being no one questioned since no one took it seriously.[25] In the late eighteenth century the British were keen on patrolling the outback in their colony of Australia,[26] and the US Army repeatedly dispatched thousands of cavalrymen to ride across the Great Plains in order to intimidate Indian tribes,[27] while in around 1900 the French sent expeditions to the inaccessible Ahaggar Mountains region merely as a way of demonstrating to the Tuareg who lived there that it was not so inaccessible after all and that they should come to terms with French authority.[28] In Africa, it was customary at the end of the nineteenth century to embark on campaigns into the bush for no other reason than to impress the local population with demonstrations of the firepower of the new machine guns.[29] Likewise the Western gunboats that patrolled the inland waterways of China in the early twentieth century were first and foremost demonstrations of military might.[30]

Clearly delimited aims also basically determined the occasional imperial military interventions on the periphery that were carried out in order to protect their own expatriate nationals and their property,[31] though sometimes the expense of the action and its unintended consequences could conspire to drive the stated aims of the mission *ad absurdum*. This is what happened, for instance, in 1867–68, when an extensive British expeditionary force sent to rescue a number of hostages being held in Abyssinia (present-day Ethiopia) invaded the country and toppled its ruler King Tewodros II;[32] and in 1907, when after attacks on Europeans French troops landed in Casablanca and proceeded to conquer Morocco;[33] and also in 1915 when, in the course of what was roughly the twentieth intervention by US troops to safeguard Western nationals on Haiti, a protectorate was established on the island.[34] Expeditions such as these therefore transitioned into imperial wars whose objectives, while still somewhat limited, took markedly more invasive forms.

Punitive expeditions

In fact, in its configuration the British war against Abyssinia in 1867–68 was a classic punitive expedition, albeit an uncommonly large-scale one given the thousands of troops deployed. Besides the freeing of the hostages (which in any event was rather improbable to achieve through military means), it had no objective other than upholding the prestige of the British Empire and 'punish[ing] an upstart ruler', nor did it have any other result—the British Army withdrew again afterwards and left the country to the chaos that had ensued as a result of Tewodros' death.[35]

These, then, are also the general characteristics of the punitive expedition, a phenomenon so typical of organized violence within the context of European expansion: punishment and maintenance of prestige as objectives; excessive force that is out of all proportion to the cause and which holds entire population groups responsible for individual attacks and serves the sole purpose of intimidation and *'encourager les autres'*; and a complete lack of interest in the consequences of the intervention. At least as far as imperial intentions were concerned, the punitive expedition was minimally invasive in the long term, in so far as it left the indigenous political and social order intact. As the adjective 'punitive' makes only too clear, its unique and exclusive purpose was to underscore demonstratively and by way of example the imperial social order, to provide a violent object lesson in superiority and inferiority in the relations between the empire and the periphery.

Punitive expeditions were the classic instrument of power on the militarized frontier, and their most striking characteristic was excessive force.[36] Examples of this are legion: in 1599, the Spanish stormed the Pueblo Acoma and in retaliation for the killing of a ten-man foraging party slaughtered 800 Indians, maimed eighty others and enslaved 500 women and children;[37] as early as the sixteenth century the Portuguese authorities in Brazil responded to attacks on settlers' property by destroying entire Indian villages;[38] resistance on the island of Ambon to corvée labour in the early seventeenth century prompted the Dutch to destroy ships and villages and most importantly to fell 10,000 clove trees (the latter action had the welcome additional effect of reinforcing the Dutch monopoly on the spice trade);[39] in 1772, in the Roggeveld Plateau region of South Africa, the Boers regarded the theft of 100 cattle and 500 sheep as sufficient grounds for slaughtering more than fifty Khoisan (Hottentots);[40] in 1832 President Andrew Jackson reacted to the killing of two US merchant seamen during a raid on Sumatra by razing a whole city to the ground and causing the death of 200 people;[41] and in 1902 in Kenya the British colonial officer Richard Meinertzhagen set light to entire villages in reprisal for isolated killings, and in at least one case had every inhabitant put to death.[42] In each of these instances, the ends—namely a demonstrative affirmation of imperial dominance—justified the means. It was inherent in this system that the actual perpetrators of the original transgression were often not among the victims of punitive expeditions (given that the innocent were always less suspicious and hence easier to apprehend), and anyhow their innocence was an irrelevance to those carrying out the retribution, who operated on the principle of collective responsibility.[43] In general punitive expeditions tended to hit, with a certain pragmatic perfidiousness, those sectors of the population who simply had the misfortune to live closest to imperial military bases.[44]

The most monumental punitive expedition of the modern age was undoubtedly the Allied intervention in the Boxer Rebellion in China in 1900–1901, when a whole people was 'punished' for the murder of a few Western diplomats.[45] Yet one of the official objectives of the invasion of Afghanistan in 2001 was also 'to make clear to the Taliban leaders and their supporters that harboring terrorists is unacceptable and carries a price'.[46] Here, too, the punitive motive is plain for all to see.

Enforcing obedience

Closely related in its structure to the punitive expedition, though somewhat more ambitious in its aims, was the kind of intervention that was designed to enforce obedience. Here, too, the immediate objective was not to wipe out or subjugate an indigenous society. Yet it was certainly intended to coercively implement measures which at least in time would alter the character or the ruling structure of that society. Incidentally, in enforcing obedience it was not always necessary to exert any force: this is the classic domain of 'gunboat diplomacy', in which a few well-positioned naval guns or machine guns, or a detachment of marines, could be very persuasive. A good example of this was the United States' opening-up of Hawaii in the 1880s.[47]

The direct and straightforward objectives of enforcing obedience included, for example, resettlement programmes[48] or collective labour services.[49] But the enforcement of obedience opens up a wide field, since the category also encompasses primarily those interventions by Western powers in non-European societies which (unlike punitive expeditions) were conducted in pursuit of concrete political goals but which, at least *prima facie*, were not intended to establish or secure sovereignty over the region in question. These were the kind of military engagements with respect to which empires were wont to claim that they were not really acting out of self-interest but in the service of higher aims, in the interest of the global community at large or at least of the West, or even on behalf of the indigenous societies that were directly affected— in other words that their motives were thoroughly altruistic. Principal among the classic motives that were adduced in this context was the multifaceted Christianizing or 'civilizing' mission,[50] which was used to justify the Spanish subjugation and enforced religious conversion of Amerindians, and similar Russian actions among the populace of Siberia.[51] In the nineteenth and early twentieth centuries, the *mission civilisatrice* became a cheap vindication of numerous obedience-enforcing interventions in the non-European world,[52] including absurdly the enslavement of Brazilian Indians,[53] and the tragic and culturally genocidal deportation of the so-called 'Five Civilized Tribes' in the southern United States in the 1830s.[54] The civilizing mission could also be used to legitimize the establishment of direct rule.[55]

The specific goals of military action aimed at enforcing obedience included in particular the suppression of the slave trade,[56] the disarming of indigenous warriors,[57] the establishment of free trade,[58] order and stability,[59] the creation of legal certainty through the implementation of Western legal norms[60] and (after 1945) the introduction and safeguarding of democracy and capitalism (on the part of the West) or of socialism (by the Eastern Bloc).[61] The paternalistic—and often openly self-serving—aspect of all these supposedly noble aims is of course obvious, for exactly whose freedom to trade, stability and legal certainty was in question here? From which cultural milieu did the values that were to be implemented derive? From the Christian faith to Western international law to the dominant social models of the twentieth century, these were all export products of the West. This is strikingly evident in the Boxer Rebellion, surely the greatest obedience-enforcing expedition of all time, which in contemporary research is customarily discussed under the categories of the integration of China into the 'imperialist world order'[62] or into the 'Western-dominated global system'.[63]

One can never go far wrong if one takes a sceptical view of such appeals to higher aims. In military expeditions of this kind, motivation and legitimation can scarcely be distinguished from one another even in terms of logic. As Osterhammel concedes, genuine 'humanitarian interventions' are historically vanishingly rare and are actually predicated upon 'properly functioning international organizations and the recognition of corresponding norms of international law'—in other words, the state of the world as presently constituted—otherwise the actors always ultimately act only out of self-interest.[64] However, that is to apply double standards—namely mistrusting past discourses about legitimation because we can assess the practical results from a historical perspective, while implicitly believing those of the present-day since we cannot yet assess them (sufficiently reliably). I would venture to doubt that egoistical motives were simply more prevalent in conflict situations in the past, as Osterhammel suggests.[65] After all, we still live in a world in which the international community is made up of nation-states all acting from their own security interests. As Thoralf Klein and Frank Schumacher have rightly pointed out:

> The legitimation strategies that have been used in the fight against Islamist terror [...] are suspiciously similar to those models of argumentation underpinning European expansion in the age of high imperialism. Whereas in former times, the talk was of the spreading of Western civilization, now the spread of democracy and human rights is at the forefront of the discourses justifying intervention.[66]

Certainly, George W. Bush, on the occasion of his swearing-in for his second term as US president in 2005, seriously (or at least publicly) took the view that US forces were in Iraq to safeguard freedom and democracy and to combat tyranny.[67] Who apart from American neo-conservatives could possibly believe that? Likewise, the primary reasons for Western troops being deployed in Afghanistan, and from 2013 on in Mali too, are not to liberate women from Islamist oppression[68] or to save the world's cultural heritage from destruction[69]—any more than the principal objective of German troops in Kosovo as part of the NATO-led peacekeeping force in the 1990s was their introduction of waste separation to the former Yugoslav territory.[70] Formal legitimation by the international community only succeeds in temporarily creating a procedural veil for the implementation of national or collectively Western economic and security interests, whose dressing-up as altruism does not, in and of itself, command any greater claim to credibility than, say, couching such motives in terms of the Christian/ Western community of values in the Early Modern period, or the 'civilizing mission' of the nineteenth century. So far, no historical research has successfully attempted to prove the contrary.

In my opinion, a similarly confusing contrasting of modern rhetoric with the (alleged) practice of past centuries is also evident in the argument put forward by Odd Arne Westad, namely that in the Cold War the superpowers were motivated by a genuinely anti-imperialist sense of responsibility for the people of the Third World: 'Different from the European expansion that started in the early modern period, Moscow's and Washington's objectives were not exploitation or subjection, but control and improvement.'[71] But in its interventions in the Third World in the Cold War did the US really have the wellbeing of the populations as its main concern, or rather the need to secure the regions in question for the West in the zero-sum game of the Cold War?[72] In any case, the containment of communism as part of the 'domino theory' played a far greater role in the US involvement in Southeast Asia than democracy and human rights, which were only seen as the bases for a long-term remedy to the region's problems.[73] And for the colonial powers Great Britain, France and Portugal this aim, when intervening in Third World countries, of bringing them within the West's orbit was at any rate outwardly the dominant one, especially since it could be peddled as a greater good, common to the entire West, as compared to mere national interest.[74] At least in the case of France in Algeria, a modernizing civilizing mission also came into play in the context of the programme of enforced resettlement, which was an additional measure designed to secure the region for the West in an even more profound sense.[75]

As Westad himself concedes, the distinction between 'exploitation' and 'improvement' was somewhat academic at the 'receiving end',[76] and that was also true of previous centuries—the supposed civilizing mission of the West was rarely seen as such by its intended beneficiaries,[77] especially when it was hidden behind the barrel of a machine gun. Apart from that, as the preceding sections have shown, 'exploitation and subjection' (particularly the latter) were not actually the sole motives for imperialist military missions in earlier centuries, even if these missions did, time and again, and even sometimes quite unintentionally, result in precisely that situation. Of course, this is why the establishment of 'open colonial conditions'[78] has never been a prerequisite for imperial or Western civilizing missions—either today or a hundred years ago. We are dealing here in debating terms with a straw man, a specious argument that casts historical practice in a clichéd light in order to make our own age appear more positive.

Regime change

The toppling of despotic and unjust regimes, as seen most recently in Afghanistan[79] and Iraq[80]—though this justification was also advanced in the past for the subjugation of the Aztecs in 1519 and the Maya of Itza in 1697,[81] for the conquest of the West African state of Benin in 1896 (on the grounds of human sacrifice and cannibalism)[82] and for the reconquest of the Sudan in 1898 (the alleged need to end the tyrannical and brutal rule of Muslim fanatics)[83]—is actually just a special instance of the apparently altruistic enforcement of obedience. As the stated aim of a military action, it is clearly more invasive than other forms of such enforcement, which in the normal run of things leave the indigenous political and social order intact in principle—that is, if we disregard the socioeconomic and political consequences of far-reaching changes like resettlements or the abolition of slavery,[84] which are mostly unintentional. In contrast, a regime change has the aim of creating a lasting relationship of dependency, in order to prolong the enforcement of obedience without the effort of an enduring military deployment.[85]

This is essentially a classic instrument of empire building: a form of indirect rule that chimed with imperial preferences for cost-effective solutions. The militarily supported (re-)establishment or securing of cooperative governmental structures—so-called collaborationist regimes or collaborationist elites[86]—covers a wide spectrum. On a scale of increasing dependence, it begins for example with the aforementioned military assistance offered by the Dutch during the wars of succession on Java as a way of winning the favour of a particular contender for the throne[87]—which it failed to secure in the long term.[88]

The spectrum continues with the (re-)installing of a government that is well disposed to a particular empire or more broadly to the West in what was still in principle an independent country; this would generally result in advantageous trading arrangements, political privileges or the establishment of military bases. The textbook example of this is Egypt in 1882,[89] but the US interventions in Panama in 1903[90] and in Iraq exactly a century later also follow this pattern.[91] At the end of the spectrum we find the actual loss of effective independence for indigenous political entities, ranging from renouncing control over an autonomous foreign and security policy—namely, becoming a protectorate[92]—to total incorporation within an empire, retaining in the process only their internal structure of governance.[93] All these categories are not absolutely distinct from one another, especially since it was often a case of a creeping loss of autonomy that continued long after the original military intervention. On a lower level, another common objective of imperial military actions was to install 'chiefs' answerable to the empire as a means of controlling non-state institutions.[94]

Yet above and beyond being an obedience-enforcing intervention, regime change also had the potential to turn into a self-inflicted wound as a result of unintended consequences. The military action itself frequently had an extremely destabilizing effect on indigenous political structures that were none too stable in the first place. A regime is always easier to destroy than to restore, and if the intervener is not really familiar with local conditions, there is a high risk of triggering a socio-political landslide with the supposed liberation of the oppressed.[95] It is particularly difficult—as the West has found not least through its recent experiences in Iraq—to enforce democracy and human rights without endangering the stability of the entire region.[96] Even in less invasive interventions than the Iraq War of 2003, the problem arises that the cooperative regime formed by the indigenous population after the event can easily appear to be simply a puppet regime of the empire or the West, owing its very existence to the military intervention, with the result that, lacking any real support among the populace, it increasingly becomes an irrelevance or is toppled in an uprising. In any event, a second intervention leading to a more direct assumption of power then becomes necessary.[97]

The wars of decolonization post-1945 are generally regarded as a special instance of installing a cooperative regime. Certainly it is true that, in view of their dwindling ability to exert power, the growing strength of proto-nationalist independence movements and an increasingly anti-colonially minded international public (with the additional forum of the United Nations), the colonial powers at some stage began to refrain, however unwillingly, from attempting to maintain direct rule over their colonies through military means. Instead they resorted to trying to win the military struggle (through political means as well) in order to have a controlling influence over who they transferred power to: namely, a regime with a social model and a political orientation that was close to those of the West.[98] The aim was therefore to install a cooperative regime for the period following formal colonial rule.[99] The prime example of this is British Malaya.[100] France failed in a similar attempt in North Africa, where its former colonies ended up, to a greater or lesser degree, in the enemy camp.[101] The conflicts between the superpowers took a similar form: in Korea and Vietnam both sides had the objective (as did the Soviet Union in its intervention in Afghanistan from 1980 to 1988) of shoring up an existing collaborationist regime.[102]

Subjugation

While it was possible for the installation or defence of cooperative regimes as a cost-effective form of control to nonetheless unwittingly result in direct rule, there were also many imperial wars that were aimed at the expansion, intensification or defence of imperial control from the outset, and at the suppression, pacification or crushing of revolts. The direct assumption of power through military means was always a costly and risky enterprise. This explains why an aspect of exhausted patience is so often evident in campaigns of subjugation, an impulsion to callously force a deadly calm upon a region in order to finally solve a problem that had been impervious to less invasive approaches:[103] 'Let us put an end to this plague once and for all and remove the settlers from its threat, clear the land and build a city on it,' as the governor of Brasilia said in 1565 in justifying the suppression of the warlike Tamoio people.[104] Of course, such pronouncements are also self-justification on the part of the actors involved, but they occur so frequently in conjunction with the preamble to the violent incorporation of peripheral territories into empires that one cannot help but regard this motive as perfectly genuine—especially when set alongside the general propensity of the 'military mind' for 'final solutions'.[105] Peace beyond one's borders was manifestly vital for maintaining stability within them.[106]

In the course of conducting their pacification campaigns, the 'men on the spot' regularly fell into the trap of creating a self-perpetuating 'turbulent frontier', in which the elimination of hot spots through direct occupation of regions on the frontier only led to the formation of new frontiers with new trouble spots.[107] Thus, not only India as far as the Himalayas was conquered,[108] but Russia also subjugated one steppe people after another, ostensibly in order to enhance its own defensive security.[109] The Spanish wiped out the Itza kingdom of the Maya because it provided a focus for Indian resistance movements within the colonies along the coast of the Gulf of Mexico,[110] while the British conquered Zululand with the same intention.[111] The securing of Algeria against raids from the Sahara led to the French occupation of Morocco,[112] and the hinterland of Burma and Vietnam was occupied primarily in order to provide extensive protection for the European bases on the coast.[113]

The reason for the formal seizure of territory within the framework of a military operation did not always lie within that territory itself, however. On occasion, peripheral societies were forcibly integrated into an empire primarily in order to forestall a similar move by another empire, and to strategically safeguard existing interests. This was an important motivation especially in the early conquest of India (where in the seventeenth century the Dutch feared Portuguese competition, while the British sought to checkmate France in the eighteenth and Russia in the nineteenth)[114] and in the partitioning of Africa,[115] but it also played a part on the border between Spanish and Portuguese spheres of interest in South America,[116] on the northern frontier of Spanish America[117] and elsewhere.[118] Strategic considerations that went far beyond the intrinsic usefulness of a particular region naturally also played a major role in the global power struggle of the Cold War and determined for example Britain's determination to hold on to Kenya as a military base to be used against the Soviet Union in the event of global war.[119]

Alongside strategic and defensive motives, another factor in the establishment of direct rule through military means is simply the pretension to power of the state in question. This was the case for example in the final phases of administrative penetration over existing colonies, notably in the wake of the partitioning of Africa,[120] but also in the imperialization of the Spanish system of rule in Latin America in the eighteenth century (a phenomenon identified by Horst Pietschmann)[121] and not least in the wars through which the successor states of Spain's American empire sought to incorporate their respective frontier regions within the new nation-states that were then taking shape.[122]

Plunder and destruction

Conquest, subjugation, pacification and the suppression of revolts were military objectives that focused on control over individual societies, not on their eradication.[123] Precisely the opposite was the case when the indigenous society appeared superfluous to the fulfilment of the purpose of the military action or even stood in its way: namely when the imperial actors were far more interested in the resources of the region that was the focus of their armed incursion. In this case, although the destruction of the indigenous political and social organization was not the prime objective of the empire's act of violence, it was nevertheless accepted as necessary if the objective was to be attained.

This was especially true of the large-scale expeditions of theft and depredation by which the conquistadors brought the major kingdoms of Central America to their knees. The men who followed Cortés and Pizarro, and later Francisco Vázquez de Coronado and Hernando de Soto, were adventurers who were always prepared to use violence, who had burnt their bridges behind them and who had everything to gain and nothing to lose. They ruthlessly smashed Indian power and social structures through a campaign of terror, pillage and mass murder[124] and in their hunt for gold destroyed many priceless cultural artefacts: the ransom for Atahualpa alone, which basically comprised the contents of Aztec temples and works of art that today would have been of incalculable cultural and archaeological value, yielded 6.1 tonnes of gold and 11.7 tonnes of silver when melted down,[125] and had a value worth more than €200 million today.[126] Little wonder, then, that the conquistadors went on a robbing, plundering and murdering rampage through the Americas in the years that followed, from the southeast of the present-day USA to Tierra del Fuego, in the hope of being able to emulate Pizarro. However, other major prizes proved few and far between in the mostly stateless regions outside of the principal regional empires, a fact that only served to exacerbate the disappointed adventurers' propensity for violence.[127]

Another commodity that the Spanish were after, and which made the indigenous social structures (if not the people themselves) similarly expendable, was cheap labour. If a conquistador failed to find mountains of gold, he could at least hope for an *encomienda*, a kind of exploitative fiefdom over Indians. Although the Spanish Crown, in granting conquistadors the right to retain an indigenous workforce, also intended that there should be a duty of care towards people concerned, it is not difficult to guess that the reality would have been very different on the far frontier: the de facto enslaved Indians were literally worked to death on sugar plantations and in mines.[128] In Portuguese Brazil slavery was abolished in 1570, but there were legal loopholes such as the 'ransom' paid for those who had been taken prisoner in battles between Indians and who were allegedly being threatened with cannibalism by the victors—a system that was tantamount to incitement to slave hunting.[129] In the long term, Brazil became economically totally dependent upon slave labour, and for centuries it became practically an industry for the inhabitants of the frontier city of São Paulo to conduct slave raids deep into Indian territory.[130] This activity also made the Paulistas sought-after professional auxiliary troops in Indian wars.[131] Even as late as the end of the nineteenth century, the rubber boom in northwestern Brazil led to mass de facto enslavement of Indian labour, conducted with a degree of violence and a mortality rate that rivalled the notorious atrocities being perpetrated in the Belgian colony of the Congo at around the same time.[132]

In other parts of the world, abduction to a life of enforced labour was not such a key motif of imperialist violence as it was in Spanish America. Certainly, there were some instances in British North America,[133] the Cape Boers captured slave labourers in their wars against the San[134] and for centuries the Portuguese engaged in wars in Angola and the Congo with the primary objective of taking African slaves. Yet elsewhere in

Africa the imperial powers tended to let the population be enslaved by their African trading partners, from whom they would then purchase the manpower they needed.[135] Nevertheless, the hunting, trading and exploitation of slaves as labour represents in all cases a violent coercive structure, though this is more often a state or private economic matter rather than a more narrowly martial one.[136]

Indigenous manpower could be used to exploit natural resources, for example in mines. But the extraction of these resources could itself be the purpose of acts of violence against the non-European populace of a region. The classic example of this is the gold and silver rushes that took place in the US West in the mid-nineteenth century, in which uncontrollable private gold prospectors first overran the Indians of the Pacific Coast, who for the most part lived in small groups and were therefore practically defenceless, driving them out or slaughtering them,[137] and then proceeded, in states such as Colorado, New Mexico, Wyoming and Washington, to spark enduring conflicts with Indian groups that were far more capable of resistance like, for instance, the Apaches,[138] and finally, through their illegal occupation of the Black Hills of South Dakota in 1874, brought about the showdown between the US Army and the Sioux.[139] In Russian Central Asia and Siberia, it was sable pelts that caused the displacement of indigenous peoples.[140] And the search for tropical hardwoods determined among other acts of violence the final conquest of the Yucatán by Mexico and of Formosa (present-day Taiwan) by Japan, both in the early years of the twentieth century.[141]

The expansion of the Boer settlers into the interior of the Cape Colony, which triggered clashes with the local Khoisan over access to cattle, game, water and grazing pastures,[142] and the conflicts between the Spanish and Indians over access to the vast herds of wild cattle and horses on the Argentinian pampas[143] finally lead us to the natural resource which most commonly prompted empires to push indigenous societies to the margins: fertile agricultural or pastoral land. Nothing turned a conflict so quickly into a matter of life and death and made it positively explosive than disputes over land. For while with other causes of conflict there remained the fundamental potential for compromise and coexistence, colonists of the modern period could only conceive of the power of disposition over land in absolute terms.

Intensive agriculture in the modern manner effectively excluded every other form of land usage. And while that is not the case with pastoral farming, this took up such vast tracts of land, especially in marginal regions such as some frontier areas of South Africa and Australia, that all competition for water and pasturage would have been highly unwelcome in any event, even leaving aside the fact that, from the settlers' point of view the indigenous people had 'sticky fingers' where cattle were concerned.[144]

Where the acquisition and use of land was concerned, therefore, the indigenous population was manifestly an irrelevance, indeed even an impediment. Individually such people on the spot might at most be welcome as workers on plantations or cowherds on grazing lands;[145] but small-scale arable farming in the European style as practised, say, in North America, could do without such help. Correspondingly, the destruction of indigenous societies, individual or collective expulsion, and not infrequently the gradual eradication of the populaces concerned were consistently the de facto aims of violent actions on the settler frontiers of empires.[146] The actors were in many cases the colonists themselves, either acting individually, in ad hoc raiding parties or organized in militias.[147] This was facilitated by the fact that most of the older settler colonies came into existence opportunistically in places where the indigenous population was small in number, scattered, stateless and hence comparatively defenceless.[148] Only the more large-scale campaigns of expulsion were instigated by the imperial authorities and were carried out by regular forces.[149]

The displacement of the indigenous populace was mostly justified by claiming that they had no legitimate moral claims to own the land, given that they were not using it anyhow.[150] The fact that non-European land usage, for example mixed rotational crop cultivation in woodland clearings in North America and in the tropical rainforests of Africa and South America, often simply looked different to the rectangular monoculture plots of Europeans, does not play any significant part in this discourse on legitimation—the conquerors would have ridden roughshod over proof of indigenous cultivation even if they had been prepared to acknowledge it took place at all.[151] (And how those who argued that only Europeans used land effectively might have justified the presence in the highlands of Kenya of large European-style farms of up to 40,000 hectares, of which only a small proportion could be cultivated, is unfortunately not to be found on record).[152]

The displacement, expulsion or successive eradication of the autochthonous population in order to gain exclusive access to land was in theory—and also often in fact—a process that was culturally genocidal at the very least and over time amounted to an act of physical genocide as well.[153] And there were many voices—notably prevalent among the settlers themselves—which called openly for extermination. After decades of conflict against the martial Chichimeca people, Spanish frontier colonists in Central Mexico called on the viceroy in 1582 to unleash a 'war of fire and the sword' on them, which would enslave and forcibly resettle the people and destroy their culture.[154] In the mid-nineteenth century, newspapers in California regularly called for the Indian populace there to be sent to the 'happy hunting grounds;'[155] similar sentiments were aired in Tasmania.[156] 'For my part I am frank to say that I fight on the broad platform of extermination,' the settler militia leader King S. Woolsey wrote following a massacre of Apaches in Colorado in 1864.[157] And the foremost Indian-hunter in the US Army, General Philip Sheridan, is rumoured to have once said, 'The only good Indians I ever saw were dead;'[158] his colleague William Tecumseh Sherman is on record as having stated his intention of punishing the Sioux 'with vindicative earnestness ... even to their extermination.'[159] Eighty years later, the first of these infamous utterances was adapted as the slogan of white settlers in their campaign of excessive violence against the Mau-Mau revolt in Kenya:[160] 'The only good Kyuke [Kikuyu] is a dead Kyuke.'[161]

In view of such statements it may seem of little historical or pragmatic relevance to nonetheless observe that the indigenous populace was an incidental factor in the process of forcible land seizure. Where they were present, they stood in the way and had to yield. But the act of violence was aimed at gaining control over the land, not at the people affected. The objective of total war was not intentional, it was functional—leaving aside the fact that it was often not even a stated aim, since the displacement and extermination of the original users of the land was such a gradual and individual process comprising a succession of acts of violence that the 'disappearance' of the indigenous population could sometimes take decades, even centuries, and was seen by the perpetrators rather as a suprapersonal and involuntary process—as a kind of fact of Social Darwinism.[162]

The aims of total war

The same was true of 'total' war aims in general during European expansion. The conscious destruction of indigenous societies (rather than casual connivance in it) was only very rarely a stated aim of imperialist acts of violence, though in the wake of interest in the Holocaust corresponding instances of alleged genocide in colonial situations have received an above-average amount of historical attention.[163] If total war aims did exist, then they were—as in the case of the Spanish colonists and the Chichimeca—mostly of a secondary nature: the urge for 'final solutions' only came at the end of a long series of clashes over other aims, and was once more functional rather than intentional, resulting from escalation or deriving from a situational dynamism. This quite evidently accords with the logic of imperial expansion and the use of violence. Dominance on the periphery had a point, namely first and foremost an economic one; intentional campaigns of extermination were dysfunctional and too costly for this objective—at least, that was the official government perspective; settlers naturally saw things differently. For the armed forces of the state, however, repression and genocide were attractive options only when all other solutions had failed.

This is quite clearly the case regarding the destruction of North American Indian societies in the nineteenth century; although the government and army acquiesced in the de facto genocide of individual Indian peoples, it was as a means to an end.[164] This is equally true of the planned (though not executed) physical extermination of the rebellious population in the so-called Ten Years War in Cuba from 1868 to 1878; this was a reaction to years of indecisive guerrilla warfare.[165] And it applies unequivocally to the infamous extermination order issued by the German commander Lothar von Trotha in the Herero War in Southwest Africa in 1905, which arose from his frustration over the failed battle of encirclement at Waterberg (and which served retrospectively to legitimize a de facto act of slow mass murder that had already taken place, when his forces drove the Herero out into the desert to perish of thirst).[166] The same can also be said of 'total pacification' of the Mekong Delta by means of massive firepower and widespread massacring of the civilian population during Operation 'Speedy Express' in the Vietnam War: the operational goal was control, while the mass murder was merely collateral damage.[167] And finally this is also true of the alleged planned cultural genocide of the Kikuyu of Kenya during Britain's suppression of the Mau-Mau uprising in 1952–1960, though in this case the terminological sensationalizing of an interpretation constructed almost entirely on the basis of oral history would appear to go too far.[168]

This distinction may seem pedantic, as already mentioned. This much is clear: in the course of European expansion there were most definitely total war aims in the narrower sense: that is the stated and well-documented readiness to destroy indigenous societies, as classically exemplified by the campaign of extermination conducted by US Army Generals John Sullivan and James Clinton against the Iroquois nation in 1779, in which war was waged systematically against the entire civilian population, their homes and food resources, and which resulted in the complete dismantling of social structures and the mass exodus of thousands of people.[169] This was no situational escalation—this was planned. George Washington's orders to Sullivan identified the aim of the assault on the Iroquois as:

> the total destruction and devastation of their settlements, and the capture of as many prisoners of every age and sex as possible. It will be essential to ruin their crops now in the ground and prevent their planting more [...] I would recommend [...] that the country may not be merely overrun, but destroyed.[170]

Evidently, this annihilation of the Iroquois was not meant to force them to sue for peace—it was intended to precede any peace; it was itself the true war aim.[171] Yet the background to this had been years of devastation of frontier settlements by Indians in the service of the British enemy in the American War of Independence: the campaign of annihilation was a radical ultimate solution to a running sore of a security problem.[172] Moreover it was an American tradition: as early as 1636–37, in the Pequot War, settlers in New England had wiped out their indigenous rivals in a deliberately planned act of cultural genocide.[173] But even here the decision to adopt this 'final solution' was dictated by circumstance. Had it been informed, as Richard Slotkin suggests, by the notion of some struggle against quintessential evil, fuelled by Puritanical fundamentalism,[174] then the campaign, as Armstrong Starkey rightly points out, would hardly have been preceded by fifty years of peace with their Indian neighbours.[175]

Even the French administration in Canada, which was fundamentally less predisposed to exterminatory solutions due to their low settler numbers, felt so perpetually irritated in the 1730s by the diplomatically unpredictable Fox Indians who inhabited the peripheries of their trade and alliance networks that, in the Second Fox War of 1729, they openly sought—and achieved—a genocidal solution.[176] In 1839, the president of the independent Republic of Texas, Mirabeau Buonaparte Lamar, proclaimed an 'exterminating war' against the Comanches in order to put a stop to the raids they had been conducting for decades—furthermore along routes that were so well-established that they appeared on contemporary maps. According to Lamar, this war would 'admit of no compromise and have no termination except in their total extinction or expulsion.'[177]

Undoubtedly, another officially planned act of cultural genocide was the forcible resettlement of the 'Five Civilized Tribes' of the Cherokee, the Chickasaw, the Choctaw, the Creek and the Seminole from Georgia, Alabama and Mississippi to the Indian Territory west of the Mississippi, which later became the US state of Oklahoma. True, the Indian communities concerned remained intact as far as their basic structure was concerned. But as a result of their expulsion from their centres of culture, with their flourishing civilization and commerce, to wilderness marginal in agrarian terms, which in addition was already claimed by nomadic Indian groups, they of course lost their cultural roots. On top of this came the 'Trail of Tears,' the forcible eviction at gunpoint of the Cherokee, which resulted in the death of 4,000 of them from starvation, epidemics and hypothermia.[178]

In the seventeenth century the Brazilian governor-general Alexandre de Sousa Freire issued an extermination order against the Indians of the Sertão region, whose cattle-rustling activities had embroiled them in a long-lasting conflict with colonists: 'Only after being completely destroyed do they become quiet [...] All experience has shown that this public nuisance can be checked only at its origin: by destroying and totally extinguishing the villages of the barbarians.'[179] In 1808 the

Portuguese prince regent authorized the final destruction of Indian societies in Brazil with the intention of getting them to either vanish or be assimilated.[180] In the same spirit, the 'final solution' of the Indian question was called for in 1878, as a way of ending a centuries-long frontier conflict,[181] an approach also adopted by the government and setters of Tasmania in 1830.[182] There were, then, most decidedly planned total and 'final solutions'—but they were the last acts in a long-lasting process of violence which culminated in the demise of an ethnic group or of an indigenous political system.

Opportunism

In addition to the actual, declared or de facto intrinsic motives behind imperialist acts of violence, we should not omit to mention the situational, institutional or opportunistic motivations which may in each individual case have been decisive in reaching the decision to go to war or to sustain a conflict. Such motivations could encompass a wide range of circumstances: the 'men on the spot', military officers and bureaucrats who were intent on grabbing the headlines, enriching themselves through pillage or advancing their own careers (after all, the chances of promotion are greater in wartime);[183] generals and governors who had something to prove because they were newly appointed, or who conversely felt under pressure to quickly record a significant success before their recall;[184] adventurers who were desperate to succeed because they had burnt their bridges behind them or had quite literally burned their ships, like Cortés;[185] military apparatuses that did not want to admit their failures;[186] nationalistic and chauvinistic considerations of prestige, especially for imperialist parvenu nations like Germany, Italy or Japan or alternatively declining empires such as Spain;[187] credibility during the ideological conflict of the Cold War;[188] sheer optimism—conquering a region merely because the circumstances seemed favourable to do so thanks to, say, a weak adversary or rivals being distracted, or imperial troops just happening to be on the ground for other reasons;[189] downright cynical motives such as that of toughening up imperial forces in a relatively risk-free small war and trying out new weaponry;[190] social imperialism—that is, using military victories overseas to try and deflect public attention from social conflicts at home;[191] and, finally, the simple urge to take revenge for earlier humiliations.[192]

The significance of such secondary motives appeared to be heightened to the point of caricature in the Italian conquest of Libya from 1911 onwards, which came about as the result of a whole series of such impulsions. Among other reasons, it had much to do with the wish to be seen as a great power, to exact revenge for defeat at the Battle of Adowa in 1896, and to divert attention from social conflicts and shortcomings in political participation within the heterogeneous Italian nation-state. Above all, though, it was driven by a pragmatic opportunism—namely to seize what was left in the 'Scramble for Africa', and moreover a territory that was close to home.[193] The actual territory that was conquered was of secondary importance for these motivations, especially since it was the Ethiopians and not the Libyans who had defeated the Italians at Adowa. Yet the French had also managed to go to war with Prussia in 1870 with the absurd battle-cry *'Revanche pour Sadowa'* ('Revenge for Sadowa') on their lips—despite the fact that at the Battle of Sadowa/Königgrätz in 1866, it had been the Austrians, not the French, who were defeated by the Prussians. Then again, national pride is not governed by logic.

Motivations of indigenous peoples

If we are to believe older accounts of European conquests, it would appear that the indigenous opponents of imperial expansion had no compelling reasons for their acts of violence—or at least their motivations were of no interest. According to one account of the conquest of Yucatán written less than seventy years ago—in other words by no means at the zenith of chauvinistic imperialism—the conquistadors came under attack wherever they went by bloodthirsty natives, apparently for no reason.[194] A very different view is taken nowadays. Even though the ultimate cause for the violent conflict was the mostly uninvited presence of imperialist merchants, settlers, soldiers and officials on the periphery, which had the potential to result in a diffuse but largely truculent defensive attitude on the part of indigenous societies, this does not preclude there being some very specific and nameable causes of war where the adversaries of empire were concerned.

One such cause was the fact that in their activities on the periphery, expansionist Western empires frequently came into conflict with the expansion of major non-European empires, by forming alliances with their vassals or simply clashing over control of regions claimed by their indigenous enemy. Indigenous realms that became direct rivals to Western imperialism in this way included the expansionist Bantu-speaking peoples' warrior kingdoms of southeast Africa—such as the Zulu, Matabele, Nguni and Hehe.[195] Likewise, the crushing of the slave empire established by Arab merchants in the east of the Congo Basin can be interpreted as a clash of competing imperial interests.[196] The Boer republics of southern Africa fostered their own form of imperialism against the surrounding Bantu kingdoms, with the aim of creating a Great Boer Empire that would stretch to the coast; this was a fundamental cause of the conflict with the British Empire.[197] Regional empires whose expansion came into competition with that of the West also existed in West Africa, in the form of the kingdoms of the Ashanti and the Tukolor, Samori's empire and Dahomey.[198] In South Asia, the conquering empires of the Marathas and of Nepal collided head-on with British imperialism.[199] In North America, imperial conflicts broke out in the seventeenth century between the French and the Iroquois, and in the nineteenth between the United States and the Sioux.[200] Even the outbreak of the Tuscarora War in 1711, which was once seen primarily as an Indian reaction to abuses committed by white colonists and fraudulent traders, has been reinterpreted by more recent commentators as having been triggered in large part by European settlement of the region, which threatened the hegemony of the Tuscarora, who were based in the interior, over their client peoples on the Atlantic coast.[201]

One should therefore beware of the tendency to always regard the indigenous foes of Western imperialism principally as victims, whose violence was of necessity a reaction to external aggression. There existed outside of Europe many societies whose socio-political structures were predisposed to lead almost automatically to permanent conflicts with Western empires' claims to hegemony on the periphery, because for example they were based on the phenomenon of the raiding party. In particular the Apaches and the Comanches of the southwestern USA, the Tuareg of the Sahara, the Berbers of the Rif, the tribes along the Northwest Frontier of India and the nomads on the southern periphery of the Russian Empire in the Early Modern period were classically adherents of this socioeconomically determined violent activity, which they could not easily renounce without abandoning their whole social model.[202] Similarly, those indigenous societies for which war was less an controllable means to an end and more a way of life—a model we are probably justified in applying to the Sioux and many other Plains Indian peoples, the warrior monarchies of the Zulu and the Matabele (even leaving aside their expansionist tendencies), the Mapuche Indians of southern Chile[203] and the warlike Naga on the border between India and Burma[204]—also found themselves set on a course of practically inevitable violent conflict with the empires of the West.

These and other frontiers were characterized by positively systemic cycles of violence, which generally speaking remained below the threshold of all-out war and which were rooted in socioeconomic structures. Such cycles included for example the raids conducted by the nomadic faction of the Navajo people known as the Ladrones, to which the colonists of New Mexico responded with raids of their own, which inevitably hit the settled, property-owning Navajos (the Ricos), who then in their turn, now impoverished and embittered, likewise became Ladrones, thereby increasing the overall potential for violence.[205] The escalation of violence on the frontier had a long tradition in this region. As early as the seventeenth century, there existed in New Mexico a flourishing network of transcultural trade in horses, people and maize, which was primarily stimulated by the fact that from 1681 onwards the Spanish were legally obliged to buy the freedom of Indian prisoners who had been taken captive by other Indian groups—an entitlement to which in one case in 1694 a Navajo group laid claim by starting to publicly behead captured and unsold Pawnee Indian children on the market square in Santa Fe.[206]

While violent resistance to imperial expansion and its consequences had many roots and points of reference, it by no means invariably had its starting point in the political sphere, but rather often began with socioeconomic conflicts. In particular it was of course the expansion of European settlement that drove local populations to armed resistance, because it threatened their livelihoods. Farming and pasturage robbed hunter-gatherer societies of sources of food and drinking water.[207] Settlement also destroyed hunting grounds and displaced or eradicated the game animals there—the classic example of this is the slaughter of the huge bison herds of the Great Plains.[208] Colonists fenced in land and expropriated livestock herds.[209] And as their draught animals passed through indigenous lands on well-trodden routes, they would graze the verges bare.[210] Little wonder, then, that violence by non-European peoples was often directed in the first instance at the immediate socioeconomic causes of the threat to their way of life: hence the rustling of cattle and the burning of crops in the field or attacks on European farms.[211]

Yet not all causes of war in the socioeconomic sphere had to do with settlement. Sometimes trade conflicts lay at the root of the problem; a growing dependence upon European-controlled global trade could, for instance, lead to deprivation and resistance during downturns in the market. One such occasion was the collapse of the fur market and the fall in the value of wampum,[212] which formed the prelude to King Philip's War (1675–1676) in New England, or the revolt of the Yamasee against the British monopsony in the fur market in South Carolina in the early eighteenth century.[213] Occasionally the cause could be bafflingly complex, such as the impoverishment of the Rajput clans of central and northern India, which, via a circuitous route that also took in a change in ethnic preferences for recruitment to the British Indian Army, led to the Indian Rebellion of 1857.[214] The disruption of traditional economic and social structures stimulated anti-French violence in the Sahara.[215] And the British economic policy of 'second colonial occupation' after 1945 was responsible in part for the Malayan Emergency.[216]

The establishment of imperial authority over indigenous societies was followed, with a fair degree of regularity, by a secondary uprising,[217] which sometimes had the return to idyllic pre-colonial conditions as its goal only in a very vague manner,[218] but which usually focused on some very specific grievances. Indigenous peoples opposed land expropriation,[219] forced labour,[220] the seizure of their weapons,[221] taxation,[222] and the building of roads or stockades on their land.[223] They took up arms against settler brutality, slave hunters or soldiers,[224] against discriminatory laws,[225] corrupt officials,[226] and restrictions of their autonomy through the imposition of direct imperial rule.[227] The living conditions on *encomiendas* and reserves,[228] economic discrimination, for example through the proscription of traditional forms of land use,[229] and attempts at cultural assimilation and integration into the imperialist social order[230] led to violent protest. Yet participatory integration into the imperial state system could conversely be precisely the objective of armed resistance in certain cases; this occurred not least during the decolonization process,[231] but also for example at the beginning of the seventeenth century on the Dutch spice islands.[232] In some instances, it was the conditions of service among colonial troops that sparked military revolts.[233]

Indigenous resistance to imperial dominance could also be religiously motivated—in other words remaining faithful to traditional cult practices in defiance of Christianization[234]—or in some cases, in particular in the Cold War, it could even be ideologically driven.[235] The latter generally coincided with the formation of proto-nationalist independence movements, which in the main, and as a result of the experience of enduring foreign rule, embraced numerous motives for resistance and—more importantly—many different social and ethnic groups in the search for self-determination.[236] Conversely there were also a number of relatively motiveless, particularistic and sectarian resistance movements, which simply opposed any form of rule and in the final analysis were not far removed from armed criminality—at least from the perspective of the imperial power.[237] In the eighteenth and early nineteenth centuries revolts of peoples predominantly of African origin became endemic in the Caribbean, classically in opposition to both slavery and colonial rule in equal measure. It was in this context that a modern independence movement emerged on Haiti in 1804, which appealed to the principles of the French Revolution and resulted in the formation of a sovereign state.[238]

As with empires, secondary motives could be the decisive factor in the indigenous opponents of empire taking up arms. Such motives included the desire to exact retribution for insults, provocations or the breaking of treaties (which, as is well known, was not uncommon for empires in their dealings with non-European peoples) or for past defeats.[239] The problem of credibility or of institutional dynamics that proscribed the avoidance of conflict also affected some indigenous administrations. It was for this reason that the leadership of the Sikh people set itself on a course of war against the British in 1845, in order to either give its ungovernable army something to do or (in the case of defeat) to be rid of it;[240] similarly, Abd-el-Krim entered into an unwinnable war with France in 1924 because, being at the height of his power, he was convinced that his reputation would suffer irreparable harm if he was seen to climb down.[241]

Conclusion

Imperial conflicts by no means always, or even mainly, consisted in the planned and total subjugation of indigenous societies, as victims, by imperial perpetrators. If we cease to fixate upon the brutal wars of conquest by the Spanish in the Americas and of the final phase in the partitioning of the world around 1900, and cast our eye instead over the entire 500-year process of the establishment of Western global hegemony, three facts become clear:

1. The objectives of imperial acts of force were often manifestly limited, aimed solely at achieving a position of economic dominance, at enforcing obedience or at the (re-)establishing of cooperative ruling structures.
2. More ambitious war aims were frequently the result of long-term or situational escalation. These only became a reality when less invasive uses of force had evidently failed. The takeover of direct rule through conquest was at best an *ultima ratio*. Only in exceptional cases were 'final solutions' and wars of annihilation the original intention of acts of force on the part of empires, even though the rhetoric of land-hungry settlers might sometimes have given this impression.
3. The indigenous foes of empire did not solely take up arms out of some inchoate impulse to resist or in order to defend themselves but often had their own very specific motives for doing so. In actual fact, they were not infrequently the original instigators of violence. Several violent conflicts in the course of European expansion were in reality transcultural clashes between empires or the result of irreconcilable socioeconomic systems.

The use of force had many functions in the expansion of Western empires. In the most general sense it was a consequence of the presence and the claim to power of empires on the periphery, of the distortions that these produced and not least of the weakness of empires on the ground. Violence was therefore never absent for long; on the contrary, it was the ultimate form of coercion employed by imperial dominance. Violence has underpinned, accentuated, accelerated, and sometimes even seen through political, economic and social processes of change. And below the state level it has also, under special circumstances, contributed to genocidal processes of displacement.

However, this does not mean that the global dominance of the Western world in the present day is a result of colonial wars of conquest and extermination. As we saw in the foregoing chapter, the imperial instruments of power on the periphery were not generally sufficient for the effective military occupation of large, populous regions. And conquest was rarely the primary goal, since it was hard to square with the central concern of imperial control—namely a healthy cost–benefit ratio. The power interaction between the outposts of empire and the indigenous societies on the periphery, on which the hegemony of the West and its empires is based, went further and was more complex. Of necessity, limited objectives, informal dominance and the motivations of non-European actors (not to mention transcultural cooperation) characterized the military components of the imperial system just as much as its political, economic or cultural structures—on which, however, historical research has focused earlier and more effectively.

This factor is hard to register statistically, since acts of violence on the periphery were just as hard to demarcate from one another, given that the processes merged into one another and the aims represented a continuum, as this chapter has clearly shown. The violent implementation of market power verged on the enforcement of obedience, which in turn merged into formation of indirect control, which could then result in direct rule; and at some stage 'final solutions' became attractive. Violent protests against specific aspects of imperial dominance culminated in national strivings toward independence. And on a militarized frontier, all these processes were inevitably based on violence. Yet this violence was not automatically total and absolute. Rather it was the flexible function of a dynamic process of the creation of imperial dominance and control.

Above all, this insight challenges the apparently crystal-clear distinction between earlier colonial wars or imperial wars of conquest on the one hand and contemporary 'humanitarian interventions' on the other, at least where the motivations of those intervening is concerned. The enforcing of obedience and regime change in order to (re-)integrate peripheral societies into the dominant Western global system are every bit as much the objective and justification for military operations by Western powers in the non-European world today as they were throughout the preceding 500 years of European expansion. Doubtless, within a few decades a hopefully critical historical analysis will decide whether in so doing the states of the modern West have been acting without exception in an altruistic way, or whether they have been guided primarily, as they were in their earlier interventions, by a continuing imperative of national self-interest.

3

CROSSING BOUNDARIES

'Colonial military campaigns were often extremely violent. [...] Long and destructive operations were required to break the resistance of certain groups of people. In the process great suffering and destruction was inflicted.'[1] Thus David Killingray characterized imperial warfare in Africa at the end of the nineteenth century. In the same context, Michael Crowder noted that European methods of waging war in Africa were at least as 'bloodthirsty' as those of the Africans and that they would not have been countenanced in Europe at the same time.[2] With regard to Algeria, Olivier Le Cour Grandmaison spoke of a 'war without borderlines of any kind, territorial or human.'[3] Talk of 'violent excesses'[4] or 'extreme force'[5] has in recent times become almost a shorthand code for colonial warfare.[6] And even the adjective 'total' (in conjunction with words like 'warfare', 'violence', 'aims' and 'submission') is readily applied to acts of force carried out by empires against indigenous societies.[7]

I have already questioned elsewhere whether the research paradigm of 'total war' is especially apposite in describing imperial conflicts.[8] Total war, understood as the total mobilization of total resources to achieve total war aims,[9] has heuristic value mainly in contexts where the social norm is defined in other ways, namely in complex industrial societies with a tradition of regulated and contained warfare. To speak of a 'total mobilization' in a stateless society lacking a complex division of labour would be at best tautologous. Conversely, no imperial con-flict throughout history has even begun to require the mobilization of all the societal resources of an empire. Where war aims and the means to wage war are concerned, though, the term may have greater cur-rency. Yet in imperial conflicts war aims are almost always heavily asymmetrical, since the imperial society at home cannot, as we have already seen,[10] be seriously threatened by its indigenous enemy. It is certainly possible to talk where appropriate of an empire's total war aims, and perhaps also of total war in the restricted sense of a form of warfare that is directed against the entire enemy civilian population. But in the sense of a coherent total programme—even as an ideal-typical construct—I would continue to restrict applying the concept of 'Total War' (with a capital 'T') to the core region of the Western world in the era of the world wars.

There can be no doubt, however, that imperial wars throughout the centuries have been extraordinarily violent. They were hallmarked by an apparently indiscriminate brutality which was only remotely matched within the core territory of the Western world between the Thirty Years' War and the Second World War by a few exceptional situ-ations such as the revolutionary crushing of the Royalist Vendée Rebellion in France in 1793–1796.[11] The clichéd phrase about the exception that proves the rule is, exceptionally, justified in this instance: in so far, that is, as one can judge the general level of violence in imperial wars from a few campaigns, of which subsequent historical literature saw fit to note that Western customs of war were actually observed there or that imperial commanders at least issued reminders to that effect. Thus, for example, in the punitive expedition undertaken by the Dutch East India Company against Ambon in 1637, pillaging, arson, murder and rape were forbidden unless express orders were given to the contrary.[12] In Australia, on the occasion of the punitive expedition of 1816, it was ordered that Aboriginal women and chil-dren should be spared if at all possible.[13] According to David Chandler, in the British Abyssinia Expedition of 1867–1868, no women were molested and there was nothing there to pillage in any case.[14] In the late nineteenth century the British Army is reputed to have actually punished individual cases of the rape of African women with prison sentences.[15] In the Second Boer War, in the Rif War and in Indochina—

admittedly symmetrical conflicts in a certain sense—prisoners were taken and even formally treated correctly,[16] and indeed in the Boer War even the looting of enemy property contrary to orders was subject to judicial punishment.[17]

We may easily deduce from such exceptions and admonitions what the customary standards were for waging war in imperial conflicts. Even in engagements between European armies, it was hard to ascertain whether armed male combatants who surrendered were actually spared. But in imperial wars this difficult and complex intercultural point of agreement did not occur in practice.[18] If prisoners were taken at all, then they were generally executed later; the same went for defenceless enemy wounded.[19] The order issued by US Colonel James Carleton in 1862 for the conflict with the Mescalero Apaches—'The men are to be slain, whenever they can be found'[20]—was virtually the motto for all imperial wars where empires were concerned, and the approach mostly taken by the indigenous adversary, at least traditionally,[21] was not far different.[22] Indeed, according to a recurrent motif of stories from the front, it was often not even possible to take non-European warriors captive, because even when seriously wounded they would fight on to the death.[23]

It was standard practice on both sides in imperial wars to systematically loot the enemy's resources, to a degree moreover that exceeded their own supply needs: this included destroying food stocks, burning down crops, felling fruit trees, driving away or slaughtering livestock and filling in wells, all so as to deprive the enemy of the wherewithal to survive.[24] The Sullivan–Clinton Expedition of 1779 against the Iroquois alone destroyed thousands of fruit trees and over 5,600 cubic metres of grain.[25] The Australian Aborigines also killed the sheep farmed by English settlers in their thousands.[26] In the Ninth Frontier (or Xhosa) War of 1877–78, the British drove away 13,000 head of cattle belonging to their Gcaleka Xhosa enemy.[27] After taking part in a punitive expedition against the Nandi in Kenya, Richard Meinertzhagen recorded in punctilious detail in his diary the destruction of 239 grain stores and forty-six stock enclosures, the burning of almost 60 hectares of crops ('mostly millet') and the capture of fifty-four cows and 399 sheep and goats.[28] Within the space of just a week in December 1901, in the south of the island of Luzon in the Philippines, the US Army seized a million tonnes of rice, 200 water buffaloes, 700 horses and 800 cattle.[29] In Libya the Italians slaughtered livestock in their tens of thousands.[30] And according to a report by Human Rights Watch, in Afghanistan in 2006 NATO troops 'killed large numbers of livestock and destroyed numerous vineyards.'[31]

It is not hard to imagine what this kind of warfare which aimed at depleting food resources must have meant for the people concerned in regions that were already characterized by marginal subsistence farming, and resistance was guaranteed. It is therefore hardly surprising that things escalated beyond indirect violence against the enemy's civilian population. In imperial wars, houses and even whole settlements were regularly burnt down, and it would be an understatement to say that the perpetrators were not always scrupulous about sparing non-combatants.[32] For the French troops stationed in Algeria in the nineteenth century, destroying whole villages was so much the norm that Le Cour Grandmaison described such acts as 'acts of administrative destruction', which were apparently carried out according to a precise set of rules.[33] The British writer Colonel Callwell even provided instructions on how to permanently raze a village to the ground.[34]

There can be no doubt that, in such a frenzy of destruction, there must have been instances of collateral damage at least among the civilian population. Mostly it was far worse than that: ever since the Early Modern period, the burning down of villages and towns had been part and parcel of ruthless war waged on an enemy's entire society.[35] An attack by a volunteer cavalry regiment on a peaceful Indian village at Sand Creek in Colorado in 1864 during which, according to eyewitnesses, troops took obvious pleasure in cutting down women and children,[36] was one of the most notorious instances of war against the civilian population from the Indian Wars in the USA, but by no means the only one.[37] An equivalent incident in Algeria was the Dahra Massacre of 1845, in which French colonial troops suffocated to death 500 tribespeople in a cave with fire;[38] in Mexico, it was Bacúm, where 450 Yaqui civilians were incinerated inside their own church in 1868.[39] On the evidence of his own diary, Richard Meinertzhagen massacred all the inhabitants of villages on at least two occasions.[40] The situation was no different in the colonial empires of other nations.[41] In the interwar period new weapons, notably the aeroplane, made attacks on the civilian population easier.[42] During the Vietnam War, the infamous My Lai Massacre was just the tip of the iceberg.[43] In the 1980s, the Soviet Army flattened countless villages in Afghanistan, slaughtered the inhabitants and depopulated areas with cluster bombs.[44] And by now it is common knowledge that Western troops have regularly been responsible for causing collateral damage among the civilian populations of Afghanistan and Iraq.[45]

Of course, indigenous adversaries did exactly the same in response—not least because the settlers, officials and missionaries on the frontiers of empires quite rightly seemed to them to pose a very real threat to their existence. Thus, at the end of the sixteenth century the Chichimeca of Central Mexico destroyed Spanish villages and farms and indiscriminately killed women, children and slaves.[46] The first victims of the Pueblo Uprising were 380 Spaniards in settlements and on farms, especially many priests.[47] North American Indians made basically no distinction between European soldiers and civilians and invariably attacked outlying frontier farms first.[48] The same was true of the Maoris and Australian Aborigines.[49] The Maji-Maji rebels first killed planters, government officials and missionaries.[50] Both the Herero and the Algerian revolts began with the murder of European settlers.[51] Rebels in Northern Angola indiscriminately put to death 1,000 Europeans in 1961.[52] It became a deliberate strategy of proper terror campaigns such as that launched by the FLN in the Algerian rebellion to first and foremost target civilians.[53]

Nor were civilians just killed. From the Spanish conquest of the Americas to the Scramble for Africa, indigenous opponents were often enslaved—if not directly by the imperial power then by their indigenous allies, who were rewarded with war booty.[54] It was not only empires that took hostages and executed them if their demands were not met.[55] Soldiers and civilians alike were routinely tortured,[56] particularly notoriously during the French anti-insurgency campaign in Algeria,[57] where Roger Trinquier, the resourceful prophet of 'modern warfare', defended such actions as legitimate acts of force against enemy combatants.[58] Women were raped,[59] people were scalped while they were still alive,[60] branded with red-hot irons, castrated,[61] maimed by having their fingers, hands, feet, or breasts cut off,[62] beheaded,[63] burned to death,[64] or thrown to the dogs.[65] Soldiers would display severed heads, ears, noses, or genitals as hunting trophies by either wearing them about their person or presenting them to their superiors as proof of their achievements.[66] Among some indigenous peoples the torture of living captives[67] and the ritual mutilation of dead enemies were widespread practices.[68] Cannibalism also occurred, sometimes even by indigenous allies fighting on the imperial side.[69]

In suppressing the Indian Rebellion of 1857, British officers had captured rebel sepoys bound across the muzzles of cannons, which were then fired. This public annihilation of adversaries was often recounted in gruesome detail and with great relish; the perpetrators believed that they were making the death sentence complete by also desecrating the bodies of their victims,[70] while in the same breath claiming that such punishment was traditional in India.[71] This attempt to do more than just kill an enemy—somewhat orientalist in its supposedly superior cultural understanding[72]—in the belief that this would heighten its deterrent effect, crops up repeatedly: the same rationale was used when beheading alleged Boxer rebels in China and Islamists in Algeria.[73]

Other forms of religious profanation were also widespread. Again in the fight to quell the Indian Rebellion, orders were issued to ritually defile captured Indians.[74] In the Philippines, dead Muslim Moro fighters were buried alongside the carcasses of pigs.[75] Places of worship and cemeteries were desecrated.[76] The Spanish burned the mummified bodies of Inca rulers after the last surviving Inca state of Vilcabamba fell in 1572.[77] After the British conquest of the Sudan was complete, the supreme commander Sir Herbert Kitchener had the tomb of the Mahdi destroyed and initially instructed that his skull should be sent to London; however, he later rescinded this order.[78] By contrast, the Germans really did have the bones of the Hehe chief Mkwawa transported to Berlin.[79] Hand in hand with such desecration of corpses went the destruction of symbols of indigenous authority, an act that was intended to make the conquest complete: accordingly, the imperial palace at Hué was burnt down in 1885,[80] clearly in imitation of the destruction of the Chinese emperor's summer palace, which met the same fate after the Second Opium War in 1860.[81] In the last of the Ashanti Wars, in 1899–1900, the British governor of the Gold Coast Sir Frederick Hodgson demanded the surrender of the 'Golden Stool' of the Ashanti kings, in order to sit ostentatiously on it himself. Hodgson did this either in ignorance or in conscious disregard of the essential fact that the Asantehene (Ashanti rulers) never did this themselves, since the Golden Stool was not a throne but a pure cult object.[82]

In imperial wars weapons were deployed whose use was prohibited in Europe. Biological warfare, especially the deliberate infection of indigenous populations with the smallpox virus, was repeatedly advocated in both Australia and America, and in at least one case verifiably attempted. While we know that large sections of the autochthonous populations of both continents died in smallpox epidemics, only where local outbreaks are concerned is it at all plausible to suppose that there may be a connection.[83] No sooner had small-calibre firearms with a high muzzle velocity been developed in Europe at the end of the nineteenth century, which could even shoot clean through bone, than the imperial powers decided that such weapons did not have enough 'stopping power' for campaigns against 'savages' who kept on fighting even when wounded. The result was the dum-dum bullet with a soft lead nose which spread out on impact in the victim's body, thus inflicting a much more terrible wound and immediately rendering him incapable of fighting. Despite the fact that soft-tipped munitions like this contravened the intention of the 1868 St Petersburg Declaration relating to Explosive Projectiles, for some time they became standard issue for imperial conflicts.[84] Likewise, the use of poison gas became common in imperial wars in the mid-twentieth century.[85] Napalm was used by the Americans in Vietnam,[86] while the Soviet Union deployed its whole arsenal in Afghanistan, including chemical weapons and cluster bombs.[87] Settler violence against their indigenous neighbours obeyed no rules and also had little to do with open warfare, such as when mantraps and poisoned foodstuffs were used.[88]

Aside from forced relocations with ulterior motives, as already discussed in the context of political warfare, indigenous populations were collectively deported, sometimes with genocidal consequences.[89] Some imperial wars of the early twentieth century saw the introduction of what can only be described as death camps.[90] And all these measures here were still designed as means of waging war—not of planned genocide.

War without rules

What, then, is the source of the especial brutality of imperial wars, which has violated modern Western international law in so many regards? This is an interesting question, since the most common and glib answer hitherto has been that international law did not apply uniquely to such conflicts because they had been in and of themselves unregulated.

This response has a long tradition. Certainly it is irrelevant for the conquest of the Americas, for until the late seventeenth century the practices outlined above would scarcely have raised any eyebrows even in Europe. In conflicts that were played out there in the Early Modern period, there were no effective legal safeguards for people who were defenceless or non-combatants, and the acts perpetrated in the New World by the conquistadors or the settlers of New England were equally acceptable in the Old World.[91] Even as late as 1625, the classical author of international law Hugo Grotius, basing his judgement on the writings of ancient authors, was still able to justify such acts as the indiscriminate killing of prisoners of war and enemy civilians, the destruction of property, pillaging and the enslavement of captives in war, and deemed rape only morally—but not legally—questionable. Subsequently, it is true that he recommended under certain conditions that certain groups of people be spared, peasants for example or enemy soldiers who had surrendered voluntarily—but even then only as an act of clemency, not an inalienable legal right.[92]

However, in the second half of the seventeenth century, there evolved in Europe the restrictions on the conduct of war that are in principle still in force today, and which encompassed protective rights for prisoners of war above all, but also to some extent for non-combatants.[93] These were then further refined in the eighteenth and nineteenth centuries. Yet the jurisdiction of these rules was limited in two respects. Firstly they were binding only in conflicts involving legitimate belligerents, namely states, which enjoyed the *ius ad bellum*, the right to wage war: thus they did not apply to those who rebelled against a legitimate authority—and, as we have already seen, empires set great store by branding their non-European adversaries as rebels, who neither had any *ius ad bellum* nor consequently the protective rights of the *ius in bello*, the just conduct of warfare.[94] It was only logical, therefore, that in many imperial conflicts, at least the enemy commanders were treated as common criminals once captured, in other words condemned and usually executed or deported.[95]

Secondly, according to what was in practice universal opinion, Western laws of war did not apply to 'savages' or 'heathens', in short to any opponents of Europe in imperial wars.[96] The Swiss philosopher of international law Emer de Vattel hallowed this view in the mid-eighteenth century with his assertion that:

> When we are at war with a savage nation, who observe no rules, and never give quarter, we may punish them in the persons of any of their people whom we take (these belonging to the number of the guilty), and endeavour, by this rigorous proceeding, to force them to respect the laws of humanity.[97]

The decisive point here is that a 'savage nation' identifies itself as such through its failure to observe the Western laws of war: anyone who themselves (seemingly) adheres to no rules by implication leaves themselves open to any form of retribution in response. This postulate has been cited right up to the recent present as a justification for practically all brutality in war against non-Western peoples, and sanctioned in international law by the Hague Conventions on Land Warfare of 1899 and 1907.[98] It has been primarily responsible for conditioning the popular categorical assertion that international law has basically not applied in imperial conflicts,[99] a position that was in fact more a consensus of nineteenth-century military theoreticians and international jurists than a principle of international law.[100] Moreover, it is surely symptomatic that there are numerous weighty tomes on the development of protective laws in war which make not a single mention of violent conflicts on the periphery.[101]

But is it really the case that the conduct of war in indigenous societies was subject to no limitations? Much evidence suggests that the representatives of empires on the periphery were all too hasty in their assessment that Indians, Africans or Asians practised unrestricted and random violence. They read Vattel's statement back-to-front, as it were: 'savage' nations by definition adhered to no rules; or at least the slightest infringement of rules sufficed as proof positive of their 'savagery' and lawlessness; lest there were any doubt on this score, the fact that indigenous opponents avoided giving open battle was sufficient proof.[102] For the US Army in the Philippines in the period 1899–1906, the waging of guerrilla warfare and a 'people's war' was the defining criterion of an 'uncivilized' enemy, against which any form of violence was permissible.[103] Generally speaking, 'tribal war', namely guerrilla warfare, was regarded as treachery and as a justification for taking off the kid gloves (though the misleading implication of this is that they had ever been on in the first place).[104] When all was said and done, the enemy's cunning unmasked him as the ultimate form of evil, which warranted no mercy.[105] English settlers justified their violent campaign of retribution by pointing to an attack by Powhatan Indians on the colony of Virginia (the so-called 'Virginia Massacre') in 1622, which had indeed been based on deceit: 'Our hands, which before were tied with gentleness and fair usage, are now set at liberty by the treacherous violence of the Savages.'[106]

Without a doubt, North American Indians disregarded certain precepts of European customs of waging war, by ambushing non-combatants for example or by torturing prisoners.[107] But for all that, Indian war practices, in common with those of every civilization,[108] were nevertheless quite clearly regulated—it is just not true to claim that indigenous warfare basically amounted to 'war to the knife'.[109]

The Pequot War of 1636–1637, the first large-scale conflict between settlers and Indians in New England, is a well-researched example of something which in all likelihood happened regularly in the course of European expansion. The Pequot, whose rules of engagement were not dissimilar to those of the West, were initially fully prepared to contain the conflict and for instance to take prisoners or spare women and children; they even tried to reach an accord with the British on this score. However, the latter interpreted the Pequots' refusal to meet them in open combat as a breach of the rules of war, and immediately switched over to waging a brutal war of annihilation. Little wonder, then, that the Pequot and subsequently also those Indian peoples who confronted the English colonies fifty years later in King Philip's War, in their turn abandoned the now-redundant rulebook; no custom of war can survive a refusal to reciprocate.[110] The same thing happened to the Herero in 1904–1905, whose demonstrative sparing of German women and children was in no way acknowledged by the German Schutztruppe. On the contrary, the (militarily entirely sensible) irregular mode of warfare adopted by the Herero was seen as treacherous and therefore taken as an easy justification for abandoning any constraints on the use of force.[111]

These connections have not been intensively researched, simply because the idea that the transcultural conduct of warfare in the context of European expansion must have been unregulated is widely taken as a given. I strongly suspect that something similar took place in warlike first contacts between adversaries on almost every margin of empire. The Europeans disregarded or flouted existing regional sets of rules designed to contain the conduct of war within certain limits, taking its unfamiliarity as proof of total lawlessness and consequently obeying no rules themselves, either the local ones or their own European regulations. In doing so, they destroyed any hope of reciprocity in placing limitations on the conduct of war and hence themselves generated the very state of lawlessness they were complaining about and were citing as justification for their own transgressions of the rules of war.

Yet if the imperial 'men on the spot' had indeed been right—that is, if they really had encountered a state of universal lawlessness on the periphery, in which everything was permitted, would that automatically have meant that they were obliged to do everything that they were ostensibly entitled to do? Logic, let alone humanity, says No: self-imposed limitations on the way they waged war would not only have opened up the possibility of reciprocity but also have lent their own actions a legitimacy, both in the eyes of the indigenous society and in those of European public opinion.

Yet contemporaries answered this question with a resounding Yes. The notion that a less restricted mode of warfare would exert a downward pull, that one might willingly or otherwise be compelled to fall in line in order not to fall behind, was a very powerful discourse of self-vindication, which even as early as the sixteenth century was used to justify the 'war of fire and sword' against the Amerindians of Central America.[112] The brutality of the conquest of Algeria was presented by contemporary observers as the French having to match a fanatically violent enemy who flouted all human rights and codes of honour.[113] Similarly, contemporary German commentators sought to justify their troops' conduct in colonial wars by speaking in terms of an 'unavoidable adjustment to the behaviour of the native foe'. According to the Imperial Commissar for East Africa, Hermann von Wissmann, unless one used all the means at one's disposal, one would find oneself at a disadvantage to an enemy who stopped at nothing.[114] This argument had staying power. Even as late as 1961, the French pioneer of counterinsurgency Roger Trinquier had this to say: 'In modern warfare [...] it is absolutely essential to make use of all the weapons the enemy employs. Not to do so would be absurd.'[115] And a veteran of the US Special Forces mission in Afghanistan was, and presumably still is, not alone in his view that self-imposed restraints in the conduct of warfare would be counterproductive against an enemy that allegedly obeyed no such rules:

> The enemy is prepared to go to any lengths to achieve victory, terrorizing its own people, if necessary, and resorting to barbaric practices against its enemy, including decapitating people or butchering them. We are not allowed to fight them on those terms. And neither would we wish to. However, we could fight in a much more ruthless manner, stop worrying if everyone still loved us. If we did that, we'd probably win in both Afghanistan and Iraq in about a week. But we're not allowed to do that.[116]

The passage that Patrick Porter cites as evidence that Charles Callwell also advocated such a downgrading of standards to match those of the enemy—'the regular forces are compelled, whether they like it or not, to conform to the savage method of battle'[117]—in fact only relates to the tactical thinking, not to the brutal actuality of waging war. But in general, it is true to say that a subtext of Callwell's handbook *Small Wars* is that it is of course inevitable that methods of waging war should change in the face of the challenge posed by an enemy that fights in an irregular manner, especially when he claims that regular troops are 'forced to resort to [...] village burning.'[118] Porter is at least correct in his view that 'Callwell's *Small Wars* supplied a permissive ideology which enabled imperial armies to justify the level of force based on the enemy's perceived barbarity [...] To a degree it was necessary to become the enemy to defeat it.'[119]

However, as we have already seen, this was ultimately a discourse of self-vindication, albeit a very predominant one. Unless we are willing to accept that the whole brutality of violent conflicts in the context of European expansion was solely attributable to a collective self-delusion on the part of the conquering forces that no rules obtained on the periphery, and that it was therefore not only permissible, but actually vitally imperative, that every means of coercion should be used in order to secure victory, then we need to enquire after the concrete, situational causes of violence. And they were present in abundance. In fact, the escalating dynamics in imperial warfare were so numerous that the 'permissive ideology' of the conquerors was ultimately more of a self-justifying discourse than an actual condition for the brutality of the way in which those wars were conducted, a brutality that was overdetermined anyway.

Military necessity

The operational character of wars on the periphery was a key factor in their totalization. As we have seen, imperial military commanders were obsessed with trying to force their 'tribal' adversaries to engage in a decisive battle, something which, as a rule, they successfully avoided doing. The textbook solution to this problem, as expounded in Callwell's book, had been known about since the Early Modern period:

> The adoption of guerrilla methods by the enemy almost necessarily forces the regular troops to resort to punitive measures directed against the possessions of their antagonists. It must be remembered that the one way to get the enemy to fight is to make raids on his property—only the most cowardly of savages and irregulars will allow their cattle to be carried off or their homes to be destroyed without making some show of resistance.[120]

Callwell does concede that such a modus operandi was not the British way of doing things—'the proper way to deal with them [i.e. irregulars] is to kill them or to wound them, or at least to hunt them from their homes and then to destroy or carry off their belongings.'[121] But the requirement to force the enemy to give battle outweighed such moral scruples, as Winston Churchill later emphasized: 'Of course, it is cruel and barbarous, as is much else in war, but it is only an unphilosophic mind that will hold it legitimate to take a man's life, and illegitimate to destroy his property.'[122] Accordingly, the destruction of settlements, food supplies and crops with the intent of forcing a decisive outcome came to form an integral part of imperial warfare over the centuries. For Callwell, the primary motivation—at least in terms of theoretical argument—may well have

161

been to force enemy troops into a fight by threatening the very basis of their existence; just as the British supreme commander in North America understood his troops' campaign of looting and burning in Cherokee territory as a way to 'draw out the men'.[123] But as soon as one started torching the enemy's property, the intention of thereby forcing their troops to engage in battle became both practically and theoretically impossible to disengage from the wider notion of indirectly deciding the outcome of the conflict by destroying the enemy's wherewithal to live. If it proved impossible to pin down opposing fighters, then at least one could deprive them of their logistical and social support network by breaking the economy and the spirit of the enemy society.

And from that notion it was only a small step to the idea that victory was most complete if the society in question ceased to exist as a social and cultural system. At least in practice, therefore, the desire to bring about a decisive battle culminated over time in all-out warfare against the whole of the enemy society;[124] the logic of this position was akin to Italian military strategist Giulio Douhet's doctrine of strategic aerial bombing,[125] and indeed was sometimes even carried out through those very means.[126] The structural parallels to the practice of 'total war' in the later twentieth century are clear.

Constructs such as the collective responsibility of villages, indeed of entire ethnic groups, for the violent actions of individual factions or even individuals supported and radicalized this practice—regardless of the fact that such constructs were incompatible with the low level of political organization and potential for control within most indigenous societies.[127] Lord Frederick Roberts, commander-in-chief of British forces in the Second Anglo-Boer War, famously said of this notorious guerrilla conflict: 'Unless the people generally are made to suffer for the misdeeds of those in arms against us, the war will never end.'[128]

However, a key factor—as shown by the quotation from Roberts— is that intentional thoughts of extermination were not necessarily intrinsic to a war conducted against a society in its entirety. For the actors it was primarily an emergency solution for a particular situation, a circuitous route—albeit a time-consuming and unmilitary one—to achieve a military objective. The forces of empire would always have preferred a swift, decisive military conflict against indigenous warriors. It was the impossibility of achieving this that shifted the focus of the war effort from the enemy's fighting forces to domiciles, food supplies, and women and children.[129]

One could therefore subsume this logic under the multifaceted umbrella term of 'military necessity.' As far as the actors involved were concerned, this category also covered various other practices that could not be squared with the conduct of war in European theatres— for instance the execution of prisoners in cases where guarding and feeding them seemed incompatible with the objectives of a military operation,[130] or torture when it seemed a suitable way of obtaining vital intelligence and possibly averting terrorist attacks[131]—yet it was also widely favoured as a way of justifying a protracted campaign against an indigenous civilian population.[132]

This should not be misunderstood as a pure discourse of self-justification, however. The concept of 'military necessity' may derive from the legitimation of military action to a (national and international) civilian public, but what it describes are essentially situational inherent necessities whose military logic has historically been relevant as a motivation for action even when it finds itself in competition with the precepts of the law of war. And within this situation of competing claims, one was of course at liberty to interpret military logic, that is 'military necessity', as drastically as one liked, so as to justify in principle any abuse, a situation that indeed often occurred in practice. This is just the way it is, and has always been, not only in imperial wars; in individual cases, especially in the absence of reliable sources, it presents real problems of interpretation. Yet it still does not fundamentally make all appeals to military logic purely self-serving attempts to justify unacceptable behaviour.

Things are very similar regarding the fact that not just in imperial wars but in guerrilla conflicts in general[133] combatants and non-combatants often cannot reliably be distinguished from one another in combat situations, at least not readily, thanks to their lack of uniforms.[134] But reliable and fast identification is precisely what a soldier needs to decide whether he must shoot in order to avoid being shot himself, or conversely whether he is not entitled to shoot because his adversary is no longer capable of offering resistance, is in the act of surrendering or is not armed in the first place. In close-quarters combat the soldier will generally, out of a sense of self-preservation, opt to shoot in the case of doubt, which recently in Iraq has accounted for many civilian deaths at the hands of nervous US soldiers.[135] And given the absence of any set-piece battles, close-quarters fighting was and remains the dominant mode of warfare in imperial conflicts. In particular this is true of firefights that develop from ambushes and raids, which are typical of guerrilla warfare as a whole,[136] but it also the case during fighting at night[137] or in enclosed areas and strongholds[138]—all situations where one is suddenly confronted by people and has to make a split-second decision whether to kill or spare them. Under such circumstances, the situational dynamics ensured that prisoners were hardly ever taken and non-combatants often became the victims of deadly force.[139]

In a wider sense, part of the same complex of problems was the difficulty of distinguishing between friendly and hostile groups when dealing with adversaries lacking any political cohesion; this was a notorious source of violence in the Indian Wars in the USA.[140] A similar situation also existed on Russia's frontier in the Caucasus.[141]

It goes without saying that this problem of being unable to distinguish between combatants and non-combatants was often and freely cited as a justification for civilian deaths in imperial wars. Once more, Callwell is the best witness for the corresponding discourse on this subject, when he maintains: 'It is an inconvenient habit of irregular warriors that if they get a moment's respite after defeat they conceal their arms and pose as harmless people of the country, in which role they cannot well be molested by the troops.'[142] Notwithstanding the qualification that he gives at the end, this is a classic example of a dangerous 'permissive ideology'. In practice, the suggestion that 'harmless people of the country' were in fact disguised fighters effectively gave carte blanche to troops to butcher civilians, as happened in China around the time Callwell was writing his book, with the mass liquidation of peaceful village dwellers as alleged Boxer rebels.[143] The vindication of this action by a contemporary Austrian war correspondent sounds like an echo of Callwell; he reported that the troops were 'faced with completely unfair adversaries, who when a column approaches cast off their uniforms and disguise themselves as peasants. They then regroup, arm themselves to the teeth once more and attack from behind, picking off weaker units or patrols.'[144] A similar complaint was voiced by an American general in the Philippines:

> The common soldier [on the rebel side] wears the dress of the country; with his gun he is a soldier; by hiding it and walking quietly along the road, sitting down by the nearest house, or going to work in the nearest field, he becomes an 'amigo', full of good will and false information for any of our men who may meet him.[145]

In an update of this paranoid logic, which of course also tells us much about the level of mistrust and fear in the face of a genuinely elusive enemy, during the Vietnam War every dead Vietnamese was said to be Viet Cong.[146] Likewise, in a battle fought in the volcanic crater of Bud Dajo on the Philippines in 1906, that so many women and children were claimed to have been killed because they were wearing trousers seems little more than a threadbare excuse.[147]

Yet this likewise is not to say that the difficulty of identifying non-combatants would invariably have been an instance of pure self-justification. On the contrary: if this difficulty had not been real and hence credible, it could hardly have become such a commonplace excuse. Not least, the fact that among indigenous adversaries, in so far as they were non-state agents, there was often no reliable distinction between civilians and soldiers in the Western sense[148] constituted a very real problem, which viewed objectively contained the potential for escalation.[149]

In a wider sense, of course, collateral damage also falls into the broad category of 'military necessity.' Since the mid-twentieth century collateral damage has largely resulted from the frequently indiscriminate deployment of weapons with a broad impact radius but a low level of accuracy, such as artillery or aerial bombs.[150] The bombardment of villages allegedly occupied by the enemy was not a case of holding their inhabitants collectively responsible; rather, in an act of great indifference to the fate of the innocent, military aims were simply allowed to eclipse the law of war. In a continuation of this logic, US military jurists today justify the killing of innocent civilians during the 'targeted' elimination of terrorist leaders as an inevitable consequence of the fact that the latter have sneakily—from the perpetrator's perspective—sought refuge among the civilian population, and are therefore primarily responsible for their suffering, and until proof is provided to the contrary every dead person is counted as a combatant.[151]

The logistical difficulties of campaigns on the frontiers of empire[152] could also give rise to 'military necessities' whose victims were principally the civilian population of the regions in question: for example when their food supplies were seized in order to feed the troops[153] (though the logistics of the opposing side were also based on plundering);[154] or when their beasts of burden or—in malarial regions—the people themselves were pressed into the service of the imperial forces as porters, usually with fatal consequences.[155]

Severity and determination

The brutality of imperial wars was also a consequence of the weakness of the colonial state: a factor which, as we have already seen, was essentially responsible for coercive violence and the demonstrative use of force becoming a commonplace condition of society on the peripheries of empire. Unlike the modern Western state, empires did not present the indigenous populations whom they were to govern with an extensive bureaucracy, judicial system and police force to guarantee enduring social order. Instead, on the periphery the West's fragile claim to power was underpinned with selective military actions whose chief purpose was to intimidate. And these military actions became all the more violent the more state control saw itself challenged[156]—or the more self-evident the claim to hegemony became, something that incidentally made precisely the final phases of the blanket subjugation of colonies especially violent, as the residual resistance grew all the more irritating [to the colonial rulers].[157]

The 'punitive expedition' as the real instrument of colonial authority underlines this connection.[158] The term hints at the paternalistic vocabulary which the colonial masters used to express, to themselves and to the public at large, their relationship to the indigenous population. They saw themselves, as it were, as foster parents of underage children whom they had to educate. And an obligatory part of the educational process, according to the conceptions of that era, was correction, with adults imparting a 'sharp lesson' and laying down an 'example' to children, especially if their charges proved lazy, impertinent or unruly or even rebelled against the educational mission—this was a widespread image of how 'savages' behaved.[159] Of course, all this talk of education and punishment again constituted a highly loaded vocabulary, for the presumption about punishment in an authoritarian mode of education is that it is ultimately in the best interests of the one being punished, as it will make him into a better person: so it was that the punitive expedition automatically became the flip side of the civilizing mission.[160]

Yet ultimately the state's claim to power and its punitive educational mission were nothing but the proud façade of imperialism, behind which something quite different lurked, namely insecurity and fear. The 'men on the spot' were only too conscious of their numerical weakness.[161] Hence their fixation upon maintaining the credibility and prestige of the 'White Man', values which in their view of the world could only be permanently upheld by sustaining an aura of invincibility.[162] Hence also their enthusiasm for preemptively cowing indigenous societies into submission through demonstrations of Western superiority in arms technology[163] (the classic form this took in Africa was the public firing of machine-guns)[164] and the threat of violence. Any actual challenges to the authority of the empire were to be punished swiftly, decisively and ostentatiously. Revolts were to be nipped in the bud before they turned into a major conflagration. The 'natives' should not even begin to imagine that there was any real possibility of casting off European rule.[165]

These pretensions to power, the educational mission and fear of their own weakness generated a self-serving ideology that glorified decisiveness and ostentatious displays of might and ridiculed a willingness to compromise and observance of rules; according to this view of things, the 'savage' had a weak character and was easily impressed; furthermore, he only understood severity; and a lack of such strictness was seen as abject weakness which he would immediately exploit:[166] 'Uncivilized races attribute leniency to timidity' (Charles Callwell);[167] 'Savages must be *crushed* before they can be completely conquered' (US General William S. Harney).[168]

This did not just apply to claims to colonial rule that had already been established. The ideological hallowing of 'severity' was transferred to military conflicts on the periphery, where it created a cult of initiative, decisiveness and a permanent offensive as the only means of offsetting the numerical inferiority of imperial forces by demonstrating moral superiority.[169] Callwell preached:

> The lower races are impressionable. They are greatly influenced by a resolute bearing and by a determined course of action. [...] The spectacle of

an organized body of troops sweeping forward slowly but surely into their territory unnerves them. There must be no doubt as to which side is in the ascendant, no question as to who controls the general course of the war; delays must not occur, they cause the enemy to pluck up courage; every pause is interpreted as weakness, every halt gives new life to the foe.[170]

The watchword was to keep on the offensive and above all keep winning: 'This is the way to deal with Asiatics—to go for them and cow them by sheer force of will.'[171]

This cult of the offensive helped intensify imperial wars, where it readily complemented the obsession with getting the enemy to engage in battle, namely through the conviction that it was necessary, once battle had finally been joined, to ensure that it was particularly 'decisive'. Encirclements and relentless pursuit were the magic formulae by which the death of as many enemy fighters as possible might be achieved.[172] As the British commander-in-chief in India, Sir Frederick Roberts, postulated in 1887:

> When there is an enemy in arms against British rule, all arrangements must be made, not only to drive him from his position, but also to surround the position to inflict the heaviest loss possible. Resistance overcome without inflicting heavy punishment only emboldens him to repeat the game, and thus, by protracting operations, costs more lives than a severe lesson promptly administered, even though that lesson may cause some casualties on our side.[173]

Once again, the vocabulary of 'punishment' and 'lessons' is noteworthy; the indigenous adversary is made to appear like some mischievous youth who will keep on with his 'game' until someone knocks some sense into him and makes him desist. Set against this approach was the fact that the cult of the offensive caused the military to take unnecessary risks and was occasionally responsible for the defeat of imperial armies.[174]

The precepts of severity and determination both prompted the use of demonstrative force and at the same time legitimized it: in striving to make as great an impression as possible on the enemy, so as to demoralize his resistance and prevent him from becoming aware of his own numerical superiority and deploying this against the imperial forces, terror became a commonplace, tried-and-tested means of warfare on the periphery; moreover this terror was indiscriminate. Making an example precisely of innocent parties was highly effective *'pour encourager les autres'*.[175]

This applied especially to the crushing of insurrections, where it was imperative that the challenge to imperial rule and to the prestige of the 'White Man', which formed the basis of the uprising, should be snuffed out 'through the blatant use of terror and even cruelty' and 'with rivers of blood', as the German commander in Southwest Africa, Lothar von Trotha, archetypically formulated it.[176] Nowhere was that doctrine applied with greater ferocity than in the suppression of the Indian Rebellion in 1857–1858, where it was the stated aim of British officers to terrorize the civilian population into unquestioning submission by carrying out a series of genocidal massacres. It appeared that in times of crisis, the fragile control exercised by a tiny European ruling echelon, which even in normal everyday life could only be maintained through ostentatious shows of force, could only be brought back onto an even keel by monumental excesses of violence.[177]

This way of thinking was carried over into the doctrine and practice of counterinsurgency in wars of the twentieth century. There, too, it was regarded as the necessary correlate to the policy of 'winning hearts and minds', to the offer of compromise and leniency, as a way of underscoring the credibility of state authority by providing proof of how strict it could be: carrot and stick.[178] And even this credibility was based not least on violations of the law of war by abuses against the civilian population, including instances of abduction and murder.[179]

It goes without saying that intimidation by means of demonstrative, excessive violence directed mostly at innocent bystanders was by no means the preserve of empires. The deliberate terror campaigns waged by many resistance movements in the twentieth century employed the same rationale of using selective physical violence as their principal instrument of communication[180] in order to indirectly achieve more broadly defined political goals that lay far beyond their capabilities by any conventional military means. If the murder of loyalists—highly effective in terms of publicity—was designed to deter the majority of a populace from cooperating with the colonial power, if not motivate them to support the insurgency, then behind this thinking lay the very same notion of *'encourager les autres'*.[181] Terrorist violence by way of example was first and foremost a political communication strategy for both the weak colonial state and for its non-state or sub-state enemy alike.

Cultural distance

Paternalism was the outward manifestation of a cultural hierarchy constructed by imperial 'men on the spot' between themselves and their indigenous opposite numbers. The message was clear: only the person who is on a higher cultural rung, more developed, may lay claim to the role of educator. And yet inherent within paternalism is the idea that parents and children are located on the same line of development, albeit at different stages of advancement along it; in other words, that children can mature.[182] However, the cultural distance between the two opposing sides in imperial wars could be far greater. Here, the cultural difference could be construed as fundamental, seen as unbridgeable or in extreme cases even deemed to exclude the opposing side entirely from the human race. In fact, this conception of an essential culture clash was characteristic of imperial warfare as a whole, which was almost always transcultural; moreover the idea did not only develop after the emergence of a highly evolved 'scientific' form of racism in the late nineteenth century.[183] Originally this feeling of an unbridgeable culture gap dividing one from one's enemy was founded on cultural misunderstandings, and it was reciprocal. As Stephen Morillo explains:

> One or both sides fundamentally misunderstand each other in basic ways, failing to comprehend the goals, motivations and methods of their enemy. The opponents in intercultural warfare therefore often think themselves engaged in warfare with non-humans, variously conceived of as savage sub-human barbarians or being capable of superhuman feats—indeed sometimes both at the same time.[184]

Different customs of warfare, especially those involving practices regarded as cruel and inhuman, such as the torturing to death of prisoners practised by North American Indians, but also simply the outward appearance of an enemy, helped foster this idea of the essential otherness of one's foe. One need only think back to the Americas during the Spanish Conquest in order to understand this: cumbersome riders in armour on armour-clad horses (hitherto unknown in the

Americas) and with similarly armoured attack dogs versus painted, naked warriors, whose preferred method of attack was by surprise and from the rear, uttering piercing shrieks.[185] Little wonder that European and Indians alike found it difficult to regard one another as human beings.[186] In addition, in the Early Modern period religion was such an essential, fundamental cultural characteristic, that it alone had the potential to be a source of virtually insurmountable otherness.[187]

Then, in the nineteenth century, this was indeed compounded by the rise of modern racism, which in place of mutual alienation additionally posited a massive cultural hierarchy;[188] and finally Social Darwinism, which in a kind of logical circular argument provided the conclusive legitimation for exterminatory behaviour towards indigenous groups by maintaining that they were evidently condemned to die out anyway, as evinced by their successive extermination.[189] Yet these were merely new forms of an awareness of cultural distance between the representatives of empire and indigenous populations on the periphery which had for centuries been keenly felt and handed down as common wisdom.

It should anyhow be noted that racism was not primarily an ideological creation that was imported from the mother countries into frontier regions (a notion encapsulated neatly by Susanne Kuß when she talks of the 'metropolitan field pack' carried by German colonial soldiers)[190] but in many respects was a rationalization and consolidation of the collective experiences of the 'men on the spot' on the colonial margins: the fragility of the colonial presence, the logic of maintaining that presence, which positively demanded an inferior indigenous counterpart as a foil, and not least the experience of actual cultural distance all contributed to the development of a situational racism that not infrequently preempted its ideological formulation in the metropole, or in any event evolved independently of it. Nevertheless, this situational racism was subsequently handed down culturally on the periphery and, independently of people's own experiences, came to form the prevailing image of the foreigner.[191]

This fundamental cultural difference had direct ramifications for the intensity of violence used in these transcultural conflicts. For one thing, it excluded any possibility of mutuality: there could clearly be no agreement on the rules of war with non-humans. On the contrary, they were capable of anything. Anyone who tortured captives might well also butcher children—and would naturally breach any agreements. And for another, the cultural distance legitimized one's own unbounded use of violence. In place of reciprocity in factual matters—which will be discussed presently—came reciprocity in what was theoretically possible. In other words, one was entitled to do pretty much anything to those who were capable of anything:[192] as a New England pastor said of the Indians, 'They act like wolves, and are to be dealt withall as wolves.'[193] As a result of being ostracized from the human race, the indigenous adversary effectively became fair game.[194] Several of the perpetrators of the My Lai Massacre in Vietnam said of themselves that they could never have killed a *person*.[195]

Yet we should not overlook the fact that, although the feeling of essential otherness was originally based on practical experience of the enemy culture, over the centuries it transformed into part of the narrative tradition and not least a discursive strategy. In later transcultural conflicts the adversary was deliberately dehumanized precisely in order to justify inhumane practices.[196] As Geoffrey Parker explains:

> An important aim of state-sponsored propaganda before and during war is to destroy any sense of identification with the enemy by dehumanizing all adversaries so that they can be killed, mutilated, and otherwise mistreated with a clear conscience. Evidence of subhuman traits and racial inferiority, as well as alleged atrocities and supposedly implacable malice, all play their part in this process.[197]

In imperial wars, where the cultural distance could be felt and experienced directly and did not—like in conflicts within Europe—first have to be fabricated through propaganda, this process of dehumanization was all the easier. Disparaging terms like 'Gu-gus', 'Gooks,' 'Dinks' and 'Slopes', which US troops applied to their enemies in transcultural wars during the twentieth century,[198] but for which there are already parallels in preceding centuries,[199] were just the start. As late as the 1950s the British colonial administration in Kenya, by playing up through propaganda the excessive violence shown by the Mau Mau towards civilians, managed to paint them as bestial savages and as the incarnation of demonic evil.[200]

The most resonant theme of propaganda was talking about adversaries as though they were animals. This was an obvious choice, since the 'tribal' enemy's skill in guerrilla warfare already conveyed the impression that he was in league with nature, or even an integral part of it. Racist vilification could sometimes go hand-in-hand with a grudging recognition of indigenous 'bushcraft', not only by Callwell, who without any irony referred to 'irregular warriors with their aptitude for creeping about and their instinctive capacity for stalking unsuspecting adversaries'.[201] According to their British opponents, the Maori were supposedly 'able to burrow like rabbits through the high fern', darting 'from one cover to another with the quickness of monkeys', with 'their naked brown skin nearly blending with the trunks' and 'were as much at home in the water as on land.'[202] During the Second Boer War, on the one hand the Boers were dehumanized as uncivilized, primitive, Africanized foes with the herd-like instinct of animals, but on the other were admired for their courage, skill, tactical prowess and horsemanship. This even went as far as the superstitious fancy that they were natural hunters, better fighters, could see in the dark and even had magical powers.[203]

Yet both the Maori and the Boers (the latter of whom were of European origin) were regarded as being relatively highly placed in the contemporary racial hierarchy.[204] Where other adversaries were concerned, though, there was little sign of any admiration. In the Seven Years' War in North America, the British colonel Henry Bouquet begged leave to 'extirpate or remove the vermin', to which end he devised a plan, with the approval of the British supreme commander Jeffery Amherst, of deliberately infecting the Indian population with smallpox.[205] In reference to the homeland of the Seminole Indians in southern Florida, an American army doctor wrote that the swamps there were 'a perfect paradise for Indians, alligators, serpents, frogs and every other kind of loathsome reptile.'[206] In the nineteenth century, it was the general consensus of the Portuguese conquerors of Brazil that the indigenous population were somewhere between humans and orangutans,[207] an assessment that found an echo in Rhodesia (present-day Zimbabwe), where one settler considered the Africans to be 'merely superior baboons [...] and the sooner they are exterminated the better.'[208]

From their conquest of the country in the nineteenth century to the war of decolonization in the twentieth, the French in Algeria labelled

173

their Arab foes with a whole catalogue of zoological epithets: hyenas, raptors, jackals, foxes, marabous (storks), snakes, locusts, scorpions— with each term linked to the express call to deal with the enemy as one would usually with such forms of parasite.[209] In putting down the Indian Rebellion of 1857, the British, according to their own reports, were hunting down 'rats'.[210] Occasionally the indigenous adversary would slip out of the animal kingdom and drop even further down the evolutionary scale: for instance, during the Malayan Emergency one British commander, General Boucher, actually referred to the clearing of insurgents from a particular area as 'disinfection'.[211]

The use of such metaphors crossed the borderline between a permissive and an exterminatory ideology. Compared to them, Clive Turnbull's suggestion that the Aborigines of Tasmania must have appeared to the first European settlers as nothing but natural phenomena without any rights, while still dehumanizing, is really quite a harmless observation. 'To these men "savages" [...] were obstacles to be overcome, in no way differing from the obstacles of ocean, storm, forest and barren soil; that savages might have rights was no more part of their belief than that oceans and thunderstorms had rights.'[212]

However, it is worth reiterating that we should not forget that the feeling of a fundamental culture gap was mutual in imperial conflict and that dehumanization was a two-way street. In the Boxer Rebellion of 1900–1901 it was not only the Europeans who proclaimed that they were going to 'punish [...] these thoroughly subordinate creatures [...] this cowardly, treacherous rabble, terrifying when they have strength in numbers', namely the Boxers;[213] the Chinese rebels in their turn called for the 'foreign devils' to be 'slaughtered'.[214] The dehumanizing of the enemy was equally prevalent in the cultural codes of many non-European societies.[215]

Dehumanization and comparisons with animals point to an unconventional flip side to the phenomenon of cultural distance in imperial wars. In the self-image of the perpetrators, particularly in the period at the end of the nineteenth century, which was highly charged with aggressive, ostentatious ideals of manhood,[216] violent conflict on the periphery could be read as a kind of great adventure.[217] Commentators have rightly pointed to the phenomenological proximity of punitive expeditions in Africa and safaris.[218] And from this perspective, violent conflict on the fringes of empire could sometimes seem like an exhilarating pastime, which was frequently expressed in the terminology of sports,[219] but particularly shooting and big-game hunting.[220] In the Second Boer War it was common practice among cavalry officers to chase down fleeing Boers with cries of 'Tally-Ho' and to run them through with lances, an activity described as 'most excellent pig-sticking'.[221] In the Mau Mau Uprising professional big-game hunters were called in to track the 'Mickeys' (Kikuyu),[222] while army units collected the severed hands of insurgents and competed in a kind of sporting contest to see who had the biggest tally of kills.[223] The sanctioning in 1899 by the British Minister of War Lord Lansdowne of the introduction of the dum-dum bullet into colonial warfare, with the argument that 'Civilised man is much more susceptible to injury than savages [...] the savage, like the tiger, is not so impressionable, and will go on fighting even when desperately wounded', also belongs in this context, since expanding munitions were originally developed for big-game hunting.[224]

The heights of inhuman absurdity were surely reached in Tasmania, where settlers would engage in 'hunting' Aborigines as a casual pastime during Sunday picnics en famille.[225] The fact that a significant number of people could take pleasure in killing other human beings, or at least threatening them with death—provided that there was a sufficiently large cultural gap and that an extremely asymmetrical constellation of power guaranteed the perpetrator immunity—should not be underestimated.[226] Simply for recreation, US troops in North Africa in 1942 would also take potshots at Arabs who had no involvement whatever in the desert war between the Allies and Germans.[227]

'Indian Country'

The skill in guerrilla warfare shown by indigenous adversaries engendered a range of strong emotions among imperial troops: admiration (rarely), condescension (frequently) but almost always negative feelings of frustration, anxiety and not least fear—a constant emotion anyway when stationed at frontiers.

Frustration—a failure to fulfil expectations—was a typical experience of bush campaigns against an elusive enemy.[228] Living conditions were miserable, and endless marching in a state of constant tension and readiness for battle frequently only resulted in stress, health problems and death. As Bernd Greiner has pointed out in reference to the Vietnam War:

> In the jungle and paddy-fields all expectations and hopes were abruptly dashed. The enemy was either nowhere in evidence or dictated the time and place of combat at his choosing, superior weaponry brought no advantages, losses were incurred without being able to inflict any appreciable damage on the enemy in return, the front was everywhere and nowhere, and death out of the blue in the form of land mines, booby traps or snipers hung over everyone the whole time.[229]

When imperial commanders decided to extend the violent conflict to the local civilian population, such escalation was very often born, alongside pragmatic considerations, of sheer frustration at the lack of any decisive outcomes in the exhausting conflict.[230]

Many other reasons prompted these negative feelings too. Certainly, war in any event is a sphere of intensely focused intimidation and fear, but indigenous warriors, whose outward appearance—naked, their bodies painted, uttering chilling war cries, brandishing edged weapons and spoiling for hand-to-hand combat—made them seem out of all control, fanatical and terrifying, instilled especial dread in imperial troops; this was particularly the case with American Indians and Zulus,[231] who were feared all the more for their habit of literally butchering their enemies on the battlefield and finally cutting open their stomachs.[232] Many indigenous warriors would make great play of this 'savagery' as a way of instilling sheer terror in their European adversaries, brutally executing captured soldiers in full view of the enemy camp, displaying mutilated corpses, and having body parts of dead prisoners—especially heads—delivered to their surviving comrades.[233] It was not hard to predict how the recipients of such messages would react.

Rumours and cultural stereotypes ensured that this fear of the terror meted out by 'savages' also affected those who had not yet come into contact with them: Western soldiers in colonial wars would often already be intimidated even before they arrived at the theatre of operations. They went in dread of being killed in battle in a gruesome way. Yet they were even more terrified at the prospect of being taken alive, which in the Indian Wars in North America was proverbially seen as 'a fate worse than death'—hence the clichéd advice to 'save the last bullet for yourself'.[234] British troops who took part in 'small wars' after 1900 would perhaps have gone into battle with the verses of the principal cheerleader of British imperialism, Rudyard Kipling, ringing in their ears, whose 'Young British Soldier' ended his short career at a particularly fateful theatre of war on the fringes of the Empire:

> When you're wounded and left on Afghanistan's plains,
> And the women come out to cut up what remains,
> Jest roll to your rifle and blow out your brains
> An' go to your Gawd like a soldier.[235]

French foreign legionnaires were toughened up by their comrades with stories of atrocities 'which in the colonial discourse also came up in many other contexts, for instance the cutting off of noses, ears and heads, ritual castration by "young womenfolk" or homosexual rape.'[236] The training of US conscripts preparing to go to Vietnam included indoctrination in the grisly methods of warfare employed by the Viet Cong.[237]

Of course, horror stories about alleged atrocities by indigenous adversaries had the potential to themselves become the cause of excessive violence—doing to the enemy what you could expect from him if the boot was on the other foot. But in the first instance, grisly rumours made for a state of permanently high tension and strained nerves, which characterized life, and above all military operations, on the frontier.

In general it is fair to say that fear was the prevailing emotion among European troops on the periphery, who almost invariably found themselves faced with a numerically vastly superior indigenous population and so lived 'with a permanent siege mentality;'[238] fear of a hidden and incomprehensible threat that they could do nothing to actively combat—'much to fear, but no one to fight.'[239] Nor was it just in settler colonies that Europeans (not always groundlessly) lived in constant mistrust of the indigenous population, seeing plots everywhere, and with wild rumours flying around at the slightest provocation about a supposedly imminent mass uprising.[240] These were structurally very similar circumstances to those which played such a large part in prompting fear-driven excesses of violence against African-Americans in the US South during the nineteenth century.[241]

One indication of this permanent state of fear was the irrational panic which could sometimes grip entire settler colonies, causing their whole population to take flight.[242] But another sign was the excessive and equally irrational force with which the colonial masters and settlers then reacted when their worst fears seemed about to be realized, such as the actions of the whites in Kenya during the Mau Mau Uprising:

> After the murders [of several Europeans] white Kenyans and their govern-
> ment were united in the conviction that the Mau Mau were bestial savages,
> crazed by unspeakable oaths, void of all human restraint, and beyond the
> reach of decency or redemption. They believed that Mau Mau would kill
> women, children, anyone, in sheer animal frenzy. There could be no
> understanding 'animals' like these; there could be no mercy, there could
> be no forgiveness.[243]

The archetypal locus of terror for Western soldiers in imperial wars was the primeval forest. It appeared to be a thoroughly partisan environment: for the foreigner—the European—completely inscrutable, impenetrable and hostile; for the native—the non-European—not only accessible and comprehensible but positively in league with him against the interloper. Spencer Chapman described British soldiers' fear of the Malayan jungle in the following terms: 'To them the jungle seemed predominantly hostile, being full of man-eating tigers, deadly fevers, venomous snakes and scorpions, natives with poisoned darts, and a host of half-imagined nameless terrors [...] in this green hell they expected to be dead within a few weeks—and as a rule they were.'[244]

Here, we have come full-circle back to the animal metaphors of the previous section: in the final analysis, they all come down to the sense that indigenous fighters were an intrinsic element of a landscape Europeans found intensely hostile, living creatures every bit as much at home in the jungle as tigers, snakes or tropical diseases.[245] This was particularly so with regard to the kind of 'tribal warfare' practised by indigenous warriors, with their preference for ambushes from deep cover, for which the jungle was tailor-made. Like jungle predators and tropical diseases the indigenous adversary was an invisible yet ever-present danger; he could, quite literally, be lurking behind every tree,[246] or in the Congo in every swamp.[247] Just by virtue of living in the jungle, non-Europeans were the very antithesis of Westerners: the virgin forest, like the indigenous foe himself, had a quintessential otherness about it, which was by definition hostile.[248]

Although it is well documented in studies on the subject that US troops in Vietnam described the jungle there stereotypically as 'Indian

Country', this has generally only been seen as an instance of the cultural transference of war experiences and conceptions of the enemy: in other words, the use of the Indian Wars as a yardstick for gauging the war in Indochina.[249] However, this is only the half of it. We need, perhaps, to delve back into literature to understand what 'Indian Country' really denoted and still denotes: the indissoluble unity of a foe and a hostile landscape. 'Indian Country' did not mean first and foremost that the tract of land in question belonged to the 'Indians' (i.e. the enemy) or was controlled by them. Rather, it signalled that they were completely at one with this landscape in an organic way that was not only unattainable and incomprehensible, but above all deadly, to the outsider.[250] 'Indian Country' described a feeling of utter helplessness in the face of an alien environment that conspired against the interloper:

> The landscape was anomalously beautiful and hostile. It was desolate and unforgiving [...] Above all, it was wild, definitively wild. And it was inhabited by a people who were to him [i.e. the European] altogether alien and inscrutable, who were essentially dangerous and deceptive, often invisible, who were savage and unholy—and who were perfectly at home.[251]

This passage by the American Indian author Scott Momaday conveys the conquerors' view of the American West. No one, though, has captured the symbolic sense of 'Indian Country' as vividly as Philip Caputo in his eponymous novel about a Vietnam veteran:

> Often it was difficult to tell which were real bushes and which camouflaged North Vietnamese, and so he fired his rifle at both. The woods became an evil thing, with the power of conscious deadly intent and he didn't care if his bullets were hitting vegetation or people—he wanted it all destroyed, leveled, flattened, blown to bits, the bits to dust, the dust to vapor.[252]

Like Caputo's anti-hero Christian Starkmann, in imperial conflicts many Western soldiers, but also settlers, sought to overcome their sense of powerless exposure to a thoroughly hostile environment through self-empowerment in the form of blind destructive rage.[253] The fact that hyper-nervous soldiers—especially inexperienced conscripts—would at the slightest provocation fire wildly into the undergrowth or basically at anything that moved, was the least of it.[254] Pent-up frustration, tension, nerves, and the fear of atrocities and of being heavily outnumbered by the indigenous population regularly erupted into outrages against the innocent—except that the flip side of the feeling of being in 'Indian Country' was that there were no innocent parties. Anyone who felt at home in 'Indian Country' was by definition part of the hostile landscape, and so was a logical and ultimately legitimate target of the violence through which all the pent-up negative feelings sought an outlet. If no enemy soldier could be found, then anyone you came across counted as the enemy. This was not new to Vietnam; it has applied to imperial wars and imperial rule since the beginnings of the Spanish Conquest.[255]

Discourses on retribution

In the main, tension, fear and frustration took effect subconsciously, impelling individuals or small groups of men to commit atrocities as an outlet for negative emotions. Though retribution was of a more explicit nature, it could manifest itself in a similar way, as direct revenge by combatants for the use of excessive violence against their comrades.[256] Mutilations or the desecration of bodies, for example, have the potential to excite an extreme thirst for revenge, not least due to the perpetrators' awareness of their own vulnerability.[257] But sometimes, just personal humiliation, a straightforward defeat or heavy losses in a battle could be enough to spark a violent reaction that was out of all proportion.[258] Direct retribution, though, was somewhat uncommon, if only for the fact that precisely in imperial wars it was virtually impossible when facing 'tribal' adversaries to find a direct object to take revenge on—for this reason, vengeful violence was usually directed at non-combatants.[259] For instance, on the Californian frontier it was common practice for ranchers to massacre several Indians living nearby in retribution for livestock that had apparently been rustled (but which in many cases had simply wandered off)[260]—another example of the principle of collective responsibility being applied.

Mostly, however, the urge to take 'an eye for an eye' was mediated through the passage of time, a change of location or hearsay—in other words, neither the perpetrators nor the victims of vengeance had anything to do with the original act of violence or its immediate aftermath. This makes retribution as a vindication of a person's own transgression of boundaries primarily a discursive factor; that is, it required rumours circulating among troops or settlers at the frontier,[261] or uproar among the public and in the media over real or imagined enemy outrages, for its increasingly violent effect to unfold.

Perhaps the most relevant example of a collective discourse on violent retribution was the reaction to the Cawnpore Massacre during the Indian Rebellion, in which some 200 captured European women and children were literally slaughtered on the night of 15–16 July 1857, by butchers armed with meat cleavers. Cawnpore unleashed a clamour for retribution, particularly in Britain. The British press revelled in lurid accounts of the butchery committed by the 'black satyrs' against innocent women and children, and called for a crusade of extermination in revenge; this press campaign played a part in making the violence meted out in the suppression of the mutiny all the more intense and ruthless. Above all, though—a fact clearly corroborated by the chronology of events—the Cawnpore Massacre legitimized excessive violent practices that had been commonplace before Cawnpore and which in their turn were initial knee-jerk responses to the challenge to British rule posed by the uprising. Even prior to the massacre, British troops had executed entire enemy regiments, burnt down villages and put to death all their inhabitants. It is even highly probable that Cawnpore was itself a reaction to these British outrages.[262]

Yet the fact that the hysteria over Cawnpore was also a discourse on legitimation does not mean that it was not at the same time quite genuine. Certainly it is clear that the desire for revenge for this and other atrocities would have motivated British soldiers to take part in massacres of Indian civilians—and of course this would equally have applied to the rebels vis-à-vis the European population. Revenge, especially since it tends as a rule towards overreaction,[263] has a habit of triggering a chain-reaction of escalating violence[264]—underpinned by the negative attitudes discussed in the previous section.

The most direct result of discourses on retribution was a general lifting of restraints on the conduct of warfare, as evidenced in William Tecumseh Sherman's call for the Sioux to be shown no mercy, 'for they grant no quarter nor ask for it,'[265] or Cecil Rhodes's exhortation to white settlers in Rhodesia regarding the Matabele, who had just murdered 100 Europeans: 'Kill all you can!'[266] The refusal to take any pris-

oners is the particular form of outrage most frequently cited, in contemporary reports and in scholarly accounts, as a justification for
adopting the same practice toward an adversary.[267] Terror also represents a transgressing of accepted boundaries which legitimizes counter-
terror and sets in train spirals of violence.[268] In the wars of decolonization in Kenya and Algeria in the 1950s, the colonial authorities
deliberately released pictures of the mutilated and dismembered bodies
of the victims of African violence in order to justify their own repres-
sive measures[269]—and in the process doubtless furnished their own
security forces with the legitimation and motive or even possibly the
template for their own, often very similar, acts of terror.

In its rhetorically most insidious form, violent retribution could
even present itself as a preventative measure. The Methodist preacher
and volunteer colonel John M. Chivington, who at the head of his unit
of 700 volunteer cavalrymen positively gleefully massacred a group of
around 200 Arapaho and Cheyenne, comprising mainly women and
children, at Sand Creek in Colorado on 29 November 1864,[270] subsequently maintained that he was certain that it was 'right and honorable
to use any means under God's heaven to kill Indians that would kill
women and children.'[271] This subjunctive formulation was an example
of the logic of preventative elimination of a threat, as later popularized
in the metaphorical dictum 'Nits make lice,' which also legitimized the
murder of children.[272] The fact that Sand Creek really was construed
by the perpetrators as an act of revenge for past white victims of Indian
violence[273] and that the massacre in its turn unleashed a wave of escalating revenge attacks across the American West[274] obeys the general
pattern outlined here. We can see a later continuation of this logic in
the ongoing 'War on Terror' post-9/11, in which the United States
regards as legitimate the targeted assassination of people in the Third
World who are merely suspected of terrorist activities as an ostensible
safeguard against the future threat they might pose.[275]

Traditions of violence

It was not only through otherness and cultural distance that the clash
of two different cultures of violence conspired to generate unchecked
violence. Sometimes the roots of the high degree of brutality were to

be found within the violent civilizations involved themselves—or at least it was the case that, in claiming this, the actors concerned created new realities in perpetuity.

Thus, the Spanish and Portuguese conquistadors' propensity for excessive violence in the Americas and Asia alike has been attributed to the legacy of the Reconquista (the long-running struggle against the Moors to regain control over the Iberian Peninsula), while that of the English settlers and particularly the soldiers amongst them is traced back to the experience of the Wars of Religion in Europe and the conquest of Ireland. In addition to certain tactical and strategic innovations such as ways of dealing with a guerrilla war in Ireland,[276] both of these realms of conflict taught their veterans a lesson in the radical abuse of the human rights of those whose cultures were different or seen as different, particularly if in doing so they could invoke the will of God: by this reckoning, heathens and heretics deserved no mercy. Presumably a general desensitizing and brutalizing effect must also have been evident, at least among those who were personally involved in these earlier conflicts.[277]

The problem with these interpretations, if we were to rely solely upon them, would be that this would implicitly efface the dynamics of escalation evident within imperial conflict. Nonetheless, these individual traditions of violence should certainly be taken into account as a background factor here—or, to revisit that resonant phrase, a 'metropolitan field pack.' In any event, it would not take much to convince a veteran of the brutal warfare of the first decades of the Early Modern period in Europe that burning down Indian villages and massacring the people who lived in them was something quite inconsequential. Nor—and in this Clive Turnbull is quite right—could one have expected the serious criminals who were deported to Tasmania ('brutalised persons, child-slaughterers and even potential cannibals') to show much sensitivity for the human rights of the local population, especially when one bears in mind that, at the start of the nineteenth century in Great Britain human life was cheap and even minors were hanged for the pettiest of crimes.[278]

Later, too, these traditions of violence within individual societies were adduced as a foil for categorizing new, supposedly similar violent conflicts: a habit particularly prevalent in frontier societies like the United States. At the same time, this suggested that the solutions of

183

those older conflicts were likewise correct, given the nature of the clashes at any given time with an alien adversary, and above all—qua those traditions—were legitimate. At least in the estimation of Joanna Bourke, a corresponding process of socialization could even begin in kindergarten: 'Australian lads imaginatively cleared primitive Aborigines from artificial bushlands; American kids fought off wild Indians in suburban backyards; English boys slaughtered beastly blacks on playing fields.'[279] In the Philippines War fought by the USA from 1899 onwards, there is clear evidence that references to the Indian Wars served to vindicate the current conflict and the brutal way in which it was resolved.[280] However, such public legitimation is not only retrospective rationalization. In a protracted conflict, it generates a new reality among the perpetrators of the violence themselves; thus, if they come to regard a conflict in a certain light, then that is also how they will henceforth conduct it.

Isabel Hull's argument concerning German military culture surely also belongs in this context; namely, that the tradition of the Prussian General Staff and the experience of the wars of 1864 to 1871 that led to German unification predisposed it to 'military extremism' and to an absolutizing of operational decisions with all means at its disposal[281]— even though this military culture ultimately had only limited scope, having its institutional roots within the Prussian-German army leadership rather than more generally within the Western culture of violence. Similar caveats should also be placed on the equally interesting suggestion that the brutality of the way the Italians waged colonial warfare in Libya had its origins in the generally high propensity for violence within fascism.[282]

Conversely, the traditions of violence that existed within non-European cultures were also responsible de facto for practices that, at least when measured against Western customs of waging war, must be regarded as beyond the pale. Several references have already been made to individual brutality of Indian conduct in warfare.[283] In sub-Saharan Africa, the enemy's entire society including all its economic and personal resources became the target of any war effort: looting was paramount, women were enslaved and sold, men massacred or mutilated, and villages razed to the ground.[284] As a point of principle, Zulus never gave any quarter.[285] In Southeast Asia not just the Spanish and Portuguese routinely burned down settlements and slaughtered all the inhabitants, but their adversaries behaved likewise as a direct result of their own traditions of violence.[286] There is a particularly curious case involving a Japanese expedition that was ambushed on the island of Formosa (present-day Taiwan), and the ensuing punitive expedition. Both parties, the Japanese and Taiwanese alike, were in the habit of beheading their fallen adversaries—yet quite independently of one another: for the former it was a legacy of their samurai tradition, whereas for the latter it was an offshoot of the Southeast Asian culture of headhunting.[287]

Yet this chance convergence of what to our mind are excessively violent practices was the exception. As a general rule, of course, an interaction took place between the cultures of violence, in the form of an adoption of enemy practices.

Sometimes this assimilation was simply institutional on the imperial side, namely through the integration of indigenous allies or auxiliary troops into its own military apparatus. Should these auxiliaries then proceed to follow the norms of their own culture of violence, this would often be the subject of official expressions of regret as an unavoidable evil that one just had to put up with if one was to enjoy the advantages of indigenous manpower, and their familiarity with the terrain and bushcraft. At the same time, unofficially, the possibility of turning the indigenous enemy's own weapons against him, and what is more without getting one's own hands dirty, was welcomed. In case of doubt the uncontrollable indigenous allies (and sometimes the equally uncontrollable settlers) could be blamed for all abuses; this somewhat apologetic stance can still occasionally be found in scholarly analyses of colonialism even today.[288]

Yet the rather sanctimonious commitment to the common good, if not to the specific legitimacy of indigenous fighting practices, leads on to a further discourse. This postulated that transcultural imperial wars could only be won if imperial forces consciously embraced the regional culture of violence. Naturally this idea went hand in hand with the suggestion discussed at the start of this chapter—that the conduct of warfare outside of Europe was fundamentally lawless, and hence that anyone who abided by European rules in a war against non-European peoples would be at a distinct disadvantage. Nevertheless, imperial officers on the periphery clearly cherished the anecdotal notion of a specific Indian, African, or Arab culture of violence with certain rules, to which they could appeal in order to vindicate their own use of force, which would have appeared disproportionate when measured with the yardstick of modern European standards of warfare.[289] A contemporary quotation on the conquest of Algeria illustrates the connotation of unrestricted violence and the indigenous culture of violence: 'Gradually, slipping on the unfeeling slope that can so quickly lead a civilized person back to a state of barbarism, our soldiers began to adopt Arab practices. They killed without mercy, they hit out for no reason and they mutilated people as a punishment.'[290]

The fact that in doing this, imperial officers were succumbing to an orientalist worldview which gave them the illusion that they understood the opposing side's culture of violence well enough to be able to turn the tables[291] underlines the primarily legitimizing character of this discourse. Above all, the key thing was to legitimize their own transgression of boundaries by pointing to allegedly inherent necessities.[292] As one contemporary historian has put it: '"Africanization" of warfare meant [...] focusing not on a real enemy but on an image of the enemy that did not derive so much from any face-to-face experience of the Other as it did from a monologue of the colonial power with itself.'[293]

Yet once again this is not to say that this discourse did not, by virtue of its public presence and institutional tradition, create new realities. European officers in Africa may well have genuinely believed that by waging war in the brutal way they did against enemy civilians and their resources, they were simply conforming to an African mode of warfare—and their metropolitan critics may occasionally even have believed this too.[294] Certainly, they were far less conscious of the fact that the military forces of empire had for centuries been behaving in exactly the same way in theatres of war that had absolutely nothing to do with Africa. What is less comprehensible is the way in which research literature has continued, to some extent even to the present day, to present this self-serving ideology as a real process of adjustment to regional practices.[295]

Institutional dynamics

Conditions on the periphery created a set of dynamics which for particular groups of actors made the attainment of their objectives by means of unrestricted violence toward the indigenous population both urgent and (thanks to poor communications) possible. The 'men on the spot' often saw themselves as being under implicit pressure to succeed, which compelled them to quickly and brutally bring about faits accomplis before resistance had a chance to take shape, and above all before their superiors intervened to take control. According to Wayne Lee, the conquistadors were men 'imbued with a crusading ideology, an energizing greed for hidden mineral wealth and a profound, ends-of-the-earth, succeed-or-die desperation.'[296] Similarly driven were the military imperialists who defied orders and conquered French West Africa in order to further their careers,[297] or the imperial commanders who believed that a swift, resounding success was expected of them.[298]

The peripheral group of actors for whom ruthless violence virtually untroubled by any legal or human qualms became a positive role model were, as we have already seen, the settlers. Their claim on fertile agricultural land turned their relationship with the indigenous population into an existential one: 'us or them'. This situation was not just responsible for the permanent and often, in both intention and outcome, genocidal processes of displacement and extermination that were conducted on a lower organizational level. Settlers also became a dangerous escalation factor in imperial wars, where, acting in the capacity of militias, hunting parties or terror squads, they were responsible for numerous abuses and massacres that were for the most part unintended by the respective military high commands. Settlers were the ultimate uncontrollable and most murderous element within the imperial system.[299]

Finally, one specific institutional dynamic was also the de facto selling into slavery of the Indians of Brazil, which came about through settler pressure, weak government and a general lawlessness at the frontier; slavery invariably went hand in hand with murder, rape and other forms of violation.[300] This phenomenon is also interesting in so far as the primary original economic motive of imperialism—the exploitation of resources on the periphery—has a direct connection here to unrestrained violence. Consequently, this action was geared to much the same end as campaigns whose objective was primarily to destroy the economic wherewithal of competitors in global trade. Such actions could easily develop a transgressive dynamic of their own: generally speaking, it is not a big step from burning down houses and crops to murdering civilians.

States of exception

Violence did not always have to have specific, situational causes. Exotic theatres of war, the fundamental strangeness of the enemy, and a constantly high level of violence had the capacity in imperial conflict to create the general feeling of a state of exception, in which one was free to consider all rules as temporarily and locally suspended without questioning their otherwise universal validity. Joachim Bergmann has presented such an argument regarding the Spanish conquistadors, in which he points to the fact that, after their adventures in the Americas, they were able to be easily reintegrated into Spanish society. In other words, their excessive propensity for violence was reserved for the exceptional circumstances of the Conquista.[301] But elsewhere too it is often easy to diagnose in violent conflicts on the fringes of empire a collective temporary blurring of the very notion that violence had to have clearly defined borders. Within the particular fragile constellation of power at the periphery, the idea that exceptional circumstances admitted of no regulation could, in the long term, come to characterize the norm. Imperial conflict was a permissive environment hallmarked by a permanent state of overexcitement and exception.[302]

Over time, unrestricted violence produced its own set of norms. Whatever is done repeatedly ultimately becomes a routine that requires no further explanation. The Spanish, who in the sixteenth century went in search of the legendary Seven Cities of Gold in what are now the southern states of the USA, evidently regarded it as perfectly normal to demand food, gold and sexual favours from the Indians free of charge, as evidenced by the frequency and the matter-of-fact way that this is reported in the sources. For them, the instinctive response to resistance, but also to simple cultural misunderstandings, was to shout 'Santiago!' and ride down the Indians.[303] The sources recount with the same laconic casualness how, during the conquest of Peru, in every Indian village the community leaders were tortured, hanged or thrown to the dogs.[304] In time, and through constant repetition, many of the excessively violent practices of imperial warfare became the norm.[305]

After 300 years of bitter experience, the Mapuche Indians in the south of present-day Chile would surely have agreed that torching villages, driving away livestock, killing and maiming the men and abducting women and children was simply the Spanish way of waging war, all the more so since the independent nation of Chile carried on in much the same way.[306] The cave massacre at Dahra in 1845 was just as much 'standard operating procedure'[307] as the routine destruction of villages by Meinertzhagen in Kenya[308] or the mass murder perpetrated at My Lai, which Bernd Greiner has referred to as 'the business of killing.'[309] According to Le Cour Grandmaison, to call such actions 'excesses' is to miss the point, since they are precisely not 'born of chaos, anarchy or anomie.'[310] This assertion is both correct and incorrect—in truth, serial massacre is a state of chaos, anarchy and anomie that has become normality and hence the (temporary and local) norm. Contemporary euphemisms that were generally recognized and understood, such as 'dispersal' for the Australian practice of the summary killing of Aboriginal groups by the native police, point clearly to the normality of excess.[311]

There were certain situational structures in imperial wars that played a key role in reinforcing the sense of a state of exception. It is true of every kind of war that containment of violence, to the extent that it works at all, works best at the centre of the war effort, under the gaze of the high command and the world's public, for, as Harold Selesky has rightly observed, 'control over the use of violence slips away on the margins', that is in small wars and at the frontiers of empire.[312] In both these respects—functional and geographic—imperial conflict was the classic 'margin' and hence predestined for a use of force that was difficult to circumscribe. Moreover, it was frequently shaped by violent protagonists who would act individually or in small groups: this too helped promote the feeling of operating within an exceptional environment devoid of all responsibility.[313]

The ultimate state of exception would thus arise in imperial conflicts when all-out warfare against an entire enemy society became the true objective of all war efforts. Admittedly this situation was less common than has often been suggested. But when it did occur, then it became clear to those involved that basically any abuse was not only permitted but could be construed as positively expedient: the permissive system in its purest form.

Conclusion

It should be noted in passing that some escalation factors in imperial wars ultimately had little to do with the specific situation of peripheral violent conflicts, but instead spilled over from the imperial centre. In the twentieth century it was hard to avoid concluding that some Western powers were trying out their military doctrines, and above all their latest weaponry, in the relatively permissive environment of the fringes of empire (which, moreover, was conveniently hidden from public gaze)—this was especially true of the deployment of aerial carpet bombing and poison gas.[314]

The emotionally highly charged atmosphere fomented by the ideological clash of the Cold War doubtless intensified the level of violence in some wars of decolonization; not least in Algeria, where the French 'centurions'[315] summarily and wrongly identified the liberation front with communism, so giving themselves de facto licence to exact revenge for the defeat in Indochina.[316] Yet here, as in Vietnam or in Malaya, where the insurrectionists were stubbornly identified as 'Communist Terrorists,'[317] the global struggle between competing ideologies was only a supplementary element contributing to the generally transgressive situation.

And this is ultimately true of almost everything that has been cited in this chapter as a factor contributing to the rise of unrestricted violence in imperial wars: no one factor was alone sufficient to achieve this, and none was indispensable for producing the disinhibited nature of the violent conflict on the periphery. The factors behind the brutalization process complemented one another, entered into semantic and structural relationships, and in the perception of contemporaries—in as much as they reported on it at all—became virtually inseparable from one another analytically, and remain so today. Accordingly, the suggestion of general lawlessness on the periphery (a legalistic discourse), the alleged adaptation to local traditions of violence (a cultural and orientalist discourse) and the premiss of violence as revenge (a pragmatic discourse) are all closely related; in the final analysis, these are all forms of negative reciprocity. In turn, vengeful violence is to all practical intents and purposes barely distinguishable from excesses fuelled by feelings of anxiety ('Indian Country'), especially since both

are frequently conveyed through the medium of rumour. Their separation is based solely on the fact that in the one case, the enemy atrocity
had already been presumed to have taken place, whereas in the other it
was still anticipated; that retribution makes its motivation explicit,
whereas murder as an outlet for frustration is guided by the subconscious; and that the one escalation factor is mediated socially and collectively, whereas the other gained its momentum within small groups
or individuals. Equally hard to separate are revenge and punishment—
here, the difference resides mainly in the paternalistic weighting of the
latter mechanism.

Empirically all this can seldom be distinguished so clearly. This is
why it is presumably also fitting that scholarly literature on the subject
has generally not even made the attempt to differentiate. One should
surely best proceed from the notion of a cloud of radicalized tendencies, permissive ideologies and situational dynamics, which coalesced
into different forms in each individual instance, but which in all cases
billowed up over the phenomenon of imperial war. This does not
exclude the possibility that empirical works, based principally on the
personal testimonies of perpetrators, might in future make a more
concerted attempt to analyse the conditions for the escalation of violence in each particular case; perhaps this chapter can provide some
impetus to this. In each case one will be in a position to conclude that,
in view of there being so many factors contributing to the transgression of boundaries, the brutality of imperial war was in almost every
respect overdetermined.

Even so, it is important to point out that there were also some
retarding factors at work—circumstances which had the effect of lim-
iting violence: otherwise, the history of imperial warfare would be
nothing but the history of massacres and genocide. And, for all the
attention that such incidents have quite rightly attracted, in the main
it is most decidedly not that. For all the tendency of violence to escalate, such an interpretation would be manifestly incompatible with the
generally very limited objectives of the use of force by empires. As has
been correctly pointed out on many occasions, imperial war aims
were primarily control, exploitation and forced modernization, and
only very rarely extermination.[318] This was a pragmatically containing
factor, for something had to be spared in the first place in order for it

to be kept and exploited. To cite a specific instance, many settler colonies were reliant upon the manpower of the indigenous population, a fact that conflicted with the exterminatory ideas of the colonists.[319] On top of this came the pressure, especially post-1945, of having to justify imperial power to a critical global public and, at least officially, of abiding by the precepts of international military law.[320] There were therefore good reasons why not all imperial wars basically descended into orgies of unchecked devastation and destruction—a fact that is perhaps just as remarkable.

ASYMMETRY, ADAPTATION AND LEARNING

A recent history of the Battle of Britain, which was fought in the summer of 1940, compares the rigid, geometrically organized tactical formations of RAF fighter squadrons with 'Fenimore Cooper's Redcoats', namely the British regular soldiers fighting in the Seven Years' War in North America, and the swarms of 'free hunting' attacking German Messerschmitts with the Indians 'waiting in the undergrowth to ambush the end of the line.'[1] The general comprehensibility of this metaphor, which refers to another period, another place and a completely different set of circumstances, illustrates how strongly our image of the conflict between European and non-European cultures of violence is characterized by dichotomies which are embedded in our cultural tradition; here it turns upon the contrast between order, discipline and control on the one hand, and individuality, personal initiative and (apparent) lack of structure on the other. With remarkable consistency, right up to the present day, in depictions of battles on the fringes of empire the indigenous adversaries are invariably portrayed as an indistinct mass, as a disordered, frantic, agitated, fanatical 'swarm,'[2] as a 'great black wave,'[3] breaking over the stoical, iron-disciplined battle formations of the regular armies of the West.[4] The motif of the 'handful against the horde'[5] is rooted in this image, but also the sense of the moral superiority of the West and the professional superiority of its military specialists. It has pervaded modern popular culture, as epitomized most notably by the epic British war film *Zulu* (1964), directed by the American Cy Endfield.[6]

However, implicit within this image is a further semantic thread, at least as influential, which is also impressively and archetypically on display in *Zulu*: the technological superiority of the West. The Martini-Henry rifle of the British infantry, which enabled a force of 152 men to hold off 4,000 Zulu warriors, outshines Michael Caine as the true hero of the movie.[7] There is a general consensus in the literature on imperial conflict that, alongside such martial virtues as discipline, it was above all modern weapons technology that allowed the 'handful' to ward off the 'horde'. Nor has this been the case only since the advent of industrialization; it may go as far back as the beginnings of European expansion overseas.[8]

This image of cultural and technological dichotomies has yet another subtext, namely the suggestion that two so fundamentally different cultures of violence could in no way comprehend one another or learn anything from each other. There seems to be no common ground between Braddock's columns of soldiers and the Indians' 'skulking way of war', between redcoats and redskins. Empires and their indigenous foes may have spent a great deal of time slaughtering one another but they inhabited separate worlds, and embodied diametrically opposed world views: a clash of violent cultures in its purest dichotomous form.

Of course, there is some truth in all these notions. The forces of the modern West, that is from the time of the military reforms enacted by Maurice of Orange in the Netherlands in the late sixteenth century,[9] really were organized according to rational principles, which made discipline and control paramount, and this did indeed manifest itself in the form of close formations, at least until the revolution in weapons technology in the late nineteenth century. Armies outside Europe were as a general rule less rigidly structured and for the most part presented tactically a less regimented picture. Indian or Africans rarely had anything comparable to counter the fortresses, cannons or machine guns of Western forces, to say nothing of steamships, railways and aeroplanes. And frequently the cultures of violence on both sides remained separate. In particular, Western commanders not infrequently found it a completely absurd notion that they should try in any way to adapt to the 'native' mode of waging war or that they might learn anything from that quarter.

Nevertheless, in many respects the familiar cliché really is misleading. It was far from being the case that all imperial troops on the periphery were highly disciplined and professional, if only because they were often neither regular soldiers nor did they come from the imperial centre. And conversely, some thoroughly well-organized and virtually regular armed forces were to be found among the opponents of empire. The idea that they always attacked in undisciplined 'swarms' may well also be a cultural stereotype of the West, which was designed to emphasize its own moral superiority and which has come to characterize our image of violent conflicts on the periphery largely as a result of there being so few historical sources on the opposing side. Besides, a 'swarm' could well have had some tactical organization about it, which the arrogant or terrified adversary simply failed to appreciate.[10] In a global historical context, a clear superiority in weapons technology on the part of the West was an exceptional situation, which only lasted from the mid-nineteenth to the mid-twentieth century; and even in this phase much depended upon actually being able to deploy those weapons on the battlefield, which on the periphery was not always simple even from a logistical perspective.

Finally and principally the history of violent contact between the empires of the West and non-Western cultures were characterized to at least as great an extent by adaptation and learning as they were by a blinkered refusal to learn. In certain parts, it is even fair to speak of a veritable synthesis of cultures of violence.

Armed forces

We have already had cause to quote Hew Strachan's contention that 'many opponents outside Europe were not soldiers, but warriors,'[11] and that is undoubtedly correct in the first instance: the abundance of acephalous and tribal societies with which Western empires repeatedly came into conflict did not maintain any armies in the Western sense of the term. North American Indians, nomads from the Central Asian steppes or tribal warriors from the Northwest Frontier of India did without a hierarchical structure and organized themselves for military campaigns on an ad hoc basis with an improvised leadership[12]—though this emphatically did not mean that they had no organization whatsoever or did not plan battles in meticulous detail.[13] Their mode of warfare was based on individual bravery and on a warrior ethos that was inculcated in them socially from earliest childhood and sometimes even rooted in special warrior castes,[14] as well as on charismatic leadership rather than bureaucratic principles.

It was far from being the case that all the adversaries who opposed empires were stateless. And correspondingly, almost the only indisputable generalization regarding the organization of their armed forces is that one cannot generalize.[15] Even just in nineteenth-century Africa, military structures ran the whole gamut, from tribal contingents brought together in an ad hoc fashion to a general draft in times of war[16] and standing cadre-based armies, plus everything in-between.[17] Besides, this should not be understood as a simple scale ranging from primitive to modern or from unorganized to governmental; the reality was much more complex. Staying with Africa for the moment, the only indigenous force which for a long time was able to resist European conquest, namely the Ethiopian army, was organized according to a system of princely retinues, but thanks to a presiding imperial dictatorship that was committed to modernization, it was superbly well-armed and trained in modern warfare,[18] whereas the radically centralized Zulu tribal army, which was organized around age-group cadres (*intanga*)[19] succumbed relatively quickly after an initial success against the British, despite its high level of training.[20] Its ultimate defeat was due not least to its antiquated weaponry. Statehood, modernity and a complexity in military organization did not necessarily coincide. The traditional military monarchies of West Africa had armies with a thoroughly hierarchical structure, a sophisticated tactical leadership and elements of regularity that were completely recognizable to Western observers, and which were commensurate with those polities' developed sense of statehood, yet precisely for that reason they were also comparatively inflexible and resistant to modernization.[21] By contrast, a tribal military organization like that of the Maori was in many respects eminently capable of modernizing,[22] while the same was true of the jihad states of Central Africa, which comprised various tribal contingents.[23]

The example of Ethiopia, however, already provides the first pointer to transcultural adaptation: over the course of the centuries of

European expansion, the Western empires found themselves increasingly confronted by enemy armed forces that were at least in part organized along the lines of the modern Western military system, namely with a hierarchical command structure, division into modular units, formalized training, discipline and drill and based at their core around infantry, supported by cavalry and artillery. Even as early as the eighteenth century, standing mercenary armies based on the European pattern evolved on the African Slave Coast,[24] and in the nineteenth century the army of Samori Touré was reorganized completely on the Western model, including drilling and bugle calls,[25] and, according to the testimony of a French officer, fought 'exactly like Europeans.'[26]

The adoption of Western principles took place especially early and was particularly far-reaching on the Indian subcontinent, with the modernized military monarchies of the Marathas, Mysore and the Sikhs extensively regularizing their military systems, largely through the assistance of British or French instructors.[27] During the British conquest of the Punjab in 1845–1849, two armies faced one another that had barely any fundamental discernible differences between them in terms of their organization, external appearance and tactics.[28] Granted, Randolf Cooper has pointed out that disciplined and well-drilled infantry armies which were organized into standing units already existed in antiquity in South Asia;[29] the fact remains, however, that the armies of the larger Indian princely states at the time of the British and French conquest of the subcontinent had a distinctly European character.

In general, though, the adoption of Western military structures by traditional non-European societies remained only superficial and limited. A military system is always closely bound up with its socioeconomic background and cannot simply be exchanged summarily without stirring up tensions within a society. Once again, the most pertinent example here is India, where the traditionally dominant feudal cavalry was closely associated with the social system and above all with the opportunity for upward social mobility. Under such circumstances modern infantry troops represented an unpopular alien body within the state structure.[30] The military discipline that European officers tried to inculcate in the regular units of the princely states came into conflict with the traditional flexibility of the Indian military labour market, where soldiers were accustomed to having a free hand to look around for new employers. In the event of war, tradition tended to gain the upper hand, at least when things looked bleak: the troops were not prepared to take up arms against the British East India Company, especially not when their British officers had already switched their allegiance.[31] Similar circumstances hampered the successful adoption of Western military organization in most traditional societies.[32] Even in the best case, this remained only superficial, and primarily confined to model units, around which the rest of the traditional military establishment carried on as before, largely unimpressed;[33] this pattern, incidentally, reflected the division of the army in many societies into a core standing force and a largely disorganized general levy.[34]

Ultimately it transpired that the command structure of post-Mauritian European troops, which was based on bureaucratic principles and military discipline, could not be simply replicated elsewhere—it was anchored in the Western culture of military force. As a result, even after indigenous armies had partially adopted Western military principles, they remained beset by the classic problem of leadership by charismatic individuals, leading to a sudden and irrevocable collapse if the commander fell in battle.[35] In India, if the king's elephant should suddenly charge off in the wrong direction, this was enough to cause a rout.[36] Likewise, maintaining discipline in the event of defeat was a challenge, which almost always overtaxed even modern non-European armies.[37] Yet where indigenous armies did display a high level of tactical cohesion and incontestable persistence even in the face of defeat, those on the imperial side often tended to ascribe this not to their military competence but rather their 'fanaticism'.[38] In any event, rational operation planning for larger armies remained for the most part a 'trade secret' known only to the West[39]—even though the self-satisfied attitude of Western observers may have led them to overlook some impressive feats of coordination and leadership among peoples such as the Maori.[40]

Above all, it was those non-European states that were amenable to root-and-branch modernization of society as a whole which succeeded in adopting Western military principles in a truly systematic, far-reaching fashion; these nations thus also bought into the substructure of their new military system, including bureaucratic centralization for the mobilization of resources (standing armies on the Western model were very expensive), depriving traditional elites of their power and the introduction of universal conscription. As David Ralston has noted, this military modernization—albeit with significant exceptions such as Japan[41]—often made the state in question more capable of defending itself only on paper, laying it wide open instead to being completely infiltrated by the West.[42] The prime example of this is the collapse of the forcibly modernized Khedivate of Egypt, whose army had been equipped and trained by Europeans.[43]

Basically, it was the anticolonial insurgencies of the nineteenth and especially the twentieth centuries which, as a result of their overall socially revolutionary agenda, were also most successful in adopting the Western military model. Armies on the borderline between partially modernized tradition and a modern national army on the Western model were the armed forces of the Yaqui Republic in Mexico in the late nineteenth century, which adapted the Western military system in the form of a communal-democratic militia,[44] and those of the Rif state in the 1920s, which combined a well-armed Western core army complete with service regulations and badges of rank and drill, with irregular tribal contingents.[45] But by the time Vo Nguyen Giap began in the early 1950s to reform the guerrilla fighters of the Viet Minh into regular army units, which went on to face the French Army in open battle, the process of adoption of Western military principles by an indigenous nation was complete. Such symmetrization did not necessarily have to be the ultimate solution, since the Vietnamese suffered significantly greater losses in these set-piece battles than in guerrilla warfare;[46] rather it was, as we have already noted, principally conditioned by political and legitimational necessities and has for similar reasons also recurred in more recent conflicts on the periphery.[47]

Besides, there were also several instances of the opposite occurring: in its war against the USA in 1898 following the defeat of the Spanish colonial power, the Philippines Republic at first ostentatiously put a regular army in the field to demonstrate their claim to statehood and hence to international legitimacy,[48] and ultimately only transformed this force extremely reluctantly during the course of the conflict against the conventionally superior United States Army into a decentralized guerrilla force from 1899 onwards[49]—even this represented an adaptation to the enemy, albeit not a symmetrical one. Small fighting units and terror cells were and remain generally an important option for resistance movements on the periphery of the global system to organize their armed struggle.[50]

Certainly those indigenous states that maintained standing armies or even regularized them along Western lines received more attention from European observers and hence also figure more prominently in research literature.[51] In military terms, though, they mostly played into the hands of empires who, thanks to their superior resources and their specific culture of violence, benefitted from a symmetrical conflict involving set-piece battles—a mode of warfare towards which regular armed forces necessarily incline. Although, as John Pemble has argued, it was probably only through copying the Western military system that the Indian princely states were even able to resist the military machine of the British East India Company in the first place,[52] they still lost in the end. The same applies to the genuinely European or European-trained armies that the British Empire found itself confronted by in putting down the 1857 Indian Rebellion[53] and in the Second Boer War.[54]

There can be little doubt that the military system of the modern West, which was based on bureaucracy, discipline and systems of uniform training and organization, offered significant advantages not only for the symmetrical battlefield wars of Europe, but also in principle for violent conflicts on the periphery[55]—at least in those cases where the enemy really did stand and fight. There are countless instances in which European-trained troops, in the most confused situations, under the greatest possible numerical disadvantage and despite incurring heavy losses, and even having lost their commander, nevertheless maintained their tactical cohesion and ultimately emerged victorious.[56] Yet also in operational and logistical terms (precisely in view of the difficulty of the terrain on the periphery), rational bureaucratic work within the Western army staff system enabled the war to be waged in a decisive, methodical manner; this in turn allowed pressure to be brought to bear on indigenous societies for considerably longer than most of them were able to withstand it.[57] Western armies owed their 'greater persistence in slaughtering their enemies'[58] not primarily to any cultural advantage (even though it has been repeatedly argued that indigenous opponents were

culturally overstretched by this methodical doggedness),[59] but above all
to their tighter military organization, as Michael Howard explains:

> The European armies which fought [colonial] campaigns consisted of
> disciplined professionals of a kind developed in 17th–18th century
> European warfare: regularly paid, relatively well supplied, trained in the
> complex manipulation of weapons, strongly cohesive in battle. It were
> these qualities, developed in the womb of the European state system, that
> enabled small European forces to overwhelm far larger indigenous ones
> overseas. Sustaining them was a comparatively reliable administrative and
> logistical infrastructure—also the product of eighteenth-century Euro-
> pean culture.[60]

We should resist any temptation to idealize this situation (as has
admittedly often happened). It is almost as easy to cite instances argu-
ing against the professionalism of Western armies on the periphery as
it is to find evidence for it: cases, in other words, in which the leadership was evidently lacking, where training, morale and discipline were
wretched, and where troops failed to respond well in battle or even
deserted before the engagement began.[61] This had a number of causes,
which were however generally not systematic but situational, for
example the catastrophic leadership weakness exhibited by the aged
and spineless general Sir William Elphinstone during the British retreat
from Kabul in 1842, which led to the destruction of his entire army.[62]
At best these counterexamples were due to particular military and
political combinations of circumstances, such as the excessive parsi-
mony of US defence policy in the eighteenth and nineteenth century,
with its ideological aversion to professional standing armies[63] or, one
hundred years later, the attempt to fight a protracted imperial war with
an army of conscripts serving only short terms in the military.[64] Only
in exceptional cases was this failure on the part of the Western military
system so dramatic that its fundamental structural superiority was
called into question. Yet when that did happen, the consequences could
sometimes be catastrophic—even though one should mistrust the teleology which, in attempting to explain unexpected defeats of the West
in imperial wars, understandably tends to exaggerate the causes.[65]

Two further qualifications are necessary: for one thing, it was quite
uncommon for metropolitan core troops to actually take part in imperial wars. Thanks to the setting of priorities in favour of the imperial

centre, as we have already discussed, the periphery of the empire was usually also the periphery of the military system.[66] A bewildering variety of different violent actors were mustered there,[67] whose only common denominator was, generally speaking, that their sole rationale for being there was to save the valuable regular armed forces of the imperial heartland or mother country for deployment against enemy troops of the same status. As we have already seen,[68] the initial result of this rationale was the extensive use of indigenous confederates, auxiliaries and colonial troops, of whom only the latter were trained in the European manner. But elsewhere too, imperial warfare was and is the domain of locally raised units, settler militias,[69] soldier-peasants (not just in Russia),[70] private mercenaries (especially in the Early Modern period, occasionally in the 'Scramble for Africa' and recently once more in Afghanistan and Iraq),[71] marine landing parties[72] and last but not least—thanks to the inadequate demarcation line between war and peace—paramilitary police units.[73] European regular troops, even (from the nineteenth century on) conscripts, were therefore only used to any great extent on the margins of empire when all local resources had been exhausted or when the stakes were sufficiently high to justify their deployment.[74] In particular this applied where a transcultural conflict also took on a dimension of conflict between Western empires, as for instance was the case in the French and Indian Wars, the North American theatre of the Seven Years' War in the mid-eighteenth century.[75]

Although these local and organizationally often ad hoc violent actors were in principle organized along Western lines, in practice they were by no means all at the cutting edge of European warfare. Europe's 'military revolution' was in evidence in its offshoots at the fringes of empire at best in a watered-down form. However, the fundamental superiority of the Western military system at the periphery was questionable in another respect. Very often, imperial forces found themselves facing an asymmetric opponent who was not inclined to do them the courtesy of engaging in a set-piece battle. And in such instances, a modern military in the Western mode was not necessarily ideally organized. Its rigid leadership structure, its hierarchical, closed units, its formal training and its drill, indeed even its discipline, which penalized individual initiative as a negative trait, not to mention its elaborate logistics, made it ponderous and inflexible when trying to hunt down a loosely organized adversary that was hard to find and which specialized in ambushes. Quite apart from the fact that regular troops dispatched directly from the metropole were of course unfamiliar with the combat conditions on the ground.

A military force in the Western style in its purest form was therefore de facto not the primary violent actor present on the periphery nor unequivocally the most suitable one for this task. The prerequisite for tactical adaptation to the peripheral theatre of war and to an indigenous enemy (which will form the subject of the following section) was thus an initial adjustment in terms of organization: namely, breaking down complex, hierarchical structures in favour of smaller, more flexible units that could gear themselves to local conditions and liberate themselves from the requirements of an apparatus designed for fighting large-scale wars. It was within this field of tension that the adaptability of the imperial military apparatus began to accommodate itself to the demands of colonial warfare.

The metropolitan regular army largely excluded itself from such processes of adaptation. But were local military organizations on the frontier in and of themselves better equipped to undertake campaigns against an irregular opponent? Settlers were keen to suggest this, claiming that their own paramilitary squads and militias were genuinely specialist units in jungle or bush warfare, not least in order to secure for themselves primacy in conflicts against the indigenous population.[76] The real situation often looked very different.[77] Many local European units continued to follow the military logic of the metropole, and were trained like regular troops in the tactical forms of Western large-scale conflicts.[78] Certainly, they were used to the climatic and geographical conditions of 'their' theatre of war, and had arguably become more familiar with their indigenous adversary by dint of having lived in the region for a long time. They also possibly provided somewhat more fertile ground for tactical adaptation— undoubtedly all the more so the more irregular they were, the closer to the frontier they had been recruited and the less subject they were to centralized control.[79] An example of locally established units operating very effectively in a small war were the *Cazadores de Balmaceda*, recruited by the Spanish colonel Valeriano Weyler during the Ten

Years' War on Cuba (1868–1878). They fought in the guerrilla style, but primarily derived their military efficacy and their dubious posthumous fame from the ruthless brutality with which they waged war.[80] This points to the disinhibited flip side of unconventional warfare: the absence of central control over violence.[81]

Of course, this held even truer for those violent actors on the imperial side who really were born to fight colonial warfare: the indigenous allies. They were acclimatized, familiar with the countryside and its people and, crucially, they were also part of the local culture of violence. They were the real specialists in the struggle for mastery over any given frontier region. Yet in the Western commanders' way of thinking, the indigenous allies were simply too irregular. They pursued their own interests and only went to war when they could see some concrete gains from it for themselves. They were difficult to control and, furthermore, they were actually virtually useless for the intensive set-piece battle after which imperial commanders were constantly striving.

The inevitable consequence of this was the regularization of indigenous allies, initially into auxiliary troops and later into proper colonial troops, and even—in the case of the British Indian Army—into a full imperial military organization. These attempts to get the best of both worlds were naturally problematic. For to the extent that the indigenous specialists submitted to the formal order of the Western military system and were drilled by European officers in rapid volley fire in rank and file, they began to sacrifice their suitability for local fighting conditions. In the conflict of objectives between an 'ethnic army' and a pool of manpower for an indigenous colonial army along Western lines, Western commanders' need to keep full control almost always prevailed. While regular units recruited from among the indigenous population, such as the *Schutztruppe* in Germany's African colonies, the West African Frontier Force in British-controlled Nigeria or the French *Tirailleurs Sénégalais*, continued to be cheaper and more acclimatized to tropical conditions, they were tactically hardly more suited to fighting a bush war than the most alien battalion of regular metropolitan troops.[82] During the interwar years, the British Indian Army finally mutated into a fully motorized main battle army, barely suited any longer for controlling the mountainous Northwest Frontier.[83] Only occasionally was this conflict of objectives explicitly voiced within the imperial military, but even when it was, the regular army drill was usually the winner.[84]

Certainly, one can identify in this a certain professional persistence on the part of the Western military system. In the long term, it tended to assimilate new elements into its own logic, for instance by turning specialist irregular troops into regular ones, only to then discover a need for new irregular troops, and so on ad infinitum—a process that may also incidentally be observed in Europe in the Early Modern period.[85] This trend towards regularization with the aim of consolidating forces in preparation for a decisive battle was always stronger than the impulse towards organizational adaptation to peripheral deployment.[86]

In the nineteenth century this tendency converged with the tightening of the imperial centres' grip on the fringes of their empires, facilitated by, amongst other things, the rise of modern communications technology,[87] and culminated in the almost universal creation of metropolitan imperial troops. The purpose of this was to bring the projection of Western power on the periphery under central control and to pursue it through the deployment of regular troops, without having to have recourse to the metropolitan standing army. In this way, the latter's command structure would not be weakened by constant detachment of personnel, its units would not be demoralized by service in the tropics and fighting small wars, nor would they thereby be rendered unfit for fighting large-scale conflicts. Almost as important, especially in view of the expansion of both compulsory military service and political participation, was the isolation of colonial conflicts from the political discourse in the metropole. From the marine battalions of the German Empire, the *Troupes Coloniales* (the marine units of the French Army) and the Italian *Corpo Speciale*,[88] to the French and Spanish Foreign Legions, the overseas expeditionary corps of the major powers had first and foremost this common purpose, namely to fight dirty little wars on the fringes of empire with effective regular forces but to keep them at arm's length from the general public and from the metropolitan military system.[89]

Accordingly, the logic behind these Western imperial troops, notwithstanding the occasional suggestion that they constituted 'specialized armies [...] structured, trained and armed for unconventional warfare,'[90] was conspicuously metropolitan: they were primarily devised for the military and political needs of the imperial centre, not for the place of deployment at the periphery. In terms of their structure, training and equipment they emulated the metropolitan regular troops and often had scant knowledge of the peripheral theatre of war and its particular demands. This was not always as chronic a situation as with the German marine battalions, which on their arrival in Africa proved not only to be poorly equipped and tactically completely inexperienced but also, and above all, not fit to serve in the tropics.[91] Yet these metropolitan expeditionary corps were of necessity considerably further from a genuine organizational adaptation to the peripheral theatres of war than regional units precisely because they were primarily conceived for worldwide deployment.

Considering this professional persistence of the imperial military apparatus, it is hardly surprising that proper special units played only a very limited role in small wars on the periphery. The classic example is the Rangers in North America. Created in the eighteenth century as a fighting unit dedicated to forest warfare on the frontier, they were viewed with mistrust by the regular forces as an irregular foreign body, and were regularly disbanded when conflicts ended.[92] A contemporaneous unit that was somewhat more highly esteemed was the French *Troupes de la Marine*, which despite their somewhat misleading name were actually woodland combat experts trained in Canada.[93] Only in the twentieth century did units specialized in fighting small wars, for example the British Special Air Service (SAS), become permanently integrated into the structure of armies,[94] whereas in the US Army special units for peripheral conflict remained only an ad hoc phenomenon, especially during the Vietnam War, where they gained a reputation less for bushcraft and more for the unchecked brutality of their operations.[95] On the other hand, although the US Marine Corps liked to present itself as the best counterinsurgency unit in the world,[96] even in the Vietnam War, where such skills would have been useful, it saw its primary role as undertaking classic amphibious landings in the style of the Pacific War of 1941–1945; it carried out more than sixty such assaults over the course of the conflict.[97] Portugal raised *caçadores especiais* (special hunters) units for small war duties in its wars of decolonization.[98] Overall, however, after 1945, as a result of dwindling colonial empires and the dominance of the Cold War in the Northern Hemisphere, the general trend was towards unitary armies without any pronounced local or functional specializations.[99] An interesting synthesis of the later trend towards creating special forces units and the universal rationale of exploiting local manpower—and at the same time a partial counter-reaction to the tendency to regularize them—was the establishment in 1970 in the Portuguese colonies of special units consisting almost exclusively of African recruits.[100]

Alongside the formation of proper special units came the less radical organizational restructuring of regular troops into a kind of light infantry so as to make them more suitable for jungle warfare operations:[101] a concept that was still in evidence in the wars of decolonization,[102] but which is rooted historically just as much in European developments within the military system towards the end of the eighteenth century—the tradition of the 'small war'—as it is in a genuine orientation towards the peripheral theatre of operations.[103] Formations of small groups, which as 'countergangs' copied the organizational form and the tactics of the insurgents (and which took in defectors) were one of the innovative adaptation concepts devised by the British during their wars of decolonization,[104] yet as a form of temporary improvisation they belong more to the realm of tactical adaptation.

Likewise the formation of mobile mounted units also enabled imperial forces to control larger areas and to adapt to the requirements of colonial warfare.[105] At the same time, this adjustment also represented a retrograde step back to the pre-modern era, contributing to the fact that the armies of nations with empires, even in Europe, found themselves saddled with an anachronistic burden that proved fatal in the era of mechanized warfare in the twentieth century, in the form of an absurdly high proportion of cavalry regiments in the overall composition of forces; however, this is a different story.[106]

In practice, for centuries a hybrid state of affairs held sway at the periphery, enabling the imperative of the local theatre of war to be squared with the institutional preference for a decisive clash involving regular troops. Around a hard core of regular or even metropolitan troops, imperial forces gathered a multiplicity of locally recruited contingents, irregular units and indigenous auxiliary troops and allies in wildly varying ratios. Not infrequently, as we have already seen,[107] the indigenous element was predominant, but even where this was not the case, no army on the fringes of empire could manage without auxiliary troops, or at the very least a number of guides and scouts who were familiar with the region.[108] And at least in the ideal case this varied mix was not conditioned solely by fiscal or pragmatic considerations but by an insight into the usefulness of such functional heterogeneity.[109]

Tactics

The cultural dichotomies of imperial warfare also appeared to be sharply pronounced in the field of tactics—namely the ways and means by which battles are fought. Almost always the violent confrontation between Europeans and non-Europeans took place within an area of tension between the concept of pitched battles and that of 'tribal' or irregular warfare. The organizational forms and the cultural character of the imperial military conditioned its preference for the modern Western age's intensive style of waging war; closed formations to produce a concentrated shock effect, heavy weapons for maximum firepower, methodical advances in search of an enduring decisive outcome, and determined pursuit of a beaten enemy in order to seal the victory. The location for this kind of warfare is the open, set-piece battle. It therefore requires a symmetrical opponent who is willing to engage in this form of combat.

Yet non-European and moreover non-state armed forces are overwhelmingly culturally conditioned by 'tribal' warfare; loose formations to lessen the impact of the enemy's firepower, light weapons to maximize mobility, using the terrain for cover, conducting raids and ambushes to minimize losses, and a permanent extensive use of violence instead of an intensive search for a decisive outcome. This style of warfare and the imperial one are manifestly incompatible. And that above all presents a problem for the military apparatus of empires, for if one side in a war chooses to avoid pitched battles, the other side cannot as a general rule force them to take place—unless, that is, it manages to surprise the enemy in a situation in which he is left with no choice but to join battle. Yet in the ponderous, methodical mode of warfare espoused by the West, the element of surprise was at a premium.[110]

Not all the adversaries of the West on the periphery were tribal, though. As a rule, states and empires had at their disposal standing armies which on the basis of their internal functioning logic necessarily preferred set-piece battles.[111] Similarly, the monarchies of South and

East Africa, which were based around tribal groupings and warrior castes, favoured the open massed assault,[112] while in Morocco guerrilla warfare was clearly regarded as unmanly.[113] Even intrinsically 'tribal' adversaries like the North American Indians would occasionally let themselves be drawn into open battle.[114] Thus, time and again, indigenous opponents would appear who did empires the favour of entering into what tactically tended to be a symmetrical conflict with them. Yet even in these instances the 'tribal' method of warfare could mostly still be seen in all its fundamental traits, with for instance mobility, using the terrain as cover and surprise continuing to play a major role.

Processes of adaptation could also be seen in the realm of tactics. Basically, four important instances can be differentiated. The logic of the first is asymmetrical. Indigenous societies whose armies proved inferior to those of the Western empires in open battle or who avoided engaging in such clashes with good reason switched to a form of guerrilla warfare in difficult terrain,[115] which incidentally in many cases only meant reverting to a cultural preference that was prevalent among non-European societies anyway. The most successful instance of this kind of adaptation was that of the woodland-dwelling Indian tribes of North America, who prior to the European invasion had been no strangers to set-piece battles, but who in response to the deadlier effect of firearms compared to throwing spears or bows and arrows abandoned this practice and developed instead their 'skulking' style of warfare. Another interesting aspect of this particular case is that this tactical transformation was not primarily prompted by direct conflict with the forces of empire but perhaps initially by their experience with the use of firearms in clashes with other Indian groups[116]—in which case this would be in the first instance a symmetrical realignment to new technological conditions and only secondarily an asymmetrical adaptation to the requirements of imperial warfare.[117] A move in a similar direction was the adoption of looser tactical forms of organization by African armies that prior to the introduction of firearms in the seventeenth century had fought in much more closed formations.[118]

By contrast, the logic of the second process of adaptation is symmetrical: namely, indigenous forces moving closer to European field warfare. This transformation largely coincided with the instances we have already cited of adoption of Western military structures, which went hand in hand with the use of corresponding tactics. This could either take the form of a symmetrical perfecting of a home-grown tradition of field warfare, as happened in the eighteenth and partly also the nineteenth centuries in South and Southeast Asia,[119] or conversely it was a correlate of the aforementioned regularization process undertaken in the twentieth century by resistance movements in order to give themselves a stronger aura of statehood, for reasons of legitimation. An integral part of this process was that they should henceforth wage war in a Western way—i.e. openly and in regular fashion—and refrain from using tactics which in the eyes of the West were considered deceitful, such as the surprise attack or guerrilla warfare.[120] We have already noted that this tactical transformation was often militarily counterproductive, given the material superiority of the imperial military apparatuses.[121]

On occasion, it may simply have been a flawed learning process that motivated indigenous societies to copy Western tactics. Thus, along with Western muskets, the Maori also adopted the closed formations and the set-piece battles that were associated with this weapon. This tactic worked well so long as it was a case of Maori versus Maori (though it hugely increased the death toll in such encounters). But it was a sure-fire recipe for disaster when the Maori battle lines came up against the professionally drilled British line infantry. Little wonder that the Maori swiftly rethought their tactics and switched over to waging a highly effective guerrilla war.[122]

The third instance of tactical adaptation was once again a symmetrical one. Confronted with an enemy that could not be coerced into fighting a set-piece battle, the forces of empire found themselves obliged to assimilate some irregular elements into their tactical repertoire. These included fundamentally better reconnaissance and screening measures while on the march in order to avoid being ambushed, deployment in self-reliant small units that were more lightly equipped for greater mobility, the use of the terrain as cover, and of course, as a basic concept conditioning all these measures, a renunciation of large, closed formations and elaborate logistical support. Targeted firing (instead of volley fire), night-time operations and laying their own traps and ambushes were further tactical innovations that were designed to enable imperial troops to fight their 'tribal' enemy on equal terms. The fact that these types of reform were in many respects alien to the traditionalism of the Western military apparatus, with its 'big war mindset,'[123] and indeed in the opinion of many officers jeopardized the possibility of a decisive outcome, explains the difficulties their introduction encountered, as well as their mostly limited scope and duration.[124] Very often, as we have already seen, these unconventional tactics were therefore hived off and made the domain of irregular forces or indigenous troops.[125] Other forms of symmetrical adaptation to the realities of the peripheral battlefield, especially in Africa, were the temporary fortification of overnight camps with thornbush entanglements, wooden palisades or later barbed wire,[126] a practice that met with all the reservations mentioned above.[127]

The fourth instance of adaptation was again asymmetrical: when waging colonial wars empires retained or revived certain tactical concepts of open field battle that had already become obsolete in European wars. The classic example of this is the infantry square, a closed formation with all four fronts facing outwards, that was designed to repel cavalry attack; with the 'breech-loader revolution' in European field warfare, the square had by the mid-nineteenth century already become far too concentrated and vulnerable a target, yet against numerically superior 'swarms' of comparatively lightly armed indigenous adversaries in imperial wars it continued to yield results even well into the twentieth century, and was even used offensively.[128] As a tactical solution to the operational problem of hugely inadequate troop strengths in large tracts of territory in which the enemy was waging an irregular war, the square was even developed further on the periphery into a marching formation, in which the combat forces would protect the vulnerable field guns and baggage trains on all sides. Yet this meant that the whole unwieldy unit could only advance at a snail's pace, which in turn raised tactical problems of another kind.[129]

In addition, there was a multitude of smaller, somewhat anecdotal-sounding but for all that no less interesting adaptations to asymmetrical military confrontation, which included creative individual responses to the enemy's use of firearms. The Zulu for example switched to rushing from one piece of cover to the next during their attacks,[130] a tactic that would doubtless have struck a European infantryman of the mid-twentieth century as very familiar, yet it was decidedly not one that the Zulu had copied from the British line infantry of the 1870s, which still fought inflexibly in rank and file. Before the discharge of a British field gun—clearly signalled by the gun crew stepping aside—they would throw themselves to the ground.[131] The Australian Darug were also in the habit of ducking when British musketeers fired and attacking them immediately afterwards when they were busy reloading their weapons.[132] A few indigenous societies adopted the tactic of field fortifications,[133] sometimes even during conflicts with other indigenous groups.[134] There were even some effective tactics that were deployed against modern Western weapons of war. The Rif rebels, for instance, neutralized Spanish armoured cars by flinging themselves to the ground and shooting through the vehicles' observation slits at close range, or setting the petrol tanks on fire.[135] But devising such techniques for dealing with unfamiliar weapons systems or tactics was not a monopoly of the indigenous side. In Mexico in the Early Modern period, the Spanish used mobile wooden fortresses to protect convoys of wagons against Indian attacks.[136] In Southeast Asia in the same period, the Spanish and the Portuguese countered poison arrows with protective screens made of sailcloth and by advancing at a swift pace while often and rapidly changing direction. They would also put war elephants to flight by igniting gunpowder under their trunks.[137] In response, indigenous societies developed countermeasures against the Western trump card in mobility, the horse.[138]

There were therefore a great number of tactical transformations on both sides. Yet not all these processes were informed by the same logic. Symmetrical adaptation as an emulation of enemy practices is something fundamentally different from asymmetrical adaptation as a way of acquiring a strength in an area where the enemy is weak.[139] According to the context, one and the same adaptation could have quite different effects—the 'skulking way of war' of the North American Indians was a form of symmetrical adaptation where intra-cultural conflict was concerned, but asymmetrical for transcultural conflict. But what all these adaptation processes have in common is that the encounter between manifestly different cultures of violence demanded that both sides should adjust to the peculiarities of this confrontation; for the empires there was the additional factor of having to adapt to the peripheral theatre of war.

Technology

Hardly any image of imperial warfare is as deeply embedded in our collective consciousness as the technological superiority of the West, especially in the field of armaments. Slingshots versus arquebuses, spears versus breech-loading guns, matchlocks versus machine guns, Kalashnikovs versus Phantom fighter-bombers—if any one thing characterizes war on the periphery in the public mind it is asymmetry in weapons technology, epitomized nowhere so iconically as in the Battle of Omdurman on 2 September 1898, where 11,000 Mahdists armed partly with spears and partly with sawn-off muskets were mown down by machine gun bullets and naval shells (and another 16,000 were taken prisoner), whereas the Anglo-Egyptian force ranged against them sustained casualties of just forty-eight dead.[140] Michael Crowder is not alone in his assertion that: 'Disciplined troops with rapid-fire rifles and fortified with Gatling and Maxim guns, could mow down opponents with vastly superior numbers, whether foot soldiers or cavalry.'[141] Another contemporary historian comes to the same resigned insight with regard to the conquest of the Sokoto Caliphate in Nigeria: 'In the last resort [...] no tactics, no personal courage and no resistance would have prevailed, since the "Europeans" [...] had the Maxim gun and the artillery and the Caliphate had not.'[142]

Again, much of this image is accurate. In a brief historical phase roughly between the mid-nineteenth and the mid-twentieth centuries Western empires were indeed streets ahead of their indigenous foes in weapons technology, to the extent that, under at least halfway favourable conditions, the smallest European troop contingents could really slaughter hordes of considerably less well armed opponents. The reason for this lay primarily in the dramatic acceleration in the development of weapons technology which came with the rise of industrialization. The 'breech-loader revolution,' which began in the 1840s, multiplied the rate of fire and the range of handguns and rifles within the space of a few decades, while at the same time massively increasing the cost of such weapons. In the process, the West gained a huge technological lead in killing power, which non-industrialized countries were no longer able to match through their own efforts and which, even by means of the trickle-down of weapons technology that had been customary up to that time (which always found its way to the periphery, albeit gradually), they could only slowly rival.[143]

Yet this was, as noted, an exceptional situation in historical terms. In the Early Modern period, there was mostly no question of any such superiority of the West in weapons technology, especially not where early firearms were concerned.[144] If anything, it was the durable steel swords produced in Europe, combined with steel armour and the shock effect of horses (which gave their riders mobility and a height advantage over horseless societies), that granted the conquerors of the Americas and Asia a small but sometimes tactically decisive technological edge.[145] In tropical Africa, the Portuguese had to make do with the sword alone.[146] By contrast, the hand guns of the seventeenth and eighteenth centuries were cumbersome to use and hence had a slow rate of fire (even among core European troops in the late eighteenth century, only real professionals could achieve several shots per minute);[147] they were also unreliable (especially in wet weather, which also made them rust) and above all they had a very short range and poor accuracy.[148] Using one of the smooth-bore, muzzle-loading muskets that were still the norm in the armies of the West until the mid-nineteenth century, even a practised marksman would be fortunate to hit a barn door at 50 metres.[149] The same was true of field guns, except they were also so heavy and immobile that they principally were able to justify their existence behind fortress walls and on major warships; against tribal opponents who did not mass into large tactical formations, artillery pieces were useless at all times anyway.[150] Basically, against indigenous peoples, who had no firearms of their own, the main effect of guns and artillery was a psychological one: in any event, during initial encounters their noise and fire and the terror of 'invisible death' that they spread had a considerably greater effect than the actual impact of the projectiles, even when they managed to hit anything.[151]

In terms of weapons technology, therefore, imperial troops of the Early Modern period were less impressive than is often assumed. In particular—and this was a key factor—their weapons had none of the effects of the products of the breech-loading revolution, which proved so decisive towards the end of the nineteenth century: the power to kill at a distance and the ability to multiply their effectiveness through rapid fire. Even if the terrain and the tactical situation had not stood in the way of realizing these advantages—which still happened often later thanks to the tactical configuration of imperial warfare—the first centuries of European expansion on the periphery were dominated by hand-to-hand combat between individuals, which had a very equalizing effect where weapons technology was concerned. In those circumstances, the edged weapons produced by many non-European societies were perfectly competitive—not to mention the various long-ranged weapons that existed in many different parts of the world (arrows, blowpipes, slingshots and spear throwers.[152]

More importantly, though, contact between different cultures of violence immediately triggered a process of adaptation; the indigenous adversaries of empires began to acquire Western weapons technology—especially, but not exclusively, firearms.[153] The quickest and most successful such adaptation was by the Woodland Indians of North America, who not least thanks to the rivalry between different European empires could always find ready suppliers of weapons. Within a few generations, they had swapped their deadly accurate bows and arrows for modern European firearms, namely flintlocks, which were more suitable for use in inclement weather than arquebuses, and increasingly long-range rifled weapons. These latter guns were more in keeping with their 'skulking' style of warfare than the more rapidly firing but less long-range or accurate muskets. Even by the early eighteenth century, therefore, most Indian groups were superior to their European opponents in long-distance marksmanship.[154]

The situation was once again quite different in South and Southeast Asia, since firearms had been known about there for a long time before the arrival of the first Europeans. As early as the sixteenth century, hand-held guns and rifles found their way to the Indian Ocean region via the Ottoman Empire[155] and the Mughal Empire. Even though the monarchies there had a fatal predilection for the display and shock value of firearms and so favoured above all monstrous cannons that were completely immobile and ineffectual, at least the primitive hand-held firearms used by Europeans in the Early Modern period did not represent much of an advantage over their technology.[156] When their conquest of India got into full swing in the mid-eighteenth century, the British found themselves confronted by principalities which, thanks to their permanent contact with various European and Asian sources, had at their disposal guns that were easily a match for, or even better than, those of the British, and in some cases excellent artillery as well. In particular, the artillery pieces of the Marathas were extremely mobile.[157] In the First Afghanistan War—as with the Woodland Indians of North America—the long-range rifles used by the Pashtun mountain fighters were clearly superior to the smooth-bore muskets of the British infantry.[158] Even in the early nineteenth century, European armies in South and Southeast Asia found themselves facing indigenous forces using admittedly somewhat outmoded but still completely serviceable hand-held firearms and in some cases even field guns, partly acquired as war booty and partly of their own manufacture.[159] On Russia's Central Asian frontier, too, firearm use spread over the centuries among the nomadic peoples despite the Czarist empire's best efforts to prevent it.[160]

Further east, two societies were particularly enthusiastic about adopting firearms: by the seventeenth century Japan was home to thousands of guns, manufactured by domestic gunsmiths using the model of two matchlock arquebuses taken from a shipwrecked Portuguese vessel.[161] Within the space of just a few years, the Maori of New Zealand equipped all their warriors with European muskets by trading food and services to European whalers in return for weapons.[162]

As a result of the slave trade, the coastal kingdoms of West Africa began to acquire European firearms from the eighteenth century onwards. After the end of the Napoleonic Wars, a glut of newly superfluous firearms from Europe found their way to the Slave Coast, where they contributed to the rise of the great military monarchies of West Africa, some of which held out against European imperial encroachment until the late nineteenth century.[163] For the same reason, when the French set out to conquer Algeria, they did not enjoy any great superiority in weapons technology.[164] It is a little-known fact that up to a third of the Zulu army that defeated the British at Isandhlwana in 1879 were equipped with guns, whereas 90 per cent of the indigenous auxiliary troops fighting on the British side had only edged weapons.[165]

Even so, this assimilation of Western weapons technology by non-Western societies did have certain limits. It was not enough to simply purchase (or capture) hand-held firearms or field guns; they also had to be properly used and maintained if they were to be deployed effectively over a long period.[166] This often proved beyond the capabilities of indigenous societies, and the firearms of non-European armies were not infrequently so poorly maintained and cleaned that the only thing they were fit for was producing a spectacular flash of gunpowder.[167] The repair of guns and cannon called for artisanal skills that were rarely available to non-Europeans[168] (with some notable exceptions, especially from the period before the arrival of the complex products of industrial manufacture)[169] and making gunpowder remained a mystery to most firearms users, at least outside of South Asia, so that they were dependent upon shipments from the West and/or made do with very poor-quality powder.[170]

Even when non-European warriors managed to actually discharge guns, their effective deployment on the battlefield still required firearms training and formal instruction in tactics, a facility that was intrinsically bound up with the organizational forms of modern Western armed forces. Ultimately, this was the actual crux of indigenous societies' assimilation of weapons technology: as a general rule, the traditions of non-European cultures of violence—even when, as indeed happened in some cases,[171] they did not shun firearms out of hand from the outset as dishonourable—were simply incompatible with the formal drill and the bureaucratic organization which alone made it possible to deploy at least hand-held firearms in a tactically effective way.[172] This was why the opponents of empire (again with some significant exceptions like the North American Woodland Indians and the Pashtun of the Northwest Frontier) were generally very bad shots.[173] Furthermore, many indigenous societies regarded firearms primarily as a symbolic power resource, indeed even as cult objects, and as such did not even think of actually using them in combat. Instead, such societies tended to hoard rifles especially, and later machine guns, at the seat of power rather than distributing them to their fighters.[174]

An additional factor which came into play was that non-European armies did not have access to the most modern examples of the West's weapons technology, and had to make do instead with second-hand and often already obsolete equipment.[175] In the West, it was deliberate policy to offer as barter goods so-called 'trade guns' that were fit for the scrap heap.[176] And the fact that indigenous societies mostly received such substandard weaponry and hence acquired a very eclectic assortment of guns generated further problems in the supply of ammunition and in training.[177]

Notwithstanding this, up until the mid-nineteenth century non-European forces were still perfectly able to keep pace with the empires of the West in weapons technology. This all changed, as we have seen, with the Industrial Revolution in the West. Breech-loading guns, automatic weapons, steamships, railways and before long aircraft too revolutionized warfare, even on the margins of empire, and for several decades furnished the imperial powers with an almost unassailable technological advantage. The machine gun in particular, which according to the testimony of contemporary observers could supplant the firepower of an entire company of infantry[178] (which, with repeating rifles, was not inconsiderable in itself), represented an exponential increase in power.

Yet even the deployment of modern weapons technology on the periphery had its limits. It was by no means simple taking heavy equipment into difficult, undeveloped terrain; this was especially true of artillery pieces, unless they had been expressly built for mobile deployment.[179] The British 75-mm field gun required a carrier party of 200 porters to transport it in Africa; its barrel alone weighed 100 kilograms.[180] In any case, apart from the bombardment of fortified positions (and the more mobile and hence lighter they were, the less well-suited they were for this task)[181] field guns were as good as useless against an uncooperative enemy—namely, one that refused to expose itself to their fire in closed formations.[182] Not to mention the fact that, at least in one exceptional case—the Maori Wars of the 1860s—the adversary had such sophisticated fortified emplacements that even the heaviest and most modern field guns proved ineffectual.[183] Early machine guns were extremely unreliable and likewise only portable to a very limited degree.[184] The Gardner gun, an American-made machine gun deployed by the British in the Sudan, weighed over 600 kilograms including all its accessory components, and jammed repeatedly in sandy conditions.[185]

In North America, at least, the gap in weapons technology between the US Army—which, aside from the occasional use of mountain howitzers, was scarcely able to bring superior new weaponry to bear in combat on the frontier—and the Indians west of the Mississippi, who even as early as 1870 were equipped with repeating rifles and revolvers,[186] was never so pronounced as it was, say, between Europeans and kingdoms across large parts of Africa.

Besides, many empires consciously refrained from deploying their most up-to-date weapons technology (which was also their most costly and complex) in their wars of expansion outside of Europe[187]—especially when it was a question of equipping colonial troops with it.[188] And declining empires like that of Spain in the twentieth century were quite simply not in a position to do so anyhow.[189]

Over time, while still lagging some decades behind, the adversaries of empire began to close the gap once more.[190] Even before the turn of the twentieth century, European armies were occasionally confronted with an enemy equipped with modern rifles, machine guns and even artillery. This situation did not just apply to the independent Ethiopian Empire[191] and the Boer Republics,[192] which were most definitely special cases, but also for example to Samori Touré, who acquired first-class firearms from the most diverse sources to arm his jihad state on the Upper Niger and Senegal; when it was finally defeated in 1898, his army was found to have more than 4,000 repeating rifles.[193] The Senussi, who during the First World War rose up against the British and the Italians in the border region between Egypt and Libya, were supplied with modern weapons by the German and Ottoman empires.[194] On the Northwest Frontier of India in 1939, the Pashtun were able to deploy more than 230,000 breech-loading rifles—and furthermore, just like a century before, these were primarily long-range precision weapons[195]—supplemented with light machine guns and 'home-made' artillery pieces.[196] Another instance that fits into this same picture is that of the Rif Republic; thanks to the state-capitalist endeavours of its leader Abd-el-Krim, its standing army, which in structural terms was not far short of the Western standard anyway, was equipped with modern weaponry, including hundreds of thousands of state-of-the-art Mauser rifles, 200 field guns, several hundred machine guns, three armoured cars and even three aeroplanes (though they never flew).[197]

At the same time the marginal utility of innovations in weapons technology in imperial warfare began to run out. Aside from machine guns there were hardly any other increments in killing power that were truly relevant for the conduct of warfare on the periphery.[198] Small wars in challenging terrain did not provide mission profiles for the deployment of tanks, armoured personnel carriers, heavy artillery, bombers or fighter-bombers—not to mention atomic weapons. To a limited extent, niches were found for armoured reconnaissance vehicles and light (especially airlift-capable) tanks as well as for slow-flying aircraft, particularly (from the 1950s onwards) helicopters.[199]

In imperial wars post-1945, the confrontation between the two superpower blocs ensured that anticolonial resistance movements could count on being supplied with relatively modern weaponry by either of the opposing camps.[200] Through the use of automatic weapons such as the AK-47 to anti-aircraft and rapid-fire guns[201]—indeed from the 1970s onwards even shoulder-launched anti-tank and surface-to-air (SAM) missiles, which effectively countered the last high-tech advantage of the West that was suitable for deployment on the periphery, namely the helicopter[202]—the adversaries of empire to all intents and purposes regained parity in weapons technology.[203]

It is therefore possible to read the history of technology in imperial warfare primarily as one of adaptation by indigenous societies to the West through the adoption of weaponry. Conversely the empires have only very rarely adopted non-Western weapons, since they already had at their disposal almost every type of close-quarters or long-range weapon that their enemies also had access to, and hence had nothing to gain by doing so. Even so, the quilted cotton armour that was commonly used by the Aztecs was far better suited to the Mesoamerican climate than the cumbersome and rust-prone metal armour worn by the conquistadors, and so was widely adopted by them instead.[204] Then there was the *bola*, which Spanish cavalrymen adopted from the Indios on the Pampas of Argentina.[205] Otherwise, though, the imperial powers' assimilation of weapons technology consisted primarily in retaining or reintroducing weapons already obsolete in large-scale wars within Europe, notably the lance, which made it easier for cavalrymen to hunt down elusive enemies.[206] During the Cuban War of Independence, the Spanish military discussed introducing the machete, possibly in response to the myth that this type of cleaver, which was widespread on this sugarcane-producing island and had a fearsome reputation, was a highly effective weapon in the hands of the insurgents.[207]

Weapons were not the only technologies that were exchanged across cultural borders in the course of imperial wars. Here and there, imperial forces made use of indigenous transport technologies that were well adapted to the prevailing lie of the land and local climate. The prime example of this were the light birch-bark canoes and snowshoes used by the Woodland Indian tribes of North America.[208] But in India too in the eighteenth century, the British took over the wagon-building workshops, the breeding stations for draught animals and the superior harness technology of the princely states in order to improve their own modes of transport on the subcontinent.[209] Sometimes colonial troops would also copy or adapt local clothing, which was much more comfortable to wear in harsh climatic conditions; however, because this practice contravened military regulations, it was largely confined to local initiatives or was found mainly among irregular forces. Alternatively, imperial troops would at least try to modify their uniforms to suit the local climate.[210] Conversely indigenous fighters would sometimes adopt the non-weapons-related military technology of the West: during their last stand against the US Army the Apaches, for instance, came to value the usefulness of field glasses and also found the practical McClellan saddle used by the US Cavalry much to their liking.[211]

The introduction of beasts of burden that were widely used by the enemy or at least well suited to the local environment can also be seen as a form of technological adaptation. The classic example is the horse, which particularly in open terrain, less so in mountains or forest, yielded a huge advantage both tactically and in terms of mobility, and so was readily adopted by previously horseless societies, yet none as enthusiastically (and occasionally counterproductively) as the Indians of the Great Plains of the American West.[212] In their turn, imperial forces began using camels in Africa and Asia and even North America,[213] while for difficult terrain where forage was scarce the mule proved indispensable—admittedly not a transcultural adoption, but certainly an adaptation to the theatre of war.[214] Last but not least, in South and Southeast Asia the elephant became an important feature of imperial campaigns, not just because of the great symbolic value it had for indigenous societies but also as an extremely powerful beast of burden.[215]

Incidentally, in view of the great significance of technological adaptation, it is no wonder that empires would sometimes try, though rarely with much success, to prevent enemies from acquiring certain technologies. These measures included arms embargoes (which were always circumvented, if not by European rivals, then by their own arms dealers),[216] a refusal to train colonial troops in the use of modern weapons systems to try and stop such know-how from leaking to the rest of the indigenous population,[217] and occasionally the destruction of strategic resources before they could fall into enemy hands: during their withdrawal from Goa in 1510, for example, the Portuguese not only killed all the Muslims they had taken prisoner, but also all the surplus horses.[218]

Fortifications

One special field of technology in which the West appeared to have a very pronounced edge for a long period was fortress warfare. All empires built numerous fortresses along all of their frontiers—this was, as we have already seen,[219] simply a functional necessity in the light of the problem of controlling large areas with comparatively small numbers of troops. Fortifications were also vital in providing protection for coastal sea routes and inland waterways, ports and trading stations.[220]

Not all of these fortified emplacements were impressive edifices. Where only a moderate level of threat existed, it was deemed sufficient to erect comparatively ramshackle palisades, which would barely have withstood a really determined assault; this was the standard defensive ploy along the US frontiers with 'Indian Country', but even so the forts built there rarely fell to attackers, and then only mainly due to the negligence of the commanding officer.[221] Yet basically, following the 'military revolution' empires had the technical and material potential at their disposal to build fortresses that could only be captured by indigenous forces in the rarest of circumstances (and which in any event, at least for those built on the coast, were primarily for defence against other empires). Certainly, the modern artillery fortress, along with effective heavy guns and their most efficient support systems, large men-of-war, may be counted among the European key achievements in military technology that were basically invincible even in the Early Modern period. And fortresses in the European style were mostly able to hold out against assaults on the fringes of empire for longer than the generally less efficient indigenous armies were able to bring the necessary organizational and logistical support to bear to sustain these attacks.[222]

Beyond Europe, fortresses were an unmistakeable status symbol of nation-states and empires. As a rule, non-state societies had neither the resources and organizational structure to build such large complexes, nor did they have enough possessions worth protecting to justify the expense involved.[223] Great empires, on the other hand, built in many cases mighty fortifications primarily in order to guard their cities. Famous examples are the megalomaniacally huge city walls of China, the towering castles of Japan and the mighty fortresses of India.[224] Less well known, perhaps, is the fact that the jihad states of West Africa constructed huge defensive walls; those of the city of Kano in the Sokoto Caliphate were 13 metres thick and between 10 and 15 metres high, and encompassed an area of more than 25 square kilometres, equivalent to almost half of the island of Manhattan.[225]

Walls such as this could not be breached with cannons; the customary siege tactics were to starve a city into submission or to tunnel under the fortifications. This may have been the reason why, outside of Europe, no truly effective siege artillery was ever developed.[226] Equally, though, even the modern field guns that Western armies took with them to the frontiers of their empires had great difficulties with such cyclopean masonry.[227] More often, fortresses fell by being stormed in mass attacks that caused huge casualties—just the kind of assault that Western armies were able to mount thanks to their specializing in intensive warfare.[228]

In a figurative sense, too, fortress warfare was rather a static affair. There was scarcely any reason for the forces of empire to assimilate their enemies' practices; their own strongholds were easily sufficient to meet the demands of waging war on the periphery.[229] Conversely virtually no non-European society that already possessed fortresses adopted the European style of fortification, which was primarily geared towards defence against the heaviest siege cannons, armaments which as a general rule did not even exist in peripheral warfare.[230] In addition, the construction of a large artillery fort in the modern Western style would in all likelihood have overstretched the capacity of any indigenous society, except large-scale empires, to marshal the necessary resources and taken many years to complete—a timeframe that was mostly not available in conflicts with expanding Western empires.

On the other hand, there are a number of indications that non-European societies transformed their primitive fortified positions—fortified villages or small forts—so as to better withstand assaults by enemies equipped with firearms. As early as the eighteenth century the Tuscarora in present-day North Carolina and the Susquehannock in what is now Pennsylvania already had palisades with covered ditches, parapets and even bastions, betraying a European influence that was unmistakeable, at least to contemporary observers. The same was true of the Creek Indians in the nineteenth century. Although it has been mooted that the autochthonous Mississippian mound-builder civilization (which admittedly had died out several centuries previously) may have provided the original inspiration for these fortifications, the fact remains that the Susquehannock had cannons, which were of course of European provenance, strongly suggesting that their fortification architecture came from the same source.[231] By contrast, the stone-built and wooden forts of the New England Indian tribes in the seventeenth century were clearly original, but also much less sophisticated.[232]

In Africa too there were forts that integrated elements of the European art of fortification.[233] In sixteenth-century India, evidently in the light of the growing challenge posed by Western navies, the art of building harbour defences spread throughout the subcontinent via intra-Indian knowledge transfer.[234] Yet probably the most interesting case is that of the Maori. They had their own tradition of fort-building; their home-grown fortification known as a Pa was a high palisade with a fighting platform, from which rocks were hurled. James Belich has shown convincingly how the Maori drastically transformed these structures to make them more resistant to Europeans armed with rifles and cannons, making them into an earthwork with trenches and bunkers that could withstand even the heaviest artillery bombardment.[235] There is no plausible evidence to suggest that this tactical remodelling by the Maori had its roots in Europe—as the British claimed at the time—especially since the Pa was a piece of fortification technology that was decades ahead of the standard Western fort of that era. Once again, then, here was an instance of asymmetrical adaptation—'an antidote to European techniques rather than a copy of them.'[236]

War at sea

The way in which war at sea was waged resembled fortress warfare to a certain extent. Here, too, the imperial powers enjoyed a considerable technological advantage that gave them little reason to adapt or assimilate. At the very beginning of European expansion, it was only the states of Western and Northern Europe which possessed vessels that could sail in all weathers, were ocean-going and could carry cannons. These ships ensured the nations of the West dominion over the oceans and so provided the basis for Western hegemony throughout the world.[237] Sea power alone—in the face of all the difficulties discussed so far—facilitated the worldwide projection of military power by empires whose heartland comprised what on a continental scale was a tiny conglomerate of nation-states on the westernmost fringes of Eurasia.[238] It provided a way for the comparatively small armed forces of those empires to augment their military impact,[239] enabling large guns to be deployed in conflicts overseas without the need to expend any disproportionate effort.[240] Sea power facilitated strategic mobility, which indigenous land forces could do nothing to counter, making possible operations on a continental scale and landings behind enemy lines, and above all creating the ability to withdraw at will from critical situations.[241] The strategic risk for empires of waging war on the periphery was thus minimized—at least so long as the expeditionary forces remained within range of the ships' guns. Sea power had considerable potential to intimidate and was eminently suitable as a means of exerting asymmetric pressure on coastal states in the framework of gunboat diplomacy.[242] It enabled (and required) the maintenance along foreign coasts of military bases and settlements that were not economically autonomous and could not be defended with their own resources; in the long run, these places became the entry points for European invasion and conquest.[243] Sea power cut off indigenous empires from the outside world and so laid the foundations for the system of imperial rule.[244] And finally, sea power made continental expansion possible—at least wherever there were inlets and estuaries, or rivers deep enough to allow 6 feet of water beneath a ship's keel.[245]

On the high seas, Western imperial naval power was not generally susceptible to any effective challenge—in any event not once China, for internal political reasons, had ceased building ocean-going junks from the mid-fifteenth century on.[246] For a long time, however, the situation in coastal waters was quite another matter. In South Asia during the Early Modern period, the Portuguese came face-to-face with heavily armed war galleys deployed by the coastal kingdoms of the region, which, thanks to their high degree of manoeuvrability independent of any wind, proved to be formidable adversaries, though their shallow draft meant that they dared not venture far out to sea.[247] In narrow stretches of water—around archipelagos, river estuaries or inland waterways—large sailing ships could either not be deployed at all or found themselves virtually defenceless against attacks from smaller indigenous sailing boats or craft propelled by human muscle power such as canoes. The naval dominance of empires ended where their ships ran out of deep enough water and room to manoeuvre.[248]

At least, this was the situation up until the middle of the nineteenth century. At a stroke, the arrival of the steamship altered the centuries-old balance between European dominion over the oceans and indigenous control over coastal and inland waters. The steamship was fast, powerful (indeed so powerful that it was capable of towing mighty sailing vessels in places where they could not venture under sails), manoeuvrable and, being independent of the wind, could penetrate everywhere where there was at least a passable waterway. It was also far superior to any indigenous craft. The steamship brought the kind of strategic mobility that empires had enjoyed for centuries on the open ocean, plus the firepower of naval guns and all the other advantages that were associated with sea power, into the interior. As a result, its introduction was followed in relatively short order by the conquest or at least the forcible opening up of all those regions of the world reachable by great rivers, which had for centuries hitherto resisted imperial control, in particular West Africa and Southeast Asia as well as large parts of China.[249] Small steam vessels that could be broken down into prefabricated sections could even be portaged over land and reassembled on an inland lake or other stretch of water that did not have direct access from the sea. In this way, imperial naval power could be projected far from the world's oceans[250]—a concept that the Spanish had already successfully applied using wooden ships during their conquest of the Americas in the sixteenth and seventeenth centuries.[251] Ships on inland bodies of water continued to give the West a vital advantage in terms of logistics and mobility even in the wars of decolonization in the later twentieth century.[252]

There were some attempts by indigenous societies to copy this successful Western model. In the Arab coastal regions, India, and Southeast Asia as well as along the coasts of China, Portuguese and Dutch seafarers found themselves repeatedly confronted up to the eighteenth century by adversaries who had built their own ocean-going ships in response to Western seaborne power. In the case of the Kingdom of Aceh on Sumatra, these vessels could carry up to fifty guns; the Arab state of Oman is even said to have possessed a warship with over 100 guns.[253] At least nominally these ships were a match for anything that the Europeans could dispatch to Southeast Asia—though in reality the picture looked somewhat different.[254] As early as the nineteenth century, the Kingdom of Vietnam embarked, with the assistance of French experts, on the construction of frigates based on the European model[255]—albeit too late to really put up any effective resistance against the burgeoning and rapidly overwhelming naval power of the West. Burma even bought steamships in Europe and in the war of 1885 against Great Britain they had more of these vessels than their foe (twenty-seven as against twenty-three ships), though the guns on board the Burmese ships were no match for the British.[256] West African rulers would sometimes fit out war canoes with cannon—no doubt a very ingenious synthesis of military technologies.[257] Once more there were also instances of technical innovation which were not copies of Western practices, despite the fact that they were bound to have looked like that to contemporary observers: the principle of the hand-driven paddle-boat warships that China deployed in the Battle of Wusong on the Yangtse River in 1842 had been known about there since the eighth century.[258] An example of asymmetrical adaptation that may be cited here was the stakes that were driven into the bed of Lake Tenochtitlán by the Aztecs as a defensive measure against Spanish brigantines.[259]

The imperial powers had, as we have seen, little reason to adapt on the high seas. Until the introduction of the steamship, the situation in coastal and inland waters looked very different, however. There, the navies of the West would sometimes adopt the various smaller water-borne craft that were commonplace in any particular region so as to keep on level terms with the enemy: canoes in North and Central America as well as in West Africa, and praus in Southeast Asia.[260] In Brazil in the Early Modern period the Portuguese deployed fortified rafts on inland rivers as a countermeasure against the canoe fleets of the Indios.[261]

War in the air

If the asymmetry in weapons technology on the high seas, and after the advent of the steamship also on inland waterways, was pronounced, in the air it was absolute. To date it has only ever been in a few isolated conventional confrontations with modern states (North Korea, North Vietnam, Iraq in 1991) that the West has found itself facing an indigenous enemy with its own air force.

Almost immediately after its invention, the aeroplane was deployed in imperial conflicts, giving Western forces a decisive advantage.[262] Until the adversaries of empire during the Cold War began to be supplied with modern anti-aircraft weaponry by one or other bloc, there were no defensive measures against the West's air superiority on the periphery. Aircraft made reconnaissance easier and revealed the enemy's military assets, which up till then had been impossible to identify.[263] They made it possible to attack targets from the air that were extremely hard to reach by land due to the difficult terrain or the long distances involved.[264] This was particularly true of mountainous regions, where aircraft robbed indigenous opponents of the advantage of occupying the high ground, as in the final phase of the conquest of Morocco.[265] But aircraft also meant that war now had the potential to affect the entire population; the extremely poor accuracy of aerial bombing, long a feature of air power, represented a necessarily indiscriminate and completely asymmetrical deployment of deadly force.[266] Through their ability to transport troops by air, aeroplanes achieved a hitherto unknown degree of operational mobility,[267] from which, say, French forces in Indochina repeatedly profited.[268] Aircraft could also facilitate the logistical support of forward units by airdropping supplies and reinforcements.[269] In the 1970s, the advent of long-range transport aircraft already ensured strategic mobility to a certain extent.[270]

However, the excessively optimistic future expectations of the most enthusiastic protagonists of air power were not fulfilled in the long term. Contrary to the promises made by the 'air control' lobby within the British Royal Air Force, reprisal raids from the air were not enough to ensure control over areas on the margins of empire. What was already in the case of land-based punitive expeditions a highly dubious way of suggesting that imperial control had been achieved—namely the exercising of force as an example rather than putting an enduring physical military presence on the ground—proved to have virtually no effect from the air; indeed, in worst-case scenarios this indiscriminate use of force could even escalate the conflict.[271] Overall, the effect of aerial bombing on locally organized groups of indigenous fighters who used the terrain as cover was only minimal.[272] In Malaya the RAF needed to fly on average thirty sorties in order 'to help'[273] eliminate a single insurgent. The most effective method was to launch air strikes against concentrated civilian targets, that is larger settlements and towns, as in the notorious French bombardment of Damascus in 1945.[274] Airborne logistics and mobility were likewise of only limited value in difficult terrain (and if the enemy had effective anti-aircraft guns, like the Viet Minh did at Dien Bien Phu, such missions could be utter failures).[275] Only the advent of the helicopter, which could land virtually anywhere, brought a significant advantage in this area[276]—but once again, only under conditions of (almost) total air superiority. The experience of US forces in Somalia[277]—captured on film in the descriptively titled Hollywood movie *Black Hawk Down*[278]—showed that just a few simple rocket-propelled grenades (RPGs) could make a helicopter sortie impossible.

Yet the greatest impediment to the use of aircraft of all kinds on the periphery was the fact that they were expensive and required a lot of maintenance and hence were rarely available in sufficient numbers.[279] Merely the trend we have already mentioned—namely that from the 1940s onwards at the latest, the most up-to-date technological developments were no longer usable in imperial conflicts—stood in the way of their deployment. Even if they had been able to operate from anything other than purpose-built airfields, nuclear bombers and jet fighters were completely useless against ground targets that were hard to find, small or, due to their lack of elaborate infrastructure, not very vulnerable to begin with. Accordingly, apart from helicopters, colonial warfare was and remains a decidedly 'low tech'[280] domain where aero-space is concerned.

Western adaptation to aerial warfare on the periphery therefore consisted at most of the realization that it was of limited use, that slow-flying, robust and cheap aircraft which could use short runways were the most useful and that air power would never for the foreseeable future supplant boots on the ground.[281] Indigenous opponents likewise had only limited opportunities to adapt to aerial warfare. Aside from acquiring anti-aircraft weapons, their principal adaptive achievements resided in managing to overcome the initial shock effect of aircraft in general and aerial bombing in particular, in appreciating that aero-planes were generally less dangerous than they appeared and in devel-oping effective methods of spotting, camouflage and defence against air attacks—something that even the politically loosely organized tribes who were the victims of British 'air control' in Iraq and along the Northwest Frontier of India learned to do within just a few years.[282]

At present, it seems improbable that unmanned drones, which for the past few years have been used for detailed reconnaissance and for elimi-nating pinpoint targets, will herald a general trend towards the effective use of high-tech weaponry in wars on the margins as well. Despite some spectacular, media-friendly individual successes such as the assassinations of enemy leaders, which are claimed to have a demonstrably negative impact on the structure and effectiveness of terrorist networks,[283] in the medium term drones may actually remain irrelevant for the de facto control of peripheral regions, and more importantly they create the same false impression of omnipotence that the aeroplane once inspired when it was first introduced.[284] Currently, it seems that remotely controlled attacks once again require the presence of personnel on the spot in order to properly identify targets, that they lower the threshold of inhibitions for interventions by the West and that, as a result of the civilian deaths they cause, they tend rather to have the effect of escalating violence and strengthening resistance.[285]

Cultures of violence in conflict

Establishing the fact that there has been a degree of adaptation in such realms as army organization, technology, weapons, and tactics, however hard it may sometimes have been to achieve, ultimately only high-lights the pragmatism of the military: one simply adapts to difficult circumstances, and anything that makes sense and gives one an edge is—ideally—adopted. Initially, this has to do with the transcultural nature of imperial warfare only indirectly—in as much as different cultures of violence also organize, equip and deploy their armed forces in different ways, hence generating these problems of assimilation when they come into contact with each other.

Yet how exactly do diverse cultures of violence interact when they actually clash with one another? How do they respond to each other? Is there any mutual understanding? What part do knowledge, ignorance and wilful refusal to learn play in these interactions and in violent con-flicts themselves? And how, as a result of these conditions, do adapta-tion and learning actually function in a transcultural context? The remainder of this chapter will attempt to give a provisional response to these questions, hard though they are to answer if only for the paucity of source material.

The first reaction to coming face to face with a very different cul-ture of violence was often initially irritation and shock—more pro-nounced on the indigenous side, which usually had little experience of such encounters, whereas Europe had long since absorbed them into its collective subconscious over years of expansion.[286] A classic form of this culture shock was non-European peoples' first encounter with firearms, archetypically represented by the 'battle' which took place at what was later named Lake Champlain on 21 July 1609, in which the French explorer Samuel Champlain put an entire army of terrified Mohawk Indians to flight with two shots from his match-lock.[287] Admittedly, most indigenous societies evidently got used to firearms very quickly; within a few decades of this first encounter the Mohawk, with the help of European guns, became the leading power in the Great Lakes region. But the shock effect was subsequently repeated time and again in a variety of other locations, with ever more spectacular weaponry: field guns, machine guns, rockets, armoured cars or aircraft.[288] Similarly, metal armour, steel swords and the horse apparently had the same effect at other first contacts[289]—though some peoples, to the amazement of the Europeans, remained totally immune to this shock.[290]

The way in which war was waged and the violent practices employed could trigger more deep-seated and enduringly unsettling feelings of shock that went far beyond the pyrotechnic effect of fire-arms. Thus, Europeans appeared horrified by acts of ruthless torture and ritual cannibalism as well as by violence against women and children, all of which formed normal aspects of warfare among North American Indians,[291] and for centuries the fear of such violations of the rules of war conditioned their feeling of deep insecurity in an unfamiliar environment. Conversely the methodical and relentless strategy of subjugation enacted by expanding empires—which rode roughshod over the cultural boundaries of warfare, purposefully exacted a high death toll in battle, often resulted in total war against entire populations, and aimed at eventually establishing permanent rule rather than a temporary hegemony—must have been deeply disruptive to non-European societies that were accustomed to more limited war aims and methods of warfare; in any event, this is what many European authors have suggested.[292]

Less extreme than culture shock, but all the more frequent and obvious, was cultural misunderstanding in violent transcultural conflicts.[293] We have already encountered this in its simplest and at the same time most serious form: namely, as a failure to comprehend the opposing culture of violence or the enemy's social structure. One example of this was the inability (or even unwillingness) of Europeans to grasp the strictly regulated nature, and hence also the definite limitations, of indigenous acts of violence. In other words, they construed as totally without rules something which in fact simply obeyed a different set of rules. Similarly, the fact that indigenous societies often had no appreciation of the importance that expanding empires attached to borders and treaties (at least where these were supposed to be binding on the opposing side), and therefore in the eyes of their adversaries often behaved in a 'treacherous' manner, is further prima facie evidence of cultural misunderstanding. The same applies conversely to the enduring myth peddled by empires that an agreement with a political authority—often imagined by the imperialists—representing the opposing side was binding on a society in its entirety, which in the main was only very loosely organized. These were classic problems which beset not just the Indian Wars in the USA.[294] During the conquest of

Mexico both sides clearly believed that the other wanted to submit themselves to them as their vassals.[295] A lack of insight into an indigenous culture of violence could also lead to imperial commanders being disappointed in their indigenous allies, who failed to comply with their military discipline, had no conception of the niceties of the European laws of war (for instance accepting the surrender of a besieged fortress in return for allowing the defenders safe passage) and who simply melted away and returned home once they thought the war objective had been achieved.[296]

Although these were the largest and most classic misunderstandings arising from the encounter between the European and non-European cultures of violence, many smaller, situational ones, but no less disastrous for that, were ever-present in the centuries-long history of European expansion: from the Pueblo Indians of North America, who greeted the Spanish conquistadors with (justifiably) mistrustful but in any event visibly harmless ceremonies of incantation and for their pains were ridden down with hysterical cries of 'Santiago!'[297] to the Australian Aborigines who approached a group of settlers holding twigs in their hands—a widespread symbol of peace in many cultures—whereupon the Europeans panicked and took to their heels, only to return later and take revenge for this supposed assault.[298] Perhaps the most obvious reaction when confronted with another culture of violence—yet one which precludes from the outset any cultural understanding—was and remains to simply regard the opposing side as primitive and irrational.[299]

Undoubtedly there were some attempts, at least on first meeting, to integrate the adversary with his alien culture into one's own worldview through rituals or their reinterpretation; however, these were as a rule very hesitant and doomed to failure.[300] Paradoxically, at least on the imperial side, one thing that often stood in the way of a deeper understanding of the opponent's culture of violence was the firm conviction that their own cultural superiority meant that they knew everything worth knowing about their adversary anyhow. Such arrogance not only lay at the root of recommendations that it was vital for non-Europeans to be divested of their cannon and flags in order to demoralize them,[301] but also justified excessive use of force in combat (to match supposed indigenous fighting practices).[302] A similar orientalism was also on display in the justification of corporal punishment, gruesome executions and desecration of corpses, each backed up by supposed knowledge of the special deterrent value of particular practices within the enemy's culture, and somewhat stereotypically on the idea that animists, Buddhists or Muslims would have no hope of redemption if their bodies did not remain intact after death.[303] We should not be surprised if these insights into the 'traditional' values of the opponent's culture appear in the main to derive less from some body of authoritative knowledge than from contemporary adventure writers like Karl May: popular heroes of this time like George A. Custer or General Charles G. Gordon of Khartoum,[304] who were praised by their contemporaries as being great experts in other cultures, in fact had only the most superficial understanding of the societies they allegedly knew inside-out.[305] Likewise, the supposed adoption or imitation of an indigenous warrior culture—for instance when Americans saw themselves as Indians in their fight for independence against Europe, as embodied by the British,[306] or when the British themselves fancied that they might be able to send, instead of genuine indigenous auxiliary fighters, Highland Scots, whom they also regarded as 'barbaric,' into the primeval forests of North America[307]—also betrays definite traits of orientalism in its naïve notion of the essence of 'wildness'.

On the other hand, there was also occidentalism, of course. Patrick Porter has suggested that the fact Saddam Hussein came to believe that modern American society was timid and averse to taking casualties from watching *Black Hawk Down* may have determined his intransigent course of action prior to the 2003 invasion of Iraq.[308] This is by no means implausible if we stop to consider that similar fantasies clearly conditioned the actions of the Axis powers in the Second World War.[309]

From time to time the imperial powers would also come across cultures of violence in which they recognized similar tendencies to their own: the conquistadors of the Early Modern period and Southeast Asian warrior cultures clearly shared a martial ethos that had its roots in religion. Yet this superficial similarity primarily had the effect of actually precluding any deeper understanding of the actual cultural differences, which were of course enormous.[310]

Knowledge and ignorance

The orientalist (or occidentalist) refusal to engage with a deeper understanding of the opponent's culture of violence, and the disinclination to acquire knowledge, fed by the conviction that understanding was possible without knowledge (a self-satisfied European perspective which informs the depictions of Cortés, which can still be found even nowadays, as the great, omniscient manipulator of the helpless Mexicans)[311] highlight the more general significance of knowledge and ignorance for the encounter between European and non-European cultures of violence on the periphery.

In this context, two factors should be borne in mind. Firstly, knowledge was distributed asymmetrically. Thanks to their intensive interaction with one another—even in the Early Modern period Europe had been the kind of knowledge culture community that existed nowhere else in the world except perhaps in South Asia and the Far East—and as a result of their experiences with various cultures of violence on the most diverse continents, the imperial powers of the West had a global knowledge of the world in its entirety,[312] which no indigenous culture that was more isolated and less communicative could possibly hope to possess, or to rapidly acquire. This knowledge of the world brought with it certain strategic, political and military advantages. It made it possible to formulate standard techniques for solving particular problems, techniques that in any individual instance may have been appropriate or inappropriate but which in all cases were reassuring and promoted self-confidence.[313]

Compared with this, the indigenous adversaries of empire naturally possessed knowledge that was locally relevant: they knew the political and social structures of their homeland, its cultural and military traditions, its economic and population potential, its geography and climate, and its foods and medicines. Such information would have been decisive for any form of warfare, but was particularly so for the most promising form of combat when fighting imperial powers: guerrilla warfare.[314]

By rights, this asymmetry of knowledge relevant to waging war might suggest that the two sides would have taken great pains to acquire the knowledge that each of them was lacking and which conversely their adversary possessed. Yet curiously—and this is the second general factor to be borne in mind—not uncommonly the opposite was in fact the case. For a long time, the imperial armed forces showed an astonishing lack of interest in gathering any intelligence whatsoever about the people against whom they were fighting or about the environment in which the conflict was being fought. The latter in particular was of course often of direct military significance, which made the incapacity of the representatives of the West to furnish themselves with reliable information all the more perplexing. To be sure, the fact that, in the Early Modern period, European conceptions especially of the inland geography of great continents were fantastically wrong is neither unfamiliar nor surprising; thus, in North America the Spanish evidently believed in all seriousness that their colony of New Mexico was situated very close to Roanoke in North Carolina and that both were not very far from the Pacific.[315] But that was in the seventeenth century, when knowledge of the world in general was still extremely nebulous and shaped at least as much by the Christian creation myth as it was by the scientific principles of geography. What is much more astonishing is that it was still quite common on the eve of the twentieth century for imperial armies fighting in jungles, mountainous terrain or in the desert to get themselves hopelessly lost; this could even sometimes occur in open country as well.[316]

Until the twentieth century, for many theatres of war there were no maps available, or at best only confusingly inaccurate ones, and in general knowledge of the hinterland of a country beyond the immediate coastal region was very scant indeed.[317] The Italian defeat at the Battle of Adowa in 1896 can be explained not least by the fact that their commander in chief General Oreste Baratieri planned his tactical approach using an absurdly vague sketch map which even with the best will in the world no observer could ever have squared with the real terrain[318] and which in its turn was based on a general overview map 'riddled with crass errors'[319] on the scale of 1:400,000 (some sources even claim 1:1,000,000)[320]—the kind of thing that not even a modern tourist would attempt to use on a well-signposted road. Yet with this as his guide, Baratieri confidently dispatched his columns into an inhospitable landscape where there were no roads or milestones but instead a plethora of place names repeated within a confusingly short distance of one another, and where even tiny streams changed their name five times within the space of a few kilometres. Its extremely rugged and fissured topography, which stymied any attempts at orientation, earned this region the nickname of the 'Ethiopian Switzerland.'[321]

Such conditions—impenetrable and inaccessible terrain plus total geographical ignorance—were only atypical for imperial wars fought in the twentieth century to the extent that Baratieri was in possession of a map, albeit a completely useless one. Around the same time, the German campaign strategy in South West Africa was based primarily on guides who were familiar with local terrain,[322] yet whom military commanders apparently mistrusted as a point of principle.[323] This was a common prejudice of the period, as Callwell makes clear in his *Small Wars*: 'The ordinary native found in theatres of war peopled by coloured races lies simply for the love of the thing and his ideas of time, numbers, and distance are of the vaguest, even when he is trying to speak the truth.'[324] It is clear from this that contemporary racism may well, at least subconsciously, have stood in the way of a search for knowledge. Of course, some expeditions were indeed misled,[325] for which local guides, who in many cases had been pressed into service, were invariably blamed; the Spanish conquistadors regularly garrotted their guides whenever their forces went astray.[326] Understandably, the Spanish sources cannot be considered a credible testimony on whether these punishments were justified. What is certain beyond all dispute is that from the Early Modern period, European expansion through North America was largely dependent upon the Indians' own knowledge of the country; they even drew maps for the European interlopers.[327] By contrast, in the mapping and dividing up of Africa from the 1880s on, indigenous geographical knowledge was arrogantly ignored.[328]

If knowledge on the imperial side about even the most banal and in operational terms most directly relevant circumstances of a particular theatre of war was often 'practically nil,'[329] then the situation regarding intelligence on the size, whereabouts, equipment, organization or plans of the enemy forces was mostly no better.[330] Occasionally imperial forces on the periphery did not have the faintest idea of precisely whom they were actually going to war against, and hence failed entirely to locate the enemy.[331] Waging an imperial war was like attempting to hit midges with a sledgehammer in a dark room. Nowhere has this comprehensive ignorance been better summarized than by Jap de Moor in his account of the Dutch in Indonesia: 'Without precautions, unacquainted with political conditions, military skills of the enemy, and terrain, in short: ignorant of the social and geographical theatre of war, the army time and again invaded unknown areas only to discover that it had made a new mistake.'[332]

Moreover, this ignorance had direct consequences when imperial forces fabricated for themselves a totally false picture of the political conditions on the ground. The delusion of conquerors that the great mass of the indigenous population is just waiting to be liberated from the yoke of tyranny, which we can observe in the nineteenth, twentieth and twenty-first centuries alike, at the very least made it extremely difficult to reliably assess the sheer effort involved in conquering a territory.[333]

Deficient intelligence only exacerbated the problem. As a general rule, commanders on the periphery consciously eschewed any attempt to use scouts to gather information on the enemy, and it was quite normal for nobody in the invading army to speak the language of the country being invaded.[334] Even protecting columns tactically through the use of vanguards, rearguards and flanking detachments, and the guarding of camps by sentries—absolutely self-evident aspects of warfare in large-scale conflicts in the West—was thoroughly uncommon in imperial wars. This neglect was directly responsible for such catastrophic defeats as that of Braddock on the Monongahela in 1755, Custer on the Little Bighorn in 1876, Chelmsford at Isandlwana in 1879 and the German East African *Schutztruppe* under Emil Zelewski at Rugaro in 1891.[335]

This complete inability of imperial commanders on the periphery to equip themselves with some knowledge about a theatre of war that was alien to them in the most fundamental of ways, knowledge which, if viewed dispassionately, would have been vital for the successful prosecution of a war there, can in all honesty only be interpreted as wilful ignorance. Yet how are we to explain this glaring failure, this disregard for acknowledged military precautions?

The short answer to this is hubris. Across the board and down the ages, imperial military commanders on the periphery have been guilty of hopelessly underestimating their indigenous adversaries. Racist feelings of superiority, which denied a priori that the enemy might be capable of military competence, discipline, tactical acumen or the ability for rational planning, played just as great a role in this as a blind faith in the weapons technology, discipline and morale of their own troops and, of course, the experience of past victories. At root, the imperial actors expected to score a swift and comprehensive success; or at least they had nothing to fear from an enemy who anyhow was notorious for avoiding giving battle.[336] Indeed, advance scouting might actually alert the enemy to one's own presence; it was this notion, encouraged by his surprise victory on the Washita in 1868, that had been directly responsible for Custer's readiness to attack without hesitation the largest Indian encampment of all time with just a small detachment of cavalry.[337] A man who believes that his greatest problem is to get a 'weak, constantly elusive enemy'[338] to stand and fight naturally has no great interest in the aims and capabilities of this enemy

A few examples may serve to illustrate this widespread mindset. Braddock, for example, claimed of the Indians: 'These Savages may indeed be a formidable Enemy to your raw American Militia; but upon the King's regular and disciplin'd Troops [...] it is impossible they should make any Impression.'[339] Custer said of the Indians: 'There are not Indians enough in the country to whip the Seventh Cavalry',[340] and Zelewski remarked on the Hehe: 'the fellows haven't even got guns, just shields and spears.'[341] Chelmsford, too, was convinced that the Zulus, whom he saw as 'hopelessly inferior [...] to us in fighting power'[342] would be doing him no greater favour than to launch an attack on his army, 'which will save a great deal of trouble,'[343] since he believed that the very first salvo from their Martini-Henry rifles, which had highly effective stopping power, would demoralize the entire enemy force.[344] As a result, he did not seriously consider that the Zulus would prove to be so audacious and thus neglected to fortify or protect his camp in any way, offering instead the confident prediction: 'My troops will do all the attacking.'[345] Likewise General Gordon maintained that the British expeditionary force in the Sudan would 'not encounter any enemies worth the name in an [sic] European sense of the word,'[346] and convinced himself that the highly motivated mass armies of the Mahdi would be completely demoralized by small parties of forty to sixty British soldiers.[347]

While this may read like a wilful cherry-picking of pithy sayings to which a lie was lent in very short order—after all, the five commanders quoted here were responsible for some of the most spectacular defeats of the West in imperial wars—it is worth remembering that similar statements by contemporaries would actually fill whole volumes. All in all, Western military leaders on the periphery clearly had difficulty in taking their opponents seriously.[348] In this context, John Pemble rightly speaks of 'an excess of self-confidence and an impatience that caused real dangers to be minimized and scientific principles to be violated', in addition to engendering a 'lax attitude'.[349]

In general, non-European peoples were regarded by colonial officials and commanders as 'pusillanimous,'[350] while their leaders were seen as simple 'native chiefs,' an attitude clearly expressed in this public statement by the French foreign minister Aristide Briand on Abd-el-Krim, the creator of the Rif Republic: 'These native chiefs [...] we know them well. They are really simple fellows. Properly handled, they respond to kindness. There is, of course, not the slightest chance that this one will ever attack us. It would be madness.'[351] Even the French defeat at Dien Bien Phu in 1954 was based on a catastrophic and arrogant underestimation of the logistical capabilities (and the artillery) of the Viet Minh.[352]

'Groupthink'—the self-reinforcement of prevailing opinions espoused by a closed group of actors who overestimate their own importance[353]—even immunized the extremely small officer corps of armies on the fringes of empire from quite legitimate doubts concerning both the supposed harmlessness of the indigenous foe and the imperial forces' own military and moral superiority. Warnings about offensive concentrations of enemy fighters were ignored or dismissed as alarmist prophesies of doom.[354]

Self-aggrandizement and contempt for the enemy—fuelled, as we have seen, by supposed military experience and by racist predispositions—therefore stood squarely in the way of a willingness to learn. As far as contemporaries were concerned it was both unnecessary to take any interest in such an inferior enemy and impossible to learn anything from him.[355] Empires saw the periphery as a tabula rasa, a clean slate onto which they could project their own models of society.[356] From their perspective, if there was anything to be learnt from this intercultural encounter, then it was the representatives of the West who would be educating a backward indigenous society as part of their civilizing mission; they had come there in order to teach, not to learn. Ignorance was therefore not just intentional—it was an essential proof-positive of one's own superiority.

Even so, there were some exceptions. Once in a while, imperial armies on the frontier would make an effort to acquire local knowledge, especially if they recognized in it an instrument of domination. If troops were deployed long-term to the same region to fight an insurrection, they almost automatically got to know the natural environment there, its people and the local customs.[357] Local leaders, interpreters, missionaries, settlers, indigenous allies and auxiliaries were all sources of indispensable knowledge about local conditions and could act as middlemen in acquiring such knowledge—provided, that is, that the imperial military was prepared to use them in this role.[358] Successful commanders realized the importance of effective intelligence-gathering on the enemy and espionage.[359] Over and above individual initiatives, empires would sometimes institutionalize the gathering of reliable information on the geography and culture of their peripheries—such endeavours were especially prevalent after defeats or setbacks such as the Indian Rebellion of 1857. In general, anthropology and colonial geography grew hugely in significance from the late nineteenth century onwards, furnishing empires with—aside from transparent legitimations of their rule—a wealth of at least potentially militarily useful insights into possible future theatres of war and adversaries (as well as ethnographic and statistical material on how to identify and recruit allies from 'warrior races').[360] Ultimately, within the framework of the counterinsurgency debate of the late twentieth century, the acquisition of reliable information on the command and control structure of insurgent groups, intelligence and espionage, and in particular the use of information gleaned from defectors became acknowledged key instruments in any successful fight against an insurgency.[361/362] For the present-day United States the 'War on Terror' is also primarily an information war—albeit (as one might expect) with a stress on quantifiable pieces of intelligence that do not necessarily contribute to a transcultural understanding of complex social realities.[363]

In turn, during the twentieth century the indigenous opponents of empire began to acquire the global knowledge they had been previously lacking. In part, the empires themselves were responsible for this, by granting indigenous elites access to Western educational systems; but in part it was simply a consequence of the process of globalization that was stimulated by European expansion, which ensured that information became available worldwide through the communications media. This global information was in one respect absolutely central, in that it facilitated, through the mobilization techniques and ideology of nationalism, the formation of potent transethnic alliances, which were able to lobby successfully on an international stage for recognition of the legitimacy of the anticolonial resistance movement.[364]

Of course, ethnic groups who tended rather toward isolation continued to exist throughout the world, just as there was a continuing supply of ignorant, arrogant Western commanders in imperial wars. But generally speaking, over the course of the twentieth century empires came to know more about their opponents and about local conditions, while for their part those opponents gained more knowledge about the world in general than ever before. This was a particular defining feature of the wars of decolonization.

Learning

However, for a long time, knowledge was distributed asymmetrically, and at least the imperial actors gave little sign of having any incentive to change this. In light of this, it is astonishing that any lessons at all were learnt from imperial wars or for imperial wars—if we understand learning to be a conscious collective acquisition of knowledge that transcends the immediate instance of application, in other words that amounts to more than simple adaptation to present circumstances.[365] Learning of this kind required two cognitive preconditions on the part of empires: the recognition that wars on the periphery had something in common that distinguished them from European warfare, namely that they were sui generis; and secondly the admission that this particularity demanded that a military which had been trained to fight large-scale European wars should genuinely undergo a process of adjustment. Both of these preconditions were anything but self-evident. Indeed, for a long spell, two opposing views hampered learning on the periphery: on the one hand, the idea that in each case the local conditions were so different that no useful generalizations could be drawn from them[366] (assuming it was necessary at all to find out anything about such inferior enemies), while on the other, and more importantly, the widespread natural assumption that the small-scale was automatically contained within the larger entity, in other words that a regular army employing methods that were valid in Europe was also ideally equipped to fight 'small' wars on the periphery.[367]

This latter assumption was in line with the 'big war mentality' that has been postulated for a variety of modern armies, first and foremost the armed forces of the USA, which despite the frontier war against the Indians—virtually their only assignment during the nineteenth century—and despite their experiences in the Philippines and Vietnam (and latterly Afghanistan and Iraq) still doggedly maintained, and continue to this day to do so, that conventional means of warfare such as concentrated deployment and firepower are the answer to every military challenge.[368] There are, of course, good reasons for this inertia of the big war doctrine: the greater security relevance of conventional threats to the mother country compared to irregular conflicts on the periphery;[369] the instructional, technological and psychological advantages of a unified doctrine, reinforced by the institutional weight of traditional conceptions in a thoroughly hierarchical institution such as the military, which rewards conformity and hence concentrates orthodox thinking at its head;[370] and last but not least (and related to the previous point) the idea of a hierarchy of types of conflict, in which 'small wars' are seen as irregular and relatively uncomplicated and technically and operationally primitive, as well as being political and therefore 'unmilitary' and unworthy of any particular intellectual attention.[371] Quite the opposite, in fact: concerning oneself with such aberrations can even be regarded as positively harmful to institutional cohesion and defence policy, given that the primary internal impulse is always to lobby for procurement of the most up-to-date and expensive armaments for waging a conventional war against other major powers and to keep the armed forces as a whole in a fit state to fight such a conflict.[372] Nor, generally speaking, was it beneficial to a military man's career prospects to have too great an involvement with imperial wars.[373]

To some extent, therefore, those armed forces or services whose configuration was from the outset geared towards deployment on the margins of empire had an institutional advantage; this was the case for the British Army throughout the nineteenth century and later for the British infantry[374] and the metropolitan expeditionary corps of other imperial powers.[375] However, this did not preclude the conventional image of warfare from also exerting its far greater power of attraction in these institutions—the heroic quest for a decisive outcome using concentrated military force is simply much more in tune with Western military culture than long drawn-out and less ostentatious counterinsurgency operations.[376]

It is consequently no coincidence that metropolitan military apparatuses mostly 'learned' from colonial experiences when they confirmed their preconceived notion of warfare, as we have already observed with regard to the cult of the offensive, which in the run-up to the First World War was also based upon experiences on the periphery—precisely at a point in time where the development of firearms actually suggested that a switch to a defensive tactical approach would be far preferable.[377] Intimations of the importance of trenches and barbed wire from, say, the Second Boer War were ignored in the face of this exclusive focus on the offensive.[378] The occasional contention that deployments on the periphery necessarily also taught the officers who took part in these campaigns adaptability, flexibility and creativity[379] is for one thing anything but certain—on the contrary, there is much evidence to indicate that in the majority of cases imperial commanders on the frontier were far from receptive to change—and for another thing, even where this was the case, it may well have proved a double-edged sword for the metropolitan military. As we have already noted, imperial warfare has been a repository not just of weapons (like the lance) but also of tactics long obsolete in Europe (such as the infantry square).[380] Accordingly, for contemporary observers there was plenty of evidence to corroborate the idea of a hierarchy of types of conflict: at least if one thought within conventional military categories, imperial warfare could easily appear to be a primitive and poor imitation of major European wars, more archaic, brutal and 'savage'. The readiness to draw lessons from the former and apply them to the latter was not necessarily encouraged by such a view.[381] In the best case, imperial warfare was adduced as a stereotypical template for trying out military innovations that might enhance the West's capacity to wage war, as for instance when Britain's experiences of the American War of Independence on the fringes of its empire reinforced the usefulness of light infantry tactics in Europe.[382]

In spite of all institutional resistance to learning within the imperial military apparatus, however, some learning did still take place. How this exactly functioned has not been investigated thus far; as a rule, most commentators have been content to reason *a posteriori*. Yet in view of the circumstances outlined above, I am disinclined to share Gerald Bryant's enthusiasm for the supposed reflectiveness and adaptability of European officers;[383] I tend rather to agree with Ian Beckett's pragmatic assumption that the transfer of experience from one generation of officers to the next necessarily meant that something was learned which amounted to an institutional response to particular problems.[384] In any event, we know that up to the eve of the twentieth century, such learning processes took place on an almost exclusively informal basis. As a result of constant deployment in the same peripheral theatre of war, armies devised numerous techniques for adapting to the specific natural environment, but above all to the enemy's culture of violence, which as a rule was geared to that environment. Tactics that were adapted to the opponent's 'tribal' warfare likewise formed part of the repertoire of learning[385]—although here the answer frequently did not lie in trying to mimic the enemy's techniques but rather in formulating a response to these techniques that generally involved raising the threshold of violence.[386] The classic example of this kind of pragmatic adaptation is the practice of 'Indian warfare' embraced by the British and the early United States armies in North America, albeit to only a limited extent and using primarily their irregular ranger forces. Furthermore, Indians themselves initially served in these units and passed on their knowledge and skills to their European comrades—an example of direct transfer of technical know-how from fighter to fighter.[387] Conversely, when an army was intent on deploying its soldiers and officers to a theatre of war on only a short-term basis, like the US Army in Vietnam, the process of learning from experience was of course severely impaired.[388]

Such learning becomes historically comprehensible when it transcended the specific location where it was first applied, that is when generalizable lessons could be drawn from it that were then applied to other conflicts—possibly even on other continents.[389] At this juncture we can see that the historical actors developed an awareness that imperial warfare was a very specific form of conflict, namely sui generis, and that its techniques, equipment and tactics were transferable. This has been studied especially comprehensively in the case of Great Britain, where the methods employed by British troops in the Frontier War in North America were said to have been influenced by those used in the conquest of Ireland[390] and where above all in the twentieth century the experiences gleaned from the Irish Civil War of 1919–1921 played into the way in which the smaller frontier wars of the interwar period were conducted. These were adopted once more in Palestine before culminating in Malaya during the Emergency in the creation of a modern counterinsurgency strategy, which was handed down to those involved in suppressing the Mau Mau Uprising in Kenya and subsequently to other conflicts.[391]

Similarly, as early as the nineteenth century the French colonial army also had a general doctrine of colonial warfare, which was based on the seemingly successful mobile campaign of terror conducted by Thomas-Robert Bugeaud in Algeria in the 1840s.[392] At the start of the twentieth century, partly through the involvement of the same central personalities in these diverse theatres of conflict, the French Army carried its experience from Vietnam and Madagascar over to the conquest of Morocco.[393] Yet even in the Early Modern period, the Spanish had applied their repeatedly successful policy of sowing division and blackmailing rulers to conquering a series of indigenous societies—in the Caribbean, Mexico and Peru.[394] During the nineteenth century there evolved among the Spanish officer corps an informal catalogue of methods of waging irregular warfare, which were then subsequently applied in Cuba and elsewhere.[395] In the case of Portugal, too, it has been suggested that the methods it used to combat nationalist uprisings in its African colonies from 1961 to 1974 were based on 500 years of experience in overseas conflicts since the beginning of the Modern Age,[396] and more specifically that even as early as the sixteenth century Portugal's progressive incursion into Asia had helped foster its development of generalizable techniques and adaptability to alien cultures.[397] Until the mid-nineteenth century the Russian Army proved remarkably resistant to learning and insisted upon waging every frontier war using a classic 'sledgehammer to crack a nut' strategy, which even in the seventeenth and eighteenth centuries regularly failed thanks to the logistical difficulties of the theatre of war and the guerrilla warfare skills of their adversaries.[398] However, from the 1850s it began to make efforts to actively encourage the study of peripheral conflicts and awareness of their specific features, and from this to develop a general doctrine of colonial warfare.[399] It is less clear to what extent its tenets were actually applied to the practice of Russian war strategy, especially since the big war mentality clearly continued to predominate.[400] Likewise, the Soviet Union supposedly learned lessons for the conduct of future peripheral conflicts from its experience in Afghanistan, though at present this is still difficult to corroborate from a historical perspective.[401]

Institutional learning through personal practical experience clearly functioned less well in Imperial Germany[402] and the US armies[403] in the nineteenth and twentieth centuries, where the big war mentality was apparently especially prevalent and institutional memory especially short.

Besides, two potential problems attached to the transference of lessons from previous conflicts to later ones: firstly that the insights gained were either inappropriate in the first instance or that, while perfectly applicable to the past war, they were of little or no use for the future conflict. This was true, for example, of the French officers who believed that in the Algerian FLN, they were dealing essentially with a copy of the communist Viet Minh insurgents in Indochina. This attitude actually prevented them from gaining a deeper understanding of the Algerian conflict (and contributed to its brutality).[404] Similarly, the supposedly experience-based but in actual fact ideologically motivated obsession with 'bringing the enemy to battle' proved itself on occasion to be a dangerous false doctrine.[405]

In addition, it was not always the peripheral theatre of war and its culture of violence that was responsible for providing solutions to peripheral problems: techniques for fighting 'small wars' could just as easily be transferred from Europe to non-European locations, based for instance on the relevant experiences from the Vendée Rebellion (1793–1796) and the Peninsular War (1808–1814).[406] Likewise, the fact that irregular tactics evolved almost contemporaneously in Europe and North America in the second half of the eighteenth century is an analytical problem that exercises Anglo-American scholars in particular and makes the question of which direction the transfer flowed in hard to answer historically.[407]

There is an unofficial Spanish handbook on the conduct of colonial warfare dating from 1599 whose recommendations for carrying out guerrilla-style attacks and ambushes under cover of darkness while operating in small groups have a remarkably modern feel to them.[408] Yet in general, lessons drawn from imperial wars for application in future imperial wars were only formalized in writing for military consumption and institutionalized as doctrine from the mid-nineteenth century onwards. This process began with short pamphlets and occasional books by individual officers, whose publication was generally at best tolerated by the authorities, and only really found its way via official publications into service manuals by the mid-twentieth century; it was only in a very few cases that these lessons ended up being actually incorporated into the formal training programme for a particular mission. And even in this process of institutionalizing learning, the individual theatre of war still took precedence. Once again, the British military is the most frequently studied example.[409] The British Indian Army blazed a trail in this respect with its formalizing of mountain warfare techniques drawn from the experience of the protracted conflict along the Northwest Frontier.[410] The rare case of a military manual that attained the status of a classic was the legendary *The Conduct of Anti-Terrorist Operations in Malaya* of 1954[411]—the Bible of the counter-insurgency in Malaya, which among other things had a major influence on the formulation of a similar directive for dealing with the Mau Mau Uprising.[412] Its twenty-three chapters cover every last detail of counterinsurgency, from survival in the jungle to the tactics of the ambush and the deployment of tracker dogs.

Of a far more general nature was the magnum opus of Colonel Charles Callwell, which I have already cited on several occasions—the extensive treatise entitled *Small Wars*, which was based on the study of a huge number of what were at that time recent conflicts on all continents and from all contemporary overseas empires. From these Callwell drew practical lessons, which once again addressed the whole gamut of issues including logistics, the minutiae of tactics and security measures. First appearing in 1896, in later editions it was granted the honour of being published at least nominally under the auspices of the British Army General Staff, not however without the caveat in the preface that it should in no way be 'regarded as [...] an expression of official opinion on the subjects of which it treats.'[413] Even today, despite his evident obsession with the cult of the offensive (which he refers to on numerous occasions), military historians continue to use Callwell's work as a reliable portrayal of all colonial war around 1900, at least in its operational and tactical form.[414] And to some extent this is justified, since the views that he expounded were undoubtedly representative of contemporary practice (and of a handful of less prominent earlier written treatments of the same subject).[415] The factual, manual-like character of *Small Wars*—the content of certain chapters even found their way into the Field Service Regulations of 1929[416]—plus the fact that no such comprehensive treatment of warfare on the periphery appeared thereafter, then ensured that this practice was perpetuated until well into the twentieth century. This is a topic in its own right that research has perhaps still devoted too little attention to.[417] Another classic, General Charles Gwynn's *Imperial Policing* (1934), which likewise inspired a service regulation of the same name[418] and which shaped practice in this area until 1939,[419] confined itself to treating the use of the military in maintaining civil order, a role that at least formally remained below the threshold of war operations.[420] Gwynn's treatise is to the present day still commonly associated with having established the principle of 'minimum force' in dealing with internal unrest of a political nature. Yet the British Army would have to wait until after 1945 for an official formalization of regulations for the conduct of war on the periphery.[421]

In France, the programmatic forty-page pamphlet written by the future Marshal Hubert Lyautey, *Du Rôle colonial de l'armée* of 1900, should be regarded first and foremost as a propagandistic and stylized self-portrait of the French colonial officer corps at variance with the metropolitan military and political elite. Relying on key statements by his mentor Joseph Gallieni, deriving from the conquest of Vietnam and Madagascar, in his pamphlet Lyautey praised the policy of so-called peaceful pacification by soldiers acting as aid workers,[422] expressed familiarly in the image of the 'drop of oil', yet which in the estimation of Ian Beckett was far removed from the reality of the often extremely brutal pacification of territories by the French military, especially in Morocco.[423] A work which appeared in 1905, written by Lieutenant-Colonel Albert Ditte,[424] treated the organizational and logistical challenges of colonial warfare; Ditte clearly aspired to be the French Callwell but failed in his ambition, and the work lapsed into obscurity. By contrast, the theory of the *guerre révolutionnaire*, which was formulated in the 1960s in response to the Algerian War of Independence, was highly influential, and became the French alternative blueprint to the British doctrine of counterinsurgency. Both concepts were united in their diagnosis that modern imperial war was primarily a political conflict. Yet from this insight, the French theory drew a conclusion that was totally at variance with the British notion of winning 'hearts and minds', with its stress on political and psychological solutions: namely, that it was, precisely for that reason, the job of the military to exert massive force to nip any impending revolt in the bud.[425] Initially developed by contemporary military practitioners,[426] the theory of the *guerre révolutionnaire* became known worldwide primarily through the works of Roger Trinquier (who in 1961 justified the use of torture in Algeria as a legitimate and necessary tool of war)[427] and the American French émigré Lieutenant-Colonel David Galula.

Incidentally, Galula's truly uninspiring textbook *Counterinsurgency Warfare* of 1964,[428] together with the likewise somewhat cursory and popular work *Defeating Communist Insurgency* (1967) by the British Lieutenant-Colonel Roger Thompson,[429] which was nonetheless based on his experiences on the staff of the British commander-in-chief during the Malayan Emergency, represent to date virtually the sole theoretical basis for the US formalization of doctrines for conducting small wars on the periphery, as reflected in the celebrated *Field Manual No. 3–24* of 2006.[430] This only serves to highlight the relatively short history of the American military's serious engagement with the theories and methods of imperial warfare, unless one counts the 1940 *Small Wars Manual* of the US Marine Corps in this context. This work, however, focused very narrowly on the requirements of gunboat diplomacy in Latin America[431] and emphasized above all firepower, control of the local population and collaboration with local regimes regardless of their international or internal legitimacy—a true blueprint for Vietnam.[432]

The Spanish armed forces could refer back to a standard work of the 1880s, which like Callwell (but predating him) primarily dealt with the practical aspects of irregular warfare, but in doing so did not distinguish systematically between European and colonial conflicts.[433] Apart from that, the formalization of doctrines of imperial warfare was clearly not well developed within the Spanish military.[434] It was a similar story in the Netherlands and the Soviet Union.[435]

In any event, the limited scope of such written explanations of techniques, methods and theories of warfare must always be borne in mind. The ideas contained in these works only very rarely found themselves applied in the actual training for specific military missions on the periphery—and it is only such training courses which prove that a military apparatus has really adopted a particular doctrine. In the British case, one can point to the training centre of the Far Eastern Land Forces at Johore Bahru near Singapore, better known as the 'Jungle Warfare Training School', where in the 1950s British soldiers learnt the techniques of counterinsurgency for the Malaya campaign.[436] Things were taken much further in France, where the theory of the *guerre révolutionnaire* inspired the creation of the 'Centre for the Teaching of Pacification and Counter-Guerrilla' (Centre d'Instruction à la Pacification et à la Contre-Guérilla) at Arzew in Algeria, where no fewer than 10,000 officers were instructed in the methods of violent suppression of uprisings.[437] Similarly, the Portuguese troops engaged in the wars of decolonization benefitted from training courses both at home and at training centres overseas based on the British model.[438]

Learning lessons from imperial wars about how best to conduct other imperial wars and the formalization of general doctrines for imperial warfare already point to the fact that, over time, empires amassed a fund of transferable practical knowledge for peripheral conflicts,[439] which supplemented their already extensive global knowledge with a new insight into specific military techniques. This fact becomes all the more clear when one takes into account that the learning process had from the outset been an international discourse—empires learnt not just from their own individual experiences but also from one another. Even the very first reports by the French explorer Jacques Cartier on his journeys around North America in the sixteenth century were eagerly devoured in Europe and scoured for tips on Indian fighting techniques.[440] Callwell, as already noted, digested a wide spectrum of foreign literature on military matters, including French accounts of the war in Algeria.[441] Generally speaking, empires began to take note of their mutual experiences in imperial conflicts from the beginning of the Scramble for Africa at the latest, and in particular the smaller nations took keen notice of foreign writings on the subject.[442]

After 1945, this transfer of knowledge intensified within the context of NATO, whose focus on international war in the Northern Hemisphere represented on the one hand something of a handicap to a specialization of the militaries of its member states in peripheral conflicts,[443] but on the other provided an institutional framework for cooperation, exchange of experiences and the discussion of doctrines. The collaboration between the British, French and Americans in this forum was particularly intensive[444]—although the way in which the United States conducted its war in Vietnam does not necessarily suggest that the American side benefitted to any great extent from the know-how of its European allies.[445] Generally, we should probably take a critical view of the scope of such interactions between empires: the British theory of counterinsurgency and the French notion of *guerre révolutionnaire* were simply too divergent to constitute a unified Western doctrine of imperial warfare. Not to mention the lack of conclusive proof that these consultations had any real practical relevance at all, an assumption that is anyhow placed in doubt a priori by the fact that those who participated in them generally carried very little institutional weight within their respective national military organizations.[446] For example, British forces post-1945 were dominated in both their military structure and in terms of defence policy by nuclear deterrence and their contribution to NATO. Even in the British Army, where the overseas role had traditionally carried the most weight, the protagonists of such deployments were at best equally matched by the lobby advocating large-scale mechanized warfare within the framework of the BAOR (British Army of the Rhine).[447] Proponents of counterinsurgency by special forces units were clearly marginalized.[448] Such priorities were set even more explicitly in France.[449]

It was the Portuguese who carried out the most intensive evaluation of the experiences of others. Their doctrine of combatting insurrections, which was formally expounded in a five-volume handbook published in 1963, was based, alongside their own traditions, primarily on the intensive study over many years of British and French methods through observing those two countries' policy in action, reading their war studies and ensuring that Portuguese officers attended courses held at military training facilities abroad.[450]

Even so, this international exchange still does not prove that the recurrence of tactical conceptions for waging imperial wars was based primarily on this exchange—especially since this only began to happen in an intensive and verifiable way in the twentieth century. Christian Gerlach has noted that with regard to, say, the policy of resettlement and the recruitment of local manpower in the colonial fight against uprisings, 'the wheel has been reinvented time and again since the 1940s.'[451] Attempts to solve recurrent problems were in each individual case mostly developed through a laborious process of trial and error on the ground rather than being applied as panaceas via directives from above[452]—a procedure completely in line with the imperial system, in which the 'men on the spot' always enjoyed great freedom of action. Accordingly, a Portuguese military practitioner, General Kaúlza de Arriaga (supreme commander in Mozambique from 1970 to 1973) substantially relativized the importance of theoretical learning from the experience of others when he explained that 'comparable minds naturally produce similar solutions under comparable circumstances'.[453] It is primarily the similarity of circumstances, the military logic of the situation on the periphery, which explains why the individual manifestations of imperial warfare over several centuries and across different continents and empires have remained so strikingly consistent.

What, then, has been the overall result? We can say without doubt that empires' arrogant refusal to learn stood at the forefront for a long time and that every attempt to adapt to the particular circumstances of imperial conflict was thwarted by the inertia of metropolitan military apparatuses. If lessons were learnt at all, then this happened very tentatively, belatedly and above all superficially. In the search for generalizations and globally applicable panaceas the particular circumstances of any individual conflict sometimes got left by the wayside. In every case, learning was geared to its immediate applicability and above all to military solutions: armaments, techniques or tactics. A deeper understanding of the enemy's culture of violence was seldom on the agenda. On the ground, imperial warfare continued to be conducted in a situational and practical manner.

Where the adversaries of empire were concerned, it is historically extremely difficult to glean even halfway reliable findings about their efforts to learn from violent encounters with the West. To begin with, the problem of available sources militates against this: almost every-thing that we know about the overwhelming majority of indigenous societies throughout the history of European expansion is viewed through a European lens. And almost across the board, Western observ-ers refused to consider 'savages' capable of any form of learning.

The best proof of this is the persistent way in which indigenous successes in learning or indeed any notable military technologies at all were attributed to European defectors. Especially the independently developed art of fortress-building by the North American Indians or the Maori could, according to contemporary sources, be traced back to instruction by European deserters or the influence of Western writ-ings on the subject.[454] If a non-European army had a recognizably regu-lar appearance, it was blithely assumed that European influences must have been the driving force behind their creation.[455] If we are to believe the sources of the Early Modern period, even such genuinely indige-nous weapons technologies as shields or war clubs, or tactics like ambushes and feigned retreats, could not possibly have been indepen-dently devised by the Indians.[456] Western puppet masters were stereo-typically suspected as being behind inexplicable military successes on the part of the enemy.[457] According to British reports from the eigh-teenth century, Haidar Ali, the founder of the aggressively modernizing military monarchy of Mysore in Southern India, was actually a French deserter, while in the nineteenth century the legendary Burmese gen-eral Maha Bandula, who successfully resisted the British in the First Burmese War, was thought to be an illegitimate son of the former Governor General of India, Warren Hastings.[458] In similar vein, the Spanish explained the military victories of the Rif Republic in the 1920s as being down to the alleged presence of European staff officers in the service of Abd-el-Krim.[459]

There are certainly some instances in which knowledge can be shown to have been transferred by individual Europeans working for the indigenous side or by indigenous deserters from colonial armies, not least in the regularization of the armies of the Indian princely states in the eighteenth century and of the Southeast Asian kingdoms in the nineteenth,[460] as well as in the modernization of Samori Touré's forces[461] (plus the Rif Berbers really did employ a former French foreign legionnaire as an artillery commander and surveyor).[462] Nevertheless, from an unreconstructed Western perspective of the kind that claims for its own culture a monopoly on all capacity to innovate and learn, little in the way of plausible fact will be learned about the adaptability of their indigenous opponents.

In this absence of sources, if one attempts instead to deduce something about the indigenous learning process from the degree of success enjoyed, then a few indigenous societies possibly appeared to be habitually more willing to learn than others. Yet we should take into account here that more recent scholarly literature has only just begun to overcome the traditional condescending European perspective which portrays the non-European world as fundamentally static. We may therefore perhaps assume that the societies that have not thus far been described as more than averagely capable of learning have simply not yet found a sympathetic historiographer.[463]

However little one may say about actual learning processes, one thing remains clear: namely that it is not true, once again in contradiction of Eurocentric assumptions, to claim that in every case learning by indigenous peoples in preparation for war against empires was simply to be equated with learning from those empires. New weapons, technology and tactics could also be acquired through observation,[464] or in conflict with indigenous neighbours, who were themselves in the main—though not always—the direct recipients of Western innovations. Up to the mid-eighteenth century the Indian princely states learnt primarily from one another, not from the British or the French,[465] and in any case their military system was structurally similar enough to the European one that the subsequent conflict with the imperial powers was for a long time almost symmetrical. The same applied to the island of Java. A particularly interesting form of transcontinental transfer of military knowledge has been identified by John Thornton in the revolution on Haiti (1791–1804): the rebellious slaves there clearly fell back on their own experiences in West and Central African armies like that of the Kingdom of the Kongo or Dahomey.[466]

As for the empires, so for their indigenous adversaries the demands of intercultural and transcultural warfare could sometimes find themselves competing with one another, thus giving rise to a complex situation of contradictory doctrines and technologies. In the eighteenth century the Cherokee found themselves obliged to retain their traditional strongholds in conflicts with their Indian neighbours although these had become obsolete when fighting against regular European armies equipped with artillery.[467] The Maori, too, fought against other Maori in serried ranks—an eighteenth-century mode of open battle, and in itself already a tactical innovation brought about by the adoption of firearms—but against British soldiers armed with artillery this style of warfare was suicidal, which is why the Maori also developed in parallel the modern Pa system.[468]

If the Western empires were in many regards a knowledge community, the same cannot for a long time be said of their opponents, who instead were essentially isolated and restricted to their own resources—not least as a result of European dominion over the oceans. Supraregional exchange of knowledge and technology clearly existed principally within the Islamic cultural region of South and Southeast Asia. Only in the late nineteenth century did anticolonial resistance movements or at least their elites (not infrequently in cooperation with Western leftist intellectuals) develop a strong consciousness of the universality of their struggle against Western domination, which then resulted in the medium term in institutional collaboration.[469] In this context the opponents of empire did not merely copy tactics that had been developed elsewhere—the Philippine guerrillas in the war against the USA took their cue from Cuban and Boer models[470]—they also read and critiqued theories of guerrilla warfare including, alongside those of Western provenance, the writings of Mao Zedong especially,[471] which after 1945 came to form the basis of armed 'revolutionary' campaigns worldwide, despite the fact that the applicability of Mao's theories anywhere other than in China always remained questionable.[472] Nevertheless, augmented by adaptations such as those of Vo Nguyen Giap, Che Guevara and Carlos Marighela[473] these works at least provided their users with an important fund—at least in terms of morale—of anti-imperial warfare techniques, whose universal validity was presumably no less than that of the Western panaceas for fighting imperial conflicts. Traces of these anti-imperialist theories can still be observed in transnational terrorist groups of the present day.[474]

What should have become clearly apparent by now is that indigenous societies' capacity to learn lessons for fighting imperial wars was
often hampered by the close interrelationship between a warrior culture, its weapons technology and its social mode, which either completely precluded innovations or at the very least restricted them to
superficial copies of Western models, whose military effectiveness then
often left a lot to be desired. On top of this came attempts at active
obstruction by the imperial powers, who undermined the transfer of
knowledge by refusing, among other things, to train indigenous auxiliary troops either at all or specifically in the use of certain weapons. In
the long term, however, such strategies had only limited success.[475]

For many isolated societies engaged in violent conflict with Western
empires, the most serious impediment to effective learning was the
frequently short duration of this encounter. Empires that swiftly collapsed, such as those of the Aztecs and the Incas, simply had no time to
develop a more intensive process of adaptation or enduring learning,
even if—and this is something that has been doubted time and again,
though with no attempt to prove it—they had been culturally capable
of an innovative response to new military challenges.[476] Much the same
can undoubtedly be said of many other non-European societies.[477]

Conversely this means that those indigenous cultures which remained
in contact with expansionist empires over a long period without suffering
a catastrophic and terminal military defeat stood the best chance of
adapting and learning over the long term. Essentially this applied most
readily to intensively interrelated societies from the same cultural region,
provided that region also displayed a great strategic depth, for example
the American continent. Although the Aztecs, the Incas and the unfortunate coastal peoples of the North American continent all collapsed in the
sixteenth and seventeenth centuries under the Western onslaught, they
did in the process buy time for their neighbours in the interior, who were
able over the ensuing centuries to come to terms with the European
challenge, which on a continent-wide scale only expanded slowly.[478] The
same was true of Southeast Asia, where the Western presence was confined to the coastal strip until the mid-nineteenth century.

In the course of these cultural contacts over centuries, the imperial
side also had good opportunity—and cause—to adjust to their adversaries' style of waging war. Even if whole empires or armies did not
manage to do so, then at least individual actors adapted to the condi-

tions of the theatres of war and adopted the technologies and methods of the indigenous culture of violence. In North America[479] and Southeast Asia[480] but also for instance in India[481] (where it was only less obvious because the conflict was in the first instance more symmetrical) and occasionally also elsewhere,[482] a 'middle ground'[483] emerged from the encounter between Europe and the rest of the world, in which weapons, equipment and modes of warfare merged into a synthesis of cultures of violence that was genuinely new. Representatives of this realm include such diverse figures as the North American ranger[484] and the Southeast Asian buccaneer[485]—both of whom could be of European, indigenous, or mixed extraction.[486] The fact that, in the long run, empires were more often the ultimate beneficiaries of this military melting pot is another matter, as John Lynn has explained with regard to India in the eighteenth century:

> The sepoy fought so well because even though he carried European weapons and wore a European uniform, he was inspired by very South Asian ideals. European military culture merged with South Asian religious, social, and village values and practices to produce a new military culture unique to India and the sepoy.[487]

The same can be said of many colonial military units.[488]

Over and above all this, however, we should not on the other hand ignore the limits of such synthesis, especially not on the Western side: the adoption of indigenous attributes could also simply be a superficial mannerism,[489] and fear of the stigma of 'going native'[490] was never far from people's minds.

Conclusion

The asymmetry between empires and indigenous peoples in the violent conflicts arising from European expansion was pronounced, but it was neither universal nor unbroken. Both regionally and sometimes thoroughly symmetrical constellations would appear, especially before the middle of the nineteenth century and in particular in South and Southeast Asia (for very different reasons in each case). More importantly, though, the representatives of such diverse cultures of violence who encountered each other on the periphery interacted with one another. They adapted to one another, developed new techniques for transcultural conflict, and at least occasionally merged to create something new. This insight challenges the commonplace notion of a catastrophic clash between two completely incompatible elements and corroborates Patrick Porter's reminder that war is always a cultural exchange as well, albeit under extreme conditions:

> Warfare has a reciprocal dynamic. Rather than being the by-product of separate and discrete autonomous cultures, it is shaped also by the reactive processes of competition, imitation and globalisation. Culture is shaped by externalities, such as the interpenetration of ideas and influences across boundaries. While the rhetoric of war may be one of hostility and mutual abhorrence, the practice of war is often convergence.[491]

On the other hand, one should not overplay this caveat and especially not misconstrue the violent encounter as some transcultural idyll between equal partners. The fact remains that for long periods, it was the imperial powers who were calling the tune in this clash between cultures of violence and that as a rule the pressure to assimilate was stronger for the indigenous cultures, if only because they ran the greater risk in the form of an immediate threat to their survival. One might conclude from this that non-Europeans' adaptation and difficulties in adapting have had a greater historical impact than the ability (or failure) of representatives of the West to learn lessons.

Framed in this way, however, the question of the relationship between learning and military success is irrational and sterile. It implies that the side that is better at learning is the one that wins[492]— the US Army, of all armed forces, explicitly states as much;[493] and yet it is immediately apparent that even successful learning cannot guarantee that one will overcome a developmental advantage on the part of the enemy.[494] For example, the Indian princely states adapted remarkably quickly and extensively to the European style of warfare and yet were still defeated. Before 1945, the imperial powers often dispensed with any learning process or adaptation, revelled in their ignorance of local conditions and yet still conquered the world. And after 1945, despite developing sophisticated theories of counterinsurgency and 'revolutionary war,' they still lost their colonies.

Adoption of weapons technology, assimilation, knowledge and learning are just some of the many factors that decide a military conflict. The original resource potentials presumably play a considerably greater role, especially in an asymmetrical constellation. And besides, the outcome of any particular war is down to a myriad of situational factors that cannot be generalized. In the final analysis, however, European expansion throughout the world was not primarily a military conflict. At most, force of arms supported and underpinned decisions that had been taken at a political and social level—cooperation, alliances and structures that maintained the fragile edifice of imperialism. Likewise, the colonial empires were not primarily conquered on the battlefield, nor were those empires as a rule lost on the field of combat; rather, they declined in spite of military victories. In this context, adaptation, knowledge and learning in the military realm were merely a footnote.

The question of the mechanisms of the encounter between two such different cultures of violence is above all of interest to the historian of military cultures. Empirical studies in this realm are unfortunately still very thin on the ground. In particular, on the questions of how the indigenous side coped with a massively asymmetrical and threatening conflict, or who first highlighted shortcomings or prompted innovations, and the difficulties with which their implementation was confronted, academic studies have very little to say. Conclusions drawn from the outcome permit only the vaguest assumptions. A great task lies ahead for historians, sociologists and anthropologists of violence.

CONCLUSION

It seems to be obligatory to conclude every war history with a discussion of who won, and why. The question of the recipe for military success, of the reasons for failures, of strength and weakness and of victors and vanquished appears to exert a huge fascination, particularly in generalized accounts of global history such as that by Lawrence Keeley: 'A broad survey of warfare indicates that (in the short term or tactically) superior numbers or fortifications and (in the long term or strategically) a larger population and logistics are the keys to victory.'[1] However, this assertion would completely exclude the possibility of smaller armies defeating larger ones with larger populations behind them by having better morale and/or weapons technology. It would not only cast fundamental doubt on the whole raison d'être of Prussian-German military strategy from at least Frederick II onwards,[2] but also flatly contradict the entire body of evidence from 500 years of imperial warfare, in which the 'handful' was pitted against the 'horde'; besides, at least where more recent history is concerned, it can clearly be disproved statistically.[3] More specifically as regards the topic of this current work, it would fly in the face of the observations cited in the first chapter of this book about the general invincibility of empires, say by Jürg Helbling:

> Wars of resistance almost always ended with victory for the colonial state, particularly if it had acquired a clear advantage in weapons technology, was in a position to pursue a 'divide and rule' strategy, was resolute in its suppression of the native populace and was prepared to pay the price for this, whatever the cost.[4]

I regard generalizations like this, especially such sweeping ones as Keeley's, as problematic. The circumstances (from the political state of both sides and their relative military strengths—numerical, material, and in terms of morale—to the theatre of war) are just too diverse, the outcome of individual battles and whole conflicts is simply too dependent upon situational factors (one need only think of such broadly contingent elements like the weather or the leadership qualities of individual commanders), and finally it is all too easy to find a host of examples to demonstrate the opposite.

This is not to say that I am against generalizations per se—otherwise I would never have been able to write this book. But looking for patterns and recurrent conditions in the course of violent conflicts is quite different to making one-dimensional generalizations about their outcomes. Absolute statements of this kind, which reduce whole combinations of conditions to a simple common denominator, tend towards teleology or even towards the application of prescriptive solutions—a quest for recipes for victory that can be applied beyond the individual case—or at least hint at some predictability. Even some more cautious viewpoints concerning the wars of a particular era or region, such as that of Robert Utley, who maintains that during the Indian Wars in the USA, the Indians enjoyed 'military success' whenever they stuck to their traditional fighting methods, as did the 'whites' when they employed the same methods,[5] have the problem that it is totally unclear what is meant by 'military success' and how far it extended (quite apart from the fact that in this specific case there is a logical gap in Utley's analysis with respect to what happened if both of these premises were true).

What, then, do victory or defeat or 'military success' mean in the violent history of European expansion? The question of who 'won' can hardly be dealt with globally, and even in each individual case can only be tentatively answered through recourse to non-military factors. If one wanted to identify a trend, then one would at least need to distinguish between settler colonies and colonies of domination: in the first case, the indigenous population undoubtedly 'lost' in the long run, albeit in large part as a result of demographic shifts and the destruction of the natural environment, processes in which force of arms played at best a supporting role.

CONCLUSION

In the case of colonies of domination, with a majority indigenous population, providing any meaningful answer is fundamentally more difficult. In many places, there existed for a long time a military balance, in which the empires held sway along the coast and in more accessible regions, whereas indigenous societies controlled the interior and undeveloped areas. As a result, in large parts of the world, notably Africa and South Asia, 'conquest' mostly happened in the late nineteenth century. Yet on the one hand this was accompanied by regular military setbacks for the empires,[6] when the indigenous side would sometimes prevail not only in individual battles but even win wars, and on the other it was based at least as much on the policy of 'divide and rule' as it was on military operations—even though these often benefitted from a clear superiority in weapons technology. Above all, imperial rule in these colonies remained unstable for a protracted period, as evidenced by the frequent succession of disturbances and 'uprisings' that lasted far into the twentieth century. As is well known, despite their military 'victories,' in the mid-twentieth century the empires of the West did not manage to keep hold of their colonies, which once again goes to show that 'military success' is a category of extremely dubious global validity, to say the least. As I have stated on several occasions, imperial wars were first and foremost political confrontations, which defied the intrinsic military logic of victory and defeat, of 'bending the enemy to our will'. Nor is this insight the final word on the subject, for despite the formal independence of former colonies, we clearly now inhabit a world that is shaped politically, economically, legally and culturally by the dominance of the West. So who really 'won'?[7]

Globally, therefore, the question of who was the 'victor' in imperial conflicts cannot be answered in any serious and unequivocal way. At most, looking back at 500 years of European expansion with military support, all that can be offered is a list of factors that favoured either the imperial or the indigenous protagonist, a comparison of the specific strengths and weaknesses of both sides—with the provisos that such a synopsis can have no claim to comprehensiveness, that the weighting and combination of these factors varied in each individual case and that the outcome of individual conflicts was additionally—perhaps even primarily—determined by situational circumstances.

Thus, in a global context, empires profited from:

- their modern and stable statehood;
- their superior ability to mobilize resources;
- their global knowledge and their experience of expansion;
- their control over the seas;
- the asymmetry of risk in an imperial conflict;
- their bureaucratic and professional military system;
- their possession of (at times) superior transport, communications and weapons technology and horses;
- their art of fortress building;
- local alliance partners.

Meanwhile, the negative factors affecting empires were:

- the deployment of inadequate resources due to the setting of priorities in defence policy;
- the difficulties of projecting power across oceans or continents;
- the cumbersome nature of heavily armed forces with complex logistics;
- the lie of the land; that is, the extent and undeveloped nature of the peripheral landscape, the defensive qualities of the prevailing terrain and the climatic and pathological challenges they faced, especially in the tropics;
- ignorance of the physical and social geography of the theatre of war;
- the institutional inability to adapt on the part of the military apparatus, with its 'big war mentality.'

The factors that favoured the indigenous side in imperial conflicts included:

- their mostly superior numbers;
- their skill at fighting small wars ('tribal wars');
- their high degree of mobility and straightforward logistics;
- their acclimatization and resistance to local pathogens;
- their local knowledge;
- support among the populace;
- the defensive qualities of the peripheral landscape.

The disadvantages facing indigenous armies were:

- the fragility of their statehood (if it even existed in the first place);
- their political fragmentation, which furnished the empires with alliance partners;
- their mostly inadequate strategic depth and ability to mobilize resources;
- their lack of global knowledge, which meant that they experienced a culture shock on first encountering Westerners;
- their military organization, which, being based on the charismatic leadership of individuals, lacked bureaucratic planning elements and institutional stability;
- the incompatibility of their social structure with a complete adoption of Western military technology.

Such lists tell us nothing about the weighting of these different factors in each individual case, nor do they provide any definitive answers, with much remaining ambivalent. Thus, the political fragmentation of non-state societies could at least occasionally become a trump card, since societies of this kind provided Western modes of warfare, which were intent upon decisive outcomes, with little purchase. And although copying the Western military system was largely a successful strategy, it could sometimes actually counteract the ability to wage guerrilla warfare, so was not an unqualified advantage. Hence, all these speculations are to be taken with a pinch of salt.

However, suggesting reasons for victory or defeat or offering patent solutions for 'military success' are not the primary concern of this book. Rather, it was my intention to discern the pattern of conflict that was typical of imperial warfare, to understand its internal logic and to try and grasp what characteristics make it a form of sui generis conflict that is highly relevant to the modern era. The book's main thesis and findings can be briefly summarized as follows:

1. The internal logic of imperialism, the setting of defence policy priorities and logistical actualities (both globally and on the spot) restricted the imperial deployment of resources at the periphery to such an extent that, in the face of a vast, unexploited space that favoured defenders and a politically often only loosely organized enemy, who in addition shunned set-piece battles, it was frequently impossible to achieve a swift and decisive operational result of the

kind expected by modern Western war strategy. Imperial wars were therefore hallmarked as temporally, spatially and structurally open-ended, primarily political conflicts in which indigenous cooperation played a crucial role.

2. The aims of imperial acts of violence were often very limited and blurred into one another to form an escalating continuum (which does not preclude a meaningful typology, though it does make it difficult). In the process, the subjugation or destruction of indigenous communities was more of a functional *ultima ratio* than an intentional war aim. Acts of violence by the enemy were not always primarily a reaction but could have independent intrinsic motives.

3. The obsession of imperial commanders with trying to force a decisive military outcome, in spite of the circumstances noted above, and the difficulties when dealing with politically less complex societies and in distinguishing between combatants and non-combatants under conditions of irregular war, was a key element of warfare on the periphery in that these factors encouraged the violation of accepted limits on the legitimate use of force. This was backed up with discourses about harshness, decisiveness and punishment, which were prompted by the physical weakness of the colonial state; by the permissive ideology arising from the enemy's alleged lack of rules and supposedly brutal local methods of warfare, to which the imperial side necessarily had to adapt; by a deeply felt cultural distance; by strong emotions such as fear, prompted by exposure to a profoundly alien and hostile environment; by discourses on retribution; and lastly by an institutional dynamic and the suggestion of a permanent state of exception on the periphery. All these factors complemented and overlapped one another and ultimately provided a multitude of predetermined excuses for the use of unrestricted violence on the margins of empire.

4. As a general rule, the periphery witnessed the meeting of cultures of violence whose military organization, style of warfare, technologies and tactics were radically different, although there were some notable exceptions to this situation of extreme asymmetry. Above all the conflict between cultures of violence was characterized by cultural exchange, adaptation and learning, even though these processes had limits and met with psychological and sociocultural difficulties.

CONCLUSION

In the final analysis, imperial conflict thus turns out to be a form of warfare whose defining characteristic is that it does not follow the logic of large-scale wars fought in the West. The huge significance of space, the temporal open-endedness and low operational intensity of warfare—if only thanks to the limited resources deployed—the for a long time limited objectives, and the irregularity arising from a confrontation with a 'tribal' martial culture all make imperial warfare a qualitatively 'different' kind of conflict—one that is primarily political, in which transcultural cooperation is more important than the quest for a decisive military outcome. The fact that these very elements are also responsible for producing the contrary trend towards more brutal tactics is an interesting contradiction, yet one which is easily resolved if one considers that such 'solutions' to the military-political problem can at best, under what are ideal surrounding circumstances from an imperial point of view (such as in North America in the eighteenth century), have more than just a temporary effect, but usually only contribute to an escalation of violence and to raising the costs of controlling a region, and hence must be seen primarily as an institutional inability on the part of the military to recognize the true nature of the conflict. The transcultural character of imperial warfare reinforces this process of brutalization through a sense of otherness and a lack of understanding; this insight can, and should, be taken alongside an awareness of the oft-stated transcultural efforts to learn and assimilate.[8]

It need hardly be said that this very general characterization of the logic of imperial conflict represents an abstraction of the highest order—an ideal type, as it were. But on closer inspection, a number of important variables can be identified in the general logic, which might make for a more nuanced account in terms of typology and periodization. (In the list below, I have broadly followed the sequence of chapters in the book.)

1. One of the most important variables has already been mentioned, namely the character of the particular peripheral region, which is not entirely covered by the distinction of settler colonies versus colonies of domination, but should perhaps instead focus directly on the demographic relationship between the European presence and the indigenous population. Where empires achieved a demographic preponderance, the character of the imperial conflict

changed permanently in so far as military control was made considerably easier by the prevailing environmental conditions.

2. In cases where peripheral conflicts were assigned a high prestige value by empires or where, as a result of the geographical proximity of the theatre of war to the imperial motherland or because of its strategic importance, they were deemed to be of extraordinary relevance to security, the mobilization for imperial conflicts could far exceed the usual level. This was increasingly the case after 1945, when the Cold War, through the paradigms of the zero-sum game and credibility, invested peripheral conflicts with an unprecedented importance for empires.[9]

3. The political organization and the military potential of the indigenous society or societies played an important role. Where a complex indigenous state body existed, which put a regular army in the field, the conflict tended from the outset to be far more symmetrical and also more likely to be characterized by reciprocal adaptation, which made the war even more symmetrical. The outcome then depended on the durability of the indigenous state; if it survived a defeat relatively intact, an imperial conflict could reach a comparatively clear conclusion through a transition to a collaborationist regime. If, on the other hand, it disintegrated, the more common condition of an imperial war against a fragmented and either sub-state or stateless enemy would ensue.

4. As a special variable in this context, the capacity of indigenous elites to create stable transethnic intracultural alliances is relevant. In the twentieth century, these alliances benefitted hugely from the internally mobilizing and internationally legitimizing ideology of nationalism and people's right to self-determination, and hence transformed into successful anticolonial liberation movements with proto-state aspirations, which increasingly divested transcultural alliances with the respective empire of any legitimacy (which is not to say that these failed to emerge).

5. Space, terrain and climate were similarly relevant. In particular the accessibility by sea of the theatre of war was central to the imperial projection of power, but also a limited size of the theatre of war and a comparative high degree of openness and development could deprive an imperial war of one of its defining aspects. Much the same

was also true of social geography: high population densities and intensive agriculture tended to make an imperial war more like a European large-scale war, especially since those circumstances almost always went hand in hand with strong indigenous statehood.

6. The broader geopolitical climate was crucial to the chances of the indigenous side of forming alliances and hence to their ability to withstand a conflict that would have overstretched them had they been isolated. Eras and regions of intensive imperial rivalry (North America and India in the eighteenth century, and the world as a whole between 1945 and 1991) created far better initial conditions for this than unchallenged spheres of influence (large parts of Spanish America, Australia, New Zealand, the US West after 1812) or periods of de facto imperial cartels against the rest of the world (1880–1914).

7. In connection with this, a secondary variable resides on the legal status and the legitimation of the indigenous parties to a conflict. It is of only minor significance here that indigenous statehood was recognized on paper as legitimate in the Early Modern period,[10] since this basic fact did not prevent empires from engaging without compunction in wars of annihilation then any more than in the late nineteenth century, when no notice whatsoever was taken of indigenous political organization anymore (as evidenced by the construct of the *terra nullius* and the summary carving-up of Africa by the European powers after 1880) and indigenous acts of violence were generally criminalized as insurrections. However it is relevant that this situation changed fundamentally after 1945 with the formation of the United Nations, the development of a globally dominant anticolonial ideology and the legal recognition of non-state liberation movements.

8. A key factor in the character of imperial warfare is of course the imperial war aim, though it should be borne in mind that this was not always clearly articulated, that war aims could blur together on an escalating scale and develop their own dynamic (the collapse of collaborationist regimes, situational 'final solutions'), and that the operational and tactical logic of warfare, that transcended limitations on the acceptable use of force, could frustrate the strategic objective.

9. An absolutely central variable—for many observers, the one which alone precludes the application of any overarching logic to imperial conflict—is technology, in particular weapons technology. In the Early Modern period, any technological advance on the part of empires, except for at sea, had little relevance. But in the second half of the nineteenth century, the revolution in breech-loading guns, steamships and railways gave the West for a time a massive technological edge, which began to level off again after 1900 and since 1945 has played a significantly smaller role.

10. For the ability to learn and adapt, particularly of the indigenous side, the duration of contact was a key variable. Intensive violent first contacts with little forewarning could result in a catastrophic culture shock; by contrast longer-lasting contacts, buffered by strategic distance, stood a high chance of resulting in military adaptation and cultural synthesis.

11. Conversely, the imperial military's readiness to adapt was characterized above all by how great a priority or how much in the way of resources the metropolitan military establishment assigned to operations on the periphery. Armed forces, or particular units within a military, that were geared to imperial warfare were markedly better placed in this regard than a unitary metropolitan military conditioned to large-scale warfare.

12. The asymmetry of knowledge was subject to certain obvious changes. The global knowledge of empires was always pronounced, but the twentieth century saw them also gain local knowledge, and likewise witnessed the acquisition of global knowledge by indigenous societies.

Although some of these variables are regional or situational, it is nonetheless striking that others change with the passage of time. In particular, this applies to the status of indigenous societies, which began in the twentieth century, and ever more rapidly post-1945, to profit from increasingly global knowledge, the ideology of nationalism and international legitimacy—three elements which of course are closely linked. Other factors that underwent radical change over the course of time were the imperialists' technological advantage and the general international situation, as well as the relative importance of peripheral conflicts (at least during the Cold War).

CONCLUSION

At an early stage of this project, I was still convinced that these variables over time could form the basis of a periodization of violent conflicts during European expansion, which would look something like this:

1. Pre-classic (or Early Modern) imperial warfare (up to the mid-nineteenth century): the enemy enjoys, at least on paper, a certain legitimacy. There is intense imperial rivalry, which gives the indigenous side the chance to form alliances. Technological asymmetry is minimal.
2. Classic imperial warfare (c. mid-nineteenth to the early/mid-twentieth century): the enemy has almost no legitimacy. Empires cooperate; the enemy is isolated. Technological asymmetry is pronounced.
3. Post-classic imperial warfare (from the mid-twentieth century on): the legitimacy of the enemy is markedly greater. Effective transethnic liberation movements benefit from global knowledge, making empires pay a heavier price for their colonial rule. The Cold War provides these liberation movements with an automatic alliance partner, who also supplies them with modern weaponry; technological asymmetry tails off.

There is no denying that that this kind of periodization has a certain explanatory value; at the very least, it helps give a plausible account of why the West's conquest of the world in the 'classic' phase from around 1850 to 1930 became so intensified. Ultimately, though, the boundaries are not watertight enough to make a truly meaningful division into distinct phases. The shift in the overall geopolitical environment only partially coincides with that in weapons technology and while, taken as a whole, the chances for indigenous societies of forming alliances after 1945 were good, this depended very much on which part of the world was involved.[11] As regards weapons technology, the first conflicts in which 'post-classic' elements became apparent were probably the Italian invasion of Ethiopia (which contemporaries also registered as epoch-changing)[12] and the Second Boer War;[13] and where the configuration of the resistance movement and the imperial response was concerned, undoubtedly the US conquest of the Philippines—all were conflicts that occurred around 1900.[14] Similarly, imperial mobilization for individual imperial wars increased sharply at precisely this time too. Yet at the same time, even after the Treaty of Versailles, the international constellation remained relatively favourable to the imperial powers for some decades, and in many places quite classic, small, isolated imperial wars were waged with minimal use of resources, at least until 1945. This attempted periodization should, then, be taken with a pinch of salt at best. This kind of analysis does, however, indicate that the 'classic' phase was short and somewhat atypical of the entire course of the history of violence within European expansion. And in any event it should be noted that the conflict pattern of imperial warfare, notwithstanding certain important variables, has most definitely been of relevance, in its overarching logic and in many of its concrete manifestations, for the total course of European expansion.

How do things stand regarding more recent violent conflicts on the periphery after the end of the wars of decolonization and the Cold War? Initially, of course, it is the differences that are most apparent, especially with the 'classic' imperial wars of the nineteenth to early twentieth centuries. The bases for legitimation appear to have changed in part; humanitarian considerations are now mostly paramount, at least officially. Interventions are more often collective enterprises and undertaken with the blessing of the international community. And the West is no longer establishing any overseas empires—at least none that involve any formal dominion or re-colouring of the world map.

But how relevant are these differences when seen from a historically informed and long-term perspective? If one is to believe their contemporary protagonists, almost all imperial conflicts were humanitarian in one way or another: toppling unjust regimes or bringing the benefits of Christianity, civilization, free trade or liberty—nowadays the gift of democracy is most commonly cited. In truth, though, the actual reasons for going to war in those days were, and remain today, far more tangible: economic interests, regional stability and warding off potential threats. At its core, Afghanistan is first and foremost a 'turbulent frontier' (in John Galbraith's sense of the term)[15] within the global system. Anyhow, the West's humanitarian concern is highly selective and its application determined by opportunism. To date, no Western statesman has seriously mooted the idea of intervening by force to redress human rights abuses in the People's Republic of China. Besides, the altruistic intention, even if it is genuine in itself, is patently driven by a paternalistic urge to impart Western values unbidden to the non-European world—an impulse which, when all is said and done, is typical of imperialism.

Collective interventions were not uncommon in earlier times—the Boxer Rebellion in China is merely the most famous example. However, it is questionable what analytical difference an alliance between Western nations makes to the structure of the intervention. At best it is proof of the fact that, compared to earlier phases of European expansion—most recently the Cold War—the rivalry nowadays among Western nations vis-à-vis the rest of the world has diminished markedly. Above all, though, collective intervention primarily serves to justify the action to the international public and to mask national self-interest—and the same holds good for procedural legitimation via the United Nations, which likewise can do little to disguise the fact that ultimately it is most frequently the leading powers within the global system who engage in military action essentially in order to safeguard their own interests. The extent to which this is also the case even without such fig leaves of legitimation is demonstrated not just by the 2003 American-British invasion of Iraq but also by France's military intervention in its former colony of Mali;[16] this operation was wholly unauthorized to begin with and, despite a subsequent UN mandate and symbolic troop contributions from other Western and African allies, remained essentially a unilateral intervention. This is just the latest in a long line of military operations that have been undertaken since decolonization on the territory of the former French West Africa, which France, in spite of assurances to the contrary, continues to regard as lying within its sphere of influence.[17]

Finally, only in exceptional cases was the establishment of formal colonial rule historically the objective of Western military action on the periphery, nor generally speaking was it the immediate result of such action, even though repeated interventions and the collapse of discredited collaborationist regimes could ultimately have this as their (unintended) consequence. For the most part, however, the very same supposedly limited aims of the most recent armed interventions in the non-Western world—to enforce compliance or bring about a change of regime or social system—were also the predominant motivations for the use of force by empires over the last 500 years. Apart from that, as yet no one has any idea what will happen in the long term to the de facto Western protectorates in various places including Afghanistan, in the event that it proves impossible year after year for decades to come—just as happened in the British invasion of Egypt in 1882—to withdraw without leaving the country in chaos. Certainly, at present, colonial rule has been sufficiently discredited in global historical terms that one can confidently discount any possibility of these countries formally losing their independence or Western geographers repainting the map of the world in the colours of their motherlands. But in truth, right now Afghanistan is no more independent than Morocco or the Indian princely states were at the beginning of the twentieth century— a sovereign state on paper, but de facto a peripheral dependency of Western empires (and of the Western global system in any case).

Yet in the final analysis such questions of legitimacy and niceties of international law are only really of concern to political scientists. Where the history of conflict is concerned the structural continuities of transcultural, peripheral conflicts weigh far more heavily in the balance. These modern imperial wars continue to be shaped primarily by the realities of the lie of the land and by the transcultural and asymmetrical constellation of adversaries. They remain at root local civil wars, in which Western forces constitute merely one (albeit dominant) power factor among many others, and they are still, as they always have been, devoid of temporal, spatial and structural boundaries of any kind. Again, the most recent example of this is Mali, where the ethnic and factional conflict underlying the events of 2012–13 has continued to flare up time and again for decades.[18] And as before, Western troops are—to varying degrees—far removed from any real understanding of the societies in which they are waging war: Iraq and Afghanistan are prime examples of this. The Western military machine continues to be tormented by its inability to find a decisive military solution to a political conflict or to tempt into open battle an enemy who has no reason to engage in one and who relies instead on guerrilla warfare and terrorism, to which the conventionally trained Western forces still have no real answer. Little wonder that the armed forces of the West are starting to reflect anew on peripheral conflicts of the past, especially the wars of decolonization—or at least to invoke them in their rhetoric.[19] All the same, in the West's projection of power on the periphery, it continues to be its limitations that are most in evidence.

Where the reality of warfare is concerned, and from the perspective of those at the 'receiving end'—namely, for the most part, the civilian populace of the theatre of war—the checks and balances preventing an escalation of the violence (largely the result of a critical international public with access to almost real-time mass media) are surely the most crucial difference from a time when the armed forces of the Western powers and their local allies could indulge in massacres virtually unchecked on the periphery. Despite continuing (and revealing) attempts to screen interventions in the Third World from the gaze of the world's press (as the French army did most recently in Mali in January 2013),[20] human rights violations can no longer as a rule be hushed up in the age of the Internet. The heightened sensitivity not just to losses on one's own side, but also to civilian casualties, plus the strict political control that is now exerted over military operations overseas from the metropolitan centre have had the effect of shifting the nature of warfare in imperial conflicts. Yet even so, the price for any attempt to solve political problems by military means, and to enforce a dominant foreign influence (albeit not formal foreign rule) with insufficient resources, is still paid by the civilian population on the ground. Recently, this trend has only been exacerbated by the deployment of remotely guided weapons designed to minimize Western casualties. If there is one thing above all else that continues to characterize imperial conflict, it is this: its asymmetry.

ACKNOWLEDGEMENTS

My thanks are due first to Thoralf Klein and Frank Schumacher, who invited me to deliver the opening lecture at the conference on 'Colonial Wars' held in Erfurt in January 2003, which marked the beginning of my involvement in this field of scholarship. As chairman of the Hamburg Institute for Social Research (HIS), Jan Philipp Reemtsma has been responsible for providing funding for my work on this project since 2007. In the process, he has shown great forbearance towards several postponements on my part occasioned by spells of paternity leave and my appointment to a visiting professorship; without this support this book would never have appeared. Martin Bauer, Managing Editor of the Institute's journal *Mittelweg 36* repeatedly encouraged me to publish various preliminary studies for this book in the form of articles; the interest he showed was a real morale-booster, too. I would also like to thank the librarians at the HIS for fulfilling my numerous requests for interlibrary loans, reprints of newspaper articles and new acquisitions (the bibliography that follows gives some idea of the work I put them to). In particular, I am much obliged to Christoph Fuchs for his research into the reception of Charles Callwell's works and to Ingwer Schwensen for material associated with the deployment of drones in war. Likewise, the student assistants of the former working group on the theory and history of violence supported me with countless small ancillary tasks, especially Katrin Radtke over many years, and subsequently Klaas Voss, who in the meantime has become a valued colleague at the Institute; Laura Haloschan, whose knowledge of Spanish were very useful in evaluating sources on the Conquista; and finally Yves Schmitz, who researched the conflict in Mali on my behalf. I would also like to thank Birgit Otte at Hamburger Edition for her knowledgeable and careful preparatory reading of my text for publication.

Where its contents are concerned, this book has undoubtedly benefitted most from my long-standing academic and personal contacts with the chair of modern general history at the University of Bern. My interest in imperialism and war was first stimulated by my academic tutor Stig Förster, for which I thank him wholeheartedly. My collaboration with Tanja Bührer has proved particularly fruitful; among other joint undertakings, we published an anthology in 2011 on the theme of 'Wars of Empire,' while her work on the German Schutztruppe in East Africa has considerably broadened my understanding of how war was waged in Africa. Andreas Stucki, a colleague of mine at the HIS since 2012, and Flavio Eichmann took on the task of reading the text of this book in its entirety and gave me the benefit of their extensive comments. I am extremely grateful to them not only for raising various points of criticism and clarifying certain concepts but also for providing some valuable pointers to supplementary information from their own special fields of expertise, the later Spanish and Portuguese colonial empires and French military involvement in the Caribbean. I have also profited enormously from their knowledge of the debates surrounding imperialism and empires.

My thanks are also due to a host of other colleagues for the tips they offered me, the rewarding discussions I had with them, and for their encouragement, cooperation and criticism. They include James Belich, Arndt Brendecke, Moritz Feichtinger, Wolfgang Gabbert, Bernd Greiner, Matthias Häußler, Nadin Hée, Jürg Helbling, Ulrike von Hirschhausen, Konrad Jarausch, Jonas Kreienbaum, Birthe Kundrus, Dieter Langewiesche, Wolfgang Reinhard, Ute Schüren, Hew Strachan and more generally all those who took part in the 2009 conferences on 'Wars of Empire' and 'Transcultural Learning in Imperial Wars', held in Potsdam and Hamburg respectively, whose insights are reflected at many points in this book. It goes without saying that, as always, any shortcomings or errors in my account are entirely of my own making.

As is customary, I have saved my most important debt of gratitude till last. No one has played a bigger part in bringing this work to fruition (and no one aside from me has suffered as much) than my wife Birgit

ACKNOWLEDGEMENTS

Albrecht. During the seemingly interminable writing phase, she shouldered a disproportionally heavy burden of the household duties and childcare. Yet alongside this she also somehow found the time to read and correct various draft versions of the text and to constantly urge me to give it a more logical structure and explain ideas more lucidly. She did this not just in her capacity as a scholar of linguistics but also as an interested and informed reader, who for long periods found herself wedded just as much to wars of empire as she was to me. This work would never have seen the light of day had it not been for her unstinting support and loyalty. To her and to my daughters Charlotte and Pauline, who for far too long had to put up with a father whose thoughts were often far away on the Spice Islands, I dedicate this book.

NOTES

INTRODUCTION

1. Kaldor, *New and Old Wars*; Münkler, *Die neuen Kriege*; Jäger, *Komplexität der Kriege*.
2. Thomas/Moore/Butler, 'Conclusion', p. 411f.; Wendt, *Vom Kolonialismus zur Globalisierung*, pp. 326–330, 349–362.
3. Wallerstein, *Modern World System*.
4. Gallagher/Robinson, 'Imperialism of Free Trade'; Cain/Hopkins, *British Imperialism*; Cain/Hopkins, 'Gentlemanly Capitalism I'.
5. Reinhard, *Geschichte der europäischen Expansion*.
6. Ribas, 'Eclipse and Collapse'.
7. Jalée, *Impérialisme en 1970*; Magdoff, *Imperialism*; Nkrumah, *Neo-Colonialism*.
8. Robinson, 'Excentric Idea of Imperialism'; Robinson, 'Non-European Foundations'.
9. Smith, *Pattern of Imperialism*, p. 85.
10. Beissinger, 'Rethinking Empire', p. 29f.; Burbank/Cooper, *Empires in World History*, pp. 453–459; Darwin, *After Tamerlane*, pp. 482–485; Go, 'Entangled Empires'; Howe, *Empire*, pp. 114–116; Münkler, *Imperien*, pp. 224–254; Parrott, 'Transformation of the Soviet Union', p. 11f.; Zielonka, *Europe as Empire*; McCoy/Fradera/Jacobson, *Endless Empire*.
11. Eichmann, 'Expansion und imperiale Herrschaft', pp. 89–91; Osterhammel/Petersson, *Geschichte der Globalisierung*; Wendt, *Vom Kolonialismus zur Globalisierung*.
12. Mommsen, *Imperialismustheorien*.
13. Headrick, *Tools of Empire*, p. 83. Almost identical wording in Trotha, 'Genozidaler Pazifizierungskrieg', p. 41. Cf. Osterhammel, *Verwandlung der Welt*, p. 663; Osterhammel, 'Entdeckung und Eroberung', p. 408f.; Peers, 'Introduction', p. xv; Porch, 'Introduction', p. v; Trotha, *Koloniale Herrschaft*, p. 33.
14. Bitterli, *Die "Wilden" und die "Zivilisierten"*, pp. 130–136; Raudzens, 'Why Did Amerindian Defences Fail?', p. 345.
15. Gallagher/Robinson, 'Imperialism of Free Trade', p. 5.
16. Bryant, 'Asymmetric Warfare', p. 431.
17. Kundrus/Walter, 'Anpassung und Lernen', pp. 19–22.
18. Hirsch, 'Collision of Military Cultures', p. 1211.
19. Utley, 'Cultural Clash', p. 91. Gordon, 'Limited Adoption', p. 229.

20. Schröfl/Pankratz, *Asymmetrische Kriegführung*. See also Heuser. *Rebellen—Partisanen—Guerilleros*.

21. Klose, '"Antisubversiver Krieg"'; Charters/Tugwell, *Armies in Low-Intensity Conflict*; Beckett/Pimlott, *Armed Forces and Counter-Insurgency*.

22. For example Hull, *Absolute Destruction*; Zimmerer, 'Geburt des "Ostlandes"'.

23. Le Cour Grandmaison, *Coloniser, Exterminer*, pp. 146–152. Zur Kritik Meynier/Vidal-Naquet, 'Coloniser Exterminer'.

24. Kuß, *Deutsches Militär*.

25. Balandier, 'Situation Coloniale'.

26. Stucki, 'Bevölkerungskontrolle in asymmetrischen Konflikten', p. 257f.

27. Gerwarth/Malinowski, 'Holocaust als "kolonialer Genozid"?', p. 447f.

28. Stucki, 'Bevölkerungskontrolle in asymmetrischen Konflikten', p. 259.

29. Beckett, *Modern Insurgencies*, p. 213; Boot, *Savage Wars of Peace*, pp. 336–341; Clayton, *Wars of French Decolonization*, p. 186; Feichtinger/Malinowski, 'Konstruktive Kriege?', p. 276; Keeley, *War Before Civilization*, p. 79–81; Kiernan, *Colonial Empires*, p. 230; Porch, 'Myths and Promise of COIN', p. 241; Porch, 'Introduction', pp. v, vii, xii, xvii; Schmidl, '"Asymmetrische Kriege"'.

30. Bradford, 'Preface', p. xvii.

31. Gat, *War in Human Civilization*, pp. 542–557; Keegan, *History of Warfare*. A few scattered references to the conquest of America, the Spanish method of waging war on Cuba and the Boer Wars in addition (rather curiously) to several pages on the French conquest of Morocco and the Italian invasion of Ethiopia in 1935/36 can be found in Jones, *Art of War*, pp. 317f., 418f., 495–501. Strachan, *European Armies*, pp. 76–89, contains a chapter on the importance of the experience of fighting colonial conflicts for European techniques of warfare. Even in the context of guerrilla wars, there is not a single mention of conflicts on the periphery in Best, *Humanity in Warfare*. Perhaps not surprising in view of the book's title, but certainly surprising given its author's British nationality, is the complete absence of any treatment of military actions outside the European sphere in Howard, *War in European History*.

32. Marshall, 'Western Arms in Maritime Asia', p. 13.

33. Keeley, *War Before Civilization*.

34. Beckett, *Modern Insurgencies*; Hahlweg, *Guerilla*; Laqueur, *Guerrilla Warfare*.

35. Vandervort, *Indian Wars*; Vandervort, *Wars of Imperial Conquest*.

36. Killingray, 'Guardians of Empire'; Klein/Schumacher, *Kolonialkriege*; Bradford, *Military and Conflict*; Moor/Wesseling, *Imperialism and War*.

37. Lee, *Empires and Indigenes*; Raudzens, *Technology, Disease and Colonial Conquests*; Peers, *Warfare and Empires*.

38. Walter/Kundrus, *Waffen Wissen Wandel*; Bührer/Stachelbeck/Walter, *Imperialkriege*; Kortüm, *Transcultural Wars*; Ferguson/Whitehead, *War in the Tribal Zone*.

39. See, among other works, Boot, *Savage Wars of Peace*; Kuß, *Deutsches Militär*; Bond, *Victorian Military Campaigns*; Crowder, *West African Resistance*.

40. Hochgeschwender, 'Kolonialkriege als Experimentierstätten?'; Schmidl, 'Kolonialkriege'; Vandervort, 'Colonial Wars'.

41. Osterhammel, *Geschichtswissenschaft jenseits des Nationalstaats*, p. 291.

42. Monographs continue to treat the same case studies—the British conquest of India, the French subjugation of Algeria, the end phase of the Indian Wars in the

USA, the Herero War in South West Africa, the Philippines War and the more significant wars of decolonization (Indochina, Malaya, Algeria). In most cases, there is a marked unwillingness to venture into new empirical territory.

43. Raudzens, 'Why Did Amerindian Defences Fail?', pp. 331, 333.

44. Osterhammel, *Geschichtswissenschaft jenseits des Nationalstaats*, p. 291.

45. Baberowski, 'Diktaturen der Eindeutigkeit', p. 40.

46. For parallels, see Aksan, 'Ottoman War and Warfare', p. 167; Eberspächer, 'Chinas imperiale Kriege'; Hack, 'Imperial Systems of Power', pp. 17–26; Simpson, 'Indonesiens Kolonialkrieg'; Wade, 'Chinese Colonial Armies'. Eichmann, 'Expansion und imperiale Herrschaft', identifies structural similarities in the history of the ancient world.

47. Deutscher, *Through the Language Glass*.

48. Daase, *Kleine Kriege*, pp. 103–105.

49. Callwell, *Small Wars*, p. 21f.

50. For a full explanation of this choice of terminology, see Walter, 'Imperialkriege', pp. 1–21.

51. Brower, *Desert Named Peace*, p. 4. From the eighteenth to the twentieth century, the losses among indigenous populations as a consequence of European expansion are thought to have been a hundred times greater than those among Europeans; 95 per cent of these deaths were civilians. Etemad, *Possession du monde*, p. 134f. It goes without saying that such rough sets of figures should be treated with the utmost caution.

52. Helbling, 'Tribale Kriege und expandierende Staaten', pp. 61–63; Lappas, 'Lernen inmitten des Blutvergießens', p. 154f.

53. Häußler, 'Asymmetrie tribaler und staatlicher Kriegführung', p. 177f.; Ricklefs, *War, Culture and Economy*, p. 1f.; Robson, *Fuzzy-Wuzzy*, p. xviii; Strachan, 'Typology of Transcultural Wars', p. 91.

54. Guilmartin, 'Cutting Edge', p. 46; Hemming, *Conquest of the Incas*, p. 62. Yet as Gabbert, 'Kultureller Determinismus', p. 280, explains, the range of these sources is also limited. Cf. on New Zealand Belich, *Victorian Interpretation*, p. 334.

55. Starkey, 'Lernen im Kolonialkrieg', p. 141.

56. Ferguson/Whitehead, 'Violent Edge of Empire', pp. 2–15.

57. In the French of the colonial period, at least, even the term 'indigène' tended to be pejorative, perhaps comparable with the word 'native' in English or 'eingeboren' in German. Brower, *Desert Named Peace*, p. 19f.

58. Middleton/Lombard, *Colonial America*, p. 4.

1. WAR ON THE PERIPHERY

1. Hérisson, *Chasse à l'homme*, p. X.

2. Daase, *Kleine Kriege*, pp. 11–14.

3. Wesseling, 'Colonial Wars', p. 2. Wesseling's second premiss was the separability of war and peace.

4. Gottmann, 'Bugeaud, Galliéni, Lyautey', p. 234.

5. Ditte, *Guerre dans les Colonies*, p. 11.

6. Callwell, *Small Wars*, pp. 21, 23. There have also been some fundamentally more banal definitions, such as 'conflict between white military forces (or at least forces

commanded by white men) and non-white groups'. Jeffery, 'Colonial Warfare', p. 24. According to this definition, the Russo-Japanese War of 1904/1905 and the Pacific War of 1941–1945 would also have been colonial wars.

7. Gottmann, 'Bugeaud, Galliéni, Lyautey', p. 234f. A very similar exposition is given in François, *Kriegführung in Süd-Afrika*, p. 5.

8. For example Hochgeschwender, 'Kolonialkriege als Experimentierstätten?', pp. 276–282; Kuß, *Deutsches Militär*, pp. 15–18.

9. Lincoln, *Conquest of a Continent*, pp. 45, 55.

10. Gann/Duignan, *Rulers of Belgian Africa*, p. 54f.

11. Thomas, 'Order Before Reform', p. 202.

12. Hemming, *Conquest of the Incas*, p. 90.

13. Hemming, *Red Gold*, p. 385f.

14. Porch, *Conquest of the Sahara*, p. 165f.

15. Vandervort, *Indian Wars*, pp. 213–215.

16. Guinea (modern Guinea-Bissau), the smallest of Portugal's three African colonies, which the Portuguese fought to keep hold of until the mid-1970s, was only about the size of Switzerland, though with some very challenging terrain. Cann, *Counterinsurgency in Africa*, p. 2.

17. Callwell, *Small Wars*, pp. 115–124; Ditte, *Guerre dans les Colonies*, p. 15f.

18. Callwell, *Small Wars*, p. 44. Similarly in Chacón, *Guerras Irregulares*, Vol. 1, p. 5.

19. Brower, *Desert Named Peace*, p. 95; Clayton, *France, Soldiers and Africa*, p. 17.

20. Utley, *Frontier Regulars*, p. 171f.

21. Vandervort, *Indian Wars*, p. 192.

22. Utley, *Frontier Regulars*, p. 276.

23. Vandervort, *Indian Wars*, pp. 134–136.

24. Girard, *Slaves Who Defeated Napoleon*, p. 118.

25. Coates, *Suppressing Insurgency*, pp. 143–145.

26. Gann/Duignan, *Rulers of Belgian Africa*, pp. 53–55.

27. Buckley, *Slaves in Red Coats*, pp. 121–123; Kiernan, *Colonial Empires*, p. 33.

28. Hemming, *Conquest of the Incas*, p. 156f.

29. Girard, *Slaves Who Defeated Napoleon*, p. 118f.

30. Utley, *Frontier Regulars*, p. 76f.

31. Linn, *Counterinsurgency in the Philippine War*, p. 2f.

32. Williams, 'Egyptian Campaign', p. 266.

33. James, *Savage Wars*, p. 217.

34. Porch, *Conquest of the Sahara*, p. xii.

35. Cann, *Counterinsurgency in Africa*, p. 171.

36. Scott/McCone/Mastroianni, 'US Combat Units in Iraq', p. 61f.

37. Duffy, 'British Attitudes to West Indian Colonies', p. 86f.; Eichmann, 'Cooperation in a Subversive Colony', p. 18; Geggus, 'Slavery, War, and Revolution', p. 24.

38. Girard, *Slaves Who Defeated Napoleon*, pp. 159–180.

39. Stucki, *Aufstand und Zwangsumsiedlung*, pp. 185, 188.

40. Curtin, *Disease and Empire*, pp. 12–27; Headrick, *Tools of Empire*, pp. 59–70.

41. Keegan, 'Ashanti Campaign', p. 184.

42. Headrick, *Tools of Empire*, p. 69f.

43. Vandervort, *Wars of Imperial Conquest*, p. 100.

44. Curtin, *Disease and Empire*, pp. 187–190; Paillard, 'Expedition to Madagascar', p. 183f.

45. Black, *War in the World*, p. 176; Fourniau, 'Colonial Wars before 1914', p. 83; Moreman, *Army in India*, p. 11; Mostert, *Military System*, p. 20; Stucki, *Aufstand und Zwangsumsiedlung*, p. 188; Vandervort, *Indian Wars*, p. 130.

46. Abler, 'Beavers and Muskets', p. 166f.; Charters, 'Disease, Wilderness Warfare, and Imperial Relations', pp. 8–13; Connor, *Australian Frontier Wars*, p. 74; Utley, *Frontiersmen in Blue*, p. 316.

47. Jones, *Conquest of the Last Maya Kingdom*, p. 38.

48. Utley, *Frontiersmen in Blue*, pp. 275–279. Cf. Ibid., p. 329f., also Utley, *Frontier Regulars*, p. 159.

49. Porch, *Conquest of the Sahara*, pp. 235–238, also p. 170.

50. Macrory, *Signal Catastrophe*, p. 86.

51. Gould, *Imperial Warriors*, p. 37.

52. Fynn, 'Ghana–Asante', p. 34f.

53. Killingray, 'Colonial Warfare', p. 150.

54. Girard, *Slaves Who Defeated Napoleon*, p. 180.

55. Belich, *Victorian Interpretation*, p. 122.

56. Chandler, 'Expedition to Abyssinia', pp. 134–147, Quotation: p. 136.

57. Moreman, *Army in India*, p. 10.

58. Jones, *Graveyard of Empires*, p. 91f.

59. Calloway, *Winter Count*, p. 197f.

60. Utley, *Frontier Regulars*, pp. 200–203.

61. Bandini, *Italiani in Africa*, p. 161; Clayton, *Wars of French Decolonization*, p. 114; Hemming, *Conquest of the Incas*, pp. 104f., 137; Powell, *Soldiers, Indians and Silver*, p. 35f.; Utley, *Frontier Regulars*, p. 379; Woolman, *Rebels in the Rif*, p. 18f.

62. Coates, *Suppressing Insurgency*, pp. 143–145; Gregorian, '"Jungle Bashing" in Malaya', p. 345f.

63. Beckett, *Modern Insurgencies*, p. 124; Fall, *Hell in a Very Small Place*, pp. 68–72; Gann/Duignan, *Rulers of Belgian Africa*, p. 52; Greiner, *Krieg ohne Fronten*, p. 201; Hemming, *Amazon Frontier*, p. 98; Kiernan, *Colonial Empires*, pp. 43–46; Killingray, 'Colonial Warfare', pp. 149–151; Linn, *Counterinsurgency in the Philippine War*, p. 120; Moor, 'Warmakers in the Archipelago', pp. 52–54; Ricklefs, *War, Culture and Economy*, p. 7; Thornton, 'Warfare, Slave Trading and European Influence', p. 131f.

64. Kopperman, *Braddock at the Monongahela*, pp. 3–7, 50, 57–59. A more famous engagement called the 'Battle of the Wilderness' was fought in Virginia in 1864 during the American Civil War.

65. Falls, 'Reconquest of the Sudan', pp. 288, 292; Horne, *Savage War of Peace*, pp. 263–267; James, *Savage Wars*, pp. 91f., 100–103; Porch, *Conquest of the Sahara*, pp. 129, 163–180.

66. Macrory, *Signal Catastrophe*, pp. 127–129.

67. Utley, *Frontier Regulars*, p. 171f.

68. Porch, *Conquest of the Sahara*.

69. Vandervort, *Indian Wars*, pp. 213–215.

70. Wickwire/Wickwire, *Cornwallis*, p. 156.

71. Ricklefs, *War, Culture and Economy*, p. 143f.

72. Killingray, 'Colonial Warfare', p. 150.
73. Hemming, *Amazon Frontier*, p. 20.
74. Girard, *Slaves Who Defeated Napoleon*, p. 118.
75. Bührer, *Kaiserliche Schutztruppe*, pp. 237–245; Ditte, *Guerre dans les Colonies*, p. 14f.; Fynn, 'Ghana–Asante', p. 40f.; Gann/Duignan, *Rulers of British Africa*, p. 115f.; Hassig, *Mexico and the Spanish Conquest*, p. 61; Hemming, *Red Gold*, p. 222f.; James, *Savage Wars*, pp. 174–180; Kopperman, *Braddock at the Monongahela*, pp. 57–59; Linn, *Counterinsurgency in the Philippine War*, pp. 102f., 106; Robson, *Fuzzy-Wuzzy*, pp. 13–15; Schmidt, *Araberaufstand in Ost-Afrika*, pp. 311–317; Utley, *Frontiersmen in Blue*, pp. 133–135.
76. Macrory, *Signal Catastrophe*, p. 141f.; Moreman, *Army in India*, pp. 10–13; Woolman, *Rebels in the Rif*, p. 107.
77. Beckett, *Modern Insurgencies*, p. 211.
78. Gottmann, 'Bugeaud, Galliéni, Lyautey', p. 252f.
79. Hemming, *Conquest of the Incas*, p. 186.
80. Guilmartin, 'Cutting Edge', p. 49.
81. Lock/Quantrill, *Zulu Victory*, p. 150.
82. Isby, *War in a Distant Country*, p. 86f.
83. Beckett, *Modern Insurgencies*, p. 2; Laqueur, *Guerrilla Warfare*, p. 393f.
84. Powell, *Soldiers, Indians and Silver*, p. 35f.
85. Howe, *What Hath God Wrought*, p. 100f.
86. Kiernan, *Colonial Empires*, pp. 43–46. A recent example from 2013 is the desert and mountainous region of Northern Mali. Morgan, 'Remote mountains of northern Mali'.
87. Lettow-Vorbeck, *Mein Leben*, p. 84.
88. Connor, *Australian Frontier Wars*, pp. 53, 56f.; Hemming, *Red Gold*, p. 399f.; Penn, *Forgotten Frontier*, pp. 125–135; Potempa, 'Raum und seine Beherrschung', p. 451.
89. François, *Kriegführung in Süd-Afrika*, p. 7. I am indebted to Kuß, *Deutsches Militär*, p. 262, for the quotation.
90. Utley, 'Cultural Clash', p. 96.
91. Calloway, *Winter Count*, pp. 126–149.
92. Starkey, *European and Native American Warfare*, p. 124.
93. François, *Kriegführung in Süd-Afrika*, pp. 6–10.
94. Bond, 'South African War', pp. 216, 233; Butlin, *Geographies of Empire*, p. 453f.; Connor, *Australian Frontier Wars*, p. 13; Ditte, *Guerre dans les Colonies*, p. 14f.; Eichmann, *Sklaverei, Weltkrieg und Revolution*; James, *Savage Wars*, p. 48; Utley, *Frontier Regulars*, p. 158; Ward, '"European Method of Warring"', p. 255f. Even the sugar-producing islands of the Caribbean, with their intensive agriculture, still had no roads around 1800, since all trade was conducted across the seas. Gliech, *Saint-Domingue und die französische Revolution*, pp. 63–65.
95. Bailes, 'Technology and Imperialism', p. 88f.
96. Guy, *Destruction of the Zulu Kingdom*, p. 57; James, *Savage Wars*, pp. 39f., 44; Lock/Quantrill, *Zulu Victory*, pp. 46f., 66–70, 96, 132
97. James, *Raj*, p. 144.
98. Callwell, *Small Wars*. According to information from North America, a pack horse could carry enough forage to feed itself for a distance of around 300 kilometres.

Vandervort, *Indian Wars*, pp. 218–220. A mule could last forty days in the same way. Brower, *Desert Named Peace*, p. 77.

99. Bryant, 'Asymmetric Warfare', p. 462f.; Cook, *Sikh Wars*, p. 33f.; Cooper, 'Culture, Combat, and Colonialism', p. 540f.

100. Macrory, *Signal Catastrophe*, p. 85f.

101. Pemble, 'Resources and Techniques', pp. 290–292.

102. Chandler, 'Expedition to Abyssinia', pp. 124f., 129. On the northwest frontier of India, cf. Moreman, *Army in India*, p. 11.

103. Vandervort, *Indian Wars*, pp. 55–57.

104. Utley, *Frontier Regulars*, pp. 48–50.

105. Chuchiak, 'Forgotten Allies', p. 192; Hassig, *Mexico and the Spanish Conquest*, p. 84f.; Hemming, *Conquest of the Incas*, pp. 349–358; Oudijk/Restall, 'Mesoamerican Conquistadors', p. 38f.

106. Fourniau, 'Colonial Wars before 1914', p. 84; Ricklefs, *War, Culture and Economy*, p. 146.

107. Bailes, 'Technology and Imperialism', p. 95; Bührer, *Kaiserliche Schutztruppe*, p. 236f.; James, *Savage Wars*, pp. 265–272; Killingray, 'Colonial Warfare', pp. 156, 162–165.

108. Kanya-Forstner, 'French Marines', p. 138.

109. Gann/Duignan, *Rulers of British Africa*, p. 149. Indigenous auxiliary workers also perished in large numbers during the conquest of Mexico and New Mexico. Altman, 'Conquest, Coercion, and Collaboration', pp. 147–159.

110. On the Western mode of warfare, see: Beckett, *Modern Insurgencies*, pp. 184–187; Hanson, *Western Way of War*, p. xxivf.; James, *Raj*, pp. 20, 122; Parker, 'Introduction', pp. 2–5; Peers, 'Introduction', p. xxiif.; Weigley, *Age of Battles*; Wilson, 'European Warfare', p. 187.

111. Gelpi/Feaver/Reifler, 'Success Matters'; Merom, *How Democracies Lose Small Wars*, pp. 15, 230; Porter, *Military Orientalism*, p. 81.

112. Vandervort, 'Colonial Wars', p. 167.

113. Griffith, *Forward into Battle*, pp. 105–136.

114. Eder/Hofbauer, 'Operation Enduring Freedom', p. 58; Gustenau/Feichtinger, 'Krieg in und um Kosovo', p. 475f.

115. Over the last decade, unmanned drones have taken the principle of applying technology in order to minimize the risks to one's own troops to a whole new level. In the process, civilian losses at the target site continue to be accepted as 'collateral damage', though it should be said that these are presumably considerably fewer than would be the case with conventional bombing. The precise extent of casualties is disputed. Dowd, 'Drone Wars', pp. 11–14; Kennedy, 'Drones', p. 26; Müller/Schörnig, 'Drohnenkrieg', pp. 19–21; Taj, 'Drone Misinformation'.

116. Grau, *Bear Over the Mountain*, p. 205f.

117. Calloway, *Winter Count*, pp. 214–219; Malone, 'Changing Military Technology', p. 243; Starkey, *European and Native American Warfare*, p. 19.

118. Vandervort, *Indian Wars*, p. 202f.

119. Vandervort, *Wars of Imperial Conquest*, p. 117.

120. Paillard, 'Expedition to Madagascar', pp. 177f., 183f.

121. Connor, *Australian Frontier Wars*, pp. 48–53, 62–71, 78f., 105–107; Keeley, *War Before Civilization*, p. 74; Nasson, *South African War*, p. 150f.; Porch, 'French Colonial Forces', pp. 164–167; Robson, *Fuzzy-Wuzzy*, pp. 161, 176.

122. For a more extensive discussion of the how military structures adapt to the theatre of war on the periphery, see chapter 4.

123. Ikime, 'Nigeria—Ebrohimi', pp. 222–226; Keegan, 'Ashanti Campaign', p. 184; Lock/Quantrill, *Zulu Victory*, pp. 93–95; Paillard, 'Expedition to Madagascar', p. 183f.; Ricklefs, *War, Culture and Economy*, p. 143f.; Vandervort, *Indian Wars*, p. 118; Ward, '"European Method of Warring"', p. 255f.

124. Jones, *Conquest of the Last Maya Kingdom*, pp. 111–113, 251.

125. Steele, *Betrayals*, p. 35.

126. Hemming, *Amazon Frontier*, p. 111.

127. Clayton, *Wars of French Decolonization*, p. 126; Moreman, *Army in India*, pp. 160–166.

128. Lemke, 'Kolonialgeschichte als Vorläufer?', p. 293f.

129. James, *Savage Wars*, p. 124.

130. Hack, 'Imperialism in Southeast Asia', p. 241. The construction of a road had a similarly decisive effect in helping overthrow the Yaqui Republic in Mexico in 1886. Vandervort, *Indian Wars*, p. 233f.

131. Khodarkovsky, 'Krieg und Frieden', p. 216.

132. Walter, 'Kolonialkrieg, Globalstrategie und Kalter Krieg', p. 131.

133. Kelly, *Warless Societies*, p. 84.

134. Jones, *Counterinsurgency and the SAS*, pp. 126, 129.

135. Griffith, *Forward into Battle*, p. 111f.

136. Gerlach, *Extremely Violent Societies*, p. 186; Klose, *Menschenrechte im Schatten kolonialer Gewalt*, p. 186f.

137. Lee, 'Projecting Power', p. 11.

138. Butlin, *Geographies of Empire*, pp. 471–489.

139. Headrick, *Tools of Empire*, p. 182f.; Utley, *Frontier Regulars*, p. 93f.

140. Hull, *Absolute Destruction*, pp. 22, 33–42; Kuß, *Deutsches Militär*, pp. 82f., 85.

141. Potempa, 'Raum und seine Beherrschung', p. 455.

142. James, *Savage Wars*, p. 94f., 100–103; Robson, *Fuzzy-Wuzzy*, pp. 90–94; Williams, 'Egyptian Campaign', p. 251.

143. Vandervort, *Indian Wars*, p. 241.

144. Utley, *Frontiersmen in Blue*, pp. 272, 275.

145. Headrick, *Tools of Empire*, pp. 74–76; James, *Savage Wars*, p. 91f.

146. Miège, 'Conquest of Morocco', p. 207; Moreman, *Army in India*, p. 141.

147. Cann, *Counterinsurgency in Africa*, pp. 174–177.

148. Gann/Duignan, *Rulers of British Africa*, p. 77.

149. Ward, '"European Method of Warring"', p. 257.

150. Corum/Johnson, *Airpower in Small Wars*, p. 171f.

151. Isby, *War in a Distant Country*, pp. 59–66.

152. Cann, *Counterinsurgency in Africa*, pp. 129–134.

153. Fall, *Hell in a Very Small Place*, pp. 185, 243–249.

154. Woolman, *Rebels in the Rif*, p. 178.

155. Vandervort, *Wars of Imperial Conquest*, p. 117.

156. Clausewitz, *On War*, ed. and transl. by Michael Eliot Howard and Peter Paret p. 586 (Book 8, chapter 3.B).

157. Keeley, *War Before Civilization*, p. 48.

158. A short exposition on the character and ambivalence of Japanese imperialism can be found in Hée, *Imperiales Wissen*, pp. 29–39.

159. Osterhammel, 'Entdeckung und Eroberung', p. 414.

160. Michels, '"Ostasiatisches Expeditionskorps"', p. 401.

161. Kiernan, *Colonial Empires*, p. 205.

162. Hassig, 'Aztec and Spanish Conquest', pp. 85–90; Hemming, *Conquest of the Incas*, p. 52f.; Reinhard, *Geschichte der europäischen Expansion*, Vol. 2, pp. 22–31.

163. Jones, *Conquest of the Last Maya Kingdom*, pp. 60–107.

164. Kanya-Forstner, 'Mali—Tukulor', p. 53.

165. Vandervort, *Wars of Imperial Conquest*, p. 166f.

166. Marx, *Geschichte Afrikas*, pp. 60–66; Muffett, 'Nigeria—Sokoto Caliphate', pp. 270–272; Person, 'Guinea', pp. 113–121; Vandervort, *Wars of Imperial Conquest*, pp. 16–18, 74–79, 194f.

167. Kanya-Forstner, 'Mali—Tukulor', p. 75f.; Vandervort, *Wars of Imperial Conquest*, p. 78f.

168. Barua, 'Military Developments in India', pp. 600–613.

169. Reid, *Europe and Southeast Asia*, p. 6.

170. Keegan, 'Ashanti Campaign', p. 167f.; Law, 'Warfare on the Slave Coast', pp. 121–125; Ross, 'Dahomey', pp. 144–146; Vandervort, *Wars of Imperial Conquest*, pp. 14–16.

171. Knight, *Anatomy of the Zulu Army*, pp. 46–88.

172. Arnold, 'Schlacht bei Rugaro', pp. 97, 105f.; Bührer, 'Hehe und Schutztruppe', pp. 217–222, 268–270; Fage/Tordoff, *History of Africa*, pp. 311–322.

173. The Islamic kingdoms of North Africa may be cited as examples of this kind of traditional monarchical state. Cf. Abun-Nasr, 'Staat im Maghrib', pp. 190–196.

174. Ricklefs, *War, Culture and Economy*, pp. 2–13.

175. Bührer, *Kaiserliche Schutztruppe*, pp. 212–216; Ikime, 'Nigeria—Ebrohimi', pp. 205–211; Law, 'Warfare on the Slave Coast', pp. 105–107.

176. Vandervort, *Wars of Imperial Conquest*, pp. 140–144.

177. Dahlmann, 'Sibirien', pp. 58–64; Hemming, *Amazon Frontier*, p. 10; Lincoln, *Conquest of a Continent*, pp. 45–56; Palmer, *Colonial Genocide*, p. 129; Utley, *Frontiersmen in Blue*, pp. 92–96.

178. Abler, 'Beavers and Muskets', pp. 152–154; Belich, *Victorian Interpretation*, p. 21f.; Dunn, *Resistance in the Desert*, pp. 263–271.

179. Sahlins, *Tribesmen*, pp. 5–20.

180. Ferguson/Whitehead, 'Violent Edge of Empire', pp. 13–15; Helbling, *Tribale Kriege*, p. 288f.; Whitehead, 'Tribes Make States', p. 128f.

181. Khodarkovsky, 'Krieg und Frieden', pp. 200–208; Porch, *Conquest of the Sahara*, pp. 65–70.

182. Calloway, *Winter Count*, p. 174f.; Knaut, *Pueblo Revolt*; Weber, *Spanish Frontier*, p. 134.

183. Starkey, *European and Native American Warfare*, pp. 156–159; Vandervort, *Indian Wars*, p. 68.

184. Ranger, 'African Reactions', pp. 312–318. For further examples of transethnic alliances, see: Belich, *Victorian Interpretation*, pp. 89–91; Billington, *Westward Expansion*, p. 143f.; Knaap, 'Crisis and Failure', pp. 157–161; Powell, *Soldiers, Indians and Silver*, pp. 75–78; Ramsey, '"Something Cloudy in Their Looks"', pp. 44, 70–73; Utley, *Frontier Regulars*, p. 262; Utley, *Frontiersmen in Blue*, pp. 300–310.

185. Vandervort, *Indian Wars*, pp. 157–159.

186. Bodley, *Weg der Zerstörung*, p. 66.

187. Beez, 'Wasser gegen Gewehre'.

188. Maloba, *Mau Mau and Kenya*, pp. 114–133.

189. Bührer, *Kaiserliche Schutztruppe*, pp. 225–235; Calloway, *Winter Count*, p. 186f.

190. Some authors have highlighted the connections between older resistance movements and modern nationalism. It was undoubtedly in empires' interests to brand resistance as atavistic. Ellis, 'Conclusion'; Ranger, '"Primary Resistance" Movements'.

191. Kramer, 'Race-Making and Colonial Violence', pp. 172f., 181f.

192. Frey, *Geschichte des Vietnamkrieges*, pp. 11–16, 72–79.

193. Derradji, *Algerian Guerrilla Campaign*.

194. Woolman, *Rebels in the Rif*, pp. 111, 116f.

195. Andreopoulos, 'National Liberation Movements'; Darwin, 'Geopolitics of Decolonization'; Malinowski, 'Modernisierungskriege', p. 214; McMahon, 'Heiße Kriege', pp. 30–33; Walter, 'Warum Kolonialkrieg?', p. 41f.; Westad, *Global Cold War*, pp. 86–89. Zu Algerien Connelly, 'Cold War and Decolonization'; Klose, *Menschenrechte im Schatten kolonialer Gewalt*, pp. 256–267.

196. Thomas/Moore/Butler, 'Conclusion', pp. 419–421.

197. Beckett, *Modern Insurgencies*, p. 158; Cann, *Counterinsurgency in Africa*, p. 29f.; Clayton, *Wars of French Decolonization*, p. 158; Gates, 'Two American Wars', p. 68; Groen, 'Militant Response', p. 41f.

198. Beckett, *Modern Insurgencies*, pp. 187–189; Linn, *Counterinsurgency in the Philippine War*, pp. 132–138.

199. Clayton, *Wars of French Decolonization*, p. 123f. Barth, '"Partisan" und "Partisanenkrieg"', p. 93; Daase, *Kleine Kriege*, pp. 220–228; Münkler, 'Wandel der Weltordnung', p. 87f.; Walter, 'Kolonialkrieg, Globalstrategie und Kalter Krieg', p. 25.c. Burkhardt, *Dreißigjähriger Krieg*.

200. Clayton, *Wars of French Decolonization*, pp. 52–55; Jones, *Graveyard of Empires*, pp. 210–220; Klose, *Menschenrechte im Schatten kolonialer Gewalt*, pp. 154–158; Kramer, 'Race-Making and Colonial Violence', pp. 177, 196; Linn, *Counterinsurgency in the Philippine War*, pp. 12–16; Selesky, 'Colonial America', p. 75.

201. Vandervort, *Indian Wars*, pp. 230–236.

202. Pennel, *Country with a Government*, pp. 123–151, 234–237; Woolman, *Rebels in the Rif*, pp. 146–149, 157–159.

203. Vandervort, *Wars of Imperial Conquest*, pp. 22–25.

204. Nasson, *South African War*, pp. 61–69.

205. Walter, 'Der nordamerikanische Imperialkrieg'.

206. Bryant, 'Asymmetric Warfare', pp. 444–447, 467; Fynn, 'Ghana—Asante', p. 41f.; Hassig, *Mexico and the Spanish Conquest*, pp. 126–130; Hemming, *Conquest of the*

Incas, pp. 93–97; Kanya-Forstner, 'Mali—Tukulor', pp. 60–68; Keegan, 'Ashanti Campaign', p. 195f.; Marshall, 'Western Arms in Maritime Asia', p. 20f.; Paillard, 'Expedition to Madagascar', p. 182f.; Pietschmann, 'Imperialkriege Spaniens', p. 83f.; Porch, 'Introduction', p. xv; Vandervort, *Wars of Imperial Conquest*, p. 151f.

207. Exceptions such as the Fall of France in 1940 perhaps only serve to prove the general rule. Cf. Bloch, *Étrange Défaite*.

208. Hemming, *Conquest of the Incas*, pp. 48, 66–70; Lee, 'Projecting Power', p. 6f.

209. The classic idealization of the advantages of a state opponent can be found in: Callwell, *Small Wars*, pp. 34–42.

210. Bührer, *Kaiserliche Schutztruppe*, p. 261; Eberspächer, '"Albion zal hier"', p. 189f.; James, *Savage Wars*, pp. 180–183; Kiernan, *Colonial Empires*, pp. 43–46, 53f.; Linn, *Counterinsurgency in the Philippine War*, p. 16f.; Moor, 'Warmakers in the Archipelago', pp. 68–70; Porch, *Conquest of the Sahara*, p. 234; Potempa, 'Raum und seine Beherrschung', pp. 456–458; Raudzens, 'Why Did Amerindian Defences Fail?', p. 347f.; Vandervort, *Indian Wars*, pp. 230–239; Vandervort, *Wars of Imperial Conquest*, p. 131f.

211. Woolman, *Rebels in the Rif*, pp. 21–30, 186–196.

212. One need only compare, say, the centuries-long resistance of the nomadic Apaches with the fate of the Navajo in the same cultural region (the southwestern USA), who were defeated by the Spanish primarily because they had become sedentary and hence vulnerable as a result of having adopted settled farming, livestock herding and textile-making. Calloway, *Winter Count*, p. 198f.

213. Beckett, *Modern Insurgencies*, p. 123; Black, 'European Overseas Expansion', p. 17f.; Crowder, 'Introduction', p. 4f.; Ferguson/Whitehead, 'Violent Edge of Empire', p. 19; Hemming, *Red Gold*, pp. 90–96; Powell, *Soldiers, Indians and Silver*, p. 43f.

214. Porch, *Conquest of the Sahara*, p. xvi.

215. Charney, *Southeast Asian Warfare*, p. 263f.; Cocker, *Rivers of Blood*, p. 144; James, *Savage Wars*, pp. 122–124; Keeley, *War Before Civilization*, pp. 76–78; Wesseling, 'Colonial Wars', p. 3f.

216. Gordon, 'Limited Adoption', p. 244f.; Helbling, 'Tribale Kriege und expandierende Staaten', p. 74.

217. Utley, *Frontiersmen in Blue*, pp. 81–83.

218. Cf. chapter 3, 'Military necessity'.

219. Clausewitz, *Vom Kriege*, pp. 799–806 (Book 6, chapter 26); Goltz, *Volk in Waffen*; Moltke, 'Rede vor dem deutschen Reichstag, 14. Mai 1890', p. 638.

220. Strachan, 'Typology of Transcultural Wars', p. 88f. Also: Hahlweg, *Guerilla*, pp. 218–220; Wesseling, 'Colonial Wars', p. 4f.

221. Helbling, *Tribale Kriege*.

222. Turney-High, *Primitive War*.

223. Lappas, 'Lernen inmitten des Blutvergießens', p. 171; Starkey, *European and Native American Warfare*, pp. 25–30.

224. Hirsch, 'Collision of Military Cultures', p. 1207f.; Karr, '"Why Should You Be So Furious?"', p. 878f. Cf. chapter 3, 'War without rules'.

225. Porter, *Military Orientalism*, p. 30f.

226. Connor, 'Briten und Darug', p. 226f.; Helbling, *Tribale Kriege*, p. 277f., 425;

Khodarkovsky, *Russia's Steppe Frontier*, p. 17; Ricklefs, *War, Culture and Economy*, p. 10; Sahlins, *Tribesmen*, p. 5; Woolman, *Rebels in the Rif*, p. 24–30.

227. Starkey, *European and Native American Warfare*, p. 27f.

228. Bührer, *Kaiserliche Schutztruppe*, pp. 256–258; Keeley, *War Before Civilization*, p. 176; Lappas, 'Lernen inmitten des Blutvergießens', p. 172.

229. Hunt, *Wars of the Iroquois*, p. 97f.; Keeley, *War Before Civilization*, p. 93.

230. Hakami, 'Clash of Structures', p. 163; Hirsch, 'Collision of Military Cultures', p. 1191f.; Keeley, *War Before Civilization*, p. 91f.

231. Helbling, *Tribale Kriege*, pp. 58f., 63; Keeley, *War Before Civilization*, pp. 65–69; Turney-High, *Primitive War*, pp. 113–116.

232. Etwa Porch, 'French Colonial Forces', p. 166.

233. Bryant, 'Asymmetric Warfare', p. 447f.

234. Bührer, 'Hehe und Schutztruppe', p. 275.

235. Hassig, *Aztec Warfare*, p. 101.

236. Wilson, 'European Warfare', p. 187.

237. Knight, *Anatomy of the Zulu Army*, pp. 187–223.

238. The Zulu had an utter dread of close combat against European troops wielding fixed bayonets on their rifles. Knight, *Zulu*, p. 110.

239. Charney, *Southeast Asian Warfare*, pp. 17–22.

240. Hemming, *Red Gold*, p. 388; Reid, *Europe and Southeast Asia*, pp. 1–4.

241. Malone, *Skulking Way of War*, p. 23.

242. Even some non-European peoples with complex state systems and standing armies, such as the Fon in Dahomey, sometimes avoided engaging in set-piece battles. Ross, 'Dahomey', p. 155.

243. For examples of ritualized battles and the avoidance of losses as elements of 'tribal' warfare, see: Belich, 'Krieg und transkulturelles Lernen', p. 242; Connor, 'Briten und Darug', pp. 222–227; Connor, *Australian Frontier Wars*, pp. 1–7; Häußler, 'Asymmetrie tribaler und staatlicher Kriegführung', pp. 181–183; Lee, 'Fortify, Fight, or Flee', pp. 719–724; Meuwese, 'Ethnic Soldiering', p. 194f.; Morris, *Washing of the Spears*, pp. 37–39; Starkey, *European and Native American Warfare*, pp. 17–19; Whitehead, 'Tribes Make States', p. 142f.

244. Laqueur, *Guerrilla Warfare*, p. 75.

245. Bührer, *Kaiserliche Schutztruppe*, p. 261; Donnelly, *Conquest of Bashkiria*, p. 26f.; Fourniau, 'Colonial Wars before 1914', p. 82f.; Hemming, *Amazon Frontier*, pp. 20–22, 83–88; Hemming, *Red Gold*, pp. 90–96; Hull, *Absolute Destruction*, p. 67; Kuß, *Deutsches Militär*, p. 84f.; Lemke, 'Kolonialgeschichte als Vorläufer?', p. 290f.; Moor, 'Warmakers in the Archipelago', p. 66; Palmer, *Colonial Genocide*, pp. 125–132; Penn, *Forgotten Frontier*, pp. 123f., 131; Porch, *Conquest of Morocco*, p. 169f.; Powell, *Soldiers, Indians and Silver*, p. 32f.; Slatta, '"Civilization" Battles "Barbarism"', p. 134, 144; Starkey, *European and Native American Warfare*, pp. 83–91, 97–101; Utley, *Frontiersmen in Blue*, p. 142f.; Vandervort, *Indian Wars*, p. 152; Whitehead, 'Tribes Make States', pp. 144, 148.

246. This is why I doubt that 'coloured and underdeveloped peoples' first had to learn guerrilla warfare from the 'whites', as Werner Hahlweg postulates. Hahlweg, *Guerilla*, p. 149f.

247. Nasson, *South African War*, p. 200f.

248. Linn, *Counterinsurgency in the Philippine War*, pp. 100, 138f.

249. Woolman, *Rebels in the Rif*, pp. 74–83, 155.

250. Beckett, *Modern Insurgencies*, pp. 124–127, 187–190; Cann, *Counterinsurgency in Africa*, pp. 80, 190; Clayton, *Wars of French Decolonization*, pp. 48–54; Furedi, 'Kenya', p. 151.

251. Grau, *Bear Over the Mountain*, pp. 200–204; Jones, *Graveyard of Empires*, p. 34.

252. Connell, *Son of the Morning Star*, p. 149.

253. Häußler, 'Asymmetrie tribaler und staatlicher Kriegführung', p. 194f.; Hirsch, 'Collision of Military Cultures', p. 1208; Hull, *Absolute Destruction*, p. 10f.; Karr, '"Why Should You Be So Furious?"', p. 878f.; Kiernan, *Colonial Empires*, p. 39; Klein, 'Straffeldzug im Namen der Zivilisation', p. 170; Rickey, *Forty Miles a Day*, p. 283; Schmidl, 'Kolonialkriege', p. 117.

254. Laqueur, *Guerrilla Warfare*, p. 3.

255. Helbling, *Tribale Kriege*, p. 67.

256. In particular among the North American Indians: Hirsch, 'Collision of Military Cultures', p. 1203; Steele, *Betrayals*, p. 90; Utley, *Frontiersmen in Blue*, pp. 320–322.

257. Lee, 'Fortify, Fight, or Flee', p. 722.

258. Guilmartin, 'Ideology and Conflict', p. 1f.

259. Fynn, 'Ghana—Asante', p. 38; Gordon, 'Limited Adoption', p. 232f.; Khodarkovsky, *Russia's Steppe Frontier*, pp. 17, 19; Lappas, 'Lernen inmitten des Blutvergießens', p. 168f.; Ross, 'Dahomey', p. 153; Thornton, 'Firearms, Diplomacy, and Conquest', p. 172; Thornton, 'Art of War in Angola', pp. 90–92; Utley, 'Cultural Clash', pp. 94–96; Vandervort, *Indian Wars*, p. 49; Vandervort, *Wars of Imperial Conquest*, pp. 9f., 22–25, 131f.

260. Ferguson/Whitehead, 'Violent Edge of Empire', p. 19.

261. Fynn, 'Ghana—Asante', p. 38; Gordon, 'Limited Adoption', p. 232f.; Khodarkovsky, *Russia's Steppe Frontier*, pp. 17, 19; Lappas, 'Lernen inmitten des Blutvergießens', p. 168f.; Ross, 'Dahomey', p. 153; Thornton, 'Firearms, Diplomacy, and Conquest', p. 172; Thornton, 'Art of War in Angola', pp. 90–92; Utley, 'Cultural Clash', pp. 94–96; Vandervort, *Indian Wars*, p. 49; Vandervort, *Wars of Imperial Conquest*, pp. 9f., 22–25, 131f.

262. Guilmartin, 'Light Troops in Classical Armies', p. 26.

263. Keeley, *War Before Civilization*, p. 55.

264. Füssel, 'Händler, Söldner und Sepoys', p. 310f.; Macrory, *Signal Catastrophe*, p. 141f.; Selby, 'Third China War', pp. 83f., 88; Utley, *Frontiersmen in Blue*, p. 7f.; Vandervort, *Indian Wars*, p. 6f.

265. Knight, *Anatomy of the Zulu Army*, pp. 178–181, 212f.; Lock/Quantrill, *Zulu Victory*, pp. 61–64.

266. Hassig, 'Aztec and Spanish Conquest', p. 85.

267. Bryant, 'Asymmetric Warfare', p. 462f.

268. Charney, *Southeast Asian Warfare*.

269. Porch, *Conquest of Morocco*, p. 99f.

270. Bryant, 'Asymmetric Warfare', pp. 456–458; Pemble, 'Resources and Techniques', pp. 290–292.

271. Thornton, 'Firearms, Diplomacy, and Conquest', p. 171f.

272. Guilmartin, 'Cutting Edge', p. 48.

273. See chapter 4.

274. Fall, *Hell in a Very Small Place*, pp. 125–134, 451–453.

275. Belich, *Victorian Interpretation*, p. 22; Crowder, 'Introduction', p. 16; Keeley, *War Before Civilization*, p. 75; Lee, 'Fortify, Fight, or Flee', p. 767; Palmer, *Colonial Genocide*, p. 129; Raudzens, 'Why Did Amerindian Defences Fail?', pp. 331f., 342–344.

276. Black, *European Warfare 1660–1815*, p. 236; Childs, *Armies and Warfare*, pp. 5–20; Duffy, 'Introduction'; Gat, *War in Human Civilization*, pp. 449–511; Jones, 'Military Revolution'; Kennedy, *Rise and Fall*, pp. 76–86; Parker, *Military Revolution*, pp. 45–79; Reinhard, *Geschichte des modernen Staates*, pp. 70f., 76–82, 97–103; Roberts, *Military Revolution*, p. 21f.

277. Cooper, 'Culture, Combat, and Colonialism', p. 542; Crowder, 'Introduction', p. 16; Parker, 'Introduction', pp. 6–8; Peers, 'Introduction', p. xxixf.; Strachan, 'Typology of Transcultural Wars', p. 93; Vandervort, *Indian Wars*, pp. 12–14.

278. Ferguson/Whitehead, 'Violent Edge of Empire', p. 19.

279. Moor, 'Warmakers in the Archipelago', p. 54. Similarly Knaap, 'Crisis and Failure'; Mostert, *Military System*, p. 122.

280. Bergmann, 'Dynamik der Conquista', pp. 216–221, 226. A less dramatic, though presumably just as decisive, reason behind the early advances made by the Boer commandos against the Khoikhoi of South Africa was the Boers' access to the farming resources of the Cape Colony. Penn, *Forgotten Frontier*, pp. 108–112.

281. Bryant, 'Asymmetric Warfare', p. 432f.

282. Barua, 'Military Developments in India', p. 613, 616; Bryant, 'Asymmetric Warfare', p. 468f.; Marshall, 'Western Arms in Maritime Asia', p. 27f.

283. Hack/Rettig, 'Demography in Southeast Asia', pp. 62, 240–246.

284. Hemming, *Conquest of the Incas*, pp. 203, 212f.

285. Robson, *Fuzzy-Wuzzy*, pp. xvif., 184f.

286. Walter, 'Asymmetrien in Imperialkriegen'.

287. Cipolla, *Guns, Sails, and Empires*; Clayton, 'Iberian Advantage'; McNeill, *Age of Gunpowder Empires*.

288. Khodarkovsky, *Russia's Steppe Frontier*.

289. Knaut, *Pueblo Revolt*, pp. 3–15.

290. Lenman, *England's Colonial Wars*, pp. 231f., 249.

291. Ramsey, '"Something Cloudy in Their Looks"', p. 44.

292. Silver, *Our Savage Neighbors*, p. 69; Ward, '"European Method of Warring"', p. 247f.

293. Meuwese, 'Ethnic Soldiering', p. 215.

294. Hassig, *Mexico and the Spanish Conquest*, pp. 63f., 77; Restall, *Myths of the Spanish Conquest*, p. 144.

295. Barkawi, 'Pedagogy of "Small Wars"', p. 25.

296. Cf. chapter 4, 'Armed forces' and 'Technology'.

297. Bryant, 'Asymmetric Warfare', p. 445.

298. Dahlmann, 'Sibirien', p. 70.

299. Cooper, 'Culture, Combat, and Colonialism', p. 542.

300. Crawford, 'Sikh Wars', pp. 49–65. The same thing happened to Madagascar in 895–1896, except without the need for a second war. Paillard, 'Expedition to Madagascar', pp. 186–188.

301. Moor, 'Warmakers in the Archipelago', p. 50.

302. Charney, *Southeast Asian Warfare*, p. 257f.
303. Vandervort, *Wars of Imperial Conquest*, p. 134f.
304. Bond, 'South African War', pp. 212, 217, 221, 234–236.
305. Slatta, '"Civilization" Battles "Barbarism"', p. 130.
306. Brooks, 'Impact of Disease', p. 128.
307. Billington, *Westward Expansion*, pp. 15–28
308. For example the four Mysore Wars 1766–1769, 1780–1784, 1789–1792 and 1799, three Burma Wars 1823–1826, 1852–1853 and 1885, four Ashanti Wars 1823–1831, 1863/64, 1873/74 and 1894–1896, and three Afghanistan Wars 1838–1842, 1878–1880 and 1919. Bruce, *Burma Wars*; Förster, *Mächtige Diener*, pp. 50–166; Fynn, 'Ghana—Asante'; Richards, *The Savage Frontier*.
309. Reid, *Europe and Southeast Asia*, p. 5.
310. Helbling, 'Tribale Kriege und expandierende Staaten', p. 70.
311. Kanya-Forstner, 'French Marines', p. 137.
312. Marshall, 'Western Arms in Maritime Asia', p. 13. Cf. Bitterli, *Die "Wilden" und die "Zivilisierten"*, p. 175; Laqueur, *Guerrilla Warfare*, p. 392. An updated new formulation of this same argument can be found in Merom, *How Democracies Lose Small Wars*, pp. 15, 230.
313. Whitehead, 'Tribes Make States', p. 136.
314. Burroughs, 'Imperial Institutions', p. 176f.
315. Bond, 'Editor's Introduction', p. 20.
316. Galbraith, '"Turbulent Frontier"', p. 151.
317. Belich, *Victorian Interpretation*, p. 123; Fieldhouse, *Economics and Empire*, p. 80f.; Förster, *Mächtige Diener*; Galbraith, '"Turbulent Frontier"'; Killingray, 'Guardians of Empire', p. 9; Trotha, 'Was war Kolonialismus?', p. 63f.; Zirkel, 'Military Power', p. 93. 'Men on the spot' also existed in ancient Rome: Eichmann, 'Expansion und imperiale Herrschaft', pp. 97–101.
318. Hull, 'Military Culture and "Final Solutions"', p. 143.
319. Kanya-Forstner, 'French Marines', p. 121f.; Brower, *Desert Named Peace*, p. 39.
320. Porch, *Conquest of the Sahara*, p. 134. The expression 'fit of an absence of mind' was coined by Seeley, *Expansion of England*, p. 17.
321. Kanya-Forstner, *Conquest of the Sudan*, pp. 176–178.
322. Porch, *Conquest of the Sahara*, p. 261.
323. James, *Raj*, p. 105f. The recapture of Lucknow during the Indian Rebellion of 1857 is likewise rumoured to have given rise to Sir Colin Campbell's (probably equally apocryphal) message: 'Nunc fortunatus sum' ('I am in luck now').
324. Hemming, *Conquest of the Incas*, p. 149; Lee, 'Projecting Power', p. 5; Pietschmann, 'Imperialkriege Spaniens', pp. 89–91.
325. Hassig, *Mexico and the Spanish Conquest*, pp. 68–70.
326. See the later section 'Grey areas'.
327. Eichmann, '"Freibeuter der Moderne"', p. 107, argues very plausibly that it was precisely the fringes of empire that attracted such headstrong, nonconformist adventurers and provided them with a field of operation.
328. James, *Savage Wars*, p. 55f.; Lock/Quantrill, *Zulu Victory*, pp. 19–27, 31–35; Utley, *Frontiersmen in Blue*, p. 284f.
329. Thornton, 'Firearms, Diplomacy, and Conquest', p. 180.
330. Lincoln, *Conquest of a Continent*, p. 42.

331. Förster, *Mächtige Diener*.

332. Eskildsen, 'Civilization and Savages', pp. 388, 403f.; Fynn, 'Ghana—Asante', pp. 20–24; Moor, 'Warmakers in the Archipelago', p. 61; Muffett, 'Nigeria—Sokoto Caliphate', p. 290f.; Vandervort, *Wars of Imperial Conquest*, pp. 191–195; Woolman, *Rebels in the Rif*, p. 58, 65, 72; Zirkel, 'Military Power', pp. 92–97.

333. Howard, 'Colonial Wars', pp. 219–221.

334. On settlers in general, but especially on their exterminatory ideology, see Veracini, *Settler Colonialism*.

335. Bodley, *Weg der Zerstörung*, p. 69f.; Connor, *Australian Frontier Wars*, pp. 103–105; Elkins/Pedersen, 'Settler Colonialism', p. 2; Finzsch, '"The Aborigines ... were never annihilated"', p. 254; Hemming, *Red Gold*, pp. 34–40; Penn, *Forgotten Frontier*, pp. 27–55.

336. Palmer, *Colonial Genocide*, pp. 5–10; Utley, *Frontiersmen in Blue*, pp. 100–102.

337. Cocker, *Rivers of Blood*, pp. 144–157; Häußler, 'Settlers in South West Africa', p. 7; Helbling, *Tribale Kriege*, p. 287; Hemming, *Red Gold*, pp. 69–89, 346–358; Lonsdale, 'Conquest State of Kenya', p. 115; Moses, *Genocide and Settler Society*, p. 33; Powell, *Soldiers, Indians and Silver*, pp. 172–176; Utley, *Frontiersmen in Blue*, pp. 346–349.

338. Porter, *Lion's Share*, p. 34f.

339. On the motives of the combatants in wars of empire, see chapter 2.

340. Fourniau, 'Colonial Wars before 1914', p. 78; Headrick, *Tools of Empire*, p. 84; Jones, 'Muscovite-Nomad Relations', p. 119; Osterhammel, *Verwandlung der Welt*, p. 608; Porch, *French Foreign Legion*, p. xviiif.; Vandervort, *Wars of Imperial Conquest*, p. 38f.; Wesseling, 'Colonial Wars', p. 5f.

341. Cf. chapter 2, 'Regime change'.

342. Fieldhouse, *Economics and Empire*, p. 79f.; Fieldhouse, *Colonial Empires*, pp. 207–241, 380–394; Gallagher/Robinson, 'Imperialism of Free Trade'; Osterhammel, *Verwandlung der Welt*, p. 655; Reinhard, *Geschichte der europäischen Expansion*, Vol. 4, p. 208; Robinson, 'Excentric Idea of Imperialism', p. 270f.

343. Marshall, 'Western Arms in Maritime Asia', p. 23f.; Meuwese, 'Ethnic Soldiering', p. 211; Mostert, *Military System*, p. 10f.; Reinhard, *Geschichte der europäischen Expansion*, Vol. 1, p. 214f.

344. Clayton, *France, Soldiers and Africa*, p. 4; Etemad, *Possession du monde*, p. 79f.; Killingray, 'Guardians of Empire', p. 6; Ranger, 'African Reactions', pp. 293–297; Wesseling, 'Colonial Wars', p. 7f.

345. Bührer, *Kaiserliche Schutztruppe*, p. 126; Cann, *Counterinsurgency in Africa*, p. 87; Fourniau, 'Colonial Wars before 1914', p. 78; Gann/Duignan, *Rulers of Belgian Africa*, p. 63.

346. Powell, *Soldiers, Indians and Silver*, p. 32.

347. Calloway, *Winter Count*, p. 163; Kennedy, *Rise and Fall*, pp. 41–55.

348. Cann, *Counterinsurgency in Africa*, pp. 1–10. Portugal's military budget sometimes reached 48 per cent of its GDP, a larger allocation than that of the USA. Ibid., p. 10.

349. Starkey, *European and Native American Warfare*, p. 141f.; Utley, *Frontiersmen in Blue*, pp. 12–17; Weigley, *History of the United States Army*, pp. 74–292.

350. Cipolla, *Guns, Sails, and Empires*, p. 134; Glete, 'Warfare at Sea', p. 32f.; Marshall, 'Western Arms in Maritime Asia', p. 16. At the start of the nineteenth century,

even for the short sea passage to the Caribbean, losses of 10 per cent as a result of epidemics were quite normal. In 1702, 80 per cent of the 5,000 soldiers died on a troop transport sailing in the opposite direction. Buckley, *Slaves in Red Coats*, pp. 4, 99.

351. Thornton, 'Warfare, Slave Trading and European Influence', p. 135f.

352. Hack/Rettig, 'Demography in Southeast Asia', p. 48.

353. Bond, 'Editor's Introduction', p. 20.

354. Ditte, *Guerre dans les Colonies*, p. 12f.; Potempa, 'Raum und seine Beherrschung', pp. 454–456.

355. Chandler, 'Expedition to Abyssinia', p. 124f.

356. Walter, *Dschungelkrieg und Atombombe*, pp. 125–127.

357. Eder/Hofbauer, 'Operation Iraqi Freedom', pp. 478f., 481f.

358. Marshall, *Russian General Staff*, pp. 46f., 76, 81, 131f.

359. Hack/Rettig, 'Demography in Southeast Asia', pp. 55–59. A number of similar ratios are given there for other Southeast Asian colonies—universally, for every one soldier there were around 1,000 indigenous inhabitants. See also Taylor, 'Colonial Forces in British Burma', p. 197.

360. Gann/Duignan, *Rulers of British Africa*, p. 84f.

361. Vandervort, *Wars of Imperial Conquest*, p. 190. On Southern Rhodesia, see Gann/Duignan, *Rulers of British Africa*, p. 127.

362. Vandervort, *Wars of Imperial Conquest*, p. 42.

363. Trotha, *Koloniale Herrschaft*, p. 41.

364. Gann/Duignan, *Rulers of German Africa*, pp. 115–118.

365. Utley, *Frontiersmen in Blue*, p. 16.

366. Utley, *Frontier Regulars*, p. 174.

367. Vandervort, *Indian Wars*, p. 204f.

368. Cann, *Counterinsurgency in Africa*, p. 62. Other examples: Coates, *Suppressing Insurgency*, p. 150; Linn, *Counterinsurgency in the Philippine War*, pp. 52f., 98–106; Petillo, 'Leaders and Followers', pp. 194–198.

369. Meinertzhagen, *Kenya Diary*, p. 32.

370. Not five times the size, as stated in Grau, *Bear Over the Mountain*, p. xii.

371. Jones, *Graveyard of Empires*, p. 34f.

372. Grau, *Bear Over the Mountain*, pp. xi–xiii.

373. Jones, *Graveyard of Empires*, pp. 238–255.

374. Peers, 'Revolution, Evolution, or Devolution', p. 83.

375. Mostert, *Military System*, p. 19.

376. Crowder, 'Introduction', p. 6. Many similar such statistics are also given here.

377. Vandervort, *Wars of Imperial Conquest*, p. 142.

378. Gann/Duignan, *Rulers of British Africa*, p. 123f.

379. Osterhammel, 'Entdeckung und Eroberung', p. 403.

380. Jobst, 'Expansion des Zarenreiches', p. 67f.

381. Brooks, 'Impact of Disease', p. 128.

382. Charney, 'Iberier und Südostasiaten', p. 180.

383. Kuß, *Deutsches Militär*, pp. 53, 59, 82, 107–113.

384. Groen, 'Militant Response', p. 35.

385. Deenon, 'Understanding Settler Societies', p. 512.

386. Crosby, *Ecological Imperialism*, pp. 196–216, 281–287.

387. Brooks, 'Impact of Disease', pp. 136–159; Newson, 'Pathogens, Places and Peoples'.

388. Raudzens, 'Outfighting or Outpopulating?', pp. 47–50; Starkey, *European and Native American Warfare*, p. 7. Elsewhere pathogens had a clear negative impact on indigenous societies' ability to resist, for example by fatally weakening the Aztec elite and, even before the arrival of the Spanish in Peru, through the untimely death there by disease of the Inca ruler Huayna Capac, both of which sparked civil wars in the respective empires. Hassig, *Mexico and the Spanish Conquest*, p. 124f.; Restall, *Myths of the Spanish Conquest*, p. 140f.

389. Raudzens, 'Outfighting or Outpopulating?', pp. 36–56.

390. Raudzens, 'Why Did Amerindian Defences Fail?', p. 346.

391. Starkey, *European and Native American Warfare*, p. 68.

392. Ibid., p. 63f.

393. Nester, *Frontier War*, p. 13.

394. Wood, *The American Revolution*, p. 4.

395. Kennedy, *Population of the United States in 1860*, p. 598; Utley, *Frontiersmen in Blue*, p. 4.

396. Cocker, *Rivers of Blood*, pp. 144–157.

397. Bodley, *Weg der Zerstörung*, p. 70f.

398. Belich, 'Krieg und transkulturelles Lernen', p. 248.

399. Raudzens, 'Outfighting or Outpopulating?'.

400. Utley, 'Cultural Clash', p. 103f.; Utley, *Frontier Regulars*, pp. 409–411.

401. Hassig, *Mexico and the Spanish Conquest*, pp. 184–193; Knaut, *Pueblo Revolt*, p. 186f.; Raudzens, 'Why Did Amerindian Defences Fail?', p. 345f.

402. Hemming, *Amazon Frontier*, pp. 6f., 283, 286; Hemming, *Conquest of the Incas*, pp. 335–338; Whitehead, 'Tribes Make States', pp. 140–142.

403. Penn, *Forgotten Frontier*, p. 286f.

404. Broome, *Aboriginal Australians*, p. 48; Connor, 'Briten und Darug', p. 232f.; Palmer, *Colonial Genocide*, pp. 87–101.

405. Khodarkovsky, *Russia's Steppe Frontier*, p. 221f.

406. Rink, 'Kleiner Krieg', p. 438.

407. Stora, 'Pieds Noirs', p. 226.

408. Le Cour Grandmaison, *Coloniser, Exterminer*, p. 188.

409. Clayton, *Wars of French Decolonization*, p. 108.

410. Ibid., pp. 108–112.

411. Elkins/Pedersen, 'Settler Colonialism', p. 3f.

412. Delmas/Masson, 'Interventions Extérieures', p. 524; Vandervort, *Wars of Imperial Conquest*, p. 62.

413. Jobst, 'Expansion des Zarenreiches', pp. 68–70; Laqueur, *Guerrilla Warfare*, pp. 73–75.

414. Stucki, *Aufstand und Zwangsumsiedlung*, pp. 122, 240.

415. Nasson, *South African War*, pp. 68, 279.

416. Woolman, *Rebels in the Rif*, pp. 105, 204. However, the fact that Spain had a standing army of 150,000 men in Morocco during the Second World War was prompted by foreign policy considerations that had nothing to do with maintaining control over the protectorate. Fleming, 'Decolonization and the Spanish Army', p. 123f.

417. Brogini-Künzi, 'Wunsch nach einem blitzschnellen Krieg', p. 276f.
418. Thompson, *Defeating Communist Insurgency*, p. 47f.
419. Bodin, 'Adaptation des hommes', p. 114f.
420. Mollenhauer, 'Gesichter der pacification', p. 337.
421. Greiner, *Krieg ohne Fronten*, p. 53.
422. Cann, *Counterinsurgency in Africa*, pp. 5–8. In Portuguese Guinea it was 43,000 soldiers against 7,000 insurgents. MacQueen, 'Portugal's First Domino', p. 226.
423. Moreman, '"Watch and Ward"', p. 150.
424. Jacobson, 'Imperial Ambitions', pp. 87–91; McCoy/Fradera/Jacobson, *Endless Empire*, p. 18f.
425. This was the case in Cuba, despite the geographical distance. Stucki, 'Weylers Söldner', p. 223.
426. Robinson/Gallagher/Denny, *Africa and the Victorians*, pp. 410–472.
427. Greiner, *Krieg ohne Fronten*, pp. 56–73; Nissimi, 'Illusions of World Power'; Stockwell, '"A widespread and long-concocted plot"'; Walter, 'Kolonialkrieg, Globalstrategie und Kalter Krieg', pp. 133–137; Westad, *Global Cold War*, p. 180.
428. For examples, see Boot, *Savage Wars of Peace*; Clayton, *Wars of French Decolonization*, pp. 33–38, 79–85, 88–104; Dewey, *Brush Fire Wars*.
429. Lee, 'Fortify, Fight, or Flee', p. 770. Other examples: Fynn, 'Ghana—Asante', p. 41f.; Linn, *Counterinsurgency in the Philippine War*, p. 106; Nasson, *South African War*, p. 171f.; Starkey, *European and Native American Warfare*, p. 152; Utley, *Frontier Regulars*, p. 93f.; Wickwire/Wickwire, *Cornwallis*, pp. 169–321.
430. Bond, 'Editor's Introduction', p. 21
431. Callwell, *Small Wars*, p. 117f.; Chandler, 'Expedition to Abyssinia', p. 129; James, *Raj*, p. 120f.; Strachan, *European Armies*, p. 81f.; Vandervort, *Wars of Imperial Conquest*, p. 120f.
432. Belich, *Victorian Interpretation*, p. 162; Fynn, 'Ghana—Asante', p. 41f.; Hemming, *Conquest of the Incas*, p. 93; James, *Savage Wars*, p. 91f.; Kopperman, *Braddock at the Monongahela*, pp. 9–13; Paillard, 'Expedition to Madagascar', p. 181; Utley, *Frontiersmen in Blue*, pp. 205f., 272.
433. Belich, *Victorian Interpretation*, pp. 162–165; Fynn, 'Ghana—Asante', pp. 31f., 38f.; Grau, *Bear Over the Mountain*, p. 204; Utley, *Frontier Regulars*, pp. 50f., 253f.; Utley, *Frontiersmen in Blue*, pp. 139f., 242, 254, 270–272, 323–332.
434. Porch, *Conquest of Morocco*, p. 171.
435. Kuß, *Deutsches Militär*, pp. 88–90.
436. Callwell, *Small Wars*, p. 108.
437. Bryant, 'Asymmetric Warfare', p. 458; James, *Savage Wars*, p. 152; Porch, *Conquest of the Sahara*, pp. 265–267; Utley, *Frontiersmen in Blue*, pp. 324–326.
438. Lock/Quantrill, *Zulu Victory*, pp. 86–90, 147–149, 176–179.
439. Utley, *Custer*, pp. 156–162.
440. Beckett, *Modern Insurgencies*, pp. 114–116; Black, *Beyond the Military Revolution*, p. 111f.; Bodley, *Weg der Zerstörung*, pp. 69f., 78–80; Callwell, *Small Wars*, p. 134f.; Charney, *Southeast Asian Warfare*, pp. 271–273; Clayton, *Wars of French Decolonization*, pp. 56f., 61, 135f.; Dahlmann, 'Sibirien', p. 60; Donnelly, *Conquest of Bashkiria*, pp. 16, 49–53, 161–172; Hemming, *Amazon Frontier*, pp. 97f., 179f.; Khodarkovsky, *Russia's Steppe Frontier*, pp. 131f., 215–220; Moor, 'War-makers in the Archipelago', p. 51f.; Powell, *Soldiers, Indians and Silver*, pp. 141–157; Ricklefs,

War, Culture and Economy, p. 146; Schindler, *Bauern und Reiterkrieger*, pp. 30–35; Slatta, '"Civilization" Battles "Barbarism"', p. 132f.; Star-key, *European and Native American Warfare*, p. 41; Utley, *Frontier Regulars*, pp. 121–125, 281, 288; Utley, *Frontiersmen in Blue*, pp. 248–258, 274f.; Vandervort, *Wars of Imperial Conquest*, p. 120f.; Woolman, *Rebels in the Rif*, p. 141.

441. Nasson, *South African War*, p. 210f.; Rose, '"Unsichtbare Feinde"', p. 233f. In the 1900s, Japan employed a similar system on Taiwan. Bodley, *Weg der Zerstörung*, pp. 78–80.

442. Clayton, *Wars of French Decolonization*, p. 135; Horne, *Savage War of Peace*, pp. 263–267.

443. Mattioli, 'Kolonialverbrechen des faschistischen Italien', p. 219f. The American equivalent was the McNamara Line along the demilitarized zone (DMZ) in North Vietnam. Beckett, *Modern Insurgencies*, p. 193. In the wars between 1868 and 1898 Cuba was divided on several occasions by North–South fortified military lines known as *trochas*, which were intended to facilitate Spanish efforts to quell uprisings. Stucki, *Aufstand und Zwangsumsiedlung*, pp. 41–43.

444. Connor, *Australian Frontier Wars*, p. 46f.; Utley, 'Cultural Clash', p. 92f.; Utley, *Frontiersmen in Blue*, pp. 42f., 53–57, 71–74, 86–88, 346–349; Vandervort, *Indian Wars*, p. 51f.

445. Stokes, *Peasant Armed*, pp. 17–48.

446. Stucki, *Aufstand und Zwangsumsiedlung*, p. 80f.

447. Beckett, *Modern Insurgencies*, p. 91.

448. Bodin, 'Adaptation des hommes'.

449. Mollenhauer, 'Gesichter der pacification', p. 337; Thomas, 'Order Before Reform', pp. 204–212.

450. Gwynn, *Imperial Policing*, p. 19.

451. *Field Manual 3–24*, pp. 1–13.

452. Schmidl, 'Kolonialkriege', p. 116f. Hendrik Wesseling, however, takes a diametrically opposed view; he posits precisely the ability to delimit war and peace on the periphery as the basis for any discussion about colonial wars as a distinct phenomenon: Wesseling, 'Colonial Wars', p. 2.

453. Delmas/Masson, 'Interventions Extérieures', p. 529.

454. Brower, *Desert Named Peace*, p. 98.

455. Zahlen: Gann/Duignan, *Rulers of German Africa*, pp. 72, 118; Kirk-Greene, 'Thin White Line', pp. 26, 38. Cf. Burroughs, 'Imperial Institutions', p. 177; Wirz, 'Körper, Kopf und Bauch', pp. 254–256.

456. Bührer, *Kaiserliche Schutztruppe*, pp. 211, 485; Fleming, 'Decolonization and the Spanish Army'; Gallieni, *Pacification de Madagascar*; Gann/Duignan, *Rulers of Belgian Africa*, pp. 65–69, 79, 82; Hée, *Imperiales Wissen*, p. 46f.; Killingray, 'Guardians of Empire', pp. 11–13; Omissi, *Sepoy and the Raj*, pp. 197–199; Zirkel, 'Military Power', pp. 97–107; Zollmann, *Koloniale Herrschaft*, pp. 183–199.

457. Gwynn, *Imperial Policing*; Hull, *Absolute Destruction*, pp. 330–332; James, *Savage Wars*, p. 131; Le Cour Grandmaison, *Coloniser, Exterminer*, pp. 153–161, 201–262; Mann, 'Gewaltdispositiv des Kolonialismus', p. 116; Mukherjee, *Spectre of Violence*, p. 23f.; Trotha, 'Genozidaler Pazifizierungskrieg', p. 45; Trotha, *Koloniale*

Herrschaft, pp. 81–84, 155f.; Wesseling, 'Colonial Wars', p. 9f.; Zollmann, *Koloniale Herrschaft*, pp. 107–126.

458. Belich, *Victorian Interpretation*, p. 73f.; Broome, *Aboriginal Australians*, pp. 40–48; Cocker, *Rivers of Blood*, pp. 122–150; Connor, *Australian Frontier Wars*, pp. 16f., 35–40, 85–90, 114–117; Hemming, *Amazon Frontier*, pp. 174–181; Hochgeschwender, 'Last Stand', pp. 47–49; Keeley, *War Before Civilization*, pp. 152–156; Penn, *Forgotten Frontier*, pp. 27–66; Silver, *Our Savage Neighbors*, pp. 39–71; Turnbull, *Black War*, pp. 24–30; Utley, *Frontier Regulars*, pp. 174, 185f., 192f.; Utley, *Frontiersmen in Blue*, pp. 97–102, 135–138, 176–178, 227–229.

459. Hemming, *Amazon Frontier*, pp. 25–60, 296–299; Hemming, *Conquest of the Incas*, pp. 349–358; Hemming, *Red Gold*, pp. 146–160, 244–252, 380f., 402–408; Jones, *Conquest of the Last Maya Kingdom*, pp. 256–264; Kars, '"Cleansing the Land"', p. 264f.; Penn, *Forgotten Frontier*, pp. 144–147; Thomas, *Violence and Colonial Order*, pp. 22–25, 41; Trotha, *Koloniale Herrschaft*, pp. 349–365; Weber, *Spanish Frontier*, pp. 123–129.

460. Meissner/Mücke/Weber, *Schwarzes Amerika*.

461. Campbell, 'Social Structure of the Túpac Amaru', p. 213.

462. Calloway, *Winter Count*, pp. 132–149.

463. Hemming, *Red Gold*, pp. 69–89.

464. Lee, 'Fortify, Fight, or Flee', pp. 761–763.

465. Utley, *Frontiersmen in Blue*, pp. 102–121, 143f., 176–178, 238.

466. Denzer, 'Sierra Leone—Bai Bureh', pp. 250–256.

467. Clayton, *Wars of French Decolonization*, pp. 88–90.

468. Omissi, *Sepoy and the Raj*, p. 220.

469. Lonsdale, 'Conquest State of Kenya', p. 103f.

470. Zirkel, 'Military Power', p. 97.

471. Morlang, '"Die Wahehe haben ihre Vernichtung gewollt"', p. 80.

472. Utley, *Frontier Regulars*, p. 410. A very similar figure (943 battles between 1865 and 1898) appears in Weigley, *History of the United States Army*, p. 267. For other such statistics, see Beckett, *Modern Insurgencies*, pp. 31–36.

473. Haywood/Clarke, *History of the Royal West African Frontier Force*, pp. 60–80.

474. Wesseling, 'Wars and Peace', p. 56.

475. Bröchler, '"Was uns das Recht"'; Karr, '"Why Should You Be So Furious?"', pp. 881–888.

476. Calloway, *Winter Count*, p. 120; Hassig, *Mexico and the Spanish Conquest*, p. 60; Parker, 'Early Modern Europe', p. 56.

477. Pagden, *Lords of All the World*, p. 91. In the chaotic situation at Cajamarca, a Spanish priest apparently very hastily proclaimed the *Requerimiento*, before the conquistadors began slaughtering the Peruvian elite. Hemming, *Conquest of the Incas*, p. 42.

478. Calloway, *Winter Count*, pp. 244f., 250. The Portuguese in Africa, the Spanish in the Yucatan and the Russians in Central Asia all behaved in similar fashion: Donnelly, *Conquest of Bashkiria*, p. 19; Jones, *Conquest of the Last Maya Kingdom*, pp. 167–186, 291f.; Thornton, 'Firearms, Diplomacy, and Conquest', p. 178.

479. Connor, 'Briten und Darug', p. 227; Finzsch, '"The Aborigines … were never annihilated"', p. 261f.; Veracini, *Settler Colonialism*, pp. 82–84.

480. See Butlin, *Geographies of Empire*, pp. 335–344; Jureit, *Ordnen von Räumen*, pp. 75–126; and Fieldhouse, *Colonial Empires*, pp. 207–241.

481. Fourniau, 'Colonial Wars before 1914', pp. 73–75; Gann/Duignan, *Rulers of British Africa*, pp. 142–144; Kleinschmidt, *Diskriminierung durch Vertrag und Krieg*, pp. 94–111; Lombardi, *Bürgerkrieg und Völkerrecht*, pp. 86f., 126f., 173–175; Moreman, '"Watch and Ward"', p. 137f.; Paillard, 'Expedition to Madagascar', pp. 168, 171; Starkey, *European and Native American Warfare*, p. 12; Vandervort, *Indian Wars*, p. 49f.; Vandervort, *Wars of Imperial Conquest*, pp. 146–149.

482. Cf. chapter 3, 'War without rules'.

483. Münkler, *Imperien*, p. 16f.; Osterhammel, *Verwandlung der Welt*, p. 607f.

484. Callwell, *Small Wars*, pp. 25–27.

485. Ferguson/Whitehead, 'Violent Edge of Empire', p. 7.

486. Schumacher, '"Niederbrennen, plündern und töten"', p. 113.

487. Klein, 'Straffeldzug im Namen der Zivilisation', p. 169; May, 'Philippine-American War', p. 439; Michels, '"Ostasiatisches Expeditionskorps"', p. 404.

488. 491 Furedi, 'Creating a Breathing Space', p. 94; Klose, 'Legitimation kolonialer Gewalt', pp. 266–269; Klose, 'Notstand'; Mollenhauer, 'Gesichter der pacification', p. 348f.; Palmer, *Colonial Genocide*, pp. 132–134; Walter, 'Kolonialkrieg, Globalstrategie und Kalter Krieg', p. 130.

489. Kleinschmidt, *Diskriminierung durch Vertrag und Krieg*, p. 137. Strictly speaking, in my view the Hague Conventions would allow for the possibility that a non-state combatant might comply with the customs of war and hence be privy to the protection rights of the conventions; however, it is abundantly clear that such observance of the rules on the part of indigenous societies would have been collectively ignored by the Western powers anyway. Cf. chapter 3, 'War without rules'.

490. Andreopoulos, 'National Liberation Movements'.

491. Arai-Takahashi, 'Disentangling Legal Quagmires'; Dörmann, 'Legal Situation'.

492. Utley, *Frontier Regulars*, p. 45.

493. Hochgeschwender, 'Last Stand', p. 60; Utley, *Frontiersmen in Blue*, pp. 110–112, 210. The same clearly applied to the Tuareg and the nomadic peoples of Central Asia. Donnelly, *Conquest of Bashkiria*, p. 11; Porch, *Conquest of the Sahara*, pp. 94–125.

494. Howe, *What Hath God Wrought*, p. 355; Kleinschmidt, *Diskriminierung durch Vertrag und Krieg*, p. 106; Utley, *Indian Frontier*, p. 36.

495. Utley, *Frontier Regulars*, p. 21.

496. Bührer, *Kaiserliche Schutztruppe*, p. 211; Peers, 'Introduction', p. xxif.

497. Calloway, *Winter Count*, pp. 177–185; Powell, *Soldiers, Indians and Silver*, pp. 28f., 32; Vandervort, *Indian Wars*, pp. 149f., 192–199.

498. Hemming, *Amazon Frontier*, pp. 184–191.

499. Rink, 'Kleiner Krieg', p. 441; Vandervort, *Wars of Imperial Conquest*, p. 69f.

500. Le Cour Grandmaison, *Coloniser, Exterminer*, p. 184f.

501. Miège, 'Conquest of Morocco', pp. 201, 212; Porch, *Conquest of Morocco*, p. ix; Woolman, *Rebels in the Rif*, p. 14.

502. Connor, *Australian Frontier Wars*, p. 83. For other examples of long-running conflicts, see: Mattioli, 'Kolonialverbrechen des faschistischen Italien', pp. 208f., 220; Mostert, *Military System*, p. 84.

503. The war in Angola began in 1961 with an uprising led by the People's Front for the Liberation of Angola and ended in 1988 with a peace accord with South Africa. The war in Indochina lasted from the beginning of the reconquest of the region by the French in 1945 to the victory of North Vietnam in 1975.

504. Kiernan, *Colonial Empires*, pp. 46, 53f.; Linn, *Counterinsurgency in the Philippine War*, pp. 116f., 148–151; Moor, 'Warmakers in the Archipelago', pp. 68–70; Moreman, '"Watch and Ward"', p. 150; Schumacher, '"Niederbrennen, plündern und töten"', p. 112f.

505. Brogini-Künzi, 'Wunsch nach einem blitzschnellen Krieg', p. 285.

506. Bierling, *Geschichte des Irakkriegs*, pp. 124–126.

507. Hemming, *Red Gold*, pp. 361–363; Lee, 'Fortify, Fight, or Flee', pp. 738–740; Starkey, *European and Native American Warfare*, p. 155f.; Utley, *Frontier Regulars*, pp. 95–97, 131–139, 242–248; Utley, *Frontiersmen in Blue*, p. 337f.

508. Belich, *Victorian Interpretation*, p. 115f.; Bond, 'South African War', pp. 234–236; Crawford, 'Sikh Wars', pp. 49–65; Guy, *Destruction of the Zulu Kingdom*, pp. 69–246; Keegan, 'Ashanti Campaign', p. 195f.; Mostert, *Military System*, p. 91f.; Vandervort, *Wars of Imperial Conquest*, p. 81f.

509. Thornton, 'Firearms, Diplomacy, and Conquest', p. 179, 182, 185f.

510. Cann, *Counterinsurgency in Africa*, p. 80; Reis/Oliveira, 'Cutting Heads or Winning Hearts', p. 88.

511. Huntington, *Soldier and State*, p. 59–79.

512. Beckett, *Modern Insurgencies*, p. 184; Cann, *Counterinsurgency in Africa*, p. 28–31; Clayton, *Wars of French Decolonization*, pp. 140, 178f.; Corum/Johnson, *Airpower in Small Wars*, p. 82f.; Gann/Duignan, *Rulers of German Africa*, pp. 119–121; Groen, 'Militant Response', pp. 30–39; Kanya-Forstner, 'French Marines', pp. 121f., 132–137; Khodarkovsky, 'Krieg und Frieden', p. 216; Khodarkovsky, *Russia's Steppe Frontier*, p. 168f.; Schmidl, 'Kolonialkriege', p. 116; Thomas, 'Order Before Reform', p. 199; Utley, *Frontiersmen in Blue*, p. 111f.

513. Keeley, *War Before Civilization*, p. 80.

514. Jones, *Graveyard of Empires*, pp. 303–306; Pavilonis, 'Irregular War in Afghanistan'.

515. Roxborough, 'Lessons of Counterinsurgency', p. 40.

516. Kanya-Forstner, 'French Marines', p. 132.

517. Bilton/Sim, *Four Hours in My Lai*, p. 33. I am indebted to Greiner, *Krieg ohne Fronten*, p. 74, for the quotation.

518. Callwell, *Small Wars*, p. 97.

519. Ibid., p. 106.

520. Prince, *Gegen Araber und Wahehe*, p. 302. My thanks are due to Bührer, *Kaiserliche Schutztruppe*, p. 262, for the quotation.

521. Utley, *Frontiersmen in Blue*, pp. 148–152.

522. Walter, '"The Enemy Must Be Brought to Battle"'.

523. Lock/Quantrill, *Zulu Victory*, pp. 15f., 151–159; Manning, 'Learning the Trade', pp. 651–653; Utley, *Custer*, pp. 74f., 158.

524. Belich, *Victorian Interpretation*, pp. 68, 99, 142–157; Chandler, 'Expedition to Abyssinia', p. 120; Crawford, 'Sikh Wars', p. 40f.; Lock/Quantrill, *Zulu Victory*, p. 181f.; Utley, *Frontiersmen in Blue*, p. 274f.; Vandervort, *Indian Wars*, pp. 176f., 180f.; Williams, 'Egyptian Campaign', pp. 252, 262, 269.

525. Nasson, *South African War*, pp. 117–144.

526. Calloway, *Winter Count*, p. 195; James, *Savage Wars*, pp. 180–183; Linn, *Counterinsurgency in the Philippine War*, pp. 113–115; Utley, *Frontier Regulars*, pp. 20, 177–180, 196, 230, 257f., 391–393; Utley, *Frontiersmen in Blue*, p. 345; Vandervort, *Indian Wars*, pp. 134–136, 202f.; Vandervort, *Wars of Imperial Conquest*, p. 134f.

527. Fall, *Hell in a Very Small Place*, p. ix, 24–51; Navarre, *Agonie de L'Indochine*, pp. 188–200, 251–255; Tourret, 'Évolution de la tactique', pp. 178, 182f.

528. Cf. chapter 3, 'Military necessity'.

529. James, *Savage Wars*, pp. 35, 37–39, 54–57; Kanya-Forstner, 'French Marines', pp. 132–137; Kanya-Forstner, 'Mali—Tukulor', p. 75f.; Keegan, 'Ashanti Campaign', p. 179f., 189; Morlang, '"Die Wahehe haben ihre Vernichtung gewollt"', p. 90f.; Person, 'Guinea', pp. 137–140; Porch, *Conquest of the Sahara*, p. xvi; Vandervort, *Wars of Imperial Conquest*, p. 120f.

530. Ross, 'Dahomey', pp. 162–167.

531. Belich, *Victorian Interpretation*, pp. 29–36, 158. The British conquest of Sindh in present-day Pakistan in 1839 also began with the issuing of an unacceptable ultimatum. James, *Raj*, pp. 100–106.

532. In the history of conflict, 'annihilation' is an intriguing word. In the classical military sense, it means nothing more than using operational and tactical means to render an enemy incapable of fighting. In the colonial context this has sometimes led to a confusion of terminology in historiography, not least in the Herero War of 1904/05, where a military annihilation, somewhat unintentionally, turned into a physical one. Cf. Hull, *Absolute Destruction*, pp. 22–33. I use the term 'annihilation' in the ensuing discussion to denote the destruction of an indigenous society's political or social structure. When referring to physical annihilation, in other words acts of genocide, I use the term 'extermination' instead.

533. Edmunds/Peyser, *Fox Wars*, pp. 119–157; Hemming, *Conquest of the Incas*, pp. 395–438; Jones, *Conquest of the Last Maya Kingdom*, pp. 266–269; Karr, '"Why Should You Be So Furious?"', pp. 900–903; Lee, 'Fortify, Fight, or Flee', pp. 731–733.

534. Cf. chapter 2, 'Plunder and destruction' and 'Total war aims'.

535. Globally speaking, that is. Tactically, the relative strengths depended to a large extent on the operational situation. Numerous descriptions of a range of circumstances, from massive superiority to clear inferiority in numbers can be found in Utley, *Frontiersmen in Blue*.

536. In the Cape Colony in the eighteenth century, the Boer commandos (militias) of the Dutch settlers were numerically massively superior to the small hunter-gatherer groups of the San (Bushmen). Penn, *Forgotten Frontier*, p. 118f. In the Maori Wars of the 1860s the British invariably had two to five times as many men on the battlefield as their opponents. Belich, *Victorian Interpretation*, pp. 22, 91–98, 134–141. Yet because they had so much difficulty breaching the earthworks of the Maoris, they subsequently wrote in their reports that the relative strengths were precisely the opposite, a fiction which accorded with the usual situation in wars of empire. Ibid., p. 311f.

537. Fall, *Hell in a Very Small Place*, pp. 127, 133.

538. Crowder, 'Introduction', p. 6f.; Headrick, *Tools of Empire*, pp. 117–120; Killingray,

'Colonial Warfare', p. 151f.; Porch, *Conquest of Morocco*, p. 197f.; Rainero, 'Battle of Adowa', p. 200; Vandervort, *Wars of Imperial Conquest*, pp. 110f., 154f.

539. Boot, *Savage Wars of Peace*, p. 52f.; Linn, *Counterinsurgency in the Philippine War*, p. 138.

540. Bryant, 'Asymmetric Warfare', p. 439; Headrick, *Tools of Empire*, p. 89f.; James, *Raj*, p. 20.

541. Ricklefs, *War, Culture and Economy*, p. 141.

542. Cf. chapter 4, 'Armed forces' and 'Technology'.

543. Killingray, 'Colonial Warfare', p. 151.

544. Bryant, 'Asymmetric Warfare', p. 439.

545. James, *Raj*, p. 34f.

546. Glover, *Rorke's Drift*, p. 99.

547. Knight, *Zulu*, pp. 105–116.

548. Glover, *Rorke's Drift*, p. 130.

549. James, *Savage Wars*, p. 130.

550. Hemming, *Red Gold*, p. 125f.; Raudzens, 'Why Did Amerindian Defences Fail?', p. 341; Ricklefs, *War, Culture and Economy*, p. 138.

551. Hassig, *Mexico and the Spanish Conquest*, p. 50.

552. Raudzens, 'Why Did Amerindian Defences Fail?', p. 349f.

553. Unlike for the conquest of Mexico, virtually no significant indigenous sources exist on the conquest of the Inca Empire in Peru. (For this information I am grateful to Ute Schüren; cf. also Parry/Keith, *New Iberian World*, Vol. 4, p. 81.) While the well-known illustrated chronicle of Huamán Poma contains some fascinating material on the state and daily life of the Incas prior to the Spanish conquest, with the exception of the massacre at Cajamarca the conquest itself is only mentioned on very general terms on a few pages. Aside from pictorial images showing the Peruvians' fear at the conquistadors' horses, for long stretches the chronicle adopts the Spanish perspective and recounts virtually nothing that is not already known from the Spanish sources. The fact that the author seriously relates how St. James, mounted on a white horse, personally took part in the siege of the Inca capital Cuzco betrays the degree to which he was Hispanicized and Christianized. Huamán Poma, *Letter to a King*, pp. 108f., 115; Huamán Poma, *Primer nueva corónica*, pp. 385, 407.

554. Guilmartin, 'Cutting Edge', p. 46.

555. Diamond, *Guns, Germs, and Steel*, pp. 67–74; Hemming, *Conquest of the Incas*, pp. 29, 38–47.

556. Raudzens, 'Outfighting or Outpopulating?', p. 33.

557. Diamond, *Guns, Germs, and Steel*, p. 75; Hemming, *Conquest of the Incas*, pp. 101–107; Sancho, *Conquest of Peru*, pp. 67–88.

558. Guilmartin, 'Cutting Edge', p. 46.

559. Hemming, *Conquest of the Incas*, pp. 190–199.

560. Hagerman, *American Civil War*, pp. 115–148; Jones, *Right Hand of Command*; Van Creveld, *Command in War*, pp. 103–147; Van Creveld, *Supplying War*, pp. 75–108.

561. Gabbert, 'Warum Montezuma weinte', p. 35.

562. Charney, 'Iberier und Südostasiaten', p. 183f.; Flores Galindo, *In Search of an Inca*, p. 21.

563. Porter, *Military Orientalism*, p. 43.

564. Raudzens, 'Outfighting or Outpopulating?', p. 32.

565. Ibid., p. 33.

566. Director: Ridley Scott. In reference to the fierce street fighting in Mogadishu portrayed in the film, one of the US commandos who took part in the Somalia operation referred in his war memoirs to a 'swarm effect'. Casper, *Falcon Brigade*, p. 40.

567. Gabbert, 'Warum Montezuma weinte', p. 35, suggests that the conquistadors used six-figure numbers of opponents simply as a way of saying 'a lot'.

568. Guilmartin, 'Cutting Edge', pp. 50–57.

569. Hemming, *Conquest of the Incas*, pp. 57, 110. A similar account is given in: Restall, *Myths of the Spanish Conquest*, p. 143.

570. Sancho, *Conquest of Peru*, p. 121f.

571. Ibid., p. 123. Just as informative is a report by the Spanish regional council of Jauja, which at one point casually mentions 20,000 'yndios amigos' (friendly Indians), only to claim two paragraphs later that the Battle of Jauja had been won by 'some Spaniards on horseback and others on foot armed with a few crossbows' on one day and by 'eighteen riders and ten or twelve footsoldiers' on the next. 'El Ayuntamiento de Jauja al Emperador', p. 127f. Like Sancho's account, the description of the engagement by John Hemming follows these sources uncritically. In Hemming's description of the second day of the battle, the participation of 2,000 friendly Indians is mentioned in passing without finding this striking instance of a transcultural alliance in any way worthy of comment. Hemming, *Conquest of the Incas*, p. 136. Likewise, Hemming recounts how, at the Battle of Tecocajas on 3 May 1534 a handful of Spaniards defeated more than 50,000 Indians, without mentioning in this context again those 3,000 Cañari Indians who a page earlier are described as having come over to the Spanish side. Ibid., p. 152f. In the account by Huamán Poma the Peruvian allies of the Spanish are mentioned in just a single sentence. Huamán Poma, *Letter to a King*, p. 113; Huamán Poma, *Primer nueva corónica*, p. 397.

572. Gabbert, 'Warum Montezuma weinte', p. 38f.; Hemming, *Conquest of the Incas*, pp. 29–31, 93–97, 101f.

573. The Portuguese evidently took the same attitude towards their African allies around the same time. Thornton, 'Firearms, Diplomacy, and Conquest', p. 179.

574. Restall, *Myths of the Spanish Conquest*, p. 45.

575. Gabbert, 'Warum Montezuma weinte', p. 41f.; Gabbert, 'Kultureller Determinismus'; Hassig, 'Eroberung Mexikos', p. 126f.; Hassig, *Mexico and the Spanish Conquest*, pp. 179–183.

576. Restall, *Myths of the Spanish Conquest*, p. 48.

577. Abernathy, *Dynamics of Global Dominance*, pp. 39, 264–269. Examples: Black, *Beyond the Military Revolution*, p. 122f.; Brooks, 'Impact of Disease', p. 136; Connor, *Australian Frontier Wars*, p. 28; Gann/Duignan, *Rulers of Belgian Africa*, p. 55; Gann/Duignan, *Rulers of German Africa*, pp. 126, 128; Gates, 'Two American Wars', pp. 51–53; Hemming, *Red Gold*, pp. 72–75, 402–408; Hochgeschwender, 'Last Stand', p. 75f.; James, *Raj*, pp. 28–44, 58, 70f.; James, *Savage Wars*, p. 36f.; Jones, *Conquest of the Last Maya Kingdom*, pp. 223, 245; Kanya-Forstner, 'Mali—Tukulor', pp. 57–59; Khodarkovsky, *Russia's Steppe Frontier*, pp. 83–86, 149f.; Knaap, 'Crisis and Failure', pp. 171–174; Law, 'Warfare on the Slave Coast',

p. 109f.; Lonsdale, 'Conquest State of Kenya', p. 92; Macrory, *Signal Catastrophe*, pp. 17–81; Miège, 'Conquest of Morocco', p. 210f.; Moor, 'Warmakers in the Archipelago', p. 60f.; Mostert, *Military System*, p. 17; Olatunji-Oloruntimehin, 'Senegambia—Mahmadou Lamine', p. 102f.; Pemble, 'Resources and Techniques', p. 304; Penn, *Forgotten Frontier*, pp. 104–107; Ricklefs, 'Balance and Military Innovation', pp. 101–104; Ricklefs, *War, Culture and Economy*, pp. 2–13, 134–140; Ross, 'Dahomey', p. 147f.; Thornton, 'Warfare, Slave Trading and European Influence', p. 135f.; Thornton, 'Art of War in Angola', p. 82f.; Utley, *Frontiersmen in Blue*, pp. 237–243; Vandervort, *Wars of Imperial Conquest*, p. 27; Whitehead, 'Tribes Make States', pp. 137–139. The imperial expansion of ancient Rome clearly proceeded in much the same way. Eichmann, 'Expansion und imperiale Herrschaft', pp. 101–106.

578. Ferguson/Whitehead, 'Violent Edge of Empire', p. 22; Helbling, *Tribale Kriege*, p. 283f.; Lee, 'Military Revolution', pp. 65–70; Ranger, 'African Reactions', pp. 300–302.

579. Ferguson/Whitehead, 'Violent Edge of Empire', p. 21.

580. Hemming, *Red Gold*, p. 74.

581. Cooper, 'Culture, Combat, and Colonialism', p. 547.

582. Calloway, *Winter Count*, p. 176.

583. Vandervort, *Indian Wars*, p. 121.

584. Ibid., p. 209f.

585. Billington, *Westward Expansion*, p. 63f.; Kars, '"Cleansing the Land"', p. 264f.; Powell, *Soldiers, Indians and Silver*, p. 135; Silver, *Our Savage Neighbors*, pp. 46–48; Vandervort, *Indian Wars*, p. 196f.

586. Wesseling, 'Colonial Wars', p. 3.

587. Gabbert, 'Warum Montezuma weinte', p. 40.

588. Hassig, *Mexico and the Spanish Conquest*, pp. 177, 181; Oudijk/Restall, 'Mesoamerican Conquistadors', pp. 54–56.

589. Kolff, 'End of an Ancien Régime', p. 45.

590. Crowder, 'Introduction', p. 13f.; Restall, *Myths of the Spanish Conquest*, p. 141f.; Starkey, *European and Native American Warfare*, pp. 10, 60, 132f.; Vandervort, *Indian Wars*, pp. 15, 155; Wesseling, 'Colonial Wars', p. 6f.

591. Crowder, 'Introduction', p. 10f.

592. Helbling, 'Tribale Kriege und expandierende Staaten', p. 73.

593. Gabbert, 'Kultureller Determinismus', p. 284f.; Hassig, 'Eroberung Mexikos', p. 110.

594. Gabbert, 'Warum Montezuma weinte', p. 39.

595. Nester, *Frontier War*, p. 11.

596. White, 'Winning of the West', pp. 320, 342. The same was true in the South regarding the Comanche. Vandervort, *Indian Wars*, pp. 162–164.

597. Crowder, 'Introduction', p. 13f.

598. Bailes, 'Technology and Imperialism', p. 95f.; Black, 'European Overseas Expansion', pp. 23–25; Hochgeschwender, 'Kolonialkriege als Experimentierstätten?', pp. 279–282; Porch, *Conquest of the Sahara*, p. 185f.

599. Altman, 'Conquest, Coercion, and Collaboration', pp. 159–167; Calloway, *Winter Count*, p. 133f.; Chuchiak, 'Forgotten Allies', p. 206f.; Hemming, *Red Gold*, p. 75; Mostert, *Military System*, pp. 25–27; Ricklefs, *War, Culture and Economy*, pp. 138,

146; Scammell, 'Indigenous Assistance', p. 146; Thornton, 'Art of War in Angola', p. 98.

600. Bryant, 'Asymmetric Warfare', p. 452.

601. Heathcote, *Military in British India*, p. 34.

602. Omissi, *Sepoy and the Raj*, pp. 132–134.

603. Kanya-Forstner, 'French Marines', p. 138f.; Miège, 'Conquest of Morocco', pp. 208–210. Other examples: Lock/Quantrill, *Zulu Victory*, pp. 36, 81; Vandervort, *Wars of Imperial Conquest*, pp. 42–44.

604. Gann/Duignan, *Rulers of Belgian Africa*, p. 66f. Similar figures applied for the British and the German *Schutztruppe*: Bührer, *Kaiserliche Schutztruppe*, pp. 112–138; Moreman, '"Small Wars"', p. 111; Morlang, '"Die Wahehe haben ihre Vernichtung gewollt"', pp. 97–100.

605. Buckley, *Slaves in Red Coats*; Geggus, 'Slavery, War, and Revolution', p. 22f.

606. Demographically, the French settlers in North America in the seventeenth and eighteenth century only numbered around a twentieth of their British counterparts. At the time of the British conquest in 1760, only 70,000 French were living in Canada, whereas the population in British North America of European origin doubled between 1750 and 1770 from 964,000 to 1.8 million. Raudzens, *Empires*, p. 143.

607. Calloway, *Winter Count*, pp. 219–243; Raudzens, *Empires*, pp. 119–135.

608. Kopperman, *Braddock at the Monongahela*, p. 30.

609. Starkey, *European and Native American Warfare*, pp. 83–165.

610. Malone, *Skulking Way of War*, pp. 84–88; Starkey, *European and Native American Warfare*, pp. 57–135; Steele, *Betrayals*, pp. 70–75; Walter, 'Der nordamerikanische Imperialkrieg'.

611. Utley, 'Cultural Clash', pp. 100–102; Vandervort, *Indian Wars*, pp. 205–210.

612. Belich, 'Krieg und transkulturelles Lernen', p. 248.

613. Eberspächer, '"Albion zal hier"', p. 194; Nasson, *South African War*, pp. 67, 213f., 224f., 282.

614. Vandervort, *Wars of Imperial Conquest*, pp. 92f., 149, 159.

615. Vandervort, *Indian Wars*, pp. 208–210.

616. Bryant, 'Asymmetric Warfare', p. 432f.; James, *Raj*, p. 73.

617. Seeley, *Expansion of England*, p. 212; Hyam, 'British Imperial Expansion', p. 115.

618. Powell, *Soldiers, Indians and Silver*, p. 158; Matthew, 'Whose Conquest?'; Oudijk/Restall, 'Mesoamerican Conquistadors'; Pietschmann, 'Imperialkriege Spaniens', p. 84. Peru functioned in a similar way: Cahill, 'Long Conquest', p. 96.

619. Killingray, 'Colonial Warfare', p. 155. Interestingly, Douglas Porch explicitly takes issue with the notion that Morocco 'conquered itself': 'Tribes did not "conquer" other tribes, they merely raided them.' Porch, *Conquest of Morocco*, p. 186. This strikes me as rather pedantic. Although France could not immediately exploit the fragmentation of indigenous societies to assert its control on a permanent basis, it did nonetheless incite indigenous groups to attack each other in order to establish its hegemony.

620. Álvarez, *Betrothed of Death*, p. 220f.; Teitler, 'The Mixed Company', p. 160.

621. Mücke, 'Agonie einer Kolonialmacht', pp. 260–262, 265.

622. James, *Raj*, p. 122.

623. Lonsdale, 'Conquest State of Kenya', p. 92.

624. An African soldier in French service around 1900, for example, had to get by on 800 grams of rice and 24 grams of salt per day, whereas his European comrade-in-arms had access to bread, wine, tea, coffee, sugar and tinned meat. Ditte, *Guerre dans les Colonies*, p. 71.

625. At the beginning of the twentieth century, an indigenous West African *tirailleur* cost the French treasury barely 1,000 francs a year, while a French marine stationed in the same place cost 2,500 francs. Vandervort, 'Colonial Wars', p. 159. A quarter of a century later and the difference was less pronounced (700 as against 1,000 francs). Jauffret, 'Armes de "la plus grande France"', p. 59. Further figures can be found in: Etemad, *Possession du monde*, p. 78. However, the Dutch East India Company found European troops to be cheaper in the Early Modern period, because they only had to be paid for six months a year and in addition were obliged to purchase their equipment from the Company. Mostert, *Military System*, p. 25.

626. Wheeler, 'African Elements in Portugal's Armies', p. 240.

627. Buckley, *Slaves in Red Coats*, pp. 6–8; Bührer, *Kaiserliche Schutztruppe*, p. 128; Curtin, *Disease and Empire*, pp. 16–18; Etemad, *Possession du monde*, p. 73f.; Olatunji-Oloruntimehin, 'Senegambia—Mahmadou Lamine', p. 93f.

628. Bryant, 'Asymmetric Warfare', p. 435; Bührer, 'Kriegführung in Deutsch-Ostafrika', p. 214f.; Hack, 'Imperial Systems of Power', p. 9; Hée, *Imperiales Wissen*, pp. 204–235; Kars, '"Cleansing the Land"', pp. 261–268; Killingray, 'Guardians of Empire', p. 7f.; Killingray, 'Colonial Warfare', p. 154f.; Lee, 'Projecting Power', p. 10; Moor, 'Recruitment of Indonesian Soldiers', p. 54f.; Morlang, *Askari und Fitafita*, p. 137; Olatunji-Oloruntimehin, 'Senegambia—Mahmadou Lamine', p. 93f.; Plank, 'Deploying Tribes and Clans', pp. 221–223; Schumacher, '"Niederbrennen, plündern und töten"', p. 119f.; Starkey, *European and Native American Warfare*, pp. 68–71; Vandervort, *Wars of Imperial Conquest*, p. 82f.

629. Clayton, *France, Soldiers and Africa*, p. 4; Feichtinger, 'Aspekt revolutionärer Kriegführung', pp. 271–274; Gérin-Roze, '"Vietnamisation"', p. 137; Gerlach, *Extremely Violent Societies*, p. 197f.; Linn, 'Cerberus' Dilemma', p. 118f.; Martin, 'From Algiers to N'Djamena', p. 92.

630. Eichmann, *Sklaverei, Weltkrieg und Revolution*.

631. The differentiation within the military realm introduced here corresponds to that made by James Belich between 'allied collaborators', 'client collaborators', and 'collaboration agents' for the social realm as a whole (oral communication by James Belich, quoted by friendly permission).

632. Bührer, *Kaiserliche Schutztruppe*, pp. 259–261, 264f., 272; Lonsdale, 'Conquest State of Kenya', p. 110f.; Moor, 'Recruitment of Indonesian Soldiers', pp. 54–56; Omissi, *Sepoy and the Raj*, pp. 71–74, 86–93; Powell, *Soldiers, Indians and Silver*, pp. 164–166.

633. Gann/Duignan, *Rulers of British Africa*, pp. 116–120; Moor, 'Recruitment of Indonesian Soldiers', pp. 54–56.

634. Füssel, 'Händler, Söldner und Sepoys', pp. 311–317; Lynn, *Battle*, pp. 164–177; Marshall, 'Western Arms in Maritime Asia', pp. 24–27.

635. Teitler, 'The Mixed Company', pp. 158–167. Cf. chapter 4, 'Armed forces'.

636. Echenberg, *Colonial Conscripts*, pp. 15, 19–21, 118.

637. Gann/Duignan, *Rulers of Belgian Africa*, p. 83.
638. Broome, *Aboriginal Australians*, p. 49f.; Echenberg, *Colonial Conscripts*, p. 14f.; Füssel, 'Händler, Söldner und Sepoys', p. 317; Heathcote, 'Army of British India', p. 390; Killingray, 'Guardians of Empire', pp. 16–18; Kirk-Greene, '"Damnosa Hereditas"'; Linn, 'Cerberus' Dilemma', p. 118f.; Morlang, *Askari und Fitafita*, pp. 16, 25, 28, 33, 45, 47f., 54, 74, 98f., 114f., 129; Taylor, 'Colonial Forces in British Burma', p. 197f.; Trotha, *Koloniale Herrschaft*, p. 44f.; Womack, 'Ethnicity and Martial Races'.
639. Gann/Duignan, *Rulers of British Africa*, pp. 107–109; Hack, 'Imperial Systems of Power', pp. 12–17; Kiernan, *Colonial Empires*, p. 138f.; Killingray, 'Guardians of Empire', p. 14f.; Lunn, 'French Race Theory', pp. 225–228; Martin, 'From Algiers to N'Djamena', p. 95; Moor, 'Recruitment of Indonesian Soldiers', pp. 59–69; Omissi, *Sepoy and the Raj*, pp. 1–46; Streets, *Martial Races*; Taylor, 'Colonial Forces in British Burma', p. 197f.; Utley, *Frontier Regulars*, p. 378. Cf. Bourke, *History of Killing*, p. 117f.; Kennedy, *Islands of White*, p. 161.
640. Hack, 'Imperial Systems of Power', pp. 14–17; Hack, 'Imperialism in Southeast Asia', pp. 249–259; Omissi, *Sepoy and the Raj*, pp. 38–40, 153–191; Taylor, 'Colonial Forces in British Burma', pp. 195–201.
641. Vandervort, *Wars of Imperial Conquest*, p. 213f.
642. Lonsdale, 'Conquest State of Kenya', p. 92.
643. Heathcote, *Military in British India*, p. 76–78.
644. Heathcote, 'Army of British India', pp. 394–401; Kiernan, *Colonial Empires*, p. 55f.; Perry, *Commonwealth Armies*, pp. 82–120.
645. Gould, *Imperial Warriors*, pp. 58f., 69–106, 129f.; Streets, *Martial Races*, p. 76f.
646. Killingray, 'British Imperial African Army'; Walter, *Dschungelkrieg und Atombombe*, pp. 120–122
647. Their mortality rate as a result of disease was ten times less that of European soldiers, but still twice that of African troops. Buckley, *Slaves in Red Coats*, p. 95f.; Etemad, *Possession du monde*, p. 73f.
648. Kiernan, *Colonial Empires*, p. 30f.
649. Cann, *Counterinsurgency in Africa*, p. 94.
650. Lunn, 'French Race Theory', pp. 235–239.
651. Echenberg, *Colonial Conscripts*, p. 26.
652. Clayton, *Wars of French Decolonization*, pp. 4–6; Clayton, *France, Soldiers and Africa*, p. 8; Fourniau, 'Colonial Wars before 1914', p. 78; Hack/Rettig, 'Demography in Southeast Asia', pp. 59–61; Killingray, 'Guardians of Empire', pp. 2–5, 10f.; Koller, *Von Wilden aller Rassen*; Martin, 'From Algiers to N'Djamena', p. 94.
653. Furedi, 'Demobilized African Soldier'; Kiernan, *Colonial Empires*, pp. 183–190.
654. Charney, 'Iberier und Südostasiaten', p. 180.
655. Vandervort, *Wars of Imperial Conquest*, p. 27f.
656. Meuwese, 'Ethnic Soldiering', p. 204.
657. Lee, 'Projecting Power', p. 7.
658. Hemming, *Conquest of the Incas*, p. 172.
659. Hochgeschwender, 'Kolonialkriege als Experimentierstätten?', p. 282f.
660. Kramer, 'Race-Making and Colonial Violence', p. 186f.; Reis/Oliveira, 'Cutting

Heads or Winning Hearts', p. 90; Stockwell, '"A widespread and long-concocted plot"', p. 79f.; Walter, 'Kolonialkrieg, Globalstrategie und Kalter Krieg', p. 128.

661. Evans, 'Harkis', pp. 124–127; Gerlach, *Extremely Violent Societies*, p. 195.

662. Furedi, *Mau Mau War*, pp. 216–218; Smith, *Pattern of Imperialism*, pp. 85, 120, 132f. A good example is Malaya: Hack, 'Screwing down the People'; Stock-well, 'Insurgency and Decolonisation'; Walter, 'Kolonialkrieg, Globalstrategie und Kalter Krieg', pp. 119–122.

663. Beckett, *Modern Insurgencies*, p. 155; Dülffer/Frey, 'Introduction', p. 2f.; Furedi, 'Kenya', p. 145; Gates, 'Two American Wars', pp. 62–65; Hack, 'Screwing down the People'; Killingray, 'Guardians of Empire', p. 19; Smith, *Pattern of Imperialism*, p. 132f.; Walter, 'Kolonialkrieg, Globalstrategie und Kalter Krieg', pp. 133, 137–140.

664. Clayton, *Wars of French Decolonization*, p. 74.

665. Gerlach, *Extremely Violent Societies*, p. 194.

666. Evans, 'Harkis'.

667. Clayton, *Wars of French Decolonization*, p. 120.

668. Groen, 'Militant Response', p. 35.

669. Frey, *Geschichte des Vietnamkrieges*, p. 194.

670. Cann, *Counterinsurgency in Africa*, pp. 10, 88. The proportion of non-European troops may have been even greater, namely almost 70 per cent. The Portuguese government claimed a figure of 60 per cent at the time, no doubt so as to suggest that the war was being fought predominantly by the indigenous population—and hence by implication on their behalf. Wheeler, 'African Elements in Portugal's Armies', pp. 236–239.

671. Isby, *War in a Distant Country*, pp. 81–90.

672. DeFronzo, *Iraq War*, pp. 183f., 217f., 231f.; Jones, *Graveyard of Empires*, pp. 90, 129–131.

673. Ferguson/Whitehead, 'Violent Edge of Empire', p. 11.

674. Abler, 'Beavers and Muskets', p. 157f.; Billington, *Westward Expansion*, pp. 110–137; Calloway, *Winter Count*, pp. 207–211, 251–264; Gordon, 'Limited Adoption', p. 239; Hunt, *Wars of the Iroquois*, pp. 158–161; James, *Raj*, p. 24; Lee, 'Military Revolution', pp. 65–70; Marshall, 'Western Arms in Maritime Asia', pp. 24–27; Starkey, *European and Native American Warfare*, pp. 30–33, 83f., 118.

675. Hemming, *Red Gold*, pp. 283–311; Meuwese, 'Ethnic Soldiering', pp. 198–214.

676. Balfour-Paul, 'Britain's Informal Empire', p. 503. During the First World War, the allies of the German and Ottoman Empires in North and East Africa received consignments of weapons. James, *Savage Wars*, pp. 110–112. The collaboration by Southeast Asian liberation movements with Japan in the period 1941–1945 could scarcely be described as exercising an alliance option, given the lack of any freedom of choice under Japanese occupation. Stockwell, 'Imperialism and Nationalism', p. 478f.

677. Burbank/Cooper, *Empires in World History*, pp. 436–438; McMahon, 'Heiße Kriege', pp. 30–33; Westad, *Global Cold War*, pp. 86–89.

678. Andreopoulos, 'National Liberation Movements', p. 200. A less well-known instance of rivalry between empires in this period was the support given by the Spanish to the Moroccan independence movement in its struggle against France;

its fighters were given a safe haven in the Spanish-controlled area of Morocco. Fleming, 'Decolonization and the Spanish Army', p. 126. However, this situation only continued until independent Morocco set its sights on taking back the Spanish Western Sahara. Ibid., pp. 129–131.

679. Galtung, 'Structural Theory of Imperialism', p. 89.

680. Examples: Gann/Duignan, *Rulers of British Africa*, pp. 142–144; Gates, 'Two American Wars', p. 58; Nasson, *South African War*, p. 164f.; Paillard, 'Expedition to Madagascar', pp. 168, 171; Vandervort, *Wars of Imperial Conquest*, p. 149.

681. Billington, *Westward Expansion*, pp. 191–194; Pulsipher, 'Gaining the Diplomatic Edge'; Starkey, *European and Native American Warfare*, pp. 12, 155f.; Walter, 'Der nordamerikanische Imperialkrieg', p. 95f.; White, *Middle Ground*, p. xv.

682. Reid, *Europe and Southeast Asia*, p. 7f.

683. Johnson, '"Alliance Imperialism"'.

684. Beckett, *Modern Insurgencies*, p. 127f.; Clayton, *Wars of French Decolonization*, pp. 87, 105f.; Furedi, 'Creating a Breathing Space', p. 98.

685. Boot, *Savage Wars of Peace*, pp. 253–278; Michels, '"Ostasiatisches Expeditionskorps"', p. 401; Selby, 'Third China War'.

686. Boot, *Savage Wars of Peace*, p. 54f.; James, *Savage Wars*, pp. 138, 141–144; Kiernan, *Colonial Empires*, p. 120.

687. Hemming, *Amazon Frontier*, pp. 104–123.

688. Vandervort, *Indian Wars*, p. 204f.

689. Mücke, 'Agonie einer Kolonialmacht', p. 265f.; Woolman, *Rebels in the Rif*, pp. 174–179.

690. Kunz, '"Con ayuda del más dañino de todos los gases"'.

691. Fleming, 'Decolonization and the Spanish Army', pp. 129–131.

692. Jones, *Graveyard of Empires*, pp. 238–255.

693. 'Co-operation and Empire' was the theme of an international symposium held at the University of Berne in June 2013. Across the board, the papers presented there emphasized the importance of constantly renegotiated social cooperation on the periphery for the fragile Western colonial rule. The most significant pioneer of the concept of collaboration/cooperation was Robinson, 'Excentric Idea of Imperialism'; Robinson, 'Non-European Foundations'. See also Gabbert, 'Longue durée of Colonial Violence', p. 262f.; Jureit, *Ordnen von Räumen*, p. 86f.; Killingray, 'Guardians of Empire', p. 1f.; Kratoska, 'Elites in Southeast Asia', pp. 38–40; McCoy/Fradera/Jacobson, *Endless Empire*, p. 12; Osterhammel, *Verwandlung der Welt*, pp. 664–666; Trotha, 'Was war Kolonialismus?', pp. 64–66; Wirz, 'Körper, Kopf und Bauch', p. 255.

694. Wirz, 'Körper, Kopf und Bauch', pp. 254–256. Cf. Schaper, *Koloniale Verhandlungen*, p. 127f.

695. Rothermund, 'Strukturwandel des britischen Kolonialstaats'.

696. Omissi, *Sepoy and the Raj*, p. 191–199, 208–231.

697. David Omissi's assumption that the British Indian Army grew too strong after 1857 for a new Indian Mutiny to have stood any chance of success, seems to be far from the truth. How could a few hundred thousand soldiers maintain lasting control over a Subcontinent of 300 million people in the event that the majority of the populace chose not to cooperate? The fact that the Indian independence movement in the twentieth century succeeded in its aims largely with-

out the use of violence does not in my view prove that India, as Omissi suggests, could be governed purely by military means (Ibid., p. 241), but on the contrary that cooperation—or a refusal to do so—was decisive in determining whether the country was governable or not.

698. Knöbl, 'Imperiale Herrschaft und Gewalt'.

699. Cloake, *Templer*, p. 262.

700. Dixon, '"Hearts and Minds"?', p. 361.

701. Conway, 'To Subdue America', p. 381.

702. Cann, *Counterinsurgency in Africa*, p. 11; Clayton, *Wars of French Decolonization*, p. 130; Furedi, 'Creating a Breathing Space', p. 98; Lieb, 'Guerre Révolutionnaire', p. 472f.; Malinowski, 'Modernisierungskriege', p. 217.

703. Cf. chapter 3, 'Severity and determination'.

704. Clayton, *Wars of French Decolonization*, p. 130f.; Linn, *Counterinsurgency in the Philippine War*, pp. 17–20, 107–112, 117f.; Selesky, 'Colonial America', pp. 75–85; Walter, 'Der nordamerikanische Imperialkrieg', pp. 98–100.

705. Gwynn, *Imperial Policing*, p. 5.

706. Gottmann, 'Bugeaud, Galliéni, Lyautey', pp. 241–248; Lieb, 'Guerre Révolutionnaire', pp. 471, 477.

707. Galula, *Counterinsurgency Warfare*, p. 5.

708. Cf. chapter 3, 'Military necessity'. See also Mollenhauer, 'Gesichter der pacification', pp. 338–342; Reis/Oliveira, 'Cutting Heads or Winning Hearts', p. 92; Wesseling, 'Colonial Wars', p. 4f.; Whittingham, '"Savage Warfare"', pp. 597, 600f.

709. Beckett, *Modern Insurgencies*, p. 127; Bührer, 'Staatsstreich im Busch'; Cann, *Counterinsurgency in Africa*, pp. 66–70; Charters, 'Palestine to Northern Ireland', pp. 196–201; Clayton, *Wars of French Decolonization*, p. 60; Connor, *Australian Frontier Wars*, p. 95; Gallieni, *Pacification de Madagascar*, pp. 31–33; Hull, *Absolute Destruction*, p. 25; Kuß, *Deutsches Militär*, p. 83f.; Mattioli, 'Kolonialverbrechen des faschistischen Italien', p. 213f.

710. Klose, 'Notstand'.

711. Calloway, *Winter Count*, pp. 186–196; Campbell, 'Social Structure of the Túpac Amaru', p. 226f.; Utley, *Frontiersmen in Blue*, p. 208.

712. Hemming, *Amazon Frontier*, pp. 61–79.

713. Knaap, 'Crisis and Failure', pp. 163–170; Powell, *Soldiers, Indians and Silver*, pp. 181–205.

714. Coates, *Suppressing Insurgency*, p. 129.

715. Belich, *Victorian Interpretation*, pp. 119–122; Gates, 'Two American Wars', p. 49; Walter, 'Kolonialkrieg, Globalstrategie und Kalter Krieg', p. 128f.

716. Cann, *Counterinsurgency in Africa*, pp. 143–155, 162f.; Charney, *Southeast Asian Warfare*, p. 273; Feichtinger, 'Aspekt revolutionärer Kriegführung', pp. 269–271; Moor, 'Warmakers in the Archipelago', p. 51f.; Porch, 'French Colonial Forces', p. 169f.; Porch, *Conquest of Morocco*, pp. 122–130; Schumacher, '"Niederbrennen, plündern und töten"', p. 121.

717. Feichtinger, 'Aspekt revolutionärer Kriegführung', p. 278.

718. Beckett, *Modern Insurgencies*, p. 41; Hemming, *Amazon Frontier*, p. 190f.; Khodarkovsky, *Russia's Steppe Frontier*, pp. 156–162, 189–201, 221f.; Lemke, 'Kolonialgeschichte als Vorläufer?', p. 289f.; Penn, *Forgotten Frontier*, pp. 230–267, 272; Porch, 'French Colonial Forces', p. 169f.; Powell, *Soldiers, Indians and Silver*,

pp. 181–205; Slatta, '"Civilization" Battles "Barbarism"', pp. 135–139; Whitehead, 'Tribes Make States', pp. 140–142, 148.

719. Abler, 'Beavers and Muskets', p. 165; Billington/Ridge, *Westward Expansion*, pp. 29–41, 61–82; Hemming, *Red Gold*, pp. 97–118; Knaut, *Pueblo Revolt*, p. 186f.; Powell, *Soldiers, Indians and Silver*, pp. 207–212; Starkey, *European and Native American Warfare*, p. 7f.; Whitehead, 'Tribes Make States', pp. 144–149.

720. Including almost 2 million in Algeria and over a million in Kenya. Mollenhauer, 'Gesichter der pacification', p. 344; Newsinger, 'Minimum Force', p. 49.

721. As with the demand by settlers that the Chichimeca of Central Mexico be forcibly relocated in 1582: 'Experience has shown that it does no good to make peace with these Chichimecas and allow them to settle down in their own country. They should be removed to settle in Mexico City or some other place designated by the viceroy *and be mixed in with other tribes.*' Powell, *Soldiers, Indians and Silver*, p. 175 (my emphasis).

722. Hemming, *Amazon Frontier*, p. 144–150; Hemming, *Red Gold*, pp. 97–118; Jones, *Maya Resistance to Spanish Rule*, pp. 189–276.

723. Utley, *Indian Frontier*, pp. 203–252; Utley, *Frontier Regulars*, pp. 190f., 237–248.

724. Stucki, 'Bevölkerungskontrolle in asymmetrischen Konflikten', pp. 244–250.

725. Eberspächer, '"Albion zal hier"', p. 189; Nasson, *South African War*, pp. 218–224; Rose, '"Unsichtbare Feinde"', pp. 234–237.

726. Elkins, *Imperial Reckoning*.

727. May, 'Philippine-American War', p. 453.

728. Markel, 'Draining the Swamp'.

729. Herberg-Rothe, *Krieg*, p. 79; Law, *Terrorism*, p. 189. Mao's original words in his 1937 tract *On Guerrilla Warfare* were: 'Many people think it impossible for guerrillas to exist for long in the enemy's rear. Such a belief reveals lack of comprehension of the relationship that should exist between the people and the troops. The former may be likened to water, the latter to the fish who inhabit it. How may it be said that these two cannot exist together?'

730. Beckett, *Modern Insurgencies*, pp. 198–200; Cann, *Counterinsurgency in Africa*, pp. 155–159; Clayton, *Wars of French Decolonization*, pp. 121, 136f.; Cocker, *Rivers of Blood*, p. 179; Feichtinger, 'Aspekt revolutionärer Kriegführung', pp. 264–269, 278; Gerlach, *Extremely Violent Societies*, pp. 200–206; Greiner, *Krieg ohne Fronten*, pp. 100–102; Hack, 'Screwing down the People', p. 94f.; Knaap, 'Crisis and Failure', p. 171; Linn, 'Cerberus' Dilemma', p. 121; Malinowski, 'Modernisierungskriege', pp. 216f., 235–243; McCuen, *Counter-Revolutionary Warfare*, pp. 231–234; Mollenhauer, 'Gesichter der pacification', p. 344f.; Porch, 'Myths and Promise of COIN', p. 240f.; Schumacher, '"Niederbrennen, plündern und töten"', p. 122; Stucki, 'Bevölkerungskontrolle in asymmetrischen Konflikten', p. 257f.; Stucki, 'Antiguerilla-Kriegführung auf Kuba'; Thomas, 'Order Before Reform', pp. 202–204; Walter, 'Kolonialkrieg, Globalstrategie und Kalter Krieg', pp. 121, 127.

731. Beckett, *Modern Insurgencies*, p. 211; Del Boca, 'Faschismus und Kolonialismus', p. 195f.; Hemming, *Amazon Frontier*, p. 37f.; Mattioli, 'Kolonialverbrechen des faschistischen Italien', p. 218f.; Utley, *Frontier Regulars*, pp. 388–393; Vandervort, *Indian Wars*, p. 238f.

732. DeFronzo, *Iraq War*, p. 230f. Markel, 'Draining the Swamp', pp. 35–37, 45–47, recommended more far-reaching resettlements on the British model.

733. Lyautey saw indigenous auxiliary troops and their families as forming the core of civilization through settlement on the periphery. Lyautey, *Rôle colonial de l'armée*, p. 25f.

734. Barrett, *Edge of Empire*, p. 147; Billington, *Westward Expansion*, p. 54; Calloway, *Winter Count*, p. 190; Donnelly, *Conquest of Bashkiria*, pp. 161–172; Khodarkovsky, *Russia's Steppe Frontier*, pp. 215–222; Knaut, *Pueblo Revolt*, p. 186f.; Matthew, 'Whose Conquest?', p. 108; Penn, *Forgotten Frontier*, p. 135; Powell, *Soldiers, Indians and Silver*, pp. 213–216; Steele, *Warpaths*, pp. 72–77; Teitler, 'The Mixed Company', p. 159.

735. DeFronzo, *Iraq War*, p. 232f.

736. Brown/Fernandez, 'Tribe and State', pp. 179–184; Calloway, *Winter Count*, p. 153; Slatta, '"Civilization" Battles "Barbarism"', pp. 134–136.

737. Cf. chapter 4, 'Learning'.

738. Hull, *Absolute Destruction*, p. 12f.

739. Beckett, *Modern Insurgencies*, pp. 184–187, 194–204; Greiner, *Krieg ohne Fronten*, pp. 74–90; Pavilonis, 'Irregular War in Afghanistan'. The Dutch military evidently took much the same attitude: Groen, 'Militant Response', pp. 35–41.

740. Lieb, 'Guerre Révolutionnaire'.

741. Dixon, '"Hearts and Minds"?'; Porch, 'Myths and Promise of COIN'; Strachan, 'British Counter-Insurgency'.

742. MacQueen, 'Portugal's First Domino'; Reis/Oliveira, 'Cutting Heads or Winning Hearts'.

743. *Small Wars Manual*, p. 11; Andreopoulos, 'National Liberation Movements', pp. 211–213; Galula, *Counterinsurgency Warfare*, p. 4f.; Hahlweg, *Guerilla*, pp. 218–220; Hull, *Absolute Destruction*, pp. 12f., 18; Lieb, 'Guerre Révolutionnaire', p. 478; Strachan, *European Armies*, p. 80.

744. Clausewitz, *On War*, p. 75. (Book 1, chapter 1.2).

745. Killingray, 'Guardians of Empire', pp. 1–2, 19.

746. Walter, 'Kolonialkrieg, Globalstrategie und Kalter Krieg', pp. 119–122.

747. Clayton, *Wars of French Decolonization*, pp. 133–135, 155–158; Thomas, 'Order Before Reform', pp. 204–212.

748. Cann, *Counterinsurgency in Africa*, pp. 187, 194. On the contrary, MacQueen, 'Portugal's First Domino', pp. 224–226, maintains that Portugal was on the verge of losing the war in Guinea militarily in 1973.

2. OBJECTIVES AND LEGITIMATION

1. Belich, *Victorian Interpretation*, p. 19.

2. Charney, 'Iberier und Südostasiaten', p. 179f.; Hemming, *Red Gold*, pp. 1–23, 242; Raudzens, 'Why Did Amerindian Defences Fail?', pp. 334–339; Turnbull, *Black War*, pp. 5–13.

3. Raudzens, 'Why Did Amerindian Defences Fail?', p. 342.

4. Belich, *Victorian Interpretation*, p. 21; Bitterli, *Die "Wilden" und die "Zivilisierten"*, pp. 81–95; Calloway, *Winter Count*, pp. 132–149; Hemming, *Red Gold*, pp. 34–40; Lappas, 'Lernen inmitten des Blutvergießens', pp. 157–162.

5. Bryant, 'Asymmetric Warfare', p. 447f.

6. Lee, 'Fortify, Fight, or Flee', pp. 731–733.

7. Belich, *Victorian Interpretation*, pp. 29–36.

8. Wesseling, 'Colonial Wars', p. 3. Repeated largely verbatim though without being flagged up as a quotation in Kuß, *Deutsches Militär*, p. 14.

9. Utley, *Frontier Regulars*, pp. 401–404; Vandervort, *Indian Wars*, pp. 110–115, 142f.

10. Ramsey, '"Something Cloudy in Their Looks"', pp. 46–70.

11. Bührer, *Kaiserliche Schutztruppe*, pp. 225–235; Kuß, *Deutsches Militär*, pp. 102–107.

12. Osterhammel, *Geschichtswissenschaft jenseits des Nationalstaats*, p. 294.

13. Callwell, *Small Wars*, pp. 25–28.

14. Bodley, *Weg der Zerstörung*, p. 62.

15. Osterhammel, *Geschichtswissenschaft jenseits des Nationalstaats*, pp. 303–319.

16. Hochgeschwender, 'Kolonialkriege als Experimentierstätten?', p. 276.

17. Cf. chapter 1, 'Grey areas'.

18. Thornton, 'Firearms, Diplomacy, and Conquest', p. 172f.; Thornton, 'Warfare, Slave Trading and European Influence', p. 135f.

19. Calloway, *Winter Count*, pp. 219–243; Lappas, 'Lernen inmitten des Blutvergießens', p. 167f.

20. Ricklefs, 'Balance and Military Innovation', pp. 101–104.

21. Ricklefs, *War, Culture and Economy*, pp. 134–142.

22. Bryant, 'Asymmetric Warfare', pp. 444–447, 467; James, *Raj*, pp. 28–44, 58.

23. Hassig, *Mexico and the Spanish Conquest*, pp. 94–98.

24. Black, 'Introduction', p. 12; Ikime, 'Nigeria—Ebrohimi', pp. 205–220; James, *Savage Wars*, pp. 25–27, 117, 124–126; Marshall, 'Western Arms in Maritime Asia', pp. 20–24; Mostert, *Military System*, pp. 10f., 15–17, 84–92; Watson, 'Fortifications', pp. 60–66.

25. Jones, *Conquest of the Last Maya Kingdom*, pp. 29–38.

26. Connor, *Australian Frontier Wars*, pp. 31–33.

27. Utley, *Frontiersmen in Blue*, pp. 64f., 115f., 270–272.

28. Porch, *Conquest of the Sahara*, p. 260.

29. James, *Savage Wars*, pp. 120–122; Trotha, *Koloniale Herrschaft*, p. 38.

30. Boot, *Savage Wars of Peace*, p. 259f. Incidentally, pure demonstrations cannot logically be clearly separated from actual interventions, since in the latter case simply the threat of violence was enough to achieve imperialist objectives.

31. Ibid., p. 60f.; Osterhammel, *Geschichtswissenschaft jenseits des Nationalstaats*, p. 308.

32. Chandler, 'Expedition to Abyssinia'.

33. Porch, *Conquest of Morocco*, pp. 147–182.

34. Boot, *Savage Wars of Peace*, pp. 156–167.

35. Chandler, 'Expedition to Abyssinia', p. 142f., 149f.

36. Bodley, *Weg der Zerstörung*, pp. 62–64; James, *Savage Wars*, p. 174f.; Kuß, *Deutsches Militär*, pp. 243–251.

37. Calloway, *Winter Count*, pp. 147–149.

38. Hemming, *Red Gold*, p. 81.

39. Knaap, 'Crisis and Failure', pp. 152–157.

40. Penn, *Forgotten Frontier*, p. 101.

41. Howe, *What Hath God Wrought*, p. 363.

42. Meinertzhagen, *Kenya Diary*, pp. 39f., 50–52.

43. Utley, *Frontiersmen in Blue*, pp. 152–157.

44. Kuß, *Deutsches Militär*, pp. 247–249; Porch, 'French Colonial Forces', p. 173f.

45. Klein, 'Straffeldzug im Namen der Zivilisation', pp. 163–167.

46. 'Rumsfeld Briefing'.

47. Edwards, *New Spirits*, pp. 254–256.

48. Billington/Ridge, *Westward Expansion*, pp. 300–315; Jones, *Conquest of the Last Maya Kingdom*, pp. 143–146; Jones, *Maya Resistance to Spanish Rule*, pp. 48–50; Meinertzhagen, *Kenya Diary*, pp. 251, 264f.; Utley, *Frontier Regulars*, pp. 153–157, 193–198, 242–248, 296–300; Utley, *Frontiersmen in Blue*, pp. 227–229, 237–248; Vandervort, *Indian Wars*, pp. 126–132.

49. Lonsdale, 'Conquest State of Kenya', p. 108; Trotha, *Koloniale Herrschaft*, pp. 349–365.

50. Osterhammel, *Civilizing Mission*; Osterhammel, '"Uplifting Mankind"'. Besides, the civilizing mission was not exclusively Western: Japan also cited this as the reason for its expansive actions in the twentieth century. Hée, *Imperiales Wissen*, pp. 29–35, 51–87.

51. Dahlmann, 'Sibirien'.

52. Bertrand, 'Violences impériales', p. 138f.; Bitterli, *Die "Wilden" und die "Zivilisierten"*, p. 135; Bodley, *Weg der Zerstörung*, p. 65; Eskildsen, 'Civilization and Savages'; Fynn, 'Ghana—Asante', p. 28f.; Schumacher, '"Niederbrennen, plündern und töten"', p. 130; Williams, 'Egyptian Campaign', p. 249.

53. Hemming, *Red Gold*, p. 354.

54. Hurt, *Indian Frontier*, pp. 137–163.

55. Brogini-Künzi, 'Wunsch nach einem blitzschnellen Krieg', p. 286; James, *Savage Wars*, pp. 3–17; Jones, *Conquest of the Last Maya Kingdom*, p. xxi; Khodarkovsky, *Russia's Steppe Frontier*, pp. 185–201; Pagden, *Lords of All the World*, pp. 86–91.

56. James, *Savage Wars*, pp. 126, 140–144; Vandervort, *Wars of Imperial Conquest*, pp. 140–144.

57. Gann/Duignan, *Rulers of German Africa*, p. 119f.; Lonsdale, 'Conquest State of Kenya', p. 105f.

58. Boot, *Savage Wars of Peace*, pp. 54f., 257; James, *Raj*, p. 31; Miège, 'Conquest of Morocco', pp. 202–207; Muffett, 'Nigeria—Sokoto Caliphate', p. 285; Selby, 'Third China War', pp. 71–75; Smith, 'Nigeria—Ijebu', pp. 170–177, 182; Vandervort, *Wars of Imperial Conquest*, p. 87.

59. James, *Raj*, p. 73; Kolff, 'End of an Ancien Régime', p. 31f.; Linn, 'Cerberus' Dilemma', p. 115; Whitehead, 'Tribes Make States', p. 129.

60. Klein, 'Straffeldzug im Namen der Zivilisation', p. 165f.; Michels, '"Ostasiatisches Expeditionskorps"', p. 401; Osterhammel, *Geschichtswissenschaft jenseits des Nationalstaats*, p. 305.

61. Westad, *Global Cold War*, pp. 8–38, 66–72.

62. Klein, 'Straffeldzug im Namen der Zivilisation', p. 147.

63. Michels, '"Ostasiatisches Expeditionskorps"', p. 401. Susanne Kuß mentions the contemporary view that China needed to be forced to 'abide by the rules of the "Western" and the "civilized" world'. Kuß, *Deutsches Militär*, p. 49.

64. Osterhammel, *Geschichtswissenschaft jenseits des Nationalstaats*, p. 316.

65. Ibid., pp. 316–318.

66. Klein/Schumacher, 'Einleitung', p. 7.

67. Bierling, *Geschichte des Irakkriegs*, p. 162f.

68. Feichtinger/Malinowski, 'Konstruktive Kriege?', pp. 298–300.

69. Uppermost among the official Western war objectives in all three cases were the West's security and the stability of the region; humanitarian motives either had the lowest priority (Afghanistan) or gained in importance over the course of the conflict as a way of legitimizing the West's involvement (Iraq, Mali). 'Hollande: l'opération au Mali'; '9 questions about the Mali conflict'; 'Rumsfeld Briefing'; Bellamy/Wheeler, 'Humanitarian Intervention', pp. 518–520; Harding, 'French troops continue operation'. Humanitarian aims were not quite so obviously secondary in the interventions of the 1990s, though even there we may safely assume 'mixed motives'. Bellamy/Wheeler, 'Humanitarian Intervention', pp. 514–517.

70. Apparently the Bundeswehr really was responsible for introducing waste recycling to Kosovo, an achievement to which the former NATO General Klaus Reinhard accorded great significance at a conference in Augsburg in 2002. Max Boot also regards waste disposal as an important civilizing outcome of the 'generally well-meaning' American occupation in small wars on the periphery: Boot, *Savage Wars of Peace*, p. 345.

71. Westad, *Global Cold War*, p. 5.

72. Kanet, 'Sowjetische Militärhilfe', p. 66.

73. Frey, 'Vereinigte Staaten und Dritte Welt', pp. 47–55; Gates, 'Two American Wars', p. 66f.; Greiner, *Krieg ohne Fronten*, pp. 59–62.

74. Clayton, *Wars of French Decolonization*, p. 59f.; McMahon, 'Heiße Kriege', pp. 30–33; Mollenhauer, 'Gesichter der pacification', pp. 338–342, 348–353; Stockwell, '"A widespread and long-concocted plot"'; Walter, 'Kolonialkrieg, Globalstrategie und Kalter Krieg', pp. 133–137.

75. Feichtinger, 'Aspekt revolutionärer Kriegführung', p. 278; Malinowski, 'Modernisierungskriege'.

76. Westad, *Global Cold War*, p. 5.

77. Barkawi, 'Pedagogy of "Small Wars"', p. 27.

78. Osterhammel, '"Uplifting Mankind"', p. 422.

79. Eder/Hofbauer, 'Operation Enduring Freedom', p. 58.

80. Feichtinger, 'Aspekt revolutionärer Kriegführung', p. 278; Osterhammel, '"Uplifting Mankind"', pp. 381–386, 366f.

81. Jones, *Conquest of the Last Maya Kingdom*, pp. 290, 302–335.

82. James, *Savage Wars*, p. 122; Osterhammel, *Geschichtswissenschaft jenseits des Nationalstaats*, p. 306; Pagden, *Lords of All the World*, p. 97.

83. James, *Savage Wars*, p. 99.

84. Lonsdale, 'Conquest State of Kenya', p. 92.

85. Osterhammel, *Geschichtswissenschaft jenseits des Nationalstaats*, p. 307f.

86. Robinson, 'Excentric Idea of Imperialism'; Robinson, 'Non-European Foundations'.

87. Law, 'Warfare on the Slave Coast', p. 109f.; Mostert, *Military System*, p. 15–17, 92f.

88. Moor, 'Warmakers in the Archipelago', p. 60f.

89. James, *Savage Wars*, pp. 74–81.

90. Boot, *Savage Wars of Peace*, p. 133f.

91. Bierling, *Geschichte des Irakkriegs*, pp. 121–129. Other examples: Edwards, *New Spirits*, pp. 254–256; James, *Raj*, pp. 24, 29, 40; Macrory, *Signal Catastrophe*, pp. 17–67; Ricklefs, *War, Culture and Economy*, p. 141f.; Thornton, 'Firearms, Diplomacy, and Conquest', pp. 181–183.

92. Boot, *Savage Wars of Peace*, pp. 156–167; Crawford, 'Sikh Wars', pp. 49–65; James, *Savage Wars*, p. 140; Miège, 'Conquest of Morocco', p. 212; Paillard, 'Expedition to Madagascar', pp. 168–179.

93. Cahill, 'Long Conquest'; Hack, 'Imperialism in Southeast Asia', p. 244; Herold, 'Fliegendes Kreuzergeschwader', p. 391; James, *Raj*, pp. 70–73; James, *Savage Wars*, p. 45; Kanya-Forstner, 'Mali—Tukulor', p. 72; Knaap, 'Crisis and Failure', pp. 152–170; Morlang, '"Die Wahehe haben ihre Vernichtung gewollt"', pp. 85–88; Muffett, 'Nigeria—Sokoto Caliphate', p. 284f.; Porch, *Conquest of the Sahara*, p. 272; Ross, 'Dahomey', pp. 162–167; Vandervort, *Wars of Imperial Conquest*, p. 144.

94. Penn, *Forgotten Frontier*, p. 120; Utley, *Frontiersmen in Blue*, p. 118. On the significance of 'chiefs' in the colonial system of rule, see Schaper, *Koloniale Verhandlungen*, pp. 110–127; Trotha, 'Utopie staatlicher Herrschaft', pp. 230–233.

95. Moor, 'Warmakers in the Archipelago', pp. 66–68.

96. Osterhammel, '"Uplifting Mankind"', p. 374.

97. Guy, *Destruction of the Zulu Kingdom*, pp. 69–246; Hassig, *Mexico and the Spanish Conquest*, pp. 105–113, 177; James, *Raj*, p. 38f.; James, *Savage Wars*, p. 136; Kanya-Forstner, 'French Marines', pp. 141–143; Keegan, 'Ashanti Campaign', p. 195f.

98. Clayton, *Wars of French Decolonization*, pp. 161–173; Feichtinger, 'Aspekt revolutionärer Kriegführung', p. 278; Furedi, 'Creating a Breathing Space', p. 94; Furedi, *Mau Mau War*, pp. 216–218; Groen, 'Militant Response', p. 31f.

99. Smith, *Pattern of Imperialism*, pp. 85, 132f.

100. Hack, 'Screwing down the People'; Stockwell, 'Insurgency and Decolonisation'; Walter, 'Kolonialkrieg, Globalstrategie und Kalter Krieg', pp. 111f., 120, 133–137.

101. Clayton, *Wars of French Decolonization*, p. 178f. Spain too had little success with this policy in North Africa. Fleming, 'Decolonization and the Spanish Army'.

102. Bechtol, 'Paradigmenwandel des Kalten Krieges'; Gibbs, 'Sowjetische Invasion in Afghanistan'; Reilly, 'Cold War Transition'.

103. Nester, *Frontier War*, pp. 251–268; Penn, *Forgotten Frontier*, pp. 114, 117f.; Utley, *Frontier Regulars*, pp. 143–147.

104. Hemming, *Red Gold*, p. 133f.

105. Howard, 'Colonial Wars', p. 220; Kanya-Forstner, 'French Marines', p. 132.

106. Fynn, 'Ghana—Asante', p. 35.

107. Galbraith, '"Turbulent Frontier"'.

108. James, *Raj*, p. 63; Kolff, 'End of an Ancien Régime', p. 31f.; Lemke, 'Kolonialgeschichte als Vorläufer?', p. 289f.; Mockaitis, *British Counterinsurgency*, p. 83.

109. Jones, 'Muscovite-Nomad Relations', p. 130; Khodarkovsky, *Russia's Steppe Frontier*, p. 221.

110. Jones, *Conquest of the Last Maya Kingdom*, pp. 48–52; Jones, *Maya Resistance to*

Spanish Rule, p. 101. The subjugation of the Chichimeca in Central Mexico was a similar case. Powell, *Soldiers, Indians and Silver*, p. 90f.

111. Lock/Quantrill, *Zulu Victory*, pp. 19–23.
112. Porch, *Conquest of Morocco*, pp. 10f., 77, 90.
113. Charney, *Southeast Asian Warfare*, pp. 259–262.
114. Bryant, 'Asymmetric Warfare', p. 434; James, *Raj*, pp. 67–69; Lemke, 'Kolonialgeschichte als Vorläufer?', p. 289f.; Mostert, *Military System*, pp. 92–100.
115. Bond, 'South African War', pp. 201–208; Denzer, 'Sierra Leone—Bai Bureh', p. 235; Eberspächer, '"Albion zal hier"', p. 186f.; Falls, 'Reconquest of the Sudan', p. 286; Fynn, 'Ghana—Asante', pp. 42–44; Gann/Duignan, *Rulers of British Africa*, p. 122; James, *Savage Wars*, pp. 25–27, 52f., 97–100, 136; Mücke, 'Agonie einer Kolonialmacht', pp. 248–255; Paillard, 'Expedition to Madagascar', p. 187f.; Vandervort, *Wars of Imperial Conquest*, pp. 34, 146–149, 152f.; Zirkel, 'Military Power', p. 92.
116. Hemming, *Amazon Frontier*, pp. 25–39, 104–123.
117. Billington/Ridge, *Westward Expansion*, pp. 61–82; Calloway, *Winter Count*, pp. 207–211.
118. Boot, *Savage Wars of Peace*, pp. 156–167; Moor, 'Warmakers in the Archipelago', p. 59f.
119. Nissimi, 'Illusions of World Power'; Walter, 'Kolonialkrieg, Globalstrategie und Kalter Krieg', pp. 111–116.
120. Denzer, 'Sierra Leone—Bai Bureh', pp. 234–244; Fynn, 'Ghana—Asante', pp. 44–46; Killingray, 'Colonial Warfare', p. 166f.; Lonsdale, 'Conquest State of Kenya', p. 111.
121. Pietschmann, 'Imperialkriege Spaniens', pp. 86–89.
122. Slatta, '"Civilization" Battles "Barbarism"', pp. 143–147; Vandervort, *Indian Wars*, pp. 229f., 239–242.
123. Gottmann, 'Bugeaud, Galliéni, Lyautey', p. 234f.; Hemming, *Red Gold*, p. xivf.; Hochgeschwender, 'Kolonialkriege als Experimentierstätten?', p. 277; Strachan, 'Typology of Transcultural Wars', p. 96.
124. Bergmann, 'Dynamik der Conquista', pp. 226–232; Pietschmann, 'Imperialkriege Spaniens', p. 84f. Prior to this, the destruction of the indigenous societies on Haiti was primarily motivated by the search for gold: Bitterli, *Die "Wilden" und die "Zivilisierten"*, p. 130.
125. Hemming, *Conquest of the Incas*, p. 73f.
126. According to precious metal prices in August 2013.
127. Billington, *Westward Expansion*, pp. 29–41; Calloway, *Winter Count*, pp. 126–145; Schindler, *Bauern und Reiterkrieger*, p. 18; Whitehead, 'Tribes Make States', pp. 142–144.
128. Bergmann, 'Dynamik der Conquista', p. 217f.; Bitterli, *Die "Wilden" und die "Zivilisierten"*, pp. 132–134; Jones, *Conquest of the Last Maya Kingdom*, p. 40f.
129. Hemming, *Red Gold*, pp. 34–40, 218–221. On the dimensions of Spanish and Portuguese slave hunting in the early sixteenth century, see Gabbert, 'Longue durée of Colonial Violence', p. 258f.
130. Hemming, *Red Gold*, pp. 244–252.
131. Ibid., pp. 355–369.
132. Hemming, *Amazon Frontier*, pp. 277–301.

133. Ramsey, "'Something Cloudy in Their Looks'", p. 60f.

134. Penn, *Forgotten Frontier*, p. 117f.

135. Thornton, 'Firearms, Diplomacy, and Conquest', p. 178f.; Thornton, 'Warfare, Slave Trading and European Influence', pp. 139–142.

136. Fage/Tordoff, *History of Africa*, pp. 244–286; Reinhard, *Geschichte der europäischen Expansion*, Vol. 2, pp. 139–152; Zeuske, *Geschichte der Amistad*.

137. Lindsay, *Murder State*; Utley, *Frontiersmen in Blue*, pp. 97f., 227–229.

138. Utley, *Frontier Regulars*, pp. 333–342; Utley, *Frontiersmen in Blue*, pp. 178–181, 187–200, 248–259; Vandervort, *Indian Wars*, pp. 197–199.

139. Utley, *Frontier Regulars*, pp. 242–248; Vandervort, *Indian Wars*, p. 174f.

140. Donnelly, *Conquest of Bashkiria*, p. 49; Lincoln, *Conquest of a Continent*, pp. 46–56.

141. Bodley, *Weg der Zerstörung*, p. 78; Vandervort, *Indian Wars*, p. 239f.

142. Penn, *Forgotten Frontier*, pp. 27–55, 91–102, 108–112.

143. Slatta, '"Civilization" Battles "Barbarism"', p. 131f.

144. Broome, *Aboriginal Australians*, pp. 41–43; Lindsay, *Murder State*, pp. 179–222.

145. Penn, *Forgotten Frontier*, p. 94.

146. Broome, *Aboriginal Australians*, pp. 40–48; Connor, *Australian Frontier Wars*, pp. 103–105.

147. Connor, *Australian Frontier Wars*, p. 120f.; Lindsay, *Murder State*, pp. 179–222; Penn, *Forgotten Frontier*, pp. 108–112; Schmidl, 'Kolonialkriege', p. 127f.; Utley, *Frontiersmen in Blue*, pp. 135–138, 172f.

148. Deenon, 'Understanding Settler Societies', p. 512.

149. Keeley, *War Before Civilization*, pp. 152–156; Lonsdale, 'Conquest State of Kenya', p. 115; Palmer, *Colonial Genocide*, pp. 40–58.

150. Bailey, 'Civilization the Military Way', p. 116; Finley, 'Colonies', p. 179f.; Pagden, *Lords of All the World*, p. 76f.; Penn, *Forgotten Frontier*, p. 129.

151. Lowenthal, 'Empires and Ecologies', p. 233f.; Middleton/Lombard, *Colonial America*, pp. 11–13.

152. Walter, 'Kolonialkrieg, Globalstrategie und Kalter Krieg', p. 123.

153. Cocker, *Rivers of Blood*, pp. 176–180; Finzsch, '"Extirpate or remove"', p. 216; Moses, 'Keywords', pp. 24–29; Palmer, *Colonial Genocide*, pp. 87–101; Penn, *Forgotten Frontier*, pp. 273–287.

154. Powell, *Soldiers, Indians and Silver*, pp. 172–175.

155. Lindsay, *Murder State*, pp. 319–323.

156. Reynolds, 'Genocide in Tasmania?', pp. 141–143.

157. Utley, *Frontiersmen in Blue*, p. 256.

158. Connell, *Son of the Morning Star*, p. 179f.; Kane, 'Nits Make Lice', p. 82; Utley, 'Total War', p. 399. This attribution is almost certainly apocryphal, since the phrase 'The only good Indian is a dead Indian' is verifiably older. Mieder, '"The Only Good Indian Is a Dead Indian"'.

159. Utley, *Frontier Regulars*, p. 111.

160. Edgerton, *Mau Mau*, pp. 142–154.

161. Ibid., p. 143.

162. Barkan, 'Genocides of Indigenous Peoples'; Broome, *Aboriginal Australians*, p. 50f.; Brower, *Desert Named Peace*, p. 23; Finzsch, '"The Aborigines ... were never annihilated"', p. 253f.; Lindsay, *Murder State*, p. 332f.; Palmer, *Colonial Genocide*, p. 195; Moses, *Genocide and Settler Society*, pp. 5f., 28–35.

163. Zimmerer, 'Geburt des "Ostlandes"'; Zimmerer, 'Holocaust und Kolonialismus', pp. 1111–1118.

164. Bailey, 'Civilization the Military Way', pp. 109–127; Utley, 'Total War', pp. 399–410.

165. Stucki, 'Antiguerilla-Kriegführung auf Kuba'.

166. Hull, *Absolute Destruction*, pp. 45–66; Kuß, *Deutsches Militär*, pp. 91–93. Cf. Potempa, 'Raum und seine Beherrschung', p. 460f.

167. Greiner, *Krieg ohne Fronten*, pp. 389–414.

168. Elkins, *Imperial Reckoning*.

169. Williams, *Year of the Hangman*, pp. 188–296.

170. Nester, *Frontier War*, p. 252.

171. Ibid., pp. 251–268; Williams, *Year of the Hangman*, pp. 188–296.

172. Walter, 'Der nordamerikanische Imperialkrieg', p. 95.

173. Freeman, 'Puritans and Pequots', pp. 290–293; Karr, '"Why Should You Be So Furious?"', p. 902f.; Katz, 'Pequot War Reconsidered'.

174. Slotkin, *Regeneration Through Violence*, pp. 69–78.

175. Starkey, *European and Native American Warfare*, p. 61.

176. Edmunds/Peyser, *Fox Wars*, pp. 119–157.

177. Vandervort, *Indian Wars*, p. 162.

178. Hurt, *Indian Frontier*.

179. Hemming, *Red Gold*, p. 349.

180. Hemming, *Amazon Frontier*, pp. 89–102.

181. Bodley, *Weg der Zerstörung*, p. 69f.

182. Cocker, *Rivers of Blood*, pp. 144–157.

183. Gann/Duignan, *Rulers of British Africa*, p. 144f.; James, *Raj*, pp. 74–77; Kanya-Forstner, 'French Marines', pp. 124–132; Vandervort, *Indian Wars*, pp. 172–174.

184. Jones, *Conquest of the Last Maya Kingdom*, p. 223; Karr, '"Why Should You Be So Furious?"', p. 897f.; Walter, '"The Enemy Must Be Brought to Battle"', p. 59.

185. Hassig, *Mexico and the Spanish Conquest*, pp. 100–102; Lee, 'Projecting Power', p. 5; Pietschmann, 'Imperialkriege Spaniens', p. 84f.

186. Greiner, *Krieg ohne Fronten*, pp. 74–88; Woolman, *Rebels in the Rif*, p. 198.

187. Gann/Duignan, *Rulers of German Africa*, p. 120; Jacobson, 'Imperial Ambitions'; Klein, 'Straffeldzug im Namen der Zivilisation', p. 164; Mücke, 'Agonie einer Kolonialmacht', p. 248f.; Porch, *Conquest of the Sahara*, p. 10f.; Rose, '"Unsichtbare Feinde"', p. 239; Zirkel, 'Military Power', pp. 98–103.

188. Greiner, *Krieg ohne Fronten*, pp. 64–73; Walter, 'Kolonialkrieg, Globalstrategie und Kalter Krieg', pp. 133–137.

189. Dahlmann, 'Sibirien', p. 57; Karr, '"Why Should You Be So Furious?"', p. 898f.; Lock/Quantrill, *Zulu Victory*, p. 25f.; Porch, *Conquest of the Sahara*, p. 211f.

190. Brogini-Künzi, 'Wunsch nach einem blitzschnellen Krieg', p. 274f.; McNeill, 'European Expansion, Power and Warfare', p. 12; Paillard, 'Expedition to Madagascar', p. 186.

191. Vandervort, *Wars of Imperial Conquest*, p. 59; Woolman, *Rebels in the Rif*, pp. 31–37.

192. Chandler, 'Expedition to Abyssinia', p. 149; Charney, 'Iberier und Südostasiaten', p. 180; Vandervort, *Wars of Imperial Conquest*, p. 84f.

193. Falls, 'Reconquest of the Sudan', p. 286; Mattioli, 'Kolonialverbrechen des faschistischen Italien', p. 205f.

194. Chamberlain, *Conquest of Yucatan*, pp. 12–15.

195. Bührer, 'Hehe und Schutztruppe', pp. 268–270; Bührer, *Kaiserliche Schutztruppe*,
pp. 211–235; Glass, *Matabele War*, pp. 1–83, 269–270; Lock/Quantrill, *Zulu
Victory*, pp. 19–27; Morlang, '"Die Wahehe haben ihre Vernichtung gewollt"',
pp. 81–85.

196. Gann/Duignan, *Rulers of Belgian Africa*, pp. 55–58; James, *Savage Wars*, pp. 141–
144; Vandervort, *Wars of Imperial Conquest*, pp. 140–144.

197. Nasson, *South African War*, pp. 47–49, 56f.

198. Fynn, 'Ghana—Asante', pp. 34–39; Kanya-Forstner, 'Mali—Tukulor', pp. 57–59,
75f.; Keegan, 'Ashanti Campaign', pp. 168–178; Law, 'Warfare on the Slave
Coast', pp. 121–125; Olatunji-Oloruntimehin, 'Senegambia—Mahmadou
La-mine', pp. 87–91, 102f.; Person, 'Guinea', pp. 126–129; Ross, 'Dahomey',
p. 147f.; Vandervort, *Wars of Imperial Conquest*, pp. 84–92.

199. Gould, *Imperial Warriors*, pp. 33–43; Pemble, 'Resources and Techniques', p. 275.

200. Abler, 'Beavers and Muskets'; Vandervort, *Indian Wars*, pp. xiv, 27–29, 170f.;
White, 'Winning of the West'.

201. Lee, 'Fortify, Fight, or Flee', p. 731f.

202. Calloway, *Winter Count*, p. 162; Donnelly, *Conquest of Bashkiria*, pp. 11f., 16;
Khodarkovsky, 'Krieg und Frieden', pp. 200–208, 212f., 217; Khodarkovsky,
Russia's Steppe Frontier, pp. 8–19, 221f.; Moreman, '"Watch and Ward"', pp. 139f.,
150; Mücke, 'Agonie einer Kolonialmacht', pp. 248–255; Porch, *Conquest of the
Sahara*, pp. 65–70; Porch, *Conquest of Morocco*, pp. 64–71; Utley, *Frontier Regulars*,
pp. 172–174; Utley, *Frontiersmen in Blue*, pp. 71–74, 81–84, 158, 165f.;
Vandervort, *Indian Wars*, pp. 38f., 161–164, 194–197.

203. Schindler, *Bauern und Reiterkrieger*, pp. 18–35.

204. Bodley, *Weg der Zerstörung*, p. 73f.

205. Utley, *Frontiersmen in Blue*, p. 237f.

206. Calloway, *Winter Count*, p. 205.

207. Broome, *Aboriginal Australians*, pp. 40–48; Connor, 'Briten und Darug', p. 229f.;
Lindsay, *Murder State*, pp. 181, 183; Palmer, *Colonial Genocide*, pp. 87–101; Slatta,
'"Civilization" Battles "Barbarism"', p. 131f.; Utley, *Frontier Regulars*, p. 323f.

208. Utley, *Frontiersmen in Blue*, pp. 5, 59f.; Vandervort, *Indian Wars*, p. 170f.

209. Hull, *Absolute Destruction*, p. 7f.; Penn, *Forgotten Frontier*, pp. 91–98; Ranger, *Revolt
in Southern Rhodesia*, pp. 105–113.

210. Powell, *Soldiers, Indians and Silver*, p. 27.

211. Broome, *Aboriginal Australians*, p. 42f.; Connor, 'Briten und Darug', p. 232f.;
Lindsay, *Murder State*, pp. 179–222; Palmer, *Colonial Genocide*, pp. 125–128.

212. Shell beads used as a substitute for hard currency.

213. Ramsey, '"Something Cloudy in Their Looks"', pp. 46–70; Starkey, *European and
Native American Warfare*, p. 60f.

214. Bayly, 'Editor's Concluding Note', p. 116; Stokes, *Peasant Armed*, pp. 100–
115.

215. Brower, *Desert Named Peace*, pp. 93–137.

216. Stockwell, '"A widespread and long-concocted plot"'; Stubbs, *Hearts and Minds*,
pp. 10–38.

217. Gallieni, *Pacification de Madagascar*, p. 9f.; Porch, *Conquest of the Sahara*, p. 223f.; Ranger, *Revolt in Southern Rhodesia*, p. 98.

218. Campbell, 'Social Structure of the Túpac Amaru', pp. 213–225.

219. Belich, *Victorian Interpretation*, p. 21; Billington, *Westward Expansion*, pp. 206–208; Connor, *Australian Frontier Wars*, p. 55f.; Häußler, 'Asymmetrie tribaler und staatlicher Kriegführung', pp. 183–186; Mattioli, 'Kolonialverbrechen des faschistischen Italien', p. 210f.; Rainero, 'Battle of Adowa', pp. 197–200; Ranger, *Revolt in Southern Rhodesia*, pp. 101–105; Utley, *Frontier Regulars*, p. 98f.; Vandervort, *Indian Wars*, pp. 110–115, 141–149.

220. Boot, *Savage Wars of Peace*, pp. 171–176; Calloway, *Winter Count*, p. 177f.; Fourniau, 'Colonial Wars before 1914', p. 84; Helbling, *Tribale Kriege*, p. 287; Hemming, *Amazon Frontier*, pp. 25–39; Jones, *Conquest of the Last Maya Kingdom*, pp. 40f., 397–405; Jones, *Maya Resistance to Spanish Rule*, pp. 189–276; Killingray, 'Colonial Warfare', p. 165; Knaap, 'Crisis and Failure', pp. 152–159; Olatunji-Oloruntimehin, 'Senegambia—Mahmadou Lamine', p. 83; Trotha, *Koloniale Herrschaft*, pp. 81–84; Weber, *Spanish Frontier*, pp. 122–141.

221. Ranger, 'African Reactions', p. 306.

222. Denzer, 'Sierra Leone—Bai Bureh', pp. 250–256; Donnelly, *Conquest of Bashkiria*, p. 21f.; Hack, 'Imperialism in Southeast Asia', p. 241; James, *Savage Wars*, pp. 45, 134; Knaut, *Pueblo Revolt*, pp. 153–159; Kuß, *Deutsches Militär*, pp. 102–107.

223. Jones, *Conquest of the Last Maya Kingdom*, pp. 135–142; Utley, *Frontier Regulars*, pp. 98–107, 121–125; Utley, *Frontiersmen in Blue*, p. 274f.; Woolman, *Rebels in the Rif*, pp. 31–36.

224. Helbling, *Tribale Kriege*, p. 287; Hemming, *Conquest of the Incas*, pp. 173–180; Hemming, *Red Gold*, pp. 69–71; Kars, '"Cleansing the Land"', p. 264f.; Penn, *Forgotten Frontier*, pp. 56–66; Utley, *Frontiersmen in Blue*, p. 227f.; Woolman, *Rebels in the Rif*, pp. 56, 71.

225. Kuß, *Deutsches Militär*, p. 80f.; Starkey, *European and Native American Warfare*, p. 66f.

226. Donnelly, *Conquest of Bashkiria*, p. 21f.; Khodarkovsky, *Russia's Steppe Frontier*, p. 172.

227. Belich, *Victorian Interpretation*, p. 32f.; Denzer, 'Sierra Leone—Bai Bureh', pp. 234–244; Gabbert, 'Longue durée of Colonial Violence', pp. 262–264; Hack, 'Imperialism in Southeast Asia', p. 244.

228. Hemming, *Amazon Frontier*, pp. 33–38; Jones, *Maya Resistance to Spanish Rule*, pp. 41–52; Utley, *Frontier Regulars*, pp. 370f., 401f.; Vandervort, *Indian Wars*, p. 215f.

229. Omissi, *Sepoy and the Raj*, p. 221f.; Walter, 'Kolonialkrieg, Globalstrategie und Kalter Krieg', p. 125.

230. Clayton, *Wars of French Decolonization*, p. 79f.; Gates, 'Two American Wars', pp. 51–53; Hemming, *Amazon Frontier*, p. 190f.; Morillo, 'Typology of Transcultural Wars', p. 36; Vandervort, *Indian Wars*, p. 111; Westad, *Global Cold War*, p. 399f.

231. Mollenhauer, 'Gesichter der pacification', pp. 329–333; Walter, 'Kolonialkrieg, Globalstrategie und Kalter Krieg', pp. 117–119.

232. Knaap, 'Crisis and Failure', p. 157.

233. Heathcote, *Military in British India*, pp. 61, 63, 88–91; James, *Savage Wars*, p. 150f.; Omissi, *Sepoy and the Raj*, p. 5.

234. Calloway, *Winter Count*, pp. 165–167, 175f., 196f.; Jobst, 'Expansion des Zarenreiches', p. 68f.; Jones, *Conquest of the Last Maya Kingdom*, pp. 43–52; Lemke, 'Kolonialgeschichte als Vorläufer?', p. 295; Linn, *Counterinsurgency in the Philippine War*, pp. 45–49; Miège, 'Conquest of Morocco', p. 210f.; Starkey, *European and Native American Warfare*, p. 66.

235. Gates, 'Two American Wars', pp. 62–65.

236. Cann, *Counterinsurgency in Africa*, pp. 18–26; Clayton, *Wars of French Decolonization*, pp. 79–84, 88–90, 93–98; Derradji, *Algerian Guerrilla Campaign*, pp. 61–106; Fourniau, 'Colonial Wars before 1914', pp. 73–75; Gates, 'Two American Wars', pp. 51–53; James, *Savage Wars*, pp. 112f., 144–146; Linn, *Counterinsurgency in the Philippine War*, pp. 3–5; Mücke, 'Agonie einer Kolonialmacht', p. 259; Rainero, 'Battle of Adowa', pp. 197–200; Ranger, 'African Reactions', pp. 312–318; Thomas, 'Order Before Reform', p. 204; Woolman, *Rebels in the Rif*, pp. 74–83.

237. Boot, *Savage Wars of Peace*, pp. 162–165; Linn, 'Cerberus' Dilemma', p. 116f.; Miège, 'Conquest of Morocco', p. 210f.; Paillard, 'Expedition to Madagascar', p. 188.

238. Fick, 'Revolution in Saint Domingue'; Geggus, 'Slavery, War, and Revolution'; Gliech, *Saint-Domingue und die französische Revolution*. Isolated slave revolts also took place in the south of British-controlled North America and the USA. Howe, *What Hath God Wrought*, pp. 160–163, 323–327; Middleton/Lombard, *Colonial America*, pp. 362–366; Wood, *Empire of Liberty*, pp. 534–537.

239. Boot, *Savage Wars of Peace*, p. 58; Broome, *Aboriginal Australians*, p. 45; De-Fronzo, *Iraq War*, pp. 212–214; Hemming, *Amazon Frontier*, p. 178; Hemming, *Conquest of the Incas*, pp. 181–183; Knaap, 'Crisis and Failure', p. 157f.; Moreman, '"Watch and Ward"', p. 149; Utley, *Frontiersmen in Blue*, pp. 120f., 285–287, 300–310; Vandervort, *Indian Wars*, pp. 171–175, 178, 201f.

240. Heathcote, *Military in British India*, p. 84f.

241. Woolman, *Rebels in the Rif*, p. 171f.

3. CROSSING BOUNDARIES

1. Killingray, 'Colonial Warfare', p. 157.

2. Crowder, 'Introduction', p. 16.

3. Le Cour Grandmaison, *Coloniser, Exterminer*, p. 184f.

4. Kreienbaum, 'Koloniale Gewaltexzesse', p. 172.

5. Kuß, *Deutsches Militär*, p. 11.

6. Cf. Hull, *Absolute Destruction*, p. 1.

7. Elkins, *Imperial Reckoning*, p. 272; Hochgeschwender, 'Kolonialkriege als Experimentierstätten?', p. 277; Malone, 'Changing Military Technology', p. 242; May, 'Philippine-American War'; Mukherjee, *Spectre of Violence*, p. 34; Peers, 'Introduction', p. xxiif.; Porch, 'French Colonial Forces', p. 166; Starkey, *European and Native American Warfare*, p. 164; Trotha, '"The Fellows Can Just Starve"'; Utley, 'Total War'; Utley, *Frontiersmen in Blue*, p. 346; Wesseling, 'Colonial Wars', p. 5.

8. Walter, 'Warum Kolonialkrieg?', pp. 36–40.

9. For a summary, see Förster, 'Einleitung'. See also the edited volumes in the series 'The Age of Total War' and especially the introductions by the editors: Chickering/Förster/Greiner, *World at Total War*; Chickering/Förster, *Shadows of Total War*;

Chickering/Förster, *Great War*; Boemeke/Chickering/Förster, *Anticipating Total War*; Förster/Nagler, *Road to Total War*.

10. Cf. chapter 1, 'The power of empires'.

11. Bell, *First Total War*, pp. 154–185.

12. Knaap, 'Crisis and Failure', p. 161.

13. Connor, *Australian Frontier Wars*, pp. 49–51.

14. Chandler, 'Expedition to Abyssinia', p. 132.

15. James, *Savage Wars*, p. 236.

16. Fall, *Hell in a Very Small Place*, pp. 228–230, 250–252; Nasson, *South African War*, pp. 12, 206–208; Woolman, *Rebels in the Rif*, pp. 200, 206f.

17. James, *Savage Wars*, pp. 225–228.

18. Walter, 'Kein Pardon'.

19. Both here and in the following footnotes, I offer just a few examples in evidence: Belich, *Victorian Interpretation*, p. 43; Bührer, *Kaiserliche Schutztruppe*, p. 265f.; Connor, *Australian Frontier Wars*, p. 83; Crawford, 'Sikh Wars', pp. 45, 63, 64; Fall, *Hell in a Very Small Place*, p. 83; Greiner, *Krieg ohne Fronten*, pp. 219–223; Hemming, *Conquest of the Incas*, p. 195; Hemming, *Red Gold*, pp. 285, 302; James, *Savage Wars*, p. 207f.; Kiernan, *Colonial Empires*, p. 164; Linn, 'Cerberus' Dilemma', p. 122; Mücke, 'Agonie einer Kolonialmacht', p. 262f.; Nasson, *South African War*, p. 88f.; Starkey, *European and Native American Warfare*, p. 122f.; Streets, *Martial Races*, p. 40f.; Utley, *Frontiersmen in Blue*, pp. 135, 156f., 168; Vandervort, *Indian Wars*, pp. 120, 135, 151, 154.

20. Utley, *Frontiersmen in Blue*, p. 235.

21. Hemming, *Red Gold*, p. 29; Keeley, *War Before Civilization*, pp. 83–88.

22. Edgerton, *Mau Mau*, p. 124f.; Hassig, 'Eroberung Mexikos', p. 118f.; Knight, *Anatomy of the Zulu Army*, pp. 221–227; Mostert, *Military System*, p. 107; Porch, *Conquest of Morocco*, p. 178; Rickey, *Forty Miles a Day*, p. 316; Robson, *Fuzzy-Wuzzy*, p. 52.

23. Gordon, *Khartoum Journal*, p. 141; Hull, *Absolute Destruction*, p. 14f.; James, *Savage Wars*, p. 172; Klose, *Menschenrechte im Schatten kolonialer Gewalt*, p. 184; Woolman, *Rebels in the Rif*, p. 154f.

24. Altman, 'Conquest, Coercion, and Collaboration', p. 166; Barrett, *Edge of Empire*, p. 156; Belich, *Victorian Interpretation*, p. 105f.; Billington, *Westward Expansion*, p. 53f.; Brower, *Desert Named Peace*, p. 22; Calloway, *Winter Count*, pp. 114f., 198f.; Callwell, *Small Wars*, pp. 133, 145–149; Chet, *Conquering the Wilderness*, p. 22; Connor, 'Briten und Darug', p. 232f.; Hull, *Absolute Destruction*, p. 195f.; Khodarkovsky, 'Krieg und Frieden', p. 216; Malone, *Skulking Way of War*, p. 96; Nasson, *South African War*, p. 211f.; Penn, *Forgotten Frontier*, p. 123f.; Porch, *Conquest of Morocco*, p. 178f.; Powell, *Soldiers, Indians and Silver*, p. 40; Starkey, *European and Native American Warfare*, p. 41f.; Stucki, 'Bevölkerungskontrolle in asymmetrischen Konflikten', p. 244f.

25. Nester, *Frontier War*, p. 267.

26. Broome, *Aboriginal Australians*, p. 45; Connor, *Australian Frontier Wars*, pp. 115–117.

27. James, *Savage Wars*, p. 36.

28. Meinertzhagen, *Kenya Diary*, p. 282f.

29. Linn, *Counterinsurgency in the Philippine War*, p. 157f.

30. Mattioli, 'Kolonialverbrechen des faschistischen Italien', p. 218.

31. Jones, *Graveyard of Empires*, p. 218.

32. Altman, 'Conquest, Coercion, and Collaboration', p. 158; Charney, 'Iberier und Südostasiaten', p. 183f.; Gann/Duignan, *Rulers of British Africa*, pp. 142–144; Greiner, *Krieg ohne Fronten*, pp. 92–95; Hemming, *Red Gold*, pp. 69–89; Hirschfeld, 'Kriegsgreuel im Dekolonisierungsprozess', p. 363; Ikime, 'Nigeria—Ebrohimi', p. 220; Kuß, *Deutsches Militär*, pp. 65–77; Mukherjee, *Spectre of Violence*, p. 31; Nester, *Frontier War*, p. 267; Smith, 'Nigeria—Ijebu', p. 185f.; Utley, *Frontier Regulars*, pp. 50–52; Utley, *Frontiersmen in Blue*, p. 111f.

33. Le Cour Grandmaison, *Coloniser, Exterminer*, pp. 146–152.

34. Callwell, *Small Wars*, pp. 308–310.

35. Calloway, *Winter Count*, pp. 147–149; Hemming, *Conquest of the Incas*, pp. 199–202; Starkey, *European and Native American Warfare*, pp. 74–77.

36. Utley, *Frontiersmen in Blue*, pp. 290–297; Vandervort, *Indian Wars*, p. 172f.

37. Utley, *Custer*, p. 74f.; Utley, *Frontier Regulars*, p. 192f., 347–349; Utley, *Frontiersmen in Blue*, pp. 125–133, 152–157, 342–346.

38. Porch, 'French Colonial Forces', p. 166f.

39. Vandervort, *Indian Wars*, p. 147f.

40. Meinertzhagen, *Kenya Diary*, pp. 39f., 50–52.

41. Bertrand, 'Violences impériales', pp. 134–136; Cocker, *Rivers of Blood*, p. 3f.; Klein, 'Straffeldzug im Namen der Zivilisation', pp. 156–161; Koller, 'Französische Fremdenlegion', p. 380; Moor, 'Warmakers in the Archipelago', p. 59; Morlang, '"Die Wahehe haben ihre Vernichtung gewollt"', p. 84f.; Porch, *Conquest of the Sahara*, pp. 181–197.

42. Corum/Johnson, *Airpower in Small Wars*, p. 79; Lemke, 'Kolonialgeschichte als Vorläufer?', p. 284.

43. Bourke, *History of Killing*, pp. 171–183; Greiner, *Krieg ohne Fronten*, pp. 90–119.

44. Grau, *Bear Over the Mountain*, p. 207f.; Jones, *Graveyard of Empires*, p. 29.

45. Bierling, *Geschichte des Irakkriegs*, p. 173f.; Jones, *Graveyard of Empires*, pp. 303–306.

46. Powell, *Soldiers, Indians and Silver*, pp. 53, 74.

47. Calloway, *Winter Count*, pp. 174–176.

48. Hochgeschwender, 'Last Stand', p. 76; Lee, 'Fortify, Fight, or Flee', p. 732f.; Starkey, *European and Native American Warfare*, p. 27; Utley, *Frontiersmen in Blue*, pp. 262–265.

49. Belich, *Victorian Interpretation*, p. 82; Connor, 'Briten und Darug', p. 232f.; Connor, *Australian Frontier Wars*, pp. 40–43.

50. Kuß, *Deutsches Militär*, p. 107.

51. Clayton, *Wars of French Decolonization*, p. 118f.; Häußler, 'Asymmetrie tribaler und staatlicher Kriegführung', pp. 183–186.

52. Cann, *Counterinsurgency in Africa*, p. 27.

53. Cahn, 'Kriegsgreuel im Algerienkrieg', pp. 372–374.

54. Bührer, *Kaiserliche Schutztruppe*, pp. 256–258; Calloway, *Winter Count*, pp. 126–132, 148f.; Dahlmann, 'Sibirien', p. 62f.; Hemming, *Red Gold*, pp. 134–138; Kanya-Forstner, 'French Marines', p. 140f.; Karr, '"Why Should You Be So Furious?"', p. 899; Khodarkovsky, 'Krieg und Frieden', p. 216; Lee, 'Fortify, Fight, or Flee', p. 743f.; Powell, *Soldiers, Indians and Silver*, pp. 106–111; Starkey, *European and*

Native American Warfare, p. 80f.; Vandervort, *Indian Wars*, p. 120f.; Vandervort, *Wars of Imperial Conquest*, p. 145.

55. Bührer, *Kaiserliche Schutztruppe*, p. 258f.; Dahlmann, 'Sibirien', p. 62f.; Kuß, *Deutsches Militär*, pp. 122–124; Lappas, 'Lernen inmitten des Blutvergießens', pp. 157–162; Morlang, '"Die Wahehe haben ihre Vernichtung gewollt"', p. 95; Utley, *Frontier Regulars*, pp. 153–155; Vandervort, *Indian Wars*, p. 199.

56. Greiner, *Krieg ohne Fronten*, pp. 106, 111; Hemming, *Conquest of the Incas*, pp. 57, 63; Linn, *Counterinsurgency in the Philippine War*, p. 57f.

57. Cahn, 'Kriegsgreuel im Algerienkrieg', pp. 376–380; Clayton, *Wars of French Decolonization*, p. 132f.; Klose, *Menschenrechte im Schatten kolonialer Gewalt*, pp. 227–237; Mollenhauer, 'Gesichter der pacification', pp. 346–348.

58. Trinquier, *Guerre moderne*, pp. 14–21.

59. Calloway, *Winter Count*, p. 139; Clayton, *Wars of French Decolonization*, p. 85; Edgerton, *Mau Mau*, p. 159; Greiner, *Krieg ohne Fronten*, pp. 223–227; Hemming, *Amazon Frontier*, p. 177; Jobst, 'Expansion des Zarenreiches', p. 69; Kiernan, *Colonial Empires*, p. 215; Selby, 'Third China War', p. 80.

60. Utley, *Frontiersmen in Blue*, p. 295f.

61. Broome, *Aboriginal Australians*, p. 45; Edgerton, *Mau Mau*, p. 159.

62. Calloway, *Winter Count*, p. 149; Hassig, *Mexico and the Spanish Conquest*, p. 89; Hemming, *Conquest of the Incas*, p. 199; Hemming, *Red Gold*, p. 400; Penn, *Forgotten Frontier*, p. 74; Powell, *Soldiers, Indians and Silver*, pp. 83, 86; Schindler, *Bauern und Reiterkrieger*, p. 20; Vandervort, *Wars of Imperial Conquest*, p. 145.

63. Eskildsen, 'Civilization and Savages', p. 403f.; Hée, *Imperiales Wissen*, pp. 204–208.

64. Hemming, *Conquest of the Incas*, p. 215; Powell, *Soldiers, Indians and Silver*, p. 109.

65. Hemming, *Conquest of the Incas*, p. 157f.

66. Bourke, *History of Killing*, pp. 38–41; Hemming, *Amazon Frontier*, p. 357; Le Cour Grandmaison, *Coloniser, Exterminer*, p. 157; Starkey, *European and Native American Warfare*, p. 59; Vandervort, *Indian Wars*, pp. 120f., 201; Woolman, *Rebels in the Rif*, p. 201f.

67. Lappas, 'Lernen inmitten des Blutvergießens', p. 171.

68. Connell, *Son of the Morning Star*, p. 194; Edgerton, *Mau Mau*, pp. 124–126; Hull, *Absolute Destruction*, p. 10f.; Knight, *Anatomy of the Zulu Army*, pp. 224–227; Lock/ Quantrill, *Zulu Victory*, p. 228f.; Powell, *Soldiers, Indians and Silver*, pp. 50–52; Rickey, *Forty Miles a Day*, p. 314; Starkey, 'Conflict and Synthesis', pp. 69–71; Utley, *Frontiersmen in Blue*, p. 191f.

69. Steele, *Betrayals*, pp. 84–90; Thornton, 'Firearms, Diplomacy, and Conquest', p. 182; Vandervort, *Wars of Imperial Conquest*, p. 139.

70. Mukherjee, *Spectre of Violence*, pp. 41–45.

71. Lehmann, *All Sir Garnet*, p. 53.

72. Said, *Orientalism*.

73. Klein, 'Straffeldzug im Namen der Zivilisation', p. 161; Le Cour Grandmaison, *Coloniser, Exterminer*, p. 157.

74. Heathcote, *Military in British India*, p. 105.

75. Schumacher, '"Niederbrennen, plündern und töten"', p. 125.

76. Fourniau, 'Colonial Wars before 1914', p. 84; Le Cour Grandmaison, *Coloniser, Exterminer*, pp. 168–173.

77. Hemming, *Conquest of the Incas*, p. 432f.
78. Falls, 'Reconquest of the Sudan', p. 299.
79. Morlang, '"Die Wahehe haben ihre Vernichtung gewollt"', p. 95.
80. Fourniau, 'Colonial Wars before 1914', p. 84.
81. Selby, 'Third China War', pp. 76, 103.
82. Fynn, 'Ghana—Asante', p. 45f.
83. Connor, *Australian Frontier Wars*, pp. 28–31; Fenn, 'Biological Warfare'; Finzsch, '"Extirpate or remove"', pp. 221–224; Finzsch, 'Frühgeschichte der biologischen Kriegführung', pp. 13–19; Hemming, *Amazon Frontier*, p. 153; Lindsay, *Murder State*, p. 320.
84. Spiers, 'Dum Dum Bullet'.
85. Del Boca, 'Faschismus und Kolonialismus', p. 194f.; Hée, *Imperiales Wissen*, p. 203f.; Klose, *Menschenrechte im Schatten kolonialer Gewalt*, p. 186–190; Kunz, '"Con ayuda del más dañino de todos los gases"'; Mattioli, 'Kolonialverbrechen des faschistischen Italien', pp. 211f., 217.
86. The French Army, however, also deployed napalm in its joint campaign with Spain against the Moroccan expansion in 1958. Fleming, 'Decolonization and the Spanish Army', p. 131.
87. Isby, *War in a Distant Country*, p. 76; Jones, *Graveyard of Empires*, p. 29.
88. Cocker, *Rivers of Blood*, p. 140f.; Lindsay, *Murder State*, p. 320.
89. Cf. chapter 1, 'Political warfare', and chapter 2, 'Total war aims'.
90. Del Boca, 'Faschismus und Kolonialismus', p. 195f.; Hull, *Absolute Destruction*, pp. 70–90.
91. Karr, '"Why Should You Be So Furious?"', pp. 881–888; Parker, 'Early Modern Europe', pp. 40–50.
92. Grotius, *De jure belli ac pacis*, pp. 447–532 (Book 3, chapters 4–14).
93. Parker, 'Early Modern Europe', pp. 51–55.
94. Cf. chapter 1, 'Grey areas'.
95. Anderson, *Histories of the Hanged*, p. 6f.; Bailey, 'Civilization the Military Way', p. 111; Bührer, *Kaiserliche Schutztruppe*, p. 274; Calloway, *Winter Count*, pp. 177–185; Campbell, 'Social Structure of the Túpac Amaru', p. 227; Clayton, *Wars of French Decolonization*, pp. 86, 103f.; Denzer, 'Sierra Leone—Bai Bureh', p. 263; Heathcote, *Military in British India*, p. 63; Hemming, *Conquest of the Incas*, p. 162; Howe, *What Hath God Wrought*, p. 102; Howe, *Empire*, p. 97; Hull, *Absolute Destruction*, p. 18f.; Ikime, 'Nigeria—Ebrohimi', p. 227f.; Kanya-Forstner, 'French Marines', p. 141; Lehmann, *All Sir Garnet*, p. 53; Marshall, *Russian General Staff*, p. 122f.; Mockaitis, *British Counterinsurgency*, p. 67f.; Penn, *Forgotten Frontier*, p. 106f.; Person, 'Guinea', p. 139f.; Powell, *Soldiers, Indians and Silver*, pp. 106–111; Vandervort, *Indian Wars*, p. 228.
96. Fenn, 'Biological Warfare', p. 1573f.; Kiernan, *Colonial Empires*, p. 154f.; Parker, 'Early Modern Europe', p. 56f.
97. Vattel, *Droit des gens*, Vol. 2, p. 107f. (Book 3, chapter 8, § 141).
98. Kleinschmidt, *Diskriminierung durch Vertrag und Krieg*, p. 137.
99. Hull, 'Military Culture and "Final Solutions"', p. 153; Klose, 'Legitimation kolonialer Gewalt', p. 266f.; Strachan, 'Typology of Transcultural Wars', p. 91.
100. Kleinschmidt, *Diskriminierung durch Vertrag und Krieg*, pp. 113–137.
101. Best, *Humanity in Warfare*.

102. Greiner, '"First to Go"', p. 252; Hirsch, 'Collision of Military Cultures', pp. 1207–1209; Hull, 'Military Culture and "Final Solutions"', p. 153; Karr, '"Why Should You Be So Furious?"', pp. 900–903; Kiernan, *Colonial Empires*, pp. 155–157; Klein, 'Straffeldzug im Namen der Zivilisation', pp. 158, 170; Kleinschmidt, *Diskriminierung durch Vertrag und Krieg*, pp. 24, 124; Schmidl, 'Kolonialkriege', p. 117f.

103. Kramer, 'Race-Making and Colonial Violence', pp. 198–201, 205.

104. James, *Savage Wars*, p. 184f.

105. Bourke, *History of Killing*, p. 229.

106. Bitterli, *Die "Wilden" und die "Zivilisierten"*, p. 140.

107. Starkey, *European and Native American Warfare*, pp. 26–28.

108. Hakami, 'Clash of Structures', p. 163.

109. Keeley, *War Before Civilization*, p. 176; Porch, 'French Colonial Forces', p. 166.

110. Hirsch, 'Collision of Military Cultures'; Karr, '"Why Should You Be So Furious?"'.

111. Häußler, 'Asymmetrie tribaler und staatlicher Kriegführung', p. 194f.; Hull, *Absolute Destruction*, p. 10f.

112. Powell, *Soldiers, Indians and Silver*, pp. 50–52, 107f.

113. Le Cour Grandmaison, *Coloniser, Exterminer*, p. 195.

114. Bührer, *Kaiserliche Schutztruppe*, p. 270; Kuß, *Deutsches Militär*, pp. 189–198, 349f.

115. Trinquier, *Guerre moderne*, p. 105.

116. Luttrell, *Lone Survivor*, p. 312.

117. Callwell, *Small Wars*, p. 31.

118. Ibid, p. 40.

119. Porter, *Military Orientalism*, pp. 40, 42.

120. Callwell, *Small Wars*, p. 145. Cf. also Chacón, *Guerras Irregulares*, Vol. 1, pp. 20–23, 63–89. I am indebted to Andreas Stucki for providing me with this reference.

121. Callwell, *Small Wars*, p. 146.

122. Churchill, *Frontiers and Wars*, p. 110.

123. Sir Jeffery Amherst, 1760, quoted in Lee, 'Fortify, Fight, or Flee', p. 766.

124. Bührer, *Kaiserliche Schutztruppe*, p. 258f.; Denzer, 'Sierra Leone—Bai Bureh', pp. 256–262; Grenier, *First Way of War*, p. 1; Howe, *What Hath God Wrought*, p. 516f.; James, *Savage Wars*, pp. 36–37, 184; Jobst, 'Expansion des Zarenreiches', pp. 68–70; Karr, '"Why Should You Be So Furious?"', pp. 899–901; Le Cour Grandmaison, *Coloniser, Exterminer*, p. 173; Linn, *Counterinsurgency in the Philippine War*, pp. 57–60; Potempa, 'Raum und seine Beherrschung', p. 453; Raudzens, 'Why Did Amerindian Defences Fail?', p. 338; Rink, 'Kleiner Krieg', p. 437f.; Starkey, *European and Native American Warfare*, pp. 122–125; Stucki, 'Bevölkerungskontrolle in asymmetrischen Konflikten', p. 244f.; Utley, *Frontiersmen in Blue*, p. 345f.; Vandervort, *Indian Wars*, pp. 128, 134–135. However, as a rule the precise mechanisms of this successive extension of the accepted limits of the use of legitimate force have not been studied, either in individual cases or in general. Far more research is required in this field.

125. Douhet, *Dominio dell'aria*, pp. 7–27.

126. Kunz, '"Con ayuda del más dañino de todos los gases"'.

127. Barrett, *Edge of Empire*, pp. 155f., 165; Clayton, *Wars of French Decolonization*, p. 118f.; Grau, *Bear Over the Mountain*, p. 207; Klose, *Menschenrechte im Schatten kolonialer Gewalt*, pp. 173–175, 180–182; Le Cour Grandmaison, *Coloniser,*

Exterminer, pp. 207–223; Linn, *Counterinsurgency in the Philippine War*, pp. 152–154; Mattioli, 'Kolonialverbrechen des faschistischen Italien', pp. 208, 214; Palmer, *Colonial Genocide*, pp. 50–55; Porch, *Conquest of Morocco*, pp. 122–127; Utley, *Frontiersmen in Blue*, pp. 111f., 165f., 237–248.

128. Nasson, *South African War*, p. 217f.; Rose, '"Unsichtbare Feinde"', p. 230f.

129. Hull, *Absolute Destruction*, pp. 45–66, 195–196; Kuß, *Deutsches Militär*, pp. 91–93; Potempa, 'Raum und seine Beherrschung', p. 460f.

130. Bourke, *History of Killing*, p. 190; Greiner, *Krieg ohne Fronten*, p. 221f.; Steele, *Betrayals*, p. 74; Utley, *Frontiersmen in Blue*, p. 168.

131. Clayton, *Wars of French Decolonization*, p. 132f.

132. Hirschfeld, 'Kriegsgreuel im Dekolonisierungsprozess', p. 366f.; James, *Savage Wars*, pp. 173, 207f.

133. Andreopoulos, 'National Liberation Movements', p. 195; Best, *Humanity in Warfare*, pp. 118–120; Strachan, 'Typology of Transcultural Wars', p. 90.

134. Hull, 'Military Culture and "Final Solutions"', p. 153; Schmidl, 'Kolonialkriege', p. 118; Utley, *Frontier Regulars*, p. 407f. Cf. Pretorius, 'Uniform and not so Uniform'.

135. Bierling, *Geschichte des Irakkriegs*, p. 173f.

136. Barth, '"Partisan" und "Partisanenkrieg"', p. 94; Bourke, *History of Killing*, p. 188; Laqueur, *Guerrilla Warfare*, p. 399; Penn, *Forgotten Frontier*, pp. 58–61; Walter, 'Der nordamerikanische Imperialkrieg', p. 104.

137. Connor, *Australian Frontier Wars*, pp. 46–52.

138. Bührer, *Kaiserliche Schutztruppe*, pp. 246–256; Kuß, *Deutsches Militär*, pp. 256–258; Porch, *Conquest of the Sahara*, pp. 200–207.

139. Utley, *Custer*, p. 74f.

140. Hochgeschwender, 'Last Stand', p. 60; Starkey, *European and Native American Warfare*, pp. 68–71; Utley, *Frontier Regulars*, p. 190f.; Utley, *Frontiersmen in Blue*, pp. 154, 311f.

141. Khodarkovsky, 'Krieg und Frieden', p. 216.

142. Callwell, *Small Wars*, p. 210.

143. Klein, 'Straffeldzug im Namen der Zivilisation', p. 160; Kuß, *Deutsches Militär*, p. 69.

144. Klein, 'Straffeldzug im Namen der Zivilisation', p. 170.

145. Linn, *Counterinsurgency in the Philippine War*, p. 119.

146. Greiner, *Krieg ohne Fronten*, p. 119.

147. Petillo, 'Leaders and Followers', p. 202; Schumacher, '"Niederbrennen, plündern und töten"', p. 126.

148. Cf. chapter 1, 'The enemies of empire'.

149. Wesseling, 'Colonial Wars', p. 4f.

150. Cann, *Counterinsurgency in Africa*, p. 28; Grau, *Bear Over the Mountain*, p. 208; Greiner, *Krieg ohne Fronten*, pp. 92–95; Jones, *Graveyard of Empires*, pp. 303–306.

151. Cullen, 'Targeted Killing', p. 25; McCrisken, 'Obama's Drone War', p. 115.

152. Cf. chapter 1, 'Spatial conditions' und 'Logistics and mobility'.

153. Brower, *Desert Named Peace*, p. 77f.; Calloway, *Winter Count*, pp. 126–149; James, *Savage Wars*, pp. 225–228; Jones, *Conquest of the Last Maya Kingdom*, p. 365; Lock/Quantrill, *Zulu Victory*, p. 78f.; Michels, '"Ostasiatisches Expeditionskorps"',

pp. 406–412; Moor, 'Warmakers in the Archipelago', pp. 57–59; Selby, 'Third China War', p. 87.

154. Belich, *Victorian Interpretation*, pp. 104–107; Connor, 'Briten und Darug', p. 232f.; Connor, *Australian Frontier Wars*, pp. 40–43; Gordon, 'Limited Adoption', p. 233.

155. Fourniau, 'Colonial Wars before 1914', p. 84; Gann/Duignan, *Rulers of British Africa*, pp. 148–150; Kanya-Forstner, 'French Marines', p. 140f.; Kiernan, *Colonial Empires*, p. 127; Porch, *Conquest of the Sahara*, pp. 187, 235–239.

156. Gann/Duignan, *Rulers of British Africa*, p. 120f.; Trotha, *Koloniale Herrschaft*, pp. 41–44.

157. Lonsdale, 'Conquest State of Kenya', pp. 111, 115; Pietschmann, 'Imperialkriege Spaniens', p. 92; Whitehead, 'Tribes Make States', p. 144f.

158. Bodley, *Weg der Zerstörung*, pp. 62–64; Kuß, *Deutsches Militär*, pp. 243–251. Cf. chapter 2, 'Punitive expeditions'.

159. Bailey, 'Civilization the Military Way', pp. 109–127; Belich, *Victorian Interpretation*, pp. 92, 328; Dabringhaus, 'Army on Vacation?', p. 469; Herold, 'Fliegendes Kreuzergeschwader', p. 399f.; Kuß, *Deutsches Militär*, pp. 118f., 124; Lemke, 'Kolonialgeschichte als Vorläufer?', p. 285; Mann, 'Gewaltdispositiv des Kolonialismus', pp. 113–115; Mockaitis, *British Counterinsurgency*, pp. 63–65.

160. Osterhammel, '"Uplifting Mankind"', pp. 366f., 372.

161. Vann, 'Fear and Loathing'.

162. Furedi, 'Demobilized African Soldier'; Gottmann, 'Bugeaud, Galliéni, Lyautey', p. 258f.; Kiernan, *Colonial Empires*, p. 157f.; Vandervort, *Indian Wars*, pp. 208–210; Vandervort, *Wars of Imperial Conquest*, p. 92f.

163. Chet, *Conquering the Wilderness*, p. 19f.; Marshall, *Russian General Staff*, p. 61f.; Mostert, *Military System*, pp. 32–34.

164. James, *Savage Wars*, pp. 120–122; Trotha, *Koloniale Herrschaft*, p. 38.

165. Belich, *Victorian Interpretation*, pp. 82, 99; Gwynn, *Imperial Policing*, p. 15; Lemke, 'Kolonialgeschichte als Vorläufer?', p. 285.

166. Bailey, 'Civilization the Military Way', p. 114; Hull, *Absolute Destruction*, p. 177; Linn, 'Cerberus' Dilemma', p. 122; Morlang, '"Die Wahehe haben ihre Vernichtung gewollt"', p. 91; Trotha, *Koloniale Herrschaft*, p. 155f.; Vandervort, *Indian Wars*, p. 76f.

167. Callwell, *Small Wars*, p. 148.

168. Longacre, *John Buford*, p. 43.

169. Boot, *Savage Wars of Peace*, p. 163; Bryant, 'Asymmetric Warfare', p. 465f.; Gann/Duignan, *Rulers of British Africa*, p. 76f.; Hemming, *Conquest of the Incas*, p. 110; James, *Raj*, p. 64; Marshall, *Russian General Staff*, p. 73; Potempa, 'Raum und seine Beherrschung', p. 458, 460f.; Utley, *Custer*, p. 158; Wesseling, 'Wars and Peace', pp. 67–69.

170. Callwell, *Small Wars*, p. 72f.

171. Ibid, p. 82. Cf. Whittingham, '"Savage Warfare"', pp. 592, 594–598. The glorification of the permanent offensive can sometimes be found reflected uncritically even in modern scholarly treatments: 'Indecision, any show of weakness would be absolutely fatal in Algeria.' Singer/Langdon, *Cultured Force*, p. 76. See also: Boot, *Savage Wars of Peace*, p. 347.

172. Callwell, *Small Wars*, pp. 106, 150f., 159–176, 194; Kiernan, *Colonial Empires*,

p. 49f.; Meinertzhagen, *Kenya Diary*, pp. 251, 264f., 292–295; Nasson, *South African War*, p. 117. Indeed, this is positively a leitmotif in Callwell.

173. Quoted in Charney, *Southeast Asian Warfare*, p. 269.

174. Walter, '"The Enemy Must Be Brought to Battle"'.

175. Brower, *Desert Named Peace*, pp. 16f., 22, 83f.; Calloway, *Winter Count*, pp. 147–149, 177–185; Clayton, *Wars of French Decolonization*, p. 129f.; Connor, *Australian Frontier Wars*, pp. 62–67, 107–111; Gallois, 'Dahra and the History of Violence'; Hassig, *Mexico and the Spanish Conquest*, p. 89; Hemming, *Conquest of the Incas*, pp. 215, 198f.; Hemming, *Red Gold*, pp. 349, 358; Hirschfeld, 'Kriegsgreuel im Dekolonisierungsprozess', pp. 363–368; Hochgeschwender, 'Kolonialkriege als Experimentierstätten?', p. 283f.; Hochgeschwender, 'Last Stand', p. 76; Hull, *Absolute Destruction*, p. 26f.; Isby, *War in a Distant Country*, p. 56; James, *Savage Wars*, p. 184f.; Kiernan, *Colonial Empires*, p. 160f.; Le Cour Grandmaison, *Coloniser, Exterminer*, pp. 146–161; Marshall, *Russian General Staff*, p. 62; Morlang, '"Die Wahehe haben ihre Vernichtung gewollt"', pp. 93–97; Penn, *Forgotten Frontier*, pp. 67–77; Slatta, '"Civilization" Battles "Barbarism"'.

176. Quoted in Drechsler, *Südwestafrika unter Kolonialherrschaft*, p. 156.

177. Mukherjee, *Spectre of Violence*, pp. 23–34; Kiernan, *Colonial Empires*, p. 117f. Cf. chapter 3, 'Discourses on retribution'.

178. Cf. chapter 1, 'Political warfare'.

179. Gates, 'Two American Wars', pp. 47–51; Lieb, 'Guerre Révolutionnaire'.

180. Waldmann, *Terrorismus und Bürgerkrieg*, p. 38.

181. Beckett, *Modern Insurgencies*, pp. 88f., 155, 188; Cahn, 'Kriegsgreuel im Algerienkrieg', pp. 372–374; Clayton, *Wars of French Decolonization*, p. 127f.; Hirschfeld, 'Kriegsgreuel im Dekolonisierungsprozess', pp. 363; Law, *Terrorism*, pp. 188–214; Linn, *Counterinsurgency in the Philippine War*, pp. 133–135; Maloba, *Mau Mau and Kenya*, p. 119. Cf. Schneckener, *Transnationaler Terrorismus*, p. 22f.

182. Osterhammel, '"Uplifting Mankind"', p. 365.

183. Bradford, 'Preface', pp. xviii, xx.

184. Morillo, 'Typology of Transcultural Wars', p. 34.

185. Powell, *Soldiers, Indians and Silver*, p. 46.

186. Hemming, *Conquest of the Incas*, p. 198f.; Hunt, *Wars of the Iroquois*, p. 135; Starkey, *European and Native American Warfare*, p. 14.

187. Calloway, *Winter Count*, p. 175f.; Campbell, 'Social Structure of the Túpac Amaru', p. 226f.; Hering Torres, 'Fremdheit', Para. 1227; Hochgeschwender, 'Last Stand', pp. 47–49; Kramer, 'Empires, Exceptions, and Anglo-Saxons', pp. 1320–1335; Malone, *Skulking Way of War*, p. 75; Rüther, 'Religiöse Interaktion', Sp. 1166; Slotkin, *Regeneration Through Violence*, pp. 37–42. On the connection between religion and racism in the Early Modern period, cf. Kidd, *Forging of Races*, pp. 54–78.

188. Barth, 'Grenzen der Zivilisierungsmission', p. 202f.; Barth, '"Partisan" und "Partisanenkrieg"', p. 98; Finzsch, 'Frühgeschichte der biologischen Kriegführung', pp. 21–25; Gay, *Cultivation of Hatred*, pp. 68–95; Hochgeschwender, 'Last Stand', p. 73f.; Mann, 'Gewaltdispositiv des Kolonialismus', p. 114f.; Michels, '"Ostasiatisches Expeditionskorps"', pp. 412–416; Mücke, 'Agonie einer Kolonialmacht', p. 263f.; Osterhammel, *Verwandlung der Welt*, pp. 1214–1224; Osterhammel, '"Uplifting Mankind"', p. 420; Petillo, 'Leaders and Followers', pp. 186–193; Schumacher, '"Niederbrennen, plündern und töten"', p. 129.

189. Barkan, 'Genocides of Indigenous Peoples'; Broome, *Aboriginal Australians*, p. 50f.; Cocker, *Rivers of Blood*, pp. 173f., 178, 360–364; Hawkins, *Social Darwinism*; Hemming, *Amazon Frontier*, p. 287; Palmer, *Colonial Genocide*, pp. 75–80.

190. Kuß, *Deutsches Militär*, p. 232.

191. On the ways in which this situational racism functioned and became a tradition, see especially Kennedy, *Islands of White*, pp. 128–166. Also: Belmessous, 'Assimilation and Racialism'; Grenier, *First Way of War*, p. 11f.; Hull, *Absolute Destruction*, pp. 330–332; Kramer, 'Race-Making and Colonial Violence', pp. 189–192; Penn, *Forgotten Frontier*, p. 64; Strachan, 'Typology of Transcultural Wars', p. 99. Situational racism was also evident in the definition of so-called 'warrior races', where pragmatic preferences were later rationalized through pseudo-scientific arguments. Killingray, 'Guardians of Empire', pp. 14–16; Streets, *Martial Races*, pp. 6–10. Cf. Omissi, *The Sepoy and the Raj*, pp. 23–34.

192. Edgerton, *Mau Mau*, p. 142; Koller, 'Französische Fremdenlegion', pp. 372–376, 379f.

193. Quoted in Hirsch, 'Collision of Military Cultures', p. 1208.

194. Greiner, '"First to Go"', p. 249; Kramer, 'Race-Making and Colonial Violence', p. 192.

195. Bourke, *History of Killing*, p. 205.

196. Kiernan, *Colonial Empires*, pp. 155–157. I fail to grasp Michael Hochgeschwender's objection ('Although the dehumanization of the enemy in colonial warfare was structurally anchored in cultural patterns of perception, in practice it was only invoked temporarily and even in wartime was mostly cushioned by the ideal of the paternalistic civilizing mission.' Hochgeschwender, 'Kolonialkriege als Experimentierstätten?', p. 289).

197. Parker, 'Early Modern Europe', p. 56.

198. Bourke, *History of Killing*, p. 232; Greiner, '"First to Go"', p. 249; Kramer, 'Race-Making and Colonial Violence', pp. 192–194.

199. The Spanish called their most stubborn opponents in Central Mexico the '*Chichimeca*', which can be translated as 'dirty, uncivilized dog'. Powell, *Soldiers, Indians and Silver*, p. 33.

200. Klose, *Menschenrechte im Schatten kolonialer Gewalt*, pp. 251–256.

201. Callwell, *Small Wars*, p. 253.

202. All these quotations appear in: Belich, 'Krieg und transkulturelles Lernen', p. 254f.

203. Nasson, *South African War*, pp. 241–243, 251f. The Mahdists in the Sudan were also reputed to be able to see in the dark as a result of their 'cat-like eyes'. Falls, 'Reconquest of the Sudan', p. 296.

204. Belich, *Victorian Interpretation*, p. 327f.; Nasson, *South African War*, p. 250.

205. Finzsch, '"Extirpate or remove"', p. 223. The Boers of the Cape Colony were also regarded as 'vermin' to be exterminated. Penn, *Forgotten Frontier*, p. 122.

206. Quoted in Vandervort, *Indian Wars*, p. 130.

207. Hemming, *Amazon Frontier*, p. 136.

208. Quoted in Kennedy, *Islands of White*, p. 130.

209. Le Cour Grandmaison, *Coloniser, Exterminer*, pp. 89–94.

210. Stokes, *Peasant Armed*, p. 79f.

211. Coates, *Suppressing Insurgency*, p. 148.

212. Turnbull, *Black War*, p. 28f.

213. German soldier's letter, quoted in Klein, 'Straffeldzug im Namen der Zivilisation', p. 167.

214. Ibid., p. 163.

215. Schmidl, 'Kolonialkriege', p. 118.

216. Edwards, *New Spirits*, pp. 121–124; Gay, *Cultivation of Hatred*, pp. 95–127.

217. Dawson, *Soldier Heroes*; James, *Savage Wars*, pp. 3–17; Kuß, *Deutsches Militär*, p. 369; Streets, *Martial Races*, p. 12f.; Wesseling, 'Wars and Peace', p. 68f.

218. Headrick, *Tools of Empire*, pp. 115–117; Kuß, *Deutsches Militär*, p. 243.

219. Cf. on sport and aggression: Gay, *Cultivation of Hatred*, pp. 434–443.

220. Bourke, *History of Killing*, pp. 62, 233; Greiner, *Krieg ohne Fronten*, p. 324; Hérisson, *Chasse à l'homme*; James, *Raj*, p. 262; James, *Savage Wars*, pp. 3–17, 159–162, 166; Kennedy, *Islands of White*, p. 130; Klose, *Menschenrechte im Schatten kolonialer Gewalt*, pp. 175, 179; Kramer, 'Race-Making and Colonial Violence', p. 203f.; Mattioli, 'Kolonialverbrechen des faschistischen Italien', p. 212; Meinertzhagen, *Kenya Diary*, p. 284; Palmer, *Colonial Genocide*, p. 44f.; Schumacher, '"Niederbrennen, plündern und töten"', p. 132; Utley, *Frontiersmen in Blue*, p. 234f. A revealing photograph of 1896, showing Europeans posing with their 'hunting bag' of dead Ndebele, can be found in Howe, *Empire*, p. 96.

221. James, *Savage Wars*, p. 204.

222. Edgerton, *Mau Mau*, p. 151.

223. Klose, *Menschenrechte im Schatten kolonialer Gewalt*, p. 177f.

224. Spiers, 'Dum Dum Bullet', p. 7.

225. Cocker, *Rivers of Blood*, p. 148.

226. Brower uses the phrase 'ecstatic sadism' in reference to French excesses during their conquest of the Sahara. Brower, *Desert Named Peace*, p. 81.

227. Atkinson, *Army at Dawn*, p. 462.

228. Bührer, *Kaiserliche Schutztruppe*, p. 267; Hochgeschwender, 'Kolonialkriege als Experimentierstätten?', p. 283; Hochgeschwender, 'Last Stand', p. 58; Slatta, '"Civilization" Battles "Barbarism"', p. 144.

229. Greiner, *Krieg ohne Fronten*, p. 35.

230. Mattioli, 'Kolonialverbrechen des faschistischen Italien', p. 207f.; Olatunji-Oloruntimehin, 'Senegambia—Mahmadou Lamine', p. 100f.; Utley, *Frontiersmen in Blue*, p. 111f. Cf. Andreopoulos, 'National Liberation Movements', p. 195; Bergmann, 'Dynamik der Conquista', p. 230f.; Bourke, *History of Killing*, p. 203f.; Cahn, 'Kriegsgreuel im Algerienkrieg', p. 378; Fourniau, 'Colonial Wars before 1914', p. 84f.; Greiner, *Krieg ohne Fronten*, pp. 179–200, 254–257; Hull, *Absolute Destruction*, p. 51; Hull, 'Military Culture and "Final Solutions"', p. 152f.; James, *Savage Wars*, pp. 183–186; Kiernan, *Colonial Empires*, p. 215; Kuß, *Deutsches Militär*, pp. 69, 76; Laqueur, *Guerrilla Warfare*, p. 399; Linn, *Counterinsurgency in the Philippine War*, pp. 26f., 151–160; Newsinger, 'Minimum Force'; Palmer, *Colonial Genocide*, p. 132; Porch, *Conquest of Morocco*, pp. 177–180; Utley, *Frontiersmen in Blue*, pp. 152–157; Walter, 'Der nordamerikanische Imperialkrieg', p. 104.

231. Hirsch, 'Collision of Military Cultures', p. 1206f.; Lock/Quantrill, *Zulu Victory*, p. 58f.; Powell, *Soldiers, Indians and Silver*, p. 46; Vandervort, *Indian Wars*, p. 154.

232. Knight, *Anatomy of the Zulu Army*, pp. 221–227.

233. Greiner, *Krieg ohne Fronten*, p. 51; Hassig, 'Eroberung Mexikos', p. 118f.; Mostert, *Military System*, p. 107; Powell, *Soldiers, Indians and Silver*, p. 51; Silver, *Our Savage Neighbors*, pp. 42, 45, 51; Vandervort, *Wars of Imperial Conquest*, p. 127.

234. Quotations from: Vandervort, *Indian Wars*, p. 96f. See also Chet, *Conquering the Wilderness*, p. 15; Kopperman, *Braddock at the Monongahela*, pp. 71–76; Rickey, *Forty Miles a Day*, pp. 314–318.

235. Kipling, 'Young British Soldier', p. 39.

236. Koller, 'Französische Fremdenlegion', p. 379. Similar fears haunted soldiers of the German *Schutztruppe* in Africa. Bührer, *Kaiserliche Schutztruppe*, p. 270.

237. Greiner, '"First to Go"', p. 248f.

238. Mann, 'Gewaltdispositiv des Kolonialismus', p. 116.

239. Silver, *Our Savage Neighbors*, pp. 39–71. Quotation: Ibid., p. 48.

240. Freeman, 'Puritans and Pequots', p. 284f.; Häußler, 'Settlers in South West Africa', p. 5; Hirsch, 'Collision of Military Cultures', pp. 1205, 1207; Jones, *Conquest of the Last Maya Kingdom*, p. 386; Karr, '"Why Should You Be So Furious?"', p. 897; Kennedy, *Islands of White*, pp. 128–137; Palmer, *Colonial Genocide*, p. 131f.; Ranger, 'African Reactions', pp. 308–310; Starkey, *European and Native American Warfare*, p. 70.

241. Howe, *What Hath God Wrought*, pp. 323–327.

242. Kopperman, *Braddock at the Monongahela*, p. 124f.; Lee, 'Fortify, Fight, or Flee', p. 733; Penn, *Forgotten Frontier*, p. 64f.; Powell, *Soldiers, Indians and Silver*, p. 50; Silver, *Our Savage Neighbors*, pp. 47, 49, 52, 69; Starkey, *European and Native American Warfare*, p. 77f.; Steele, *Betrayals*, pp. 124–128; Vandervort, *Indian Wars*, pp. 194, 217.

243. Edgerton, *Mau Mau*, p. 142.

244. Chapman, *The Jungle is Neutral*, p. 125.

245. Belich, *Victorian Interpretation*, p. 135; Callwell, *Small Wars*, p. 304; Kuß, *Deutsches Militär*, p. 249; Linn, *Counterinsurgency in the Philippine War*, pp. 102–107; Stucki, 'Bevölkerungskontrolle in asymmetrischen Konflikten', p. 245. During the Herero Wars, a German officer referred to the 'living' bush. Häußler/Trotha, 'Brutalisierung "von unten"', p. 76. Cf. also the common Spanish characterization of the climate and yellow fever during the Cuban War of Independence as the Cubans' best generals. Stucki, *Aufstand und Zwangsumsiedlung*, p. 182.

246. Hemming, *Amazon Frontier*, p. 85.

247. Gann/Duignan, *Rulers of Belgian Africa*, p. 53f.

248. Jones, *Maya Resistance to Spanish Rule*, p. 1. Cf. Slotkin, *Regeneration Through Violence*, pp. 26–93.

249. Bourke, *History of Killing*, p. 25; Espey, 'America and Vietnam'; Keeley, *War Before Civilization*, p. 80; Porter, *Military Orientalism*, p. 44f.; Vandervort, *Indian Wars*, p. 247f. Cf. chapter 3, 'Traditions of violence'.

250. Greiner, '"First to Go"', p. 251f.

251. Momaday, *Man Made of Words*, p. 91.

252. Caputo, *Indian Country*, p. 136. Cf. the definition of 'Indian Country' at the beginning of this book.

253. Incidentally, the struggle against Nature through road-building and forest-clearing can be read as at least a subconscious reaction to the pervading sense of helplessness of Westerners in 'Indian Country'.

254. Bierling, *Geschichte des Irakkriegs*, p. 173f.; Bourke, *History of Killing*, p. 198; Häußler/Trotha, 'Brutalisierung "von unten"', p. 78; Jones, *Conquest of the Last Maya Kingdom*, p. 239; Kuß, *Deutsches Militär*, p. 285f.; Michels, '"Ostasiatisches Expeditionskorps"', p. 414; Porch, *Conquest of the Sahara*, p. 116.

255. Andreopoulos, 'National Liberation Movements', p. 195; Bergmann, 'Dynamik der Conquista', p. 230f.; Bourke, *History of Killing*, p. 203f.; Cahn, 'Kriegsgreuel im Algerienkrieg', p. 378; Fourniau, 'Colonial Wars before 1914', p. 84f.; Greiner, *Krieg ohne Fronten*, pp. 179–200, 254–257; Hull, *Absolute Destruction*, p. 51; Hull, 'Military Culture and "Final Solutions"', p. 152f.; James, *Savage Wars*, pp. 183–186; Kiernan, *Colonial Empires*, p. 215; Kuß, *Deutsches Militär*, pp. 69, 76; Laqueur, *Guerrilla Warfare*, p. 399; Linn, *Counterinsurgency in the Philippine War*, pp. 26f.,151–160; Newsinger, 'Minimum Force'; Palmer, *Colonial Genocide*, p. 132; Porch, *Conquest of Morocco*, pp. 177–180; Utley, *Frontiersmen in Blue*, pp. 152–157; Walter, 'Der nordamerikanische Imperialkrieg', p. 104.

256. Kramer, 'Race-Making and Colonial Violence', p. 202.

257. Häußler/Trotha, 'Brutalisierung "von unten"', pp. 60–66; Meinertzhagen, *Kenya Diary*, pp. 50–52; Rickey, *Forty Miles a Day*, pp. 314–316.

258. James, *Savage Wars*, p. 167; Porch, *Conquest of the Sahara*, p. 205; Vandervort, *Indian Wars*, p. 135.

259. Bourke, *History of Killing*, pp. 182, 227; Brower, *Desert Named Peace*, p. 16; Clayton, *Wars of French Decolonization*, p. 118f.; Horne, *Savage War of Peace*, pp. 187–192; Reis/Oliveira, 'Cutting Heads or Winning Hearts', p. 82f.

260. Lindsay, *Murder State*, pp. 179–195.

261. Penn, *Forgotten Frontier*, p. 65f.; Rickey, *Forty Miles a Day*, p. 317; Vandervort, *Indian Wars*, p. 77f.

262. James, *Raj*, pp. 251–253; Streets, *Martial Races*, pp. 30, 37–44. It was evidently a similar situation regarding the Spanish 'revenge' for the defeat at Annual in Morocco in 1921. Mücke, 'Agonie einer Kolonialmacht', pp. 262–264.

263. Waldmann, *Terrorismus und Bürgerkrieg*, p. 174.

264. Hochgeschwender, 'Last Stand', pp. 59f., 76; Starkey, *European and Native American Warfare*, pp. 122–125; Thomas, 'Order Before Reform', p. 217f.

265. Quoted in Utley, *Frontier Regulars*, p. 114.

266. Quoted in James, *Savage Wars*, p. 57, also pp. 173, 190.

267. Crawford, 'Sikh Wars', pp. 45, 63f.; Gordon, *Khartoum Journal*, p. 141; Keeley, *War Before Civilization*, p. 83f.; Kuß, *Deutsches Militär*, p. 218. Alternatively, reference was (and still is) made to the sheer impossibility of taking prisoner opponents who fight to the death, a more subtle form of reasoning with the same effect. Cf. above and Hassig, *Mexico and the Spanish Conquest*, pp. 94–98.

268. Cahn, 'Kriegsgreuel im Algerienkrieg', p. 378f.; Hirschfeld, 'Kriegsgreuel im Dekolonisierungsprozess', p. 363f.; Hochgeschwender, 'Kolonialkriege als Experimentierstätten?', p. 283f.; Law, *Terrorism*, pp. 200–206.

269. Klose, *Menschenrechte im Schatten kolonialer Gewalt*, pp. 251–256, 272–274.

270. Utley, *Frontiersmen in Blue*, pp. 290–297.

271. Quoted in Ibid., p. 294.

272. It would appear that this turn of phrase dates from the British conquest of Ireland, a further indication of culturally transmitted tradition or legitimations of violence. Kane, 'Nits Make Lice', p. 83f.

273. Hochgeschwender, 'Last Stand', p. 64.

274. Vandervort, *Indian Wars*, pp. 172–174.

275. Chalk/Brandt, 'Drone Wars', p. 26; Dowd, 'Drone Wars', p. 12f. General prevention, in other words deterrence, of course also plays a role here.

276. Starkey, 'Conflict and Synthesis', p. 75.

277. Charney, 'Iberier und Südostasiaten', p. 183f.; Grenier, *First Way of War*, p. 21f.; Malone, *Skulking Way of War*, p. 75; Pagden, *Lords of All the World*, p. 73f.; Slotkin, *Regeneration Through Violence*, pp. 37–42; Starkey, *European and Native American Warfare*, p. 25f.; Weigl, 'Fall Tenochtitlans', pp. 178–186.

278. Turnbull, *Black War*, p. 24f. Quotation: Ibid., p. 24. Cf. Langford, 'Eighteenth Century', p. 436.

279. Bourke, *History of Killing*, p. 16.

280. Petillo, 'Leaders and Followers', p. 202; Schumacher, '"Niederbrennen, plündern und töten"', p. 133.

281. Hull, *Absolute Destruction*, pp. 1–3.

282. Mattioli, 'Kolonialverbrechen des faschistischen Italien', p. 221f.

283. Lappas, 'Lernen inmitten des Blutvergießens', p. 171f.; Starkey, *European and Native American Warfare*, pp. 25–30.

284. Bührer, *Kaiserliche Schutztruppe*, p. 256f.

285. Knight, *Anatomy of the Zulu Army*, p. 225.

286. Charney, 'Iberier und Südostasiaten', p. 184.

287. Eskildsen, 'Civilization and Savages', p. 403f.

288. Altman, 'Conquest, Coercion, and Collaboration', pp. 158, 166; Barrett, *Edge of Empire*, pp. 147–166; Bührer, *Kaiserliche Schutztruppe*, pp. 259–261, 264–269, 272; Füssel, 'Händler, Söldner und Sepoys', p. 320f.; Hée, *Imperiales Wissen*, pp. 185–201, 204–208, 220–223; Hemming, *Conquest of the Incas*, p. 215; Kramer, 'Race-Making and Colonial Violence', p. 207f.; Mattioli, 'Kolonialverbrechen des faschistischen Italien', p. 222; Meinertzhagen, *Kenya Diary*, p. 143f.; Mockaitis, *British Counterinsurgency*, pp. 44–57; Palmer, *Colonial Genocide*, p. 55; Porch, *Conquest of the Sahara*, p. 185f.; Selesky, 'Colonial America', p. 80f.; Starkey, *European and Native American Warfare*, pp. 101–103; Steele, *Betrayals*, pp. 78–90; Strachan, 'Typology of Transcultural Wars', pp. 93f., 96f.; Thornton, 'Firearms, Diplomacy, and Conquest', p. 182; Trotha, *Koloniale Herrschaft*, pp. 44–58; Vandervort, *Wars of Imperial Conquest*, p. 139.

289. Brower, *Desert Named Peace*, p. 35; Bührer, *Kaiserliche Schutztruppe*, pp. 270–272; Hull, *Absolute Destruction*, p. 26; Kuß, *Deutsches Militär*, p. 164; Morlang, '"Die Wahehe haben ihre Vernichtung gewollt"', p. 104f.

290. Gaffarel, *Algérie*, p. 283.

291. James, *Savage Wars*, p. 172.

292. Strachan, 'Typology of Transcultural Wars', p. 94.

293. Häußler, 'Asymmetrie tribaler und staatlicher Kriegführung', p. 195.

294. Porch, 'French Colonial Forces', p. 167f.

295. Bührer, *Kaiserliche Schutztruppe*, p. 258f.; Kanya-Forstner, 'French Marines', p. 140f.

296. Lee, 'Projecting Power', p. 5.

297. Porch, *Conquest of the Sahara*, pp. 181–197.

298. Mattioli, 'Kolonialverbrechen des faschistischen Italien', pp. 213, 221f.; Walter, '"The Enemy Must Be Brought to Battle"', p. 59.

299. Beckett, *Modern Insurgencies*, p. 128f.; Billington, *Westward Expansion*, p. 63f.; Clayton, *Wars of French Decolonization*, pp. 84–85, 93, 99; Connor, *Australian Frontier Wars*, pp. xii, 16–17, 93–95, 119–121; Edgerton, *Mau Mau*, p. 153f.; Grenier, *First Way of War*, p. 12; Häußler, 'Settlers in South West Africa', pp. 4–10; Hemming, *Amazon Frontier*, pp. 89–102; Hemming, *Red Gold*, pp. 134–138; Hochgeschwender, 'Kolonialkriege als Experimentierstätten?', p. 284; Hull, *Absolute Destruction*, p. 19; Kennedy, *Islands of White*, p. 142f.; Penn, *Forgotten Frontier*, pp. 67–77; Schmidl, 'Kolonialkriege', p. 127f.; Steele, *Betrayals*, p. 37f.; Stucki, *Aufstand und Zwangsumsiedlung*, p. 33f.

300. Hemming, *Amazon Frontier*, pp. 90f., 119–111, 174–181.

301. Bergmann, 'Dynamik der Conquista', pp. 226–232. Bertrand ('Violences impériales', p. 132f.) indicates that Portuguese possessions in Asia were also an acknowledged realm of unrestricted violence of a kind that was unacceptable in the pacified motherland.

302. Klose, 'Notstand'.

303. Calloway, *Winter Count*, pp. 132–145.

304. Hemming, *Conquest of the Incas*, pp. 57, 63, 156–158, 162.

305. Jones, *Maya Resistance to Spanish Rule*, pp. 41–52; Khodarkovsky, *Russia's Steppe Frontier*, pp. 21–26; Porch, *Conquest of the Sahara*, pp. 181–197.

306. Schindler, *Bauern und Reiterkrieger*, pp. 18–35.

307. Brower, *Desert Named Peace*, pp. 75–89; Gallois, 'Dahra and the History of Violence'; Le Cour Grandmaison, *Coloniser, Exterminer*, pp. 138–143.

308. Gann/Duignan, *Rulers of British Africa*, p. 120f.; Meinertzhagen, *Kenya Diary*.

309. Bourke, *History of Killing*, pp. 171–183; Greiner, *Krieg ohne Fronten*, pp. 321–333.

310. Le Cour Grandmaison, *Coloniser, Exterminer*, pp. 138–143.

311. Palmer, *Colonial Genocide*, pp. 49–55.

312. Selesky, 'Colonial America', p. 85. Cf. Laqueur, *Guerrilla Warfare*, p. 399.

313. Greiner, *Krieg ohne Fronten*, pp. 231–255.

314. Hée, *Imperiales Wissen*, p. 203f.; Hull, *Absolute Destruction*, p. 3; Kunz, '"Con ayuda del más dañino de todos los gases"'; Mattioli, 'Kolonialverbrechen des faschistischen Italien', pp. 211f., 221f.; May, 'Philippine-American War', p. 457; Strachan, 'Typology of Transcultural Wars', p. 97.

315. Lartéguy, *Centurions*.

316. Cahn, 'Kriegsgreuel im Algerienkrieg', p. 378f.; Fall, *Hell in a Very Small Place*, pp. 440–442.

317. Stockwell, '"A widespread and long-concocted plot"', p. 79f.

318. Gottmann, 'Bugeaud, Galliéni, Lyautey', p. 234f.; Hochgeschwender, 'Kolonialkriege als Experimentierstätten?', p. 284; Strachan, 'Typology of Transcultural Wars', p. 96.

319. Brower, *Desert Named Peace*, p. 24; Palmer, *Colonial Genocide*, pp. 20, 67f., 102–110.

320. Gerwarth/Malinowski, 'Holocaust als "kolonialer Genozid"?', p. 454f.; Malinowski, 'Modernisierungskriege', p. 217; Strachan, 'Typology of Transcultural Wars', p. 101.

4. ASYMMETRY, ADAPTATION AND LEARNING

1. Bungay, *Most Dangerous Enemy*, p. 262.
2. Casper, *Falcon Brigade*, p. 40.
3. Wylde, *'83 to '87 in the Soudan*, Vol. 1, p. 153.
4. Chandler, 'Expedition to Abyssinia', pp. 139–141; Clayton, *Wars of French Decolonization*, p. 84; Peers, 'Introduction', p. xvii; Porch, *Conquest of the Sahara*, p. 171f.; Porch, 'French Colonial Forces', p. 178; Porch, *Conquest of Morocco*, pp. 68–71; Utley, *Frontiersmen in Blue*, p. 335.
5. Raudzens, 'Outfighting or Outpopulating?', p. 32. Cf. chapter 1, 'Cooperation'.
6. For a more extensive treatment of this, see Walter, 'Warum Kolonialkrieg?', p. 14f.
7. Also remarked upon by Vandervort, *Indian Wars*, p. 11.
8. Bitterli, *Die "Wilden" und die "Zivilisierten"*, p. 175.
9. Walter, 'Heeresreformen', col. 285f.
10. Malone, *Skulking Way of War*, p. 21.
11. Strachan, 'Typology of Transcultural Wars', p. 88.
12. Denzer, 'Sierra Leone—Bai Bureh', pp. 244–246; Donnelly, *Conquest of Bashkiria*, p. 27; Khodarkovsky, 'Krieg und Frieden', pp. 200–208, 212f.; Moreman, *Army in India*, p. 11; Vandervort, *Indian Wars*, pp. 39, 80–86.
13. Helbling, *Tribale Kriege*, p. 60f.; Lappas, 'Lernen inmitten des Blutvergießens', p. 169.
14. Mostert, *Military System*, p. 93f.
15. Bond, 'Editor's Introduction', p. 18f.; Callwell, *Small Wars*, pp. 29–33; Moor, 'Warmakers in the Archipelago', p. 65.
16. Smith, 'Nigeria—Ijebu', pp. 179–181.
17. Vandervort, *Wars of Imperial Conquest*, pp. 3–6.
18. Ibid., pp. 22–25.
19. Knight, *Anatomy of the Zulu Army*, pp. 46–88. The military system of the East African Hehe functioned according to much the same model. Arnold, 'Schlacht bei Rugaro', pp. 97, 105f.; Bührer, 'Hehe und Schutztruppe', pp. 268–270.
20. Lock/Quantrill, *Zulu Victory*, pp. 58–64.
21. Fynn, 'Ghana—Asante', pp. 25–27; Killingray, 'Colonial Warfare', pp. 159–161; Ross, 'Dahomey', pp. 148–152; Thornton, 'Art of War in Angola', pp. 83–89.
22. Belich, *Victorian Interpretation*, pp. 21–25.
23. Kanya-Forstner, 'Mali—Tukulor', p. 57; Person, 'Guinea', pp. 116–126, 133f.; Vandervort, *Wars of Imperial Conquest*, pp. 74–79.
24. Law, 'Warfare on the Slave Coast', pp. 114–118.
25. Person, 'Guinea', p. 134.
26. Vandervort, *Wars of Imperial Conquest*, p. 132.
27. Barua, 'Military Developments in India'; Pemble, 'Resources and Techniques', pp. 275–287.
28. Cook, *Sikh Wars*; Kiernan, *Colonial Empires*, pp. 40–43. In the late eighteenth century the configuration and training of the army of the Kingdom of Nepal likewise followed the model of the British Indian Army. Streets, *Martial Races*, p. 76f.
29. Cooper, 'Culture, Combat, and Colonialism', pp. 536–540; Cooper, 'Wellington and the Marathas', pp. 305–307.
30. Gordon, 'Limited Adoption', pp. 230–237, 241f.

31. Cooper, 'Culture, Combat, and Colonialism', p. 543; Cooper, 'Wellington and the Marathas', p. 311f.; Kolff, 'End of an Ancien Régime', pp. 33–41.

32. Marshall, *Russian General Staff*, p. 72.

33. Belich, *Victorian Interpretation*, p. 292; Charney, *Southeast Asian Warfare*, pp. 213–242; James, *Savage Wars*, pp. 110–112; Marshall, *Russian General Staff*, p. 77f., 80f., 83f.; Porch, *Conquest of Morocco*, pp. 98–100; Vandervort, *Wars of Imperial Conquest*, pp. 166–168, 174; Williams, 'Egyptian Campaign', pp. 271, 275.

34. Aksan, 'Ottoman War and Warfare', pp. 150–152, 159–170; Reid, *Europe and Southeast Asia*, p. 6; Ricklefs, *War, Culture and Economy*, p. 13f.; Thornton, 'Firearms, Diplomacy, and Conquest', p. 171f.

35. Arnold, 'Schlacht bei Rugaro', p. 102; Belich, *Victorian Interpretation*, p. 62f.; Bryant, 'Asymmetric Warfare', p. 447; Füssel, 'Händler, Söldner und Sepoys', p. 310; Gordon, 'Limited Adoption', p. 232; Gould, *Imperial Warriors*, p. 55; Hemming, *Conquest of the Incas*, pp. 203–206; Kiernan, *Colonial Empires*, p. 44; Thornton, 'Firearms, Diplomacy, and Conquest', p. 185f.; Vandervort, *Wars of Imperial Conquest*, p. 12f.

36. Heathcote, *Military in British India*, p. 9.

37. Callwell, *Small Wars*, pp. 88, 159; James, *Raj*, pp. 20, 34f.; Kiernan, *Colonial Empires*, p. 144; Klein, 'Straffeldzug im Namen der Zivilisation', p. 156; Porch, 'French Colonial Forces', p. 178f.; Ricklefs, *War, Culture and Economy*, p. 141; Ross, 'Dahomey', p. 154; Thornton, 'Art of War in Angola', p. 89; Williams, 'Egyptian Campaign', p. 275.

38. Charney, *Southeast Asian Warfare*, pp. 14–22; Falls, 'Reconquest of the Sudan', p. 293; James, *Savage Wars*, pp. 95, 106–108, 163–166; Robson, *Fuzzy-Wuzzy*, p. 52; Schumacher, '"Niederbrennen, plündern und töten"', p. 126; Woolman, *Rebels in the Rif*, p. 154f.

39. Charney, *Southeast Asian Warfare*, pp. 278–280; Kiernan, *Colonial Empires*, p. 36; Rose, '"Unsichtbare Feinde"', p. 223f.

40. Belich, *Victorian Interpretation*, pp. 128–132.

41. Parker, *Military Revolution*, pp. 136–142; Varley, 'Warfare in Japan', pp. 64–70.

42. Ralston, *Importing the European Army*, pp. 173–180.

43. Ibid., pp. 79–106.

44. Vandervort, *Indian Wars*, pp. 230–236.

45. Pennel, *Country with a Government*, pp. 130–132; Woolman, *Rebels in the Rif*, pp. 149–151.

46. Clayton, *Wars of French Decolonization*, pp. 54–65.

47. Beckett, *Modern Insurgencies*, pp. 187–190; Clayton, *Wars of French Decolonization*, p. 122; Groen, 'Militant Response', p. 35; Jones, *Graveyard of Empires*, pp. 227–230.

48. Kramer, 'Race-Making and Colonial Violence', p. 178f.

49. Ibid., pp. 194–197; Linn, *Counterinsurgency in the Philippine War*, pp. 38–41.

50. Beckett, *Modern Insurgencies*, pp. 153–155, 188f.; Clayton, *Wars of French Decolonization*, p. 112f.; Derradji, *Algerian Guerrilla Campaign*, pp. 160–166; Hirschfeld, 'Kriegsgreuel im Dekolonisierungsprozess', p. 359f. Of course, al-Qaeda also functions in the same way. Schneckener, *Transnationaler Terrorismus*, pp. 67–86.

51. Thornton, 'African Soldiers in the Haitian Revolution', p. 70.

52. Pemble, 'Resources and Techniques', pp. 275–287. Cf. Headrick, *Tools of Empire*, p. 89f.

53. Kiernan, *Colonial Empires*, p. 48f.; Stokes, *Peasant Armed*, pp. 57, 69–71, 75, 98f.

54. Nasson, *South African War*, pp. 61–69.

55. Bryant, 'Asymmetric Warfare', pp. 439–441.

56. Bond, 'Editor's Introduction', p. 27; Bührer, *Kaiserliche Schutztruppe*, pp. 273–275; Chandler, 'Expedition to Abyssinia', pp. 139–141; Fynn, 'Ghana—Asante', p. 40f.; Guilmartin, 'Cutting Edge', pp. 55–57; Häußler, 'Asymmetrie tribaler und staatlicher Kriegführung', pp. 191–194; James, *Savage Wars*, pp. 168–171; Kanya-Forstner, 'Mali—Tukulor', p. 73; Kiernan, *Colonial Empires*, pp. 34–36; Martin, 'From Algiers to N'Djamena', p. 83; Mostert, *Military System*, pp. 19–22, 125; Porch, *Conquest of Morocco*, p. 177f.; Smith, 'Nigeria—Ijebu', p. 194; Stokes, *Peasant Armed*, p. 98f.; Utley, *Custer*, p. 74f.; Utley, 'Cultural Clash', p. 96.

57. Belich, *Victorian Interpretation*, pp. 23, 123–127; Chandler, 'Expedition to Abyssinia', pp. 119, 122, 128; Charney, *Southeast Asian Warfare*, pp. 278–280; Falls, 'Reconquest of the Sudan', pp. 288, 292; Headrick, *Tools of Empire*, p. 89f.; Howard, 'Colonial Wars', p. 219; Hull, *Absolute Destruction*, pp. 33–45; James, *Savage Wars*, pp. 100–103; Ross, 'Dahomey', pp. 158–162; Starkey, *European and Native American Warfare*, p. 153.

58. Reid, *Europe and Southeast Asia*, p. 5.

59. Bryant, 'Asymmetric Warfare', p. 447f.; Kiernan, *Colonial Empires*, p. 49f.; Kundrus/Walter, 'Anpassung und Lernen', p. 22; Marshall, 'Western Arms in Maritime Asia', p. 17.

60. Howard, 'Colonial Wars', p. 219.

61. Beckett, *Modern Insurgencies*, p. 191f., 211–213; Bond, 'South African War', pp. 209–211; Gould, *Imperial Warriors*, pp. 44–47; Grau, *Bear Over the Mountain*, p. 207; James, *Savage Wars*, pp. 82–84; Kopperman, *Braddock at the Monongahela*, pp. 67–77, 82f.; Michels, '"Ostasiatisches Expeditionskorps"', p. 414f.; Starkey, *European and Native American Warfare*, p. 73; Vandervort, *Wars of Imperial Conquest*, p. 144; Veltzé, *Schlacht bei Adua*, pp. 28, 75; Woolman, *Rebels in the Rif*, pp. 83–102.

62. Macrory, *Signal Catastrophe*, pp. 156–237.

63. Starkey, *European and Native American Warfare*, pp. 141–146; Utley, *Frontier Regulars*, pp. 18–28, 41f., 98–100; Utley, *Frontiersmen in Blue*, pp. 37–41.

64. Greiner, *Krieg ohne Fronten*, pp. 127–131.

65. Cf. for example the deconstruction of cheap criticism of Braddock in Kopperman, *Braddock at the Monongahela*, pp. 93–121.

66. Cf. chapter 1, 'Limits to the projection of power'.

67. Eckert, 'Double-Egded Swords'; Gann/Duignan, *Rulers of British Africa*, pp. 73–76; Kiernan, *Colonial Empires*, pp. 15–32; Vandervort, *Indian Wars*, pp. 63–65.

68. Cf. chapter 1, 'Cooperation'.

69. Gann/Duignan, *Rulers of British Africa*, pp. 122–124, 126–128; Killingray, 'Guardians of Empire', p. 13f.; Penn, *Forgotten Frontier*, pp. 108–112; Starkey, *European and Native American Warfare*, pp. 37–43; Stucki, *Aufstand und Zwangsumsiedlung*, p. 33f.; Utley, *Frontiersmen in Blue*, pp. 100–102; Vandervort, *Indian Wars*, p. 62f.

70. Billington, *Westward Expansion*, p. 54; Khodarkovsky, *Russia's Steppe Frontier*, p. 131f.; Marshall, *Russian General Staff*, pp. 57–60; Teitler, 'The Mixed Company', p. 159.

71. Bergmann, 'Dynamik der Conquista', pp. 216–221, 226; Bierling, *Geschichte des Irakkriegs*, pp. 153–156; Bührer, *Kaiserliche Schutztruppe*, pp. 35–86; Cupp/Latham, 'Role of Contractors', p. 138f.; DeFronzo, *Iraq War*, pp. 237–242; Hemming, *Red Gold*, pp. 345–376; James, *Savage Wars*, p. 118f.; Jones, 'Muscovite-Nomad Relations', p. 119; Lincoln, *Conquest of a Continent*, pp. 33–45; Morlang, *Askari und Fitafita*, p. 19; Pietschmann, 'Imperialkriege Spaniens', pp. 89–91; Powell, *Soldiers, Indians and Silver*, pp. 62–66, 124–128. The mercenaries employed by Europe around 1800 are a borderline case: Tzoref-Ashkenazi, 'Deutsche Hilfstruppen in Imperialkriegen', pp. 345–352.

72. Connor, *Australian Frontier Wars*, p. 10; Herold, 'Fliegendes Kreuzergeschwader', pp. 389–396; Kiernan, *Colonial Empires*, p. 32f.; Klein, 'Straffeldzug im Namen der Zivilisation', p. 153f.; Vandervort, *Wars of Imperial Conquest*, p. 52f.

73. Bührer, *Kaiserliche Schutztruppe*, pp. 204–209; Fourniau, 'Colonial Wars before 1914', pp. 78–80; Gann/Duignan, *Rulers of British Africa*, pp. 122–124, 126–128; Hack/Rettig, 'Demography in Southeast Asia', p. 60; Killingray, 'Guardians of Empire', pp. 11–13; Moreman, '"Small Wars"', pp. 121–124; Ranger, *Revolt in Southern Rhodesia*, pp. 118f., 125; Trotha, *Koloniale Herrschaft*, pp. 44–58; Vandervort, *Indian Wars*, p. 229f.; Womack, 'Ethnicity and Martial Races'; Woolman, *Rebels in the Rif*, p. 44.

74. Crowder, 'Introduction', p. 7f.; Fynn, 'Ghana—Asante', p. 38f.; Killingray, 'Guardians of Empire', p. 7f.; Linn, *Counterinsurgency in the Philippine War*, p. 14. Conscripts were deployed to fight in Italy's colonies (Ethiopia 1896 and 1935/36), and in those of Spain (Cuba 1895–1898), the Netherlands (Indonesia 1945–1949), the USA (Vietnam 1965–1973), and Portugal (in all its African colonies in the period 1961–1975) as well as in the Soviet Army (Afghanistan 1979–1988)—all of course instances which far exceeded the effort required in a normal imperial war. Beckett, *Modern Insurgencies*, p. 191f.; Cann, *Counterinsurgency in Africa*, pp. 88–90; Gates, 'Two American Wars', p. 58f.; Grau, *Bear Over the Mountain*, p. xiv; Greiner, *Krieg ohne Fronten*, pp. 160–162; Groen, 'Militant Response', p. 35; Kiernan, *Colonial Empires*, p. 202f; Stucki, *Aufstand und Zwangsumsiedlung*, pp. 189–191; Vandervort, *Wars of Imperial Conquest*, p. 159. Great Britain, which, apart from during the two world wars, only had conscription from 1945 to 1962, deployed its conscripts in such war zones as Malaya (1948–1960) and Kenya (1952–1960). Charters, 'Palestine to Northern Ireland', p. 204; Walter, 'Kolonialkrieg, Globalstrategie und Kalter Krieg', p. 130. From 1870 onwards in France, conscripts could be sent without their consent to fight in Algeria, whose three coastal *départements* were an integral part of the motherland; however, only volunteers fought in France's colonial units, and in the conflict in Indochina (1945–1954) and later interventions in Africa. Clayton, *Wars of French Decolonization*, p. 56; Clayton, *France, Soldiers and Africa*, p. 16; Fall, *Hell in a Very Small Place*, p. ix; Kiernan, *Colonial Empires*, pp. 214, 218; Martin, 'From Algiers to N'Djamena', p. 122. Belgium outlawed the deployment of conscripts overseas. Gann/Duignan, *Rulers of Belgian Africa*, p. 63. The German Empire was something of a curiosity in this regard; while not stationing any regular troops in its colonies, at the last minute in 1913 it conscripted its settlers into the *Schutztruppe*. Bührer, *Kaiserliche Schutztruppe*, p. 357. Argentina pressed its frontier settlers into service for its wars

against the Indians, also without doubt a unique case. Slatta, '"Civilization" Battles "Barbarism"', pp. 147–150.

75. Starkey, *European and Native American Warfare*, pp. 54–56.

76. The urge to monopolize relations with the indigenous population and to exclude policies imposed by the motherland is a defining characteristic of settler societies. Veracini, *Settler Colonialism*, pp. 30–32.

77. Starkey, 'Lernen im Kolonialkrieg', p. 142; Vandervort, *Indian Wars*, pp. 7–9, 163f.

78. This most definitely applied to the colonist militias in North America: Chet, *Conquering the Wilderness*, pp. 7–12; Malone, *Skulking Way of War*, pp. 52–66; Starkey, 'Conflict and Synthesis', pp. 74–76; Starkey, *European and Native American Warfare*, pp. 68–74. See also Connor, *Australian Frontier Wars*, p. 11f.

79. The organizational range of such local troops is illustrated in, say, Lock/Quantrill, *Zulu Victory*, p. 42f. See also Gann/Duignan, *Rulers of British Africa*, p. 75; Killingray, 'Guardians of Empire', pp. 11–13; Stucki, *Aufstand und Zwangsumsiedlung*, p. 127f.

80. Stucki, 'Weylers Söldner', pp. 225–229.

81. A corresponding case from the Early Modern period were the Paulistas in Brazil, generations of whom hunted down Indians in the country's forests in order to sell them into slavery. Hemming, *Red Gold*, pp. 355–369.

82. Cf. chapter 1, 'Cooperation' and the instances cited there, and also Bührer, *Kaiserliche Schutztruppe*, pp. 140, 481; Echenberg, *Colonial Conscripts*, p. 10; Haywood/Clarke, *History of the Royal West African Frontier Force*, p. 31f. The point is also emphasized by the ease with which indigenous colonial troops have been deployed in both world wars. Cf. Perry, *Commonwealth Armies*, pp. 199–210. Likewise, the ranger troops of African origin who fought in the Caribbean for Great Britain in the 1790s were subsequently regularized as line infantry. Buckley, *Slaves in Red Coats*, pp. 92–94.

83. Moreman, *Army in India*, pp. 141f., 177f.; Moreman, '"Small Wars"', pp. 122–124.

84. Teitler, 'The Mixed Company', pp. 161–164.

85. Over time, the numerous 'ethnic' cavalry units especially in the Austrian army— Pandurs (Croatia), Husars (Hungary), Ulans (Poland), etc.—were all regularized and by the nineteenth century were only distinguishable from the line cavalry by their picturesque uniforms. Wagner, 'K. (u.) k. Armee', pp. 206–209. The irregular frontier units were also subsumed within the Austrian army as line infantry in the late eighteenth century. Fiedler, *Taktik der Kabinettskriege*, pp. 80–85.

86. The preference for the regular was also reflected in the relative social prestige of frontier troops and forces from the motherland. While officers could still make a career in the colonial army, simply because it offered frequent combat missions, heavy losses, and the chance of swift promotion for those who survived, the rank and file who served there continued to be regarded as the dregs of the empire. Bührer, *Kaiserliche Schutztruppe*, pp. 121–123; Clayton, *France, Soldiers and Africa*, p. 9f.; Gann/Duignan, *Rulers of Belgian Africa*, pp. 59–65; Gann/Duignan, *Rulers of British Africa*, pp. 89–98, 112–114; Gann/Duignan, *Rulers of German Africa*, pp. 107–114; James, *Savage Wars*, pp. 249–251; Kanya-Forstner, 'French Marines', p. 122f.; Kiernan, *Colonial Empires*, pp. 15–32, 204; Kuß, *Deutsches Militär*, pp. 128–149; Marshall, *Russian General Staff*, pp. 39–45, 50f.; Porch, 'French Colonial

Forces', p. 167f.; Teitler, 'The Mixed Company', p. 155; Vandervort, *Wars of Imperial Conquest*, pp. 45–47.

87. Burbank/Cooper, *Empires in World History*, pp. 287–329; Kubicek, 'Empire and Technological Change'.

88. Which unconventionally was made up of conscripts. Vandervort, 'Colonial Wars', p. 155.

89. Álvarez, *Betrothed of Death*; Clayton, *France, Soldiers and Africa*, pp. 6–8; Fourniau, 'Colonial Wars before 1914', p. 78; Gottmann, 'Bugeaud, Galliéni, Lyautey', p. 245; Jauffret, 'Armes de "la plus grande France"', pp. 52–58; Koller, 'Französische Fremdenlegion', p. 365f.; Kuß, *Deutsches Militär*, pp. 386–393; Michels, '"Ostasiatisches Expeditionskorps"', pp. 402–405; Porch, 'French Colonial Forces', pp. 172; Porch, *French Foreign Legion*, pp. xviiif., 1–6; Vandervort, *Wars of Imperial Conquest*, p. 44f.; Wesseling, 'Wars and Peace', p. 67; Woolman, *Rebels in the Rif*, p. 67f. Basically the only empire that did not raise such forces was the British—thanks to the prevailing image of war there, the entire army without distinction was designed for colonial service, and was structured accordingly: Connor, *Australian Frontier Wars*, p. 14; Gann/Duignan, *Rulers of British Africa*, p. 78; Strachan, 'British Way in Warfare', pp. 146–243; Williams, 'Egyptian Campaign', p. 250. The US Marines must be regarded as a hybrid: On the one hand they were primarily deployed in small wars overseas, while on the other remaining part of the homeland military apparatus, Accordingly, they did not follow their own organizational logic. Boot, *Savage Wars of Peace*, pp. 46–49, 52f., 57–59, 156–167; Fischer, 'Suppen, Messer und Löffel', p. 511; Weigley, *American Way of War*, pp. 254f., 463f. Mixed forms with indigenous colonial armies were the French Armée d'Afrique (technically the XIX Army Corps deployed in the Algeria military region) and the colonial army of the Netherlands, since both included large numbers of indigenous troops and were stationed in the region of deployment. Even so, their European components were made up of line troops recruited for service on the periphery. Clayton, *France, Soldiers and Africa*, p. 6f.; Jauffret, 'Armes de "la plus grande France"', pp. 43–52; Teitler, 'The Mixed Company', p. 156. Likewise by 1914, 50 per cent of the French *Troupes Coloniales*, who were originally recruited in the home country, were men from West Africa, Madagascar and Indochina, a total of 48,700 troops. Jauffret, 'Armes de "la plus grande France"', pp. 58–62.

90. Vandervort, 'Colonial Wars', p. 153f.

91. Bührer, *Kaiserliche Schutztruppe*, p. 295f.; Kuß, *Deutsches Militär*, pp. 149–156.

92. Grenier, *First Way of War*, pp. 33–39, 53–77, 124–139; Maninger, '"Rangers"'; Sarkesian, 'American Response', pp. 27–37; Starkey, 'Conflict and Synthesis', p. 79f.; Starkey, *European and Native American Warfare*, p. 101; Steele, *Betrayals*, pp. 70–75.

93. Steele, *Betrayals*, p. 92f.

94. Geraghty, *Who Dares Wins*; Jones, *Counterinsurgency and the SAS*.

95. Beckett, *Modern Insurgencies*, pp. 195–197; Greiner, *Krieg ohne Fronten*, pp. 163–168, 231–255; Weigley, *American Way of War*, pp. 456–467.

96. Fischer, 'Suppen, Messer und Löffel', p. 511.

97. Beckett, *Modern Insurgencies*, pp. 184–187.

98. Cann, *Counterinsurgency in Africa*, p. 72.

99. Charters, 'Palestine to Northern Ireland', pp. 229–234; Martin, 'From Algiers to N'Djamena', pp. 100–123; Walter, *Dschungelkrieg und Atombombe*, pp. 123–158.

100. Wheeler, 'African Elements in Portugal's Armies', p. 242f.

101. Starkey, 'Lernen im Kolonialkrieg', p. 143f.; Starkey, *European and Native American Warfare*, pp. 150f.

102. Cann, *Counterinsurgency in Africa*, pp. 70–74.

103. Grenier, *First Way of War*, pp. 87–114; Kunisch, *Der kleine Krieg*; Strachan, *European Armies*, pp. 27–32.

104. Edgerton, *Mau Mau*, p. 139; Jones, *Counterinsurgency and the SAS*, p. 132; Kitson, *Gangs and Counter-gangs*; Maloba, *Mau Mau and Kenya*, pp. 94–96.

105. Connor, *Australian Frontier Wars*, p. 53; Nasson, *South African War*, p. 150f.; Stucki, *Aufstand und Zwangsumsiedlung*, p. 43.

106. Strachan, *European Armies*, p. 84; Walter, *Preußische Heeresreformen*, p. 55. Callwell praised the cavalry as that branch of the armed forces which, because of its effect on morale, embodied the true principle of colonial warfare. Callwell, *Small Wars*, p. 404. Even in Portugal's wars of decolonization in the period 1961–1975 mounted cavalry units were still regarded as a better option than motorized troops, on the grounds of logistics and mobility. Cann, *Counterinsurgency in Africa*, pp. 134–140.

107. Cf. chapter 1, 'Cooperation'.

108. On the ethnic and organizational heterogeneity of imperial armies, see: Belich, *Victorian Interpretation*, p. 125f.; Cann, *Counterinsurgency in Africa*, pp. 95–102; Fleming, 'Decolonization and the Spanish Army', p. 134; Fourniau, 'Colonial Wars before 1914', pp. 78–80; Fynn, 'Ghana—Asante', p. 44f.; Gann/Duignan, *Rulers of British Africa*, pp. 73–76; Lock/Quantrill, *Zulu Victory*, pp. 27–31, 36–46; Lonsdale, 'Conquest State of Kenya', p. 91f.; Miège, 'Conquest of Morocco', pp. 208–210, 214f.; Moreman, '"Watch and Ward"', pp. 142–151; Olatunji-Oloruntimehin, 'Senegambia—Mahmadou Lamine', p. 93f.; Powell, *Soldiers, Indians and Silver*, pp. 62–66; Ricklefs, *War, Culture and Economy*, p. 17; Schumacher, '"Niederbrennen, plündern und töten"', pp. 115–120; Steele, *Betrayals*, pp. 45–48; Utley, *Frontiersmen in Blue*, pp. 125–133; Vandervort, *Indian Wars*, pp. 208–210; Vandervort, *Wars of Imperial Conquest*, p. 150.

109. Plank, 'Deploying Tribes and Clans', pp. 221–223; Schmidl, 'Kolonialkriege', p. 116.

110. For some graphic examples of the difficulties arising from this, see Connor, *Australian Frontier Wars*, pp. 91–93; Plank, 'Deploying Tribes and Clans', p. 221.

111. Cooper, 'Culture, Combat, and Colonialism', pp. 536–540; Fynn, 'Ghana—Asante', pp. 32, 49; Gordon, 'Limited Adoption', p. 232; Hassig, *Mexico and the Spanish Conquest*, pp. 59–62; Hassig, *Aztec Warfare*, pp. 95–109; Hemming, *Conquest of the Incas*, p. 152f.; Kanya-Forstner, 'Mali—Tukulor', pp. 70f., 73f.; Kiernan, *Colonial Empires*, p. 202f.; Killingray, 'Colonial Warfare', p. 153; Muffett, 'Nigeria—Sokoto Caliphate', pp. 291–294; Smith, 'Nigeria—Ijebu', p. 192f.; Thornton, 'Art of War in Angola', pp. 86–89; Thornton, 'African Soldiers in the Haitian Revolution', pp. 65–70; Vandervort, *Wars of Imperial Conquest*, pp. 11f., 192–195; Wesseling, 'Colonial Wars', p. 3f.

112. Bührer, 'Hehe und Schutztruppe', pp. 268–270; Gann/Duignan, *Rulers of British Africa*, p. 124f.; Knight, *Anatomy of the Zulu Army*, pp. 187–223.

113. Porch, 'French Colonial Forces', pp. 176–179; Porch, *Conquest of Morocco*, pp. 192–199.

114. Utley, 'Cultural Clash', pp. 98–100; Utley, *Frontiersmen in Blue*, pp. 122f., 205–207, 210, 272f.; Vandervort, *Indian Wars*, p. 199f. In the French conquest of Vietnam, a single set-piece battle took place at Badhin in 1886. Fourniau, 'Colonial Wars before 1914', p. 82f.

115. Bührer, *Kaiserliche Schutztruppe*, p. 261; Eberspächer, '"Albion zal hier"', p. 189f.; Ferguson/Whitehead, 'Violent Edge of Empire', p. 25f.; Gann/Duignan, *Rulers of British Africa*, pp. 124–126; Hemming, *Amazon Frontier*, p. 20; Isby, *War in a Distant Country*, p. 106f.; James, *Savage Wars*, pp. 57, 154, 180; Kuß, *Deutsches Militär*, p. 109f.; Linn, *Counterinsurgency in the Philippine War*, p. 16f.; Morlang, '"Die Wahehe haben ihre Vernichtung gewollt"', p. 92f.; Porch, *Conquest of the Sahara*, p. 234; Potempa, 'Raum und seine Beherrschung', pp. 456–458; Vandervort, *Indian Wars*, p. 199f.; Vandervort, *Wars of Imperial Conquest*, pp. 131, 186; Weigl, 'Fall Tenochtitlans', p. 187; Whittingham, '"Savage Warfare"', p. 599.

116. Lee, 'Military Revolution', pp. 56–59; Starkey, *European and Native American Warfare*, p. 24f.

117. Not all indigenous societies managed the transition from the kind of open field warfare they originally preferred to irregular warfare. This was due to a variety of reasons, but at root almost certainly had to do with the established central authority's fear of losing control. Economic difficulties also played a role. Guy, *Destruction of the Zulu Kingdom*, p. 56f.; Kanya-Forstner, 'Mali—Tukulor', p. 73f.; Knight, *Anatomy of the Zulu Army*, p. 188; Muffett, 'Nigeria—Sokoto Caliphate', pp. 291–294.

118. Black, *Beyond the Military Revolution*, p. 119f.

119. Crawford, 'Sikh Wars'; Kiernan, *Colonial Empires*, pp. 40–43; Pemble, 'Resources and Techniques', pp. 275–287; Vandervort, *Wars of Imperial Conquest*, p. 131f.; Williams, 'Egyptian Campaign', pp. 251–275.

120. Kramer, 'Race-Making and Colonial Violence', p. 177.

121. Beckett, *Modern Insurgencies*, pp. 115, 190; Clayton, *Wars of French Decolonization*, pp. 60–65; Isby, *War in a Distant Country*, pp. 106–111; Jones, *Graveyard of Empires*, pp. 210–220; Linn, *Counterinsurgency in the Philippine War*, pp. 12f., 23.

122. Belich, 'Krieg und transkulturelles Lernen', p. 246f.; Belich, *Victorian Interpretation*, pp. 44–46, 134–141.

123. Boot, *Savage Wars of Peace*, pp. 282–284; Fischer, 'Suppen, Messer und Löffel', p. 508.

124. Bryant, 'Asymmetric Warfare', p. 453; Bührer, 'Hehe und Schutztruppe', p. 273; Charney, *Southeast Asian Warfare*, p. 271; Clayton, *Wars of French De-colonization*, pp. 154f., 159f.; Gann/Duignan, *Rulers of British Africa*, pp. 75f., 115f.; Gann/Duignan, *Rulers of German Africa*, p. 123; Grau, *Bear Over the Mountain*, p. 203f.; Haywood/Clarke, *History of the Royal West African Frontier Force*, p. 94f.; Helbling, *Tribale Kriege*, pp. 142; James, *Savage Wars*, pp. 36, 176–183; Keeley, *War Before Civilization*, pp. 74, 79–81; Khodarkovsky, 'Krieg und Frieden', p. 218; Kopperman, *Braddock at the Monongahela*, p. 126f.; Kuß, *Deutsches Militär*, p. 86; Lehmann, *All Sir Garnet*, pp. 94–96; Lemke, 'Kolonialgeschichte als Vorläufer?',

p. 290f.; Linn, *Counterinsurgency in the Philippine War*, pp. 58, 112f.; Malone, *Skulking Way of War*, pp. 88–94; Malone, 'Changing Military Technology', p. 243; Moor, 'Warmakers in the Archipelago', pp. 51f., 69; Moreman, *Army in India*, pp. 17–19,77f.,173; Nasson, *South African War*, p. 150f.; Schmidl, 'Kolonialkriege', p. 116; Schmidt, *Araberaufstand in Ost-Afrika*, pp. 311–317; Smith, 'Nigeria—Ijebu', p. 200; Starkey, 'Lernen im Kolonialkrieg', pp. 142–144; Starkey, 'Conflict and Synthesis', p. 79f.; Starkey, *European and Native American Warfare*, pp. 57–59, 99–101, 107–109, 133–135; Thornton, 'Art of War in Angola', p. 98; Utley, *Frontier Regulars*, pp. 52–56, 172f., 178–180; Utley, *Frontiersmen in Blue*, pp. 234, 342f.; Whitehead, 'Tribes Make States', p. 142f.

125. Cf. the earlier section 'Armed forces' as well as Maloba, *Mau Mau and Kenya*, pp. 94–96; Starkey, *European and Native American Warfare*, pp. 78, 81; Utley, 'Cultural Clash', pp. 100–102.

126. Callwell, *Small Wars*, pp. 277–285; Gann/Duignan, *Rulers of Belgian Africa*, p. 74f.; James, *Savage Wars*, pp. 92, 169, 180f.; Moreman, *Army in India*, p. 18; Porch, *Conquest of the Sahara*, p. 139; Starkey, *European and Native American Warfare*, p. 153.

127. Spiers, *Late Victorian Army*, p. 299. A classic instance of this is Lord Chelmsford in Zululand. Lock/Quantrill, *Zulu Victory*, pp. 94f., 130–134, 165; Manning, 'Learning the Trade', pp. 651–653.

128. Bond, 'Editor's Introduction', p. 25; Bührer, *Kaiserliche Schutztruppe*, p. 239; Callwell, *Small Wars*, pp. 256–276; Haywood/Clarke, *History of the Royal West African Frontier Force*, p. 96; Headrick, *Tools of Empire*, p. 121f.; James, *Savage Wars*, pp. 86–88, 92–94, 127, 129f., 154, 169; Lehmann, *All Sir Garnet*, p. 96f.; Muffett, 'Nigeria—Sokoto Caliphate', pp. 290, 292; Porch, 'French Colonial Forces', p. 180; Porch, *Conquest of Morocco*, pp. 169, 197f.; Spiers, *Late Victorian Army*, p. 289f.; Strachan, *European Armies*, p. 85f.; Vandervort, *Wars of Imperial Conquest*, pp. 64f., 153–156, 192, 194.

129. Callwell, *Small Wars*, pp. 352–358; Gann/Duignan, *Rulers of British Africa*, p. 104f.; James, *Savage Wars*, p. 169; Killingray, 'Colonial Warfare', p. 156; Marshall, *Russian General Staff*, p. 52f.; Porch, *Conquest of the Sahara*, pp. 174, 219; Robson, *Fuzzy-Wuzzy*, pp. 47f., 58f.; Ross, 'Dahomey', p. 160; Utley, *Frontiersmen in Blue*, p. 277; Vandervort, *Wars of Imperial Conquest*, pp. 97–99, 110f.

130. Knight, *Anatomy of the Zulu Army*, p. 212f.

131. Lock/Quantrill, *Zulu Victory*, p. 206. This was a tactic that had already been used by the Aztecs during the *Conquista* and the Seminoles in Florida in the nineteenth century. Gabbert, 'Kultureller Determinismus', p. 277; Vandervort, *Indian Wars*, p. 133.

132. Connor, 'Briten und Darug', p. 231; Connor, *Australian Frontier Wars*, p. 47f.

133. Denzer, 'Sierra Leone—Bai Bureh', p. 248f.; James, *Savage Wars*, p. 104; Person, 'Guinea', p. 134; Robson, *Fuzzy-Wuzzy*, p. 50f.; Vandervort, *Indian Wars*, p. 152; Whitehead, 'Tribes Make States', p. 143.

134. Law, 'Warfare on the Slave Coast', p. 110.

135. Woolman, *Rebels in the Rif*, p. 105.

136. Powell, *Soldiers, Indians and Silver*, p. 66.

137. Charney, 'Iberier und Südostasiaten', p. 192f.

138. Gabbert, 'Warum Montezuma weinte', p. 34f.; Hassig, 'Eroberung Mexikos',

pp. 111, 109, 118; Hemming, *Conquest of the Incas*, pp. 154, 189f.; Powell, *Soldiers, Indians and Silver*, p. 46.

139. Belich, *Victorian Interpretation*, p. 291.
140. Falls, 'Reconquest of the Sudan', p. 299; James, *Savage Wars*, pp. 106–108; Vandervort, *Wars of Imperial Conquest*, pp. 166–168, 174.
141. Crowder, 'Introduction', p. 9.
142. Muffett, 'Nigeria—Sokoto Caliphate', p. 294.
143. Crowder, 'Introduction', p. 8f.; Fynn, 'Ghana—Asante', pp. 40f., 49; Gann/ Duignan, *Rulers of British Africa*, p. 124f.; Headrick, *Tools of Empire*, pp. 96–103, 117–122; James, *Savage Wars*, pp. 129f., 260–265; Kanya-Forstner, 'Mali— Tukulor', pp. 69–73; Kiernan, *Colonial Empires*, pp. 123–126; Kuß, *Deutsches Militär*, pp. 109f.; Marshall, *Russian General Staff*, pp. 63; McNeill, 'European Expansion, Power and Warfare', pp. 12; Olatunji-Oloruntimehin, 'Senegambia— Mahmadou Lamine', p. 94; Slatta, '"Civilization" Battles "Barbarism"', pp. 133f., 151f.; Utley, *Frontier Regulars*, pp. 69–73; Utley, *Frontiersmen in Blue*, pp. 25–28; Vandervort, *Wars of Imperial Conquest*, pp. 113–115.
144. Black, 'European Overseas Expansion'; Brooks, 'Impact of Disease', pp. 129f., 134.
145. Guilmartin, 'Cutting Edge', pp. 50–53; Hassig, *Mexico and the Spanish Conquest*, p. 61f.; Hemming, *Conquest of the Incas*, pp. 110–115; Hemming, *Red Gold*, pp. 81, 222f.; Jones, *Conquest of the Last Maya Kingdom*, p. 139; Raudzens, 'Why Did Amerindian Defences Fail?', p. 339f.; Restall, *Myths of the Spanish Conquest*, p. 142f.; Scammell, 'Indigenous Assistance', p. 142f.
146. Thornton, 'Art of War in Angola', p. 96f.
147. Jany, *Geschichte der Preußischen Armee*, Vol. 1, p. 814; Luh, *Ancien Régime Warfare*, p. 141.
148. Headrick, *Tools of Empire*, p. 85; Jones, *Conquest of the Last Maya Kingdom*, p. 139; Thornton, 'Art of War in Angola', p. 94f.
149. As the American General Ulysses S. Grant famously said of this weapon, which was still in widespread use at the start of the American War of Independence: 'At the distance of a few hundred yards, a man might fire at you all day without your finding it out.' Grant, *Personal Memoirs*, Vol. 1, p. 95.
150. Keeley, *War Before Civilization*, p. 55; Scammell, 'Indigenous Assistance', p. 141f.; Thornton, 'Art of War in Angola', p. 95f. In the Early Modern era, Portuguese cannon too proved entirely ineffective against African earthworks. Black, *War in the World*, p. 176.
151. Abler, 'Beavers and Muskets', pp. 155–157; Charney, *Southeast Asian Warfare*, p. 266f.; Chet, *Conquering the Wilderness*, p. 19f.; Lappas, 'Lernen inmitten des Blutvergießens', p. 170f.; Marshall, *Russian General Staff*, p. 61f.; Paillard, 'Expedition to Madagascar', p. 183; Steele, *Warpaths*, p. 64f. However, Vogt, 'Saint Barbara's Legion', pp. 75–78, contends that Portuguese cannons played a major part in the conquest of Morocco in the fifteenth century.
152. Black, 'Introduction', p. 18f.; Charney, *Southeast Asian Warfare*, pp. 23–41; Connor, *Australian Frontier Wars*, pp. 4–6, 88f.; Hassig, *Mexico and the Spanish Conquest*, pp. 31–33, 46–49; Hemming, *Amazon Frontier*, pp. 287f., 294–296; Hemming, *Conquest of the Incas*, pp. 101–107, 185–190; Hemming, *Red Gold*, pp. 26–31, 357–360; Howard, 'Colonial Wars', p. 221; Knight, *Anatomy of the Zulu Army*,

pp. 101f., 109f.; Malone, *Skulking Way of War*, pp. 14–19; Peers, 'Revolution, Evolution, or Devolution', p. 96; Penn, *Forgotten Frontier*, p. 50f.; Powell, *Soldiers, Indians and Silver*, pp. 47–50; Thornton, 'Firearms, Diplomacy, and Conquest', pp. 176–185; Thornton, 'Warfare, Slave Trading and European Influence', pp. 132–135; Thornton, 'Art of War in Angola', pp. 84f., 88f.; Vandervort, *Indian Wars*, p. 142.

153. The Chichimeca of Central Mexico, for example, adopted the Spanish steel sword, as did the Incas. Hemming, *Conquest of the Incas*, pp. 207–209; Powell, *Soldiers, Indians and Silver*, pp. 45–50. The use of iron arrowheads became widespread in North America. Lappas, 'Lernen inmitten des Blutvergießens', p. 165f. The Brazilian Indians, meanwhile, adopted from the Europeans virtually everything that could be used as an edged weapon: arrowheads, swords, bayonets, daggers, etc. Hemming, *Amazon Frontier*, p. 191.

154. Hunt, *Wars of the Iroquois*, pp. 165–175; Malone, *Skulking Way of War*, pp. 31–36, 42–73; Malone, 'Changing Military Technology', pp. 231–239, 242f.; Starkey, 'Lernen im Kolonialkrieg', p. 145f.; Starkey, 'Conflict and Synthesis', pp. 64–68; Starkey, *European and Native American Warfare*, pp. 20–23, 71f. Why the Indians exchanged their bows and arrows in the first place for firearms that were, when all was said and done, more unreliabale and slower, remains the subject of speculation to this day. The most plausible assumption is that the greater kinetic energy of the musket-ball was the deciding factor. Unlike arrows, musket balls were not deflected by hitting tree branches, it was impossible to dodge them, and they inflicted wounds that instantly put a combatant out of action. Lee, 'Military Revolution', p. 56f.; Starkey, *European and Native American Warfare*, p. 20f. Incidentally, the early adoption by the Mohawks of firearms of predominantly Dutch origin (via New Amsterdam) was the key reason for the rise of the expansionist Iroquois Confederacy in the seventeenth century. Abler, 'Beavers and Muskets', pp. 158–160.

155. The Ottoman Empire had a number of cannons and guns at its disposal from the fourteenth century, while by the late seventeenth century its forces were extensively equipped with firearms of a Western pattern. Aksan, 'Ottoman War and Warfare', pp. 151–154, 164.

156. Bryant, 'Asymmetric Warfare', pp. 438, 458–460; Charney, 'Iberier und Südostasiaten', pp. 187–191; Charney, *Southeast Asian Warfare*, pp. 42–61; Knaap, 'Crisis and Failure', p. 162; Mostert, *Military System*, pp. 32–34; Parker, *Military Revolution*, pp. 125–129; Ricklefs, *War, Culture and Economy*, pp. 13f., 130f.

157. Bryant, 'Asymmetric Warfare', p. 443; Cooper, 'Culture, Combat, and Colonialism', p. 540; Cooper, 'Wellington and the Marathas', p. 308f.; Gommans, 'Warhorse and Gunpowder', p. 118f.; Peers, 'Revolution, Evolution, or Devolution', p. 93; Pemble, 'Resources and Techniques', pp. 282–287.

158. Fortescue, *History of the British Army*, Vol. 12, p. 193; Macrory, *Signal Catastrophe*, p. 141.

159. Barua, 'Military Developments in India', pp. 609–613; Charney, *Southeast Asian Warfare*, pp. 244–250, 265; Headrick, *Tools of Empire*, p. 91; Kiernan, *Colonial Empires*, p. 44f.; Moor, 'Warmakers in the Archipelago', p. 53; Reid, *Europe and Southeast Asia*, p. 6.

160. Donnelly, *Conquest of Bashkiria*, p. 27f.; Khodarkovsky, *Russia's Steppe Frontier*, p. 19f.

161. Varley, 'Warfare in Japan', pp. 64–70. It is well known that Japan subsequently outlawed the use of firearms during its self-imposed period of isolation. Parker, *Military Revolution*, p. 144.

162. Belich, 'Krieg und transkulturelles Lernen', pp. 242–246.

163. Fynn, 'Ghana—Asante', pp. 25–27, 47; Headrick, *Tools of Empire*, p. 106; Inikori, 'Import of Firearms'; Kanya-Forstner, 'Mali—Tukulor', p. 57; Killingray, 'Colonial Warfare', p. 160; Smith, 'Nigeria—Ijebu', p. 181f.

164. Headrick, *Tools of Empire*, p. 91f.; Vandervort, *Wars of Imperial Conquest*, p. 62.

165. Lock/Quantrill, *Zulu Victory*, p. 63f.

166. Kiernan, *Colonial Empires*, p. 142f.; Peers, 'Introduction', p. xxviiif.

167. Killingray, 'Colonial Warfare', p. 152f.; Marshall, *Russian General Staff*, p. 72; Thornton, 'Warfare, Slave Trading and European Influence', p. 137.

168. Vandervort, *Wars of Imperial Conquest*, p. 76.

169. Belich, 'Krieg und transkulturelles Lernen', p. 246; Malone, *Skulking Way of War*, pp. 67–72; Starkey, *European and Native American Warfare*, p. 23.

170. Hassig, 'Eroberung Mexikos', p. 108; Knight, *Anatomy of the Zulu Army*, p. 169; Pietschmann, 'Imperialkriege Spaniens', p. 88; Starkey, *European and Native American Warfare*, p. 23; Vandervort, *Indian Wars*, p. 240.

171. Connor, 'Briten und Darug', p. 231; Khodarkovsky, 'Krieg und Frieden', p. 201; Vandervort, *Wars of Imperial Conquest*, p. 8f.; Whitehead, 'Tribes Make States', p. 148.

172. Black, 'Introduction', p. 11; Charney, 'Iberier und Südostasiaten', p. 190; Hassig, 'Eroberung Mexikos', p. 108; Khodarkovsky, *Russia's Steppe Frontier*, p. 19f.; Peers, 'Introduction', p. xxix; Vandervort, *Wars of Imperial Conquest*, p. 88.

173. Knight, *Anatomy of the Zulu Army*, pp. 213–215; Law, 'Warfare on the Slave Coast', p. 119; Muffett, 'Nigeria—Sokoto Caliphate', p. 289; Smith, 'Nigeria—Ijebu', p. 181f.; Vandervort, *Indian Wars*, pp. 44–47; Vandervort, *Wars of Imperial Conquest*, p. 174.

174. Bührer, 'Hehe und Schutztruppe', p. 276f.; Charney, 'Iberier und Südostasiaten', p. 190; Moor, 'Warmakers in the Archipelago', p. 64; Muffett, 'Nigeria—Sokoto Caliphate', pp. 286–289; Paillard, 'Expedition to Madagascar', p. 183; Peers, 'Introduction', p. xxix. On the Slave Coast of Africa, another factor was clearly that it was impossible, in the absence of horses and wagons, to transport heavy cannons. Law, 'Warfare on the Slave Coast', p. 120f.

175. Charney, *Southeast Asian Warfare*, p. 246; Knight, *Anatomy of the Zulu Army*, p. 168f.; Law, 'Warfare on the Slave Coast', p. 119.

176. Denzer, 'Sierra Leone—Bai Bureh', p. 250; Fage/Tordoff, *History of Africa*, p. 290; Headrick, *Tools of Empire*, p. 105f.; Law, 'Warfare on the Slave Coast', pp. 110–112; Smith, 'Nigeria—Ijebu', pp. 179, 181f. The miserable quality of these guns is (somewhat) relativized by Inikori, 'Import of Firearms', pp. 261–268.

177. Charney, *Southeast Asian Warfare*, pp. 42–72; Porch, *Conquest of Morocco*, p. 99f.

178. Schmidt, *Araberaufstand in Ost-Afrika*, p. 314f.

179. Callwell, *Small Wars*, p. 438f.; Kuß, *Deutsches Militär*, pp. 174–178; Porch, *Conquest of the Sahara*, p. xii; Utley, *Frontier Regulars*, p. 72; Weigley, *History of the United States Army*, p. 269; Wesseling, 'Colonial Wars', p. 6.

180. Vandervort, *Wars of Imperial Conquest*, p. 50f.

181. In February 1889 the French bombarded the Tukulor fortress of Koundian for eight hours with 80-mm mountain howitzers before finally managing to breach the walls; at Djenné in 1892, despite firing 560 shells, they failed to make any impact whatsoever, since Major Archinard had left his heaviest field guns behind due to their relative lack of mobility. Kanya-Forstner, 'Mali—Tukulor', p. 69, 71. Even the makeshift ramparts built by the Temne in Sierra Leone withstood British 7-pounder guns: Denzer, 'Sierra Leone—Bai Bureh', p. 248f. In the light of this, Kanya-Forstner's previously quoted claim is surprising: 'In the long run, the economic and technological resources of a modern European state could always be translated into an overwhelming local military superiority wherever the state was prepared to make the necessary commitment.' Kanya-Forstner, 'Mali—Tukulor', p. 73. Maybe they could be so translated, in theory; but as a rule, in practice they were not.

182. Keeley, *War Before Civilization*, p. 55; Vandervort, *Indian Wars*, p. 132f.

183. Belich, 'Krieg und transkulturelles Lernen', pp. 246–249.

184. Callwell, *Small Wars*, p. 440f.; Porch, *Conquest of the Sahara*, p. xii; Utley, *Frontier Regulars*, p. 72f.; Vandervort, *Wars of Imperial Conquest*, p. 49f.

185. Robson, *Fuzzy-Wuzzy*, pp. 72f., 161, 176.

186. Utley, *Frontier Regulars*, p. 71f.; Vandervort, *Indian Wars*, p. 194; Weigley, *History of the United States Army*, p. 269.

187. Gann/Duignan, *Rulers of German Africa*, p. 118f.; Moor, 'Warmakers in the Archipelago', p. 63; Smith, 'Nigeria—Ijebu', p. 179; Vandervort, *Indian Wars*, pp. 98–101. Though the opposite effect was also possible—take, for instance, Fascist Italy, which for its second invasion of Ethiopia in 1936 took a conscious decision to show off its latest military technology. Brogini-Künzi, 'Wunsch nach einem blitzschnellen Krieg', p. 276f.

188. Bührer, *Kaiserliche Schutztruppe*, pp. 141, 153; Gann/Duignan, *Rulers of German Africa*, p. 118f.; Smith, 'Nigeria—Ijebu', p. 179; Vandervort, *Wars of Imperial Conquest*, p. 48.

189. Fleming, 'Decolonization and the Spanish Army', pp. 124, 131, 135; Mücke, 'Agonie einer Kolonialmacht', p. 256.

190. Vandervort, *Wars of Imperial Conquest*, p. 185.

191. Headrick, *Tools of Empire*, p. 120; Vandervort, *Wars of Imperial Conquest*, pp. 23f., 160.

192. Nasson, *South African War*, p. 57f.

193. Headrick, *Tools of Empire*, p. 119f.; Person, 'Guinea', p. 122f.; Vandervort, *Wars of Imperial Conquest*, p. 132f. Similarly, the Fon in neighbouring Dahomey purchased a large quantity of German repeating rifles after their first defeat by the French in 1890. Ross, 'Dahomey', p. 158. Although the Mahdists in Sudan had very few firearms, they did manage to acquire a small number of Krupp artillery pieces and Gatling guns and deployed them on at least one occasion in battle (at El Teb in 1884). James, *Savage Wars*, pp. 83–88; Robson, *Fuzzy-Wuzzy*, p. 46f.; Vandervort, *Wars of Imperial Conquest*, p. 174.

194. James, *Savage Wars*, p. 111.

195. Lemke, 'Kolonialgeschichte als Vorläufer?', p. 290; Moreman, *Army in India*, pp. 58f., 77f.

196. Moreman, '"Watch and Ward"', p. 139.

197. Mücke, 'Agonie einer Kolonialmacht', p. 258; Woolman, *Rebels in the Rif*, pp. 149–156, 163. In addition, the Berber profited from the half-hearted attempts by the Spanish to 'civilize' the region, by directly reinvesting the wages that they earned from building roads for the colonial power in rifles. Ibid., p. 98.

198. It is open to doubt whether the increase in firepower that modern assault rifles gave, say, the infantry in the Vietnam War was tactically of any great help; presumably all it did was add to the wastage of ammunition. On the use of the American M-16 assault rifle in the Vietnam conflict, see Greiner, *Krieg ohne Fronten*, p. 196.

199. Beckett, *Modern Insurgencies*, pp. 210–213; Fall, *Hell in a Very Small Place*, p. 96f.; Gates, 'Two American Wars', p. 59; Griffith, *Forward into Battle*, pp. 117–123; Isby, *War in a Distant Country*, p. 59f.; Jones, *Counterinsurgency and the SAS*, p. 133; Kiernan, *Colonial Empires*, p. 196f.; Vandervort, 'Colonial Wars', p. 167. For corresponding discussions in British military circles post-1945 see for example Walter, *Dschungelkrieg und Atombombe*, pp. 135–138, 156f., 414–429, 442f., 466f.

200. Numerous examples are cited in Westad, *Global Cold War*; Greiner/Müller/Walter, *Heiße Kriege*.

201. Beckett, *Modern Insurgencies*, p. 114; Clayton, *Wars of French Decolonization*, p. 54f.; Fall, *Street Without Joy*, p. 55f.; Fall, *Hell in a Very Small Place*, pp. 101–105, 451; Griffith, *Forward into Battle*, p. 81; Isby, *War in a Distant Country*, pp. 111–117.

202. Isby, *War in a Distant Country*, p. 114f.; Jones, *Graveyard of Empires*, pp. 37–39; MacQueen, 'Portugal's First Domino', p. 224f.

203. Beckett, *Modern Insurgencies*, p. 146f.; Jones, *Graveyard of Empires*, pp. 210–220; Martin, 'From Algiers to N'Djamena', pp. 101f. The fact that there were nonetheless also some very poorly armed resistance movements after 1945 goes without saying: Clayton, *Wars of French Decolonization*, p. 84; Maloba, *Mau Mau and Kenya*, p. 131.

204. Hassig, 'Eroberung Mexikos', p. 117; Hemming, *Amazon Frontier*, p. 97f.; Weigl, 'Fall Tenochtitlans', p. 186.

205. Slatta, '"Civilization" Battles "Barbarism"', p. 133f.

206. Robson, *Fuzzy-Wuzzy*, p. 72f.; Strachan, *European Armies*, p. 84f.

207. I am indebted to Andreas Stucki for this information. Cf. Stucki, *Aufstand und Zwangsumsiedlung*, p. 43; Tone, 'Machete and the Liberation of Cuba'.

208. Calloway, *Winter Count*, pp. 214–219; Lappas, 'Lernen inmitten des Blutvergießens', pp. 175–177; Malone, 'Changing Military Technology', p. 243; McNab/Hodgins/Standen, '"Black with Canoes"'; Starkey, *European and Native American Warfare*, p. 19.

209. Cooper, 'Culture, Combat, and Colonialism', p. 540.

210. Bond, 'Editor's Introduction', p. 23; Gann/Duignan, *Rulers of British Africa*, p. 75; Isby, *War in a Distant Country*, pp. 59; Lee, 'Projecting Power', p. 7; Omissi, *Sepoy and the Raj*, p. 93; Starkey, 'Lernen im Kolonialkrieg', p. 150; Starkey, *European and Native American Warfare*, pp. 19, 127.

211. Vandervort, *Indian Wars*, p. 194.

212. Ibid., pp. 40–44; White, 'Winning of the West', pp. 323, 331. The horse came to form the basis of warrior cultures in Central and South America as well.

Hemming, *Red Gold*, pp. 387–389; Lee, 'Projecting Power', p. 7; Powell, *Soldiers, Indians and Silver*, p. 50; Schindler, *Bauern und Reiterkrieger*, p. 19.

213. James, *Savage Wars*, pp. 91f., 187–190; Kiernan, *Colonial Empires*, p. 33f.; Macrory, *Signal Catastrophe*, pp. 85–87, 208; Porch, *Conquest of the Sahara*; Robson, *Fuzzy-Wuzzy*, pp. 161, 176; Vandervort, *Indian Wars*, p. 20.

214. Moreman, *Army in India*, pp. 10f., 142; Olatunji-Oloruntimehin, 'Senegambia—Mahmadou Lamine', p. 94; Paillard, 'Expedition to Madagascar', pp. 177f., 181; Strachan, *European Armies*, p. 81; Utley, *Frontier Regulars*, pp. 48f., 196, 253, 330, 387; Utley, *Frontiersmen in Blue*, p. 234f.; Vandervort, *Indian Wars*, p. 202.

215. Charney, *Southeast Asian Warfare*, pp. 131–163; Cooper, 'Culture, Combat, and Colonialism', p. 541; Reid, *Europe and Southeast Asia*, p. 2. The whole gamut of military beasts of burden was assembled for the British Abyssinia Mission of 1867/68: alongside horses, the British shipped camels, oxen and elephants with them to the Horn of Africa. Chandler, 'Expedition to Abyssinia', p. 123.

216. Bryant, 'Asymmetric Warfare', p. 443; Donnelly, *Conquest of Bashkiria*, p. 28. Only in Australia did the policy of keeping guns away from the indigenous population actually work, albeit mainly because the Aborigines had little interest in acquiring them. Connor, *Australian Frontier Wars*, pp. 17–20.

217. This was the motivation behind the disbandment of cavalry units in the army of the British East India Company in 1765. Gordon, 'Limited Adoption', p. 239f.

218. Scammell, 'Indigenous Assistance', p. 143. The Spanish in Peru also tried to prevent the indigenous people from acquiring horses. Hemming, *Conquest of the Incas*, p. 113.

219. Cf. chapter 1, 'Controlling a region'.

220. Connor, *Australian Frontier Wars*, pp. 73–75; Mostert, *Military System*, p. 30; Thornton, 'Warfare, Slave Trading and European Influence', p. 135; Vandervort, *Wars of Imperial Conquest*, p. 141.

221. Mattison, *Army Post on the Northern Plains*, p. 4f.; Silver, *Our Savage Neighbors*, pp. 49–51; Utley, *Frontier Regulars*, pp. 46–48, 81f.; Utley, *Frontiersmen in Blue*, p. 42f.; Vandervort, *Indian Wars*, p. 116f. It was a similar situation in South America. Slatta, '"Civilization" Battles "Barbarism"', p. 132f. In the same way, the European forts on the Slave Coast of Africa were not serious defensive structures, since the local African rulers forbade the building of genuine redoubts. Law, 'Warfare on the Slave Coast', pp. 107–109.

222. Black, 'European Overseas Expansion', p. 19f.; Bührer, *Kaiserliche Schutztruppe*, pp. 247–250; Chet, *Conquering the Wilderness*, p. 19f.; Keeley, *War Before Civilization*, pp. 71–74; Lee, 'Military Revolution', p. 61; Mostert, *Military System*, pp. 14, 27–31; Parker, *Military Revolution*, p. 131; Raudzens, 'Why Did Amerindian Defences Fail?', p. 341f.; Reid, *Europe and Southeast Asia*, p. 5; Ricklefs, *War, Culture and Economy*, p. 138; Ross, 'Dahomey', p. 156; Starkey, *European and Native American Warfare*, pp. 132, 168f.; Vandervort, *Wars of Imperial Conquest*, p. 79f.; Vogt, 'Saint Barbara's Legion', pp. 76–78. Rare exceptions like the case of the Dutch fortress of Zeelandia on Formosa, which it took 25,000 Chinese soldiers equipped with several artillery pieces nine months to overrun all the same (1661/62), prove the general rule. Mostert, *Military System*, pp. 101–109. In the seventeenth century Portugal lost several strongholds in Asia and East Africa to indigenous attackers; however, by that stage it was an empire in retreat. Black,

Beyond the Military Revolution, pp. 115, 117. The 'fortress' of Dien Bien Phu (which in any case was officially described as an 'air–ground base') was more of a network of provisional field fortifications, and in any event the Viet Minh brought modern artillery to bear in attacking it. Fall, *Hell in a Very Small Place*, pp. 87–93, 110–124.

223. Keeley, *War Before Civilization*, pp. 55–58.

224. Parker, *Military Revolution*, pp. 132, 142f.; Selby, 'Third China War', pp. 91, 100; Varley, 'Warfare in Japan', p. 70.

225. Muffett, 'Nigeria—Sokoto Caliphate', p. 280. Other non-European empires also constructed impressive fortresses. Bührer, *Kaiserliche Schutztruppe*, p. 252; Charney, *Southeast Asian Warfare*, pp. 73–103; Falls, 'Reconquest of the Sudan', p. 293f.; Hemming, *Conquest of the Incas*, pp. 190, 207–209; Reid, *Europe and Southeast Asia*, p. 6. Yet many forts of non-European societies presented no real obstacle to Western military technology. Bryant, 'Asymmetric Warfare', pp. 460–462; Crowder, 'Introduction', p. 12; Killingray, 'Colonial Warfare', p. 150; Knaap, 'Crisis and Failure', pp. 162, 164; Linn, 'Cerberus' Dilemma', p. 119f.; Mostert, *Military System*, p. 30; Porch, 'French Colonial Forces', p. 178.

226. Parker, *Military Revolution*, p. 144.

227. Kanya-Forstner, 'Mali—Tukulor', pp. 69, 71, 138f.

228. Boot, *Savage Wars of Peace*, pp. 52f., 59; Bührer, *Kaiserliche Schutztruppe*, pp. 250–252; Macrory, *Signal Catastrophe*, pp. 96–104; Marshall, *Russian General Staff*, p. 60; Moor, 'Warmakers in the Archipelago', pp. 53, 65; Pemble, 'Resources and Techniques', pp. 287–289; Ricklefs, *War, Culture and Economy*, p. 144; Vandervort, *Indian Wars*, p. 234.

229. Ricklefs, *War, Culture and Economy*, p. 20.

230. Parker, *Military Revolution*, p. 132.

231. Lee, 'Military Revolution', pp. 62–65; Lee, 'Fortify, Fight, or Flee', pp. 727–731, 736–745, 749–756; Starkey, *European and Native American Warfare*, p. 23f.; Vandervort, *Indian Wars*, p. 119f.

232. Malone, 'Changing Military Technology', pp. 239–241.

233. Porch, *Conquest of the Sahara*, p. 203.

234. Charney, 'Iberier und Südostasiaten', p. 182.

235. Belich, *Victorian Interpretation*, pp. 292–298. On 29 April 1864 British artillery bombarded Gate Pa at Tauranga with twenty times the weight of shells, for the surface area of the respective targets, than they fired on the German trenches during the first week of the Somme Offensive in 1916, one of the most intensive artillery bombardments preceding a battle in the whole of the First World War. Ibid., p. 295.

236. Belich, 'Krieg und transkulturelles Lernen', p. 253.

237. Abernathy, *Dynamics of Global Dominance*, p. 32; Black, 'European Overseas Expansion', p. 19; Brooks, 'Impact of Disease', p. 134; Cipolla, *Guns, Sails, and Empires*; Clayton, 'Iberian Advantage'; Glete, 'Warfare at Sea', p. 31; Knaap, 'Crisis and Failure', p. 171; McNeill, *Age of Gunpowder Empires*; McNeill, 'European Expansion, Power and Warfare', p. 17f.

238. Bond, 'Editor's Introduction', p. 26; Selby, 'Third China War'; Vandervort, *Wars of Imperial Conquest*, p. 54.

239. James, *Savage Wars*, p. 131.

240. Charney, *Southeast Asian Warfare*, p. 256; Clayton, *Wars of French Decolonization*, p. 56f.; Killingray, 'Colonial Warfare', p. 155; Vandervort, *Wars of Imperial Conquest*, p. 52f.

241. Abernathy, *Dynamics of Global Dominance*, p. 179; Hack/Rettig, 'Demography in Southeast Asia', p. 48; Hassig, *Mexico and the Spanish Conquest*, pp. 56–59; Raudzens, 'Why Did Amerindian Defences Fail?', p. 339f.; Starkey, *European and Native American Warfare*, p. 41f.; Vandervort, *Wars of Imperial Conquest*, p. 54.

242. Bodley, *Weg der Zerstörung*, p. 63; James, *Savage Wars*, pp. 117, 140; Watson, 'Fortifications', pp. 60–66.

243. Black, *Beyond the Military Revolution*, pp. 120, 151f., 161; Black, *War in the World*, p. 147; Cipolla, *Guns, Sails, and Empires*, pp. 140–143. On the strategic depth of Bengal achieved through British sea power, see Bryant, 'Asymmetric Warfare', p. 469.

244. Charney, *Southeast Asian Warfare*, p. 121f.; Mostert, *Military System*, pp. 17–19; Reid, *Europe and Southeast Asia*, p. 7f.

245. Thornton, 'Firearms, Diplomacy, and Conquest', pp. 177, 187.

246. Clayton, 'Iberian Advantage', pp. 221–224. Although the Ottoman Empire was easily able to compete with the West in sea power in the Early Modern period, it elected to concentrate its naval forces on the Mediterranean. Aksan, 'Ottoman War and Warfare', p. 162f.; Glete, 'Warfare at Sea', p. 37f. Japan and the Mughal Empire were de facto land powers.

247. Black, *War in the World*, p. 163; Marshall, 'Western Arms in Maritime Asia', p. 17f.

248. Black, *War in the World*, p. 142; Charney, *Southeast Asian Warfare*, pp. 104–130, 251, 257f.

249. Charney, *Southeast Asian Warfare*, pp. 128–130, 253–262; Gann/Duignan, *Rulers of British Africa*, p. 117; Hack/Rettig, 'Demography in Southeast Asia', pp. 40–44; Headrick, *Tools of Empire*, pp. 20f., 45, 48–50, 54; James, *Savage Wars*, pp. 91f., 101; Linn, *Counterinsurgency in the Philippine War*, p. 113; Moor, 'War-makers in the Archipelago', p. 62f.; Muffett, 'Nigeria—Sokoto Caliphate', p. 285f.; Vandervort, *Wars of Imperial Conquest*, pp. 79f., 114, 141–143.

250. James, *Savage Wars*, pp. 141, 144.

251. Hassig, 'Eroberung Mexikos', pp. 102–105; Jones, *Conquest of the Last Maya Kingdom*, pp. 265–269.

252. Cann, *Counterinsurgency in Africa*, p. 171; Clayton, *Wars of French Decolonization*, p. 57.

253. Marshall, 'Western Arms in Maritime Asia', pp. 19–23.

254. Reid, *Europe and Southeast Asia*, p. 5.

255. Charney, *Southeast Asian Warfare*, p. 251.

256. Ibid., p. 254f.

257. Ikime, 'Nigeria—Ebrohimi', p. 213f.; Law, 'Warfare on the Slave Coast', p. 121; Thornton, 'Warfare, Slave Trading and European Influence', p. 138.

258. Headrick, *Tools of Empire*, p. 52f.

259. Hassig, 'Eroberung Mexikos', p. 116f. The same tactic was clearly known about in Southeast Asia. Charney, 'Iberier und Südostasiaten', p. 194.

260. Calloway, *Winter Count*, pp. 214–219; Charney, 'Iberier und Südostasiaten', p. 194; Smith, 'Nigeria—Ijebu', p. 183; Vandervort, *Indian Wars*, pp. 128, 134f.

261. Hemming, *Red Gold*, p. 400.

262. Corum/Johnson, *Airpower in Small Wars*, p. 1.
263. Ibid., p. 81; Zollmann, *Koloniale Herrschaft*, p. 197.
264. Clayton, *Wars of French Decolonization*, p. 85.
265. Gottmann, 'Bugeaud, Galliéni, Lyautey', p. 253.
266. Corum/Johnson, *Airpower in Small Wars*, p. 83; Jones, *Graveyard of Empires*, p. 29; Mattioli, 'Kolonialverbrechen des faschistischen Italien', p. 208; Woolman, *Rebels in the Rif*, p. 161.
267. Gregorian, '"Jungle Bashing" in Malaya', p. 348f.
268. Clayton, *Wars of French Decolonization*, pp. 48, 53, 56.
269. Coates, *Suppressing Insurgency*, p. 171.
270. Cann, *Counterinsurgency in Africa*, pp. 172–174.
271. Beckett, *Modern Insurgencies*, p. 43; James, *Savage Wars*, pp. 187–190; Kiernan, *Colonial Empires*, pp. 194–200; Lemke, 'Kolonialgeschichte als Vorläufer?', p. 284; Moreman, '"Watch and Ward"', p. 145.
272. Corum/Johnson, *Airpower in Small Wars*, p. 76.
273. Coates, *Suppressing Insurgency*, p. 173.
274. Clayton, *Wars of French Decolonization*, p. 37; Corum/Johnson, *Airpower in Small Wars*, p. 79.
275. Fall, *Hell in a Very Small Place*, pp. 134–138, 185, 243–249, 454f.
276. Cann, *Counterinsurgency in Africa*, p. 130f.; Clayton, *Wars of French Decolonization*, p. 159; Coates, *Suppressing Insurgency*, p. 170; Corum/Johnson, *Airpower in Small Wars*, pp. 171f., 215; Isby, *War in a Distant Country*, pp. 59f., 63, 66f.; Jones, *Counterinsurgency and the SAS*, p. 133.
277. Casper, *Falcon Brigade*, p. 31–42.
278. Director: Ridley Scott, 2001. The 'Black Hawk' is the familiar name for the Sikorsky UH-60, a US Army transport helicopter.
279. Cann, *Counterinsurgency in Africa*, p. 133f.; Fall, *Hell in a Very Small Place*, p. 2f.
280. Corum/Johnson, *Airpower in Small Wars*, pp. 167, 431–433; Gates, 'Two American Wars', p. 59; Vandervort, 'Colonial Wars', p. 167.
281. Kiernan, *Colonial Empires*, p. 200.
282. Corum/Johnson, *Airpower in Small Wars*, p. 84.
283. Wilner, 'Targeted Killings in Afghanistan'.
284. McCoy, 'Imperial Illusions', pp. 375, 378–386.
285. Chalk/Brandt, 'Drone Wars'; Dowd, 'Drone Wars', p. 11f.; McCrisken, 'Obama's Drone War', pp. 107–109; Müller/Schörnig, 'Drohnenkrieg', p. 21f.
286. Guilmartin, 'Cutting Edge', pp. 41f., 59, 61; Hemming, *Red Gold*, p. 222; Kundrus/Walter, 'Anpassung und Lernen', pp. 19–22; Lee, 'Projecting Power', p. 6.
287. Abler, 'Beavers and Muskets', pp. 155–157; Steele, *Warpaths*, p. 64f. Cf. Connor, *Australian Frontier Wars*, p. 24f.; Hemming, *Red Gold*, p. 222.
288. Corum/Johnson, *Airpower in Small Wars*, p. 84; Fynn, 'Ghana—Asante', p. 32; Woolman, *Rebels in the Rif*, p. 105. Cf. on the psychological effects of firearms, Cullen, 'Targeted Killing', p. 25; McCrisken, 'Obama's Drone War', p. 115.
289. Hemming, *Conquest of the Incas*, pp. 37, 110f.; Raudzens, 'Why Did Amerindian Defences Fail?', p. 348; Reid, *Europe and Southeast Asia*, p. 5.
290. Calloway, *Winter Count*, p. 129.
291. Hochgeschwender, 'Last Stand', p. 59f.; Steele, *Betrayals*, pp. 84–86.

292. Bryant, 'Asymmetric Warfare', p. 447f.; Hassig, 'Eroberung Mexikos', p. 124f.; Hassig, 'Aztec and Spanish Conquest', p. 96; Hirsch, 'Collision of Military Cultures', p. 1202f.; James, *Raj*, p. 20; Kiernan, *Colonial Empires*, pp. 34, 49f.; Kolff, 'End of an Ancien Régime', p. 45; Malone, *Skulking Way of War*, p. 78f.; Marshall, 'Western Arms in Maritime Asia', pp. 17; Oudijk/Restall, 'Mesoamerican Conquistadors', pp. 54–56; Porch, *Conquest of Morocco*, p. 177f.

293. Bitterli, *Die "Wilden" und die "Zivilisierten"*, pp. 81–91; Morillo, 'Typology of Transcultural Wars', p. 34; Osterhammel, 'Wissen als Macht'.

294. Hochgeschwender, 'Last Stand', p. 60; Utley, *Frontier Regulars*, p. 143; Utley, *Frontiersmen in Blue*, pp. 95–97, 165f.

295. Hassig, *Mexico and the Spanish Conquest*, pp. 67, 87–93.

296. Starkey, 'Conflict and Synthesis', pp. 71–73; Steele, *Betrayals*, pp. 53f., 87–90, 99–102.

297. Calloway, *Winter Count*, pp. 134, 136.

298. Palmer, *Colonial Genocide*, p. 131f.

299. Porter, *Military Orientalism*, pp. 193, 198.

300. Connor, 'Briten und Darug', p. 228f.; Hassig, *Mexico and the Spanish Conquest*, p. 67; Kundrus/Walter, 'Anpassung und Lernen', p. 21.

301. Callwell, *Small Wars*, p. 158.

302. Hull, *Absolute Destruction*, p. 26f., 33; Porter, *Military Orientalism*, pp. 40–43. Cf. chapter 3, 'Traditions of violence'.

303. Greiner, *Krieg ohne Fronten*, p. 328; James, *Savage Wars*, p. 173f.; Le Cour Grandmaison, *Coloniser, Exterminer*, p. 156f.; Lehmann, *All Sir Garnet*, p. 53; Mukherjee, *Spectre of Violence*, p. 32f.; Zollmann, *Koloniale Herrschaft*, pp. 110–113.

304. Gordon was a British officer and Governor General of Egyptian Sudan. His death at the hands of the Mahdists during their capture of Khartoum in 1885 provoked a public outcry in Great Britain.

305. Porter, *Military Orientalism*, pp. 57–59; Utley, *Custer*, pp. 166–168. Gordon himself admitted in his diary: 'I am ignorant of all that goes on, ignorant of the Arabic language, except in my style, ignorant of the Arabic customs, &c. &c.' Gordon, *Khartoum Journal*, p. 126. According to one of his biographers, Gordon wandered around 'in a mist of incomprehension'. Trench, *Charley Gordon*, p. 224.

306. Starkey, *European and Native American Warfare*, pp. 17–19.

307. Plank, 'Deploying Tribes and Clans'.

308. Porter, *Military Orientalism*, p. 57.

309. Kennedy, *Freedom from Fear*, pp. 512, 518, 615; Weinberg, 'Hitler's Image of the United States'.

310. Charney, 'Iberier und Südostasiaten', p. 194f.; Ricklefs, *War, Culture and Economy*, pp. 22f., 129.

311. Bergmann, 'Dynamik der Conquista', p. 228f.; Todorov, *Eroberung Amerikas*, pp. 69–151. Cf. for a critique of this perspective Gabbert, 'Kultureller Determinismus', pp. 275–279; Hassig, *Mexico and the Spanish Conquest*, p. 3.

312. Wendt, *Vom Kolonialismus zur Globalisierung*, pp. 97–104, 207–220.

313. Abernathy, *Dynamics of Global Dominance*, p. 33f.; Headrick, *Tools of Empire*, p. 207f.; Mostert, *Military System*, p. 15; Ricklefs, *War, Culture and Economy*, p. 129f.

314. Beckett, *Modern Insurgencies*, p. 2; Calloway, *Winter Count*, pp. 9–13; Callwell, *Small Wars*, pp. 53–56; Connor, 'Briten und Darug', p. 235; Ditte, *Guerre dans les Colonies*, p. 16f.; Headrick, *Tools of Empire*, p. 84; Horne, *Savage War of Peace*, p. 184; James, *Savage Wars*, p. 163; Jobst, 'Expansion des Zarenreiches', p. 69; Moreman, *Army in India*, p. 12; Powell, *Soldiers, Indians and Silver*, p. 32f.; Ward, '"European Method of Warring"', p. 251; Woolman, *Rebels in the Rif*, p. 80f.; Zollmann, *Koloniale Herrschaft*, p. 193.

315. Weber, *Spanish Frontier*, p. 82. In actual fact Santa Fe lies some 2,700 km from the Atlantic coastline of North Carolina and around 1,500 km from the Pacific; on the line of latitude, the distance from Roanoke to the Pacific is over 4,000 km. In the same way, the Spanish in Mexico had only the vaguest idea of the geography of the Yucatán. Jones, *Conquest of the Last Maya Kingdom*, p. 248.

316. Bond, 'Editor's Introduction', p. 20f.; Bührer, *Kaiserliche Schutztruppe*, p. 245; Lock/Quantrill, *Zulu Victory*, p. 75f.; Nasson, *South African War*, p. 123; Utley, *Frontiersmen in Blue*, p. 332.

317. Chandler, 'Expedition to Abyssinia', p. 115; Clayton, *Wars of French Decolonization*, p. 58; Girard, *Slaves Who Defeated Napoleon*, p. 118; Gould, *Imperial Warriors*, p. 37; Lock/Quantrill, *Zulu Victory*, p. 47f.; Marshall, *Russian General Staff*, p. 132f.; Porch, *Conquest of the Sahara*, p. 134; Porch, *Conquest of Morocco*, p. 29; Potempa, 'Raum und seine Beherrschung', p. 448f.; Stucki, *Aufstand und Zwangsumsiedlung*, p. 73; Woolman, *Rebels in the Rif*, p. 18f.; Laband, *Zululand Campaign*, p. 191.

318. 'Here it is no question of pedantic hairsplitting: it is enough to look at the map in question. Nearly everything that is shown on the map is wrong, displaced or invented by its drawer.' Rainero, 'Battle of Adowa', p. 195.

319. Veltzé, *Schlacht bei Adua*, p. 75.

320. Rainero, 'Battle of Adowa', p. 195.

321. Bandini, *Italiani in Africa*, p. 161.

322. Lock/Quantrill, *Zulu Victory*, p. 47f.

323. François, *Kriegführung in Süd-Afrika*, p. 5f.; Kuß, *Deutsches Militär*, pp. 232–238.

324. Callwell, *Small Wars*, p. 49f.

325. Fynn, 'Ghana—Asante', p. 30f.

326. Calloway, *Winter Count*, p. 141.

327. Ibid., pp. 9–13.

328. Butlin, *Geographies of Empire*, pp. 335–344.

329. Rainero, 'Battle of Adowa', p. 195.

330. Callwell, *Small Wars*, pp. 47–53; Crowder, 'Introduction', p. 9; Fourniau, 'Colonial Wars before 1914', p. 76; Prince, *Gegen Araber und Wahehe*, p. 79; Starkey, *European and Native American Warfare*, p. 146; Vandervort, *Wars of Imperial Conquest*, p. 95.

331. Arnold, 'Schlacht bei Rugaro', pp. 95–97; Starkey, 'Conflict and Synthesis', p. 77.

332. Moor, 'Warmakers in the Archipelago', p. 67.

333. Ibid.; Porter, *Military Orientalism*, p. 56f.; Vandervort, *Wars of Imperial Conquest*, p. 206.

334. Bierling, *Geschichte des Irakkriegs*, p. 144f.; Bührer, 'Hehe und Schutztruppe', p. 265; Bührer, *Kaiserliche Schutztruppe*, p. 237; Clayton, *Wars of French Decolonization*, pp. 58, 116; Grau, *Bear Over the Mountain*, p. 204; Khodarkovsky, *Russia's Steppe Frontier*, p. 141; Kiernan, *Colonial Empires*, p. 45; Linn, *Counterinsurgency in the Philippine War*, p. 140f.; Nasson, *South African War*, pp. 122–128, 130–134,

200; Stucki, *Aufstand und Zwangsumsiedlung*, pp. 80–84; Utley, *Custer*, p. 74; Veltzé, *Schlacht bei Adua*, p. 75.

335. Vandervort, *Indian Wars*, p. 132; Walter, "'The Enemy Must Be Brought to Battle'".

336. Emil von Zelewski, 'Truppenführung in Ostafrika', quoted in Arnold, 'Schlacht bei Rugaro', p. 104f.

337. Utley, *Custer*, p. 158.

338. *Die Kämpfe der deutschen Truppen in Südwestafrika*, Vol. 1, p. 66.

339. Franklin, 'Autobiography', p. 1441.

340. Utley, *Custer*, p. 67.

341. Prince, *Gegen Araber und Wahehe*.

342. Lock/Quantrill, *Zulu Victory*, p. 15.

343. Ibid., p. 74.

344. Ibid., p. 40; Laband, *Zululand Campaign*, p. 31.

345. Lock/Quantrill, *Zulu Victory*, p. 134. Cf. Manning, 'Learning the Trade', pp. 651–653.

346. Gordon, *Khartoum Journal*, p. 44.

347. Ibid., p. 71.

348. Belich, *Victorian Interpretation*, pp. 120, 312–314; Bond, 'South African War', pp. 218, 227, 230; Charney, *Southeast Asian Warfare*, p. 187; Denzer, 'Sierra Leone—Bai Bureh', p. 244; Gann/Duignan, *Rulers of British Africa*, pp. 87; Hassig, 'Eroberung Mexikos', pp. 73, 110; Khodarkovsky, 'Krieg und Frieden', p. 199; Kiernan, *Colonial Empires*, p. 40; Killingray, 'Colonial Warfare', p. 147; Macrory, *Signal Catastrophe*, p. 76; Marshall, *Russian General Staff*, pp. 85, 89f.; Muffett, 'Nigeria—Sokoto Caliphate', p. 290f.; Nasson, *South African War*, pp. 12, 69–72; Pemble, 'Resources and Techniques', pp. 287–289; Porch, *Conquest of the Sahara*, p. 139f.; Powell, *Soldiers, Indians and Silver*, p. 32; Rose, "'Unsichtbare Feinde'", pp. 219–221, 226; Schumacher, "'Niederbrennen, plündern und töten'", p. 125; Starkey, *European and Native American Warfare*, p. 146f.; Vandervort, *Indian Wars*, pp. 9–11, 116, 176f.; Woolman, *Rebels in the Rif*, p. 72.

349. Pemble, 'Resources and Techniques', p. 288f.

350. Porch, *Conquest of the Sahara*, p. 86; Smith, 'Nigeria—Ijebu', p. 178.

351. 1924 interview with the US journalist Paul Scott Mowrer, as recounted in Furneaux, *Abdel Krim*, p. 161f.

352. Fall, *Hell in a Very Small Place*, pp. 49f., 101–105, 451–455.

353. Janis, *Groupthink*.

354. Lock/Quantrill, *Zulu Victory*, pp. 167–179; Porch, *Conquest of the Sahara*, pp. 224, 227f.; Starkey, *European and Native American Warfare*, p. 147; Woolman, *Rebels in the Rif*, p. 88f.

355. Beckett, *Modern Insurgencies*, p. 38; Belich, 'Krieg und transkulturelles Lernen', p. 256f.; Belich, *Victorian Interpretation*, pp. 318–325; Jones, *Conquest of the Last Maya Kingdom*, p. xxi.

356. Butlin, *Geographies of Empire*, pp. 350–395; Fourniau, 'Colonial Wars before 1914', p. 76; Honold, 'Raum ohne Volk', p. 97f.

357. Edgerton, *Mau Mau*, p. 139; Gordon, 'Limited Adoption', p. 243; Linn, *Counterinsurgency in the Philippine War*, p. 169f.

358. Ballantyne, 'Information and Intelligence', p. 177; Charney, 'Iberier und Südostasiaten', pp. 187–189; Connor, 'Briten und Darug', p. 234f.; Gould,

Imperial Warriors, p. 62; Häberlein, 'Macht und Ohnmacht', p. 87; Hassig, *Mexico and the Spanish Conquest*, p. 138; Hemming, *Conquest of the Incas*, p. 25; Hemming, *Red Gold*, p. 288; Jones, *Conquest of the Last Maya Kingdom*, pp. 233, 240; Kars, '"Cleansing the Land"', pp. 263–268; Lappas, 'Lernen inmitten des Blutvergießens', pp. 157–162, 175; Lee, 'Projecting Power', p. 9f.; Lock/Quantrill, *Zulu Victory*, p. 47f.; Morlang, *Askari und Fitafita*, p. 66; Oudijk/Restall, 'Mesoamerican Conquistadors', pp. 38–41; Palmer, *Colonial Genocide*, p. 102f.; Plank, 'Deploying Tribes and Clans', p. 223.

359. Guilmartin, 'Cutting Edge', p. 58f.; Hemming, *Conquest of the Incas*, p. 99; James, *Raj*, pp. 145–147; Jones, *Conquest of the Last Maya Kingdom*, pp. 136–139, 145f.; Penn, *Forgotten Frontier*, p. 119; Utley, *Frontier Regulars*, pp. 50, 377–381; Vandervort, *Indian Wars*, pp. 202f., 208–210. This aspect is also emphasized by Callwell, *Small Wars*, pp. 143–145.

360. Ballantyne, 'Information and Intelligence'; Bührer, 'Hehe und Schutztruppe', p. 279f.; Butlin, *Geographies of Empire*, pp. 325–349; DeFronzo, *Iraq War*, p. 215; Hée, *Imperiales Wissen*, pp. 51–120; Honold, 'Raum ohne Volk', p. 99; Kirk-Greene, '"Damnosa Hereditas"'; Kuß, *Deutsches Militär*, pp. 238–243, 379–386, 393f.; Livingstone, *Geographical Tradition*, pp. 241–245; Marshall, *Russian General Staff*, pp. 3–10, 15–30; McCoy, 'Imperial Illusions', pp. 363–367; Miège, 'Conquest of Morocco', p. 204f.; Omissi, *Sepoy and the Raj*, pp. 23–32; Osterhammel, *Verwandlung der Welt*, pp. 1158–1167; Paillard, 'Expedition to Madagascar', p. 170f.; Slatta, '"Civilization" Battles "Barbarism"', p. 142; Wendt, *Vom Kolonialismus zur Globalisierung*, p. 302f. The limitations of what intelligence can be acquired from such purely factual knowledge are stressed by Trotha, 'Was war Kolonialismus?', p. 83.

361. Beckett, *Modern Insurgencies*, p. 156f.; Cann, *Counterinsurgency in Africa*, pp. 114–125; Clayton, *Wars of French Decolonization*, pp. 61, 154f.; Coates, *Suppressing Insurgency*, p. 167f.; Fall, *Hell in a Very Small Place*, p. 104; Mockaitis, *British Counterinsurgency*, pp. 73–76; Walter, 'Kolonialkrieg, Globalstrategie und Kalter Krieg', p. 120.

362. Beckett, *Modern Insurgencies*, pp. 194–204.

363. McCoy, 'Imperial Illusions', pp. 373–378.

364. Anderson/Pols, 'Scientific Patriotism'; Beckett, *Modern Insurgencies*, p. 81; Osterhammel, *Verwandlung der Welt*, pp. 1147–1151; Wendt, *Vom Kolonialismus zur Globalisierung*, pp. 278f., 342f.

365. According to the conceptualization in Füssel, 'Lernen—Transfer—Aneignung', p. 36f.

366. Moreman, '"Small Wars"', p. 107f.

367. *Field Manual 3–24*, p. ix; Moreman, *Army in India*, pp. 140, 143–144; Roxborough, 'Lessons of Counterinsurgency', p. 40. A revisionist opposite standpoint maintains that the very notion of war on the periphery being sui generis is an instrumental myth created by colonial officers, which was meant to emphasize their own military specialization and shield their brutal activities overseas from any scrutiny or control in the motherland. Bearing in mind the role of French officers in the conquest of Africa discussed in chapter 1 it is presumably no coincidence that this viewpoint derives from a specialist in French colonial warfare: Porch, 'Myths and Promise of COIN'. The stress laid by Spanish military prac-

titioners on the 'unique character' of the fighting in Cuba was seen by contemporary critics as a transparent attempt to deflect attention away from their own failures. According to the official Spanish position, small wars remained small wars, no matter where they were fought. Stucki, *Aufstand und Zwangsumsiedlung*, pp. 33–36.

368. Beckett, *Modern Insurgencies*, pp. 184–187; Bierling, *Geschichte des Irakkriegs*, p. 165f.; Boot, *Savage Wars of Peace*, pp. 282–284; Fischer, 'Suppen, Messer und Löffel'; Greiner, *Krieg ohne Fronten*, pp. 74–90; Joes, *America and Guerrilla Warfare*; Linn, 'Cerberus' Dilemma', p. 123; Nagl, *Soup with a Knife* (2005), pp. 151–180, 217; Nagl, 'Soup with a Knife (1999)', p. 196; Pavilonis, 'Irregular War in Afghanistan'; Sarkesian, 'American Response', p. 37; Utley, *Custer*, p. 50; Utley, 'Cultural Clash', pp. 92–94, 100–102; Utley, *Frontier Regulars*, p. 46; Utley, *Frontiersmen in Blue*, pp. 33, 57; Vandervort, *Indian Wars*, pp. 53–62. On other armed forces, see: Cann, *Counterinsurgency in Africa*, pp. 61–63; Isby, *War in a Distant Country*, pp. 53–66; Porch, *Conquest of the Sahara*, pp. 223f., 227f.

369. Cf. chapter 1, 'Limits to the projection of power'.

370. On the logic of the institution of the military, see Abrahamsson, *Military Professionalization*, pp. 59–70; Elbe/Richter, 'Militär', pp. 139–143; Hagen/Tomforde, 'Militärische Organisationskultur', pp. 183–193; Huntington, *Soldier and State*, pp. 59–79; Janowitz, *Professional Soldier*, pp. 21–75.

371. Bradford, 'Preface', p. xvii; Kanya-Forstner, 'French Marines', p. 121f.; Laqueur, *Guerrilla Warfare*, p. 51; Marshall, *Russian General Staff*, p. 50f.; More-man, '"Small Wars"', p. 125; Schmidl, 'Kolonialkriege', p. 113; Starkey, *European and Native American Warfare*, p. 56; Tugwell, 'Adapt or Perish', p. 8; Whittingham, '"Savage Warfare"', p. 591f.

372. Vandervort, *Indian Wars*, p. 72f.; Walter, *Dschungelkrieg und Atombombe*, p. 52f., 126–141.

373. Beckett, *Modern Insurgencies*, p. 41f., 205; Bradford, 'Preface', p. xvii.

374. 374 Charters, 'Palestine to Northern Ireland', pp. 229–234; Strachan, *Politics of the British Army*; Strachan, 'British Way in Warfare'; Walter, *Dschungelkrieg und Atombombe*, pp. 74–77.

375. See the section 'Armed forces' above.

376. Beckett, *Modern Insurgencies*, p. 186; Connor, *Australian Frontier Wars*, p. 14; Roxborough, 'Lessons of Counterinsurgency', p. 40.

377. Gann/Duignan, *Rulers of British Africa*, p. 76f.; Kanya-Forstner, 'French Marines', p. 121f.; Kiernan, *Colonial Empires*, pp. 181–183; Porch, 'French Colonial Forces', p. 180f.; Wesseling, 'Wars and Peace', pp. 67–69.

378. Eberspächer, '"Albion zal hier"', p. 196. A more positive interpretation of what the British learnt from the Boer War is offered by Nasson, *South African War*, p. 286f.

379. Porch, 'French Colonial Forces', p. 180.

380. Bond, 'Editor's Introduction', p. 25.

381. Strachan, *European Armies*, pp. 84–88.

382. Paret, 'Colonial Experience'.

383. Bryant, 'Asymmetric Warfare', p. 440.

384. Beckett, *Modern Insurgencies*, p. 25.

385. Helbling, *Tribale Kriege*, p. 142.

386. Cf. chapter 3, 'Military necessity'.
387. Brumwell, '"Service Truly Critical"'; Grenier, *First Way of War*, 32–39; Kopperman, *Braddock at the Monongahela*, pp. 126f.; Malone, *Skulking Way of War*, p. 100; Starkey, 'Lernen im Kolonialkrieg', pp. 141–144; Starkey, *European and Native American Warfare*, pp. 82–91, 97–101, 107–109, 133–135. For other armies and theatres of war, cf. Barua, 'Military Developments in India', pp. 613, 616; Khodarkovsky, 'Krieg und Frieden', p. 218; Lemke, 'Kolonialgeschichte als Vorläufer?', p. 290f.; Mockaitis, 'Origins of British Counter-Insurgency', pp. 221–223; Moor, 'Warmakers in the Archipelago', p. 54; Moreman, *Army in India*, p. 177; Rickey, *Forty Miles a Day*, pp. 280–282; Thornton, 'Art of War in Angola', p. 97; Utley, *Frontiersmen in Blue*, pp. 342–346; Vandervort, *Indian Wars*, pp. 73f., 88f.
388. Greiner, *Krieg ohne Fronten*, pp. 127–131.
389. Connor, *Australian Frontier Wars*, p. 12; Vandervort, *Wars of Imperial Conquest*, p. 54.
390. Grenier, *First Way of War*, p. 22; Starkey, 'Conflict and Synthesis', p. 75; Starkey, *European and Native American Warfare*, pp. 41f., 81.
391. Beckett, *Modern Insurgencies*, pp. 44–48, 129; Jones, *Counterinsurgency and the SAS*, p. 128f.; Mockaitis, *British Counterinsurgency*, pp. 69–83.
392. Gottmann, 'Bugeaud, Galliéni, Lyautey', pp. 235–238; Martin, 'From Algiers to N'Djamena', pp. 81–87; Miège, 'Conquest of Morocco', p. 207; Wesseling, 'Wars and Peace', pp. 61–63.
393. Miège, 'Conquest of Morocco', p. 207; Wesseling, 'Wars and Peace', pp. 65–67.
394. Guilmartin, 'Cutting Edge', p. 56; Hassig, *Mexico and the Spanish Conquest*, p. 63f.; Lee, 'Projecting Power', p. 6; Restall, *Myths of the Spanish Conquest*, pp. 46–48.
395. Stucki, *Aufstand und Zwangsumsiedlung*, pp. 36–38.
396. Cann, *Counterinsurgency in Africa*, p. 10f.
397. Charney, 'Iberier und Südostasiaten', p. 194f.
398. Khodarkovsky, 'Krieg und Frieden', pp. 198–200.
399. Marshall, *Russian General Staff*, pp. 20f., 65f.
400. Ibid., pp. 46–51.
401. Isby, *War in a Distant Country*, p. 73.
402. Michels, '"Ostasiatisches Expeditionskorps"', p. 416.
403. Beckett, *Modern Insurgencies*, pp. 204–206; Linn, 'Cerberus' Dilemma', pp. 130–132; Sarkesian, 'American Response'; Utley, *Custer*, pp. 166–168; Vandervort, *Indian Wars*, p. 136.
404. Cahn, 'Kriegsgreuel im Algerienkrieg', p. 380; Clayton, *Wars of French Decolonization*, p. 129f.; Fall, *Hell in a Very Small Place*, pp. 440–442.
405. Crawford, 'Sikh Wars', p. 40f.; Nasson, *South African War*, pp. 117–144; Walter, '"The Enemy Must Be Brought to Battle"'.
406. Charney, *Southeast Asian Warfare*, p. 271; Rink, 'Kleiner Krieg'.
407. Chet, *Conquering the Wilderness*, pp. 1–3; Starkey, 'Lernen im Kolonialkrieg', pp. 142–144; Starkey, *European and Native American Warfare*, pp. 3f., 10–12; Strachan, *European Armies*, pp. 27–32.
408. Vargas Machuca, *Indian Militia and Description of the Indies*, pp. 81–132. Hailed as the 'first manual of guerrilla warfare ever published' by Parker, *Military Revolution*, p. 120. It is unclear, however, how wide a readership Machuca's work reached. Lane, 'Introductory Study', p. xix.

409. Beckett, 'British Counter-Insurgency', p. 784f.

410. Beckett, *Modern Insurgencies*, p. 48; Lemke, 'Kolonialgeschichte als Vorläufer?', p. 290f.; Moreman, *Army in India*, pp. 169–179; Moreman, '"Small Wars"', pp. 115–117.

411. *The Conduct of Anti-Terrorist Operations in Malaya*.

412. Jones, *Counterinsurgency and the SAS*, pp. 134–137.

413. Callwell, *Small Wars*, p. 4.

414. Gates, 'Callwell, Small Wars (Review)', p. 382.

415. Whittingham, '"Savage Warfare"', p. 592.

416. Anglim, 'Callwell versus Graziani', p. 592.

417. I am not aware of any study, either in Great Britain or internationally, which treats the question of the reception of Callwell's work, yet the fact remains that Callwell continues to be extensively cited. Gates, 'Callwell, Small Wars (Review)'. The new edition of *Small Wars*, which appeared in 1996, proclaims its author— for all its criticism of his preference for solving political problems through military means—as the 'Clausewitz of colonial warfare', who continues to be relevant even nowadays. Porch, 'Introduction', pp. v, vii, xii, xvii. The significance of Callwell, at least for the British Army in general, is relativized by Beckett, 'British Counter-Insurgency', p. 785.

418. Beckett, *Modern Insurgencies*, p. 44.

419. Anglim, 'Callwell versus Graziani', p. 592.

420. Gwynn, *Imperial Policing*.

421. Moreman, '"Small Wars"', pp. 108–110.

422. Lyautey, *Rôle colonial de l'armée*, p. 20.

423. Beckett, *Modern Insurgencies*, p. 41.

424. Ditte, *Guerre dans les Colonies*.

425. Lieb, 'Guerre Révolutionnaire'.

426. Ibid., p. 466.

427. Trinquier, *Guerre moderne*, pp. 14–21.

428. Galula, *Counterinsurgency Warfare*.

429. Thompson, *Defeating Communist Insurgency*.

430. *Field Manual 3–24*, p. viii. Cf. DeFronzo, *Iraq War*, pp. 226–229.

431. *Small Wars Manual*.

432. Beckett, *Modern Insurgencies*, pp. 48–50. For a more positive view of the *Small Wars Manual*, see Boot, *Savage Wars of Peace*, pp. 282–284.

433. Though in fact this work focused primarily on peripheral theatres of war. Chacón, *Guerras Irregulares*.

434. Stucki, *Aufstand und Zwangsumsiedlung*, pp. 38–41.

435. Beckett, *Modern Insurgencies*, p. 41f.

436. Gregorian, '"Jungle Bashing" in Malaya', pp. 346–348.

437. Klose, '"Antisubversiver Krieg"', p. 489f.

438. Cann, *Counterinsurgency in Africa*, pp. 74–78.

439. Gerwarth/Malinowski, 'Holocaust als "kolonialer Genozid"?'.

440. Lappas, 'Lernen inmitten des Blutvergießens', p. 163.

441. Callwell, *Small Wars*, p. 3; Rink, 'Kleiner Krieg', p. 442.

442. Killingray, 'Colonial Warfare', p. 156; Kuß, *Deutsches Militär*, pp. 189–198; Miège, 'Conquest of Morocco', pp. 201, 212; Potempa, 'Raum und seine Beherrschung',

pp. 446–448; Stucki, 'Bevölkerungskontrolle in asymmetrischen Konflikten', pp. 250–255; Vandervort, *Indian Wars*, pp. 17–20, 60f.

443. Cann, *Counterinsurgency in Africa*, pp. 61–63; Tugwell, 'Adapt or Perish', p. 8.

444. Klose, '"Antisubversiver Krieg"', pp. 495–499.

445. Beckett, *Modern Insurgencies*, p. 198; Clayton, *Wars of French Decolonization*, p. 181f.

446. Charters/Tugwell, *Armies in Low-Intensity Conflict*, p. 254f.

447. Strachan, *Politics of the British Army*, pp. 215–218; Walter, *Dschungelkrieg und Atombombe*.

448. Geraghty, *Who Dares Wins*, pp. 51–53.

449. Martin, 'From Algiers to N'Djamena', pp. 100–123.

450. Cann, *Counterinsurgency in Africa*, pp. 40–46, 78–81.

451. Gerlach, *Extremely Violent Societies*, p. 229.

452. Ibid., pp. 228–232.

453. Arriaga, *Guerra e politica*, p. 50. My thanks are due to Andreas Stucki for alerting me to this quotation.

454. Belich, *Victorian Interpretation*, p. 316; Lee, 'Fortify, Fight, or Flee', pp. 727–731, 736; Malone, *Skulking Way of War*, p. 75; Vandervort, *Indian Wars*, p. 119. Generally speaking, the motif of deserters as sources of indigenous military expertise appears to have frequently been associated with indigenous fortresses. For other instances of this, see Jones, *Maya Resistance to Spanish Rule*, pp. 26–28; Thornton, 'Warfare, Slave Trading and European Influence', p. 137.

455. Cooper, 'Culture, Combat, and Colonialism', p. 540; Law, 'Warfare on the Slave Coast', p. 110; Thornton, 'African Soldiers in the Haitian Revolution', p. 64f.; Vandervort, *Wars of Imperial Conquest*, p. 21.

456. Hemming, *Red Gold*, p. 30.

457. Belich, 'Krieg und transkulturelles Lernen', p. 256; Cocker, *Rivers of Blood*, p. 144.

458. Peers, 'Revolution, Evolution, or Devolution', p. 83.

459. Woolman, *Rebels in the Rif*, p. 151f.

460. Barua, 'Military Developments in India', pp. 604–613; Charney, 'Iberier und Südostasiaten', p. 197; Charney, *Southeast Asian Warfare*, pp. 237–243; Penn, *Forgotten Frontier*, p. 139; Ranger, *Revolt in Southern Rhodesia*, p. 118f.

461. Person, 'Guinea', p. 134.

462. Woolman, *Rebels in the Rif*, p. 151f.

463. The works of James Belich draw particular attention to the Maoris' capacity for learning, but also the Japanese, North American Indian peoples, the Javanese and even Australian Aborigines are now widely regarded as being open to innovations in both technology and tactics. Belich, 'Krieg und transkulturelles Lernen', pp. 250–252; Belich, *Victorian Interpretation*, pp. 292–298; Connor, *Australian Frontier Wars*, pp. 20f., 40–43; Lee 'Fortify, Fight, or Flee', pp. 715–718, 723; Ricklefs, *War, Culture and Economy*, p. 13f., 130; Starkey, *European and Native American Warfare*, pp. 71–74, 145f.; Varley, 'Warfare in Japan', pp. 64–70. On the modernizing dictatorships of the Islamic world in the eighteenth and nineteenth centuries, see chapter 1, 'The enemies of empire'. Yet to date scholarship has regarded the tactical capacity of African actors to learn as generally low, with significant exceptions such as Samori Touré. Crowder, 'Introduction', p. 14f.; Vandervort, *Wars of Imperial Conquest*, pp. 54–55, 132–133.

464. Lee, 'Fortify, Fight, or Flee', p. 744f.

465. Barua, 'Military Developments in India', p. 599f.; Bryant, 'Asymmetric Warfare', p. 442.

466. Thornton, 'African Soldiers in the Haitian Revolution'.

467. Lee, 'Fortify, Fight, or Flee', pp. 745f., 749–757, 768f.

468. Belich, 'Krieg und transkulturelles Lernen', pp. 246–249; Belich, *Victorian Interpretation*, p. 45f.

469. Anderson, *Under Three Flags*; Burbank/Cooper, *Empires in World History*, pp. 326f., 402–404; Edwards, 'Shadows of Shadows'; Feichtinger, 'Von Brüssel nach Bandung'; Malley, *Call from Algeria*, pp. 21–27; Prashad, *A People's History of the Third World*; Wendt, *Vom Kolonialismus zur Globalisierung*, p. 285f. My thanks are due here to Moritz Feichtinger for showing me the manuscript of his lecture and providing me with pointers to secondary literature. A precursor of such international cooperative efforts, albeit more limited in scope, may be identified in the anticolonial networks among Spanish-American revolutionaries at the beginning of the nineteenth century. Rinke, *Revolutionen in Lateinamerika*, pp. 44–67.

470. Kramer, 'Race-Making and Colonial Violence', p. 195; Linn, *Counterinsurgency in the Philippine War*, p. 5f. On the practical exchange of experience cf. also Gerlach, *Extremely Violent Societies*, p. 228.

471. See, among other sources, Mao, 'Über den langwierigen Krieg'; Mao, 'Strategische Probleme des Partisanenkriegs'; Mao, 'Strategische Probleme des revolutionären Krieges'.

472. Guevara, *Guerilla*; Marighela, 'Handbuch des Stadtguerillero'; Vo Nguyen Giap, *Volkskrieg, Volksarmee*. Cf. Beckett, *Modern Insurgencies*, pp. 70–81; Gates, 'Two American Wars', pp. 59, 62–65; Heuser. *Rebellen—Partisanen—Guerilleros*, pp. 97–109.

473. Beckett, *Modern Insurgencies*, pp. 79–81, 170f., 174–176.

474. Porter, *Military Orientalism*, p. 62f.

475. Bryant, 'Asymmetric Warfare', p. 433f.; Mostert, *Military System*, p. 25. Cf. p. 220f., especially the comments on efforts to prevent the spread of weapons and horses.

476. Guilmartin, 'Cutting Edge'; Hassig, 'Eroberung Mexikos', pp. 107–109.

477. In other cases the European influence may have been so sporadic and temporary, that for a long time it did not seem to necessitate any attempt at assimilation, as has been noted regarding the Dutch influence in India. Moor, 'Warmakers in the Archipelago', p. 66.

478. Jones, *Conquest of the Last Maya Kingdom*, pp. xxi; Lee, 'Projecting Power', p. 6f.; Lee, 'Fortify, Fight, or Flee', pp. 731, 745f.

479. Lappas, 'Lernen inmitten des Blutvergießens', pp. 175–178; Malone, *Skulking Way of War*, p. 100; Plank, 'Deploying Tribes and Clans', pp. 221–223; Starkey, 'Conflict and Synthesis', p. 82.

480. Ricklefs, *War, Culture and Economy*, pp. 128–130.

481. Bryant, 'Asymmetric Warfare', p. 462f.; Cooper, 'Culture, Combat, and Colonialism', pp. 540f., 546; Gordon, 'Limited Adoption', p. 243; Heathcote, *Military in British India*, pp. 21–37.

482. Lee, 'Projecting Power', p. 7; Thornton, 'Art of War in Angola', p. 81f.; Whitehead, 'Tribes Make States', p. 142f.
483. White, *Middle Ground*, pp. ix–xv. Cf. Bitterli, *Die "Wilden" und die "Zivilisierten"*, pp. 161–173; Morillo, 'Typology of Transcultural Wars', p. 36; Petillo, 'Leaders and Followers', p. 184; Porter, *Military Orientalism*, p. 19.
484. Lappas, 'Lernen inmitten des Blutvergießens', p. 174; Starkey, 'Lernen im Kolonialkrieg', pp. 141, 150; Starkey, *European and Native American Warfare*, pp. 57–59.
485. Charney, 'Iberier und Südostasiaten', p. 197.
486. This also applies to the Portuguese frontier fighters in the early period of the colonization of Brazil: Hemming, *Red Gold*, p. 223.
487. Lynn, *Battle*, p. 176f.
488. Gann/Duignan, *Rulers of Belgian Africa*, p. 80f.; Gann/Duignan, *Rulers of German Africa*, pp. 114f., 123; Kiernan, *Colonial Empires*, pp. 183–190; Teitler, 'The Mixed Company', pp. 158–167.
489. Starkey, *European and Native American Warfare*, pp. 125–129.
490. Trotha, 'Was war Kolonialismus?', p. 73.
491. Porter, *Military Orientalism*, p. 19.
492. See also Bryant, 'Asymmetric Warfare', p. 433.
493. *Field Manual 3–24*, p. ixf.
494. Füssel, 'Lernen—Transfer—Aneignung', p. 41.

CONCLUSION

1. Keeley, *War Before Civilization*, p. 81.
2. Citino, *German Way of War*.
3. Arreguín-Toft, 'How the Weak Win Wars', p. 96f.
4. Helbling, 'Tribale Kriege und expandierende Staaten', p. 70. Similarly Kanya-Forstner, 'French Marines', p. 137; Marshall, 'Western Arms in Maritime Asia', p. 13.
5. Utley, 'Cultural Clash', p. 92.
6. Beaumont, 'Introduction', p. 11; Killingray, 'Colonial Warfare', p. 147; Walter, '"The Enemy Must Be Brought to Battle"'.
7. Besides, even this distinction between colonies of settlement and domination should also, however unclear the answer is even for the second category, take account of hybrid forms like South Africa, where the demise of the Khoisan in the Early Modern period matches one model, while by contrast the de facto decolonization post-1990, where power was handed over to the Bantu majority population, fits the other.
8. Kundrus/Walter, 'Anpassung und Lernen', p. 32.
9. Another variable concerning Western engagement in imperial conflicts is the imperative, at least in Western democracies over the past few decades, of avoiding casualties on one's own side. Yet because this avoidance of casualties is achieved through an intensification of firepower it is ultimately a relatively neutral factor in the pattern of conflict. Gil Merom's assertion that democracies were unable to win peripheral wars because they were not fully prepared to deploy intensive force ruthlessly not only glorifies violence ('brutality pays') but above all falsely implies that the

stronger side ultimately had the capacity to prevail in every conflict if it just took off the kid gloves. Merom, *How Democracies Lose Small Wars*, pp. 15, 42–47, 230.

10. Pagden, *Lords of All the World*, pp. 31–52, 73–86, 91–102.

11. To a certain extent this was also true of subsequent decades: while the Cold War affected Asia immediately after 1945, it took until around 1960 in Africa, and even longer in Latin America, before the bipolar world order began to determine the imperial constellation in general within those regions. For an overview see (among others) Westad, *Global Cold War*.

12. Rainero, 'Battle of Adowa', p. 189f.

13. Nasson, *South African War*, pp. xiv, 7.

14. Linn, *Counterinsurgency in the Philippine War*, pp. 17–20. For the completely opposite view, cf. Gates, 'Two American Wars', pp. 58f., 68.

15. Galbraith, '"Turbulent Frontier"'.

16. Delaporte, 'Lessons from Mali'; Lussato, 'Mali'.

17. Aldrich, 'When Did Decolonization End?', pp. 223–228.

18. Trotha, 'Utopie staatlicher Herrschaft', pp. 228, 245.

19. Feichtinger/Malinowski, 'Konstruktive Kriege?', pp. 290–305. For an example cf. Markel, 'Draining the Swamp'

20. Marthoz, 'War "without images and without facts"'; Ryan, 'Mali journalists despair'.

BIBLIOGRAPHY

'9 questions about the Mali conflict. Who started it, and what's it all about?', in: *CBC News World*, 14 January 2013. URL: http://www.cbc.ca/news/world/story/2013/01/14/f-mali-faq.html [17. 07. 2013].

Abernathy, David B., *The Dynamics of Global Dominance. European Overseas Empires 1415–1980*, New Haven, CT 2000.

Abler, Thomas S., 'Beavers and Muskets. Iroquois Military Fortunes in the Face of European Colonization', in: R. Brian Ferguson and Neil L. Whitehead (eds), *War in the Tribal Zone. Expanding States and IndigenousWarfare*, Santa Fe, NM 1992, pp. 151–174.

Abrahamsson, Bengt, *Military Professionalization and Political Power*, Beverly Hills, CA 1972.

Abun-Nasr, Jamil M., 'Der Staat im Maghrib und seine Entwicklung nach 1830', in: Wolfgang Reinhard (ed.), *Verstaatlichung derWelt? Europäische Staatsmodelle und außereuropäische Machtprozesse* (Schriften des Historischen Kollegs, Kolloquien, vol. 47), 1999, pp. 189–205.

Aksan,Virginia H., 'OttomanWar andWarfare 1453–1812', in: Jeremy Black (ed.), *War in the Early ModernWorld, 1450–1815*, London 1998, pp. 147–175.

Aldrich, Robert, 'When Did Decolonization End? France and the Ending of Empire', in: AlfredW. McCoy, Josep M. Fradera and Stephen Jacobson (eds), *Endless Empire. Spain's Retreat, Europe's Eclipse, America's Decline*, Madison,WI 2012, pp. 216–229.

Alexander, Martin S., Martin Evans and John F. V. Keiger (eds), *The AlgerianWar and the French Army, 1954–62. Experiences, Images,Testimonies*, Basingstoke 2002.

Altman, Ida, 'Conquest, Coercion, and Collaboration. Indian Allies and the Campaigns in Nueva Galicia', in: Laura E. Matthew and Michel R. Oudijk (eds), *Indian Conquistadors. Indigenous Allies in the Conquest of Mesoamerica*, Norman, OK 2007, pp. 145–174.

Álvarez, José E., *The Betrothed of Death.The Spanish Foreign Legion during the Rif Rebellion, 1920–1927*, Westport, CT 2001.

Anderson, Benedict, *UnderThree Flags. Anarchism and the Anti-Colonial Imagination*, London 2005.

Anderson, David, *Histories of the Hanged. Britain's DirtyWar in Kenya and the End of Empire*, London 2005.

Anderson,Warwick, and Hans Pols, 'Scientific Patriotism. Medical Science and National Self-Fashioning in Southeast Asia', in: AlfredW. McCoy, Josep M. Fradera and Stephen

BIBLIOGRAPHY

Jacobson (eds), *Endless Empire. Spain's Retreat, Europe's Eclipse, America's Decline*, Madison, WI 2012, pp. 262–275.

Andreopoulos, George J., 'The Age of National Liberation Movements', in: Michael Howard, George J. Andreopoulos and Mark R. Shulman (eds), *The Laws of War. Constraints on Warfare in the Western World*, New Haven, CT 1994, pp. 191–213.

Andrien, Kenneth J., and Rolena Adorno (eds), *Transatlantic Encounters. Europeans and Andeans in the Sixteenth Century*, Berkeley, CA 1991.

Anglim, Simon, 'Callwell versus Graziani. How the British Army Applied "Small Wars" Techniques in Major Operations in Africa and the Middle East, 1940–41', in: *Small Wars and Insurgencies* 19 (2008), H. 4, pp. 588–608.

Antlöv, Hans, and Stein Tønnesson (eds), *Imperial Policy and Southeast Asian Nationalism. 1930–1957* (Studies in Asian Topics, vol. 19), Richmond 1995.

Arai-Takahashi, Yutaka, 'Disentangling Legal Quagmires. The Legal Characterisation of the Armed Conflicts in Afghanistan since 6/7 October 2001 and the Question of Prisoner of War Status', in: *Yearbook of International Humanitarian Law* 5 (2002), pp. 61–105.

Arnold, Bernd, 'Die Schlacht bei Rugaro 1891 (Tansania, Iringa). Verlauf der Kämpfe und Ursachen der Niederlage des Expeditionskorps der kaiserlichen Schutztruppe für Deutsch-Ostafrika', in: Peter Heine and Ulrich van der Heyden (eds), *Studien zur Geschichte des deutschen Kolonialismus in Afrika. Festschrift zum 60. Geburtstag von Peter Sebald*, Pfaffenweiler 1995, pp. 94–113.

Arreguín-Toft, Ivan, 'How the Weak Win Wars. A Theory of Asymmetric Conflict', in: *International Security* 26 (2001), H. 1, pp. 93–128.

Arriaga, Kaúlza de, *Guerra e politica. Em nome da verdade os anos decisivos*, Lisboa 1988.

Atkinson, Rich, *An Army at Dawn. The War in North Africa, 1942–1943*, New York 2002.

Auch, Eva-Maria, and Stig Förster (eds), *"Barbaren" und "Weiße Teufel". Kulturkonflikte und Imperialismus in Asien vom 18. bis zum 20. Jahrhundert*, Paderborn 1997.

Baberowski, Jörg (ed.), *Moderne Zeiten? Krieg, Revolution und Gewalt im 20. Jahrhundert*, Göttingen 2006.

Baberowski, Jörg, 'Diktaturen der Eindeutigkeit. Ambivalenz und Gewalt im Zarenreich und in der frühen Sowjetunion', in: Ibid. (ed.), *Moderne Zeiten? Krieg, Revolution und Gewalt im 20. Jahrhundert*, Göttingen 2006, pp. 37–59.

Bailes, Howard, 'Technology and Imperialism. A Case Study of the Victorian Army in Africa', in: *Victorian Studies* 24 (1980), H. 1, pp. 82–104.

Bailey, John W., 'Civilization the Military Way. The Generals' View of the Plains Indians, 1866–91', in: James C. Bradford (ed.), *The Military and Conflict between Cultures. Soldiers at the Interface*, College Station, TX 1997, pp. 109–129.

Balandier, Georges, 'La Situation Coloniale. Approche Théorique', in: *Cahiers Internationaux de Sociologie* 11 (1951), pp. 44–79.

Balfour-Paul, Glen, 'Britain's Informal Empire in the Middle East', in: Judith M. Brown and William Roger Louis (eds), *The Oxford History of the British Empire*, vol. 4: *The Twentieth Century*, Oxford 1999, pp. 490–514.

Ballantyne, Tony, 'Information and Intelligence in the Mid-Nineteenth-Century Crisis in the British Empire', in: Alfred W. McCoy, Josep M. Fradera and Stephen Jacobson (eds), *Endless Empire. Spain's Retreat, Europe's Eclipse, America's Decline*, Madison, WI 2012, pp. 169–181.

Bandini, Franco, *Gli Italiani in Africa. Storia delle guerre coloniali 1882–1943* (Il Mondo Nuovo, vol. 98), Milano 1971.

BIBLIOGRAPHY

Barany, Zoltan D., and Robert G. Moser (eds), *Ethnic Politics after Communism*, Ithaca, NY 2005.

Barkan, Elazar, 'Genocides of Indigenous Peoples. Rhetoric of Human Rights', in: Robert Gellately and Ben Kiernan (eds), *The Specter of Genocide. Mass Murder in Historical Perspective*, Cambridge 2003, pp. 117–139.

Barkawi, Tarak, 'On the Pedagogy of "Small Wars"', in: *International Affairs* 80 (2004), H. 1, pp. 19–37.

Barrett, Thomas M., *At the Edge of Empire. The Terek Cossacks and the North Caucasus Frontier, 1700–1860*, Boulder, CO 1999.

Barth, Boris, 'Die Grenzen der Zivilisierungsmission. Rassenvorstellungen in den europäischen Siedlungskolonien Virginia, den Burenrepubliken und Deutsch-Südwestafrika', in: Boris Barth and Jürgen Osterhammel (eds), *Zivilisierungsmissionen. Imperiale Weltverbesserung seit dem 18. Jahrhundert*, Konstanz 2005, pp. 201–228.

———, '"Partisan" und "Partisanenkrieg" in Theorie und Geschichte. Zur historischen Dimension der Entstaatlichung von Kriegen', in: *Militärgeschichtliche Zeitschrift* 64 (2005), H. 1, pp. 69–100.

Barth, Boris, and Jürgen Osterhammel (eds), *Zivilisierungsmissionen. Imperiale Weltverbesserung seit dem 18. Jahrhundert*, Konstanz 2005.

Barua, Pradeep, 'Military Developments in India, 1750–1850', in: *Journal of Military History* 58 (1994), H. 4, pp. 599–616.

Baylis, John, Steve Smith and Patricia Owens (eds), *The Globalization of World Politics. An Introduction to International Relations*, 5th edn., Oxford 2011.

Bayly, Christopher Alan, 'Editor's Concluding Note', in: Eric Stokes, *The Peasant Armed. The Indian Revolt of 1857*, ed. by Christopher Alan Bayly, Oxford 1986, pp. 116–118.

Beaumont, Roger, 'Introduction. Cross-Cultural Military Relations', in: James C. Bradford (ed.), *The Military and Conflict between Cultures. Soldiers at the Interface*, College Station, TX 1997, pp. 3–14.

Bechtol, "Bruce E., 'Paradigmenwandel des Kalten Krieges. Der Koreakrieg 1950–1953', in: Bernd Greiner, Christian Th. Müller and Dierk Walter (eds), *Heiße Kriege im Kalten Krieg* (Studien zum Kalten Krieg, vol. 1), Hamburg 2006, pp. 141–166.

Becker, Felicitas, and Jigal Beez (eds), *Der Maji-Maji-Krieg in Deutsch-Ostafrika 1905–1907*, Berlin 2005.

Beckett, Ian F. W., 'British Counter-Insurgency. A Historiographical Reflection', in: *Small Wars and Insurgencies* 23 (2012), H. 4–5, pp. 781–798.

———, *Modern Insurgencies and Counter-Insurgencies. Guerrillas and their Opponents since 1750*, London 2001.

Beckett, Ian F. W., and John Pimlott (eds), *Armed Forces and Modern Counter-Insurgency*, New York 1985.

Beez, Jigal, 'Mit Wasser gegen Gewehre. Die Maji-Maji-Botschaft des Propheten Kinjikitile', in: Felicitas Becker and Jigal Beez (eds), *Der Maji-Maji-Krieg in Deutsch-Ostafrika 1905–1907*, Berlin 2005, pp. 61–74.

Beissinger, Mark R., 'Rethinking Empire in the Wake of Soviet Collapse', in: Zoltan D. Barany and Robert G. Moser (eds), *Ethnic Politics after Communism*, Ithaca, NY 2005, pp. 14–45.

Belich, James, 'Krieg und transkulturelles Lernen in Neuseeland im 19. Jahrhundert', in: Dierk Walter and Birthe Kundrus (eds), *Waffen Wissen Wandel. Anpassung und Lernen in transkulturellen Erstkonflikten*, Hamburg 2012, pp. 239–257.

371

BIBLIOGRAPHY

————, *The Victorian Interpretation of Racial Conflict. The Maori, the British, and the New Zealand Wars*, Montreal 1986.

Bell, David A., *The First Total War. Napoleon's Europe and the Birth of Modern Warfare*, London 2007.

Bellamy, Alex J., and Nicholas J. Wheeler, 'Humanitarian Intervention in World Politics', in: John Baylis, Steve Smith and Patricia Owens (eds), *The Globalization of World Politics. An Introduction to International Relations*, 5th edn., Oxford 2011, pp. 510–525.

Belmessous, Saliha, 'Assimilation and Racialism in Seventeenth and Eighteenth-Century French Colonial Policy', in: *American Historical Review* 110 (2005), H. 2, pp. 322–349.

Bergmann, Joachim, 'Die Dynamik der Conquista', in: Christof Dipper and Martin Vogt (eds), *Entdeckungen und frühe Kolonisation* (Wissenschaft und Technik, vol. 63), Darmstadt 1993, pp. 211–239.

Bertrand, Romain, 'Norbert Elias et la question des violences impériales. Jalons pour une histoire de la "mauvaise conscience" coloniale', in: *Vingtième Siècle* (2010), H. 106, pp. 127–140.

Best, Geoffrey, *Humanity in Warfare. The Modern History of the International Law of Armed Conflicts*, London 1983.

Beyrau, Dietrich, Michael Hochgeschwender and Dieter Langewiesche (eds), *For-men des Krieges. Von der Antike bis zur Gegenwart* (Krieg in der Geschichte, vol. 37), Paderborn 2007.

Bierling, Stephan G., *Geschichte des Irakkriegs. Der Sturz Saddams und Amerikas Albtraum im Mittleren Osten*, Munich 2010.

Billington, Ray Allen, and Martin Ridge, *Westward Expansion. A History of the American Frontier*, 6th edn., Albuquerque, NM 2001.

Billington, Ray Allen, *Westward Expansion. A History of the American Frontier*, 4th edn., New York 1974.

Bilton, Michael, and Kevin Sim, *Four Hours in My Lai*, New York 1992.

Bitterli, Urs, *Die "Wilden" und die "Zivilisierten". Grundzüge einer Geistes- und Kulturgeschichte der europäisch-überseeischen Begegnung*, 2nd edn., Munich 1991.

Black, Jeremy (ed.), *European Warfare, 1815–2000*, Basingstoke 2002.

————, *War in the Early Modern World, 1450–1815*, London 1998.

Black, Jeremy, 'European Overseas Expansion and the Military Revolution', in: George Raudzens (ed.), *Technology, Disease and Colonial Conquests, Sixteenth to Eighteenth Centuries. Essays Reappraising the Guns and Germs Theories*, Leiden 2001, pp. 1–30.

————, 'Introduction', in: Ibid. (ed.), *War in the Early Modern World, 1450–1815*, London 1998, pp. 1–23.

————, *Beyond the Military Revolution. War in the Seventeenth-Century World*, Basingstoke 2011.

————, *European Warfare, 1660–1815*, London 1994.

————, *War in the World. A Comparative History, 1450–1600*, Basingstoke 2011.

Bloch, Marc, *L'étrange défaite. Témoignage écrit en 1940*, Paris 1990 [1946].

Bodin, Michel, 'L'adaptation des hommes en Indochine (1945–1954)', in: Maurice Vaïsse (ed.), *L'Armée française dans la guerre d'Indochine (1946–1954). Adaptation ou inadaptation?*, Bruxelles 2000, pp. 111–131.

Bodley, John H., *Der Weg der Zerstörung. Stammesvölker und die industrielle Zivilisation*, Munich 1983.

BIBLIOGRAPHY

Boemeke, Manfred F., Roger Chickering and Stig Förster (eds), *Anticipating Total War. The German and American Experiences, 1871–1914*, Cambridge 1999.

Bond, Brian (ed.), *Victorian Military Campaigns*, London 1994.

Bond, Brian, 'Editor's Introduction', in: Ibid. (ed.), *Victorian Military Campaigns*, London 1994, pp. 3–29.

——, 'The South African War, 1880–1', in: Ibid. (ed.), *Victorian Military Campaigns*, London 1994, pp. 201–240.

Boot, Max, *The Savage Wars of Peace. Small Wars and the Rise of American Power*, New York 2002.

Bourke, Joanna, *An Intimate History of Killing. Face-to-Face Killing in Twentieth-Century Warfare*, London 2000.

Bowen, Wayne H., and José E. Alvarez (eds), *A Military History of Modern Spain. From the Napoleonic Era to the International War on Terror*, Westport, CT 2007.

Bradford, James C. (ed.), *The Military and Conflict between Cultures. Soldiers at the Interface*, College Station, TX 1997.

Bradford, James C., 'Preface', in: Ibid. (ed.), *The Military and Conflict between Cultures. Soldiers at the Interface*, College Station, TX 1997, pp. ix–xxi.

Bröchler, Anja, '"Was uns das Recht unseres Glaubens erlaubt zu tun". Kriegsgreuel in den Eroberungen Amerikas', in: Sönke Neitzel and Daniel Hohrath (eds), *Kriegsgreuel. Die Entgrenzung der Gewalt in kriegerischen Konflikten vom Mittelalter bis ins 20. Jahrhundert* (Krieg in der Geschichte, vol. 40), Paderborn 2008, pp. 137–154.

Brogini-Künzi, Giulia, 'Der Wunsch nach einem blitzschnellen und sauberen Krieg. Die italienische Armee in Ostafrika (1935/36)', in: Thoralf Klein and Frank Schumacher (eds), *Kolonialkriege. Militärische Gewalt im Zeichen des Imperialismus*, Hamburg 2006, pp. 272–290.

Brooks, Francis, 'The Impact of Disease', in: George Raudzens (ed.), *Technology, Disease and Colonial Conquests, Sixteenth to Eighteenth Centuries. Essays Reappraising the Guns and Germs Theories*, Leiden 2001, pp. 127–165.

Broome, Richard, *Aboriginal Australians. Black Responses to White Dominance 1788–2001*, 3rd edn., Crows Nest, NSW 2001.

Brower, Benjamin Claude, *A Desert Named Peace. The Violence of France's Empire in the Algerian Sahara, 1844–1902*, New York 2011.

Brown, Judith M., and William Roger Louis (eds), *The Oxford History of the British Empire*, vol. 4: *The Twentieth Century*, Oxford 1999.

Brown, Michael F., and Eduardo Fernandez, 'Tribe and State in a Frontier Mosaic. The Asháninka of Eastern Peru', in: R. Brian Ferguson and Neil L. Whitehead (eds), *War in the Tribal Zone. Expanding States and Indigenous Warfare*, Santa Fe, NM 1992, pp. 175–197.

Bruce, George, *The Burma Wars 1824–1886*, St. Albans 1973.

Brumwell, Steve, '"A Service Truly Critical". The British Army and Warfare with the North American Indians, 1755–1764', in: *War in History* 5 (1998), H. 2, pp. 146–175.

Bryant, Gerald J., 'Asymmetric Warfare. The British Experience in Eighteenth-Century India', in: *Journal of Military History* 68 (2004), H. 2, pp. 431–469. Buckley, Roger Norman, *Slaves in Red Coats. The British West India Regiments, 1795–1815*, New Haven, CT 1979.

Bührer, Tanja, 'Die Hehe und die Schutztruppe in Deutsch-Ostafrika. Die Schlacht bei

BIBLIOGRAPHY

Rugaro 1891', in: Dierk Walter and Birthe Kundrus (eds), *Waffen Wissen Wandel. Anpassung und Lernen in transkulturellen Erstkonflikten*, Hamburg 2012, pp. 258–281.

———, 'Kriegführung in Deutsch-Ostafrika (1889–1914)', in: Tanja Bührer, Christian Stachelbeck and Dierk Walter (eds), *Imperialkriege von 1500 bis heute. Strukturen—Akteure—Lernprozesse*, Paderborn 2011, pp. 197–215.

———, 'Staatsstreich im Busch. Paul von Lettow-Vorbeck (1870–1964)', in: Stig Förster, Markus Pöhlmann and Dierk Walter (eds), *Kriegsherren der Weltgeschichte. 22 historische Portraits*, Munich 2006, pp. 287–304.

Bührer, Tanja, Christian Stachelbeck and Dierk Walter (eds), *Imperialkriege von 1500 bis heute. Strukturen—Akteure—Lernprozesse*, Paderborn 2011.

Bührer, Tanja, *Die Kaiserliche Schutztruppe für Deutsch-Ostafrika. Koloniale Sicherheitspolitik und transkulturelle Kriegführung, 1885 bis 1918* (Beiträge zur Militärgeschichte, vol. 70), Munich 2011.

Bungay, Stephen, *The Most Dangerous Enemy. A History of the Battle of Britain*, London 2000.

Burbank, Jane, and Frederick Cooper, *Empires in World History. Power and the Politics of Difference*, Princeton, NJ 2010.

Burkhardt, Johannes, *Der Dreißigjährige Krieg*, Frankfurt/Main 1992.

Burroughs, Peter, 'Imperial Institutions and the Government of Empire', in: Andrew Porter and Alaine Low (eds), *The Oxford History of the British Empire*, vol. 3: *The Nineteenth Century*, Oxford 1999, pp. 170–197.

Butlin, Robin A., *Geographies of Empire. European Empires and Colonies c. 1880–1960*, Cambridge 2009.

Cahill, David, 'The Long Conquest. Collaboration by Native Andean Elites in the Colonial System, 1532–1825', in: George Raudzens (ed.), *Technology, Disease and Colonial Conquests, Sixteenth to Eighteenth Centuries. Essays Reappraising the Guns and Germs Theories*, Leiden 2001, pp. 85–126.

Cahn, Jean-Paul, 'Kriegsgreuel im Algerienkrieg (1954–1962)', in: Sönke Neitzel and Daniel Hohrath (eds), *Kriegsgreuel. Die Entgrenzung der Gewalt in kriegerischen Konflikten vom Mittelalter bis ins 20. Jahrhundert* (Krieg in der Geschichte, vol. 40), Paderborn 2008, pp. 371–384.

Cain, Peter J., and Anthony G. Hopkins, 'Gentlemanly Capitalism and British Expansion Overseas, I. The Old Colonial System, 1688–1850', in: *Economic History Review* 39 (1986), H. 4, pp. 501–525.

———, *British Imperialism*, vol. 1: *Innovation and Expansion, 1688–1914*, London 1993.

———, *British Imperialism*, vol. 2: *Crisis and Deconstruction, 1914–1990*, London 1993.

Calloway, Colin G., *One Vast Winter Count. The Native American West before Lewis and Clark*, Lincoln, NE 2003.

Callwell, Charles Edward, *Small Wars. Their Principles and Practice*, 3rd edn., London 1906 [1896].

———, *Small Wars. Their Principles and Practice*, ed. by Douglas Porch, 3rd edn., Lincoln, NE 1996 [1896].

Campbell, Leon G., 'Social Structure of the Túpac Amaru Army in Cuzco, 1780–1781', in: Douglas M. Peers (ed.), *Warfare and Empires. Contact and Conflict between European and non-European Military and Maritime Forces and Cultures* (An Expanding World, vol. 24), Aldershot 1997, pp. 209–227.

Cann, John P., *Counterinsurgency in Africa. The Portuguese Way of War, 1961–1974* (Contributions in Military Studies, vol. 167), Westport, CT 1997.

BIBLIOGRAPHY

Caputo, Philip, *Indian Country*, Toronto 1987.

Carlton-Ford, Steven, and Morten G. Ender (eds), *The Routledge Handbook of War and Society. Iraq and Afghanistan*, London 2011.

Cartas del Peru (1524–1543), ed. by Raul Porras Barrenecha (Coleccion de Documentos Ineditos para la Historia del Peru, vol. 3), Lima 1959.

Casper, Lawrence E., *Falcon Brigade. Combat and Command in Somalia and Haiti*, Boulder, CO 2001.

Chacón, J. I., *Guerras Irregulares*, 2 vols., Madrid 1883.

Chalk, Peter, and Ben Brandt, 'Drone Wars. Unmanned Aerial Vehicles in Counter-Terrorism', in: *Jane's Intelligence Review* 24 (2012), H. 8, pp. 24–28.

Chamberlain, Robert S., *Conquest and Colonization of Yucatan*, Washington, DC 1948.

Chandler, David Geoffrey, 'The Expedition to Abyssinia, 1867–8', in: Brian Bond (ed.), *Victorian Military Campaigns*, London 1994, pp. 107–159.

Chandler, David Geoffrey, and Ian F. W. Beckett (eds), *The Oxford Illustrated History of the British Army*, Oxford 1994.

Chapman, F. Spencer, *The Jungle is Neutral*, London 1949.

Charney, Michael W., 'Iberier und Südostasiaten im Krieg. Die Eroberung von Melaka 1511 und ihre Folgen', in: Dierk Walter and Birthe Kundrus (eds), *Waffen Wissen Wandel. Anpassung und Lernen in transkulturellen Erstkonflikten*, Hamburg 2012, pp. 179–197.

————, *Southeast Asian Warfare, 1300–1900*, Leiden 2004.

Charters, David, 'From Palestine to Northern Ireland. British Adaptation to Low-Intensity Operations', in: David Charters and Maurice Tugwell (eds), *Armies in Low-Intensity Conflict. A Comparative Analysis*, London 1989, pp. 169–249.

Charters, David, and Maurice Tugwell (eds), *Armies in Low-Intensity Conflict. A Comparative Analysis*, London 1989.

Charters, Erica M., 'Disease, Wilderness Warfare, and Imperial Relations. The Battle for Quebec, 1759–1760', in: *War in History* 16 (2009), H. 1, pp. 1–24.

Chatriot, Alain, and Dieter Gosewinkel (eds), *Koloniale Politik und Praktiken Deutschlands und Frankreichs 1880–1962* (Schriftenreihe des Deutsch-Französischen Historikerkomitees, vol. 6), Stuttgart 2010.

Chet, Guy, *Conquering the American Wilderness. The Triumph of European Warfare in the Colonial Northeast*, Amherst, MA 2003.

Chickering, Roger, Stig Förster and Bernd Greiner (eds), *A World at Total War. Global Conflict and the Politics of Destruction*, Cambridge 2005.

Chickering, Roger, and Stig Förster (eds), *Great War, Total War. Combat and Mobilization on the Western Front, 1914–1918*, Cambridge 2000.

————, *The Shadows of Total War. Europe, East Asia, and the United States, 1919–1939*, Cambridge 2003.

Childs, John, *Armies and Warfare in Europe 1648–1789*, Manchester 1982.

Chuchiak, John F., 'Forgotten Allies. The Origins and Roles of Native Mesoamerican Auxiliaries and Indios Conquistadores in the Conquest of Yucatan, 1526–1550', in: Laura E. Matthew and Michel R. Oudijk (eds), *Indian Conquistadors. Indigenous Allies in the Conquest of Mesoamerica*, Norman, OK 2007, pp. 175–225.

Churchill, Winston S., *Frontiers and Wars. His Four Early Books Covering His Life as Soldier and War Correspondent Edited into One Volume*, London 1962.

Cipolla, Carlo M., *Guns, Sails, and Empires. Technological Innovation and the Early Phases of European Expansion, 1400–1700*, New York 1965.

BIBLIOGRAPHY

Citino, Robert M., *The German Way of War. From the Thirty Years' War to the Third Reich*, Lawrence, KS 2005.

Clausewitz, Carl von, *On War*, ed. and transl. by Michael Eliot Howard and Peter Paret, Princeton 1976.

Clayton, Anthony, *France, Soldiers and Africa*, London 1988.

————, *The Wars of French Decolonization*, London 1994.

Clayton, Lawrence A., 'The Iberian Advantage', in: George Raudzens (ed.), *Technology, Disease and Colonial Conquests, Sixteenth to Eighteenth Centuries. Essays Reappraising the Guns and Germs Theories*, Leiden 2001, pp. 211–235.

Cloake, John, *Templer. Tiger of Malaya*, London 1985.

————, *Suppressing Insurgency. An Analysis of the Malayan Emergency, 1948–1954*, Boulder, CO 1992.

Cocker, Mark, *Rivers of Blood, Rivers of Gold. Europe's Conquest of Indigenous Peoples*, New York 1998.

Connell, Evan S., *Son of the Morning Star*, San Francisco 1984.

Connelly, Matthew, 'Rethinking the Cold War and Decolonization. The Grand Strategy of the Algerian War for Independence' [2001], in: Martin Shipway (ed.), *The Rise and Fall of Modern Empires*, vol. 4: *Reactions to Colonialism*, Farnham 2013, pp. 419–443.

Connor, John, 'Briten und Darug. Gewalttätige Erstkontakte in Australien 1788–1816', in: Dierk Walter and Birthe Kundrus (eds), *Waffen Wissen Wan-del. Anpassung und Lernen in transkulturellen Erstkonflikten*, Hamburg 2012, pp. 219–238.

————, *The Australian Frontier Wars, 1788–1838*, Sydney, NSW 2002.

Conway, Stephen, 'To Subdue America. British Army Officers and the Conduct of the Revolutionary War', in: *William and Mary Quarterly* 43 (1986), H. 3, pp. 381–407.

Cook, Hugh C. B., *The Sikh Wars. The British Army in the Punjab 1845–1849*, London 1975.

Cooper, Randolf G.S., 'Culture, Combat, and Colonialism in Eighteenth- and Nineteenth-Century India', in: *International History Review* 27 (2005), H. 3, pp. 534–549.

————, 'Wellington and the Marathas in 1803', in: Douglas M. Peers (ed.), *Warfare and Empires. Contact and Conflict between European and non-European Military and Maritime Forces and Cultures* (An Expanding World, vol. 24), Aldershot 1997, pp. 305–312.

Corum, James S., and Wray R. Johnson, *Airpower in Small Wars. Fighting Insurgents and Terrorists*, Lawrence, KS 2003.

Corvisier, André, and Guy Pedroncini (eds), *Histoire militaire de la France*, vol. 3: *De 1871 à 1940*, Paris 1997.

Corvisier, André, and Jean Delmas (eds), *Histoire militaire de la France*, vol. 2: *De 1715 à 1871*, Paris 1997.

Crawford, E. R., 'The Sikh Wars, 1845–9', in: Brian Bond (ed.), *Victorian Military Campaigns*, London 1994, pp. 33–68.

Crosby, Alfred W., *Ecological Imperialism. The Biological Expansion of Europe, 900–1900*, Cambridge 1986.

Crowder, Michael (ed.), *West African Resistance. The Military Response to Colonial Occupation*, New York 1972.

Crowder, Michael, 'Introduction', in: Ibid. (ed.), *West African Resistance. The Military Response to Colonial Occupation*, New York 1972, pp. 1–18.

Cullen, Peter M., 'The Role of Targeted Killing in the Campaign against Terror', in: *Joint Force Quarterly* 48 (2008), H. 1, pp. 22–29.

Cupp, O. Shawn, and William C. Latham, 'Role of Contractors and Other Non-Military

Personnel in Today's Wars', in: Steven Carlton-Ford and Morten G. Ender (eds), *The Routledge Handbook of War and Society. Iraq and Afghanistan*, London 2011, pp. 137–148.

Curtin, Philip D., *Disease and Empire. The Health of European Troops in the Conquest of Africa*, Cambridge 1998. Daase, Christopher, *Kleine Kriege, große Wirkung. Wie unkonventionelle Kriegführung die internationale Politik verändert* (Weltpolitik im 21. Jahrhundert, vol. 2), Baden-Baden 1999.

Dabag, Mihran, Horst Gründer and Uwe-Karsten Ketelsen (eds), *Kolonialismus. Kolonialdiskurs und Genozid*, Munich 2004.

Dabringhaus, Sabine, 'An Army on Vacation? The German War in China, 1900–1901', in: Manfred F. Boemeke, Roger Chickering and Stig Förster (eds), *Anticipating Total War. The German and American Experiences, 1871–1914*, Cambridge 1999, pp. 459–476.

Dahlmann, Dittmar, 'Sibirien. Der Prozess der Eroberung des Subkontinents und die russische Zivilisierungsmission im 17. und 18. Jahrhundert', in: Boris Barth and Jürgen Osterhammel (eds), *Zivilisierungsmissionen. Imperiale Weltverbesserung seit dem 18. Jahrhundert*, Konstanz 2005, pp. 55–71.

Darwin, John, 'The Geopolitics of Decolonization', in: Alfred W. McCoy, Josep M. Fradera and Stephen Jacobson (eds), *Endless Empire. Spain's Retreat, Europe's Eclipse, America's Decline*, Madison, WI 2012, pp. 191–202.

———, *After Tamerlane. The Global History of Empire since 1405*, London 2007.

Dawisha, Karen, and Bruce Parrott (eds), *The End of Empire? The Transformation of the USSR in Comparative Perspective* (The International Politics of Eurasia, vol. 9), Armonk, NY 1997.

Dawson, Graham, *Soldier Heroes. British Adventure, Empire and the Imagining of Masculinities*, London 1994.

Deenon, Donald, 'Understanding Settler Societies', in: *Historical Studies* 18 (1979), H. 73, pp. 511–527.

DeFronzo, James, *The Iraq War. Origins and Consequences*, Boulder, CO 2010.

Del Boca, Angelo, 'Faschismus und Kolonialismus. Der Mythos von den "anständigen Italienern"', in: Irmtrud Wojak and Susanne Meinl (eds), *Völkermord und Kriegsverbrechen in der ersten Hälfte des 20. Jahrhunderts*, Frankfurt/Main 2004, pp. 193–202.

Delaporte, Murielle, 'French Lessons From Mali. Fight Alone, Supply Together' (2013). URL: http://breakingdefense.com/2013/06/17/french-lessons-from-mali-fight-alone-supply-together/ [08. 07. 2013].

Delmas, Jean, and Philippe Masson, 'Les Interventions Extérieures', in: André Corvisier and Jean Delmas (eds), *Histoire militaire de la France*, vol. 2: *De 1715 à 1871*, Paris 1997, pp. 501–533.

Denzer, La Ray, 'Sierra Leone—Bai Bureh', in: Michael Crowder (ed.), *West African Resistance. The Military Response to Colonial Occupation*, New York 1972, pp. 233–267. Derradji, Abder-Rahmane, *The Algerian Guerrilla Campaign. Strategy and Tactics*, Lewiston, NY 1997.

Deutscher, Guy *Through the Language Glass. Why the World Looks Different in Other Languages*, London 2010.

Dewey, Michael, *Brush Fire Wars. Minor Campaigns of the British Army since 1945*, 2nd edn., London 1987.

Diamond, Jared, *Guns, Germs, and Steel. The Fates of Human Societies*, 2nd edn., New York 2003.

BIBLIOGRAPHY

Die Kämpfe der deutschen Truppen in Südwestafrika, vol. 1: *Der Feldzug gegen die Hereros*, ed. by the War History Department I of the German Imperial General Staff, Berlin 1906.

Dipper, Christof, and Martin Vogt (eds), *Entdeckungen und frühe Kolonisation* (Wissenschaft und Technik, vol. 63), Darmstadt 1993.

Ditte, Albert, *Observations sur la Guerre dans les Colonies. Organisation—Exécution*, Paris 1905.

Dixon, Paul, '"Hearts and Minds"? British Counter-Insurgency from Malaya to Iraq', in: *Journal of Strategic Studies* 32 (2009), H. 3, pp. 353–381.

Donnelly, Alton S., *The Russian Conquest of Bashkiria 1552–1740. A Case Study in Imperialism*, New Haven, CT 1968.

Dörmann, Knut, 'The Legal Situation of "Unlawful/Unprivileged Combatants"', in: *International Review of the Red Cross* 85 (2003), H. 849, pp. 45–74.

Douhet, Giulio, *Il dominio dell'aria. Probabili aspetti della guerra futura e gli ultimi scritti del Gen. Giulio Douhet*, 2nd edn., Milano 1932.

Dowd, Alan W., 'Drone Wars. Risks and Warnings', in: *Parameters* 42/43 (2013), H. 4/1, pp. 7–16.

Drechsler, Horst, *Südwestafrika unter deutscher Kolonialherrschaft. Der Kampf der Herero und Nama gegen den deutschen Imperialismus (1884–1915)*, 2nd edn., Berlin 1984.

Dülffer, Jost, and Marc Frey (eds), *Elites and Decolonization in the Twentieth Century*, Basingstoke 2011.

Dülffer, Jost, and Marc Frey, 'Introduction', in: Ibid. (eds), *Elites and Decolonization in the Twentieth Century*, Basingstoke 2011, pp. 1–10.

Duffy, Michael (ed.), *The Military Revolution and the State 1500–1800* (Exeter Studies in History, vol. 1), Exeter 1980.

Duffy, Michael, 'Introduction. The Military Revolution and the State 1500–1800', in: Ibid. (ed.), *The Military Revolution and the State 1500–1800* (Exeter Studies in History, vol. 1), Exeter 1980, pp. 1–9.

———, 'The French Revolution and British Attitudes to the West Indian Colonies', in: David Barry Gaspar and David Patrick Geggus (eds), *A Turbulent Time. The French Revolution and the Greater Caribbean*, Bloomington, IN 1997, pp. 78–101.

Dunn, Ross E., *Resistance in the Desert. Moroccan Responses to French Imperialism 1881–1912*, London 1977.

Earle, Edward Mead (ed.), *Makers of Modern Strategy. Military Thought from Machiavelli to Hitler*, Princeton, NJ 1943.

Eberspächer, Cord, '"Albion zal hier ditmaal zijn Moskou vinden!". Der Burenkrieg (1899–1902)', in: Thoralf Klein and Frank Schumacher (eds), *Kolonialkriege. Militärische Gewalt im Zeichen des Imperialismus*, Hamburg 2006, pp. 182–207.

———, 'Chinas imperiale Kriege. Die militärische Expansion Chinas während der Qing-Dynastie 1644–1911', in: Tanja Bührer, Christian Stachelbeck and Dierk Walter (eds), *Imperialkriege von 1500 bis heute. Strukturen—Akteure—Lernprozesse*, Paderborn 2011, pp. 37–54.

Echenberg, Myron, *Colonial Conscripts. The Tirailleurs Sénégalais in French West Africa, 1857–1960*, Portsmouth, NH 1991.

Eckert, Henri, 'Double-Edged Swords of Conquest in Indochina. Tirailleurs Tonkinois, Chasseurs Annamites and Militias, 1883–1895', in: Karl Hack and Tobias Rettig (eds), *Colonial Armies in Southeast Asia*, London 2006, pp. 126–153.

Eder, Philipp, and Bruno Günter Hofbauer, 'Operation Enduring Freedom', in: *Österreichische Militärische Zeitschrift* 40 (2002), H. 1, pp. 54–60.

————, 'Operation Iraqi Freedom', in: *Österreichische Militärische Zeitschrift* 41 (2003), H. 4, pp. 476–486.

Edgerton, Robert B., *Mau Mau. An African Crucible*, New York 1989.

Edmunds, R. David, and Joseph L. Peyser, *The Fox Wars. The Mesquakie Challenge to New France*, Norman, OK 1993.

Edwards, Brent Hayes, 'The Shadows of Shadows', in: *Positions* 11 (2003), H. 1, pp. 11–49.

Edwards, Rebecca, *New Spirits. Americans in the Gilded Age, 1865–1905*, New York 2006.

Eichmann, Flavio, 'Expansion und imperiale Herrschaft. Zum epochenübergreifenden Charakter des Imperialismus', in: *Mittelweg 36* 21 (2012), H. 4, pp. 89–111.

————, '"Freibeuter der Moderne—Politisch-militärische Akteure an den Rändern von Souveränität und Legitimität". Kolloquium zum 60. Geburtstag von Prof. Dr. Stig Förster, 20. bis 21. Oktober 2011 in Bern', in: *Militärgeschichtliche Zeitschrift* 71 (2012), H. 1, pp. 103–107.

————, 'Local Co-operation in a Subversive Colony. Martinique 1802–1809'. Paper delivered at the conference 'Co-operation and Empire', Berne, 28 July 2013.

————, *Kolonialherrschaft zu Zeiten von Sklaverei, Weltkrieg und Revolution. Die Kleinen Antillen 1793–1815*. Dissertation, Universität Bern (2015).

'El Ayuntamiento de Jauja al Emperador. Jauja, 20 de Julio de 1534', in: *Cartas del Peru (1524–1543)*, ed. by Raul Porras Barrenecha (Coleccion de Documentos Ineditos para la Historia del Peru, vol. 3), Lima 1959, pp. 124–131.

Elbe, Martin, and Gregor Richter, 'Militär. Institution und Organisation', in: Nina Leonhard and Ines-Jacqueline Werkner (eds), *Militärsoziologie. Eine Einführung*, Wiesbaden 2005, pp. 136–156.

Elkins, Caroline, *Imperial Reckoning. The Untold Story of Britain's Gulag in Kenya*, New York 2005.

Elkins, Caroline, and Susan Pedersen (eds), *Settler Colonialism in the Twentieth Century. Projects, Practices, Legacies*, London 2005.

Elkins, Caroline, and Susan Pedersen, 'Settler Colonialism. A Concept and Its Uses', in: Ibid. (eds), *Settler Colonialism in the Twentieth Century. Projects, Practices, Legacies*, London 2005, pp. 1–20.

Ellis, Stephen, 'Conclusion', in: Martin Shipway (ed.), *The Rise and Fall of Modern Empires*, vol. 4: *Reactions to Colonialism*, Farnham 2013, pp. 69–87.

Eskildsen, Robert, 'Of Civilization and Savages. The Mimetic Imperialism of Japan's 1874 Expedition to Taiwan', in: *American Historical Review* 107 (2002), H. 2, pp. 388–418.

Espey, David, 'America and Vietnam. The Indian Subtext'. URL: http://www. english. upenn.edu/~despey/vietnam.htm [13. 05. 2011].

Etemad, Bouda, *La Possession du monde. Poids et mesures de la colonisation (XVIIIe-XXe siècles)*, Paris 2000.

Evans, Martin, 'The Harkis. The Experience and Memory of France's Muslim Auxiliaries', in: Martin S. Alexander, Martin Evans and John F. V. Keiger (eds), *The Algerian War and the French Army, 1954–62. Experiences, Images, Testimonies*, Basingstoke 2002, pp. 117–133.

Fage, John D., and William Tordoff, *A History of Africa*, 4th edn., London 2002.

Fall, Bernard B., *Hell in a Very Small Place. The Siege of Dien Bien Phu*, Philadelphia, PA 1967.

————, *Street Without Joy*, Mechanicsburg, PA 1994 [1961].

BIBLIOGRAPHY

Falls, Cyril, 'The Reconquest of the Sudan, 1896–9', in: Brian Bond (ed.), *Victorian Military Campaigns*, London 1994, pp. 281–308.

Feichtinger, Moritz, 'Ein Aspekt revolutionärer Kriegführung. Die französische Umsiedlungspolitik in Algerien 1954–1962', in: Tanja Bührer, Christian Stachelbeck and Dierk Walter (eds), *Imperialkriege von 1500 bis heute. Strukturen—Akteure—Lernprozesse*, Paderborn 2011, pp. 261–278.

————, 'Von Brüssel nach Bandung. Strategien antiimperialer Vernetzung im 20. Jahrhundert'. Paper delivered the the conference 'Strategien gegen imperiale Herrschaft: Wissenstransfers, Informationswege und Formen des Widerstandes', Berne, 5th June 2010.

Feichtinger, Moritz, and Stephan Malinowski, 'Konstruktive Kriege? Rezeption und Adaption der Dekolonisationskriege in westlichen Demokratien', in: *Geschichte und Gesellschaft* 37 (2011), H. 2, pp. 285–305.

Fenn, Elizabeth A., 'Biological Warfare in Eighteenth-Century North America. Beyond Jeffery Amherst', in: *Journal of American History* 86 (2000), H. 4, pp. 1552–1580.

Ferguson, R. Brian, and Neil L. Whitehead (eds), *War in the Tribal Zone. Expanding States and Indigenous Warfare*, Santa Fe, NM 1992.

Ferguson, R. Brian, and Neil L. Whitehead, 'The Violent Edge of Empire', in: Ibid. (eds), *War in the Tribal Zone. Expanding States and Indigenous Warfare*, Santa Fe, NM 1992, pp. 1–30.

Fick, Carolyn E., 'The French Revolution in Saint Domingue. A Triumph or a Failure?', in: David Barry Gaspar and David Patrick Geggus (eds), *A Turbulent Time. The French Revolution and the Greater Caribbean*, Bloomington, IN 1997, pp. 51–77.

Fiedler, Siegfried, *Taktik und Strategie der Kabinettskriege 1650–1792*, Augsburg 2002.

Field Manual No. 3–24 / Marine Corps Warfighting Publication No. 3–33.5 Counterinsurgency, ed. by Headquarters, Department of the Army, Washington, DC 2006.

Fieldhouse, David K., *Economics and Empire 1830–1914*, London 1973.

————, *The Colonial Empires. A Comparative Survey from the Eighteenth Century*, London 1966.

Finley, Moses I., 'Colonies. An Attempt at a Typology', in: *Transactions of the Royal Historical Society* 26 (1976), pp. 167–188.

Finzsch, Norbert, '"[…]Extirpate or remove that vermin". Genocide, Biological Warfare, and Settler Imperialism in the Eighteenth and Early Nineteenth Century', in: *Journal of Genocide Research* 10 (2008), H. 2, pp. 215–232.

————, 'Die Frühgeschichte der biologischen Kriegführung im 18. Jahrhundert. Nordamerika und Australien im Vergleich', in: Robert Jütte (ed.), *Medizin, Gesellschaft und Geschichte* (Jahrbuch des Instituts für Geschichte der Medizin der Robert Bosch Stiftung, vol. 22), Stuttgart 2004, pp. 9–29.

Finzsch, Norbert, '"The Aborigines … were never annihilated, and still they are becoming extinct". Settler Imperialism and Genocide in Nineteenth-century America and Australia', in: Anthony Dirk Moses (ed.), *Empire, Colony, Genocide. Conquest, Occupation, and Subaltern Resistance in World History*, New York 2008, pp. 253–270.

Fischer, Erik, 'Von Suppen, Messern und dem Löffel. Die US-Streitkräfte als "lernende Institution" und das Problem der Counterinsurgency', in: Tanja Bührer, Christian Stachelbeck and Dierk Walter (eds), *Imperialkriege von 1500 bis heute. Strukturen—Akteure—Lernprozesse*, Paderborn 2011, pp. 503–520.

Fleming, Shannon E., 'Decolonization and the Spanish Army, 1940–76', in: Wayne

BIBLIOGRAPHY

H. Bowen and José E. Alvarez (eds), *A Military History of Modern Spain. From the Napoleonic Era to the International War on Terror*, Westport, CT 2007, pp. 122–135. Flores Galindo, Alberto, *In Search of an Inca. Identity and Utopia in the Andes*, ed. by Carlos Aguirre, Charles F. Walker and Hiatt Willie, Cambridge 2010.

Förster, Stig (ed.), *An der Schwelle zum Totalen Krieg. Die militärische Debatte über den Krieg der Zukunft 1919–1939* (Krieg in der Geschichte, vol. 13), Paderborn 2002.

Förster, Stig, 'Einleitung', in: Ibid. (ed.), *An der Schwelle zum Totalen Krieg. Die militärische Debatte über den Krieg der Zukunft 1919–1939* (Krieg in der Geschichte, vol. 13), Paderborn 2002, pp. 15–36.

——————, Christian Jansen and Günther Kronenbitter (eds), *Die Rückkehr der Condottieri? Krieg und Militär zwischen staatlichem Monopol und Privatisierung: Von der Antike bis zur Gegenwart* (Krieg in der Geschichte, vol. 57), Paderborn 2010.

——————, *Die mächtigen Diener der East India Company. Ursachen und Hintergründe der britischen Expansionspolitik in Südasien, 1793–1819*, Stuttgart 1992.

——————, Markus Pöhlmann and Dierk Walter (eds), *Kriegsherren der Weltgeschichte. 22 historische Portraits*, Munich 2006.

——————, and Jörg Nagler (eds), *On the Road to Total War. The American Civil War and the German Wars of Unification, 1861–1871*, Cambridge 1997.

Fortescue, John W., *A History of the British Army*, vol. 12: *1839–1852*, London 1927.

Fourniau, Charles, 'Colonial Wars before 1914. The Case of France in Indochina', in: Jaap A. de Moor and Hendrik Lodewyk Wesseling (eds), *Imperialism and War. Essays on Colonial Wars in Asia and Africa*, Leiden 1989, pp. 72–86.

François, Curt von, *Kriegführung in Süd-Afrika*, Berlin 1900.

Franklin, Benjamin, 'The Autobiography', in: Ibid., *Writings*, New York 1987, pp. 1307–1469.

——————, *Writings*, New York 1987.

Freeman, Michael, 'Puritans and Pequots. The Question of Genocide', in: *New England Quarterly* 68 (1995), H. 2, pp. 278–293.

Frey, Marc, 'Die Vereinigten Staaten und die Dritte Welt im Kalten Krieg', in: Bernd Greiner, Christian Th. Müller and Dierk Walter (eds), *Heiße Kriege im Kalten Krieg* (Studien zum Kalten Krieg, vol. 1), Hamburg 2006, pp. 35–60.

——————, *Geschichte des Vietnamkrieges. Die Tragödie in Asien und das Ende des amerikanischen Traums*, 2nd edn., Munich 1999.

Füssel, Marian, 'Händler, Söldner und Sepoys. Transkulturelle Kampfverbände auf den südasiatischen Schauplätzen des Siebenjährigen Krieges', in: Tanja Bührer, Christian Stachelbeck and Dierk Walter (eds), *Imperialkriege von 1500 bis heute. Strukturen— Akteure—Lernprozesse*, Paderborn 2011, pp. 307–324.

——————, 'Lernen—Transfer—Aneignung. Theorien und Begriffe für eine transkulturelle Militärgeschichte', in: Dierk Walter and Birthe Kundrus (eds), *Waffen Wissen Wandel. Anpassung und Lernen in transkulturellen Erstkonflikten*, Hamburg 2012, pp. 34–49.

Furedi, Frank, 'Creating a Breathing Space. The Political Management of Colonial Emergencies', in: *Journal of Imperial and Commonwealth History* 21 (1993), H. 3, pp. 89–106.

——————, 'Kenya. Decolonization through Counterinsurgency', in: Anthony Gorst, Lewis Johnman and W. Scott Lucas (eds), *Contemporary British History, 1931–1961. Politics and the Limits of Policy*, London 1991, pp. 141–168.

——————, 'The Demobilized African Soldier and the Blow to White Prestige', in: David

BIBLIOGRAPHY

Killingray and David E. Omissi (eds), *Guardians of Empire. The Armed Forces of the Colonial Powers c. 1700–1964*, Manchester 1999, pp. 179–197. Furedi, Frank, *The Mau Mau War in Perspective*, London 1989.

Furneaux, Rupert, *Abdel Krim. Emir of the Rif*, London 1967.

Fynn, John Kofi, 'Ghana—Asante (Ashanti)', in: Michael Crowder (ed.), *West African Resistance. The Military Response to Colonial Occupation*, New York 1972, pp. 19–52.

Gabbert, Wolfgang, 'Kultureller Determinismus und die Eroberung Mexikos. Zur Kritik eines dichotomischen Geschichtsverständnisses', in: *Saeculum* 46 (1995), pp. 274–292.

————, 'The longue durée of Colonial Violence in Latin America', in: *Historical Social Research* 37 (2012), H. 3, pp. 254–275.

————, 'Warum Montezuma weinte. Anmerkungen zur Frühphase der europäischen Expansion in den Atlantischen Raum', in: Ulrike Schmieder and Hans-Heinrich Nolte (eds), *Atlantik. Sozial- und Kulturgeschichte in der Neuzeit* (Edition Weltregionen, vol. 20), Vienna 2010, pp. 29–47.

Gaffarel, Paul, *L'Algérie. Histoire, conquête et colonisation*, Paris 1883.

Galbraith, John S., 'The "Turbulent Frontier" as a Factor in British Expansion', in: *Comparative Studies in Society and History* 2 (1960), H. 2, pp. 150–168.

Gallagher, John, and Ronald Robinson, 'The Imperialism of Free Trade', in: *Economic History Review* 6 (1953), H. 1, pp. 1–15.

Gallieni, Joseph Simon, *La pacification de Madagascar. Opérations d'Octobre 1896 à Mars 1899*, Paris 1900.

Gallois, William, 'Dahra and the History of Violence in Early Colonial Algeria', in: Martin Thomas (ed.), *The French Colonial Mind*, vol. 2: *Violence, Military Encounters, and Colonialism*, Lincoln, NE 2011, pp. 3–25.

Galtung, Johan, 'A Structural Theory of Imperialism', in: *Journal of Peace Research* 8 (1971), H. 2, pp. 81–117.

Galula, David, *Counterinsurgency Warfare. Theory and Practice*, Westport, CT 2006 [1964].

Gann, Lewis Henry, and Peter Duignan (eds), *Colonialism in Africa 1870–1960*, vol. 1: *The History and Politics of Colonialism 1870–1914*, Cambridge 1969.

Gann, Lewis Henry, and Peter Duignan, *The Rulers of Belgian Africa, 1884–1914*, Princeton, NJ 1979.

————, *The Rulers of British Africa, 1870–1914*, Stanford, CA 1978.

————, *The Rulers of German Africa, 1884–1914*, Stanford, CA 1977.

Gaspar, David Barry, and David Patrick Geggus (eds), *A Turbulent Time. The French Revolution and the Greater Caribbean*, Bloomington, IN 1997.

Gat, Azar, *War in Human Civilization*, Oxford 2006.

Gates, John M., 'Small Wars: Their Principles and Practice, by C.E. Callwell (Review)', in: *Journal of Military History* 61 (1997), H. 2, pp. 381–382.

————, 'Two American Wars in Asia. Successful Colonial Warfare in the Philippines and Cold War Failure in Vietnam', in: *War in History* 8 (2001), H. 1, pp. 47–71. Gay, Peter, *The Cultivation of Hatred* (The Bourgeois Experience. Victoria to Freud, vol. 3), London 1993.

Geggus, David Patrick, 'Slavery, War, and Revolution in the Greater Caribbean, 1789–1815', in: David Barry Gaspar and David Patrick Geggus (eds), *A Turbulent Time. The French Revolution and the Greater Caribbean*, Bloomington, IN 1997, pp. 1–50.

Gellately, Robert, and Ben Kiernan (eds), *The Specter of Genocide. Mass Murder in Historical Perspective*, Cambridge 2003.

BIBLIOGRAPHY

Gelpi, Christopher, Peter D. Feaver and Jason Reifler, 'Success Matters. Casualty Sensitivity and the War in Iraq', in: *International Security* 30 (2005/2006), H. 3, pp. 7–46.

Geraghty, Tony, *Who Dares Wins. The Story of the SAS 1950–1982*, Glasgow 1981.

Gérin-Roze, Français, 'La "vietnamisation". La participation des autochtones à la guerre d'Indochine', in: Maurice Vaïsse (ed.), *L'Armée française dans la guerre d'Indochine (1946–1954). Adaptation ou inadaptation?*, Bruxelles 2000, pp. 137–145.

Gerlach, Christian, *Extremely Violent Societies. Mass Violence in the Twentieth-Century World*, Cambridge 2010.

Gerwarth, Robert, and Stephan Malinowski, 'Der Holocaust als "kolonialer Genozid"? Europäische Kolonialgewalt und nationalsozialistischer Vernichtungskrieg', in: *Geschichte und Gesellschaft* 33 (2007), H. 3, pp. 439–466.

Gibbs, David N., 'Die Hintergründe der sowjetischen Invasion in Afghanistan 1979', in: Bernd Greiner, Christian Th. Müller and Dierk Walter (eds), *Heiße Kriege im Kalten Krieg* (Studien zum Kalten Krieg, vol. 1), Hamburg 2006, pp. 291–314.

Girard, Philippe R., *The Slaves Who Defeated Napoleon. Toussaint Louverture and the Haitian War of Independence, 1801–1804*, Tuscaloosa, AL 2011.

Glass, Stafford, *The Matabele War*, London 1968.

Glete, Jan, 'Warfare at Sea 1450–1815', in: Jeremy Black (ed.), *War in the Early Modern World, 1450–1815*, London 1998, pp. 25–52.

Gliech, Oliver, *Saint-Domingue und die französische Revolution. Das Ende der weißen Herrschaft in einer karibischen Plantagenwirtschaft* (Lateinamerikanische Forschungen, vol. 38), Köln 2011.

Glover, Michael, *Rorke's Drift*, Ware 1997.

Go, Julian, 'Entangled Empires. The United States and European Imperial Formations in the Mid-Twentieth Century', in: Alfred W. McCoy, Josep M. Fradera and Stephen Jacobson (eds), *Endless Empire. Spain's Retreat, Europe's Eclipse, America's Decline*, Madison, WI 2012, pp. 334–343.

Goltz, Colmar Freiherr von der, *Das Volk in Waffen. Ein Buch über Heerwesen und Kriegführung in unserer Zeit*, Berlin 1883.

Gommans, Jos, 'Warhorse and Gunpowder in India c. 1000–1850', in: Jeremy Black (ed.), *War in the Early Modern World, 1450–1815*, London 1998, pp. 105–127.

Gordon, Charles George, *General Gordon's Khartoum Journal*, ed. by Godfrey Elton, London 1961.

Gordon, Stewart, 'The Limited Adoption of European-Style Military Forces by Eighteenth-Century Rulers in India', in: *Indian Economic and Social History Review* 35 (1998), H. 3, pp. 229–245.

Gorst, Anthony, Lewis Johnman and W. Scott Lucas (eds), *Contemporary British History, 1931–1961. Politics and the Limits of Policy*, London 1991.

Gottmann, Jean, 'Bugeaud, Galliéni, Lyautey. The Development of French Colonial Warfare', in: Edward Mead Earle (ed.), *Makers of Modern Strategy. Military Thought from Machiavelli to Hitler*, Princeton, NJ 1943, pp. 234–259.

Gould, Tony, *Imperial Warriors. Britain and the Gurkhas*, London 1999. Grant, Ulysses S., *Personal Memoirs*, vol. 1, New York 1885.

Grau, Lester W., *The Bear Went Over the Mountain. Soviet Combat Tactics in Afghanistan*, London 2005.

BIBLIOGRAPHY

Gregorian, Raffi, "'Jungle Bashing" in Malaya. Towards a Formal Tactical Doctrine', in: *SmallWars and Insurgencies* 5 (1994), H. 3, pp. 338–359.

Greiner, Bernd, "'First to Go, Last to Know". Der Dschungelkrieger in Vietnam', in: *Geschichte und Gesellschaft* 29 (2003), H. 2, pp. 239–261.

————, Christian Th. Müller and Dierk Walter (eds), *Heiße Kriege im Kalten Krieg* (Studien zum Kalten Krieg, vol. 1), Hamburg 2006.

————,*Krieg ohne Fronten. Die USA inVietnam*, 2nd edn., Hamburg 2007.

Grenier, John, *The FirstWay ofWar.AmericanWar Making on the Frontier*, Cambridge 2005.

Griffith, Paddy, *Forward into Battle. Fighting Tactics from Waterloo to Vietnam*, Strettington 1981.

Griffiths, Tom, and Libby Robin (eds), *Ecology and Empire. Environmental History of Settler Socities*, Edinburgh 1997.

Groen, Petra M. H., 'Militant Response. The Dutch Use of Military Force and the Decolonization of the Dutch East Indies, 1945–50', in: Robert Holland (ed.), *Emergencies and Disorder in the European Empires after 1945*, London 1994, pp. 30–44.

Grotius, Hugo, *De jure belli ac pacis libri tres. Drei Bücher vom Recht des Krieges und des Friedens*, ed. byWalter Schätzel,Tübingen 1950 [1625].

Guevara, Ernesto Che, *Guerilla.Theorie und Methode*, ed. by Horst Kuernitzky, Berlin 1968.

Guilmartin, John F., 'Ideology and Conflict. The Wars of the Ottoman Empire, 1453–1606', in: Douglas M. Peers (ed.), *Warfare and Empires. Contact and Conflict between European and non-European Military and Maritime Forces and Cultures* (An Expanding World, vol. 24), Aldershot 1997, pp. 1–27.

————, 'LightTroops in Classical Armies. An Overview of Roles, Functions, and Factors Affecting Combat Effectiveness', in: James C. Bradford (ed.), *The Military and Conflict between Cultures. Soldiers at the Interface*, College Station,TX 1997, pp. 17–48.

————, 'The Cutting Edge. An Analysis of the Spanish Invasion and Overthrow of the Inca Empire, 1532–1539', in: Kenneth J. Andrien and Rolena Adorno (eds), *Transatlantic Encounters. Europeans and Andeans in the Sixteenth Century*, Berkeley, CA 1991, pp. 40–69.

Gustenau, Gustav, and Walter Feichtinger, 'Der Krieg in und um Kosovo 1998/99— Politisch-strategische Zielsetzungen und operative Merkmale', in: Jens Reuter and Conrad Clewing (eds), *Der Kosovo-Konflikt. Ursachen—Verlauf—Perspektiven*, Klagenfurt 2000, pp. 467–484.

Guy, Jeff, *The Destruction of the Zulu Kingdom.The CivilWar in Zululand, 1879–1884*, London 1979.

Gwynn, CharlesW., *Imperial Policing*, London 1934.

Häberlein, Mark, 'Macht und Ohnmacht derWorte. Kulturelle Vermittler in gewaltsamen Konflikten zwischen Europäern und Außereuropäern', in: Dierk Walter and Birthe Kundrus (eds), *WaffenWissenWandel. Anpassung und Lernen in transkulturellen Erstkonflikten*, Hamburg 2012, pp. 76–99.

Hack, Karl, 'Imperial Systems of Power, Colonial Forces and the Making of Modern Southeast Asia', in: Karl Hack andTobias Rettig (eds), *Colonial Armies in Southeast Asia*, London 2006, pp. 3–38.

————, 'Imperialism and Decolonisation in Southeast Asia', in: Karl Hack and Tobias Rettig (eds), *Colonial Armies in Southeast Asia*, London 2006, pp. 239–265.

————, 'Screwing down the People. The Malayan Emergency, Decolonisation and

BIBLIOGRAPHY

Ethnicity', in: Hans Antlöv and Stein Tønnesson (eds), *Imperial Policy and Southeast Asian Nationalism. 1930–1957* (Studies in Asian Topics, vol. 19), Richmond 1995, pp. 83–109.

Hack, Karl, and Tobias Rettig (eds), *Colonial Armies in Southeast Asia*, London 2006.

Hack, Karl, and Tobias Rettig, 'Demography and Domination in Southeast Asia', in: Ibid. (eds), *Colonial Armies in Southeast Asia*, London 2006, pp. 39–72.

Hagen, Ulrich vom, and Maren Tomforde, 'Militärische Organisationskultur', in: Nina Leonhard and Ines-Jacqueline Werkner (eds), *Militärsoziologie. Eine Einführung*, Wiesbaden 2005, pp. 176–197.

Hagerman, Edward, *The American Civil War and the Origins of Modern Warfare. Ideas, Organizations, and Field Command*, Bloomington, IN 1988.

Hahlweg, Werner, *Guerilla. Krieg ohne Fronten*, Stuttgart 1968.

Hakami, Khaled, 'Clash of Structures. Eine Kriegs-Erklärung zwischen Sozialanthropologie und Geschichtswissenschaft', in: Thomas Kolnberger, Ilja Steffelbauer and Gerald Weigl (eds), *Krieg und Akkulturation* (Expansion—Interaktion—Akkulturation, vol. 5), Vienna 2004, pp. 153–172.

Hanson, Victor Davis, *The Western Way of War. Infantry Battle in Classical Greece*, 2nd edn., Berkeley, CA 2009.

Harding, Andrew, 'French troops continue operation against Mali Islamists', in: BBC News, 12 January 2013. URL: http://www.bbc.co.uk/news/world-africa2099 7522 [17.07.2013].

Hassig, Ross, 'Aztec and Spanish Conquest in Mesoamerica', in: R. Brian Ferguson and Neil L. Whitehead (eds), *War in the Tribal Zone. Expanding States and Indigenous Warfare*, Santa Fe, NM 1992, pp. 83–102.

————, 'Die Eroberung Mexikos. Kulturkonflikt und Konsequenzen', in: Dierk Walter and Birthe Kundrus (eds), *Waffen Wissen Wandel. Anpassung und Lernen in transkulturellen Erstkonflikten*, Hamburg 2012, pp. 100–127.

————, *Aztec Warfare. Imperial Expansion and Political Control*, Norman, OK 1988.

————, *Mexico and the Spanish Conquest*, 2nd edn., Norman 2006.

Häußler, Matthias, 'Settlers in South West Africa. Between Colonial State and Indigenous Peoples: A Two-Front Struggle'. Paper delivered at the conference on 'Co-operation and Empire', Berne, 28th July 2013.

————, 'Zur Asymmetrie tribaler und staatlicher Kriegführung in Imperialkriegen. Die Logik der Kriegführung der Herero in vor- und frühkolonialer Zeit', in: Tanja Bührer, Christian Stachelbeck and Dierk Walter (eds), *Imperialkriege von 1500 bis heute. Strukturen—Akteure—Lernprozesse*, Paderborn 2011, pp. 177–195.

Häußler, Matthias, and Trutz von Trotha, 'Brutalisierung "von unten". Kleiner Krieg, Entgrenzung der Gewalt und Genozid im kolonialen Deutsch-Südwestafrika', in: *Mittelweg 36* 21 (2012), H. 3, pp. 57–89.

Hawkins, Mike, *Social Darwinism in European and American Thought, 1860–1945. Nature as Model and Nature as Threat*, Cambridge 1997.

Haywood, Austin, and Frederick A. S. Clarke, *The History of the Royal West African Frontier Force*, Aldershot 1964.

Headrick, Daniel R., *The Tools of Empire. Technology and European Imperialism in the Nineteenth Century*, New York 1981.

Heathcote, Thomas Anthony, 'The Army of British India', in: David Geoffrey Chandler

BIBLIOGRAPHY

and Ian F. W. Beckett (eds), *The Oxford Illustrated History of the British Army*, Oxford 1994, pp. 376–401.

———, *The Military in British India. The Development of British Land Forces in South Asia, 1600–1947*, Manchester 1995.

Hée, Nadin, *Imperiales Wissen und koloniale Gewalt. Japans Herrschaft in Taiwan 1895–1945* (Globalgeschichte, vol. 11), Frankfurt/Main 2012.

Heine, Peter, and Ulrich van der Heyden (eds), *Studien zur Geschichte des deutschen Kolonialismus in Afrika. Festschrift zum 60. Geburtstag von Peter Sebald*, Pfaffenweiler 1995.

Helbling, Jürg, 'Tribale Kriege und expandierende Staaten', in: Dierk Walter and Birthe Kundrus (eds), *Waffen Wissen Wandel. Anpassung und Lernen in transkulturellen Erstkonflikten*, Hamburg 2012, pp. 50–75.

———, *Tribale Kriege. Konflikte in Gesellschaften ohne Zentralgewalt*, Frankfurt/Main 2006.

Hemming, John, *Amazon Frontier. The Defeat of the Brazilian Indians*, London 2004.

———, *Red Gold. The Conquest of the Brazilian Indians*, London 1978.

———, *The Conquest of the Incas*, London 1993.

Herberg-Rothe, Andreas, *Der Krieg. Geschichte und Gegenwart*, Frankfurt/Main 2003.

Hering Torres, Max Sebastián, 'Fremdheit', in: Friedrich Jaeger (ed.), *Enzyklopädie der Neuzeit*, vol. 3: *Dynastie—Freundschaftslinien*, Stuttgart 2006, Sp. 1226–1229.

Hérisson, Maurice le Comte d', *La chasse à l'homme. Guerres d'Algérie*, 4th edn., Paris 1891.

Herold, Heiko, 'Das Fliegende Kreuzergeschwader der Kaiserlichen Marine als Instrument der deutschen Kolonialpolitik 1886–1893', in: Tanja Bührer, Christian Stachelbeck and Dierk Walter (eds), *Imperialkriege von 1500 bis heute. Strukturen— Akteure—Lernprozesse*, Paderborn 2011, pp. 383–400.

Heuser, Beatrice, *Rebellen—Partisanen—Guerilleros. Asymmetrische Kriege von der Antike bis heute*, Paderborn 2013.

Hirsch, Adam J., 'The Collision of Military Cultures in Seventeenth-Century New England', in: *Journal of American History* 74 (1988), H. 4, pp. 1187–1212.

Hirschfeld, Gerhard, 'Kriegsgreuel im Niederländisch-Indischen Dekolonisierungsprozess. Indonesien 1945–1949', in: Sönke Neitzel and Daniel Hohrath (eds), *Kriegsgreuel. Die Entgrenzung der Gewalt in kriegerischen Konflikten vom Mittelalter bis ins 20. Jahrhundert* (Krieg in der Geschichte, vol. 40), Paderborn 2008, pp. 353–369.

Hochgeschwender, Michael, 'Kolonialkriege als Experimentierstätten des Vernichtungskrieges?', in: Dietrich Beyrau, Michael Hochgeschwender and Dieter Langewiesche (eds), *Formen des Krieges. Von der Antike bis zur Gegenwart* (Krieg in der Geschichte, vol. 37), Paderborn 2007, pp. 269–290.

———, 'The Last Stand. Die Indianerkriege im Westen der USA (1840–1890)', in: Thoralf Klein and Frank Schumacher (eds), *Kolonialkriege. Militärische Gewalt im Zeichen des Imperialismus*, Hamburg 2006, pp. 44–79. Holland, Robert (ed.), *Emergencies and Disorder in the European Empires after 1945*, London 1994.

'Hollande: l'opération au Mali "n'a pas d'autre but que la lutte contre le terrorisme"', in: *Le Monde*, 21 January 2013. URL: http://www.lemonde.fr/afrique/article/2013/01/12/la-france-demande-une-acceleration-de-la-mise-en-place-de-la-force-internationale-au-mali_1816033_3212.html [08. 07. 2013].

Honold, Alexander, 'Raum ohne Volk. Zur Imaginationsgeschichte der kolonialen Geographie', in: Mihran Dabag, Horst Gründer and Uwe-Karsten Ketelsen (eds), *Kolonialismus. Kolonialdiskurs und Genozid*, Munich 2004, pp. 95–110.

Horne, Alistair, *A Savage War of Peace. Algeria 1954–1962*, London 2002.

BIBLIOGRAPHY

Howard, Michael, 'Colonial Wars and European Wars', in: Jaap A. de Moor and Hendrik Lodewyk Wesseling (eds), *Imperialism and War. Essays on Colonial Wars in Asia and Africa*, Leiden 1989, pp. 218–223.

Howard, Michael, George J. Andreopoulos and Mark R. Shulman (eds), *The Laws of War. Constraints on Warfare in the Western World*, New Haven, CT 1994.

Howard, Michael, *War in European History*, Oxford 1976.

Howe, Daniel Walker, *What Hath God Wrought. The Transformation of America, 1815–1848* (Oxford History of the United States, vol. 5), Oxford 2007.

Howe, Stephen, *Empire. A Very Short Introduction*, Oxford 2002.

Huamán Poma, *El primer nueva corónica i buen gobernio*, 1615, København, Det Kongelige Bibliotek, GKS 2232 4°. URL: http://www.kb.dk/permalink/2006/poma/info/en/frontpage.htm [01. 08. 2013].

————, *Letter to a King. A Picture-History of the Inca Civilisation*, ed. by Christopher Dilke, London 1978 [1615].

Hull, Isabel V., 'Military Culture and the Production of "Final Solutions" in the Colonies. The Example of Wilhelminian Germany', in: Robert Gellately and Ben Kiernan (eds), *The Specter of Genocide. Mass Murder in Historical Perspective*, Cambridge 2003, pp. 141–162.

————, *Absolute Destruction. Military Culture and the Practices of War in Imperial Germany*, Ithaca, NY 2005.

Hunt, George T., *The Wars of the Iroquois. A Study in Intertribal Trade Relations*, Madison, WI 1940.

Huntington, Samuel P., *The Soldier and the State. The Theory and Politics of Civil-Military Relations*, Cambridge, MA 1957.

Hurt, R. Douglas, *The Indian Frontier, 1763–1846*, Albuquerque, NM 2002.

Hyam, Ronald, 'British Imperial Expansion in the Late Eighteenth Century', in: *Historical Journal* 10 (1967), H. 1, pp. 113–124.

Ikime, Obaro, 'Nigeria—Ebrohimi', in: Michael Crowder (ed.), *West African Resistance. The Military Response to Colonial Occupation*, New York 1972, pp. 205–232.

Inikori, Joseph E., 'The Import of Firearms into West Africa, 1750–1807. A Quantitative Analysis', in: Douglas M. Peers (ed.), *Warfare and Empires. Contact and Conflict between European and non-European Military and Maritime Forces and Cultures* (An Expanding World, vol. 24), Aldershot 1997, pp. 245–274.

Isby, David C., *War in a Distant Country. Afghanistan: Invasion and Resistance*, London 1989.

Jacobson, Stephen, 'Imperial Ambitions in an Era of Decline. Micromilitarism and the Eclipse of the Spanish Empire, 1858–1923', in: Alfred W. McCoy, Josep M. Fradera and Stephen Jacobson (eds), *Endless Empire. Spain's Retreat, Europe's Eclipse, America's Decline*, Madison, WI 2012, pp. 74–91.

Jaeger, Friedrich (ed.), *Enzyklopädie der Neuzeit*, vol. 3: *Dynastie—Freundschaftslinien*, Stuttgart 2006.

————, *Enzyklopädie der Neuzeit*, vol. 5: *Gymnasium—Japanhandel*, Stuttgart 2007.

————, *Enzyklopädie der Neuzeit*, vol. 10: *Physiologie—Religiöses Epos*, Stuttgart 2009.

Jäger, Thomas (ed.), *Die Komplexität der Kriege*, Wiesbaden 2010.

Jalée, Pierre, *L'impérialisme en 1970*, Paris 1970.

James, Lawrence, *Raj. The Making and Unmaking of British India*, London 1997.

James, Lawrence, *The Savage Wars. British Campaigns in Africa, 1870–1920*, New York 1985.

Janis, Irving L., *Groupthink*, 2nd edn., Boston, MA 1982.

BIBLIOGRAPHY

Janowitz, Morris, *The Professional Soldier. A Social and Political Portrait*, Glencoe, IL 1960.

Jany, Curt, *Geschichte der Preußischen Armee vom 15. Jahrhundert bis 1914*, vol. 1: *Von den Anfängen bis 1740*, ed. by Eberhard Jany, 2nd edn., Osnabrück 1967.

Jauffret, Jean-Charles, 'Les armes de "la plus grande France"', in: André Corvisier and Guy Pedroncini (eds), *Histoire militaire de la France*, vol. 3: *De 1871 à 1940*, Paris 1997, pp. 43–69.

Jeffery, Keith, 'Colonial Warfare 1900–39', in: Colin McInnes and Gary D. Sheffield (eds), *Warfare in the Twentieth Century. Theory and Practice*, London 1988, pp. 24–50.

Jobst, Kerstin S., 'Die transkontinentale Expansion des Zarenreichs', in: Tanja Bührer, Christian Stachelbeck and Dierk Walter (eds), *Imperialkriege von 1500 bis heute. Strukturen—Akteure—Lernprozesse*, Paderborn 2011, pp. 55–71.

Joes, Anthony James, *America and Guerrilla Warfare*, Lexington, KY 2000.

Johnson, Courtney, '"Alliance Imperialism" and Anglo-American Power after 1898. The Origins of Open-Door Internationalism', in: Alfred W. McCoy, Josep M. Fradera and Stephen Jacobson (eds), *Endless Empire. Spain's Retreat, Europe's Eclipse, America's Decline*, Madison, WI 2012, pp. 122–135.

Jones, Archer, *The Art of War in the Western World*, New York 1987.

Jones, Colin, 'The Military Revolution and the Professionalisation of the French Army under the Ancien Regime', in: Michael Duffy (ed.), *The Military Revolution and the State 1500–1800* (Exeter Studies in History, vol. 1), Exeter 1980, pp. 29–48.

Jones, David R., 'Muscovite-Nomad Relations on the Steppe Frontier before 1800 and the Development of Russia's "Inclusive" Imperialism', in: Wayne E. Lee (ed.), *Empires and Indigenes. Intercultural Alliance, Imperial Expansion, and Warfare in the Early Modern World*, New York 2011, pp. 109–140.

Jones, Grant D., *Maya Resistance to Spanish Rule. Time and History on a Colonial Frontier*, Albuquerque, NM 1989.

———, *The Conquest of the Last Maya Kingdom*, Stanford, CA 1998.

Jones, R. Steven, *The Right Hand of Command. Use and Disuse of Personal Staffs in the American Civil War*, Mechanicsburg, PA 2000. Jones, Seth G., *In the Graveyard of Empires. America's War in Afghanistan*, New York 2010.

Jones, Tim, *Postwar Counterinsurgency and the SAS, 1945–1952. A Special Type of Warfare*, London 2001.

Jütte, Robert (ed.), *Medizin, Gesellschaft und Geschichte* (Jahrbuch des Instituts für Geschichte der Medizin der Robert Bosch Stiftung, vol. 22), Stuttgart 2004.

Jureit, Ulrike, *Das Ordnen von Räumen. Territorium und Lebensraum im 19. und 20. Jahrhundert*, Hamburg 2012.

Kaldor, Mary, *New and Old Wars. Organized Violence in a Global Era*, Cambridge 1999.

Kane, Katie, 'Nits Make Lice. Drogheda, Sand Creek, and the Poetics of Colonial Extermination', in: *Cultural Critique* 42 (1999), pp. 81–103.

Kanet, Roger E., 'Sowjetische Militärhilfe für nationale Befreiungskriege', in: Bernd Greiner, Christian Th. Müller and Dierk Walter (eds), *Heiße Kriege im Kalten Krieg* (Studien zum Kalten Krieg, vol. 1), Hamburg 2006, pp. 61–83.

Kanya-Forstner, Alexander Sydney, 'Mali—Tukulor', in: Michael Crowder (ed.), *West African Resistance. The Military Response to Colonial Occupation*, New York 1972, pp. 53–79.

———, 'The French Marines and the Conquest of the Western Sudan, 1880–1899', in:

BIBLIOGRAPHY

Jaap A. de Moor and Hendrik Lodewyk Wesseling (eds), *Imperialism and War. Essays on Colonial Wars in Asia and Africa*, Leiden 1989, pp. 121–145.

————, *The Conquest of the Western Sudan. A Study in French Military Imperialism*, Cambridge 1969.

Karr, Ronald Dale, '"Why Should You Be So Furious?". The Violence of the Pequot War', in: *Journal of American History* 85 (1998), H. 3, pp. 876–909.

Kars, Marjoleine, '"Cleansing the Land". Dutch-Amerindian Cooperation in the Suppression of the 1763 Slave Rebellion in Dutch Guiana', in: Wayne E. Lee (ed.), *Empires and Indigenes. Intercultural Alliance, Imperial Expansion, and Warfare in the Early Modern World*, New York 2011, pp. 251–275.

Katz, Steven T., 'The Pequot War Reconsidered', in: *New England Quarterly* 64 (1991), H. 2, pp. 206–224.

Keegan, John, 'The Ashanti Campaign, 1873–4', in: Brian Bond (ed.), *Victorian Military Campaigns*, London 1994, pp. 163–198.

————, *A History of Warfare*, London 1993.

Keeley, Lawrence H., *War Before Civilization*, New York 1996.

Kelly, Raymond C., *Warless Societies and the Origin of War*, Ann Arbor, MI 2000.

Kennedy, David M., *Freedom from Fear. The American People in Depression and War, 1929–1945* (Oxford History of the United States, vol. 9), New York 1999.

Kennedy, Dane Keith, *Islands of White. Settler Society and Culture in Kenya and Southern Rhodesia, 1890–1939*, Durham, NC 1987.

Kennedy, Greg, 'Drones. Legitimacy and Anti-Americanism', in: *Parameters* 42/43 (2013), H. 4/1, pp. 25–28.

Kennedy, Joseph P., *Population of the United States in 1860. Compiled from the Original Returns of the Eighth Census under the Direction of the Secretary of the Interior*, ed. by Bureau of the Census Library, Washington, DC 1864.

Kennedy, Paul, *The Rise and Fall of the Great Powers. Economic Change and Military Conflict from 1500 to 2000*, New York 1987.

Khodarkovsky, Michael, 'Krieg und Frieden. Was Russland an seinen asiatischen Frontiers (nicht) lernte', in: Dierk Walter and Birthe Kundrus (eds), *Waffen Wissen Wandel. Anpassung und Lernen in transkulturellen Erstkonflikten*, Hamburg 2012, pp. 198–218.

————, *Russia's Steppe Frontier. The Making of a Colonial Empire, 1500–1800*, Bloomington, IN 2002.

Kidd, Colin, *The Forging of Races. Race and Scripture in the Protestant Atlantic World, 1600–2000*, Cambridge 2006.

Kiernan, Victor G., *Colonial Empires and Armies, 1815–1960*, Montreal 1998.

Killingray, David, 'Colonial Warfare in West Africa, 1870–1914', in: Jaap A. de Moor and Hendrik Lodewyk Wesseling (eds), *Imperialism and War. Essays on Colonial Wars in Asia and Africa*, Leiden 1989, pp. 146–167.

————, 'Guardians of Empire', in: David Killingray and David E. Omissi (eds), *Guardians of Empire. The Armed Forces of the Colonial Powers c. 1700–1964*, Manchester 1999, pp. 1–24.

————, 'The Idea of a British Imperial African Army', in: *Journal of African History* 20 (1979), H. 3, pp. 421–436.

Killingray, David, and David E. Omissi (eds), *Guardians of Empire. The Armed Forces of the Colonial Powers c. 1700–1964*, Manchester 1999.

BIBLIOGRAPHY

Kipling, Rudyard, 'The Young British Soldier', in: Ibid., *The Writings in Prose and Verse*, vol. 11, New York 1899, pp. 37–39.

———, *The Writings in Prose and Verse*, vol. 11, New York 1899.

Kirk-Greene, Anthony H. M., '"Damnosa Hereditas". Ethnic Ranking and the Martial Races Imperative in Africa', in: *Ethnic and Racial Studies* 3 (1980), H. 4, pp. 393–414.

———, 'The Thin White Line. The Size of the British Colonial Service in Africa', in: *African Affairs* 79 (1980), H. 314, pp. 25–44.

Kitson, Frank, *Gangs and Counter-gangs*, London 1960.

Klein, Thoralf, 'Straffeldzug im Namen der Zivilisation. Der "Boxerkrieg" in China (1900–1901)', in: Thoralf Klein and Frank Schumacher (eds), *Kolonialkriege. Militärische Gewalt im Zeichen des Imperialismus*, Hamburg 2006, pp. 145–181.

Klein, Thoralf, and Frank Schumacher (eds), *Kolonialkriege. Militärische Gewalt im Zeichen des Imperialismus*, Hamburg 2006.

Klein, Thoralf, and Frank Schumacher, 'Einleitung', in: Ibid. (eds), *Kolonialkriege. Militärische Gewalt im Zeichen des Imperialismus*, Hamburg 2006, pp. 7–13.

Kleinschmidt, Harald, *Diskriminierung durch Vertrag und Krieg. Zwischenstaatliche Verträge und der Begriff des Kolonialkriegs im 19. und frühen 20. Jahrhundert* (Historische Zeitschrift, Beihefte [Neue Folge], vol. 59), Munich 2013.

Klose, Fabian, '"Antisubversiver Krieg". Militärstrategische Transferprozesse im Zeichen der Dekolonisierungskriege', in: Tanja Bührer, Christian Stachelbeck and Dierk Walter (eds), *Imperialkriege von 1500 bis heute. Strukturen—Akteure—Lernprozesse*, Paderborn 2011, pp. 484–501.

———, 'Notstand und die Entgrenzung kolonialer Gewalt', in: *Francia* 34 (2007), H. 3, pp. 39–61.

———, 'Zur Legitimation kolonialer Gewalt. Kolonialer Notstand, antisubversiver Krieg und humanitäres Völkerrecht im kenianischen und algerischen Dekolonisationskrieg', in: *Archiv für Sozialgeschichte* 48 (2008), pp. 249–274.

———, *Menschenrechte im Schatten kolonialer Gewalt. Die Dekolonisierungskriege in Kenia und Algerien 1945–1962* (Veröffentlichungen des Deutschen Historischen Instituts London, vol. 66), Munich 2009.

Knaap, Gerrit J., 'Crisis and Failure. War and Revolt in the Ambon Islands, 1636–1637', in: Douglas M. Peers (ed.), *Warfare and Empires. Contact and Conflict between European and non-European Military and Maritime Forces and Cultures* (An Expanding World, vol. 24), Aldershot 1997, pp. 151–175.

Knaut, Andrew L., *The Pueblo Revolt of 1680. Conquest and Resistance in Seventeenth-Century New Mexico*, Norman, OK 1995.

Knight, Ian, *The Anatomy of the Zulu Army from Shaka to Cetshwayo 1818–1879*, London 1999. Knight, Ian, *Zulu. Isandlwana and Rorke's Drift 22nd—23rd January 1879*, London 1992. Knöbl, Wolfgang, 'Imperiale Herrschaft und Gewalt', in: *Mittelweg 36* 21 (2012), H. 3, pp. 19–44.

Kolff, Dirk H. A., 'The End of an Ancien Régime. Colonial War in India 1798–1818', in: Jaap A. de Moor and Hendrik Lodewyk Wesseling (eds), *Imperialism and War. Essays on Colonial Wars in Asia and Africa*, Leiden 1989, pp. 22–49.

Koller, Christian, 'Die französische Fremdenlegion als transkultureller Erfahrungsraum', in: Tanja Bührer, Christian Stachelbeck and Dierk Walter (eds), *Imperialkriege von 1500 bis heute. Strukturen—Akteure—Lernprozesse*, Paderborn 2011, pp. 363–381.

———, *Von Wilden aller Rassen niedergemetzelt. Die Diskussion um die Verwendung von*

BIBLIOGRAPHY

Kolonialtruppen in Europa zwischen Rassismus, Kolonial- und Militärpolitik (1914–1930), Stuttgart 2001.

Kolnberger, Thomas, Ilja Steffelbauer and Gerald Weigl (eds), *Krieg und Akkulturation* (Expansion—Interaktion—Akkulturation, vol. 5), Vienna 2004.

Kopperman, Paul E., *Braddock at the Monongahela*, Pittsburgh, PA 1977.

Kortüm, Hans-Henning (ed.), *Transcultural Wars from the Middle Ages to the 21st Century*, Berlin 2006.

Kramer, Paul A., 'Empires, Exceptions, and Anglo-Saxons. Race and Rule between the British and United States Empires, 1880–1910', in: *Journal of American History* 88 (2002), H. 4, pp. 1315–1353.

————, 'Race-Making and Colonial Violence in the U.S. Empire. The Philippine-American War as Race War', in: *Diplomatic History* 30 (2006), H. 1, pp. 169–210.

Kratoska, Paul H., 'Elites and the Construction of the Nation in Southeast Asia', in: Jost Dülffer and Marc Frey (eds), *Elites and Decolonization in the Twentieth Century*, Basingstoke 2011, pp. 36–55.

Kreienbaum, Jonas, 'Koloniale Gewaltexzesse. Kolonialkriege um 1900', in: Alain Chatriot and Dieter Gosewinkel (eds), *Koloniale Politik und Praktiken Deutschlands und Frankreichs 1880–1962* (Schriftenreihe des Deutsch-Französischen Historikerkomitees, vol. 6), Stuttgart 2010, pp. 155–172.

Kubicek, Robert, 'British Expansion, Empire, and Technological Change', in: Andrew Porter and Alaine Low (eds), *The Oxford History of the British Empire*, vol. 3: *The Nineteenth Century*, Oxford 1999, pp. 247–269.

Kundrus, Birthe, and Dierk Walter, 'Anpassung und Lernen in transkulturellen Erstkonflikten. Fragen—Hintergründe—Befunde', in: Ibid. (eds), *Waffen Wissen Wandel. Anpassung und Lernen in transkulturellen Erstkonflikten*, Hamburg 2012, pp. 7–33.

Kunisch, Johannes, *Der kleine Krieg. Studien zum Heerwesen des Absolutismus* (Frankfurter Historische Abhandlungen, vol. 4), Wiesbaden 1973.

Kunz, Rudibert, '"Con ayuda del más dañino de todos los gases". Der Gaskrieg gegen die Rif-Kabylen in Spanisch-Marokko 1922–1927', in: Irmtrud Wojak and Susanne Meinl (eds), *Völkermord und Kriegsverbrechen in der ersten Hälfte des 20. Jahrhunderts*, Frankfurt/Main 2004, pp. 153–191.

Kuß, Susanne, *Deutsches Militär auf kolonialen Kriegsschauplätzen. Eskalation von Gewalt zu Beginn des 20. Jahrhunderts* (Studien zur Kolonialgeschichte, vol. 3), Berlin 2010.

Laband, John P. C. (ed.), *Lord Chelmsford's Zululand Campaign 1878–1879*, Stroud 1994.

Lane, Kris, 'Introductory Study', in: Bernardo de Vargas Machuca, *The Indian Militia and Description of the Indies*, ed. by Kris Lane, Durham, NC 2008, pp. xvii–lxxiv.

Langford, Paul, 'The Eighteenth Century (1688–1789)', in: Kenneth O. Morgan (ed.), *The Oxford History of Britain. Revised Edition*, Oxford 2010, pp. 399–469.

Lappas, Thomas J., 'Lernen inmitten des Blutvergießens. Französisch-indianische Interaktionen in der Erkundungsphase in Nordamerika', in: Dierk Walter and Birthe Kundrus (eds), *Waffen Wissen Wandel. Anpassung und Lernen in transkulturellen Erstkonflikten*, Hamburg 2012, pp. 151–178.

Laqueur, Walter, *Guerrilla Warfare. A Historical & Critical Study*, New Brunswick, NJ 1998.

Lartéguy, Jean, *Les Centurions*, Paris 1960.

Law, Randall D., *Terrorism. A History*, Cambridge 2009.

Law, Robin, 'Warfare on the West African Slave Coast, 1650–1850', in: R. Brian Ferguson

BIBLIOGRAPHY

and Neil L. Whitehead (eds), *War in the Tribal Zone. Expanding States and Indigenous Warfare*, Santa Fe, NM 1992, pp. 103–126.

Le Cour Grandmaison, Olivier, *Coloniser, Exterminer. Sur la guerre et l'état colonial*, Paris 2005.

Lee, Wayne E. (ed.), *Empires and Indigenes. Intercultural Alliance, Imperial Expansion, and Warfare in the Early Modern World*, New York 2011.

Lee, Wayne E., 'Fortify, Fight, or Flee. Tuscarora and Cherokee Defensive Warfare and Military Culture Adaptation', in: *Journal of Military History* 68 (2004), H. 3, pp. 713–770.

———, 'Projecting Power in the Early Modern World. The Spanish Model?', in: Ibid. (ed.), *Empires and Indigenes. Intercultural Alliance, Imperial Expansion, and Warfare in the Early Modern World*, New York 2011, pp. 1–16.

———, 'The Military Revolution of Native North America. Firearms, Forts, and Politics', in: Ibid. (ed.), *Empires and Indigenes. Intercultural Alliance, Imperial Expansion, and Warfare in the Early Modern World*, New York 2011, pp. 49–79.

Lehmann, Joseph H., *All Sir Garnet. A Life of Field-Marshal Lord Wolseley*, London 1964.

Lemke, Bernd, 'Kolonialgeschichte als Vorläufer für modernes "Nation-Building"? Britische Pazifikationsversuche in Kurdistan und der North-West Frontier Province 1918–1947', in: Tanja Bührer, Christian Stachelbeck and Dierk Walter (eds), *Imperialkriege von 1500 bis heute. Strukturen—Akteure—Lernprozesse*, Paderborn 2011, pp. 279–300.

Lenman, Bruce P., *England's Colonial Wars 1550–1688. Conflicts, Empire and National Identity*, Harlow 2001.

Leonhard, Nina, and Ines-Jacqueline Werkner (eds), *Militärsoziologie. Eine Einführung*, Wiesbaden 2005.

Lettow-Vorbeck, Paul von, *Mein Leben*, Biberach/Riß 1957.

Lieb, Peter, 'Guerre Révolutionnaire. Die französische Theorie zur Aufstandsbekämpfung in Algerien 1954–1962', in: Tanja Bührer, Christian Stachelbeck and Dierk Walter (eds), *Imperialkriege von 1500 bis heute. Strukturen—Akteure—Lernprozesse*, Paderborn 2011, pp. 463–481.

Lincoln, W. Bruce, *The Conquest of a Continent. Siberia and the Russians*, Ithaca, NY 1994.

Lindsay, Brendan C., *Murder State. California's Native American Genocide, 1846–1873*, Lincoln, NE 2012.

Linn, Brian McAllister, 'Cerberus' Dilemma. The US Army and Internal Security in the Pacific, 1902–1940', in: David Killingray and David E. Omissi (eds), *Guardians of Empire. The Armed Forces of the Colonial Powers c. 1700–1964*, Manchester 1999, pp. 114–136.

———, *The U.S. Army and Counterinsurgency in the Philippine War, 1899–1902*, Chapel Hill, NC 1989.

Livingstone, David N., *The Geographical Tradition. Episodes in the History of a Contested Enterprise*, Oxford 1992.

Lock, Ron, and Peter Quantrill, *Zulu Victory. The Epic of Isandlwana and the Cover-Up*, London 2002.

Lombardi, Aldo Virgilio, *Bürgerkrieg und Völkerrecht. Die Anwendbarkeit völkerrechtlicher Normen in nicht-zwischenstaatlichen bewaffneten Konflikten* (Schriften zum Völkerrecht, vol. 53), Berlin 1976.

Longacre, Edward, *General John Buford. A Military Biography*, Conshohocken, PA 1996.

BIBLIOGRAPHY

Lonsdale, John, 'The Conquest State of Kenya', in: Jaap A. de Moor and Hendrik Lodewyk Wesseling (eds), *Imperialism and War. Essays on Colonial Wars in Asia and Africa*, Leiden 1989, pp. 87–120.

Lowenthal, David, 'Empires and Ecologies. Reflections of Environmental History', in: Tom Griffiths and Libby Robin (eds), *Ecology and Empire. Environmental History of Settler Socities*, Edinburgh 1997, pp. 229–236.

Luh, Jürgen, *Ancien Régime Warfare and the Military Revolution. A Study* (Baltic Studies, vol. 6), Groningen 2000.

Lunn, Joe, 'French Race Theory, the Parisian Society of Anthropology, and the Debate over la Force Noire, 1909–1912', in: Martin Thomas (ed.), *The French Colonial Mind*, vol. 2: *Violence, Military Encounters, and Colonialism*, Lincoln, NE 2011, pp. 221–247.

Lussato, Céline, 'Mali. La France un peu moins isolée … Un peu', in: *Le nouvel observateur*, 21 January 2013. URL: http://tempsreel.nouvelobs.com/guerre-aumali/20130121.OBS6101/mali-la-france-un-peu-moins-isolee-un-peu.html [08. 07. 2013].

Luttrell, Marcus, *Lone Survivor. The Eyewitness Account of Operation Redwing and the Lost Heroes of SEAL Team 10*, New York 2007.

Lyautey, Louis Hubert Gonzalve, *Du rôle colonial de l'armée*, Paris 1900.

Lynn, John A., *Battle. A History of Combat and Culture*, Boulder, CO 2003.

MacQueen, Norrie, 'Portugal's First Domino. "Pluricontinentalism" and Colonial War in Guiné-Bissau, 1963–1974', in: *Contemporary European History* 8 (1999), H. 2, pp. 209–230.

Macrory, Patrick, *Signal Catastrophe. The Story of the Disastrous Retreat from Kabul 1842*, London 1966.

Magdoff, Harry, *Imperialism. From the Colonial Age to the Present*, New York 1978.

Malinowski, Stephan, 'Modernisierungskriege. Militärische Gewalt und koloniale Modernisierung im Algerienkrieg (1954–1962)', in: *Archiv für Sozialgeschichte* 48 (2008), pp. 213–248.

Malley, Robert, *The Call from Algeria. Third Worldism, Revolution, and the Turn to Islam*, Berkeley, CA 1996.

Maloba, Wunyabari O., *Mau Mau and Kenya. An Analysis of a Peasant Revolt*, Bloomington, IN 2004.

Malone, Patrick M., 'Changing Military Technology Among the Indians of Southern New England, 1600–1677', in: Douglas M. Peers (ed.), *Warfare and Empires. Contact and Conflict between European and non-European Military and Maritime Forces and Cultures* (An Expanding World, vol. 24), Aldershot 1997, pp. 229–244.

———, *The Skulking Way of War. Technology and Tactics among the New England Indians*, Lanham, MD 2000.

Maninger, Stephan, '"Rangers". Ein Konzept der Aufstandsbekämpfung in Nordamerika von 1676 bis 1850', in: Tanja Bührer, Christian Stachelbeck and Dierk Walter (eds), *Imperialkriege von 1500 bis heute. Strukturen—Akteure—Lernprozesse*, Paderborn 2011, pp. 325–344.

Mann, Michael, 'Das Gewaltdispositiv des modernen Kolonialismus', in: Mihran Dabag, Horst Gründer and Uwe-Karsten Ketelsen (eds), *Kolonialismus. Kolonialdiskurs und Genozid*, Munich 2004, pp. 111–135.

Manning, Stephen, 'Learning the Trade. Use and Misuse of Intelligence during the British Colonial Campaigns of the 1870s', in: *Intelligence and National Security* 22 (2007), H. 5, pp. 644–660.

BIBLIOGRAPHY

Mao Tse-Tung, 'Strategische Probleme des Partisanenkriegs gegen die japanische Aggression' [1938], in: Ibid., *Ausgewählte Werke*, vol. 2: *Die Periode des Widerstandskriegs gegen die japanische Aggression (I)*, ed. by the Commission of the Central Committee of the Communist Party of China for the Publication of the Selected Works of Mao Tse-Tung, Peking 1968, pp. 83–125.

————, 'Strategische Probleme des revolutionären Krieges in China' [1936], in: Ibid., *Ausgewählte Werke*, vol. 1: *Die Periode des ersten revolutionären Bürgerkriegs*, ed. by the Commission of the Central Committee of the Communist Party of China for the Publication of the Selected Works of Mao Tse-Tung, Peking 1968, pp. 209–298.

————, 'Über den langwierigen Krieg' [1938], in: Ibid., *Ausgewählte Werke*, vol. 2: *Die Periode des Widerstandskriegs gegen die japanische Aggression (I)*, ed. by the Commission of the Central Committee of the Communist Party of China for the Publication of the Selected Works of Mao Tse-Tung, Peking 1968, pp. 127–228.

————, *Ausgewählte Werke*, vol. 1: *Die Periode des ersten revolutionären Bürgerkriegs*, ed. by the Commission of the Central Committee of the Communist Party of China for the Publication of the Selected Works of Mao Tse-Tung, Peking 1968.

————, *Ausgewählte Werke*, vol. 2: *Die Periode des Widerstandskriegs gegen die japanische Aggression (I)*, ed. by the Commission of the Central Committee of the Communist Party of China for the Publication of the Selected Works of Mao Tse-Tung, Peking 1968.

————, 'Repel the Attacks of the Bourgeois Rightists (July 9, 1957)', in: Ibid., *The Writings of Mao Zedong*, vol. 2: *1949–1976*, ed. by John K. Leung and Michael Y. M. Kau, Armonk, NY 1992, pp. 620–637.

————, *The Writings of Mao Zedong*, vol. 2: *1949–1976*, ed. by John K. Leung and Michael Y. M. Kau, Armonk, NY 1992.

Marighela, Carlos, 'Handbuch des Stadtguerillero', in: Ibid., *Zerschlagt die Wohlstandsinseln der Dritten Welt*, ed. by Conrad Detrez and Márcio M. Alves, Reinbek 1971, pp. 39–84.

————, *Zerschlagt die Wohlstandsinseln der Dritten Welt*, ed. by Conrad Detrez and Márcio M. Alves, Reinbek 1971.

Markel, Wade, 'Draining the Swamp. The British Strategy of Population Control', in: *Parameters* 36 (2006), H. 1, pp. 35–48.

Marshall, Alex, *The Russian General Staff and Asia, 1800–1917*, London 2006.

Marshall, Peter James, 'Western Arms in Maritime Asia in the Early Phases of Expansion', in: *Modern Asian Studies* 14 (1980), H. 1, pp. 13–28.

Marthoz, Jean-Paul, 'In Mali, a war "without images and without facts"', in: *CPJ Journalist Security Blog*, 25th January 2013. URL: http://cpj.org/security/2013/01/in-mali-a-war-without-images-and-without-facts.php [07. 08. 2013].

Martin, Michel L., 'From Algiers to N'Djamena. France's Adaptation to Low-Intensity Wars, 1830–1987', in: David Charters and Maurice Tugwell (eds), *Armies in Low-Intensity Conflict. A Comparative Analysis*, London 1989, pp. 77–138.

Marx, Christoph, *Geschichte Afrikas. Von 1800 bis zur Gegenwart*, Paderborn 2004.

Matthew, Laura E., 'Whose Conquest? Nahua, Zapoteca, and Mixteca Allies in the Conquest of Central America', in: Laura E. Matthew and Michel R. Oudijk (eds), *Indian Conquistadors. Indigenous Allies in the Conquest of Mesoamerica*, Norman, OK 2007, pp. 102–126.

BIBLIOGRAPHY

Matthew, Laura E., and Michel R. Oudijk (eds), *Indian Conquistadors. Indigenous Allies in the Conquest of Mesoamerica*, Norman, OK 2007.

Mattioli, Aram, 'Die vergessenen Kolonialverbrechen des faschistischen Italien in Libyen 1923–1933', in: Irmtrud Wojak and Susanne Meinl (eds), *Völkermord und Kriegsverbrechen in der ersten Hälfte des 20. Jahrhunderts*, Frankfurt/Main 2004, pp. 203–226.

Mattison, Ray H., *The Army Post on the Northern Plains 1865–1885*, Gering, NE 1962.

May, Glenn Anthony, 'Was the Philippine-American War a "Total War"?', in: Manfred F. Boemeke, Roger Chickering and Stig Förster (eds), *Anticipating Total War. The German and American Experiences, 1871–1914*, Cambridge 1999, pp. 437–457.

McCoy, Alfred W., 'Imperial Illusions. Information Infrastructure and the Future of U.S. Global Power', in: Alfred W. McCoy, Josep M. Fradera and Stephen Jacobson (eds), *Endless Empire. Spain's Retreat, Europe's Eclipse, America's Decline*, Madison, WI 2012, pp. 360–386.

McCoy, Alfred W., Josep M. Fradera and Stephen Jacobson (eds), *Endless Empire. Spain's Retreat, Europe's Eclipse, America's Decline*, Madison, WI 2012.

McCrisken, Trevor, 'Obama's Drone War', in: *Survival* 55 (2013), H. 2, pp. 97–122.

McCuen, John J., *The Art of Counter-Revolutionary Warfare. The Strategy of Counter-Insurgency*, London 1966.

McInnes, Colin, and Gary D. Sheffield (eds), *Warfare in the Twentieth Century. Theory and Practice*, London 1988.

McMahon, Robert J., 'Heiße Kriege im Kalten Krieg', in: Bernd Greiner, Christian Th. Müller and Dierk Walter (eds), *Heiße Kriege im Kalten Krieg* (Studien zum Kalten Krieg, vol. 1), Hamburg 2006, pp. 16–34.

McNab, David, Bruce W. Hodgins and Dale S. Standen, '"Black with Canoes". Aboriginal Resistance and the Canoe. Diplomacy, Trade and Warfare in the Meeting Grounds of Northeastern North America, 1600–1821', in: George Raudzens (ed.), *Technology, Disease and Colonial Conquests, Sixteenth to Eighteenth Centuries. Essays Reappraising the Guns and Germs Theories*, Leiden 2001, pp. 238–292.

McNeill, William H., 'European Expansion, Power and Warfare since 1500', in: Jaap A. de Moor and Hendrik Lodewyk Wesseling (eds), *Imperialism and War. Essays on Colonial Wars in Asia and Africa*, Leiden 1989, pp. 12–21.

——, *The Age of Gunpowder Empires 1450–1800*, Washington, DC 1989.

Meinertzhagen, Richard, *Kenya Diary (1902–1906)*, Edinburgh 1957.

Meissner, Jochen, Ulrich Mücke and Klaus Weber, *Schwarzes Amerika. Eine Geschichte der Sklaverei*, Munich 2008.

Merom, Gil, *How Democracies Lose Small Wars. State, Society, and the Failures of France in Algeria, Israel in Lebanon, and the United States in Vietnam*, New York 2003.

Meuwese, Mark, 'The Opportunities and Limits of Ethnic Soldiering. The Tupis and the Dutch-Portuguese Struggle for the Southern Atlantic, 1630–1657', in: Wayne E. Lee (ed.), *Empires and Indigenes. Intercultural Alliance, Imperial Expansion, and Warfare in the Early Modern World*, New York 2011, pp. 193–220.

Meynier, Gilbert, and Pierre Vidal-Naquet, 'Coloniser Exterminer. De vérités bonnes à dire à l'art de la simplification idéologique', in: *Esprit* 320 (2005), pp. 162–177.

Michels, Eckard, 'Das "Ostasiatische Expeditionskorps" des Deutschen Reiches in China 1900/01', in: Tanja Bührer, Christian Stachelbeck and Dierk Walter (eds), *Imperialkriege von 1500 bis heute. Strukturen—Akteure—Lernprozesse*, Paderborn 2011, pp. 401–416.

BIBLIOGRAPHY

Middleton, Richard, and Anne Lombard, *Colonial America. A History to 1763*, 4th edn., Chichester 2011.

Mieder, Wolfgang, '"The Only Good Indian Is a Dead Indian". History and Meaning of a Proverbial Stereotype', in: *Journal of American Folklore* 106 (1993), H. 419, pp. 38–60.

Miège, Jean-Louis, 'The French Conquest of Morocco. The Early Period, 1901–1911', in: Jaap A. de Moor and Hendrik Lodewyk Wesseling (eds), *Imperialism and War. Essays on Colonial Wars in Asia and Africa*, Leiden 1989, pp. 201–217.

Mockaitis, Thomas R., 'The Origins of British Counter-Insurgency', in: *Small Wars and Insurgencies* 1 (1990), H. 3, pp. 209–225. Mockaitis, Thomas R., *British Counterinsurgency, 1919–60*, London 1990.

Mollenhauer, Daniel, 'Die vielen Gesichter der pacification. Frankreichs Krieg in Algerien (1954–1962)', in: Thoralf Klein and Frank Schumacher (eds), *Kolonialkriege. Militärische Gewalt im Zeichen des Imperialismus*, Hamburg 2006, pp. 329–366.

Moltke, Helmuth von, 'Rede vor dem deutschen Reichstag, 14. Mai 1890', in: Ibid., *Vom Kabinettskrieg zum Volkskrieg. Eine Werkauswahl*, ed. by Stig Förster, Bonn 1992, pp. 638–641.

——, *Vom Kabinettskrieg zum Volkskrieg. Eine Werkauswahl*, ed. by Stig Förster, Bonn 1992.

Momaday, Navarre Scott, *The Man Made of Words. Essays, Stories, Passages*, New York 1997.

Mommsen, Wolfgang J., *Imperialismustheorien. Ein Überblick über die neueren Imperialismusinterpretationen*, 3rd edn., Göttingen 1987.

Mommsen, Wolfgang J., and Jürgen Osterhammel (eds), *Imperialism and After. Continuities and Discontinuities*, London 1986.

Moor, Jaap A. de, 'The Recruitment of Indonesian Soldiers for the Dutch Colonial Army, c. 1700–1950', in: David Killingray and David E. Omissi (eds), *Guardians of Empire. The Armed Forces of the Colonial Powers c. 1700–1964*, Manchester 1999, pp. 53–69.

——, 'Warmakers in the Archipelago. Dutch Expeditions in Nineteenth Century Indonesia', in: Jaap A. de Moor and Hendrik Lodewyk Wesseling (eds), *Imperialism and War. Essays on Colonial Wars in Asia and Africa*, Leiden 1989, pp. 50–71.

Moor, Jaap A. de, and Hendrik Lodewyk Wesseling (eds), *Imperialism and War. Essays on Colonial Wars in Asia and Africa*, Leiden 1989.

Moreman, Timothy R., '"Small Wars" and "Imperial Policing". The British Army and the Theory and Practice of Colonial Warfare in the British Empire, 1919–1939', in: *Journal of Strategic Studies* 19 (1996), H. 4, pp. 105–131.

——, '"Watch and Ward". The Army in India and the North-West Frontier, 1920–1939', in: David Killingray and David E. Omissi (eds), *Guardians of Empire. The Armed Forces of the Colonial Powers c. 1700–1964*, Manchester 1999, pp. 137–156.

——, *The Army in India and the Development of Frontier Warfare, 1849–1947*, Basingstoke 1998.

Morgan, Andy, 'The remote mountains of northern Mali—perfect for guerrillas', in: BBC News, 5 February 2013. URL: http://www.bbc.co.uk/news/worldafrica-21326831 [08. 07. 2013].

Morgan, Kenneth O. (ed.), *The Oxford History of Britain. Revised Edition*, Oxford 2010.

Morillo, Stephen, 'A General Typology of Transcultural Wars. The Early Middle Ages and Beyond', in: Hans-Henning Kortüm (ed.), *Transcultural Wars from the Middle Ages to the 21st Century*, Berlin 2006, pp. 29–42.

Morlang, Thomas, '"Die Wahehe haben ihre Vernichtung gewollt". Der Krieg der "Kaiserlichen Schutztruppe" gegen die Hehe in Deutsch-Ostafrika (1890–1898)', in:

BIBLIOGRAPHY

Thoralf Klein and Frank Schumacher (eds), *Kolonialkriege. Militärische Gewalt im Zeichen des Imperialismus*, Hamburg 2006, pp. 80–108.

————, *Askari und Fitafita. "Farbige" Söldner in den deutschen Kolonien* (Schlaglichter der Kolonialgeschichte, vol. 8), Berlin 2008.

Morris, Donald R., *The Washing of the Spears. A History of the Rise of the Zulu Nation under Shaka and Its Fall in the Zulu War of 1879*, New York 1965.

Moses, Anthony Dirk (ed.), *Empire, Colony, Genocide. Conquest, Occupation, and Subaltern Resistance in World History*, New York 2008.

————, *Genocide and Settler Society. Frontier Violence and Stolen Indigenous Children in Australian History* (Studies on War and Genocide, vol. 6), New York 2004.

Moses, Anthony Dirk, 'Empire, Colony, Genocide. Keywords and the Philosophy of History', in: Ibid. (ed.), *Empire, Colony, Genocide. Conquest, Occupation, and Subaltern Resistance in World History*, New York 2008, pp. 3–54.

Mostert, Tristan, *The Military System of the Dutch East India Company, 1655–1663*. Master's dissertation, Universität Leiden 2007. URL: http://vocwarfare.net/pdf/chain-of-command-complete.pdf [27. 03. 2014].

Mücke, Ulrich, 'Agonie einer Kolonialmacht. Spaniens Krieg in Marokko (1921–1927)', in: Thoralf Klein and Frank Schumacher (eds), *Kolonialkriege. Militärische Gewalt im Zeichen des Imperialismus*, Hamburg 2006, pp. 248–271.

Müller, Harald, and Niklas Schörnig, 'Drohnenkrieg. Die konsequente Fortsetzung der westlichen Revolution in Military Affairs', in: *Aus Politik und Zeitgeschichte* (2010), H. 50, pp. 16–23.

Münkler, Herfried, 'Wandel der Weltordnung durch asymmetrische Kriege', in: Josef Schröfl and Thomas Pankratz (eds), *Asymmetrische Kriegführung. Ein neues Phänomen der Internationalen Politik?*, Baden-Baden 2004, pp. 85–93.

————, *Die neuen Kriege*, Reinbek 2002.

————, *Imperien. Die Logik der Weltherrschaft—vom Alten Rom bis zu den Vereinigten Staaten*, Berlin 2005.

Muffett, David J. M., 'Nigeria—Sokoto Caliphate', in: Michael Crowder (ed.), *West African Resistance. The Military Response to Colonial Occupation*, New York 1972, pp. 268–299.

Mukherjee, Rudrangshu, *Spectre of Violence. The 1857 Kanpur Massacres*, New Delhi 2008.

Nagl, John A., 'Learning to Eat Soup with a Knife. British and American Army Counterinsurgency Learning during the Malayan Emergency and the Vietnam War', in: *Foreign Affairs* 161 (1999), H. 4, pp. 193–199.

————, *Learning to Eat Soup with a Knife. Counterinsurgency Lessons from Malaya and Vietnam*, Chicago, IL 2005.

Nasson, Bill, *The South African War 1899–1902*, London 1999.

Navarre, Henri, *Agonie de L'Indochine (1953–1954)*, Paris 1956.

Neitzel, Sönke, and Daniel Hohrath (eds), *Kriegsgreuel. Die Entgrenzung der Gewalt in kriegerischen Konflikten vom Mittelalter bis ins 20. Jahrhundert* (Krieg in der Geschichte, vol. 40), Paderborn 2008.

Nester, William R., *The Frontier War for American Independence*, Mechanicsburg, PA 2004.

Newsinger, John, 'Minimum Force, British Counter-Insurgency and the Mau Mau Rebellion', in: *Small Wars and Insurgencies* 3 (1992), H. 1, pp. 47–57.

Newson, Linda, 'Pathogens, Places and Peoples. Geographical Variations in the Impact of Disease in Early Spanish America and the Philippines', in: George Raudzens (ed.),

BIBLIOGRAPHY

Technology, Disease and Colonial Conquests, Sixteenth to Eighteenth Centuries. Essays Reappraising the Guns and Germs Theories, Leiden 2001, pp. 167–210.

Nissimi, Hilda, 'Illusions of World Power in Kenya. Strategy, Decolonization, and the British Base, 1946–1961', in: *International History Review* 23 (2001), H. 4, pp. 824–846.

Nkrumah, Kwame, *Neo-Colonialism. The Last Stage of Imperialism*, New York 1965.

Olatunji-Oloruntimehin, Benjamin, 'Senegambia—Mahmadou Lamine', in: Michael Crowder (ed.), *West African Resistance. The Military Response to Colonial Occupation*, New York 1972, pp. 80–110.

Omissi, David, *The Sepoy and the Raj. The Indian Army, 1860–1940*, Basingstoke 1998.

Osterhammel, Jürgen, 'Entdeckung und Eroberung, Neugier und Gewalt', in: Christof Dipper and Martin Vogt (eds), *Entdeckungen und frühe Kolonisation* (Wissenschaft und Technik, vol. 63), Darmstadt 1993, pp. 399–429.

——, '"The Great Work of Uplifting Mankind". Zivilisierungsmission und Moderne', in: Boris Barth and Jürgen Osterhammel (eds), *Zivilisierungsmissionen. Imperiale Weltverbesserung seit dem 18. Jahrhundert*, Konstanz 2005, pp. 363–425.

——, 'Wissen als Macht. Deutungen interkulturellen Nichtverstehens bei Tzvetan Todorov and Edward Said', in: Eva-Maria Auch and Stig Förster (eds), *"Barbaren" und "Weiße Teufel". Kulturkonflikte und Imperialismus in Asien vom 18. bis zum 20. Jahrhundert*, Paderborn 1997, pp. 145–169.

——, *Die Verwandlung der Welt. Eine Geschichte des 19. Jahrhunderts*, 3rd edn., Munich 2009.

——, *Europe, the "West" and the Civilizing Mission*, London 2006.

——, *Geschichtswissenschaft jenseits des Nationalstaats. Studien zu Beziehungsgeschichte und Zivilisationsvergleich* (Kritische Studien zur Geschichtswissenschaft, vol. 147), Göttingen 2001.

Osterhammel, Jürgen, and Niels P. Petersson, *Geschichte der Globalisierung. Dimensionen, Prozesse, Epochen*, Munich 2003.

Oudijk, Michel R., and Matthew Restall, 'Mesoamerican Conquistadors in the Sixteenth Century', in: Laura E. Matthew and Michel R. Oudijk (eds), *Indian Conquistadors. Indigenous Allies in the Conquest of Mesoamerica*, Norman, OK 2007, pp. 28–63.

Owen, Roger, and Bob Sutcliffe (eds), *Studies in the Theory of Imperialism*, London 1972.

Pagden, Anthony, *Lords of All the World. Ideologies of Empire in Spain, Britain and France c. 1500—c. 1800*, New Haven, CT 1995.

Paillard, Yvan-Georges, 'The French Expedition to Madagascar in 1895. Program and Results', in: Jaap A. de Moor and Hendrik Lodewyk Wesseling (eds), *Imperialism and War. Essays on Colonial Wars in Asia and Africa*, Leiden 1989, pp. 168–188.

Palmer, Alison, *Colonial Genocide*, Adelaide 2000.

Paret, Peter, 'Colonial Experience and European Military Reform at the End of the Eighteenth Century', in: Douglas M. Peers (ed.), *Warfare and Empires. Contact and Conflict between European and non-European Military and Maritime Forces and Cultures* (An Expanding World, vol. 24), Aldershot 1997, pp. 357–369.

Parker, Geoffrey (ed.), *The Cambridge Illustrated History of Warfare. The Triumph of the West*, Cambridge 1995.

Parker, Geoffrey, 'Early Modern Europe', in: Michael Howard, George J. Andreopoulos and Mark R. Shulman (eds), *The Laws of War. Constraints on Warfare in the Western World*, New Haven, CT 1994, pp. 40–58.

BIBLIOGRAPHY

————, 'Introduction. The Western Way of War', in: Ibid. (ed.), *The Cambridge Illustrated History of Warfare. The Triumph of the West*, Cambridge 1995, pp. 2–9.

————, *The Military Revolution. Military Innovation and the Rise of the West, 1500–1800*, 2nd edn., Cambridge 1996.

Parrott, Bruce, 'Analyzing the Transformation of the Soviet Union in Comparative Perspective', in: Karen Dawisha and Bruce Parrott (eds), *The End of Empire? The Transformation of the USSR in Comparative Perspective* (The International Politics of Eurasia, vol. 9), Armonk, NY 1997, pp. 3–29.

Parry, John H., and Robert G. Keith (eds), *New Iberian World. A Documentary History of the Discovery and Settlement of Latin America to the Early 17th Century*, vol. 4: *The Andes*, New York 1984.

Pavilonis, Brigid Meyers, 'Fighting the Irregular War in Afghanistan. Success in Combat; Struggles in Stabilization', in: Steven Carlton-Ford and Morten G. Ender (eds), *The Routledge Handbook of War and Society. Iraq and Afghanistan*, London 2011, pp. 20–31.

Peers, Douglas M. (ed.), *Warfare and Empires. Contact and Conflict between European and non-European Military and Maritime Forces and Cultures* (An Expanding World, vol. 24), Aldershot 1997.

Peers, Douglas M., 'Introduction', in: Ibid. (ed.), *Warfare and Empires. Contact and Conflict between European and non-European Military and Maritime Forces and Cultures* (An Expanding World, vol. 24), Aldershot 1997, pp. xv–xxxiv.

————, 'Revolution, Evolution, or Devolution. The Military and the Making of Colonial India', in: Wayne E. Lee (ed.), *Empires and Indigenes. Intercultural Alliance, Imperial Expansion, and Warfare in the Early Modern World*, New York 2011, pp. 81–106.

Pemble, John, 'Resources and Techniques in the Second Maratha War', in: Douglas M. Peers (ed.), *Warfare and Empires. Contact and Conflict between European and non-European Military and Maritime Forces and Cultures* (An Expanding World, vol. 24), Aldershot 1997, pp. 275–304.

Penn, Nigel, *The Forgotten Frontier. Colonist and Khoisan on the Cape's Northern Frontier in the 18th Century*, Athens, OH 2005.

Pennel, C. R., *A Country with a Government and a Flag. The Rif War in Morocco 1921–1926*, Wisbech 1986.

Perry, Frederick William, *The Commonwealth Armies. Manpower and Organisation in Two World Wars*, Manchester 1988.

Person, Yves, 'Guinea—Samori', in: Michael Crowder (ed.), *West African Resistance. The Military Response to Colonial Occupation*, New York 1972, pp. 111–143.

Petillo, Carol Morris, 'Leaders and Followers. A Half-Century of the U.S. Military in the Philippine Islands', in: James C. Bradford (ed.), *The Military and Conflict between Cultures. Soldiers at the Interface*, College Station, TX 1997, pp. 183–213.

Pietschmann, Horst, 'Frühneuzeitliche Imperialkriege Spaniens. Ein Beitrag zur Abgrenzung komplexer Kriegsformen in Raum und Zeit', in: Tanja Bührer, Christian Stachelbeck and Dierk Walter (eds), *Imperialkriege von 1500 bis heute. Strukturen— Akteure—Lernprozesse*, Paderborn 2011, pp. 73–92.

Plank, Geoffrey, 'Deploying Tribes and Clans. Mohawks in Nova Scotia and Scottish Highlandes in Georgia', in: Wayne E. Lee (ed.), *Empires and Indigenes. Intercultural Alliance, Imperial Expansion, and Warfare in the Early Modern World*, New York 2011, pp. 221–249.

Porch, Douglas, 'French Colonial Forces on the Sahara Rim', in: James C. Bradford (ed.),

BIBLIOGRAPHY

The Military and Conflict between Cultures. Soldiers at the Interface, College Station, TX 1997, pp. 163–182.

————, 'Introduction to the Bison Books Edition', in: Charles Edward Callwell, *Small Wars. Their Principles and Practice*, ed. by Douglas Porch, 3rd edn., Lincoln, NE 1996, pp. v–xviii.

————, 'The Dangerous Myths and Dubious Promise of COIN', in: *Small Wars and Insurgencies* 22 (2011), H. 2, pp. 239–257.

————, *The Conquest of Morocco*, New York 1983.

————, *The Conquest of the Sahara*, New York 2005.

————, *The French Foreign Legion. A Complete History*, London 1991.

Porter, Andrew, and Alaine Low (eds), *The Oxford History of the British Empire*, vol. 3: *The Nineteenth Century*, Oxford 1999.

Porter, Bernard, *The Lion's Share. A Short History of British Imperialism 1850–2004*, Harlow 2004.

Porter, Patrick, *Military Orientalism. Eastern War Through Western Eyes*, London 2009.

Potempa, Harald, 'Der Raum und seine tatsächliche Beherrschung als zentrales Problem von Imperialkriegen. Die Perzeption des Kleinen Krieges durch deutsche Streitkräfte im Zeitraum 1884 bis 1914 im Spiegel des "Militär-Wochenblattes"', in: Tanja Bührer, Christian Stachelbeck and Dierk Walter (eds), *Imperialkriege von 1500 bis heute. Strukturen—Akteure—Lernprozesse*, Paderborn 2011, pp. 443–462.

Powell, Philip Wayne, *Soldiers, Indians and Silver. North America's First Frontier War*, Tempe, AZ 1975.

Prashad, Vijay, *A People's History of the Third World*, New York 2007.

Pretorius, Fransjohan, 'Uniform and not so Uniform. Boer Combatants in the Second Anglo-Boer War, 1899–1902', in: Erwin A. Schmidl (ed.), *Freund oder Feind? Kombattanten, Nichtkombattanten und Zivilisten in Krieg und Bürgerkrieg seit dem 18. Jahrhundert*, Frankfurt/Main 1995, pp. 45–87.

Prince, Tom v., *Gegen Araber und Wahehe. Erinnerungen aus meiner ostafrikanischen Leutnantszeit 1890–1895*, Berlin 1914.

Pulsipher, Jenny Hale, 'Gaining the Diplomatic Edge. Kinship, Trade, Ritual, and Religion in Amerindian Alliances in Early North America', in: Wayne E. Lee (ed.), *Empires and Indigenes. Intercultural Alliance, Imperial Expansion, and Warfare in the Early Modern World*, New York 2011, pp. 19–47.

Rainero, Romain H., 'The Battle of Adowa on 1st March 1896. A Reappraisal', in: Jaap A. de Moor and Hendrik Lodewyk Wesseling (eds), *Imperialism and War. Essays on Colonial Wars in Asia and Africa*, Leiden 1989, pp. 189–200.

Ralston, David B., *Importing the European Army. The Introduction of European Military Techniques and Institutions into the Extra-European World, 1600–1914*, Chicago, IL 1996.

Ramsey, William L., '"Something Cloudy in Their Looks". The Origins of the Yamasee War Reconsidered', in: *Journal of American History* 90 (2003), H. 1, pp. 44–75.

Ranger, Terence Osborn, 'African Reactions to the Imposition of Colonial Rule in East and Central Africa', in: Lewis Henry Gann and Peter Duignan (eds), *Colonialism in Africa 1870–1960*, vol. 1: *The History and Politics of Colonialism 1870–1914*, Cambridge 1969, pp. 293–324.

————, 'Connexions between "Primary Resistance" Movements and Modern Mass Nationalism in East and Central Africa' [1968], in: Martin Shipway (ed.), *The Rise and Fall of Modern Empires*, vol. 4: *Reactions to Colonialism*, Farnham 2013, pp. 39–67.

BIBLIOGRAPHY

————, *Revolt in Southern Rhodesia 1896–7. A Study in African Resistance*, London 1967.

Rauchensteiner, Manfred, and Erwin A. Schmidl (eds), *Formen des Krieges. Vom Mittelalter zum "Low-Intensity-Conflict"* (Forschungen zur Militärgeschichte, vol. 1), Graz 1991.

Raudzens, George (ed.), *Technology, Disease and Colonial Conquests, Sixteenth to Eighteenth Centuries. Essays Reappraising the Guns and Germs Theories*, Leiden 2001.

Raudzens, George, 'Outfighting or Outpopulating? Main Reasons for Early Colonial Conquests, 1493–1788', in: Ibid. (ed.), *Technology, Disease and Colonial Conquests, Sixteenth to Eighteenth Centuries. Essays Reappraising the Guns and Germs Theories*, Leiden 2001, pp. 31–57.

————, 'Why Did Amerindian Defences Fail? Parallels in the European Invasions of Hispaniola, Virginia and Beyond', in: *War in History* 3 (1996), H. 3, pp. 331–352.

————, *Empires. Europe and Globalization 1492–1788*, Stroud 1999.

Reid, Anthony, *Europe and Southeast Asia. The Military Balance* (South East Asian Studies Committee Occasional Paper, vol. 16), Townsville, Queensland 1982.

Reilly, Brett, 'Cold War Transition. Europe's Decolonization and Eisenhower's System of Subordinate Elites', in: Alfred W. McCoy, Josep M. Fradera and Stephen Jacobson (eds), *Endless Empire. Spain's Retreat, Europe's Eclipse, America's Decline*, Madison, WI 2012, pp. 344–359.

Reinhard, Wolfgang (ed.), *Verstaatlichung der Welt? Europäische Staatsmodelle und außereuropäische Machtprozesse* (Schriften des Historischen Kollegs, Kolloquien, vol. 47), Munich 1999.

Reinhard, Wolfgang, *Geschichte der europäischen Expansion*, vol. 1: *Die Alte Welt bis 1818*, Stuttgart 1983.

————, *Geschichte der europäischen Expansion*, vol. 2: *Die Neue Welt*, Stuttgart 1985.

————, *Geschichte der europäischen Expansion*, vol. 3: *Die Alte Welt seit 1818*, Stuttgart 1988.

————, *Geschichte der europäischen Expansion*, vol. 4: *Dritte Welt Afrika*, Stuttgart 1990.

————, *Geschichte des modernen Staates. Von den Anfängen bis zur Gegenwart*, Munich 2007.

Reis, Bruno C., and Pedro A. Oliveira, 'Cutting Heads or Winning Hearts. Late Colonial Portuguese Counterinsurgency and the Wiriyamu Massacre of 1972', in: *Civil Wars* 14 (2012), H. 1.

Restall, Matthew, *Seven Myths of the Spanish Conquest*, Oxford 2003.

Reuter, Jens, and Conrad Clewing (eds), *Der Kosovo-Konflikt. Ursachen—Verlauf— Perspektiven*, Klagenfurt 2000.

Reynolds, Henry, 'Genocide in Tasmania?', in: Anthony Dirk Moses (ed.), *Genocide and Settler Society. Frontier Violence and Stolen Indigenous Children in Australian History* (Studies on War and Genocide, vol. 6), New York 2004, pp. 127–149.

Ribas, Josep M. Delgado, 'Eclipse and Collapse of the Spanish Empire, 1650–1898', in: Alfred W. McCoy, Josep M. Fradera and Stephen Jacobson (eds), *Endless Empire. Spain's Retreat, Europe's Eclipse, America's Decline*, Madison, WI 2012, pp. 43–54.

Richards, Donald S., *The Savage Frontier. A History of the Anglo-Afghan Wars*, London 1990.

Rickey, Don, *Forty Miles a Day on Beans and Hay. The Enlisted Soldier Fighting the Indian Wars*, Norman, OK 1963.

Ricklefs, Merle C., 'Balance and Military Innovation in Seventeenth-Century Java', in: Douglas M. Peers (ed.), *Warfare and Empires. Contact and Conflict between European and non-European Military and Maritime Forces and Cultures* (An Expanding World, vol. 24), Aldershot 1997, pp. 101–108.

BIBLIOGRAPHY

————, *War, Culture and Economy in Java, 1677–1726. Asian and European Imperialism in the Early Kartasura Period*, St. Leonards 1993.

Rink, Martin, 'Kleiner Krieg—Guerilla—Razzia. Die Kriege des französischen "Imperiums" 1808 bis 1848', in: Tanja Bührer, Christian Stachelbeck and Dierk Walter (eds), *Imperialkriege von 1500 bis heute. Strukturen—Akteure—Lernprozesse*, Paderborn 2011, pp. 425–442.

Rinke, Stefan, *Revolutionen in Lateinamerika. Wege in die Unabhängigkeit 1760–1830*, Munich 2010.

Roberts, Michael, *The Military Revolution 1560–1660. An Inaugural Lecture Delivered before the Queen's University of Belfast*, Belfast 1956.

Robinson, Ronald, 'Non-European Foundations of European Imperialism. Sketch for a Theory of Collaboration', in: Roger Owen and Bob Sutcliffe (eds), *Studies in the Theory of Imperialism*, London 1972, pp. 117–142.

————, 'The Excentric Idea of Imperialism, with or without Empire', in: Wolfgang J. Mommsen and Jürgen Osterhammel (eds), *Imperialism and After. Continuities and Discontinuities*, London 1986, pp. 267–289.

Robinson, Ronald, John Gallagher and Alice Denny, *Africa and the Victorians. The Official Mind of Imperialism*, 2nd edn., London 1981.

Robson, Brian, *Fuzzy-Wuzzy. The Campaigns in the Eastern Sudan 1884–85*, Tunbridge Wells 1993.

Rose, Andreas, '"Unsichtbare Feinde". Großbritanniens Feldzug gegen die Buren (1899–1902)', in: Tanja Bührer, Christian Stachelbeck and Dierk Walter (eds), *Imperialkriege von 1500 bis heute. Strukturen—Akteure—Lernprozesse*, Paderborn 2011, pp. 217–239.

Ross, David, 'Dahomey', in: Michael Crowder (ed.), *West African Resistance. The Military Response to Colonial Occupation*, New York 1972, pp. 144–169.

Rothermund, Dietmar, 'Der Strukturwandel des britischen Kolonialstaats in Indien 1757–1947', in: Wolfgang Reinhard (ed.), *Verstaatlichung der Welt? Europäische Staatsmodelle und außereuropäische Machtprozesse* (Schriften des Historischen Kollegs, Kolloquien, vol. 47), Munich 1999, pp. 69–86.

Roxborough, Ian, 'Learning the Lessons of Counterinsurgency', in: Steven Carlton-Ford and Morten G. Ender (eds), *The Routledge Handbook of War and Society. Iraq and Afghanistan*, London 2011, pp. 32–43.

Rüther, Kirsten, 'Religiöse Interaktion, globale', in: Friedrich Jaeger (ed.), *Enzyklopädie der Neuzeit*, vol. 10: *Physiologie—Religiöses Epos*, Stuttgart 2009, Sp. 1165–1188.

'Rumsfeld and Myers Briefing on Enduring Freedom. US Department of Defense News Transcript', 7 October 2001. URL: http://www.defense.gov/transcripts/transcript.aspx?transcriptid=2011 [17. 07. 2013].

Ryan, Yasmine, 'Mali journalists despair over "invisible war". Reporters struggle to work as travel bans are enforced and official information, such as death tolls, are not released', in: *Al-Jazeera*, 27 January 2013. URL: http://www.aljazeera.com/indepth/features/2013/01/2013127154355125483.html [07. 08. 2013].

Sahlins, Marshall D., *Tribesmen*, Englewood Cliffs, NJ 1968.

Said, Edward W., *Orientalism*, New York 1978.

Sancho, Pedro, *An Account of the Conquest of Peru*, ed. by Philip Ainsworth Means (Documents and Narratives Concerning the Discovery and Conquest of Latin America, vol. 2), New York 1917.

Sarkesian, Sam C., 'The American Response to Low-Intensity Conflict. The Formative

BIBLIOGRAPHY

Period', in: David Charters and Maurice Tugwell (eds), *Armies in Low-Intensity Conflict. A Comparative Analysis*, London 1989, pp. 19–48.

Scammell, Geoffrey Vaughan, 'Indigenous Assistance in the Establishment of Portuguese Power in Asia in the Sixteenth Century', in: Douglas M. Peers (ed.), *Warfare and Empires. Contact and Conflict between European and non-European Military and Maritime Forces and Cultures* (An Expanding World, vol. 24), Aldershot 1997, pp. 139–149.

Schaper, Ulrike, *Koloniale Verhandlungen. Gerichtsbarkeit, Verwaltung und Herrschaft in Kamerun 1884–1916*, Frankfurt/Main 2012.

Schindler, Helmut, *Bauern und Reiterkrieger. Die Mapuche-Indianer im Süden Amerikas*, Munich 1990.

Schmidl, Erwin A. (ed.), *Freund oder Feind? Kombattanten, Nichtkombattanten und Zivilisten in Krieg und Bürgerkrieg seit dem 18. Jahrhundert*, Frankfurt/Main 1995.

Schmidl, Erwin A., '"Asymmetrische Kriege". Alter Wein in neuen Schläuchen?', in: Josef Schröfl and Thomas Pankratz (eds), *Asymmetrische Kriegführung. Ein neues Phänomen der Internationalen Politik?*, Baden-Baden 2004, pp. 121–132.

——, 'Kolonialkriege. Zwischen großem Krieg und kleinem Frieden', in: Manfried Rauchensteiner and Erwin A. Schmidl (eds), *Formen des Krieges. Vom Mittelalter zum "Low-Intensity-Conflict"* (Forschungen zur Militärgeschichte, vol. 1), Graz 1991, pp. 111–138.

Schmidt, Rochus, *Geschichte des Araberaufstandes in Ost-Afrika. Seine Entstehung, seine Niederwerfung und seine Folgen*, Frankfurt/Oder 1892.

Schmieder, Ulrike, and Hans-Heinrich Nolte (eds), *Atlantik. Sozial- und Kulturgeschichte in der Neuzeit* (Edition Weltregionen, vol. 20), Vienna 2010.

Schneckener, Ulrich, *Transnationaler Terrorismus. Charakter und Hintergründe des "neuen" Terrorismus*, Frankfurt/Main 2006.

Schröfl, Josef, and Thomas Pankratz (eds), *Asymmetrische Kriegführung. Ein neues Phänomen der Internationalen Politik?*, Baden-Baden 2004.

Schumacher, Frank, '"Niederbrennen, plündern und töten sollt ihr". Der Kolonialkrieg der USA auf den Philippinen (1899–1913)', in: Thoralf Klein and Frank Schumacher (eds), *Kolonialkriege. Militärische Gewalt im Zeichen des Imperialismus*, Hamburg 2006, pp. 109–144.

Scott, Wilbur J., David R. McCone and George R. Mastroianni, 'Two US Combat Units in Iraq. Psychological Contracts when Expectations and Realities Diverge', in: Steven Carlton-Ford and Morten G. Ender (eds), *The Routledge Handbook of War and Society. Iraq and Afghanistan*, London 2011, pp. 56–67. Seeley, John Robert, *The Expansion of England. Two Courses of Lectures*, Leipzig 1884.

Selby, John, 'The Third China War, 1860', in: Brian Bond (ed.), *Victorian Military Campaigns*, London 1994, pp. 71–104.

Selesky, Harold E., 'Colonial America', in: Michael Howard, George J. Andreopoulos and Mark R. Shulman (eds), *The Laws of War. Constraints on Warfare in the Western World*, New Haven, CT 1994, pp. 59–85.

Shipway, Martin (ed.), *The Rise and Fall of Modern Empires*, vol. 4: *Reactions to Colonialism*, Farnham 2013.

Silver, Peter, *Our Savage Neighbors. How Indian War Transformed Early America*, New York 2008.

Simpson, Brad, 'Indonesiens Kolonialkrieg in Osttimor 1975–1999', in: Bernd Greiner, Christian Th. Müller and Dierk Walter (eds), *Heiße Kriege im Kalten Krieg* (Studien zum Kalten Krieg, vol. 1), Hamburg 2006, pp. 339–375.

BIBLIOGRAPHY

Singer, Barnett, and John Langdon, *Cultured Force. Makers and Defenders of the French Colonial Empire*, Madison, WI 2004.

Slatta, Richard W., '"Civilization" Battles "Barbarism". The Limits of Argentine Indian Frontier Strategies', in: James C. Bradford (ed.), *The Military and Conflict between Cultures. Soldiers at the Interface*, College Station, TX 1997, pp. 130–159.

Slotkin, Richard, *Regeneration Through Violence. The Mythology of the American Frontier, 1600–1860*, Middleton, CT 1973. *Small Wars Manual*, ed. by United States Marine Corps, Washington, DC 1940.

Smith, Robert, 'Nigeria—Ijebu', in: Michael Crowder (ed.), *West African Resistance. The Military Response to Colonial Occupation*, New York 1972, pp. 170–204.

Smith, Tony, *The Pattern of Imperialism. The United States, Great Britain, and the Late-Industrializing World since 1815*, Cambridge 1981.

Spiers, Edward M., 'The Use of the Dum Dum Bullet in Colonial Warfare', in: *Journal of Imperial and Commonwealth History* 4 (1975), H. 1, pp. 3–14.

———, *The Late Victorian Army 1868–1902*, Manchester 1992.

Starkey, Armstrong, 'Conflict and Synthesis. Frontier Warfare in North America, 1513–1813', in: George Raudzens (ed.), *Technology, Disease and Colonial Conquests, Sixteenth to Eighteenth Centuries. Essays Reappraising the Guns and Germs Theories*, Leiden 2001, pp. 59–84.

———, 'Lernen im Kolonialkrieg. Englisch-Nordamerika', in: Dierk Walter and Birthe Kundrus (eds), *Waffen Wissen Wandel. Anpassung und Lernen in transkulturellen Erstkonflikten*, Hamburg 2012, pp. 128–150.

———, *European and Native American Warfare, 1675–1815*, Norman, OK 1998.

Steele, Ian Kenneth, *Betrayals. Fort William Henry and the Massacre*, New York 1990.

———, *Warpaths. Invasions of North America*, New York 1994.

Stockwell, Anthony J., '"A widespread and long-concocted plot to overthrow government in Malaya?". The Origins of the Malayan Emergency', in: Robert Holland (ed.), *Emergencies and Disorder in the European Empires after 1945*, London 1994, pp. 66–88.

———, 'Imperialism and Nationalism in South-East Asia', in: Judith M. Brown and William Roger Louis (ed.), *The Oxford History of the British Empire*, vol. 4: *The Twentieth Century*, Oxford 1999, pp. 465–489.

———, 'Insurgency and Decolonisation during the Malayan Emergency', in: *Journal of Commonwealth & Comparative Politics* 25 (1987), H. 1, pp. 71–81.

Stokes, Eric, *The Peasant Armed. The Indian Revolt of 1857*, ed. by Christopher Alan Bayly, Oxford 1986.

Stora, Benjamin, 'The "Southern" World of the Pieds Noirs. References to and Representations of Europeans in Colonial Algeria', in: Caroline Elkins and Susan Pedersen (eds), *Settler Colonialism in the Twentieth Century. Projects, Practices, Legacies*, London 2005, pp. 225–241.

Strachan, Hew, 'A General Typology of Transcultural Wars. The Modern Ages', in: Hans-Henning Kortüm (ed.), *Transcultural Wars from the Middle Ages to the 21st Century*, Berlin 2006, pp. 85–103.

———, 'British Counter-Insurgency from Malaya to Iraq', in: *RUSI Journal* 152 (2007), H. 6, pp. 8–11.

———, 'The British Way in Warfare', in: David Geoffrey Chandler and Ian F. W. Beckett (eds), *The Oxford Illustrated History of the British Army*, Oxford 1994, pp. 417–434.

———, *European Armies and the Conduct of War*, London 1983.

BIBLIOGRAPHY

————, *The Politics of the British Army*, Oxford 1997.

Streets, Heather, *Martial Races. The Military, Race and Masculinity in British Imperial Culture, 1857–1914*, Manchester 2004.

Stubbs, Richard, *Hearts and Minds in Guerilla Warfare. The Malayan Emergency, 1948–1960*, Singapore 2004.

Stucki, Andreas, 'Bevölkerungskontrolle in asymmetrischen Konflikten. Zwangsumsiedlung und spanische Antiguerilla auf Kuba, 1868–1898', in: Tanja Bührer, Christian Stachelbeck and Dierk Walter (eds), *Imperialkriege von 1500 bis heute. Strukturen—Akteure—Lernprozesse*, Paderborn 2011, pp. 243–259.

————, 'Die spanische Antiguerilla-Kriegführung auf Kuba 1868–1898. Radikalisierung—Entgrenzung—Genozid?', in: *Zeitschrift für Geschichtswissenschaft* 56 (2008), H. 2, pp. 123–138.

————, 'Weylers Söldner. Guerillabekämpfung auf Kuba, 1868–1898', in: Stig Förster, Christian Jansen and Günther Kronenbitter (eds), *Die Rückkehr der Condottieri? Krieg und Militär zwischen staatlichem Monopol und Privatisierung: Von der Antike bis zur Gegenwart* (Krieg in der Geschichte, vol. 57), Paderborn 2010, pp. 223–235.

————, *Aufstand und Zwangsumsiedlung. Die kubanischen Unabhängigkeitskriege 1868–1898*, Hamburg 2012.

Taj, Farhat, 'The Year of the Drone Misinformation', in: *Small Wars and Insurgencies* 21 (2010), H. 3, pp. 529–535.

Taylor, Robert H., 'Colonial Forces in British Burma. A National Army Postponed', in: Karl Hack and Tobias Rettig (eds), *Colonial Armies in Southeast Asia*, London 2006, pp. 195–209.

Teitler, Gerke, 'The Mixed Company. Fighting Power and Ethnic Relations in the Dutch Colonial Army, 1890–1920', in: Karl Hack and Tobias Rettig (eds), *Clonial Armies in Southeast Asia*, London 2006, pp. 154–168.

The Conduct of Anti-Terrorist Operations in Malaya, ed. by HQ Malaya Command, 2nd edn., Kuala Lumpur 1954.

Thomas, Martin (ed.), *The French Colonial Mind*, vol. 2: *Violence, Military Encounters, and Colonialism*, Lincoln, NE 2011.

Thomas, Martin, 'Order Before Reform. The Spread of French Military Operations in Algeria, 1954–1958', in: David Killingray and David E. Omissi (eds), *Guardians of Empire. The Armed Forces of the Colonial Powers c. 1700–1964*, Manchester 1999, pp. 198–220.

Thomas, Martin, Bob Moore and Lawrence J. Butler (eds), *Crises of Empire. De-colonization and Europe's Imperial States, 1918–1975*, London 2008.

Thomas, Martin, Bob Moore and Lawrence J. Butler, 'Conclusion. Changing Attitudes to the End of Empire', in: Ibid. (eds), *Crises of Empire. Decolonization and Europe's Imperial States, 1918–1975*, London 2008, pp. 411–428.

Thomas, Martin, *Violence and Colonial Order. Police, Workers and Protest in the European Colonial Empires, 1918–1940*, Cambridge 2012.

Thompson, Robert, *Defeating Communist Insurgency. Experiences from Malaya and Vietnam* (Studies in International Security, vol. 10), London 1967.

Thornton, John K., 'African Soldiers in the Haitian Revolution', in: *Journal of Caribbean History* 25 (1991), H. 58–80.

————, 'Firearms, Diplomacy, and Conquest in Angola. Cooperation and Alliance in West Central Africa, 1491–1671', in: Wayne E. Lee (ed.), *Empires and Indigenes.*

BIBLIOGRAPHY

Intercultural Alliance, Imperial Expansion, and Warfare in the Early Modern World, New York 2011, pp. 167–191.

———, 'The Art of War in Angola, 1575–1680', in: Douglas M. Peers (ed.), *Warfare and Empires. Contact and Conflict between European and non-European Military and Maritime Forces and Cultures* (An Expanding World, vol. 24), Aldershot 1997, pp. 81–99.

———, 'Warfare, Slave Trading and European Influence. Atlantic Africa 1450–1800', in: Jeremy Black (ed.), *War in the Early Modern World, 1450–1815*, London 1998, pp. 129–146.

Todorov, Tzvetan, *Die Eroberung Amerikas. Das Problem des Anderen*, Frankfurt/Main 1985.

Tone, John Lawrence, 'The Machete and the Liberation of Cuba', in: *Journal of Military History* 62 (1998), H. 1, pp. 7–28.

Tourret, Hubert, 'L'évolution de la tactique du corps expéditionnaire français en Extrême-Orient', in: Maurice Vaïsse (ed.), *L'Armée française dans la guerre d'Indochine (1946–1954). Adaptation ou inadaptation?*, Bruxelles 2000, pp. 173–184.

Trench, Charles Chenevix, *Charley Gordon. An Eminent Victorian Reassessed*, London 1978.

Trinquier, Roger, *La guerre moderne*, Paris 2008 [1961].

Trotha, Trutz von, 'Genozidaler Pazifizierungskrieg. Soziologische Anmerkungen zum Konzept des Genozids am Beispiel des Kolonialkriegs in Deutsch-Südwestafrika, 1904–1907', in: *Zeitschrift für Genozidforschung* 4 (2003), H. 2, p. 30–57.

———, '"The Fellows Can Just Starve". On Wars of "Pacification" in the African Colonies of Imperial Germany and the Concept of "Total War"', in: Manfred F. Boemeke, Roger Chickering and Stig Förster (eds), *Anticipating Total War. The German and American Experiences, 1871–1914*, Cambridge 1999, pp. 415–435.

———, 'Über den Erfolg und die Brüchigkeit der Utopie staatlicher Herrschaft. Herrschaftssoziologische Betrachtungen über den kolonialen und nachkolonialen Staat in Westafrika', in: Wolfgang Reinhard (ed.), *Verstaatlichung der Welt? Europäische Staatsmodelle und außereuropäische Machtprozesse* (Schriften des Historischen Kollegs, Kolloquien, vol. 47), Munich 1999, pp. 223–251.

———, 'Was war Kolonialismus? Einige zusammenfassende Befunde zur Soziologie und Geschichte des Kolonialismus und der Kolonialherrschaft', in: *Saeculum* 55 (2004), pp. 49–95.

———, *Koloniale Herrschaft. Zur soziologischen Theorie der Staatsentstehung am Beispiel des "Schutzgebietes Togo"*, Tübingen 1994.

Tugwell, Maurice, 'Adapt or Perish. The Forms of Evolution in Warfare', in: David Charters and Maurice Tugwell (eds), *Armies in Low-Intensity Conflict. A Comparative Analysis*, London 1989, pp. 1–17.

Turnbull, Clive, *Black War. The Extermination of the Tasmanian Aborigines*, Melbourne 1948.

Turney-High, Harry Holbert, *Primitive War. Its Practice and Concepts*, 2nd edn., Columbia, SC 1971 [1949].

Tzoref-Ashkenazi, Chen, 'Deutsche Hilfstruppen in Imperialkriegen 1776–1808', in: Tanja Bührer, Christian Stachelbeck and Dierk Walter (eds), *Imperialkriege von 1500 bis heute. Strukturen—Akteure—Lernprozesse*, Paderborn 2011, pp. 345–361.

Utley, Robert Marshall, 'Cultural Clash on the Western North American Frontier. Military Implications', in: James C. Bradford (ed.), *The Military and Conflict between Cultures. Soldiers at the Interface*, College Station, TX 1997, pp. 91–108.

———, 'Total War on the American Indian Frontier', in: Manfred F. Boemeke, Roger

BIBLIOGRAPHY

Chickering and Stig Förster (eds), *Anticipating Total War. The German and American Experiences, 1871–1914*, Cambridge 1999, pp. 399–414.

————, *Custer. Cavalier in Buckskin*, Norman, OK 2001.

————, *Frontier Regulars. The United States Army and the Indian, 1866–1891*, Lincoln, NE 1973.

————, *Frontiersmen in Blue. The United States Army and the Indian, 1848–1865*, Lincoln, NE 1967.

————, *The Indian Frontier of the American West 1846–1890*, Albuquerque, NM 1984.

Vaïsse, Maurice (ed.), *L'Armée française dans la guerre d'Indochine (1946–1954). Adaptation ou inadaptation?*, Bruxelles 2000.

Van Creveld, Martin, *Command in War*, Cambridge, MA 1985.

————, *Supplying War. Logistics from Wallenstein to Patton*, Cambridge 1977.

Vandervort, Bruce, 'Colonial Wars, 1815–1960', in: Jeremy Black (ed.), *European Warfare 1815–2000*, Basingstoke 2002, pp. 147–171. Vandervort, Bruce, *Indian Wars of Mexico, Canada and the United States, 1812–1900*, New York 2006.

————, *Wars of Imperial Conquest in Africa, 1830–1914*, Bloomington, IN 1998.

Vann, Michael G., 'Fear and Loathing in French Hanoi. Colonial White Images and Imaginings of "Native" Violence', in: Martin Thomas (ed.), *The French Colonial Mind*, vol. 2: *Violence, Military Encounters, and Colonialism*, Lincoln, NE 2011, pp. 52–76.

Vargas Machuca, Bernardo de, *The Indian Militia and Description of the Indies*, ed. by Kris Lane, Durham, NC 2008 [1599].

Varley, Paul, 'Warfare in Japan 1467–1600', in: Jeremy Black (ed.), *War in the Early Modern World, 1450–1815*, London 1998, pp. 53–86.

Vattel, Emer de, *Le droit des gens ou Principes de la loi naturelle. Appliqués à la conduit & aux affaires des Nations & des Souverains*, vol. 2, London 1758.

Veltzé, Alois, *Die Schlacht bei Adua. 1. März 1896*, Vienna 1904.

Veracini, Lorenzo, *Settler Colonialism. A Theoretical Overview*, Basingstoke 2010.

Vo Nguyen Giap, *Volkskrieg, Volksarmee*, Munich 1968.

Vogt, John, 'Saint Barbara's Legion. Portuguese Artillery in the Struggle for Morocco, 1415–1578', in: Douglas M. Peers (ed.), *Warfare and Empires. Contact and Conflict between European and non-European Military and Maritime Forces and Cultures* (An Expanding World, vol. 24), Aldershot 1997, pp. 73–79.

Wade, Geoff, 'Ming Chinese Colonial Armies in Southeast Asia', in: Karl Hack and Tobias Rettig (eds), *Colonial Armies in Southeast Asia*, London 2006, pp. 73–104.

Wagner, Walter, 'Die k. (u.) k. Armee. Gliederung und Aufgabenstellung', in: Adam Wandruszka and Peter Urbanitsch (eds), *Die Habsburgermonarchie 1848–1918*, vol. 5: *Die bewaffnete Macht*, Vienna 1987, pp. 142–633.

Waldmann, Peter, *Terrorismus und Bürgerkrieg. Der Staat in Bedrängnis*, Munich 2003.

Wallerstein, Immanuel, *The Modern World System*, vol. 1: *Capitalist Agriculture and the Origins of the European World-Economy in the Sixteenth Century*, Berkeley, CA 2011 [1974].

————, *The Modern World System*, vol. 2: *Mercantilism and the Consolidation of the European World Economy 1600–1750*, Berkeley, CA 2011.

————, *The Modern World System*, vol. 3: *The Second Era of Great Expansion of the Capitalist World Economy 1730–1840s*, Berkeley, CA 2011 [1989].

————, *The Modern World System*, vol. 4: *Centrist Liberalism Triumphant, 1789–1914*, Berkeley, CA 2011.

BIBLIOGRAPHY

Walter, Dierk, 'Asymmetrien in Imperialkriegen. Ein Beitrag zum Verständnis der Zukunft des Krieges', in: *Mittelweg 36* 17 (2008), H. 1, pp. 14–52.

————, 'Der nordamerikanische Imperialkrieg 1775–1783. Anmerkungen zum Charakter des amerikanischen Unabhängigkeitskrieges', in: Tanja Bührer, Christian Stachelbeck and Dierk Walter (eds), *Imperialkriege von 1500 bis heute. Strukturen—Akteure—Lernprozesse*, Paderborn 2011, pp. 93–109.

————, 'Heeresreformen', in: Friedrich Jaeger (ed.), *Enzyklopädie der Neuzeit*, vol. 5: *Gymnasium—Japanhandel*, Stuttgart 2007, Sp. 277–289.

————, 'Imperialkriege. Begriff, Erkenntnisinteresse, Aktualität (Einleitung)', in: Tanja Bührer, Christian Stachelbeck and Dierk Walter (eds), *Imperialkriege von 1500 bis heute. Strukturen—Akteure—Lernprozesse*, Paderborn 2011, pp. 1–29.

————, 'Kein Pardon. Zum Problem der Kapitulation im Imperialkrieg', in: *Mittelweg 36* 21 (2012), H. 3, pp. 90–111.

————, 'Kolonialkrieg, Globalstrategie und Kalter Krieg. Die Emergencies in Malaya und Kenia 1948–1960', in: Bernd Greiner, Christian Th. Müller and Dierk Walter (eds), *Heiße Kriege im Kalten Krieg* (Studien zum Kalten Krieg, vol. 1), Hamburg 2006, pp. 109–140.

————, '"The Enemy Must Be Brought to Battle". Westliche Schlachtenniederlagen in Imperialkriegen', in: *Mittelweg 36* 20 (2011), H. 1, pp. 55–80.

————, 'Warum Kolonialkrieg?', in: Thoralf Klein and Frank Schumacher (eds), *Kolonialkriege. Militärische Gewalt im Zeichen des Imperialismus*, Hamburg 2006, pp. 14–43.

————, *Preußische Heeresreformen 1807–1870. Militärische Innovation und der Mythos der "Roonschen Reform"* (Krieg in der Geschichte, vol. 16), Paderborn 2003.

Walter, Dierk, and Birthe Kundrus (eds), *Waffen Wissen Wandel. Anpassung und Lernen in transkulturellen Erstkonflikten*, Hamburg 2012.

Walter, Dierk, *Zwischen Dschungelkrieg und Atombombe. Britische Visionen vom Krieg der Zukunft 1945–1971*, Hamburg 2009.

Wandruszka, Adam, and Peter Urbanitsch (eds), *Die Habsburgermonarchie 1848–1918*, vol. 5: *Die bewaffnete Macht*, Vienna 1987.

Ward, Matthew C., '"The European Method of Warring Is Not Practiced Here". The Failure of British Military Policy in the Ohio Valley, 1755–1759', in: *War in History* 4 (1997), H. 3, pp. 247–263.

Watson, I. Bruce, 'Fortifications and the "Idea" of Force in Early English East India Company Relations with India', in: Douglas M. Peers (ed.), *Warfare and Empires. Contact and Conflict between European and non-European Military and Maritime Forces and Cultures* (An Expanding World, vol. 24), Aldershot 1997, pp. 55–72.

Weber, David J., *The Spanish Frontier in North America*, New Haven, CT 1992.

Weigl, Gerald, 'Der Fall Tenochtitlans. Challenge and Response an der neuen "Frontera"', in: Thomas Kolnberger, Ilja Steffelbauer and Gerald Weigl (eds), *Krieg und Akkulturation* (Expansion—Interaktion—Akkulturation, vol. 5), Vienna 2004, pp. 175–199.

Weigley, Russell F., *History of the United States Army*, New York 1967.

————, *The Age of Battles. The Quest for Decisive Warfare from Breitenfeld to Waterloo*, Bloomington, IN 1991.

————, *The American Way of War. A History of United States Military Strategy and Policy*, Bloomington, IN 1977.

BIBLIOGRAPHY

Weinberg, Gerhard L., 'Hitler's Image of the United States', in: *American Historical Review* 69 (1964), H. 4, pp. 1006–1021.

Wendt, Reinhard, *Vom Kolonialismus zur Globalisierung. Europa und die Welt seit 1500*, Paderborn 2007.

Wesseling, Hendrik Lodewyk, 'Colonial Wars and Armed Peace, 1870–1914', in: *Itinerario* 5 (1981), H. 2, pp. 53–73.

————, 'Colonial Wars. An Introduction', in: Jaap A. de Moor and Hendrik Lodewyk Wesseling (eds), *Imperialism and War. Essays on Colonial Wars in Asia and Africa*, Leiden 1989, pp. 1–11.

Westad, Odd Arne, *The Global ColdWar. ThirdWorld Interventions and the Making of Our Times*, Cambridge 2005.

Wheeler, Douglas L., 'African Elements in Portugal's Armies in Africa (1961–1974)', in: *Armed Forces and Society* 2 (1976), H. 2, pp. 233–250.

White, Richard, 'The Winning of the West. The Expansion of the Western Sioux in the Eighteenth and Nineteenth Centuries', in: *Journal of American History* 65 (1978), H. 2, pp. 319–343.

————, *The Middle Ground. Indians, Empires, and Republics in the Great Lakes Region, 1650–1815*, Cambridge 1991.

Whitehead, Neil L., 'Tribes Make States and States Make Tribes. Warfare and the Creation of Colonial Tribes and States in Northeastern South America', in: R. Brian Ferguson and Neil L. Whitehead (eds), *War in the Tribal Zone. Expanding States and Indigenous Warfare*, Santa Fe, NM 1992, pp. 127–150.

Whittingham, "Daniel, "'Savage Warfare". C.E. Callwell, the Roots of Counter-Insurgency, and the Nineteenth Century Context', in: *Small Wars and Insurgencies* 23 (2012), H. 4–5, pp. 591–607.

Wickwire, Franklin, and Mary Wickwire, *Cornwallis and the War of Independence*, London 1971.

Williams, Glenn F., *Year of the Hangman. George Washington's Campaign Against the Iroquois*, Yardley, PA 2006.

Williams, M. J., 'The Egyptian Campaign of 1882', in: Brian Bond (ed.), *Victorian Military Campaigns*, London 1994, pp. 243–278.

Wilner, Alex S., 'Targeted Killings in Afghanistan. Measuring Coercion and Deterrence in Counterterrorism and Counterinsurgency', in: *Studies in Conflict and Terrorism* 33 (2010), H. 4, pp. 307–329.

Wilson, Peter, 'European Warfare 1450–1815', in: Jeremy Black (ed.), *War in the Early Modern World, 1450–1815*, London 1998, pp. 177–206.

Wirz, Albert, 'Körper, Kopf und Bauch. Zum Problem des kolonialen Staates im subsaharischen Afrika', in: Wolfgang Reinhard (ed.), *Verstaatlichung der Welt? Europäische Staatsmodelle und außereuropäische Machtprozesse* (Schriften des Historischen Kollegs, Kolloquien, vol. 47), Munich 1999, pp. 253–271.

Wojak, Irmtrud, and Susanne Meinl (eds), *Völkermord und Kriegsverbrechen in der ersten Hälfte des 20. Jahrhunderts*, Frankfurt/Main 2004.

Womack, Sarah, 'Ethnicity and Martial Races. The Garde indigène of Cambodia in the 1880s and 1890s', in: Karl Hack and Tobias Rettig (eds), *Colonial Armies in Southeast Asia*, London 2006, pp. 107–125.

Wood, Gordon S., *Empire of Liberty. A History of the Early Republic, 1789–1815* (Oxford History of the United States, vol. 4), Oxford 2009.

BIBLIOGRAPHY

————, *The American Revolution. A History*, London 2003.

Woolman, David S., *Rebels in the Rif. Abd el Krim and the Rif Rebellion*, Stanford, CA 1968.

Wylde, Augustus B., *'83 to '87 in the Soudan. With an Account of Sir William Hewett's Mission to King John of Abyssinia*, vol. 1, London 1888.

Zeuske, Michael, *Die Geschichte der Amistad. Sklavenhandel und Menschenschmuggel auf dem Atlantik im 19. Jahrhundert*, Stuttgart 2012.

Zielonka, Jan, *Europe as Empire. The Nature of the Enlarged European Union*, Oxford 2007.

Zimmerer, Jürgen, 'Die Geburt des "Ostlandes" aus dem Geiste des Kolonialismus. Die nationalsozialistische Eroberungs- und Beherrschungspolitik in (post-)kolonialer Perspektive', in: *Sozial. Geschichte* 19 (2004), H. 1, pp. 10–43.

————, 'Holocaust und Kolonialismus. Beitrag zu einer Archäologie des genozidalen Gedankens', in: *Zeitschrift für Geschichtswissenschaft* 51 (2003), H. 12, pp. 1098–1119.

Zirkel, Kirsten, 'Military Power in German Colonial Policy. The Schutztruppen and Their Leaders in East and South-West Africa, 1888–1918', in: David Killingray and David E. Omissi (eds), *Guardians of Empire. The Armed Forces of the Colonial Powers c. 1700–1964*, Manchester 1999, pp. 91–113.

Zollmann, Jakob, *Koloniale Herrschaft und ihre Grenzen. Die Kolonialpolizei in Deutsch-Südwestafrika 1894–1915* (Kritische Studien zur Geschichtswissenschaft, vol. 191), Göttingen 2010.

INDEX

INDEX

INDEX

INDEX

INDEX

INDEX